Psychology A2

The Exam Companion

Mike Cardwell

•

Cara Flanagan

Published in 2005 by:
Nelson Thornes Ltd
Delta Place
27 Bath Road
CHELTENHAM
GL53 7TH
United Kingdom

05 06 07 08 09 / 10 9 8 7 6 5 4 3 2 1

A catalogue record for this book is available from the British Library

ISBN 0 7487 9262 7

Page make-up by GreenGate Publishing Services, Tonbridge

Printed and bound in China by Midas

ACKNOWLEDGEMENTS

The team at Nelson Thornes never ceases to amuse and tolerate us. We have been through the usual stormy waters (mostly nothing to do with the book itself) but our impressive production editor Clare Wheelwright has brought the ship safely to port! Stalwarts Nigel Harriss and the unsinkable Rick Jackman have always been on hand. Thank you.

CONTENTS

HOW TO USE THIS BOOK

This *Exam Companion* covers the most popular subsections of the A2 specification. Each of the subsections (chapters) has been further broken down into divisions following the structure of the AQA A specification, and we have broken each division down into topics similar to the topics in the *A2 Complete Companion*.

For each topic there are a range of probable and possible exam questions that could be set. This is not an exhaustive list but gives you the gist of what you may be asked and there are examiner's comments for each exam question to give you ideas about how to answer them.

On the division page there are also diagrammatic summaries for each topic to give you a visual picture of the content of that topic area. Each subsequent spread deals with one topic at a time. On the left-hand side of the spread we show you the essential points you might cover in response to two of the essays on that topic. On the right-hand side, one of these essay titles is answered, showing you how the diagrammatic summaries and bullet points can be expanded into a full A-grade answer. Shading has been used to show which parts of the answer are AO2.

There are two other important parts of this book. On the next five pages we outline the 'rules of the game' (the 'exam guide') – the details of how examination questions are set and marked, and how they should be answered. At the end of the book is a section which provides you with revision lists – lists of exactly what you need to cover for each subsection in order to be fully prepared to answer all likely questions in the examination.

> Please note that there have been some minor specification changes since the first edition of the *A2 Complete Companion* (see http://www.aqa.org.uk/equal/gcease/psya.html for the latest version of the AQA A specification). We have incorporated these changes into this exam companion which means there are some small discrepancies between this book and the *A2 Complete Companion*. The changes relate to exams from January 2006 onwards.

EXAM GUIDE

The A2 specification

The A2 specification, unlike the AS specification, is not entirely compulsory. You are offered some choice of what you can study.

Unit 4 (PYA4)

This unit contains five *sections*: Social Psychology, Physiological Psychology, Cognitive Psychology, Developmental Psychology and Comparative Psychology.

Each section is broken down into three *subsections*. Social Psychology, for example, is divided into Social Cognition, Relationships, and Pro- and Anti-social Behaviour.

You may study all three subsections from Social Psychology or may not study any of them! There are just two requirements regarding the subsections you study for Unit 4:

1. You must study a minimum of three *subsections*. In the exam, you have to answer three questions, and one question is set on every subsection (five sections each with three subsections meaning there are 15 questions in total). You must ensure that you study every topic in your chosen subsection so that you can answer whatever question is set for your subsection. If you study more than three subsections, you will have a choice in the exam.

2. You must study subsections from at least two *sections* of the specification. For example, if you study only three subsections, they cannot all be from Social Psychology, but you could study all three subsections in Social Psychology plus one other subsection. In the exam, you would be able to answer only two Social Psychology questions.

There are five sections to the Unit 4 exam, each divided into three subsections, making a total of 15 subsections. In the exam, one question is set on each subsection. Question 1 is always on social cognition. Question 2 is always on relationships, and so on. For example, if you have studied relationships, cognitive development and animal cognition in class, you should answer questions 2, 10 and 14.

Section A: Social Psychology
1. Social Cognition
2. Relationships
3. Pro- and Anti-social Behaviour

Section B: Physiological Psychology
4. Brain and Behaviour
5. Biological Rhythms, Sleep and Dreaming
6. Motivation and Emotion

Section C: Cognitive Psychology
7. Attention and Pattern Recognition
8. Perceptual Processes and Development
9. Language and Thought

Section D: Developmental Psychology
10. Cognitive Development
11. Social and Personality Development
12. Adulthood

Section E: Comparative Psychology
13. Determinants of Animal Behaviour
14. Animal Cognition
15. Evolutionary Explanations of Human Behaviour

Unit 4: One exam of 1½ hours
30% of your A2 mark
Answer three questions

Unit 5: One exam of 2 hours
40% of your A2 mark
Answer three questions

Unit 6: Coursework
30% of your A2 mark
One piece of coursework, maximum length 2000 words

The specification is divided into:
- Units (e.g. Unit 4)
- Sections (e.g. Social Psychology)
- Subsections (each section being divided into three subsections, e.g. Relationships)
- Each subsection is further divided into three. In this book, we have called these 'divisions', and these divisions are further separated into topics (one double-page spread each).

Unit 5 (PYA5)

This is called the *synoptic paper*. With Unit 5, you have a longer time to answer each question, the questions are worth more marks and the paper contributes more to your overall A-level mark than with Unit 4 questions. Your answers are also marked in terms of how *synoptic* they are. You do not need to worry about making your answers synoptic because the questions will be set to facilitate a synoptic answer – although it helps to be aware of the fact that you will gain credit for demonstrating your psychology-wide knowledge when answering questions on this paper – relating essay content to research methods, issues, debates and/or approaches.

There are three sections in the Unit 5 exam:

Section A: Individual Differences. This is divided into three subsections: Issues in the Classification and Diagnosis of Psychological Abnormality, Psychopathology, and Treating Mental Disorders. In the exam, one question will be set for each subsection, and you have to answer one question. This means you can study just one subsection of Individual Differences.

Section B: Issues and Debates. This is divided into four issues and four debates. In the exam, there will be two questions on issues and two questions on debates. You have to answer one question (either issues or debates). If you only study three issues, you will be able to do one question in the exam. The same applies to debates.

Section C: Approaches. This question is different from the others and is discussed in Chapter 11. You are examined on your general understanding of different approaches in psychology.

What is synopticity, and why is it?

Synopticity refers to providing a broad view of the whole of psychology. As this is an advanced-level qualification, it seems reasonable that, at the end of the course, you should have a sense of what psychology is all about. You will learn, over the A-level course, about why people forget, about methods of stress management and about explanations of obedience, but what do all these bits of psychology have in common?

All these bits have a lot in common. All psychologists use similar research methods, all are concerned with ethical issues in their research, and all are also concerned with problems occurring in research (problems or issues such as gender bias). Psychologists debate topics such as how (or whether) behaviour is determined and whether nature or nurture offers a better account of behaviour in different areas of psychology. You often encounter the same explanations, such as behaviourist and evolutionary approaches. These are all synoptic topics – threads that run across the whole specification.

Unit 6 (PYA6)

Details about designing, conducting, analysing and reporting your coursework are given in Chapter 12 of the A2 textbook.

How the exam questions are written

1. Injunctions

Only injunctions from 'terms used in examination questions' are used, and these indicate when you have to provide 'AO1' and when 'AO2'. These injunctions are described on the right.

Terms used in examination questions

AO1 terms

Describe, outline, explain, define require you to provide descriptive material
Note that, in addition:
Outline involves a summary description only (more breadth than detail/depth)
Define requires you to state what is meant by a particular term

AO2 terms

Evaluate, assess, analyse, to what extent require you to provide AO2 commentary (analysis and/or evaluation)

AO1 and AO2 terms

Discuss, critically consider, compare and contrast require you to both describe (AO1) and evaluate (AO2). This may be done sequentially or concurrently. Questions may instruct you to discuss with reference to particular criteria, for example by the use of the phrase 'in terms of'.

Note that, in addition:

Compare and contrast requires you to demonstrate knowledge and understanding of the stipulated topic areas (AO1) and to consider similarities and/or differences between them (AO2).

An alternative (and equally legitimate) way of answering 'compare and contrast' questions is to demonstrate knowledge and understanding of the similarities and differences between the stipulated topic areas (**AO1**), and to evaluate these similarities and differences (**AO2**).

2. All questions are set from the specification

If the specification says 'social psychological theories of aggression (e.g. social learning theory)', questions cannot say 'Discuss the social learning theory of aggression' because social learning theory is given only as an *example*.

If the specification says 'theories of cognitive development, including Piaget', questions can say 'Discuss Piaget's theory of cognitive development' because Piaget's theory is *included* in the specification.

3. AO1 and AO2 are balanced in every question

12 marks for each in Unit 4
15 marks for each in Unit 5 (except the approaches question)

Critically consider **two or more** explanations of interpersonal attraction. (24 marks)

> In this question, there are 12 AO1 marks and 12 AO2 marks – you should *describe* your explanations and then *evaluate* them.

(a) Describe **one** study relating to media influences on anti-social behaviour. (6 marks)
(b) Discuss explanations of media influences on anti-social behaviour. (18 marks)

> In this question, there are 12 AO1 marks and 12 AO2 marks; part (a) consists of 6 AO1 marks, and part (b) consists of 6 AO1 marks and 12 AO2 marks. (Think: how would this allocation of marks affect the balance of your response?)

(a) Discuss **one** psychological theory of dreams. (12 marks)
(b) Discuss **one** neurobiological theory of dreams. (12 marks)

> In this question, part (a) consists of 6 AO1 marks and 6 AO2 marks. The same is true of part (b).

4. If a quotation is used in a question, there may be a specific instruction for it to be addressed

'Piaget's theory fails to represent the true capabilities of young children.'

Critically consider Piaget's theory of cognitive development, with reference to issues raised in the quotation above. (24 marks)

> If you are asked a question such as the one above, you will lose AO2 marks if you do not address the quotation (your AO2 marks will be limited to a maximum of 8 out of 12 on PYA4 and 9 out of 15 on PYA5). However, the question may be:

Critically consider Piaget's theory of cognitive development, with reference to issues such as those raised in the quotation above. (24 marks)

> In this case there is no requirement to address the quotation. The same is true if there is no mention of the quotation. In such cases, the quotation is there to provide you with ideas about what you might write.
>
> Always read the *question* first. Never answer the quotation.

5. Numbers are specified where appropriate

It is clearer to ask 'Discuss **two** theories of the function of sleep' than 'Discuss theories of the function of sleep' so that you have clear guidance about the number of theories to include to attract the full range of marks.

You might be asked 'Discuss **two or more** theories of the function of sleep', in which case you can achieve maximum marks if you cover only two theories, although you may do more if you wish.

How your examination essays are marked

Your essays are marked using the same assessment objectives as for AS: assessment objective 1 (AO1) and assessment objective 2 (AO2). AO1 is concerned with *description* – assessing your *knowledge and understanding* of psychological principles, perspectives and knowledge. AO2 is concerned with the *analysis and evaluation* of psychological principles, perspectives and knowledge.

The Unit 4 exam questions are marked out of 24 marks – 12 marks for each assessment objective. The Unit 5 exam questions are marked out of 30, with 15 marks for each assessment objective. The marking schemes for both papers are shown below. Although these may look daunting, it is worth remembering that you are likely to achieve a grade A if you perform at the 'slightly limited' level in both AO1 and AO2.

Partial performance

If a question asks for '**two** theories' and you discuss only one, you will be marked out of a maximum of 8 marks on AO1 and 8 marks on AO2 (for Unit 5 this is a maximum of 9 for both assessment objectives).

In practice, this means that if you are asked for two theories, they do not have to be balanced.

Parted questions

In some cases, questions are divided into two or more parts. Part (a) often covers the AO1 content of the question (e.g. 'Describe **one** theory of the function of sleep'), while part (b) covers the AO2 content (e.g. 'Evaluate the theory of the function of sleep that you described in part (a)'). If you present material in part (a) that is not creditworthy there but is relevant to part (b), the examiner will export the material to the appropriate part. However, you must be careful because, if part (b) was 'Evaluate the theory of the function of sleep in terms of research studies', the only material that would be creditworthy in part (b) would be evaluation based on research studies. General evaluation, for example in terms of applications, would not be creditworthy.

Unit 4 (PYA4) Marking allocations

UNIT 4 AO1

Marks	Content	Detail and accuracy	Organisation and structure	Breadth and depth
12–11	Substantial	Accurate and well detailed	Coherent	Substantial evidence of both and balance achieved
10–9	Slightly limited	Accurate and reasonably detailed	Coherent	Evidence of both but imbalanced
8–7	Limited	Generally accurate and reasonably detailed	Reasonably constructed	Increasing evidence of breadth and/or depth
6–5	Basic	Generally accurate, lacks detail	Reasonably constructed	Some evidence of breadth and/or depth
4–3	Rudimentary	Sometimes flawed	Sometimes focused	
2–0	Just discernible	Weak/muddled/inaccurate	Wholly/mainly irrelevant	

UNIT 4 AO2

Evaluation	Selection and elaboration	Use of material
Thorough	Appropriate selection and coherent elaboration	Highly effective
Slightly limited	Appropriate selection and elaboration	Effective
Limited	Reasonable elaboration	Reasonably effective
Basic	Some evidence of elaboration	Restricted
Superficial and rudimentary	No evidence of elaboration	Not effective
Muddled and incomplete	Wholly or mainly irrelevant	

Unit 5 (PYA5) Marking allocations

UNIT 5 AO1

Marks	Content	Detail and accuracy	Organisation and structure	Breadth/depth of content and synoptic possibilities
15–13	Substantial	Accurate and well detailed	Coherent	Substantial evidence of both
12–10	Slightly limited	Accurate and reasonably detailed	Coherent	Evidence of both
9–7	Limited	Generally accurate and reasonably detailed	Reasonably constructed	Evidence of both
6–4	Basic	Lacking detail	Sometimes focused	Little evidence
3–0	Just discernible	Weak/muddled/inaccurate	Wholly/mainly irrelevant	Little or no evidence

UNIT 5 AO2

Evaluation	Selection and elaboration	Use of material and synoptic possibilities
Thorough	Appropriate selection and coherent elaboration	Highly effective
Slightly limited	Appropriate selection and elaboration	Effective
Limited	Reasonable elaboration	Reasonably effective
Basic	Some evidence of elaboration	Restricted
Weak, muddled and incomplete	Wholly or mainly irrelevant	

Unit 5 (PYA5) The approaches question

Marks	Part (a) Content	Accuracy	Engagement	Part (b) and Part (d) Commentary	Use of material	Engagement	Part (c) Commentary	Plausibility	Engagement
6–5	Reasonably thorough	Accurate	Coherent	Reasonably thorough	Effective	Coherent	Reasonably thorough	Appropriate	Coherent
4–3	Limited	Generally accurate	Reasonable	Limited	Reasonably effective	Reasonable	Limited	Reasonably appropriate	Reasonable
2–1	Basic	Sometimes flawed/inaccurate	Muddled	Basic	Restricted	Muddled	Basic	Largely inappropriate	Muddled
0			No engagement			No engagement			No engagement

Writing grade A examination essays

How to produce good AO1 material

Try to provide depth and breadth

If you are asked to 'Discuss research studies related to social psychological theories of aggression', you might describe and evaluate 10 different studies, but in the 15 minutes allocated to AO1 in Unit 4, you would have little time to do more than give the briefest description of these studies. In other words, you would provide lots of *breadth* and little *depth* (detail). It is better to cover fewer studies and therefore more detail for each study. The examiners know how much time you have, and they accept that there must be a trade-off between breadth and depth. The best essays provide evidence of both.

Structure your essay

AO1 is not just about knowledge and understanding but about how well structured your answer is (i.e. how logically you unfold your material in response to the question). Structure is a way to demonstrate a good grasp of a subject (your knowledge and understanding) so it is reasonable to judge AO1 quality in terms of structure as well as depth and breadth of information.

How to write effective AO2 material

Effective use of material

You might be asked a part (b) AO2 question 'To what extent do research studies support the view that the media are responsible for anti-social behaviour?' In this case, you are required to select appropriate research studies and *use this material* (not just describe it) to present an argument that shows that the media are (or are not) responsible for anti-social behaviour. If you only *describe* research studies, your answer will receive a maximum of 4 marks out of 12 for AO2 (6 marks out of 15 in Unit 5).

The AO2 description trap

There are other situations in which candidates feel drawn into *describing* AO2 material rather than using it as part of a sustained critical commentary. You may be answering the question 'Discuss Piaget's theory of cognitive development' and wish to evaluate this by saying 'On the other hand, there are other theories of cognitive development, such as Vygotsky's. Vygotsky proposed that mental abilities ...'. A candidate who simply *describes* alternative theories (or appropriate research evidence) will receive very few marks for AO2 beyond 'rudimentary'.

Coherent elaboration

Coherent elaboration is another criterion used to mark AO2. There is very limited credit for presenting comments such as 'One limitation of this study is that it lacked ecological validity' or 'One strength of this theory is that it can be applied to the real world'. To attract higher marks, you must offer some *elaboration*. In the examples above, the candidate has just *identified* the criticism. What we now need is a justification of the criticism and an explanation of why this is a limitation or strength (see the illustration in the box below).

Identify criticism: *'One limitation of this study was that it lacked ecological validity'*

Justify criticism: *'because other studies conducted in different settings have generally failed to produce the same results'*

Explain criticism: *'which means that you cannot generalise the findings to other settings'*

Identify criticism: *'One strength of this theory is that it can be applied to the real world'*

Justify criticism: *'such as in teaching, where it has led to child-centred education'*

Explain criticism: *'and revolutionised primary school teaching'*.

How to put this together in the exam

There is no doubt that planning helps. In an exam, you should:

1. Look at the question and underline the key words, for example 'Describe and evaluate two explanations of the function of sleep.'

2. Decide on a structure for your answer. This may vary in relation to the question asked, as illustrated in the possible essay plans below. Each answer plan below is based on the notion that 600 words is about right for a 30-minute answer, appropriate for Unit 4.

'Discuss one theory of ...'	'Discuss one theory of ...'	'Discuss two theories of ...'	'Discuss two theories of ...'
AO1: Three paragraphs of 100 words each. In each paragraph, identify a feature of the theory.	AO1: Six paragraphs of 50 words each. In each paragraph, identify a feature of the theory.	Theory 1: AO1: Three paragraphs of 50 words each.	Theory 1: AO1: Four paragraphs of 50 words each.
AO2: Three paragraphs of 100 words each, identifying and explaining three criticisms.	AO2: After each AO1 point, write 50 words of commentary.	AO2: Three paragraphs of 50 words. Theory 2: AO1: Three paragraphs of 50 words each. AO2: Three paragraphs of 50 words	AO2: Four paragraphs of 50 words. Theory 2: AO1: Two paragraphs of 50 words each. AO2: Two paragraphs of 50 words.

AO2 exercise

'Discuss research studies relating to media influence on anti-social behaviour.'

Many studies have been carried out into the effects of the media. One was conducted by Parke et al. in 1977. This looked at a group of delinquent male adolescents living in an institution. A measure was taken of their aggression levels before the study started. One group was shown violent videos and the other group non-violent videos. The researchers found that aggression increased in the first group.

Now what AO2 statements could you provide? Below are a list of useful phrases to 'kick-start' the AO2. Try using some of them to provide appropriate commentary.

'This suggests that ...'
'Therefore we can conclude ...'
'This supports the theory that ...'
'There were flaws in the methodology, for example ...'
'An important ethical consideration is ...'
'Further support comes from ...'
'Another psychologist disagreed, arguing that ...'
'This has important applications in ...'
'One consequence of this is ...'
'The advantage of this study is ...'
'One limitation of this study is ...'
'An alternative explanation could be ...'
'Not everyone reacts the same way ...'
'This has been applied to ...'
'There may be cultural variations ....'
'The study lacked ecological validity because ...'

Being an effective learner and reviser

The layout of this book is designed to show you how to plan examination essay answers. The key lies in identifying the main points to be included in your essay. In order to do this you need a list of possible and probable essay questions for each topic (which have been provided for you in this book) *or* you can use the revision lists at the end of this book. You should then identify an appropriate number of AO1 and AO2 points to use in answering a question (selecting these points from textbooks and class notes). These AO1/AO2 points can be listed as bullet points. The benefit of extracting and listing appropriate points is:

1. You have to *process* the material from your textbook and class notes in order to decide what would be the best points to include. Processing material is one way to make material memorable. You probably have to be selective and decide to leave out certain things so that you have the right amount of AO1/AO2 points for a 30-minute or 40-minute essay question. You may also realise that, in some areas, you don't have enough material and need to look around for more explanations/studies, etc.

2. Reducing information to short bullet points provides *cues* for recall when you have to write an essay in an exam.

How many AO1/AO2 points do you need? Take one bullet point and elaborate this point as if you were writing an essay response. You might find that you can write about 50 words for each bullet point. In a 30-minute answer you should aim for around 600 words (a 40-minute answer would require around 800 words) and therefore can work out that you need 12 bullet points (6 AO1 points and 6 AO2 points). In some cases you may end up with more than 12 points but try to restrict these to ease the burden on your memory.

Revise by recalling the list of points and trying to recall how you might elaborate the points. Check your notes or textbook to see what else you might have included. There you are: all you have to memorise is your key points – each of these will access a rich area of recall in the exam.

What we are suggesting is a précis. A précis is a summary from which one cuts out less important material, leaving the *golden nuggets*.

When you construct your own précis or summary, you will *automatically* remember the material (at least some of it). From this précis, draw up a list of key points.

Why this works

1. Levels of processing theory: you remember things if you *process them*.
2. Cue-dependent recall: reducing the information to short bullet points provides cues for recall.
3. Selects and structures your response in the exam: having a set of bullet points ensures good breadth and depth because you make sure you remember a range of points and can elaborate each of them.

Describe **one** theory of XXX. *(30 marks)*

Rule 1: You need to know one theory in 30 minutes-worth of detail = about six points of AO1 + six points of AO2.*

Describe **two** theories of XXX. *(30 marks)*

Rule 2: You need to know one other theory in 15 minutes-worth of detail = about three points of AO1 + three points of AO2.*

Why? If you are asked a question about two theories and you describe only one theory then you incur *the partial performance penalty*. This means that the maximum AO1 mark that you can get is 8 out of 12 marks and the same for AO2. So your one theory would get you 16 marks at most – if you do know a second theory you only need 8 marks-worth on this second theory (4 marks-worth of AO1 and 4 marks-worth of AO2).

---

* The actual number of points you need is something you need to work out to have sufficient to write a 600 word essay on Unit 4 and an 800 word essay on Unit 5.

How to revise successfully

The revision tables at the end of this book (pages 206–215) list specific skills and topics that need to be revised in each division. Use these as a checklist to monitor your own revision.

- Revise actively: it is important to process information.
- Read lots of accounts: each account is different and helps you to process the information and get new ideas that are more meaningful to you.
- Be 'multisensory': work with the senses best for you – visual diagrams, word lists or even auditory cues (say it out loud).
- Work for realistic intervals: don't kid yourself that 3 hours spent in front of your books is 3 hours of revision.
- Don't gamble on topics: questions are not set to a pattern. Never leave any topic out because it came up last time.
- Revision is a skill: treat revision as a skill like any other.
- Practise with others: discussing essays and notes with others helps you process material.

Beware of the planning fallacy (Kahneman and Tversky, 1979), which states that people continue confidently to make the same plans time after time despite the fact that they know these plans have not succeeded in the past. The lesson for you is to try out some new revision strategies!

Topic 1: Explanations relating to interpersonal attraction

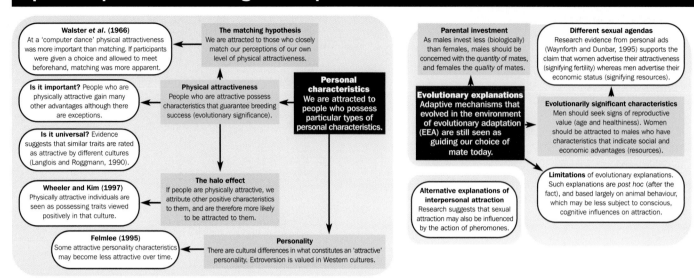

Walster et al. (1966)
At a 'computer dance' physical attractiveness was more important than matching. If participants were given a choice and allowed to meet beforehand, matching was more apparent.

The matching hypothesis
We are attracted to those who closely match our perceptions of our own level of physical attractiveness.

Personal characteristics
We are attracted to people who possess particular types of personal characteristics.

Parental investment
As males invest less (biologically) than females, males should be concerned with the *quantity* of mates, and females the *quality* of mates.

Different sexual agendas
Research evidence from personal ads (Waynforth and Dunbar, 1995) supports the claim that women advertise their attractiveness (signifying fertility) whereas men advertise their economic status (signifying resources).

Is it important? People who are physically attractive gain many other advantages although there are exceptions.

Physical attractiveness
People who are attractive possess characteristics that guarantee breeding success (evolutionary significance).

Evolutionary explanations
Adaptive mechanisms that evolved in the environment of evolutionary adaptation (EEA) are still seen as guiding our choice of mate today.

Evolutionarily significant characteristics
Men should seek signs of reproductive value (age and healthiness). Women should be attracted to males who have characteristics that indicate social and economic advantages (resources).

Is it universal? Evidence suggests that similar traits are rated as attractive by different cultures (Langlois and Roggmann, 1990).

Wheeler and Kim (1997)
Physically attractive individuals are seen as possessing traits viewed positively in that culture.

The halo effect
If people are physically attractive, we attribute other positive characteristics to them, and are therefore more likely to be attracted to them.

Alternative explanations of interpersonal attraction
Research suggests that sexual attraction may also be influenced by the action of pheromones.

Limitations of evolutionary explanations. Such explanations are *post hoc* (after the fact), and based largely on animal behaviour, which may be less subject to conscious, cognitive influences on attraction.

Felmlee (1995)
Some attractive personality characteristics may become less attractive over time.

Personality
There are cultural differences in what constitutes an 'attractive' personality. Extroversion is valued in Western cultures.

Topic 2: Explanations relating to the formation/maintenance of relationships

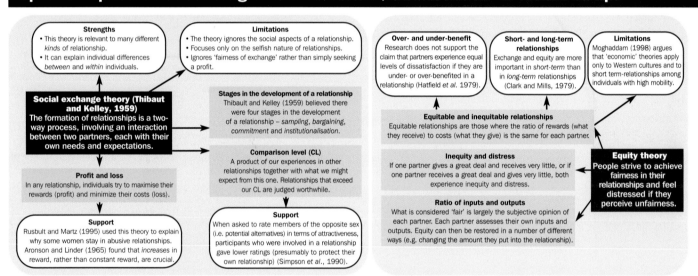

Strengths
• This theory is relevant to many different *kinds* of relationship.
• It can explain individual differences *between* and *within* individuals.

Limitations
• The theory ignores the social aspects of a relationship.
• Focuses only on the selfish nature of relationships.
• Ignores 'fairness of exchange' rather than simply seeking a profit.

Over- and under-benefit
Research does not support the claim that partners experience equal levels of dissatisfaction if they are under- or over-benefited in a relationship (Hatfield *et al.* 1979).

Short- and long-term relationships
Exchange and equity are more important in *short-term* than in *long-term* relationships (Clark and Mills, 1979).

Limitations
Moghaddam (1998) argues that 'economic' theories apply only to Western cultures and to short term-relationships among individuals with high mobility.

Social exchange theory (Thibaut and Kelley, 1959)
The formation of relationships is a two-way process, involving an interaction between two partners, each with their own needs and expectations.

Stages in the development of a relationship
Thibault and Kelley (1959) believed there were four stages in the development of a relationship – *sampling, bargaining, commitment* and *institutionalisation*.

Equitable and inequitable relationships
Equitable relationships are those where the ratio of rewards (what they receive) to costs (what they give) is the same for each partner.

Profit and loss
In any relationship, individuals try to maximise their rewards (profit) and minimize their costs (loss).

Comparison level (CL)
A product of our experiences in other relationships together with what we might expect from this one. Relationships that exceed our CL are judged worthwhile.

Inequity and distress
If one partner gives a great deal and receives very little, or if one partner receives a great deal and gives very little, both experience inequity and distress.

Equity theory
People strive to achieve fairness in their relationships and feel distressed if they perceive unfairness.

Support
Rusbult and Martz (1995) used this theory to explain why some women stay in abusive relationships. Aronson and Linder (1965) found that *increases* in reward, rather than constant reward, are crucial.

Support
When asked to rate members of the opposite sex (i.e. potential alternatives) in terms of attractiveness, participants who were involved in a relationship gave lower ratings (presumably to protect their own relationship) (Simpson *et al.*, 1990).

Ratio of inputs and outputs
What is considered 'fair' is largely the subjective opinion of each partner. Each partner assesses their own inputs and outputs. Equity can then be restored in a number of different ways (e.g. changing the amount they put into the relationship).

Topic 3: Research studies relating to interpersonal attraction

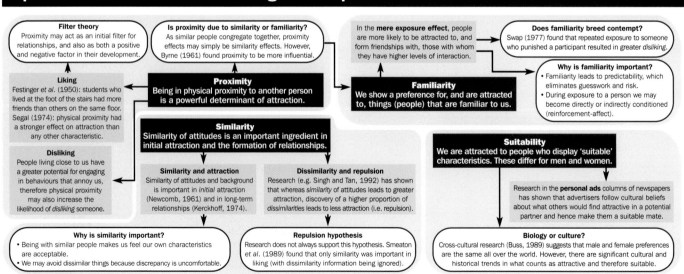

Filter theory
Proximity may act as an initial filter for relationships, and also as both a positive and negative factor in their development.

Is proximity due to similarity or familiarity?
As similar people congregate together, proximity effects may simply be similarity effects. However, Byrne (1961) found proximity to be more influential.

In the **mere exposure effect**, people are more likely to be attracted to, and form friendships with, those with whom they have higher levels of interaction.

Does familiarity breed contempt?
Swap (1977) found that repeated exposure to someone who punished a participant resulted in greater *disliking*.

Liking
Festinger *et al.* (1950): students who lived at the foot of the stairs had more friends than others on the same floor. Segal (1974): physical proximity had a stronger effect on attraction than any other characteristic.

Proximity
Being in physical proximity to another person is a powerful determinant of attraction.

Familiarity
We show a preference for, and are attracted to, things (people) that are familiar to us.

Why is familiarity important?
• Familiarity leads to predictability, which eliminates guesswork and risk.
• During exposure to a person we may become directly or indirectly conditioned (reinforcement-affect).

Disliking
People living close to us have a greater potential for engaging in behaviours that annoy us, therefore physical proximity may also increase the likelihood of *disliking* someone.

Similarity
Similarity of attitudes is an important ingredient in initial attraction and the formation of relationships.

Suitability
We are attracted to people who display 'suitable' characteristics. These differ for men and women.

Similarity and attraction
Similarity of attitudes and background is important in *initial* attraction (Newcomb, 1961) and in long-term relationships (Kerckhoff, 1974).

Dissimilarity and repulsion
Research (e.g. Singh and Tan, 1992) has shown that whereas *similarity* of attitudes leads to greater attraction, discovery of a higher proportion of *dissimilarities* leads to less attraction (i.e. repulsion).

Research in the **personal ads** columns of newspapers has shown that advertisers follow cultural beliefs about what others would find attractive in a potential partner and hence make them a suitable mate.

Why is similarity important?
• Being with similar people makes us feel our own characteristics are acceptable.
• We may avoid dissimilar things because discrepancy is uncomfortable.

Repulsion hypothesis
Research does not always support this hypothesis. Smeaton *et al.* (1989) found that only similarity was important in liking (with dissimilarity information being ignored).

Biology or culture?
Cross-cultural research (Buss, 1989) suggests that male and female preferences are the same all over the world. However, there are significant cultural and historical trends in what counts as attractive and therefore suitable.

(e.g. evolutionary explanations, matching hypothesis)

Probable questions

1. Describe and evaluate **one or more** explanations of interpersonal attraction. *(24 marks)*

2. Discuss psychological research (explanations **and/or** studies) into interpersonal attraction. *(24 marks)*

Possible questions

3. Outline and evaluate **two** explanations of interpersonal attraction. *(24 marks)*

When asked for 'one or more' you can gain maximum marks by discussing only one explanation. If you feel you do not know enough for a 30 minute answer on one explanation then there is credit for discussing other explanations. However, the more explanations you cover, the less detail you can include and detail is important for AO1 skills.

You could provide the same answer to question 2 as you did for question 1 because explanations are a legitimate way to answer this question. Alternatively you might focus solely on studies (see Topic 3) or you might present 'cut down versions' of explanations and studies (15 minutes on each).

If you only write about one explanation then your answer would be marked out of 16 marks rather than the full 24 because of 'partially performing'. If you wrote about more than two explanations then only the best two would be credited. There are no marks for additional explanations *unless* these are used as *effective* and *sustained* critical commentary.

(e.g. reward/need satisfaction, social exchange theory)

Probable questions

1. Outline and evaluate **two** theories of the formation **and/or** maintenance of relationships. *(24 marks)*

2. Outline and evaluate **two or more** theories of the formation **and/or** maintenance of relationships. *(24 marks)*

Possible questions

3. Describe and evaluate **one** theory of the formation **and/or** maintenance of relationships. *(24 marks)*

When a question requires 'two' theories, then discussion of one theory results in a partial performance penalty. The same applies to a question that requires 'two or more' theories – there would be a partial performance penalty for only one theory. But this time you would get credit for describing a third theory. 'Two or more' is used to reassure you that 'two' would be fine but you can provide more if you haven't got enough to write. The danger in writing about more than two theories is that you provide very little *depth* (detail or elaboration) for any of them. Always try to balance the depth and breadth.

In all the questions you are offered the choice of writing about theories of formation **or** maintenance **or** both. Some theories, such as social exchange theory, span both formation and maintenance.

It is less likely that the question will restrict you to just one theory but you do always need to be prepared for this possibility – and have one theory in a 30 minute version.

Probable questions

1. Describe and evaluate research studies into interpersonal attraction. *(24 marks)*

2. (a) Outline **two** explanations of interpersonal attraction. *(12 marks)*

   (b) Evaluate the **two** explanations of interpersonal attraction that you outlined in (a) in terms of relevant research studies. *(12 marks)*

Possible questions

3. (a) Outline and evaluate **one or more** explanations of interpersonal attraction. *(12 marks)*

   (b) Outline and evaluate research studies relating to interpersonal attraction. *(12 marks)*

The specification entry for interpersonal attraction refers to both explanations and research studies, thus questions may be set on either of these. In topic 1 you focused on explanations, here the focus is on research studies.

Question 1 is a straightforward question about research studies. Beware of the depth-breadth trade-off if you try to cover too many research studies. Top marks are awarded for breadth **and** depth (i.e. providing details of the studies). If you try to include too many studies (breadth) you will not have time for sufficient depth.

In such an essay you can use explanations as a form of commentary ('The implications of this study are that …'). However *descriptions* of an explanation would not attract credit.

A similar point applies to question 2. Here you have to describe explanations for AO1 and then are required to use research studies for commentary. *Descriptions* of research studies would not be creditworthy.

This question has an uncommon mark split with 6 AO1 marks and 6 AO2 marks for part (a). You are offered the opportunity to write about more than one explanation but if you do write about two that would leave you about 3 minutes to describe it and 3 minutes to evaluate it – not really enough time to get going. Better to display the depth of your understanding by focusing on one explanation only even if you know two explanations and want to impress the examiner!

Part (b) is also 6 AO1 + 6 AO2 marks but here you must cover at least two research studies (because 'studies' is in the plural).

TOPIC 1: EXPLANATIONS RELATING TO INTERPERSONAL ATTRACTION

SAMPLE ESSAY PLAN

Question 1: Describe and evaluate **one or more** explanations of interpersonal attraction. (24 marks)

EXPLANATION: PERSONAL CHARACTERISTICS

15 MINUTES WORTH OF AO1

- **PERSONAL CHARACTERISTIC (1):** People are attracted to those who are **physically attractive**.
- Physical attractiveness leads to a **positive stereotype** (**halo effect**).
- Expect physically attractive people to be sexually warmer, more socially skilled (**Feingold**, 1992).
- Important in **initial attraction** because of **evolutionary significance** → physical attractiveness signals **breeding success**.
- Men have a virtually infinite reproductive capacity and therefore seek **quantity in mating**. This is maximised with mates high in **fertility**. Indicators of fertility are age and healthiness, indicated by physical appearance (*e.g.* smooth skin, white teeth).
- May be attracted to physically attractive mates but compromise → **matching hypothesis** (**Walster et al.**, 1966).
- **PERSONAL CHARACTERISTIC (2):** an attractive **personality**.
- For example **extroversion** (**Duck**, 1999), warmth and competence (**Rubin**, 1973).
- These traits important in **initial attraction**, interaction between personalities important later.

15 MINUTES WORTH OF AO2

- Physically attractive people are **treated better** (positive stereotype) *e.g.* lighter criminal sentences (**Stewart**, 1980), better essay grades (**Landy and Sigall**, 1974).
- **Not always true** *e.g.* attractive women judged as materialistic (**Dermer and Thiel**, 1975), attractive female criminals get longer sentences (**Sigall and Ostrove**, 1975).
- **Universal support** for halo effect: physically attractive people seen as *e.g.* more extrovert, friendly, mature (**Wheeler and Kim**, 1997).
- **Evolutionary explanations** supported by personal ads (**Waynforth and Dunbar**, 1995), twice as many males than females seek youthful, physically attractive partners.
- **Universal agreement** about physical attractiveness *e.g.* large eyes, small nose and chin (**Cunningham**, 1986), supports evolutionary view.
- However, this may be explained by **baby face hypothesis** (attractiveness ensures we care for young).
- **Matching hypothesis**: physical attractiveness rather than matching at computer dance (**Walster et al.**, 1966) but no choice involved and short-term. When these factors changed there was matching (**Walster and Walster**, 1969).
- **Personality traits**: predictability may be attractive at start but later becomes boring.

Question 3: Outline and evaluate **two** explanations of interpersonal attraction. (24 marks)

EXPLANATION 1: PERSONAL CHARACTERISTICS

7½ MINUTES WORTH OF AO1

- People are attracted to those who are **physically attractive**.
- Physical attractiveness leads to a **positive stereotype** (**halo effect**).
- Expect physically attractive people to be sexually warmer, more socially skilled (**Feingold**, 1992).
- Important in **initial attraction** because of **evolutionary significance** → physical attractiveness signals **breeding success**.
- May be attracted to physically attractive mates but compromise → **matching hypothesis** (**Walster et al.**, 1966)

7½ MINUTES WORTH OF AO2

- Physically attractive people are **treated better** (positive stereotype) *e.g.* lighter criminal sentences (**Stewart**, 1980).
- **Not always true** *e.g.* attractive female criminals get longer sentences (**Sigall and Ostrove**, 1975).
- **Universal agreement** about physical attractiveness *e.g.* large eyes, small nose and chin (**Cunningham**, 1986), supports evolutionary view.
- However, this may be explained by **baby face** hypothesis (attractiveness ensures we care for young).
- **Matching hypothesis**: physical attractiveness rather than matching at computer dance (**Walster et al.**, 1966) but no choice involved and short-term. When these factors changed there was matching (**Walster and Walster**, 1969).

EXPLANATION 2: EVOLUTIONARY EXPLANATIONS

7½ MINUTES WORTH OF AO1

- Women have **limited reproductive opportunities** therefore attracted to men who can provide resources.
- Men have a virtually **infinite reproductive capacity** therefore seek **quantity in mating**. This is maximised with mates high in fertility. Indicators of fertility are age and healthiness, indicated by physical appearance (*e.g.* smooth skin, white teeth).
- Men also seek **sexual faithfulness** to be sure children are their own.

7½ MINUTES WORTH OF AO2

- **Evolutionary explanations** supported by personal ads. Women advertise attractiveness, men advertise resources (**Waynforth and Dunbar**, 1995).
- About 40% of **males seek youthful, physically attractive** partners, compared to 20% of women.
- Men showed greater physiological distress when asked to imagine scenes of sexual infidelity (**Buss et al.**, 1992).
- Evolutionary explanations **based on animal behaviour** may not apply to behaviour which is controlled by conscious factors.

An important aspect in interpersonal attraction is the possession of personal characteristics that are perceived as attractive to the observer. In particular, people are attracted to those who are physically attractive. In turn, physical attractiveness leads to a positive stereotype (halo effect), with physically attractive people being seen as being sexually warmer and more socially skilled (Feingold, 1992). Physical attractiveness, therefore, is seen as an important mediating factor in the initial stages of relationship formation. Although we may be attracted to physically attractive mates there is often a need to compromise, with the matching hypothesis (Walster et al., 1966) proposing that we are attracted to those who closely match our perceptions of our own level of attractiveness.

By mixing general statements about physical attractiveness with research studies, this adds authority to your answer, and prevents it appearing too subjective or anecdotal.

Physical attractiveness is therefore seen as important because physically attractive people gain many advantages based on this positive stereotype. Research has shown that physically attractive people receive lighter criminal sentences (Stewart, 1980), better essay grades (Landy and Sigall, 1974), and are generally seen as being nicer and happier by others (Hunsberger and Cavanagh, 1988). However, it is not always true that physically attractive people are perceived more favourably by others, e.g. attractive women are judged as materialistic (Dermer and Thiel, 1975) and attractive female criminals receive longer prison sentences (Sigall and Ostrove, 1975). There is, however, universal support for the halo effect, in that physically attractive people are seen as more extrovert, friendly and mature across a range of different cultures (Wheeler and Kim, 1997). In an investigation of the matching hypothesis, physical attractiveness appeared to be more important than matching at a computer dance (Walster et al., 1966) but no choice was involved in the selection of a partner and the study concerned short-term relationships. However, when participants were given some choice and allowed to meet beforehand, matching was apparent (Walster and Walster, 1969).

When research studies are used as AO2 all that is needed is to indicate what the study tells us; a description of the study is not relevant to commentary.

Physical attractiveness is also important in initial attraction because of its evolutionary significance, with physical attractiveness signalling potential breeding success. Men have a virtually infinite reproductive capacity therefore seek quantity in mating. This is maximised with mates high in reproductive value, i.e. fertility. Indicators of fertility are age and healthiness, both indicated by physical appearance (e.g. smooth skin, white teeth). In contrast, women should be attracted to men who have characteristics that indicate social and economic advantages. Both sexes are interested in evidence of good genetic quality in order to ensure that any offspring will survive. Youthfulness can be an indicator of robust genes. Symmetry also requires robust genes to be maintained, which may explain why symmetry is so important in attractiveness.

There are a number of evolutionary claims here and each has been sufficiently explained to ensure that enough detail is present for a higher mark.

Evolutionary explanations of physical attraction are supported by research into personal ads (Waynforth and Dunbar, 1995). This research showed that twice as many males as females seek youthful, physically attractive partners. Research has also shown universal agreement about physical attractiveness, e.g. large eyes, small nose and chin (Cunningham, 1986). This appears to support the evolutionary explanation of physical attractiveness, but the reason for this universal agreement may not be that such features indicate fertility. The baby face hypothesis provides an alternative explanation, that adults may have evolved a preference for 'baby' features because this ensures that we care for our young, and for this reason such features elicit feelings of attraction.

Note the use of 'AO2 language' ('…appears to support…', '…provides an alternative explanation…') which makes the critical commentary more obvious to an examiner.

A second personal characteristic found to be important in interpersonal attraction is personality. Some types of personality are viewed as more attractive than others within Western cultures. Extroversion is regarded more favourably than introversion because our society values sociability more than shyness (Duck, 1999). Similarly, people who are perceived as warm and competent are liked more than others (Rubin, 1973). These general traits only seem to be important in initial attraction, with individuals gradually becoming more concerned with what their partner is really like, and whether their personalities mesh together in a mutually acceptable way.

Although personality may be important in the initial stages of attraction, attractive personality traits may become less so over time, for example predictability may be attractive at the beginning of a relationship, but later becomes unattractive because it is boring (Felmlee, 1995).

It doesn't matter if there is imbalance between the different paragraph lengths, provided that an overall balance between AO1 and AO2 is apparent.

TOPIC 2: EXPLANATIONS RELATING TO THE FORMATION/MAINTENANCE OF RELATIONSHIPS

SAMPLE ESSAY PLAN

Question 1: Outline and evaluate **two** theories of the formation **and/or** maintenance of relationships. (24 marks)

THEORY 1: SOCIAL EXCHANGE THEORY (THIBAUT AND KELLEY, 1959)	7½ MINUTES WORTH OF AO1	7½ MINUTES WORTH OF AO2
	• **Interaction** between two partners. • **Profit and loss** calculated on basis of rewards and costs. • **Rewards** e.g. companionship, sex. • **Costs** e.g. effort, financial investment. • **Comparison level**: judge current relationship against other experiences. **Satisfaction** based on profit relative to expectations. • **Stages** in development of relationship: sampling, bargaining, commitment, institutionalisation.	• People involved in relationships give lower ratings to alternatives, presumably to improve **comparison level** (**Simpson et al.,** 1990). • But people leave relationships without an alternative – not predicted by comparison levels. • **Strengths**: relevant to different kinds of relationship, accounts for individual differences (personally relevant profits and losses). • **Limitations**: a selfish theory and individualist-bias, ignores fairness (as in **equity theory**).
THEORY 2: REINFORCEMENT-AFFECT (BYRNE AND CLORE, 1970)	7½ MINUTES WORTH OF AO1	7½ MINUTES WORTH OF AO2
	• Focuses on **rewards only** not interaction. • Reinforcement: people like people who are directly rewarding (**operant conditioning**). • People associated with rewards become likeable (**classical conditioning**). • **Rewarding** stimuli lead to positive affect, **punishing** stimuli lead to negative affect. • **Balance of positive and negative feelings** crucial to relationship formation.	• **Direct reinforcement**: participants (Ps) gave highest evaluations to experimenters who rated them most highly (**Griffit and Guay,** 1969). • **Association** with pleasant events: in same experiment, an onlooker was rated more highly by P when experimenter was most positive. • **Lab studies** may not reflect real-life relationship formation. • **Hays** (1985): reinforcement-affect only explores being liked by others, whereas we gain satisfaction from giving as well as receiving. • **Lott** (1974): in many cultures women are more focused on the needs of others rather than receiving reinforcement.

Question 3: Describe and evaluate **one** theory of the formation **and/or** maintenance of relationships. (24 marks)

THEORY 1: SOCIAL EXCHANGE THEORY (THIBAUT AND KELLEY, 1959)	15 MINUTES WORTH OF AO1	15 MINUTES WORTH OF AO2
	• **Interaction** between two partners. • **Profit and loss** calculated on basis of rewards and costs. • **Rewards** e.g. companionship, sex. • **Costs** e.g. effort, financial investment. • **Comparison level**: judge current relationship against other experiences. • **Satisfaction** based on profit relative to expectations. • **Stages** in development of relationship: • **Sampling**: consider potential rewards and costs and compare with other relationships; • **Bargaining**: give and receive rewards, test the future of the relationship; • **Commitment**: learn how to elicit rewards thus minimise costs; • **Institutionalisation**: relationship norms develop – patterns of rewards and costs.	• Profit vs loss can explain acceptance of **abusive relationships** (**Rusbult and Martz,** 1995). • May be that **increases** in rewards are more important than profit vs loss (**Aronson,** 1999). • People involved in relationships give lower ratings to alternatives, presumably to improve **comparison level** (**Simpson et al.,** 1990). • But people leave relationships without an alternative – not predicted by comparison levels. **Strengths:** • Relevant to **different kinds of relationship**. • Accounts for **individual differences** (personally relevant profits and losses). **Limitations:** • Ignores **social aspects** of relationship (e.g. roles). • A 'selfish' theory and **individualist**-bias. • Ignores fairness – **equity theory** suggests that receiving too little also creates distress.

Social exchange theory (Thibaut and Kelley, 1959) acknowledges that the formation of relationships is not a one-way process, but involves an interaction between two partners, each with their own needs and expectations. At the centre of this theory is the belief that all social behaviour is a series of exchanges, with individuals attempting to maximise their rewards and minimise their costs. Possible rewards from a relationship include being cared for, companionship and sex. Potential costs include effort, financial investment and missed opportunities with others. Rewards minus costs equals the outcome of the relationship, i.e. a profit or a loss. Thibaut and Kelley also introduced the concept of a comparison level, a standard against which all our relationships are judged. We judge our current relationship against previous experiences. Satisfaction is based on profit relative to expectations. Thibaut and Kelley believed that individuals went through four stages in the development of a relationship, from sampling, where people consider the costs and benefits of a new relationship, through to institutionalisation, where norms are developed which establish the patterns of rewards and costs for each partner.

Research has indeed shown that people involved in relationships give lower ratings to alternatives, presumably to improve the comparison level for their current relationship (Simpson et al., 1990). However, some people leave their current relationships without an alternative, something that would not be predicted by the notion of comparison levels. The main strengths of social exchange theory are that it is relevant to many different kinds of relationship, and can account for individual differences (i.e. personally relevant profits and losses). The main limitation of this theory is that it sees human relationships as being fundamentally selfish, suggesting that people's main interest in maintaining relationships is determined only by selfish concerns. It is also possible that such principles apply only in individualist cultures, where individuals are encouraged to become more self-focused rather than other-focused, as in collectivist cultures. The theory has also been criticised for ignoring 'fairness' in exchange, and overemphasising the profit-seeking nature of human relationships.

The reinforcement-affect model (Byrne and Clore, 1970) focuses on the ability of other people to reward (or punish) us directly (operant conditioning) or to become associated with reward or punishment (classical conditioning). In the reinforcement part of this model, some people are directly rewarding in that they produce positive feelings in us, in turn making us more likely to positively evaluate that person. We like people who are the source of a pleasant event and we also like people who are associated with a pleasant event. A previously neutral stimulus (a person we may not previously have met) can become positively valued because we meet them when we are in a happy (i.e. positive) mood. Byrne and Clore also believed that the balance of positive and negative feelings was crucial to relationship formation. Relationships in which the positive feelings outweighed the negative ones were more likely to develop and succeed, whereas relationships in which the negative feelings outweighed the positive were likely to fail.

Research has supported many of the claims of this model. On the role of direct reinforcement, Griffit and Guay (1969) found that participants gave the highest evaluations to experimenters who had given a positive evaluation of the participant's performance. The principle of liking through association was also supported in this study, as an onlooker was also rated more highly when the experimenter had given a positive evaluation of the participant's performance. Like many other studies used to support this model, this study was carried out in a laboratory, and may not necessarily show that the reinforcement-affect model applies to real life relationship formation. Hays (1985) criticises the reinforcement-affect model as focusing only on being liked by others, whereas we gain satisfaction from giving as well as receiving, particularly in the context of family relationships, which are rarely based on rewards. Lott (1994) suggests that in many cultures, women focus more on the needs of others than on receiving reinforcement.

It is easy to become tongue-tied when trying to explain this theory in an exam. It pays to practise summarising its main points, whilst maintaining some degree of detail in your answer.

Don't try to include all the stages if you are running out of time, just an extract as given here would be sufficient.

There are five points being made here. This would be the maximum number of AO2 points for a question such as this (where you have to discuss two theories). Any more would result in a lack of elaboration, and so fewer marks.

This is a lengthy model to explain at the best of times. In an outline of about 150–160 words you need to be concise, and decide what best serves the purpose of outlining the main assumptions of the model.

Each critical point is elaborated. For example, rather than just stating that the study was carried out in a lab, the consequences of this are identified. This helps to make a criticism effective.

TOPIC 3: RESEARCH STUDIES ON INTERPERSONAL ATTRACTION

SAMPLE ESSAY PLAN

Question 1: Describe and evaluate research studies into interpersonal attraction. (24 marks)

RESEARCH STUDIES INTO INTERPERSONAL ATTRACTION

15 MINUTES WORTH OF AO1

Proximity increases liking.
- **Festinger et al.** (1950): students at foot of stairs had more friends.
- **Segal** (1974): people who sat next to each other in class were more likely to form friendships.
- **Proximity** increases disliking.
- **Ebbesen et al.** (1976): if a neighbour is objectionable then proximity leads to disliking.

Similarity:
- **Newcomb** (1961): male undergraduates studied over several months, relationships developed among those who shared similar attitudes.
- **Kerckhoff** (1974): married partners typically come from similar backgrounds.
- **Drigotas** (1993): after initial attraction, the discovery of dissimilarities leads to reduced attraction (**dissimilarity-repulsion hypothesis**).

Familiarity (mere exposure effect):
- **Yinon et al.** (1977): students who had more interactions (shared facilities) formed friendships.
- **Mita et al.** (1977): Ps preferred mirror-image photos (more familiar) whereas friends preferred normal photograph.

15 MINUTES WORTH OF AO2
- **Proximity** can be explained in terms of **filter theory** – it's an initial filter but people don't form friends with everyone in near proximity.
- **May be similarity** rather than proximity (people in proximity are also similar) but **Byrne** (1961) found those seated in centre of room became more popular, therefore proximity.
- **Similarity** important because it validates our own beliefs, dissimilarity challenges our beliefs and leads to discomfort.
- **Dissimilarity** may be the driving force in attraction (**Rosenbaum**, 1986). Not supported by studies that found that variation in similar views rather than dissimilar views was more important (**Smeaton et al.**, 1989).
- But similarity may threaten one's need for uniqueness and individuality (**Snyder and Fromkin**, 1980).
- **Familiarity** may lead to liking because we like things that are predictable.
- **Familiarity** may lead to **rewarding** experiences (**reinforcement-affect model**) which increase liking.
- **Familiarity may breed contempt** – **Swap** (1977) found repeated exposure to someone who punished a Ps led to greater disliking.
- **Saegart et al.** (1973) – frequency of meeting more important in determining attraction than whether associated experience was pleasant or unpleasant.

Question 3: (a) Outline and evaluate **one or more** explanations of interpersonal attraction. (12 marks)
(b) Outline and evaluate research studies relating to interpersonal attraction. (12 marks)

(a)

7½ MINUTES WORTH OF AO1
- One explanation from topic 1.

7½ MINUTES WORTH OF AO2
- The same commentary.

(b)

7½ MINUTES WORTH OF AO1

Proximity increases liking.
- **Festinger et al.** (1950): students at foot of stairs had more friends.
- **Segal** (1974): people who sat next to each other in class were more likely to form friendships.

Similarity:
- **Newcomb** (1961): male undergraduates studied over several months, relationships developed among those who shared similar attitudes.
- **Drigotas** (1993): after initial attraction, the discovery of dissimilarities leads to reduced attraction (**dissimilarity-repulsion hypothesis**).

7½ MINUTES WORTH OF AO2
- **Proximity** can be explained in terms of **filter theory** – it's an initial filter but people don't form friends with everyone in near proximity.
- **May be similarity** rather than proximity (people in proximity are also similar) but **Byrne** (1961) found those seated in centre of room became more popular, therefore proximity.
- **Similarity** important because it validates our own beliefs, dissimilarity challenges our beliefs and leads to discomfort.
- But similarity may threaten one's need for uniqueness and individuality (**Snyder and Fromkin**, 1980).

Research has generally shown that proximity increases liking, particularly in the development of friendships. Festinger et al. (1950) studied students in a university housing complex, and found that students at the foot of the stairs (where they would interact more with people from other floors) had more friends than others on the same floor. Segal (1974) showed that physical proximity had a stronger effect on short-term attraction than any other characteristic, finding that people who sat next to each other in class were more likely to form friendships. Proximity has also been found to increase disliking as those who live close by have a greater potential to annoy us. Ebbesen et al. (1976) found that if a neighbour is objectionable then proximity leads to disliking.

Why proximity is so important in attraction can be explained in terms of filter theory. Proximity may act as an initial filter which, as shown in the Ebbesen et al. study, can be both a negative as well as a positive factor. Research suggests that proximity is a powerful determinant of liking, but an alternative interpretation of this finding is that it may be similarity rather than proximity that determines liking as similar people tend to congregate in the same place. However, when Byrne (1961) manipulated seating arrangements in a classroom, he found that those seated in the centre of the room became more popular, therefore proximity appeared to be the main determinant of others' attraction towards them.

Newcomb (1961) studied friendships among male undergraduates over a period of several months, and found that friendships were more likely to form between those who had similar attitudes. Kerckhoff (1974) discovered that married partners typically come from the same social, economic and religious groups and have the same intelligence and educational backgrounds. Drigotas (1993) found evidence for a dissimilarity-repulsion hypothesis in that after initial attraction based on similarity of attitudes, student participants who discovered more dissimilarities than similarities became less attracted to each other.

One possible interpretation of the finding that similarity is important in attraction is that it serves to validate our own beliefs, making us feel that our own characteristics are acceptable and our beliefs right. In the same way, we may avoid people who are dissimilar because dissimilarity is uncomfortable and challenges our beliefs. Contrary to research that has found that similarity is important in attraction, some psychologists believe that dissimilarity is the driving force in initial attraction (Rosenbaum). However, research where the number of dissimilar views between a participant and a hypothetical stranger were kept constant and the number of similar views varied showed that similarity was more important in influencing attraction (Smeaton et al., 1989). It is, however, possible that similarity may threaten one's need for uniqueness and individuality (Snyder and Fromkin, 1980) – positive characteristics in Western cultures – therefore making dissimilar others more attractive.

Research has also suggested that people may simply prefer things that are familiar, therefore we like things which we have had greater exposure to and are attracted to people who are more familiar to us. Yinon et al. (1977) tested this 'mere exposure effect' in a study of student residences and found that those students who had more interactions based on their living arrangements (i.e. they shared facilities) were more likely to form friendships with others in the same residential unit. Mita et al. (1977) tested the relationship between familiarity and liking, finding that participants preferred mirror-image photos of themselves (they were more familiar with this view of themselves) whereas friends preferred the normal photograph of the person for the same reason.

It is possible that familiarity leads to liking because we like things that are predictable. Familiarity may also lead to more rewarding experiences (reinforcement-affect model) which increase liking. However, familiarity may not lead to increased liking but may breed contempt for the other person, a suggestion supported by research by Swap (1977), who found repeated exposure to someone who punished a participant led to greater disliking. This was not, however, the conclusion reached by Saegart et al. (1973), who found that when participants were asked to rate the taste of drinks, the frequency of meeting other participants was more important in determining attraction than whether associated experience (the taste of the drink) was pleasant or unpleasant.

Although you are not *required* to give names of researchers, doing so, as here, does add an air of authority to your answer, and makes it sound less subjective and anecdotal.

You need to be careful when introducing other research as part of your AO2. It needs to be built into a sustained critical commentary rather than being simply extra descriptive detail.

Note that there is just enough information in each of these studies to warrant a description of 'detailed' in the AO1 marking scheme.

One way to ensure sufficient elaboration when engaging in AO2 commentary is to state your critical point, then *say something else* as a comment on the comment. Think of each point as either two sentences or a sentence with two parts.

It is okay to include some contextual detail in your AO2 material to introduce a research study.

In the textbook, four different areas are covered. In this answer we have only covered three. You should always aim for a balance of breadth *and* depth rather than trying to cram everything you know in to your answer.

Topic 1: Psychological explanations of love

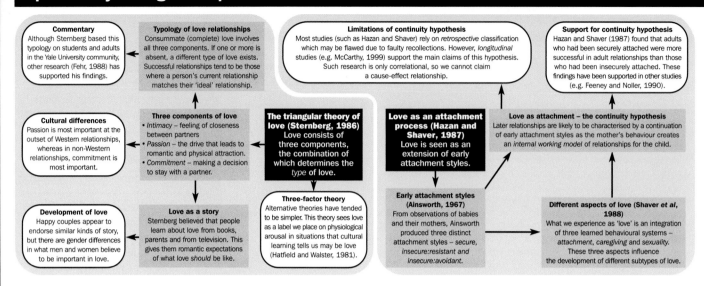

Commentary
Although Sternberg based this typology on students and adults in the Yale University community, other research (Fehr, 1988) has supported his findings.

Typology of love relationships
Consummate (complete) love involves all three components. If one or more is absent, a different type of love exists. Successful relationships tend to be those where a person's current relationship matches their 'ideal' relationship.

Limitations of continuity hypothesis
Most studies (such as Hazan and Shaver) rely on *retrospective* classification which may be flawed due to faulty recollections. However, *longitudinal* studies (e.g. McCarthy, 1999) support the main claims of this hypothesis. Such research is only correlational, so we cannot claim a cause-effect relationship.

Support for continuity hypothesis
Hazan and Shaver (1987) found that adults who had been securely attached were more successful in adult relationships than those who had been insecurely attached. These findings have been supported in other studies (e.g. Feeney and Noller, 1990).

Cultural differences
Passion is most important at the outset of Western relationships, whereas in non-Western relationships, commitment is most important.

Three components of love
• *Intimacy* – feeling of closeness between partners
• *Passion* – the drive that leads to romantic and physical attraction.
• *Commitment* – making a decision to stay with a partner.

The triangular theory of love (Sternberg, 1986)
Love consists of three components, the combination of which determines the *type* of love.

Love as an attachment process (Hazan and Shaver, 1987)
Love is seen as an extension of early attachment styles.

Love as attachment – the continuity hypothesis
Later relationships are likely to be characterised by a continuation of early attachment styles as the mother's behaviour creates an *internal working model* of relationships for the child.

Development of love
Happy couples appear to endorse similar kinds of story, but there are gender differences in what men and women believe to be important in love.

Love as a story
Sternberg believed that people learn about love from books, parents and from television. This gives them romantic expectations of what love *should* be like.

Three-factor theory
Alternative theories have tended to be simpler. This theory sees love as a label we place on physiological arousal in situations that cultural learning tells us may be love (Hatfield and Walster, 1981).

Early attachment styles (Ainsworth, 1967)
From observations of babies and their mothers, Ainsworth produced three distinct attachment styles – *secure, insecure:resistant* and *insecure:avoidant*.

Different aspects of love (Shaver *et al*, 1988)
What we experience as 'love' is an integration of three learned behavioural systems – *attachment, caregiving* and *sexuality*. These three aspects influence the development of different subtypes of love.

Topic 2: The breakdown of relationships

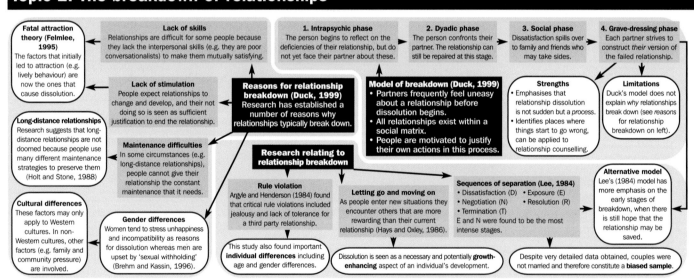

Fatal attraction theory (Felmlee, 1995)
The factors that initially led to attraction (e.g. lively behaviour) are now the ones that cause dissolution.

Lack of skills
Relationships are difficult for some people because they lack the interpersonal skills (e.g. they are poor conversationalists) to make them mutually satisfying.

1. Intrapsychic phase
The person begins to reflect on the deficiencies of their relationship, but do not yet face their partner about these.

2. Dyadic phase
The person confronts their partner. The relationship can still be repaired at this stage.

3. Social phase
Dissatisfaction spills over to family and friends who may take sides.

4. Grave-dressing phase
Each partner strives to construct *their* version of the failed relationship.

Lack of stimulation
People expect relationships to change and develop, and their not doing so is seen as sufficient justification to end the relationship.

Reasons for relationship breakdown (Duck, 1999)
Research has established a number of reasons why relationships typically break down.

Model of breakdown (Duck, 1999)
• Partners frequently feel uneasy about a relationship before dissolution begins.
• All relationships exist within a social matrix.
• People are motivated to justify their own actions in this process.

Strengths
• Emphasises that relationship dissolution is not sudden but a *process*.
• Identifies places where things start to go wrong, can be applied to relationship counselling.

Limitations
Duck's model does not explain *why* relationships break down (see *reasons for relationship breakdown* on left).

Long-distance relationships
Research suggests that long-distance relationships are not doomed because people use many different maintenance strategies to preserve them (Holt and Stone, 1988).

Maintenance difficulties
In some circumstances (e.g. long-distance relationships), people cannot give their relationship the constant maintenance that it needs.

Research relating to relationship breakdown

Alternative model
Lee's (1984) model has more emphasis on the early stages of breakdown, when there is still hope that the relationship may be saved.

Cultural differences
These factors may only apply to Western cultures. In non-Western cultures, other factors (e.g. family and community pressure) are involved.

Gender differences
Women tend to stress unhappiness and incompatibility as reasons for dissolution whereas men are upset by 'sexual withholding' (Brehm and Kassin, 1996).

Rule violation
Argyle and Henderson (1984) found that critical rule violations included jealousy and lack of tolerance for a third party relationship.

Letting go and moving on
As people enter new situations they encounter others that are more rewarding than their current relationship (Hays and Oxley, 1986).

Sequences of separation (Lee, 1984)
• Dissatisfaction (D) • Exposure (E)
• Negotiation (N) • Resolution (R)
• Termination (T)
E and N were found to be the most intense stages.

This study also found important **individual differences** including age and gender differences.

Dissolution is seen as a necessary and potentially **growth-enhancing** aspect of an individual's development.

Despite very detailed data obtained, couples were not married and therefore constitute a **biased sample**.

psychological explanations of love (e.g. triangular theory, love as attachment)

Probable questions

1. Outline and evaluate **two or more** psychological explanations of love. *(24 marks)*

2. Describe and evaluate **one or more** psychological explanations of love. *(24 marks)*

Possible questions

3. 'Psychologists have struggled to understand that most human of emotions – love.'

   Critically consider psychological research (explanations **and/or** studies) into the nature of love. *(24 marks)*

There is a distinction between 'outline' (for two theories) and 'describe' (for one theory). 'Outline' indicates that less detail is expected whereas the use of 'describe' means that both depth and breadth are required. You could answer questions 1 and 2 with the same essay (discussing two or more theories) however in question 2 the term 'describe' means that more detail is expected.

In both essays you *could* gain credit for writing about lots of theories but more theories does not mean more marks. In order to communicate knowledge and understanding, and to provide elaborated commentary, you should restrict the quantity of theories and focus on quality – especially when the injunction is 'describe'.

The use of quotations in Unit 4 exam questions is much less common than for Unit 5 questions. Such quotations are there to 'inspire' you and rarely include the requirement to 'address the quotation' in your answer. In this case the quotation suggests that psychological theories of love haven't been very successful. Do you think this is true?

The injunction is also a less common one. 'Critically consider' is an AO1+AO2 injunction which merely means that you should 'describe and evaluate'.

Unlike questions 1 and 2, here you could gain AO1 credit for describing research studies. (In questions 1 and 2 research studies would only be creditworthy if used as part of a sustained critical commentary.)

explanations (e.g. Lee; Duck) and research studies relating to the breakdown of relationships

Probable questions

1. Outline and evaluate **two or more** theories relating to the breakdown of relationships. *(24 marks)*

2. Discuss psychological research (theories **and/or** studies) into the breakdown of relationships. *(24 marks)*

3. (a) Outline **one or more** theories relating to the breakdown of relationships. *(12 marks)*

   (b) Evaluate the **one or more** theories of the breakdown of relationships that you outlined in (a) in terms of relevant research studies. *(12 marks)*

Possible questions

4. Describe and evaluate research studies into the breakdown of relationships. *(24 marks)*

If you described and evaluated two theories this would be an acceptable answer to question 1 or question 2. And, if your evaluation had been in terms of research studies this could also be a fully creditworthy answer to question 3. So, in question 1 or 2, if you know a third theory and have time, then you could discuss this. In questions 1 and 2 you can, if you wish, use other means of evaluating research beyond evidence from research studies. In question 2, if you feel you are better at *describing* research studies than describing theories, then this option is available.

In answering question 3 (b) you must take care to avoid descriptions of research studies because this would not be creditworthy. The trick is to learn how to *use* research studies as AO2 material. Further AO2 credit can be gained by criticising the research studies, for example the sample used or other aspects of the design.

One extra point that can be made relates to questions that require two theories to be described. Since you can obtain a maximum of 16 out of 24 marks for one theory (partial performance penalty is a maximum of 8 marks for AO1 and 8 marks for AO2) then the same 'rule' applies when discussing two theories. Your 'first' theory may receive a maximum of 16 marks. This means that your second theory need not be as detailed, so you could do 16 marks worth of theory 1 and 8 marks worth of theory 2. Always make sure you know a lot of detail for at least one theory.

When questions are parted you are asked to provide material appropriate to each part of the question. However the examiner will 'export' any material from the part where it is not creditworthy, if it would gain credit in the other part of the answer. This should not encourage you to put anything down in your answer but it means you should not panic if you can't work out what to put where.

In this question 'describe' is used instead of 'outline' to indicate that detail is required as well as breadth. Don't try to write about lots and lots of studies – 6 studies (50 AO1 words for each) is fine.

TOPIC 1: PSYCHOLOGICAL EXPLANATIONS OF LOVE

SAMPLE ESSAY PLAN

Question 1: Outline and evaluate **two or more** psychological explanations of love. (24 marks)

| EXPLANATION 1: TRIANGULAR THEORY (STERNBERG, 1986) | **7½ MINUTES WORTH OF AO1**
• Love is a **combination** of three factors:
1. **Intimacy**: sharing emotions, mutual self-disclosure
2. **Passion**: attraction to another and sexual involvement
3. **Commitment**: decision to stay with one person and forgo others.
• People have **two triangles**: ideal and current relationship.
• Explanation of **how** this develops: people learn different **stories about love** e.g. love as a fairy-tale.
• Such stories **learned from** books, films, parents, etc. | **7½ MINUTES WORTH OF AO2**
• Typology based on **extensive interviews** with students and adults.
• **Fehr** (1988) questioned people about love; **emergent categories** mapped on the typology.
• **Gender differences**: women prefer travel story ('love is like a journey'), men prefer art ('physical attractiveness is essential').
• **Cultural differences**: passion important in Western relationships, commitment important in arranged marriages. |
| EXPLANATION 2: LOVE AS AN ATTACHMENT PROCESS (HAZAN AND SHAVER, 1987) | **7½ MINUTES WORTH OF AO1**
• Infants learn about love from mother-figure, early relationships create **internal working model** (**Bowlby**, 1969).
• **Continuity hypothesis**: early attachment style predicts later relationships e.g. **securely attached** adults trust others and believe in enduring love, also see mother as dependable and caring.
• **Insecurely attached** (resistant) adults have trouble finding true love and remember mother as positive but rejecting.
• Love is an integration of **attachment, caregiving and sexuality** (**Shaver et al.**, 1988). | **7½ MINUTES WORTH OF AO2**
• **Love quiz**: showed that early attachment related to later attitudes to and experiences in love (**Hazan and Shaver**, 1987).
• **Supported by other studies** e.g. securely attached adults had most long-term relationships (**Feeney and Noller**, 1990).
• Such studies rely on **retrospective attachment classifications** though one longitudinal study (**McCarthy**, 1999) did find same.
• Evidence is **correlational**, continuity may be due to **innate temperament** (**Kagan**, 1984) – a person born with an easy temperament becomes securely attached and later finds relationships easier. |

Question 2: Describe and evaluate **one or more** psychological explanations of love. (24 marks)

| TRIANGULAR THEORY (STERNBERG, 1986) | **15 MINUTES WORTH OF AO1**
• Love is a **combination** of three factors:
1. **Intimacy**: sharing emotions, mutual self-disclosure.
2. **Passion**: attraction to another and sexual involvement.
3. **Commitment**: decision to stay with one person and forgo others.
• **Relative strength of each determines kind of love** e.g. companionate love is low on passion whereas romantic love is low on commitment.
• If components are absent, a different type of love may exist, e.g. passion alone is interpreted as 'having a crush'.
• People have **two triangles**: ideal and current relationship. Most successful relationships are when the two triangles are similar.
• Explanation of **how** this develops: people learn different **stories about love** e.g. love as a fairy-tale.
• Such stories **learned from** books, films, parents, etc. | **15 MINUTES WORTH OF AO2**
• Typology based on **extensive interviews** with students and adults.
• **Fehr** (1988) questioned people about love; **emergent categories** mapped on the typology.
• Couples who endorsed similar 'stories' tended to be more satisfied (**Sternberg**, 1986).
• **Gender differences**: women prefer travel story ('love is like a journey'), men prefer art ('physical attractiveness is essential').
• **Cultural differences**: passion important in Western relationships, commitment important in arranged marriages.
• **Three-factor theory** is simpler: physiological arousal is labelled as love in presence of an appropriate love object (**Hatfield and Walster**, 1981).
• Three-factor theory supported by **love on a suspension bridge** study (**Dutton and Aron**, 1974) – men expressed more interest in female when interviewed on a suspension bridge (high arousal) than low bridge.
• 'Love as stories' approach also suggests love is a **culturally learned label**. |

According to Sternberg's triangular theory, love consists of three components. The first component is intimacy, where partners share emotions and engage in mutual self-disclosure. The second component is passion, characterised by romantic and physical attraction to another and sexual involvement. The third component is commitment where an individual makes a conscious decision to stay with one person and forgo other potential partners. Sternberg believed that the relative strength of each of these three components determines the kind of love experienced, e.g. companionate love is low on passion whereas romantic love is low on commitment. According to this theory, people have two triangles, one which characterises their ideal relationship and another which characterises their current relationship. Sternberg believes that the most successful relationships are those where these two triangles are similar. Sternberg (1999) extended his theory to include an explanation of how people's attitudes about love develop. He suggested that people learn different stories about love, for example 'love as a fairy-tale'. Such stories are learned from books, films, parents and so on.

> This is potentially a very detailed theory and you could not hope to describe the whole thing here. Just concentrate on giving its central assumptions and perhaps illustrating these with a couple of examples.

Sternberg's typology of love was based on extensive interviews with students and adults in real-life relationships, unlike many studies that are based on hypothetical relationships. Further support for this theory comes from Fehr (1988), who asked people to describe love in their own words, and found that the emergent categories mapped closely onto the typology suggested by Sternberg. Sternberg also found evidence of gender differences, with women preferring the 'travel story' view of love ('love is like a journey') and men the 'art' ('physical attractiveness is essential') and pornography view ('it is important to be able to satisfy my partner's sexual desires'). Likewise, there appear to be cultural differences in this process, with passion important in the initial stages of Western relationships, and commitment important in non-Western arranged marriages.

> It is important to make each point within the context of a critical commentary. The use of phrases such as 'further support for…' and 'Despite the support for…' help you to do this.

Hazan and Shaver (1987) suggest that love represents an attachment process, with infants learning about love from their mother-figure. Later relationships are seen as a continuation of this early relationship. The mother's behaviour creates an internal working model whereby the infant expects the same experience in later relationships (Bowlby, 1969). In their continuity hypothesis, Hazan and Shaver extended Bowlby's idea that that the individual's early attachment style should predict their later relationships. For example, securely attached adults whose memories of the mother-child relationship was of a dependable and caring mother later trusted others and believed in enduring love. Insecurely attached (resistant) adults, on the other hand, have conflicting memories of the mother being both positive and rejecting, and as adults have trouble finding true love. Shaver et al. (1988) claimed that what we experience as love is actually an integration of three behavioural systems – attachment, care-giving and sexuality – which interact to produce the adult love style.

> In order to properly represent this explanation of love, it is essential that you understand it properly. Try summarising the theory in your own words, or even explaining it to someone else. Then you will be better placed to outline it in an exam answer.

Hazan and Shaver (1987) tested their expectations about the relationship between early attachment style and later relationships using a 'love quiz'. This showed that early attachment related to later attitudes to and experiences in love. Consistent with the theory they found that adults who had experienced secure attachment in infancy were more likely to have positive attitudes toward relationships and more positive experiences of them. Likewise, they were less likely to have been divorced when compared to insecurely attached individuals. This relationship is supported by other studies, e.g. securely attached adults had the most enduring long-term relationships (Feeney and Noller, 1990), and avoidantly attached people had the most short-lived and least intense relationships. A problem with studies such as these is that they rely on retrospective attachment classifications, although longitudinal studies that do not suffer from this problem (e.g. McCarthy, 1999) do tend to support these conclusions. Another issue is that evidence tends to be correlational, i.e. we cannot claim that the relationship between early attachment and later love style is one of cause and effect. Kagan (1984) suggests that this apparent continuity may be due to innate temperament: a person born with an easy temperament becomes securely attached and later, because of their easy temperament, finds relationships easier.

> This final AO2 paragraph is much longer than the previous AO2 paragraph. This is fine as both are 'elaborated' and the overall balance of AO1 to AO2 is broadly the same.

TOPIC 2: THE BREAKDOWN OF RELATIONSHIPS

SAMPLE ESSAY PLAN

Question 1: Outline and evaluate **two or more** theories relating to the breakdown of relationships. (24 marks)

THEORY 1: REASONS FOR RELATIONSHIP BREAKDOWN (DUCK, 1999)	**7½ MINUTES WORTH OF AO1**	**7½ MINUTES WORTH OF AO2**
	• **Reason 1: Lack of skills** *e.g. poor conversation.* • Means that relationship never really gets going. • **Reason 2: Lack of stimulation** *e.g.* lack of rewards (social exchange theory). • Boredom or lack of change often given as reason for breakdown (**Baxter**, 1994). • **Reason 3: Maintenance difficulties** *e.g.* due to decreased daily contact.	• These factors are converse of initial attraction (*e.g.* proximity and then lack of proximity, but **fatal attraction theory** (**Felmlee**, 1995) suggests the opposite – initial factors eventually spell disaster. • **Long-distance relationships** do survive, 70% of students have had at least one LDR. • **Cultural differences**: breakdown of arranged marriages differently explained (moving to different culture may lead to breakdown because lack of community support). • **Gender differences**: women cite incompatibility whereas men cite sexual withholding (**Brehm and Kassin**, 1996).
THEORY 2: MODEL OF BREAKDOWN (DUCK, 1999)	**7½ MINUTES WORTH OF AO1** • **Intrapsychic phase** – individual recognises problem and begins to communicate this indirectly. • **Dyadic phase** – arguments but relationship repair still possible. • **Social phase** – family and friends involved, may help repair or take sides. • **Grave-dressing phase** – after break-up each partner builds positive representation of failed relationship.	**7½ MINUTES WORTH OF AO2** • **An alternative view**: Lee (1984) dissatisfaction, exposure, negotiation, resolution attempts, termination. Focuses more on the middle of the process. • **Both models** focus on process rather than seeing breakdown as a sudden step. • At each stage Duck proposes **repair strategies**, useful for couple **counselling**. • **Doesn't explain why** (in contrast to Duck's reasons for breakdown). • Doesn't consider the **experience** of breakdown (**Akert**, 1998, studied experiences e.g. physical symptoms).

Question 4: Describe and evaluate research studies into the breakdown of relationships. (24 marks)

15 MINUTES WORTH OF AO1	**15 MINUTES WORTH OF AO2**
• **Sequences of separation** (**Lee**, 1984) surveyed 112 romantic break-ups. • **Developed stage model**: dissatisfaction, exposure, negotiation, resolution attempts, termination. • Partners who skipped through stages had been **less intimate**. Partners who went through lengthy 5 stages had had closer relationships and greatest loneliness afterwards. • **Experiences** (**Akert**, 1998) studied students, if both partners involved in decision then they had fewer physical symptoms. • **Rule violation** (**Argyle and Henderson**, 1984) leads to breakdown. Participants listed rules that were broken in lapsed relationships. • **Most common violations**: jealousy, lack of tolerance for other relationships, disclosing confidences, not offering help, public criticism. • **Breakdown is positive** (**Hays and Oxley**, 1986): studied social networks in 1st year students. • Found that relationships were constantly restructured.	• Lee's research involved **extensive interviews** but **biased** – young and uncommitted couples. • Duck's 4 stage model is an **alternative**. Also emphasises process but more on beginning and end. • Neither model looks at **why** nor do they consider the **experience** of breakdown, unlike Akert. • **Argyle and Henderson**: large sample, wide age range but focused on break-up of friendships. • **Gender differences**: women identified emotional support, men identified joking. • **Age differences**: public criticism important for young Ps whereas lack of respect important for over 20s. • **Hays and Oxley**: only students. • **Strength**: Does show how breakdown is growth-enhancing part of development process.

Duck (1999) explains the breakdown of relationships as being due to a number of factors that may individually or collectively weaken the links between the two partners. Relationships are difficult for some people because one or both partners may lack the interpersonal skills (e.g. poor conversation) to make them mutually satisfying. This may indicate to the other partner that the person is not interested and so the relationship breaks down before it really gets going. A second reason is lack of stimulation, which is one of the rewards that, according to social exchange theory, people expect from a satisfying relationship. Baxter (1994) discovered that people often quote boredom or lack of change as a reason for the breakdown of their relationship. Duck's third reason is maintenance difficulties where people find it difficult to maintain close contact (e.g. when they leave home to go to university) and so cannot maintain a relationship satisfactorily.

> You have to be realistic when outlining the 'reasons' for breakdown. Duck identified a lot more than three but you wouldn't be able to do them justice here. Three is just fine.

These factors are the converse of reasons for initial attraction (e.g. proximity leads to attraction, and then lack of proximity leads to breakdown). However, fatal attraction theory (Felmlee, 1995) suggests the opposite: factors that were important in initial attraction (e.g. being amusing) may later become annoying (e.g. not taking life seriously enough). Although maintenance difficulties are cited as a reason for relationship breakdown, there is evidence that many long-distance relationships do survive, with 70% of students having had at least one long-distance romantic relationship. The factors identified by Duck may only apply to certain cultural groups. Non-Western relationships (e.g. arranged marriages) may be formed differently and so different pressures will function in their breakdown. When people move to a different culture, this may lead to breakdown because of the lack of community support that would have been present in the parent culture. There is also evidence of gender differences in the reasons for relationship breakdown, with women more likely to stress unhappiness and incompatibility whereas men are more likely to cite sexual withholding (Brehm and Kassin, 1996).

> Commenting on a comment, as here, is a perfectly acceptable way of earning AO2 credit.

Duck (1999) also proposed a model of relationship breakdown, which described the different phases in the dissolution of a relationship. In the first phase – the intrapsychic phase – the individual recognises that there is a problem with their current relationship. Although there may be little outward show of dissatisfaction, they may begin to communicate this indirectly (e.g. through expression to a third party). In the dyadic phase, problems with the relationship are aired, perhaps through arguments and some consideration of how things might be put right. At this stage, relationship repair is still possible, although the partners recognise that they could be heading for a break-up. In the third phase – the social phase – the dissatisfaction spills over into the network of family and friends. These people may help to repair the relationship (e.g. by helping mend disputes), or they may take sides, and so speed the relationship towards breakdown. In the grave-dressing phase, which occurs after the break-up, each partner tries to build a positive representation of the failed relationship which justifies their actions and puts them in a good light.

> Don't put too much detail in when describing these phases – just enough detail for each stage so that the main points are made. This paragraph is 180 words which is perhaps slightly long for 1/4 of the essay ('long' may sound good but won't leave you sufficient time for the rest of your answer).

An alternative view (Lee, 1984) describes the breakdown process as comprising five stages: dissatisfaction, exposure, negotiation, resolution attempts, and finally termination. Lee's model focuses more on the middle of the process, whereas Duck's model is more concerned with the middle and the end of this process. Both models focus on the process of breakdown, rather than seeing it as a sudden step. A strength of both models is that at each stage they identify opportunities for repair that could be useful for couples undergoing relationship counselling. A limitation of both models is that although they explain the different stages of breakdown, they do not explain why relationships break down. In contrast, Duck's model of the reasons for breakdown offers insights into the reasons why this process is initiated in the first place. Finally, none of these approaches includes the experience of breaking up. For example, Akert (1998) found that the more that both partners were involved in decisions that had to be made, the fewer physical symptoms they experienced after break-up.

> There is a temptation to simply *describe* Lee's model instead of building it into a critical commentary. A very brief outline of its central claim followed by a comparison with the model being evaluated is an acceptable way of building up your AO2.

Topic 1: The nature of relationships in different cultures

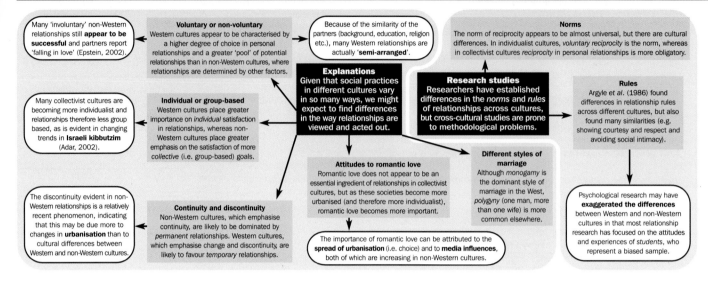

Many 'involuntary' non-Western relationships still **appear to be successful** and partners report 'falling in love' (Epstein, 2002).

Voluntary or non-voluntary
Western cultures appear to be characterised by a higher degree of choice in personal relationships and a greater 'pool' of potential relationships than in non-Western cultures, where relationships are determined by other factors.

Because of the similarity of the partners (background, education, religion etc.), many Western relationships are actually 'semi-arranged'.

Norms
The norm of reciprocity appears to be almost universal, but there are cultural differences. In individualist cultures, *voluntary reciprocity* is the norm, whereas in collectivist cultures *reciprocity* in personal relationships is more obligatory.

Many collectivist cultures are becoming more individualist and relationships therefore less group based, as is evident in changing trends in **Israeli kibbutzim** (Adar, 2002).

Individual or group-based
Western cultures place greater importance on *individual* satisfaction in relationships, whereas non-Western cultures place greater emphasis on the satisfaction of more *collective* (i.e. group-based) goals.

Explanations
Given that social practices in different cultures vary in so many ways, we might expect to find differences in the way relationships are viewed and acted out.

Research studies
Researchers have established differences in the *norms* and *rules* of relationships across cultures, but cross-cultural studies are prone to methodological problems.

Rules
Argyle et al. (1986) found differences in relationship rules across different cultures, but also found many similarities (e.g. showing courtesy and respect and avoiding social intimacy).

The discontinuity evident in non-Western relationships is a relatively recent phenomenon, indicating that this may be due more to changes in **urbanisation** than to cultural differences between Western and non-Western cultures.

Continuity and discontinuity
Non-Western cultures, which emphasise continuity, are likely to be dominated by *permanent* relationships. Western cultures, which emphasise change and discontinuity, are likely to favour *temporary* relationships.

Attitudes to romantic love
Romantic love does not appear to be an essential ingredient of relationships in collectivist cultures, but as these societies become more urbanised (and therefore more individualist), romantic love becomes more important.

Different styles of marriage
Although *monogamy* is the dominant style of marriage in the West, *polygyny* (one man, more than one wife) is more common elsewhere.

Psychological research may have **exaggerated the differences** between Western and non-Western cultures in that most relationship research has focused on the attitudes and experiences of *students*, who represent a biased sample.

The importance of romantic love can be attributed to the **spread of urbanisation** (i.e. choice) and to **media influences**, both of which are increasing in non-Western cultures.

Topic 2: Understudied relationships

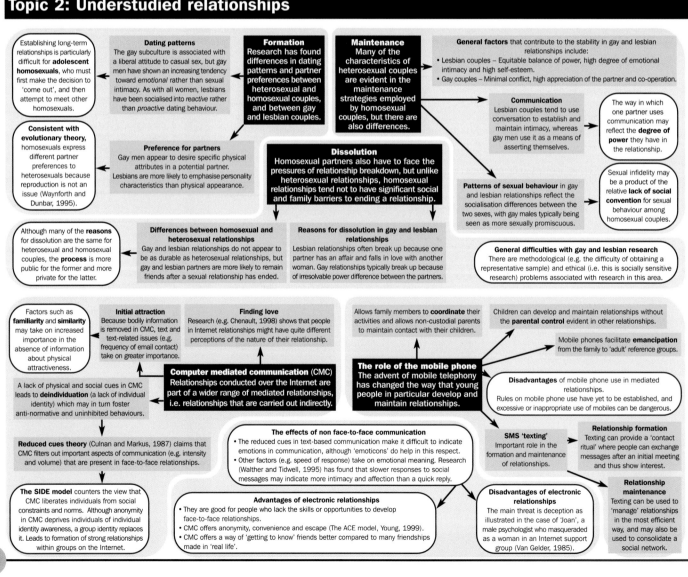

Establishing long-term relationships is particularly difficult for **adolescent homosexuals**, who must first make the decision to 'come out', and then attempt to meet other homosexuals.

Dating patterns
The gay subculture is associated with a liberal attitude to casual sex, but gay men have shown an increasing tendency toward *emotional* rather than sexual intimacy. As with all women, lesbians have been socialised into *reactive* rather than *proactive* dating behaviour.

Formation
Research has found differences in dating patterns and partner preferences between heterosexual and homosexual couples, and between gay and lesbian couples.

Maintenance
Many of the characteristics of heterosexual couples are evident in the maintenance strategies employed by homosexual couples, but there are also differences.

General factors that contribute to the stability in gay and lesbian relationships include:
• Lesbian couples – Equitable balance of power, high degree of emotional intimacy and high self-esteem.
• Gay couples – Minimal conflict, high appreciation of the partner and co-operation.

Consistent with evolutionary theory, homosexuals express different partner preferences to heterosexuals because reproduction is not an issue (Waynforth and Dunbar, 1995).

Preference for partners
Gay men appear to desire specific physical attributes in a potential partner. Lesbians are more likely to emphasise personality characteristics than physical appearance.

Communication
Lesbian couples tend to use conversation to establish and maintain intimacy, whereas gay men use it as a means of asserting themselves.

The way in which one partner uses communication may reflect the **degree of power** they have in the relationship.

Dissolution
Homosexual partners also have to face the pressures of relationship breakdown, but unlike heterosexual relationships, homosexual relationships tend not to have significant social and family barriers to ending a relationship.

Patterns of sexual behaviour in gay and lesbian relationships reflect the socialisation differences between the two sexes, with gay males typically being seen as more sexually promiscuous.

Sexual infidelity may be a product of the relative **lack of social convention** for sexual behaviour among homosexual couples.

Although many of the **reasons** for dissolution are the same for heterosexual and homosexual couples, the **process** is more public for the former and more private for the latter.

Differences between homosexual and heterosexual relationships
Gay and lesbian relationships do not appear to be as durable as heterosexual relationships, but gay and lesbian partners are more likely to remain friends after a sexual relationship has ended.

Reasons for dissolution in gay and lesbian relationships
Lesbian relationships often break up because one partner has an affair and falls in love with another woman. Gay relationships typically break up because of irresolvable power difference between the partners.

General difficulties with gay and lesbian research
There are methodological (e.g. the difficulty of obtaining a representative sample) and ethical (i.e. this is socially sensitive research) problems associated with research in this area.

Factors such as **familiarity** and **similarity** may take on increased importance in the absence of information about physical attractiveness.

Initial attraction
Because bodily information is removed in CMC, text and text-related issues (e.g. frequency of email contact) take on greater importance.

Finding love
Research (e.g. Chenault, 1998) shows that people in Internet relationships might have quite different perceptions of the nature of their relationship.

Allows family members to **coordinate** their activities and allows non-custodial parents to maintain contact with their children.

Children can develop and maintain relationships without the **parental control** evident in other relationships.

Mobile phones facilitate **emancipation** from the family to 'adult' reference groups.

A lack of physical and social cues in CMC leads to **deindividuation** (a lack of individual identity) which may in turn foster anti-normative and uninhibited behaviours.

Computer mediated communication (CMC)
Relationships conducted over the Internet are part of a wider range of mediated relationships, i.e. relationships that are carried out indirectly.

The role of the mobile phone
The advent of mobile telephony has changed the way that young people in particular develop and maintain relationships.

Disadvantages of mobile phone use in mediated relationships.
Rules on mobile phone use have yet to be established, and excessive or inappropriate use of mobiles can be dangerous.

Reduced cues theory (Culnan and Markus, 1987) claims that CMC filters out important aspects of communication (e.g. intensity and volume) that are present in face-to-face relationships.

The effects of non face-to-face communication
• The reduced cues in text-based communication make it difficult to indicate emotions in communication, although 'emoticons' do help in this respect.
• Other factors (e.g. speed of response) take on emotional meaning. Research (Walther and Tidwell, 1995) has found that slower responses to social messages may indicate more intimacy and affection than a quick reply.

SMS 'texting'
Important role in the formation and maintenance of relationships.

Relationship formation
Texting can provide a 'contact ritual' where people can exchange messages after an initial meeting and thus show interest.

The SIDE model counters the view that CMC liberates individuals from social constraints and norms. Although anonymity in CMC deprives individuals of individual identity awareness, a group identity replaces it. Leads to formation of strong relationships within groups on the Internet.

Advantages of electronic relationships
• They are good for people who lack the skills or opportunities to develop face-to-face relationships.
• CMC offers anonymity, convenience and escape (The ACE model, Young, 1999).
• CMC offers a way of 'getting to know' friends better compared to many friendships made in 'real life'.

Disadvantages of electronic relationships
The main threat is deception as illustrated in the case of 'Joan', a male psychologist who masqueraded as a woman in an Internet support group (Van Gelder, 1985).

Relationship maintenance
Texting can be used to 'manage' relationships in the most efficient way, and may also be used to consolidate a social network.

explanations and research studies relating to the nature of relationships in different cultures

Probable questions

1. Describe and evaluate research (explanations **and/or** studies) relating to the nature of relationships in different cultures. *(24 marks)*

2. (a) Outline **two** theories relating to the formation of relationships. *(12 marks)*

   (b) To what extent have research studies demonstrated variations in the nature of relationships in different cultures? *(12 marks)*

Possible questions

3. Outline and evaluate **two or more** explanations of the nature of relationships in different cultures. *(24 marks)*

4. Critically consider research studies relating to the nature of relationships in different cultures. *(24 marks)*

'understudied' relationships such as gay and lesbian and mediated relationships

Probable questions

1. Discuss research (theories **and/or** studies) into **two** types of understudied relationship. *(24 marks)*

2. Discuss research (theories **and/or** studies) into understudied relationships. *(24 marks)*

Possible questions

3. Discuss research (theories **and/or** studies) into **one** type of understudied relationship. *(24 marks)*

Questions that contain the word 'research' may appear to be a gift because they offer the opportunity to present both explanations and studies as AO1 (i.e. you have lots of things to write for AO1). But then what do you include for AO2? If you wish to use studies as AO2 you must clearly be using these as effective AO2 rather than describing the studies.

In other words, the danger is that you produce a wealth of AO1 material but end up with insufficient time and material for AO2.

Question 2 separates the AO1 and AO2 content but candidates often find it difficult to resist presenting *descriptions* of research studies. In this question there would be no AO1 credit for such descriptions. You must use such evidence to answer the question. Further AO2 credit may be gained by criticising the validity of any studies.

The AO1 content for question 2 is drawn from a different division of this subsection, which is legitimate.

Questions 3 and 4 are almost the same as question 1 except that you have been restricted to explanations (in question 3) and studies (in question 4). The specification mentions 'explanations' and 'research studies' which means that questions can be set specifically on either of these. This is not the case for understudied relationships (topics 2 and 3 below), where questions can only be set on 'research'.

In question 3 you are offered the opportunity to use more than two explanations if you wish. However, you should remember the depth-breadth trade-off. Too many explanations leave too little time for detail and/or AO2 commentary. However this may be a topic where you do not have enough material for 150 words on each explanation (300 words is about right for the AO1 content of a 24 mark essay).

One thing to remember in all four questions is to resist making rather vague statements about cultural differences and ensure that you ground your descriptions in actual research.

The specification gives examples of understudied relationships (gay and lesbian, and 'electronic' relationships). These are sometimes included in an exam question to help remind candidates about what they could include in their answer. However such examples also hinder candidates. For example, it might suggest that gay and lesbian must be treated as two different types – which would be acceptable. But they can also be grouped together as one type – homosexual relationships.

In the second question it would be acceptable to write about any kind of understudied relationship, even non-Western ones as these are understudied. However, this would not be acceptable in question 1 where you are required to write about two *types*.

Always make sure in questions about research that the AO2 material is distinctly different from the AO1. For example if you wish to use studies as AO2 instead of AO1 make sure they are being used as a critical point rather than just saying 'However ...' and then describing the study.

The difference is obvious here, warning you that you do need to have enough to write on one type of relationship in order to answer such a question. If you ignored the requirement to write about only one type of understudied relationship, and wrote about two, then all material would be read and credit given to whichever 'type' deserved more marks.

TOPIC 1: THE NATURE OF RELATIONSHIPS IN DIFFERENT CULTURES

SAMPLE ESSAY PLAN

Question 2: (a) Outline **two** theories relating to the formation of relationships. (12 marks)
(b) To what extent have research studies demonstrated variations in the nature of relationships in different cultures? (12 marks)

THEORY 1: SOCIAL EXCHANGE THEORY (THIBAUT AND KELLEY, 1959)	**(a) 7½ MINUTES WORTH OF AO1** • See page 6.	**(b) 15 MINUTES WORTH OF AO2** • **Voluntary/non-voluntary difference** e.g. non-Western societies have arranged marriages. But spouses in arranged marriages report they have **fallen in love** (**Epstein**, 2002).

THEORY 2: REINFORCEMENT-AFFECT (BYRNE AND CLORE, 1970)

(a) 7½ MINUTES WORTH OF AO1
• See page 6.
Note: If you were asked a question specifically about research studies (e.g. 'Critically consider research studies relating to the nature of relationships in different cultures.') then you could use the studies on the right, focusing on the description of these studies rather than their implications.

(b) 15 MINUTES WORTH OF AO2
• **Voluntary/non-voluntary difference** e.g. non-Western societies have arranged marriages. But spouses in arranged marriages report they have **fallen in love** (**Epstein**, 2002).
• Also about 50% of Americans say they married for reasons other than love (**Collins and Coltrane**, 1995) so difference not that great.
• **Individualist-collectivist difference**: e.g. voluntary reciprocity is the norm in **individualist cultures** whereas obligation a **collectivist** norm, **Ting-Toomey** (1986).
• May be changing e.g. **Israeli kibbutz** families have reduced in size to one couple plus parents (**Adar**, 2002).
• **Continuity-permanence difference**: Western relationships only recently non-permanent (divorce was rare until 50 years ago).
• **Different styles of marriage**: **Levine et al.** (1995) found that people in collectivist cultures more likely to marry for reasons other than love.
• **Rules**: **Argyle et al.** (1986) found cultural differences e.g. in rules for friendships but also found **similarities** e.g. important rule for courtesy and respect.
• **Cross-cultural research** prone to difficulties e.g. misinterpreting behaviour or imposing one's own standards/measurement techniques.
• Research on cultural differences **useful** to help international relationships e.g. understand appropriate rules of behaviour.

Question 3: Outline and evaluate **two or more** explanations of the nature of relationships in different cultures. (24 marks)

15 MINUTES WORTH OF AO1
• **Voluntary/non-voluntary**: Westerners live mainly in urban communities with geographical and social mobility which provides greater 'pool' of relationships.
• **Individualist-collectivist**: **Western cultures** emphasise the individual and independence.
• **Collectivist societies** foster relationships that are group-based and interdependent.
• **Continuity-permanence**: non-Western cultures emphasise heritage and are suspicious about change.
• **US culture** emphasises progress, change is important. Temporary relationships are more acceptable.
• **Attitudes to romantic love**: People in collectivist cultures more likely to marry for reasons other than love (**Levine et al.**, 1995).
• In US 2/3 of women would also marry for reasons other than love, men more romantic.
• **Different styles of marriage**: Monogamy less common in non-Western cultures possibly because of economic pressures.
• **Polyandry** (one wife, several husbands) for harsh living conditions. **Polygyny** (one husband, many wives) when resources plentiful.

15 MINUTES WORTH OF AO2
• **Voluntary/non-voluntary**: For non-Western societies arranged marriages make good sense because of lack of mobility.
• Spouses in arranged marriages report they have **fallen in love** (**Epstein**, 2002).
• **Individualist-collectivist**: In the West romantic relationships may not be group-based but friendships are.
• **Non-Western cultures** are changing, becoming more urbanised and more individualist e.g. Israeli kibbutz families have reduced in size to one couple plus parents (**Adar**, 2002).
• **Continuity-permanence**: Western relationships only recently non-permanent (divorce was rare until 50 years ago).
• **Greater urbanisation** leads to less permanence.
• **Attitudes to romantic love**: 'Hollywood style' romantic love ideals are spreading – this ideal is about having choice and marrying for love.
• **Cross-cultural research** prone to difficulties e.g. misinterpreting behaviour or imposing one's own standards/measurement techniques.
• Research on cultural differences **useful** to help international relationships e.g. understand appropriate rules of behaviour.

(a)

Social exchange theory (Thibaut and Kelley, 1959) acknowledges that the formation of relationships is not a one-way process, but involves an interaction between two partners, each with their own needs and expectations. At the centre of this theory is the belief that all social behaviour is a series of exchanges, with individuals attempting to maximise their rewards and minimise their costs. Possible rewards from a relationship include being cared for, companionship and sex. Potential costs include effort, financial investment and missed opportunities with others. Rewards minus costs equals the outcome of the relationship, i.e. a profit or a loss. Thibaut and Kelley also introduced the concept of a comparison level, a standard against which all our relationships are judged. We judge our current relationship against previous experiences. Satisfaction is based on profit relative to expectations. Thibaut and Kelley believed that individuals went through four stages in the development of a relationship, from sampling, where people consider the costs and benefits of a new relationship, through to institutionalisation, where norms are developed which establish the patterns of rewards and costs for each partner.

The reinforcement-affect model (Byrne and Clore, 1970) focuses on the ability of other people to reward (or punish) us directly (operant conditioning) or to become associated with reward or punishment (classical conditioning). In the reinforcement part of this model, some people are directly rewarding in that they produce positive feelings in us, in turn making us more likely to positively evaluate that person. We like people who are the source of a pleasant event and we also like people who are associated with a pleasant event. A previously neutral stimulus (a person we may not previously have met) can become positively valued because we meet them when we are in a happy (i.e. positive) mood. Byrne and Clore also believed that the balance of positive and negative feelings was crucial to relationship formation. Relationships in which the positive feelings outweighed the negative ones were more likely to develop and succeed, whereas relationships in which the negative feelings outweighed the positive were likely to fail.

(b)

Western and non-Western cultures are commonly thought to differ in terms of the degree to which they are considered to be voluntary (i.e. a product of romantic love) or non-voluntary (i.e. arranged for social and/or financial reasons). For example, non-Western societies frequently have arranged marriages and therefore may be considered to be largely involuntary by nature. Despite this, however, spouses in arranged marriages frequently report they have fallen in love, therefore showing the same kind of romantic love that characterises Western relationships (Epstein, 2002). Also about 50% of Americans say they married for reasons other than love (Collins and Coltrane, 1995) so the presumed difference between Western and non-Western cultures is not that great. Western and non-Western cultures are also thought to differ along the individualist-collectivist divide, for example, voluntary reciprocity is the norm in individualist cultures whereas obligation is a collectivist norm (Ting-Toomey, 1986). However, non-Western cultures are changing fast, and as they become more urbanised they become more individualist. Adar (2002) provides evidence for this showing that Israeli kibbutz families have changed from being an extended unit to being one couple and their children.

Western and non-Western cultures are also presumed to differ in terms of continuity-permanence, with the former characterised by less permanent relationships, and the latter by continuous relationships. However, the shift to non-permanent relationships in the West is a fairly recent phenomenon, with divorce being rare until 50 years ago. Despite this, research has shown some fairly consistent differences between Western and non-Western cultures, e.g. Levine et al. (1995) found that people in collectivist cultures are more likely to marry for reasons other than love. Likewise, Argyle et al. (1986) found cultural differences in rules for friendships but also found similarities e.g. both Western and non-Western cultures placed a great deal of importance on the rule for courtesy and respect. We must also exercise care when interpreting the findings from cross-cultural research. Such research is prone to difficulties e.g. misinterpreting behaviour or inappropriately imposing one's own cultural standards. However, research on cultural differences is potentially useful to help foster effective international relationships (e.g. between business people from different cultures) in that it enables people to understand appropriate rules of behaviour.

This is the same A01 material as for the question on page 7, although the A02 requirement here is quite different.

It is vital to remember that you are doing more than just *describing* ways in which relationships differ in different cultures, but you are *commenting* on whether such differences have been shown to exist.

It is acceptable to offer *some* descriptive detail, provided it is being used as the lead-in to a point of commentary as here.

You may be familiar with adverts showing how important it is to understand social customs and what is considered acceptable and unacceptable behaviour in other cultures. That is the point being made here.

TOPIC 2: UNDERSTUDIED RELATIONSHIPS

SAMPLE ESSAY PLAN

Question 1: Discuss research (theories **and/or** studies) into **two** types of understudied relationship. (24 marks)

TYPE 1: GAY AND LESBIAN

7½ MINUTES WORTH OF AO1
- **Dating patterns**: gay males 'sex first' attitude, meeting in specialised places (gay bars). Lesbians socialised to be more **reactive** than proactive in relationships.
- **Lonely hearts ads**: gay men advertise for physical attractiveness, lesbians for personality.
- **Maintenance strategies** differ in gay and lesbians. **Gays** seek minimal conflict, high appreciation of partner, cooperation (**Jones and Bates**, 1978), **lesbians** seek an equitable power balance, high emotional intimacy and high self esteem (**Eldridge and Gilbert**, 1990).
- **Dissolution**: 48% of lesbians and 36% of gays broke up within 2 years of being interviewed compared with 29% of heterosexual cohabitors (**Blumstein and Schwartz**, 1983).

7½ MINUTES WORTH OF AO2
- **Not easy to find partners**: gay bars tend to focus on casual sex.
- Comparisons of lonely hearts ads show significant **heterosexual/homosexual differences** (**Waynforth and Dunbar**, 1995).
- **Maintenance strategies**: Differences related to male-female differences e.g. men use language for dominance whereas women use it for intimacy.
- **Dissolution more frequent** because fewer barriers and less family support (**Huston and Schwartz**, 1995).
- **Process** of dissolution may be quite similar to heterosexual though tends to be more private and family/friends may be relieved.

TYPE 2: MEDIATED RELATIONSHIPS

7½ MINUTES WORTH OF AO1
Internet (CMC):
- **Reduced cues theory** (**Culnan and Markus**, 1987) important aspects of communication missing.
- Leads to **deindividuation** and anti-normative, uninhibited and more impulsive behaviour.
- **Mobile phone:**
- **Relational functions**: social coordination, parental control, emancipation (**Ling and Helmerson**, 2002).
- **Text messaging** helps find partners and maintain relationships e.g. girls say goodnight to friends (**Ling**, 2001).

7½ MINUTES WORTH OF AO2
- Physical attraction isn't only factor in relationships – **proximity and similarity** important too.
- Reduced cues compensated for with use of **emoticons** and other cues such as speed of response.
- **Advantages**: CMC relationships good for those who are shy, living alone, with physical handicaps.
- Relationships on web often deeper than 'real life' (**Lea and Spears**, 1995).
- **Disadvantages**: deception e.g. psychiatrist parading as Joan (**Van Gelder**, 1985), overuse of mobile phones.
- **Mobile phones** may be overused at the expense of more intimate ways of maintaining relationships.

Question 3: Discuss research (theories **and/or** studies) into **one** type of understudied relationship. (24 marks)

15 MINUTES WORTH OF AO1
- **Dating patterns**: 'sex first' attitude, meeting in specialised places (gay bars).
- Women socialised to be more **reactive** in relationships so lesbians less comfortable with gay bars, rely more on **mutual friends**.
- **Lonely hearts ads**: gay men advertise for physical attractiveness, lesbians for personality.
- **Maintenance strategies** differ: **Gays** seek minimal conflict, high appreciation of partner, cooperation (**Jones and Bates**, 1978), use conversation as a way to spar for dominance, have more frequent sex than any cohabiting couples (**Huston and Schwartz**, 1995), and accept lack of fidelity.
- **Lesbians** seek an equitable power balance, high emotional intimacy and high self esteem (**Eldridge and Gilbert**, 1990), use conversation for intimacy, have less sex and may tolerate sexual infidelity (**Peplau et al.**, 1978).
- **Dissolution**: Homosexual relationships **less durable** – 48% of lesbians and 36% of gays broke up within 2 years of being interviewed compared with 29% of heterosexual cohabitors (**Blumstein and Schwartz**, 1983).
- Lesbians break up because of infidelity (**Becker**, 1988), gays because of unresolvable power differences (**Huston and Schwartz**, 1995).

15 MINUTES WORTH OF AO2
- **Not easy to find partners**: gay bars tend to focus on casual sex.
- **Adolescent homosexuals** have greatest problems.
- **Hetereosexual interpersonal attraction** related to factors that increase reproduction – e.g. men seek resources and females seek physical attractiveness. Comparisons of lonely hearts ads show significant **heterosexual/homosexual differences** (**Waynforth and Dunbar**, 1995).
- **Maintenance strategies**: Differences related to male–female differences e.g. men use language for dominance whereas women use it for intimacy.
- **Homosexual infidelity** may be more common because fewer social conventions than for heterosexuals.
- **Female sexual infidelity** may anyway be more common than once thought because enhances reproductive success.
- **Dissolution more frequent** because fewer barriers and less family support (**Huston and Schwartz**, 1995).
- **Process** of dissolution may be quite similar to heterosexual though tends to be more private and family/friends may be relieved.
- **Research problems**: difficult to obtain **representative sample** (e.g. only urban homosexuals) and **socially sensitive** research (direct social consequences).

Research into dating patterns in gay relationships has suggested that gay males adopt a 'sex first' attitude to relationship formation, and establish specialised places (e.g. gay bars) where contact can be made. Women, however, have been socialised into being more reactive than proactive in relationships, meaning that for lesbians, neither woman feels comfortable making the first move, and may rely on introductions from mutual friends. Research from gay and lesbian lonely hearts ads has shown that gay men tend to advertise for physical attractiveness (e.g. an athletic body), whereas lesbians are more likely to emphasise personality rather than physical appearance. Maintenance strategies also differ in gay and lesbian relationships. Gay males seek minimal conflict, high appreciation of partner, and cooperation (Jones and Bates, 1978), whereas lesbians seek an equitable power balance, high emotional intimacy and high self esteem (Eldridge and Gilbert, 1990). When it comes to the dissolution of gay and lesbian relationships, research has shown that 48% of lesbians and 36% of gays broke up within 2 years of being interviewed compared with 29% of heterosexual cohabitors (Blumstein and Schwartz, 1983).

A problem for most gays and lesbians is the difficulty they face finding suitable partners. Although gay bars provide an opportunity for men to find partners for casual sex, these rarely lead to long-term relationships (Silverstein, 1981). The prediction from evolutionary theory that homosexual individuals would not seek or offer characteristics related to reproductive success was supported by research showing that when advertising for partners, gay men offered resources less than did heterosexual men and lesbians were less likely to offer cues of physical attractiveness (Waynforth and Dunbar, 1995). Research has also supported the prediction that maintenance strategies would also be different, with most differences being predictable from male-female differences e.g. gay men tend to use language to establish and maintain dominance whereas lesbians use it for intimacy. One explanation for why dissolution is more frequent in non-heterosexual relationships is because there are fewer barriers to breakdown, and less family support (Huston and Schwartz, 1995). Despite these differences, the process of dissolution may be quite similar to heterosexual couples, although it tends to be more private and family/friends may even be relieved at the break-up.

A second type of understudied relationship is those that are mediated, either through the Internet (computer mediated communication) or through some other medium such as the mobile phone. CMC is generally seen as being inferior to face-to-face relationships because there are fewer cues to work with when developing a relationship. Culnan and Markus (1987), in their reduced cues theory, claim that CMC filters out important aspects of communication, leaving participants in a 'social vacuum', devoid of physical and social cues. This leads to deindividuation, which in turn leads to anti-normative, uninhibited and more impulsive behaviour. Research has shown that the use of mobile phones has a number of relational functions, such as social coordination, parental control, and emancipation (Ling and Helmerson, 2002). Research in Norway has shown how the exchange of SMS messages forms part of a contact ritual in the initial stages of a new relationship (Ling and Yttri, 2002), and in the maintenance of an existing relationship.

Research in this area challenges the assumption that physical attraction is the main factor in the formation of relationships, as people become attracted to each other without face-to-face contact, demonstrating the importance of familiarity instead. The reduced cues of CMC can, however, be compensated for with the use of emoticons and other cues such as speed of response. CMC relationships can have a number of advantages, including being good for those who are shy, living or working alone, or those with physical handicaps. Lea and Spears (1995) believe that CMC relationships may even go deeper than those in 'real life' with many respondents claiming to know friends made in Internet chatrooms better than those they have known in real life for years. Disadvantages include the use of deception such as a study that involved a male psychiatrist parading as a disabled woman in an online support group (Van Gelder, 1985). The main problem with the role of mobile phones in relationships appears to be their overuse at the expense of more intimate ways of maintaining relationships.

You *could* represent gay and lesbian relationships as two separate types of relationship (and thus fulfil the requirements of the question) or present them as *one* type of understudied relationship (i.e. 'homosexual' relationships, despite the fact that there are some differences between them) as here.

There is no such thing as specific AO2 material, but rather it is what you *do* with the material that makes it into AO2. Here a prediction from evolutionary theory is interwoven with research into gay and lesbian relationships to produce effective commentary.

Here we are trying to *explain* a finding from research – this also counts as AO2 commentary.

Don't make the mistake of describing the technology (e.g. how e-mails or text messages work). Try wherever possible, as here, to include *psychological* theories and/or studies into your answer.

It would be acceptable to evaluate mediated communication in general, or just CMC, but a brief comment on the use of mobile phones is also appropriate. Try to avoid critical points that focus more on the physical dangers of mobile phone use!

Topic 1: Social–psychological theories of aggression

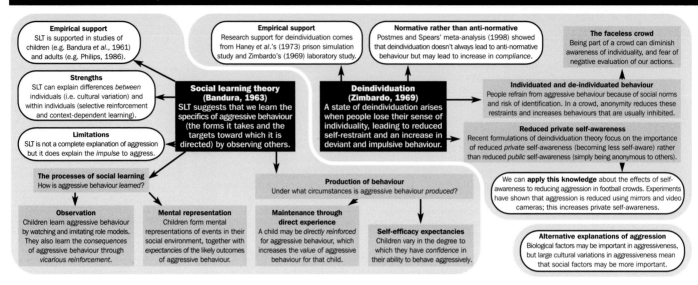

Empirical support
SLT is supported in studies of children (e.g. Bandura *et al.*, 1961) and adults (e.g. Philips, 1986).

Strengths
SLT can explain differences *between* individuals (i.e. cultural variation) and within individuals (selective reinforcement and context-dependent learning).

Limitations
SLT is not a complete explanation of aggression but it does explain the *impulse* to aggress.

Social learning theory (Bandura, 1963)
SLT suggests that we learn the specifics of aggressive behaviour (the forms it takes and the targets toward which it is directed) by observing others.

Empirical support
Research support for deindividuation comes from Haney *et al.*'s (1973) prison simulation study and Zimbardo's (1969) laboratory study.

Normative rather than anti-normative
Postmes and Spears' meta-analysis (1998) showed that deindividuation doesn't always lead to anti-normative behaviour but may lead to increase in *compliance*.

The faceless crowd
Being part of a crowd can diminish awareness of individuality, and fear of negative evaluation of our actions.

Deindividuation (Zimbardo, 1969)
A state of deindividuation arises when people lose their sense of individuality, leading to reduced self-restraint and an increase in deviant and impulsive behaviour.

Individuated and de-individuated behaviour
People refrain from aggressive behaviour because of social norms and risk of identification. In a crowd, anonymity reduces these restraints and increases behaviours that are usually inhibited.

Reduced private self-awareness
Recent formulations of deindividuation theory focus on the importance of reduced *private* self-awareness (becoming less self-aware) rather than reduced *public* self-awareness (simply being anonymous to others).

We can **apply this knowledge** about the effects of self-awareness to reducing aggression in football crowds. Experiments have shown that aggression is reduced using mirrors and video cameras; this increases private self-awareness.

The processes of social learning
How is aggressive behaviour *learned*?

Production of behaviour
Under what circumstances is aggressive behaviour *produced*?

Observation
Children learn aggressive behaviour by watching and imitating role models. They also learn the *consequences* of aggressive behaviour through *vicarious reinforcement*.

Mental representation
Children form mental representations of events in their social environment, together with *expectancies* of the likely outcomes of aggressive behaviour.

Maintenance through direct experience
A child may be *directly reinforced* for aggressive behaviour, which increases the *value* of aggressive behaviour for that child.

Self-efficacy expectancies
Children vary in the degree to which they have *confidence* in their ability to behave aggressively.

Alternative explanations of aggression
Biological factors may be important in aggressiveness, but large cultural variations in aggressiveness mean that social factors may be more important.

Topic 2: Effects of environmental stressors on aggressive behaviour

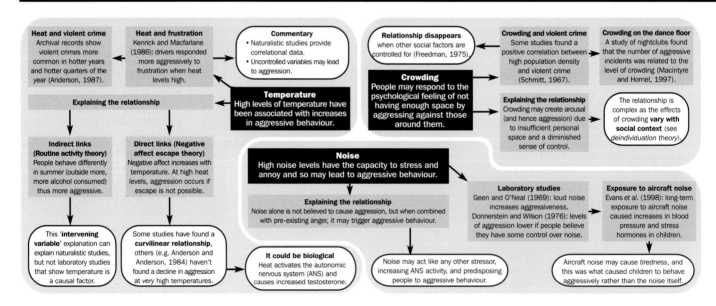

Heat and violent crime
Archival records show violent crimes more common in hotter years and hotter quarters of the year (Anderson, 1987).

Heat and frustration
Kenrick and Macfarlane (1986): drivers responded more aggressively to frustration when heat levels high.

Commentary
• Naturalistic studies provide correlational data.
• Uncontrolled variables may lead to aggression.

Relationship disappears
when other social factors are controlled for (Freedman, 1975).

Crowding and violent crime
Some studies found a positive correlation between high population density and violent crime (Schmitt, 1967).

Crowding on the dance floor
A study of nightclubs found that the number of aggressive incidents was related to the level of crowding (Macintyre and Hornel, 1997).

Explaining the relationship

Temperature
High levels of temperature have been associated with increases in aggressive behaviour.

Crowding
People may respond to the psychological feeling of not having enough space by aggressing against those around them.

Explaining the relationship
Crowding may create arousal (and hence aggression) due to insufficient personal space and a diminished sense of control.

The relationship is complex as the effects of crowding **vary with social context** (see *deindividuation theory*).

Indirect links (Routine activity theory)
People behave differently in summer (outside more, more alcohol consumed) thus more aggressive.

Direct links (Negative affect escape theory)
Negative affect increases with temperature. At high heat levels, aggression occurs if escape is not possible.

Noise
High noise levels have the capacity to stress and annoy and so may lead to aggressive behaviour.

Laboratory studies
Geen and O'Neal (1969): loud noise increases aggressiveness. Donnerstein and Wilson (1976): levels of aggression lower if people believe they have some control over noise.

Exposure to aircraft noise
Evans *et al.* (1998): long-term exposure to aircraft noise caused increases in blood pressure and stress hormones in children.

This 'intervening variable' explanation can explain naturalistic studies, but not laboratory studies that show temperature is a causal factor.

Some studies have found a **curvilinear relationship**, others (e.g. Anderson and Anderson, 1984) haven't found a decline in aggression at *very* high temperatures.

Explaining the relationship
Noise alone is not believed to cause aggression, but when combined with pre-existing anger, it may trigger aggressive behaviour.

It could be biological
Heat activates the autonomic nervous system (ANS) and causes increased testosterone.

Noise may act like any other stressor, increasing ANS activity, and predisposing people to aggressive behaviour.

Aircraft noise may cause *tiredness*, and this was what caused children to behave aggressively rather than the noise itself.

social psychological theories of aggression (e.g. social learning theory, deindividuation)

Probable questions

1. Outline and evaluate **two** social-psychological theories of aggression. *(24 marks)*

2. (a) Outline **two** social-psychological theories of aggression. *(12 marks)*

   (b) Evaluate the **two** social-psychological theories that you outlined in (a). *(12 marks)*

Possible questions

3. Describe and evaluate **one** social-psychological theory of aggression. *(24 marks)*

The answer you give to questions 1 and 2 could be identical. Both questions require you to outline and evaluate two social-psychological theories of aggression. In question 2, however, you must part your answer (separate the AO1 and AO2). In reality, if you don't part your answer the examiner will separate the material for you BUT this is dangerous because sometimes there are specific demands in part (b) (such as saying 'evaluate in terms of research studies'). Candidates often overlook the specific demands of each part of the question, and just write their prepared answer on social-psychological theories of aggression.

Questions can only be asked about research studies when they are cited in the specification. The phrase 'research studies' is not in this part of the specification for this division so the question cannot require you to use research studies – though it is likely that you would use them for evaluation.

It is possible, but less likely, that you would be asked to describe and evaluate just one theory – but you should be prepared to present a 24 mark version of one theory just in case.

Note that here the injunction is 'describe' whereas above it was 'outline' to reflect the fact that the same amount of detail is not required when two theories are asked for.

research into the effects of environmental stressors on aggressive behaviour (e.g. heat, noise, crowding)

Probable questions

1. Describe and evaluate research (explanations **and/or** studies) into the effects of **two or more** environmental stressors on behaviour. *(24 marks)*

Possible questions

2. Describe and evaluate research (explanations **and/or** studies) into the effects of **two** environmental stressors on behaviour. *(24 marks)*

In this part of the specification the word 'research' is used so questions cannot be set specifically on explanations or studies. The term 'research' gives you the option of including explanations and/or studies. It is up to you to decide whether to do one or the other or both. Remember that if you describe an explanation you may use a study as AO2, or if you *describe* a study (AO1) you could use an explanation as a form of commentary (AO2). However, you must make it clear whether material is being used as AO1 or AO2 otherwise it may all get AO1 credit and you'd end up with a low mark because of the lack of AO2 material. You can distinguish AO2 material from AO1 material by the way it is introduced and used.

At first sight you may wonder what the difference is between questions 1 and 2. There is an important difference. In question 1 you have the option of discussing more than two environmental stressors – though you can get full marks for doing just two. If you feel you haven't got enough to write about two environmental stressors then add some more – but remember that breadth often means a sacrifice of depth and this may limit your mark.

In question 2 you don't have this option – if you do write about more than two environmental stressors then the examiner would mark them all but only give credit to the best two.

SAMPLE ESSAY PLAN

Question 2: (a) Outline **two** social-psychological theories of aggression. (12 marks)
(b) Evaluate the **two** social-psychological theories that you outlined in (a). (12 marks)

THEORY 1: SOCIAL LEARNING THEORY (BANDURA, 1962)	**(a) 9 MINUTES WORTH OF AO1**	**(b) 9 MINUTES WORTH OF AO2**
	• The expression of aggression is **learned**, the **potential** for aggression is **biological**.	• SLT is supported by **empirical evidence** e.g. the **Bobo doll** studies. Children who watched an aggressive model did become more aggressive and also imitated specific acts of aggression (**Bandura et al.**, 1961).
	• **Direct** experience alone doesn't explain learning, we also learn **indirectly** (SLT).	• But aggression is towards a **doll** – however, Bandura repeated with a film of a woman hitting a clown; children hit a **live clown** when given the opportunity.
	• We **observe** aggressive behaviour and **imitate** people we identify with.	• Can explain differences between people e.g. **cultural differences:** US more violent (**Arouson**, 1999).
	• We learn through **vicarious reinforcement** – observing the consequences for others (difference between learning and performance).	• Can explain differences within people, people behave differently in different situations due to **selective reinforcement** and **context-dependent learning**.
	• The consequences create **future expectancies** (mental representation) and determine whether an individual repeats the behaviour.	

THEORY 2: DEINDIVIDUATION THEORY (ZIMBARDO, 1969)	**6 MINUTES WORTH OF AO1**	**6 MINUTES WORTH OF AO2**
	• **Deindividuation** is the loss of personal identity due to e.g. being in a crowd or wearing a uniform.	• **Empirical support** e.g. Zimbardo's **prison study**. Guards (sunglasses, uniform) behaved aggressively.
	• Deindividuated people act aggressively because loss of individuality leads to **reduced self-restraint, impulsive behaviour** and less concern over negative evaluation.	• Deindividuation **doesn't always lead to aggression**, may lead to pro-social behaviour i.e. leads to **conformity to group norms** (**Postmes and Spears**, 1998).
	• May be reduced **private** rather than **public self-awareness** i.e. becoming less self-aware rather than anonymous to others (**Prentice-Dunn and Rogers**, 1982)	• **Application:** reduce aggression in football crowds by increasing self-awareness e.g. use of video cameras.

Question 3: Describe and evaluate one social-psychological theory of aggression. (24 marks)

SOCIAL LEARNING THEORY (BANDURA, 1962)	**15 MINUTES WORTH OF AO1**	**15 MINUTES WORTH OF AO2**
	The description of theory 1 above, plus:	The evaluation of theory 1 above, plus:
	• If a behaviour is repeated then **direct reinforcement** will influence the **value** of the behaviour for that individual.	• Further empirical evidence e.g. **Bandura and Walters** (1963) showed that children may *learn* the behaviour but only repeat it if vicariously reinforced (**difference between performance and learning**).
	• Direct experience **leads** to a set of **personal expectancies**.	• **Self-efficacy** demonstrated in research studies e.g. Ps told they scored highly on test of willpower were more successful at giving up smoking (**Blittner et al.**, 1978).
	• **Self-efficacy** will affect future performance. It is derived from personal experience or observation of others.	• **Not a complete explanation** of aggression e.g. doesn't explain impulse to aggress and concerned with short-term effects.
		• Alternative **biological explanations** e.g. people with higher **testosterone** levels may be more aggressive.

In the social learning theory of aggression, Bandura (1962) believed that, although the potential for human aggression was biological, the expression of aggression is learned. Through social learning, we learn the specifics of aggressive behaviour (i.e. the forms it takes and the targets towards which it is directed). Unlike Skinner, who believed that learning takes place through direct reinforcement, Bandura suggested that we learn just by observing role models with whom we identify. By observing the consequences of others' actions, children can learn indirectly. By this process of vicarious reinforcement or punishment, children learn the likely outcome of aggressive behaviour, and so become more aware of what is considered to be appropriate (and effective) behaviour. As a result of this, they not only learn the behaviours themselves, but also whether and when such behaviours are worth repeating. In order for this social learning of aggressive acts to take place, Bandura believed that the child must form a mental representation of actions and their consequences. They must represent the possible rewards and punishments for aggressive behaviour in terms of expectancies of future outcomes. In the future, therefore, the child is likely to repeat the learned aggressive behaviour only if the expectation of reward is greater than the expectation of punishment.

Social learning theory is supported by empirical evidence e.g. the Bobo doll studies (Bandura et al., 1961). Consistent with the claims of this theory, Bandura et al. found that children who watched an aggressive model did become more aggressive and also imitated specific acts of aggression that they observed in the model. A problem for the theory is that the observed aggressive behaviour in the Bobo doll study was only towards a doll (which cannot hit back). However, Bandura repeated the study with a film of a woman hitting a live clown, discovering that children also hit a live clown when given the opportunity. A strength of this theory is that it can explain cultural differences in aggressive behaviour. Aronson (1999) notes that some societies (such as the US) are highly violent, whereas others manage to live in co-operative friendliness. Such differences must be due to social learning experiences. SLT can also explain differences within people, in that people behave differently in different situations because aggression is likely to be rewarded in some situations and not others. This means that they learn behaviours that are appropriate to particular contexts.

Zimbardo's deindividuation theory explains aggression as being a result of the loss of personal identity which results from the relative anonymity of being in a crowd or wearing a uniform. Zimbardo believed that deindividuated people are likely to behave aggressively because the loss of a sense of individuality leads to reduced self-restraint, which in turn leads to impulsive and deviant behaviour, and less concern over negative evaluation from others. Being anonymous in a crowd has the psychological consequence of reducing restraints and increasing behaviours that are usually inhibited. Recent developments of this theory have suggested that an increase in aggressive behaviour following deindividuation may be caused by reduced private rather than public self-awareness, i.e. becoming less self-aware rather than being anonymous to others (Prentice-Dunn and Rogers, 1982).

There is empirical support for deindividuation theory. In the Stanford Prison Experiment (Haney et al., 1973), Zimbardo showed how the guards who were deindividuated by wearing mirrored sunglasses and uniforms behaved aggressively toward the prisoners. A problem for the theory is that deindividuation doesn't always lead to aggression, and may actually lead to pro-social behaviour. In a meta-analysis of 60 studies of deindividuation, Postmes and Spears (1998) found that deindividuated people were more rather than less likely to comply with situational norms. Knowledge of the process of deindividuation, and its influence on aggression can be used to reduce aggression. Experiments have shown that aggression can be reduced in football crowds by increasing self-awareness, e.g. through the use of video cameras.

We have chosen (by way of variety) to cover the first theory in more detail than the second. You don't have to do this, but try to cover both in sufficient detail to avoid being assessed as 'superficial' for one of your outline descriptions.

Many students make the mistake of simply describing the Bobo doll studies in lieu of the underlying assumptions of the theory. Don't make this fundamental mistake.

It is vital, when using a study like this for evaluation, to more than just *describe* the study. You should build it into a critical commentary.

If using abbreviations (e.g. SLT), you should endeavour to use the full version at least once before switching. There are some recognised abbreviations for theories, but please don't make up your own (e.g. dndvdn theory)!

This is a slightly shorter outline of deindividuation theory than for SLT, as appropriate for the plan for this answer.

Demonstrating how a theory can be applied in real life can be a useful form of evaluation.

SAMPLE ESSAY PLAN

Question 1: Describe and evaluate research (explanations **and/or** studies) into the effects of **two or more** environmental stressors on behaviour. (24 marks)

STRESSOR 1: TEMPERATURE

5 MINUTES WORTH OF AO1

- **Routine activity theory (Cohen and Felson**, 1979): opportunities for aggression increase in hot weather, suggesting an **indirect link**.
- **Negative affect escape theory (Baron and Bell**, 1976): low levels of heat leads to negative affect (aggression), higher levels leads to desire to escape – aggression only shown if this is not possible.
- **Anderson** (1987) examined archival data and found crime more common in hot months and hotter years, relationship strongest for violent crimes.

5 MINUTES WORTH OF AO2

- Experimental evidence for a **direct link**: Ps gave more electric shocks when in a warm room (80°) but less when temperature rose to 90° (**Baron and Bell**, 1976).
- Archival studies e.g. **Baron and Ransberger** (1978) generally support a **curvilinear relationship** (as predicted by NAE).
- **Anderson and Anderson** (1984) found a **linear** relationship with no decline in aggression at higher temperatures.

STRESSOR 2: NOISE

5 MINUTES WORTH OF AO1

- Noise may **trigger** aggression but not sufficient on its own.
- **Lab study**: Ps more likely to shock confederate when in a noisy environment but only if previously aroused by watching an aggressive film (**Geen and O'Neal**, 1969).
- **Natural experiment**: children in flight path compared with children in quiet area had signs of stress (**Evans et al.**, 1998).

5 MINUTES WORTH OF AO2

- **Geen and O'Neal**'s study showed that Ps who were not angered (watched non-aggressive film) didn't behave aggressively when exposed to noise.
- **Noise does increase arousal** so should lead to aggression on own (**Bronzaft**, 1997).
- **Aircraft noise** study shows only an indirect link but supported by studies of direct link.

STRESSOR 3: CROWDING

5 MINUTES WORTH OF AO1

- Crowding may create **arousal** and a diminished sense of control.
- **Animal studies**: As **rat** population in captivity increased so did aggressiveness (**Calhoun**, 1962).
- **Correlation**: as density of **Honolulu** increased so did crime rates (**Schmitt**, 1967).

5 MINUTES WORTH OF AO2

- **Complex relationship** because effects vary with social context – crowded party leads to different effects than crowded shopping centre.
- Crowding leads to **deindividuation**, which may intensify pre-existing aggressive tendencies or positive mood.
- **Correlation**: Kelley (1985) found no relationship for assaults and that theft decreased.

Question 2: Describe and evaluate research (explanations **and/or** studies) into the effects of **two** environmental stressors on behaviour. (24 marks)

STRESSOR 1: TEMPERATURE

7½ MINUTES WORTH OF AO1

The description of stressor 1 above, plus:

- **Kenrick and MacFarlane** (1986) honking at green traffic lights positively related to outdoor temperature.
- **Baron and Bell** (1976) found corrilinear relationship in lab, **Baron and Ransberger** (1978) found same in naturalistic study.

7½ MINUTES WORTH OF AO2

The evaluation of stressor 1 above, plus:

- May be **extraneous variables** e.g. overcrowding, that cause aggression.
- Temperature-aggression link may be **biological** e.g. **testosterone** increases with heat and this may lead to aggression.
- Naturalistic studies lack control and don't demonstrate a **causal relationship**. Lab studies unrealistic because escape is possible.

STRESSOR 2: NOISE

7½ MINUTES WORTH OF AO1

The description of stressor 2 above, plus:

- **Lab study**: Ps with control over noise level reduced shocks delivered, even more so than Ps who had no noise (**Donnerstein and Wilson**, 1976).

7½ MINUTES WORTH OF AO2

The evaluation of stressor 2 above, plus:

- Natural experiments and correlations **don't demonstrate** a cause.
- **Complex relationship** because effects related to social meaning.

Temperature may be causally linked to other external factors, which are in turn causally related to aggressive behaviour. Routine activity theory (Cohen and Felson, 1979) states that opportunities for interpersonal aggression increase in hot weather as people change their normal pattern of routine activity. This suggests an indirect link between high temperatures and aggressive behaviour. In negative affect escape theory (Baron and Bell, 1976) increases in heat levels lead to increases in negative affect (aggressive feelings). Higher levels, however, lead to the desire to escape, with aggression only being shown if this is not possible. Anderson (1987) examined archival data and found that crime was more common in hot months and hotter years, with the relationship strongest for violent crimes.

> The question allows for explanations and/or studies, so there is a mixture of both of these in this first paragraph.

There is experimental evidence for a direct link between heat and aggression, with participants giving more electric shocks when in a warm stuffy room (80°) but less when temperature rose to 90° (Baron and Bell, 1976). This supports negative affect escape theory as it shows a curvilinear relationship between heat and aggression. This finding is also supported by archival studies e.g. Baron and Ransberger (1978), which showed that the number of riots in the US increased up to a temperature of 85° and declined at temperatures above that. However, Anderson and Anderson (1984) re-examined data from a number of field studies and found a linear relationship between heat and aggression, with no decline at higher temperatures.

> When evaluating an explanation with a research study, make it effective by stating how it might support or challenge the theory in question.

Noise is not thought to be sufficient on its own to cause increases in aggressiveness, but when combined with pre-existing anger, it may trigger aggression. In a lab study of the relationship between noise and aggression, participants were more likely to shock a confederate when in a noisy environment but only if previously aroused by watching an aggressive film (Geen and O'Neal, 1969). Noise may also increase stress levels which in turn lead to increases in aggressive behaviour. Evans et al. (1998) provided evidence for the stressful effects of prolonged exposure to uncontrolled noise. In this study, children in the flight path of a new airport showed significant increases in the physiological signs of stress, whereas children in quieter areas experienced no significant changes.

> It is important to make the link in this study between noise, stress levels and subsequent aggression.

Support for the claim that noise is a cue for aggressive behaviour comes from a study which showed that participants who were not angered (i.e. watched a non-aggressive film) did not behave aggressively when subsequently exposed to high levels of noise. On the other hand, there is evidence that noise acts like any other stressor, increasing the activity of the autonomic nervous system, and so, claims Bronzaft (1997), may well have a direct causal influence on aggressive behaviour. Despite the fact that Evans' study on aircraft noise only showed an indirect link between noise and aggression, this is supported by other studies that have shown a direct link.

> Introducing a research study by the phrase 'Support for the claim that… comes from a study which showed…' is a good way of representing this material as AO2.

Crowding – the psychological feeling of not having enough space – may create arousal, and so create a diminished sense of control. Animal studies have shown that crowding leads to aggression. In one such study (Calhoun, 1962), as a rat population in captivity increased so did aggressiveness. Some studies have shown a positive correlation between high population density and violent crime. Schmitt (1967) found that as the population density of Honolulu increased so did crime rates.

> There is just enough detail in this third type of stressor to justify its inclusion.

Although research suggests that crowding is related to aggression, this relationship is complex because the effects of crowding vary with the social context – a crowded party may produce different effects from a crowded shopping centre. This might be explained using the concept of deindividuation, which would predict that crowding leads to loss of personal identity. This may intensify aggressive tendencies that already exist in a group but may also intensify a crowd's positive mood. Schmitt's finding that high population density leads to increases in crime has been challenged by Kelley (1985), who found no relationship between population density and aggressive assaults and that crimes of theft were actually higher with lower urban densities.

> Deindividuation has been introduced here to *explain* a research finding, rather than just an explanation in its own right, in which case as it would have been credited as AO1 description.

Topic 1: Human altruism and bystander behaviour

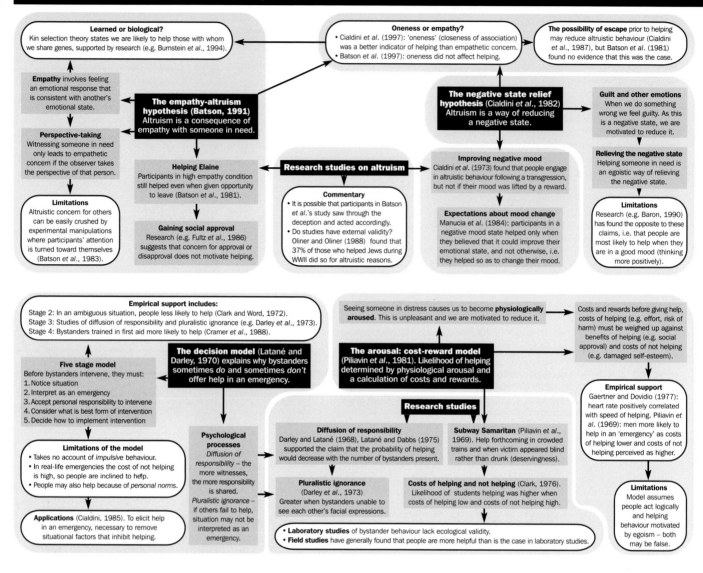

Learned or biological?
Kin selection theory states we are likely to help those with whom we share genes, supported by research (e.g. Burnstein et al., 1994).

Oneness or empathy?
• Cialdini et al. (1997): 'oneness' (closeness of association) was a better indicator of helping than empathetic concern.
• Batson et al. (1997): oneness did not affect helping.

The possibility of escape prior to helping may reduce altruistic behaviour (Cialdini et al., 1987), but Batson et al. (1981) found no evidence that this was the case.

Empathy involves feeling an emotional response that is consistent with another's emotional state.

The empathy-altruism hypothesis (Batson, 1991)
Altruism is a consequence of empathy with someone in need.

The negative state relief hypothesis (Cialdini et al., 1982)
Altruism is a way of reducing a negative state.

Guilt and other emotions
When we do something wrong we feel guilty. As this is a negative state, we are motivated to reduce it.

Perspective-taking
Witnessing someone in need only leads to empathetic concern if the observer takes the perspective of that person.

Helping Elaine
Participants in high empathy condition still helped even when given opportunity to leave (Batson et al., 1981).

Research studies on altruism

Improving negative mood
Cialdini et al. (1973) found that people engage in altruistic behaviour following a transgression, but not if their mood was lifted by a reward.

Relieving the negative state
Helping someone in need is an egoistic way of relieving the negative state.

Limitations
Altruistic concern for others can be easily crushed by experimental manipulations where participants' attention is turned toward themselves (Batson et al., 1983).

Commentary
• It is possible that participants in Batson et al.'s study saw through the deception and acted accordingly.
• Do studies have external validity? Oliner and Oliner (1988) found that 37% of those who helped Jews during WWII did so for altruistic reasons.

Gaining social approval
Research (e.g. Fultz et al., 1986) suggests that concern for approval or disapproval does not motivate helping.

Expectations about mood change
Manucia et al. (1984): participants in a negative mood state helped only when they believed that it could improve their emotional state, and not otherwise, i.e. they helped so as to change their mood.

Limitations
Research (e.g. Baron, 1990) has found the opposite to these claims, i.e. that people are most likely to help when they are in a good mood (thinking more positively).

Empirical support includes:
Stage 2: In an ambiguous situation, people less likely to help (Clark and Word, 1972).
Stage 3: Studies of diffusion of responsibility and pluralistic ignorance (e.g. Darley et al., 1973).
Stage 4: Bystanders trained in first aid more likely to help (Cramer et al., 1988).

Seeing someone in distress causes us to become **physiologically aroused**. This is unpleasant and we are motivated to reduce it.

Costs and rewards before giving help, costs of helping (e.g. effort, risk of harm) must be weighed up against benefits of helping (e.g. social approval) and costs of not helping (e.g. damaged self-esteem).

The decision model (Latané and Darley, 1970) explains why bystanders sometimes *do* and sometimes *don't* offer help in an emergency.

The arousal: cost-reward model (Piliavin et al., 1981). Likelihood of helping determined by physiological arousal and a calculation of costs and rewards.

Five stage model
Before bystanders intervene, they must:
1. Notice situation
2. Interpret as an emergency
3. Accept personal responsibility to intervene
4. Consider what is best form of intervention
5. Decide how to implement intervention

Empirical support
Gaertner and Dovidio (1977): heart rate positively correlated with speed of helping. Piliavin et al. (1969): men more likely to help in an 'emergency' as costs of helping lower and costs of not helping perceived as higher.

Research studies

Limitations of the model
• Takes no account of *impulsive* behaviour.
• In real-life emergencies the cost of not helping is high, so people are inclined to help.
• People may also help because of *personal norms*.

Psychological processes
Diffusion of responsibility – the more witnesses, the more responsibility is shared.
Pluralistic ignorance – if others fail to help, situation may not be interpreted as an emergency.

Diffusion of responsibility
Darley and Latané (1968), Latané and Dabbs (1975) supported the claim that the probability of helping would decrease with the number of bystanders present.

Subway Samaritan (Piliavin et al., 1969). Help forthcoming in crowded trains and when victim appeared blind rather than drunk (deservingness).

Applications (Cialdini, 1985). To elicit help in an emergency, necessary to remove situational factors that inhibit helping.

Pluralistic ignorance (Darley et al., 1973) Greater when bystanders unable to see each other's facial expressions.

Costs of helping and not helping (Clark, 1976). Likelihood of students helping was higher when costs of helping low and costs of not helping high.

Limitations
Model assumes people act logically and helping behaviour motivated by egoism – both may be false.

• **Laboratory studies** of bystander behaviour lack ecological validity.
• **Field studies** have generally found that people are more helpful than is the case in laboratory studies.

Topic 2: Cultural differences in pro-social behaviour

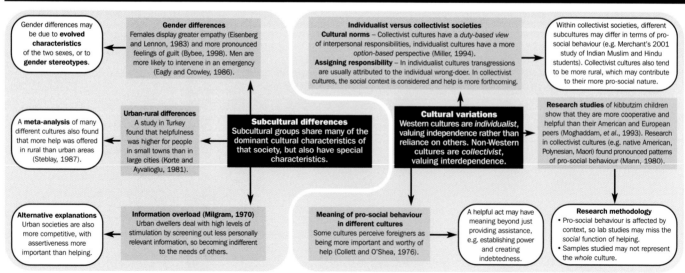

Gender differences may be due to **evolved characteristics** of the two sexes, or to **gender stereotypes**.

Gender differences
Females display greater empathy (Eisenberg and Lennon, 1983) and more pronounced feelings of guilt (Bybee, 1998). Men are more likely to intervene in an emergency (Eagly and Crowley, 1986).

Individualist versus collectivist societies
Cultural norms – Collectivist cultures have a *duty-based view* of interpersonal responsibilities, individualist cultures have a more *option-based* perspective (Miller, 1994).
Assigning responsibility – In individualist cultures transgressions are usually attributed to the individual wrong-doer. In collectivist cultures, the social context is considered and help is more forthcoming.

Within collectivist societies, different subcultures may differ in terms of pro-social behaviour (e.g. Merchant's 2001 study of Indian Muslim and Hindu students). Collectivist cultures also tend to be more rural, which may contribute to their more pro-social nature.

A **meta-analysis** of many different cultures also found that more help was offered in rural than urban areas (Steblay, 1987).

Urban-rural differences
A study in Turkey found that helpfulness was higher for people in small towns than in large cities (Korte and Ayvalioglu, 1981).

Subcultural differences
Subcultural groups share many of the dominant cultural characteristics of that society, but also have special characteristics.

Cultural variations
Western cultures are *individualist*, valuing independence rather than reliance on others. Non-Western cultures are *collectivist*, valuing interdependence.

Research studies of kibbutzim children show that they are more cooperative and helpful than their American and European peers (Moghaddam, et al., 1993). Research in collectivist cultures (e.g. native American, Polynesian, Maori) found pronounced patterns of pro-social behaviour (Mann, 1980).

Alternative explanations
Urban societies are also more competitive, with assertiveness more important than helping.

Information overload (Milgram, 1970)
Urban dwellers deal with high levels of stimulation by screening out less personally relevant information, so becoming indifferent to the needs of others.

Meaning of pro-social behaviour in different cultures
Some cultures perceive foreigners as being more important and worthy of help (Collett and O'Shea, 1976).

A helpful act may have meaning beyond just providing assistance, e.g. establishing power and creating indebtedness.

Research methodology
• Pro-social behaviour is affected by context, so lab studies may miss the *social* function of helping.
• Samples studied may not represent the *whole* culture.

Probable questions

1. Outline and evaluate **two** explanations of human altruism **and/or** bystander behaviour. *(24 marks)*

2. (a) Outline **two** explanations of human altruism **and/or** bystander behaviour. *(12 marks)*

   (b) Evaluate the **two** explanations of human altruism that you outlined in (a) in terms of relevant research studies. *(12 marks)*

Possible questions

3. Discuss **two or more** research studies relating to human altruism **and/or** bystander behaviour. *(24 marks)*

4. Discuss research (explanations **and/or** research studies) relating to human altruism **and/or** bystander behaviour. *(24 marks)*

When you are required to provide two explanations (or theories) you are not required to present these in equal measure. In fact you could do 2/3 of one and 1/3 of the other and still get full marks. The way this is worked out is as follows – if you only present one explanation when two were required then a partial performance penalty is applied. The one explanation is marked out of a total of 16 marks (8 marks maximum for AO1 and 8 marks maximum for AO2). So the same 'measure' is applied when you discuss two explanations but one is in less detail.

The answers to both questions 1 and 2 could be identical, though in question 1 you would get credit for offering evaluation that is not related to research studies.

In parted questions, such as question 2, there is no penalty for not parting the question BUT you risk overlooking the particular demands of each part of the question. You are always safer separating the parts.

In each question you are offered the choice of writing about altruism and/or bystander behaviour. Two examples are given in the specification but you do not have to use these in your essays.

In this part of the specification both explanations and research studies are mentioned so it is legitimate to ask questions that specify one or the other, or both.

Question 3 requires a minimum of two studies. If you knew enough detail about two studies (i.e. could write about 300 words describing them and 300 words evaluating them) then you could get full marks, but most candidates would do better by writing about more than two studies. However, don't go overboard – if you write about lots of studies you will end up sacrificing depth for breadth and fail to attract top marks.

Probable questions

1. Discuss research (theories **and/or** studies) relating to cultural differences in pro-social behaviour. *(24 marks)*

2. (a) Outline **one or more** explanations of human altruism **and/or** bystander behaviour. *(12 marks)*

   (b) To what extent are there cultural differences in pro-social behaviour? *(12 marks)*.

Possible questions

3. Outline **two or more** aspects of pro-social behaviour in which there are cultural differences. *(24 marks)*

Question 1 is the obvious question for this topic and very straightforward.

Question 2 is one where topics within the division have been combined. It is a less obvious question but quite appealing because it samples several areas of your knowledge. Part (b) begins with the AO2 injunction 'to what extent ...' indicating that only AO2 material will be credited in this part of the question. This is quite tricky because you haven't been offered the opportunity to *describe* the differences but must leap into considering whether there are any. Focus on the question you are being asked and provide commentary rather than description.

Question 3 is a slightly more clumsy (and therefore only possible rather than probable) attempt to combine the topics in this division. You need to identify at least two aspects of pro-social behaviour (such as altruism or bystander behaviour, or helpfulness or co-operativeness) and then describe and assess the cultural differences, if there are any.

TOPIC 1: HUMAN ALTRUISM AND BYSTANDER BEHAVIOUR

SAMPLE ESSAY PLAN

Question 3: Discuss **two or more** research studies relating to human altruism **and/or** bystander behaviour. (24 marks)

15 MINUTES WORTH OF AO1

- **Batson et al.** (1981): Those participants who watched 'Elaine' receive shocks and who were in a high empathy condition took her place, even if offered chance to escape, those in low empathy condition didn't.
- **Fultz et al.** (1986) investigated whether people help to gain social approval (rewards). Rewards don't affect behaviour in high empathy condition but people low in empathy helped more in 'public' condition.
- **Cialdini et al.** (1973): Ps made to feel guilty, those who were offered a reward to improve their mood then didn't help.
- **Manucia et al.** (1984): Ps in a negative mood state helped only when they believed that giving help could improve their emotional state.
- **Batson et al.** (1997): Empathy not oneness? Manipulated oneness by telling Ps that person in need was at same university (high oneness) or rival university. Oneness did not affect helping but degree of empathy did (when told to imagine how the other person felt).

15 MINUTES WORTH OF AO2

- Elaine study shows that predictions of empathy-altruism hypothesis are correct.
- However, empathy crushed by **self-concern**, when Ps told shocks would be painful, helping was reduced even in high empathy condition (**Batson et al.**, 1983).
- **Batson's** studies may have been affected by **demand characteristics** (e.g. guessing experiments' aims and behaving in pro-social way).
- Lab studies are **contrived**, lack **mundane realism** and **ecological validity**.
- Studies by Cialdini and Manucia support **negative state relief hypothesis**.
- **Cialdini et al.** (1997) also offered the explanation of **oneness** rather than empathy. Supported in **real life study**: most helping was due to cultural norms rather than empathy (**Oliner and Oliner**, 1988) but **challenged** by **Batson et al.** (1997),
- Negative state relief doesn't explain why people help more when in a **good mood** (Baron, 1990).

Question 1: Outline and evaluate **two** explanations of human altruism **and/or** bystander behaviour. (24 marks)

EXPLANATION 1: EMPATHY-ALTRUISM HYPOTHESIS (BATSON, 1991)

7½ MINUTES WORTH OF AO1

- **Empathy** is imagining what someone else is feeling.
- **Empathetic concern** motivates altruistic behaviour if you take the other person's perspective.
- If there is no empathetic concern then you experience **personal distress**.
- If **escape is not available** then you would still help.
- **Perspective-taking** depends on having had a similar experience, being attached to the person and/or being told to take the other person's perspective.

7½ MINUTES WORTH OF AO2

- **Empirical support**: those participants who watched 'Elaine' receive shocks and identified with her took her place, even if offered chance to escape, those in low empathy condition didn't (**Batson et al.**, 1981).
- **Helping may be motivated by social approval (rewards)**, **Fultz et al.** (1986) when potential or social evaluation manipulated (i.e. public versus anonymous helping) made no difference in high empathy condition but did in low empathy condition.
- But **Ciadlini et al.** (1987) said altruism is selfish, we help to relieve **our own negative feelings**. He found that Ps in high empathy condition would escape if offered a reward.
- Empathy may be crushed by **self-concern**, when Ps told shocks would be painful helping was reduced even in high empathy condition (**Batson et al.**, 1983).

EXPLANATION 2: THE DECISION MODEL (LATANÉ AND DARLEY, 1970)

7½ MINUTES WORTH OF AO1

- **5 stage model**: notice, interpret as an emergency, accept personal responsibility, consider what to do, act.
- At each stage **decision may inhibit helping** e.g. others present or insufficient skills.
- **Diffusion of responsibility**: presence of others means responsibility shared.
- **Pluralistic ignorance**: other non-acting bystanders indicate nothing should be done.

7½ MINUTES WORTH OF AO2

Empirical support for stages:

- Stage 1 'Notice': students who were late to lecture less likely to help (**Darley and Batson**, 1973).
- Stage 2 'Interpret': Ps heard crash in next door room helped if man shouted 'Oh my back' (**Clark and Word**, 1972).
- Stage 3 'Diffusion of responsibility': Discussion via intercom, students helped most and most quickly if they thought they were alone (**Darley and Latané**, 1968).
- But when costs of not helping are high then more rather than less help forthcoming when more people present (**Piliavin et al.**, 1969).
- Stages 4 and 5 'Action' related to characteristics of bystander and victim e.g. race, sex, skills, deservingness.
- Assumes that we think **rationally**.
- Does not explain what motivates helping which can be explained adding **personal norms** (Schwartz and Howard, 1981).

Batson et al. (1981) tested participants using a placebo drug which led participants to interpret their reactions as indicating high or low empathy. Those participants who watched a female confederate receive shocks and who were in the high-empathy condition took her place when she became distressed, even if they were offered the chance to escape, whereas those who were in the low-empathy condition took the chance to leave.

In questions such as this, it is vital to be concise when describing complicated studies.

Although the altruistic behaviour evident in Batson's study appears to be aroused in conditions where empathy is high, empathy can be easily crushed by self-concern. This was evident in a follow-up study when participants were told that the shocks would be painful. Unlike the previous study, helping was now reduced even in the high-empathy condition (Batson et al., 1983).

In this answer, smaller amounts of AO1 material are followed in turn by the related AO2 material for that study.

Fultz et al. (1986) investigated the possibility that people might only help to gain reward or avoid punishment. They found that when the potential for social evaluation was manipulated, participants in a high-empathy condition were no more or less likely to help. However, the low-empathy participants helped more in the 'public' condition than in the anonymous condition, indicating that they were motivated by social approval.

Studies such as the ones above raise important questions about the methods used. In the Batson et al. study, the student participants may have seen through the deception, guessed that the experiment was investigating helpfulness, and so behaved in a way they thought appropriate for the investigation. In other words, they may have been showing evidence of demand characteristics. The Fultz et al. study also suffers from methodological problems, as laboratory studies tend to be contrived rather than realistic representations of helping behaviours in real-life situations. Real-life studies of altruism do not always show the same importance for empathy.

It is also appropriate to include methodological limitations as AO2 commentary, but try to say more than just 'the study lacked ecological validity...'!

Cialdini et al. (1973) tested the assumption that a negative mood would be improved by receiving a reward, thus removing the need to behave altruistically for the same end. Participants were made to feel guilty (the negative state), with the result that those who were offered a reward to improve their mood showed reduced levels of helping behaviour. Manucia et al. (1984) also explored whether expectations about mood change could damage the likelihood of offering help to someone in need. They found that participants in a negative mood state helped only when they believed that giving help could improve their emotional state and not otherwise.

The studies by Cialdini et al. and Manucia et al. confirm the belief that people engage in pro-social behaviour in an attempt to overcome the negative mood that arises from harming another (the negative state relief hypothesis), but that the likelihood of helping can be subverted by manipulating the provision of rewards or expectation that helping will have any effect on negative mood. Cialdini et al. (1997) offered an alternative explanation for the results of altruism studies. He suggested that the closer a person felt to someone in need of help the more empathy and 'oneness' with the person they experienced, 'oneness' was seen as a better predictor of whether help would be offered. This explanation is supported in a real life study involving Europeans who rescued Jews during the Second World War. In this study more helping was due to cultural norms than empathy (Oliner and Oliner, 1988).

Although the concept of 'oneness' and Oliner and Oliner's research might be considered part of the AO1 component, here they are built into a sustained commentary, so would be credited as AO2.

Batson et al. (1997) explored the possibility that 'oneness' might influence the possibility of helping. In this study, the researchers manipulated levels of empathy by encouraging participants to take an objective perspective (low-empathy) or to imagine how a victim felt (high-empathy condition). They also manipulated oneness by telling participants that the person in need was at the same university (high oneness) or at a rival university. They found that oneness did not affect helping but the degree of empathy did.

The results of the Batson et al. study challenge Cialdini's view that oneness is more important in determining helping behaviour than empathy. Cialdini's finding that people are more likely to engage in pro-social behaviour when they are in a negative mood is also challenged by the finding that people are more likely to help when they are in a good mood, presumably because this causes them to think more positively about those around them (Baron, 1990).

Be careful to link evaluation to *studies* rather than explanations of helping behaviour, although in practice this distinction may be a little artificial.

TOPIC 2: CULTURAL DIFFERENCES IN PRO-SOCIAL BEHAVIOUR

SAMPLE ESSAY PLAN

Question 1: Discuss research (theories **and/or** studies) relating to cultural differences in pro-social behaviour. (24 marks)

SUBCULTURAL DIFFERENCES	**5 MINUTES WORTH OF AO1** • *Gender differences*: women display more empathy (meta-analysis by **Eisenberg and Lennon**, 1983) and greater feelings of guilt (**Bybee**, 1998). • *Urban-rural differences*: helpfulness greater in small towns (**Korte and Ayvalioglu**, 1981). • Explained in terms of **stimulus overload theory** (**Milgram**, 1970), excessive stimulation leads to indifference.	**5 MINUTES WORTH OF AO2** • **Gender differences** may be cultural (e.g. men more heroic because of socialisation) or **biological** (female caring an adaptive part of the 'tend and befriend' response, **Taylor et al.**, 2000). • **Urban-rural differences** supported by a meta-analysis of 65 populations (**Steblay**, 1987). • **Urban societies** also more industrialised and competitive which can explain low helping.
CULTURAL DIFFERENCES	**10 MINUTES WORTH OF AO1** • **Collectivist** cultures more **duty-based** view of interpersonal relations and therefore more helpful; **individualist** cultures more **option-oriented**. • Individualist cultures blame individuals rather than social context, leads to **fundamental attribution error**. • **Kibbutz** (collectivist) children more cooperative than US (**Moghaddam et al.**, 1993), same in other collectivist societies e.g. **Polynesian** (**Mann**, 1980). • In Greece **foreigners** more likely to receive help than **locals**, reverse true in Boston and Paris (**Feldman**, 1986). • Explained in terms of **social meanings**, in some cultures foreigners seen as more worthy (**Collett and Shea**, 1976).	**10 MINUTES WORTH OF AO2** • Cultural comparisons **ignore intra-cultural differences** e.g. Indians (collectivist) vary depending on whether they are **Muslim** (duty-based) or **Hindu** (option-oriented) (**Kanekar and Merchant**, 2001). • **Collectivist** societies also **more rural** and **less industrialised** which may explain pro-social behaviour. • Pro-social behaviour isn't simply about helping, it is also a **means of governing social relationships** e.g. establishing power and affirming friendships. Therefore one expects cultural differences. • **Importance of meaning** can be applied to studies of pro-social behaviour which are conducted in labs where the *meaning of the behaviour is missing* – inevitably results in an individualist picture of pro-social behaviour. • Cross-cultural studies may be hampered to some extent by the **imposed etic**.

Question 2: (a) Outline **one or more** explanations of human altruism **and/or** bystander behaviour. (12 marks)
(b) To what extent are there cultural differences in pro-social behaviour? (12 marks)

(a) 15 MINUTES WORTH OF AO1
Use two explanations from topic 1 or 2, or mixture.

(b) 15 MINUTES WORTH OF AO2
• **Evidence of differences** e.g. women display more empathy (meta-analysis by **Eisenberg and Lennon**, 1983), helpfulness greater in small towns (**Korte and Ayvalioglu**, 1981), **kibbutz** (collectivist), children more cooperative than US (**Moghaddam et al.**, 1993).
• But difficult to know the source of differences. May be social or biological (female caring an adaptive part of the 'tend and befriend' response, **Taylor et al.**, 2000).
• May be urban/rural or industrialised/non-industrialised.
• Cultural comparisons **ignore intra-cultural differences** e.g. Indians (collectivist) vary depending on whether they are **Muslim** (duty-based) or **Hindu** (option-oriented) (**Kanekar and Merchant**, 2001).
• Differences due to the **meaning** of pro-social behaviour. Pro-social behaviour isn't simply about helping, it is also a **means of governing social relationships** e.g. establishing power and affirming friendships. Therefore one expects cultural differences.
• **Importance of meaning** can be applied to studies of pro-social behaviour which are conducted in labs where the *meaning of the behaviour is missing* – inevitably results in an individualist picture of pro-social behaviour.
• Cross-cultural studies hampered to some extent by **observer bias** and use of **imposed etics**.

A meta-analysis by Eisenberg and Lennon (1983) found strong and consistent gender differences favouring greater female empathy. Males and females are also found to differ in respect to guilt, with females typically reporting greater guilt feelings than males (Bybee, 1998). Research has also established that there are urban-rural differences in helping behaviour, with helpfulness found to be higher for people in small towns than for those living in large cities (Korte and Ayvalioglu, 1981). Milgram's stimulus overload theory (Milgram, 1970) claims that people living in urban environments are exposed to excessive stimulation, which leads to emergencies being treated as everyday events. As a result, people living in urban environments develop a more indifferent attitude to the needs of others, and so are less likely to help.

> The question allows for both studies *and* theories, so both are integrated into this first paragraph.

It is difficult to treat gender differences and cultural differences as separate influences on helping behaviour. Gender differences may be an aspect of cultural influences (e.g. men may become more heroic because of socialisation differences between the sexes). Gender differences in helping behaviour might also be a product of biological differences between the sexes, with female caring being an adaptive part of the 'tend and befriend' response (Taylor et al., 2000). Although the Korte and Ayvalioglu study is limited to Turkey, the existence of urban-rural differences is supported by a meta-analysis of 65 populations (Steblay, 1987), which confirmed these differences regardless of the type of help required. Milgram's theory is only one explanation for these differences, as urban societies are also more industrialised and competitive, so assertiveness and aggression are important, which can explain low levels of helping.

> Note the use of lots of AO2 'terminology' in this paragraph e.g. 'It is difficult to…', '…is supported by…', '…is only one explanation…', '…which can explain…' etc.

Differences between cultures in terms of pro-social behaviour can be explained by the individualism-collectivism distinction. Collectivist cultures (such as the Hindu culture of India) have a more duty-based view of interpersonal relations and are therefore more helpful. On the other hand, individualist cultures (such as the US) have a more option-oriented perspective, with helping being more to do with the nature of the relationship and the magnitude of the need (Miller, 1994). A further difference between individualist and collectivist cultures lies in the assignment of responsibility. Individualist cultures tend to blame individuals without taking much notice of the social context, whereas in collectivist cultures, individual responsibility is considered alongside the social context of any transgression. This leads to the fundamental attribution error among members of individualistic cultures, where situational factors are largely ignored in favour of individual factors.

> The inclusion of the 'fundamental attribution error' could be used as AO2 commentary, but here it is included as an AO1 descriptive theory.

Research with children raised in an Israeli kibbutz has established that these children are more cooperative and helpful than their American and European peers (Moghaddam et al., 1993). Research in other collectivist cultures (e.g. Polynesia) has found a similar trend (Mann, 1980). The meaning of pro-social behaviour may also differ across different cultures. In Greece foreigners are more likely to receive help than locals, whereas the reverse is true in Boston and Paris (Feldman, 1986). Collett and Shea (1976) suggest that in some cultures foreigners may be treated differently because they are seen as more important and worthy of help.

Cultural comparisons of pro-social behaviour tend to ignore intra-cultural differences. For example, Kanekar and Merchant (2001) found that among Indian students, Muslims had a more duty-based attitude to helping, whereas Hindu students were more option-orientated. Kanekar and Merchant suggest that this difference may be due to the fact that Muslim students have a stronger social identity due to their minority status. Collectivist societies also tend to be more rural and less industrialised which may explain pro-social behaviour.

Pro-social behaviour isn't simply about helping, but may also be a means of governing social relationships, e.g. establishing power, affirming friendships and creating indebtedness. As a result, one would expect cultural differences in how and when help is given. Laboratory studies tend to show that people are less helpful whereas field studies tend to find higher levels of helpfulness. This may be explained by the fact that American participants have been socialised to behave as if they are being watched and evaluated. This results in an individualist picture of pro-social behaviour in laboratory studies. The social function of helping is also missing in laboratory studies – in the real world people seek the help of others to extend their social relationships (Moghaddam, 1998). Cross-cultural studies are also hampered to some extent by the imposed etic. The use of research methodologies developed in one culture to interpret the behaviours of another culture may mean that we draw unjustifiable conclusions about participants from that culture.

> There are a number of points being made here, so it is important to add sufficient elaboration to make each point *effective*.

Topic 1: Media influences on pro-social behaviour

Woodard (1999) found 77% of children's programmes in the US contained pro-social messages, but only 4 of the top 20 most-watched programmes did so.

Exposure to pro-social behaviour
Despite concern over the *anti-social* content in popular television programmes, there is clear evidence of a comparable level of *pro-social* content (Greenberg *et al.*, 1980).

Children are most affected by pro-social messages when **concrete pro-social** acts are demonstrated rather than more abstract messages.

Acquisition of pro-social behaviours and norms
Unlike the depiction of anti-social acts, pro-social acts tend to *represent* social norms rather than *contrast* with them. Children are more likely to be rewarded for imitating pro-social acts.

Explanations
The media has the potential to pass on positive messages to young audiences, but how does it accomplish this?

Pro-social versus anti-social effects
Children are better able to generalise from watching anti-social rather than pro-social acts on TV. Mixing the two together may have a damaging effect on any pro-social message (Silverman and Sprafkin, 1980).

Developmental factors
Skills synonymous with pro-social behaviour develop into adolescence, therefore young children are less likely to be affected by pro-social messages.

However, Mares (1996) found the weakest effect from pro-social programming was on adolescents, and strongest on primary-school children.

Mares (1996) examined all available research published between 1966 and 1995, considering four main behavioural effects of pro-social TV.

Research studies
As well as individual studies of pro-social effects, *meta-analyses* (e.g. Mares, 1996) offer a more global view of research in this area.

Pro-social effects of other media
Other media (e.g. children's books) may also carry pro-social messages, but computer games are more focused on entertainment than on pro-social messages (Media Metrix, 1999).

1. Altruism (e.g. sharing, offering help, comforting). Children who saw pro-social content behaved more altruistically than those who viewed neutral or anti-social content.

2. Positive interaction (e.g. friendly interactions, peaceable conflict resolution). Friedrich and Stein (1973): children who watched a pro-social programme behaved more positively towards each other than those who had watched a neutral programme.

3. Self-control (e.g. resistance to temptation, obedience to rules, task persistence). Children exposed to a model who demonstrated self-control later showed higher levels of self-control in their own behaviour.

4. Anti-stereotyping (e.g. counter-stereotypes of gender and ethnic groups). Johnston and Ettema (1982) found children become less stereotyped or prejudiced after watching anti-sex-role stereotyping programmes.

Problems with interpretation
• Behaviour usually measured shortly after viewing, rather than testing for long-term effects.
• When more *generalised* pro-social behaviours are measured, the effect is smaller.

Socioeconomic background of children influenced their receptiveness but this difference was only short-lived.

Other research (e.g. Pingree, 1978) has found that boys showed *stronger* sex-role stereotypes after viewing non-traditional models.

Topic 2: Media influences on anti-social behaviour

Although observational learning from specially prepared violent films has been demonstrated in Bandura's research, **evidence from real-life** scenarios are quite rare and claims often unsubstantiated.

1. Observational learning. Children observe actions of media models and may later imitate these actions, especially if they identify with the model and the model's anti-social behaviour is rewarded.

Josephson (1987) found evidence of cognitive priming among ice-hockey players following exposure to a violent film.

2. Cognitive priming. Aggressive media may trigger a network of memories involving aggression and so predispose the viewer to act in an aggressive manner.

Cumberbatch (2001) argues that although children may get 'used' to screen violence, it does not follow that they would also get used to violence in the real world.

3. Desensitisation. Under normal conditions anxiety about aggression inhibits its use. Frequent viewing of media violence desensitises viewers as to its effects and represents violence as 'normal'.

Watching violence may **increase aggressiveness** (Zillman's excitation-transfer model) or release pent-up energy (catharsis).

4. Lowered physiological arousal. Frequent viewing of media violence leads to less physiological arousal as a result of viewing violent behaviour and thus fewer inhibitions concerning its use.

The negative effects of mixed pro- and anti-social messages might be **explained** in terms of the 'good guys' having moral justification for their violence.

5. Justification. Television may provide a justification for a child's own violent behaviour. As a result, guilt and concern about consequences of violence diminish, as do inhibitions about future aggression.

Explanations
Huesmann and Moise (1996) suggest five ways in which exposure to media violence might lead to aggression.

The National Television Violence study (1994-1997)
Researchers evaluated 10,000 hours of TV, found highest proportion of violence in children's programmes, which also showed fewest long-term negative consequences of violence.

Research studies
As well as individual studies of anti-social effects, *meta-analyses* (e.g. Paik and Comstock, 1994) offer a more global view of research in this area.

Video games and aggression
A recent review of research evidence in this area concluded that exposure to video game violence increases aggressive behaviour (Dill and Dill, 1998).

Limitations
• Most studies in this area have been correlational, and do not indicate a *causal* relationship between playing violent video games and violent behaviour.
• Studies rarely distinguish between aggressive *behaviour* and aggressive *play*, which may lead to faulty conclusions.

The anti-effects lobby
• Belson (1978): boys who watched the *most* violent television were half as aggressive as those who watched moderate amounts (suggesting relationship is unpredictable).
• Hagell and Newburn (1994): violent teenage offenders watched less TV than non-offenders.

Meta-analysis of research
Paik and Comstock (1994) examined 217 studies, found highly significant relationship between television violence and aggressive behaviour, slightly higher in males.

Many earlier studies were laboratory-based, i.e. not typical of child's normal television experience.

The St. Helena study (Charlton et al., 2000)
The vast majority of measures used to assess pro- and anti-social behaviour showed no difference in either after introduction of television.

Other **natural experiments** *have* found a difference after the introduction of TV (e.g. Williams, 1986). Charlton suggests that community identity removed the need to be aggressive in St Helena.

explanations and research studies relating to media influences on pro- behaviour

Probable questions

1. Discuss research (explanations **and/or** research studies) relating to media influences on pro-social behaviour. *(24 marks)*

2. (a) Outline and evaluate **two or more** explanations relating to media influences on pro-social behaviour. *(12 marks)*

   (b) Outline and evaluate **two or more** research studies relating to media influences on pro-social behaviour. *(12 marks)*

Possible questions

3. (a) Outline **two or more** explanations relating to media influences on pro-social behaviour. *(12 marks)*

   (b) Evaluate the **two or more** explanations relating to media influences on pro-social behaviour in terms of relevant research studies. *(12 marks)*

4. Critically consider explanations **and** research studies relating to media influences on pro-social behaviour. *(24 marks)*

---

explanations and research studies relating to media influences on anti-social behaviour

Probable questions

1. Discuss research (explanations **and/or** research studies) relating to media influences on anti-social behaviour. *(24 marks)*

2. (a) Outline and evaluate research (explanations **and/or** research studies) relating to media influences on pro-social behaviour. *(12 marks)*

   (b) Outline and evaluate research (explanations **and/or** research studies) relating to media influences on anti-social behaviour. *(12 marks)*

Possible questions

3. Discuss **two or more** explanations relating to media influences on anti-social behaviour. *(24 marks)*

4. (a) Outline research studies relating to media influences on anti-social behaviour. *(12 marks)*

   (b) To what extent do these studies present conclusive evidence that the media is responsible for anti-social behaviour? *(12 marks)*

This is again a division where explanations and research studies are given in the specification which means questions can be set on one or both of them. It does mean that there are a wider range of questions that can be set, and therefore more material that you need to revise as you need 30 minutes worth of one explanation, 30 minutes of two explanations, and 30 minutes of research studies. You also need to be prepared to use your research studies as AO2.

In question 1 you are given the option of using explanations or studies. As we have said before, the danger here is that you have too much to include (since you know explanations *and* research studies). The consequence is that you either spend too much time on the whole question (and obtain lower marks on other questions on the paper), or you spend too much time on AO1 and lose marks because of too little AO2ing. The solution lies in being carefully selective about what you include.

Question 2 is again on explanations and studies and the same problem faces you. It is unlikely that you would have time for more than two explanations in part (a) because you have only 7 1/2 minutes for AO1 and 7 1/2 minutes for AO2. The option is given to you to do more than two explanations (or more than two studies) *if* you feel you don't have enough material otherwise. But two of each would be sufficient for full marks. More material doesn't necessarily mean more marks. More detail and elaboration *does* mean more marks.

Question 3 specifies that you must use research studies in your evaluation. The greatest difficulty for candidates is that they cannot resist *describing* such studies (and there is no credit for a description of the studies) and fail to *use* their knowledge as a form of evaluation. This is a *skill* that you need to practise and get down to a fine art.

The final question, question 4, is very similar to question 1 but here you must do explanations *and* studies. If you only described and evaluated studies a partial performance penalty would govern your mark (there would be a limit of 8 marks for AO1 and 8 marks for AO2). A more common failing in questions like this is that candidates describe both explanations and studies, but only evaluate one. Then their AO1 mark is assessed out of 12 but their AO2 mark is assessed out of 8.

Since the specification entry is exactly the same for topics 1 and 2 (except one says pro-social and the other says anti-social) the same set of questions can be asked, though for the sake of change some of these given here are different.

Question 2 here offers a new combination. It is legitimate to combine topics within a division in an exam question – so here part (a) is on pro-social research and part (b) is on anti-social research. Again the danger lies in having too much to write and not being sufficiently strict in what you decide to include.

Question 4 is also a new approach. Part (a) does not specify a number of research studies but since 'studies' is plural you must outline at least two (or suffer the partial performance penalty). There is no credit in part (a) for evaluation of such studies because the injunction (outline) is pure AO1. If you did provide evaluation this would not be creditworthy in part (b) and thus would not be 'exported'.

Part (b) is the less common AO2 injunction 'To what extent'. Try to focus on the question asked – do you think the media is responsible for anti-social behaviour? Yes? Then provide evidence for your opinion but *don't* spend too much time describing your evidence as there is no credit for description in this part of the question. Use your evidence and evaluate its validity. You may think that the answer is 'no'. Then do the same for this answer. Or explore both answers.

SAMPLE ESSAY PLAN

Question 1: Discuss research (explanations **and/or** research studies) relating to media influences on pro-social behaviour. (24 marks)

EXPLANATIONS

6 MINUTES WORTH OF AO1

- **Exposure to pro-social programming.** Greenberg et al. (1980) found that there are as many pro-social as anti-social acts in popular US children's programmes.
- **Social learning theory:** pro-social behaviours in the media reinforce our social norms therefore are more likely to be imitated.
- **Eisenberg** (1990) suggests a developmental explanation of the influence of pro-social media.

6 MINUTES WORTH OF AO2

- However **not all programmes are pro-social.** Woodard (1999) found that only 4 of top 20 children's programmes were.
- SLT may only explain **short-term behaviour.** Behaviours only displayed when supported by social norms.
- **Mares** (1996) found weakest effect was for adolescents and strongest for primary-school children.

RESEARCH STUDIES

9 MINUTES WORTH OF AO1

Mares (1996) meta-analysis found that for altruism:

- Children who saw more pro-social content behaved more altruistically (**Poulos et al.,** 1975).
- **Self-control:** children who watched pro-social programmes showed more self-control (higher task persistence, more obedience) than children who watched neutral or anti-social programmes (**Friedrich and Stein,** 1973).
- **Positive interaction:** Freidrich and Stein also found children positive towards each other.
- **Anti-stereotyping:** several thousand children watched pro-social TV (*Freestyle*) for 12 weeks, moderate positive effects such as less prejudged (**Johnston and Ettema,** 1982).
- **Other media:** books traditionally pro-social (**Mares,** 1998) and internet increasingly so (**Media Metrix,** 1999).

9 MINUTES WORTH OF AO2

- **Mares** (1996) reviewed relevant research 1966–1985 and concluded only a moderate effect.
- **Hearold** (1986) reviewed 230 studies and found a stronger effect possibly because programmes included in studies were specifically designed to be pro-social (**Comstock,** 1989).
- Studies measure **short-term effects.** Friedrich and Stein found effects tapered after 2 weeks, so external validity of studies poor.
- Studies also measure **specific effects,** when general levels of pro-social behaviour measured effects are reduced.
- **Individual differences,** in Friedrich and Stein study **effects stronger for lower SE** children.
- **Anti-stereotyping** may have reverse effect: teenage boys showed **stronger stereotypes** after exposure to counter-stereotypes (**Pingree,** 1978).

Question 3: (a) Outline **two or more** explanations relating to media influences on pro-social behaviour. (12 marks)
(b) Evaluate the **two or more** explanations relating to media influences on pro-social behaviour in terms of relevant research studies. (12 marks)

(a) 15 MINUTES WORTH OF AO1

The description of theory 1 above, plus:

- **Production** (as distinct from learning) is more likely than for pro- than anti-social behaviour because we already have **pro-social norms** which would lead to expectation that such behaviour would be rewarded.
- **Age may be important.** Younger children may be less affected because they lack social norms.
- Also because younger children haven't yet developed **perspective taking** (empathy) (**Eisenberg,** 1990).
- Effects enhanced when children showed exact steps for positive behaviour, e.g. showed child donating tokens (**Mares and Woodard,** 2001).
- Effects enhanced when viewing is **accompanied by follow-up discussion** in the classroom.

(b) 15 MINUTES WORTH OF AO2

The evaluation of theory 1 above, plus:

- **General levels of pro-social behaviour increased** e.g. children who watched pro-social programmes showed more self-control and more positive towards each other than children who watched neutral or anti-social programmes (**Friedrich and Stein,** 1973).

- But **short-term effects.** Friedrich and Stein found effects tapered after 2 weeks.
- **Specific acts imitated** e.g. children who watched a child rescue dog were more likely to rescue some puppies (**Poulos et al.,** 1975).
- May affect **specific but not general behaviour** e.g. when general levels of pro-social behaviour measured effects are reduced.
- However **not all programmes are pro-social.** Woodard (1999) found that only 4 of top 20 children's programmes were.
- **Mares** (1996) found strongest effects in younger children.
- **Follow-up discussion not always effective** e.g. **Rubenstein and Sprafkin** (1982) working with adolescents with psychiatric problems who took opposite view to adults.
- Pro-social research is **disappointing** compared to volume of anti-social research, possibly because anti-social effects stronger due to more concrete nature of anti-social behaviour.

Social learning theory explains the influence of the media on pro-social behaviour in terms of exposure to pro-social programming in the media. Greenberg et al. (1980) found that there are as many pro-social as anti-social acts in popular US children's programmes. The essence of this theory is that children learn by observation how to do things and whether it is acceptable to do them. They may then imitate these behaviours, particularly if they are likely to be rewarded for displaying them. Pro-social behaviours in the media are likely to reinforce our social norms rather than contrast with them, therefore are more likely to be imitated. Eisenberg (1990) suggests a developmental explanation of the relationship between pro-social media and pro-social behaviour. She claims that many of the skills associated with pro-social behaviour develop throughout childhood and adolescence, meaning that younger children will be less affected by pro-social portrayals in the media than older children.

> There are two explanations described in this first paragraph. As these theories exist independently of this context, it is important to provide a contextualised description rather than a general account of each theory.

Despite the claim that children are exposed to a great deal of pro-social media, Woodard (1999) found that only 4 of the top 20 children's programmes contained pro-social lessons. Social learning theory should predict that the portrayal of pro-social and anti-social acts in the media should have an equal effect. However, children are more able to generalise from watching aggressive than pro-social acts on television. In contrast to the portrayal of anti-social acts on television, pro-social acts are less concrete, and pro-social models may be perceived as being less attractive and weaker than anti-social models. Despite Eisenberg's claim that younger children would be least affected by pro-social programming, a meta-analysis by Mares (1996) found that the weakest effect was for adolescents and the strongest for primary-school children.

> Note how each claim is followed by a critical point that adds context to the evaluation.

Mares (1996) in a meta-analysis of research on the relationship between television and pro-social behaviour found the following. Studies that investigated the link between television and altruism tended to find that children who saw more pro-social content behaved more altruistically that who saw neutral or anti-social content, e.g. Poulos et al. (1975). Mares also found that children who watched pro-social programmes showed more self-control (higher task persistence and greater obedience) than children who watched neutral or anti-social programmes, e.g. Friedrich and Stein (1973). Friedrich and Stein also found that children behaved more positively towards each other after watching pro-social television. Johnston and Ettema (1982) studied several thousand children who watched a pro-social TV programme (Freestyle) designed to reduce sex-role stereotypes over a period of 12 weeks. They found there were substantial reductions in stereotypical attitudes and beliefs about gender roles following exposure to these programmes. Other studies have also found a moderate positive effect in studies featuring counter-stereotypical themes. Although research has focused almost exclusively on the effects of television, some research has shown the beneficial effects of other types of media. For example, Mares (1998) pointed out that many children's books carry strongly pro-social messages where good triumphs over evil. The opportunities for Internet generated media to influence pro-social behaviour appear more limited. In one study (Media Metrix, 1999), very few of the top children's sites on the Internet were pro-social in nature.

> The meta-analysis cited here is an extensive review of the area. You can only hope to give a flavour of it here.

> There are quite a few names and dates here. Although you would not be penalised for leaving them out, their inclusion does make it easier to recognise individual studies.

Despite Mares' finding that, in general, the media had a pro-social influence on children's behaviour, she concluded that this was only a moderate effect. This is in contrast to the earlier study carried out by Hearold (1986) who reviewed 230 studies and found a stronger effect for the pro-social effects of television. This is possibly because many of the programmes included in Hearold's meta-analysis were specifically designed to be pro-social and therefore the stronger effect is not surprising (Comstock, 1989). A problem with most of these studies is that they measure only short-term effects rather than enduring long-term effects. For example, in the Friedrich and Stein study, the researchers found that the positive effects of exposure to pro-social television tapered after 2 weeks, so the external validity of these studies is relatively poor. The positive relationship between programme and behaviour can also be explained by the fact that these studies tend to measure specific effects rather than more generalised pro-social behaviours. When general levels of pro-social behaviour are measured following exposure to pro-social television, these effects are reduced. Research has also established that there are important individual differences in the influence of pro-social media. In the Friedrich and Stein study, the effects were stronger for children from lower socio-economic backgrounds compared to children from higher socio-economic families. A problem for programmes attempting to reduce stereotypes is whether they work. In one study by Pingree (1978), there was a reverse effect, with teenage boys showing stronger stereotypes after exposure to counter-stereotypical models.

> There are several different forms of AO2 commentary in this paragraph, including *contrasts, interpretation, negative criticism, explanation, methodological limitations,* and *opposing research findings.*

TOPIC 2: MEDIA INFLUENCES ON ANTI-SOCIAL BEHAVIOUR

SAMPLE ESSAY PLAN

Question 4: (a) Outline research studies relating to media influences on anti-social behaviour. (12 marks)
(b) To what extent do these studies present conclusive evidence that the media is responsible for anti-social behaviour? (12 marks)

(a) 15 MINUTES WORTH OF AO1

Research studies below, plus:

- **National Violence Study** showed high risk portrayals of violence included justified and unpunished violence.
- **St Helena study found** only two significant changes in anti-social behaviour scores, both of which were lower after the introduction of television.
- **Dill and Dill** (1998) found that exposure to video game violence increases aggressive behaviour and other aggression-related behaviour.

(b) 15 MINUTES WORTH OF AO2

Yes the media is responsible:

- For example, **video games** linked to aggression e.g. **Anderson and Dill** (2000).
- But **Sacher** (1993) found only 7 out of 26 studies supported a link; **correlation** doesn't show that video games caused aggressive behaviour.
- **Lab studies lack** mundane realism because home viewing is voluntary, therefore can't generalise findings.

No the media is not responsible:

- For example, **St Helena natural experiment**.
- Earlier **natural experiment** (**Williams**, 1986) found anti-social behaviour did increase but St Helena had a strong sense of community (**strong social norms**) therefore anti-social behaviour may be learned but not produced.
- **Media effects model flawed** (**Gauntlett**, 1998): there **aren't consistent effects**, research should start with violent people and see if TV affects them rather than working backwards. **Hagell and Newburn** (1994) did this and found **negative correlation** between violence and amount of TV watched.
- Danger in **oversimplifying** a complex situation (**Livingstone**, 2001) but that's what policy-makers want.

Question 1: Discuss research (explanations **and/or** research studies) relating to media influences on anti-social behaviour. (24 marks)

EXPLANATIONS

5 MINUTES WORTH OF AO1

- **Observational learning**: children identify and imitate media models.
- **Cognitive priming**: violence on TV creates a 'script' which may be triggered at a later time.
- **Desensitisation**: aggressive behaviour becomes more acceptable and therefore more likely to be repeated.

5 MINUTES WORTH OF AO2

- **Observational learning** supported by SLT research (e.g. **Bobo doll studies**). **Anecdotal claims** of copycat behaviour may be unsubstantiated (**Cumberbatch**, 2001).
- **Cognitive priming** demonstrated by **Josephson** (1987). Hockey players imitated aggression in a film when referee holding walkie-talkie (a cue) as in film.
- **Desensitisation** from films doesn't logically follow that one is desensitised in the real world (**Cumberbatch**, 2001).

RESEARCH STUDIES

10 MINUTES WORTH OF AO1

- **National Violence Study** found highest violence in children's programmes but this genre was also least likely to show negative long-term consequences of violence.
- Meta analysis (**Paik and Comstock**, 1994) found highly significant relationship between TV violence and aggressive behaviour especially in pre-school children.
- **St Helena natural experiment** (**Charlton et al.**, 2000): effects after arrival of TV assessed, anti-social behaviour didn't significantly increase.
- **Video games** linked to aggression e.g. **Anderson and Dill** (2000) found that students who played more video games reported more aggression.
- Video game playing was found to be positively correlated with **aggressive delinquency** (**Dominick**, 1984).

10 MINUTES WORTH OF AO2

- **Lab studies lack** mundane realism because home viewing is voluntary, therefore can't generalise findings.
- Earlier **natural experiment** (**Williams**, 1986) found anti-social behaviour did increase but St Helena had a strong sense of community (strong social norms) therefore anti-social behaviour may be learned but not produced.
- Correlation doesn't show that **video games** caused aggressive behaviour.
- Other research on **video games** mostly has found no linkage (**Sacher**, 1993). Need to distinguish aggressive play and aggressive behaviour.
- **Media effects model flawed** (**Gauntlett**, 1998): there **aren't consistent effects**, research should start with violent people and see if TV affects them rather than working backwards. **Hagell and Newburn** (1994) did this and found negative correlation between violence and amount of TV watched.

(a)

The National Television Violence study evaluated television broadcasts in the US between 1994 and 1997 and found that over 60% of programmes portrayed some interpersonal violence, much of which was shown in an entertaining or glamorised manner. The researchers also found that the highest proportion of televised violence was in children's programmes although this was also the genre least likely to show the long-term negative consequences of violent behaviour. Researchers also identified those elements that increase the risk of children learning aggressive attitudes and behaviours. These high risk portrayals of violence included violence that appears justified, violence that goes unpunished and violence that has minimal consequences for the victim.

A meta-analysis of research in this area (Paik and Comstock, 1994) found a highly significant positive relationship between viewing TV violence and aggressive behaviour, especially in preschool children, with the effect being slightly higher for males than for females. A natural experiment (Charlton et al., 2000) studied the effects of recently introduced television on the island of St Helena. The researchers found that on the majority of measures used to assess pro- and anti-social behaviour there was no difference in either after the introduction of television. There were only two significant changes in anti-social behaviour scores, both of which were lower after the introduction of television (Charlton et al. 2000).

Television is not the only medium to have been studied, with video games also being linked to aggression. In one study of 15–16 year olds, video game playing was found to be positively correlated with aggressive delinquency (Dominick, 1984). Anderson and Dill (2000), in a survey of psychology undergraduates, found that those students who played more video games when younger engaged in more aggressive behaviour later on. A review of research in this area found that exposure to video game violence increases aggressive behaviour and other aggression-related behaviour (Dill and Dill, 1998).

(b)

Some research appears to conclude that the media is responsible for aggressive behaviour in those who are exposed to it. For example, violent video games have been linked to aggression, e.g. Anderson and Dill (2000) through desensitisation to violence or the acquisition of cognitive schemas that support aggressive behaviour. The general picture regarding the link between video games and aggression is, however, far from conclusive. Sacher (1993) in a review of research in this area found that of 26 studies, only 7 linked violent video games to aggressive behaviour. Those studies that have found a relationship have been correlational only, rather than suggesting a causal link between violent video games and aggressive behaviour.

A problem for many of the lab studies of media effects is that they are artificial, and fail to represent the normal viewing circumstances of the child. Home viewing tends to be a voluntary activity, whereas in the laboratory, the child is compelled to watch material that is not of their choosing. This makes it difficult to generalise findings beyond the laboratory to real life.

A number of studies have cast doubt on the claim that the media is responsible for aggressive behaviour. In the St Helena natural experiment, the researchers concluded that very little had changed following television's arrival. However, this is in contrast to an earlier natural experiment (Williams, 1986) which found that aggressive and anti-social behaviour did increase following the introduction of television into a small Canadian town. One explanation for this difference is that St Helena has a strong sense of community (i.e. strong social norms) which means that, although anti-social behaviour may be learned from watching television, it tends not to be produced in actual behaviour.

Gauntlett (1998) claims that the media effects model is flawed, arguing that research should start with people who display violent behaviour and try to see what media influences they have experienced, rather than trying to link media violence with subsequent violent behaviour. Hagell and Newburn (1994) did just this and found a negative correlation between violence and the amount of TV watched. Livingstone (2001) claims that the main danger in the media effects debate is in oversimplifying a complex situation merely to provide simple answers for policy makers and the public.

In this paragraph, rather than cramming in lots of smaller accounts of studies, a detailed account of one important study is used.

A meta-analysis is particularly useful in this context as it is a review of lots of different studies, and therefore shows general trends.

Remember there are other forms of media besides television. This shows evidence of breadth and wider reading.

You should only make this point if you *know* that the study or studies in question have been correlations rather than experiments.

If you are going to include an alternative study, make something of it. Here the difference is *explained* rather than ignored.

You may not have time to include these points, but Gauntlett and Livingstone provide an effective closing pitch for this essay.

Topic 1: Circadian, infradian and ultradian rhythms

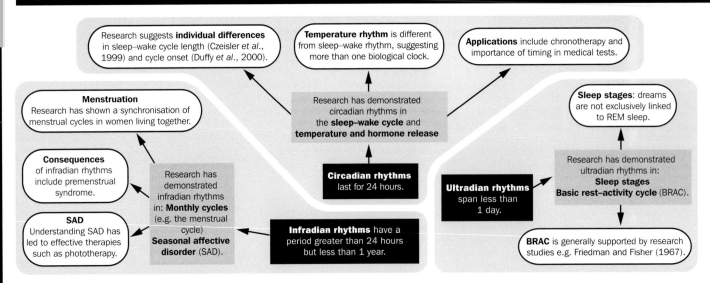

Research suggests **individual differences** in sleep–wake cycle length (Czeisler *et al.*, 1999) and cycle onset (Duffy *et al.*, 2000).

Temperature rhythm is different from sleep–wake rhythm, suggesting more than one biological clock.

Applications include chronotherapy and importance of timing in medical tests.

Menstruation
Research has shown a synchronisation of menstrual cycles in women living together.

Research has demonstrated circadian rhythms in the **sleep–wake cycle** and **temperature and hormone release**

Sleep stages: dreams are not exclusively linked to REM sleep.

Consequences of infradian rhythms include premenstrual syndrome.

Research has demonstrated infradian rhythms in: **Monthly cycles** (e.g. the menstrual cycle) **Seasonal affective disorder** (SAD).

Circadian rhythms last for 24 hours.

Ultradian rhythms span less than 1 day.

Research has demonstrated ultradian rhythms in: **Sleep stages** **Basic rest–activity cycle** (BRAC).

SAD
Understanding SAD has led to effective therapies such as phototherapy.

Infradian rhythms have a period greater than 24 hours but less than 1 year.

BRAC is generally supported by research studies e.g. Friedman and Fisher (1967).

Topic 2: The role of endogenous pacemakers and exogenous zeitgebers

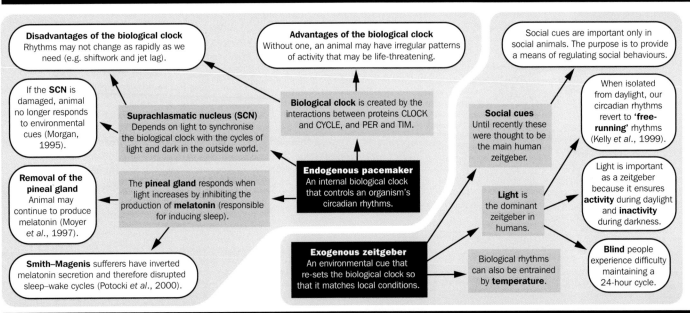

Disadvantages of the biological clock
Rhythms may not change as rapidly as we need (e.g. shiftwork and jet lag).

Advantages of the biological clock
Without one, an animal may have irregular patterns of activity that may be life-threatening.

Social cues are important only in social animals. The purpose is to provide a means of regulating social behaviours.

If the **SCN** is damaged, animal no longer responds to environmental cues (Morgan, 1995).

Suprachiasmatic nucleus (SCN)
Depends on light to synchronise the biological clock with the cycles of light and dark in the outside world.

Biological clock is created by the interactions between proteins CLOCK and CYCLE, and PER and TIM.

Social cues
Until recently these were thought to be the main human zeitgeber.

When isolated from daylight, our circadian rhythms revert to **'free-running'** rhythms (Kelly *et al.*, 1999).

Removal of the pineal gland
Animal may continue to produce melatonin (Moyer *et al.*, 1997).

The **pineal gland** responds when light increases by inhibiting the production of **melatonin** (responsible for inducing sleep).

Endogenous pacemaker
An internal biological clock that controls an organism's circadian rhythms.

Light is the dominant zeitgeber in humans.

Light is important as a zeitgeber because it ensures **activity** during daylight and **inactivity** during darkness.

Smith–Magenis sufferers have inverted melatonin secretion and therefore disrupted sleep–wake cycles (Potocki *et al.*, 2000).

Exogenous zeitgeber
An environmental cue that re-sets the biological clock so that it matches local conditions.

Biological rhythms can also be entrained by **temperature**.

Blind people experience difficulty maintaining a 24-hour cycle.

Topic 3: Consequences of disrupting rhythms

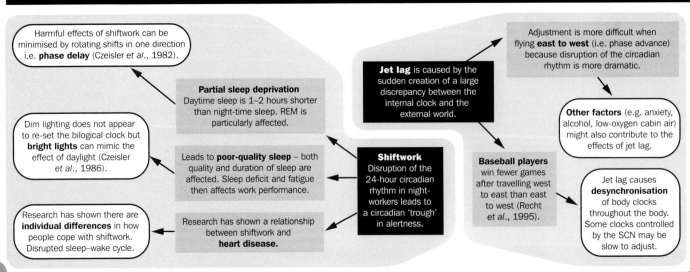

Harmful effects of shiftwork can be minimised by rotating shifts in one direction i.e. **phase delay** (Czeisler *et al.*, 1982).

Adjustment is more difficult when flying **east to west** (i.e. phase advance) because disruption of the circadian rhythm is more dramatic.

Jet lag is caused by the sudden creation of a large discrepancy between the internal clock and the external world.

Partial sleep deprivation
Daytime sleep is 1–2 hours shorter than night-time sleep. REM is particularly affected.

Dim lighting does not appear to re-set the bilogical clock but **bright lights** can mimic the effect of daylight (Czeisler *et al.*, 1986).

Leads to **poor-quality sleep** – both quality and duration of sleep are affected. Sleep deficit and fatigue then affects work performance.

Shiftwork
Disruption of the 24-hour circadian rhythm in night-workers leads to a circadian 'trough' in alertness.

Baseball players win fewer games after travelling west to east than east to west (Recht *et al.*, 1995).

Other factors (e.g. anxiety, alcohol, low-oxygen cabin air) might also contribute to the effects of jet lag.

Research has shown there are **individual differences** in how people cope with shiftwork. Disrupted sleep–wake cycle.

Research has shown a relationship between shiftwork and **heart disease.**

Jet lag causes **desynchronisation** of body clocks throughout the body. Some clocks controlled by the SCN may be slow to adjust.

Probable questions

1. Describe and evaluate research into **one or more** biological rhythm (e.g. circadian, infradian, ultradian). *(24 marks)*

2. Outline and evaluate research into **two or more** biological rhythms. *(24 marks)*

Possible questions

3. Discuss research into circadian rhythms. *(24 marks)*

4. (a) Critically consider research into infradian rhythms. *(12 marks)*

   (b) Critically consider research into ultradian rhythms. *(12 marks)*

The answers to both of these questions could be the same – discussing two rhythms.

When asked for 'one or more' you can gain maximum marks by discussing only one rhythm. However, if you feel you do not know enough for a 30 minute answer on one rhythm then there is credit for discussing other rhythms.

If a question requires you to discuss two rhythms you would be limited to 16 marks if you only discussed one rhythm (partial performance penalty).

It is possible that questions might be set on specific rhythms, since these are part of the specification content. This potentially means that you need a 30 minute answer for each of the three rhythms. In reality there is less accessible material on infradian and ultradian rhythms so that it is unlikely that a whole question would specify only one of these. Instead you might get a question such as question 4.

In all of these questions you are required to describe and evaluate 'research'. This means that it would be acceptable to discuss studies and/or explanations.

Probable questions

1. Discuss the role of endogenous pacemakers and exogenous zeitgebers. *(24 marks)*

Possible questions

2. Describe and evaluate the role of endogenous pacemakers. *(24 marks)*

3. Describe and evaluate the role of exogenous zeitgebers. *(24 marks)*

The question does not contain the word 'research' since the specification doesn't use that term. Nevertheless it is most likely that any answer would be based on research (explanations and/or studies).

One of the difficulties with this question is the overlap between AO1 and AO2. For example research studies could be AO1 or AO2. You could describe research on exogenous zeitgebers (AO1) or use this research to comment on the role of endogenous pacemakers (AO2).

This means that you need to pay careful attention to how you structure your answer and how research is *used*.

It would be permissible to ask separate questions about endogenous pacemakers or exogenous zeitgebers. Question 2 would require you to *describe* the role of the endogenous pacemakers and then evaluate them. You can *evaluate* these by considering that biological rhythms may be alternatively controlled by exogenous zeitgebers. In other words you can re-use the material from question 1 *but* you *must* use the research on exogenous zeitgebers as AO2 instead of AO1.

For question 3 you could describe the role of exogenous zeitgebers and then use AO1 material on endogenous pacemakers as AO2.

Probable questions

1. Discuss the consequences of disrupting biological rhythms (e.g. jet lag, shift work). *(24 marks)*

2. (a) Outline research into **one or more** biological rhythms. *(12 marks)*

   (b) Assess the consequences of disrupting such rhythms. *(12 marks)*

Possible questions

3. Critically consider the consequences of disrupting biological rhythms. *(24 marks)*

In question 1 the term 'research' has not been used but the most likely route to answering this question would be to describe relevant research studies and thus describe the consequences of disrupting biological rhythms. You can focus on jet lag and/or shift work and/or any other examples (e.g. seasonal changes).

AO2 might be achieved by, for example, considering strengths/limitations of any studies, contrasting research findings or the application of such knowledge.

Question 2 is an example of a question that combines more than one topic within a division (which is permissible). You have prepared the answer to part (a) in earlier questions. Part (b) is partly a repeat of the AO2 material for question 1 – except this time it is stand alone. Start by asking yourself 'What are the consequences of disrupting biological rhythms?' (for example, sleep-deprived people cause accidents). But this is not the answer for part (b). You must *assess* whether such claims are true.

This is the same question as question 1 – using a different AO1/AO2 injunction and not providing examples. Examples in questions are intended to help candidates but sometimes candidates take them too literally and feel they are required to address both examples and exclude any others. They are merely possible examples.

TOPIC 1: CIRCADIAN, INFRADIAN AND ULTRADIAN RHYTHMS

SAMPLE ESSAY PLAN

Question 2: Outline and evaluate research into **two or more** biological rhythms (e.g. circadian, infradian, ultradian). (24 marks)

CIRCADIAN RHYTHMS	**5 MINUTES WORTH OF AO1** Example – **sleep–wake cycle** is 24 hours. • Endogenous evidence from isolation studies: • (1) **Siffre** (1975) in a cave for 6 months, rhythm varied between 24 and 48 hours. • (2) **Aschoff and Wever** (1976) Ps in a bunker, rhythm varied between 24 and 29 hours. • **Exogenous zeitgebers**: bright light resets circadian rhythm, dim light may have an effect too (**Wever et al.,** 1983).	**5 MINUTES WORTH OF AO2** • **Isolation studies,** not isolated from artificial light therefore not actually testing free running cycle. • Some studies found dim lighting can reduce down to 22 hours (**Czeisler et al.,** 1999). • Some studies found artificial light is not enough e.g. submariners (**Kelly et al.,**1999). • **Individual differences**: rhythms vary from 13–65 hours. • Exogenous zeitgebers e.g. light, important to synchronise with environment.
INFRADIAN RHYTHMS	**5 MINUTES WORTH OF AO1** Description as below.	**5 MINUTES WORTH OF AO2** Evaluation as below.
ULTRADIAN RHYTHMS	**5 MINUTES WORTH OF AO1** Example – **sleep stages**, 90 minute. • **Non-REM (NREM)** sleep: stages 1&2: relaxed, 3&4 slow wave sleep (SWS) (growth hormone released). • **Rapid eye movement (REM)** sleep: possibly dreams, neurotransmitters manufactured. Example – **BRAC** (basic rest-activity cycle). • **Friedman and Fisher** (1967) gave evidence of cyclic eating, drinking behaviour.	**5 MINUTES WORTH OF AO2** • Sleep stages recorded in **artificial lab studies**. • SWS forms part of **core sleep**. • **Dreams also in NREM**, or can explain dreaming in terms of psychological rather than neurobiological function. • BRAC important for biological processes.

Question 1: Describe and evaluate research into **one or more** biological rhythm (e.g. circadian, infradian, ultradian). (24 marks)

CIRCADIAN RHYTHMS	**10 MINUTES WORTH OF AO1** Example – **sleep-wake** cycle is 24 hours. • **Endogenous** evidence from **isolation** studies: • **Siffre** (1975) in a cave for 6 months, rhythm varied between 24 and 48 hours. • **Aschoff and Wever** (1976) Ps in a bunker, rhythm varied between 24 and 29 hours. • **Folkard et al.** (1985) reduced clock speed, Ps couldn't adjust to 22 hour. Example – **temperature** rhythm, highest at 4 pm. • Leads to **improved cognitive activity**: long-term memory (LTM) better for material learned at 3pm (**Folkard et al.,** 1977). • **Exogenous zeitgebers**: bright light resets circadian rhythm but dim light may have an effect too (**Wever et al.,** 1983).	**10 MINUTES WORTH OF AO2** • **Isolation studies,** not isolated from artificial light therefore not actually testing free running cycle. • Some studies found dim lighting can reduce down to 22 hours (**Czeisler et al.,** 1999). • Some studies found artificial light is not enough e.g. submariners (**Kelly et al.,**1999). • **Individual differences**: **rhythms** vary from 13–65 hours; **cycle onset**: morning/evening types (**Duffy et al.,** 2000). • **Two biological clocks**: evidence from study of nurses (**Hawkins and Armstrong-Esther,** 1978). • **Exogenous zeitgebers** important to synchronise with environment. • **Application**, chronotherapeutics (e.g. take aspirin 11pm).
INFRADIAN RHYTHMS	**5 MINUTES WORTH OF AO1** Example – **monthly menstrual cycle**. • **Pituitary gland** → hormones, egg ripens → oestrogen. • There is a **male** cycle affecting temperature and mood, lasts 20 days (**Empson,** 1977). Example – **seasonal affective disorder**, depressed in winter. • **Melatonin** (related to depression) higher in winter months.	**5 MINUTES WORTH OF AO2** • **Menstruation** may be governed by exogenous zeitgebers – social cues transmitted through pheromones (**Russell et al.,** 1980). • A **well-controlled** (single blind) study, but small sample. • **Applications** include SAD, phototherapy.

The best known biological rhythm is the circadian cycle that occurs over the course of one day, for example the 24 hour sleep-wake cycle. One way to investigate whether the circadian sleep-wake rhythm is controlled by an internal mechanism is through the use of isolation studies where participants are cut off from all external cues about circadian rhythms (such as natural daylight and clocks).

Siffre (1972) spent 6 months inside a cave cut off from external cues. He found that his natural circadian rhythm was just over 24 hours though sometimes this would change dramatically to as much as 48 hours. Although the study of one individual is hardly a sound basis for research, the findings have been supported by other studies. Aschoff and Wever (1976) placed participants in an underground bunker, and found that most of them had a 24/25 hour rhythm though there were individual differences up to 29 hours.

One problem with these studies is that the participants were not isolated from artificial light. At one time it was thought that artificial lighting was not enough to reset the circadian rhythm but more recent research has not supported this. For example, Czeisler et al. (1999) used dim lighting to entrain participants' circadian rhythms, reducing them to 22 hours. This means that circadian rhythms in the isolation studies described above may have been controlled by exogenous zeitgebers (artificial lighting) as well as an endogenous rhythm.

On the other hand, other research has found very little effect of zeitgebers. Kelly et al. (1999) tried to entrain the circadian rhythms of people working on submarines using lighting, social cues, etc. but their rhythms remained at 24 hours. This suggests that circadian rhythms are most critically affected by internal cues but external cues are important too. For example, Wever et al. (1983) found that daylight resets the body's master clock in the superchiasmatic nucleus. This balance between internal and external control is important in adapting to one's environment but not being over controlled by it. Sensitivity to external cues ensures that we remain in step with changing seasons but only to a certain extent – otherwise Icelanders might end up sleeping all winter.

When considering research on circadian rhythms we should also consider individual differences. Czeisler et al. (1999) found that some individuals appeared to have a free-running clock of 13 hours whereas others were as long as 65 hours. There are also individual differences in terms of cycle onset. Some people are morning types – they prefer to rise early and go to bed early, whereas others are evening types (Duffy et al., 2000).

A second biological rhythm is the infradian rhythm that lasts longer than a day. One example of this is the female monthly menstrual cycle. This cycle is controlled internally by the pituitary gland which releases hormones that cause one egg to ripen in the ovaries, producing oestrogen. The biological nature of these rhythms is indicated by the universal nature of this rhythm, though there are large individual differences.

However this endogenous rhythm can also be entrained by external factors. Russell et al. (1980) took the sweat from one group of women and painted it on the upper lips of a second group. The second group's menstrual cycles became synchronised with the first group, suggesting that external factors (pheromones) can entrain the menstrual cycle. This was a well-controlled study (single blind) and it is difficult to see what else could have led to this change – though it was a very small group of women.

It appears that males have monthly cycles as well. Empson (1977) studied a group of men and found a cycle for body temperature and mood of about 20 days.

Some infradian rhythms are longer, such as seasonal affective disorder (SAD). Some people become severely depressed in winter. Research has found that melatonin levels are higher in winter months and melatonin may lead to increased depression as well as sleepiness. This understanding of SAD has led to some successful treatments involving the use of bright lights (phototherapy). The bright light lowers melatonin levels.

Research on circadian rhythms also has applications – a field called chronotherapeutics. Drug therapies may be more effective if you take the drug at the 'right' time of day, for example taking aspirin at 11pm is most effective because heart attacks are most likely in the early morning.

Notice how the essay starts with almost no preamble, so time is not wasted in getting down to creditworthy material on research studies – no outline of what will be covered and no unnecessary definitions.

There are many 'AO2 nuggets' that can be included in any essay (such as a criticism of a case study).

Notice how this AO2 point has been elaborated to satisfy the criteria for the top mark bands.

It would have been acceptable in this essay to write about only circadian rhythms but this candidate has chosen to consider two rhythms. A common problem is that, in doing so, you try to cover too much (i.e. breadth) and fail to provide sufficient detail (i.e. depth) for high AO1 marks.

This may not appear to be a description of a research study but we can assume that such 'findings' originate in research studies.

TOPIC 2: THE ROLE OF ENDOGENOUS PACEMAKERS AND EXOGENOUS ZEITGEBERS

SAMPLE ESSAY PLAN

Question 1: Discuss the role of endogenous pacemakers and exogenous zeitgebers. (24 marks)

ENDOGENOUS PACEMAKERS

7½ MINUTES WORTH OF AO1

- **Role of endogenous pacemakers** is to set free running internal rhythm.
- An endogenous pacemaker **helps animals to anticipate cyclical events** (e.g. the coming of night), and controls other neural structures over a 24-hour cycle.
- **SCN** (suprachiasmatic nucleus) in hypothalamus obtains information about light from the **optic nerve** even when eyes shut.
- **Pineal gland** exposure to light causes **melatonin** to be inhibited, melatonin induces sleep.

7½ MINUTES WORTH OF AO2

- **Evidence for SCN**: when replaced with SCN from mutant hamsters developed mutant rhythm of 20 not 24 hours (**Morgan**, 1995).
- **Destruction of the SCN** in chipmunks led to increased activity at night and greater risk of predation (**DeCoursey et al.**, 2000).
- **Evidence for melatonin**: even when the pineal gland of a lizard is removed, it continues to rhythmically produce melatonin for 10 days (**Moyer et al.**, 1997).
- However **conjoined twins** do not share circadian rhythms even though melatonin shared in blood (**Sackett and Komer**, 1993).

EXOGENOUS ZEITGEBERS

7½ MINUTES WORTH OF AO1

- **Role of exogenous zeitgebers** is to entrain biological rhythms to external cues, such as:
- **Social cues** such as meal times, social conventions.
- **Light** is dominant zeitgeber in humans, bright light suppresses melatonin but dim light may have an effect too (**Wever et al.**, 1983).
- Lack of light information causes problems for **blind** people e.g. one man who had rhythm of 24.9 hours despite clocks, social cues (**Miles et al.**, 1977).

7½ MINUTES WORTH OF AO2

- **Light cues** not always effective: artificial light is not enough to change melatonin rhythm to 18 hour day in submariners (**Kelly et al.**,1999).
- **Light important** because adaptive to sleep at night (safe from predators).
- Some **blind people** do have reduced melatonin in response to light, suggests different route to SCN besides optic nerve (**Czeisler et al.**, 1995).
- **Advantage of both endogenous and exogenous rhythms** – if solely at mercy of environmental cues the system would fluctuate too much but do need to respond to environmental changes.
- **Disadvantage** – slow to change, leads to e.g. jet lag.

Question 2: Describe and evaluate the role of endogenous pacemakers. (24 marks)

ENDOGENOUS PACEMAKERS

15 MINUTES WORTH OF AO1

The description of theory 1 above, plus:

- Run by **proteins in a feedback loop** found in many organisms (**Darlington et al.**, 1998).
- During day levels of **PER** and **TIM** increase causing decrease in **CLOCK** and **CYCLE**, this decrease then slows production of PER-TIM causing increase of CLOCK-CYCLE.
- **Pineal gland** especially important pacemaker in birds and reptiles (**third eye**).

15 MINUTES WORTH OF AO2

The evaluation of theory 1 above, plus:

- **Evidence for melatonin: Smith-Magenis syndrome:** patients fall asleep, their melatonin levels are inverted (**Potocki et al.**, 2000).
- **Body temperature rhythm** persists when both SCNs removed so there must be **another clock**. Also Kate Aldcroft in cave: 24 hour temperature rhythm and 30 hour sleep-wake cycle (**Folkard**, 1996).
- **Disadvantages** of endogenous pacemakers include their relatively slow transition in changing external circumstances.

Question 3: Describe and evaluate the role of exogenous zeitgebers. (24 marks)

EXOGENOUS ZEITGEBERS

15 MINUTES WORTH OF AO1

The description of theory 1 above, plus:

- **Menstruation** may be governed by exogenous zeitgebers – social cues transmitted through pheromones (**Russell et al.**, 1980).
- Light may also affect **cryptochromes** throughout the body (**Hall**, 2000). Explains why shining light on back of knees changes circadian rhythms (**Cambell and Murphy**, 1998).
- **Temperature** is another zeitgeber: causes leaves to drop and hibernation to commence.

15 MINUTES WORTH OF AO2

The evaluation of theory 1 above, plus:

- **Menstruation** generally an endogenous rhythm (Pituitary gland → hormones, egg ripens → oestrogen).
- Effects of light can be understood in terms of **PER-TIM protein**.
- **Can override biological system** – people told to wake up earlier have raised hormone levels just before designated time – mind over matter (**Born et al.**, 1999).

The role of endogenous pacemakers is to set the free-running internal rhythm. Most organisms have an internal biological 'clock' that matches the time passage of the 24-hour day and therefore they can control their circadian rhythm. This clock is *endogenous* in that it is part of the organism rather than being part of its environment. An endogenous pacemaker helps animals to anticipate cyclical events (e.g. the coming of night), and controls other neural structures over a 24-hour cycle.

In mammals, the main endogenous pacemaker is the suprachiasmatic nucleus (SCN) in the hypothalamus. The SCN obtains information about light from the optic nerve even when the eyes are shut. Morning light shifts the endogenous clock forwards or backwards, thus keeping the rhythm synchronised with the external world. The pineal gland also contains light-sensitive cells. Low levels of light cause melatonin to be produced by the pineal gland, which induces sleep. Exposure to light causes the inhibition of melatonin, thus promoting wakefulness.

Evidence for the importance of the SCN as an endogenous pacemaker is shown in studies where a normal SCN is replaced with a modified SCN attuned to a 20 hour cycle. Morgan (1995) found that when this was done in hamsters, they developed a mutant rhythm of 20 not 24 hours. The advantage of possessing an endogenous pacemaker was demonstrated by DeCoursey et al. (2000) who destroyed the SCN in some chipmunks and found that these animals were much more active at night than normal chipmunks, and therefore more likely to be taken by nocturnal predators.

Evidence for the importance of the pineal gland in the rhythmic production of melatonin comes from Moyer et al. (1997) who removed the pineal gland from a lizard and demonstrated that the isolated gland still produced melatonin rhythmically for up to 10 days. However, research on conjoined twins questions the role of melatonin in circadian rhythms. Conjoined twins do not share circadian rhythms even though melatonin is shared in their blood (Sackett and Komer, 1993).

The role of exogenous zeitgebers is to entrain the otherwise free-running biological rhythms to external cues. Social cues such as meal times and other social conventions are thought to entrain our biological rhythms. The dominant zeitgeber for humans is light. Bright light suppresses melatonin, meaning that daylight sets the biological clock at the beginning of each day, with dim artificial light being less effective in this function (Wever et al., 1983). Light travels from the eyes to the SCN where the main endogenous pacemaker is located.

Research has also suggested that certain proteins throughout the body (cryptochromes) detect changes in light (Hall, 2000). Campbell and Murphy (1998) found that by shining a light on the back of participants' knees, they were able to shift the participants' circadian rhythms. Lack of light information causes problems for blind people. Miles et al. (1977) report on one blind individual who had a free-running rhythm of 24.9 hours despite the presence of clocks and other social cues, and needed to take sedatives and stimulants to maintain a sleep-waking cycle that was in time with the rest of the world.

Some research challenges the view that light cues alone are sufficient to regulate the endogenous pacemaker. Artificial light was found to be insufficient to change melatonin rhythm to the required 18 hour day in submariners, with the rhythm remaining at 24 hours (Kelly et al., 1999).

Light is thought to be an important zeitgeber because it is adaptive for diurnal animals to sleep at night, at a time when they would be in danger from nocturnal predators. Because the period of daylight changes over the course of a year, it is important that an animal's circadian rhythm exactly matches the changing external conditions.

Although individuals who are blind experience difficulties adjusting to changing external conditions, this is not true of all blind people. Some blind people do show reduced melatonin in response to light, which suggests a different route to the SCN besides the optic nerve (Czeisler et al., 1995).

The advantage of having both endogenous and exogenous rhythms is that if an animal was solely at mercy of environmental cues the biological system would fluctuate too much (demonstrating the importance of an endogenous pacemaker), but they also need to respond to environmental changes (demonstrating the importance of exogenous zeitgebers). A disadvantage of this arrangement is that rhythms are slow to change when external conditions change rapidly, leading to, among other problems, jet lag and shift lag.

It is often a good idea with questions that have two or more distinct requirements (as here) to structure your answer in such a way as to deal with the two aspects one at a time. We start with the AO1 component for endogenous pacemakers.

It is important to make your AO2 look like AO2, so the use of lead-in words and phrases ('Evidence for the importance of...', 'However...' etc.) will help you to accomplish this.

The essay now moves into its second half, with a switch away from endogenous pacemakers to the role of exogenous zeitgebers. You should aim for an approximately equal balance between the two wherever possible.

Although the question does not *require* a description of research evidence, its use does add authority to your answer.

This final part draws out the advantage and disadvantage of having a system that uses *both* endogenous pacemakers *and* exogenous pacemakers. This is a useful extra bit of AO2 material if you have time at the end of your answer.

SAMPLE ESSAY PLAN

Question 1: Discuss the consequences of disrupting biological rhythms (e.g. jet lag, shift work). (24 marks)

SHIFT WORK	**15 MINUTES WORTH OF AO1** • **Artificial lighting** partially resets circadian rhythm. • But still a **circadian trough**: decreased alertness around 6am (**Boivin et al.,** 1996). • **Body temperature** rhythm takes longer to reset. • **Sleeping during the day** is difficult (daytime noises). Typically 1–2 hours less and less **REM sleep** (**Tilley and Wilkinson,** 1982). • Shift workers 3 times more likely to develop **heart disease** (**Knutsson,** 1982).	**15 MINUTES WORTH OF AO2** • **Individual differences**: some people less affected – those whose circadian rhythms are slowest to adapt (**Reinberg et al.,** 1984). • **Desynchronisation of different rhythms** may cause problem: sleep-wake cycle quicker to adjust (48 hours) (**Yamazaki et al.,** 2000). • **Disruption of social life** as well as circadian rhythms. • **Rotating shifts** are worst (**Gold et al.,** 1992). • **Phase delay** best – go to bed later and get up later. • **Bright lighting** helps reset biological clock within three days (**Czeisler et al.,** 1986). • **Application**: Czeisler et al. (1982) gave advice to US company, worker satisfaction and output increased.
JET LAG	• **Daylight and social zeitgebers** conflict with internal clock. • Biological clock not equipped to deal with **sudden changes** of time zone. • **Reduced performance**: baseballers won 37% of games when travelling west to east (**phase advance**) or 44% when east to west (**Recht et al.,** 1995).	• **Other factors**: bad sleep before travel, travel is tiring, drinking in flight. • **Application**: to help adjust: take melatonin, use bright lights, adopt social rhythms of destination (e.g. mealtimes) to entrain rhythms.
STAYING UP LATE AND GETTING UP LATE	• **Subverts** established circadian rhythms. • **Sleeping longer** has effects similar to sleeping less.	• **Evidence** from study: Ps slept 9pm–5am or 3am–11am. Both groups had **reduced alertness and vigilance** (**Taub and Berger,** 1976).

Question 2: (a) Outline research into **one or more** biological rhythms. (12 marks)
(b) Assess the consequences of disrupting such rhythms. (12 marks)

(a) 15 MINUTES WORTH OF AO1

As for Topic 1, page 42

(b) 15 MINUTES WORTH OF AO2

Example – **shift work**

• **Is it harmful? Yes**: shift workers 3 times more likely to develop **heart disease** (**Knutsson,** 1982).
• **Is it harmful? Yes**: **circadian trough** decreased alertness around 6a.m. (**Boivin et al.,** 1996).
• **Is it harmful? No**: effects may be due to other factors e.g. **sleeping during the day** is difficult (daytime noises). Typically 1–2 hours less and less **REM sleep** (**Tilley and Wilkinson,** 1982).
• **Individual differences**: some people less affected – those whose circadian rhythms are slowest to adapt (**Reinberg et al.,** 1984).

Example: **jet lag**

• **Is it harmful? Yes**: reduced performance: baseballers won 37% of games when travelling west to east (**phase advance**) or 44% when east to west (**Recht et al.,** 1995).
• **Is it harmful? No**: effects may be due to other factors e.g. bad sleep before travel, travel is tiring, drinking in flight.

Example – **staying up late and getting up late**

• **Is it harmful? Yes**: Ps slept 9pm–5am or 3am–11am. Both groups had **reduced alertness and vigilance** (**Taub and Berger,** 1976).

Night workers must be alert at a time when their endogenous pacemakers and exogenous zeitgebers instruct their bodies to be asleep. Being awake and busy at night does not shift this rhythm as it is set by exposure to daylight rather than artificial light. Because artificial light is only moderately effective in re-setting the circadian rhythm, most night workers experience a circadian trough of decreased alertness around 6a.m. during their shift (Boivin et al., 1996). Also body temperature rhythm takes longer to re-set, which may affect performance.

Shift workers who must sleep during the day experience difficulties because their body does not adjust completely, resulting in poor quality sleep and partial sleep deprivation. Sleeping during the day is difficult (because of daytime noises and other disturbances), and is typically 1–2 hours less than nocturnal sleep, with REM sleep in particular being affected (Tilley and Wilkinson, 1982). Research has also shown that there is a relationship between shift work and poor health, with shift workers three times more likely to develop heart disease (Knutsson, 1982).

Despite these findings, there are individual differences in how people cope with disrupted circadian rhythms. Some people are less affected, particularly those whose circadian rhythms are slowest to adapt. Research by Reinberg et al. (1984) confirmed this, showing that those people who gave up shift work because they could not cope tended to have rhythms that changed a lot during shift work.

The disruptive effects of shift work can be explained in terms of the sudden desynchronisation of different rhythms. Although the sleep-wake cycle adjusts fairly quickly (48 hours), other rhythms are slower to adjust, thus producing desynchronisation in many important biological rhythms (Yamazaki et al., 2000). The disruptive effects of shift work may not be solely a product of disrupted biological rhythms, but may also involve disruption due to a change in social patterns.

The type of shift system is also important when assessing the effects of shift work, with rotating shifts being associated with the most disruptive effects (Gold et al., 1992). Research has shown that the disruptive effects due to phase delay are less than those associated with phase advance. Although dim artificial lighting does not appear to re-set the biological clock, the use of bright lights helps re-set biological rhythms within three days (Czeisler et al., 1986). Importantly, bright lights appear to entrain all rhythms rather than just the sleep-waking cycle.

The disruptive effects of jet lag are caused by the sudden discrepancy between the internal clock and the external world. A sudden change in time zone means that daylight and social zeitgebers are in conflict with the internal clock. As our biological clock is not equipped to deal with sudden changes of time zone, the disruption of our circadian rhythm can be quite dramatic, particularly when travelling west to east. Recht et al. (1995) found that baseballers won 37% of their games after travelling west to east (phase advance) and 44% after travelling east to west.

The effects of jet lag attributed to air travel can also be explained by factors other than disruption of biological rhythms. These include bad sleep before travel, in-flight drinking and the fact that long-distance travel is tiring and often uncomfortable. An understanding of why long-distance travel is so disruptive has led to applications to minimise these disruptive effects. To help people adjust, it is possible to take melatonin supplements (Martin, 2002), make use of bright daylight at the destination, and adopt social rhythms of the destination (e.g. mealtimes) to entrain rhythms.

Staying up late and getting up late can also disrupt circadian rhythms because established circadian rhythms are subverted. Sleeping longer than usual has effects similar to those associated with sleeping less than usual.

Evidence to support this claim comes from Taub and Berger (1976), who displaced normal sleep patterns (midnight until 8am) of two groups of participants who slept either from 9pm–5am or from 3am–11am. Both groups had reduced alertness and vigilance, demonstrating that it is the disruption of circadian rhythms that causes problems, not simply sleep loss.

Don't make the mistake of defining or describing biological rhythms. The question is specific in its requirements, you should write only about their disruption.

The examples in the question offer a possible structure for your answer. In this essay, the first two paragraphs are AO1 material on the disruption caused by shift work.

There are many ways to evaluate this material. Demonstrating individual differences (and showing research support for such differences) is one such way.

Sometimes, as here, material may be marginally AO1 or AO2. An examiner will credit it in the way that gets you most marks. Because this is effectively *commentary* on shift work, it is being credited as AO2 here.

Here alternative explanations are offered as a form of AO2 commentary, as are applications of these insights for improving the negative consequences for air travellers.

Although this study appears as AO1 content in the main textbook, this demonstrates that any material *can* be used as AO2 provided it forms a part of a meaningful commentary on the AO1 material.

Topic 1: Function of sleep: Ecological accounts

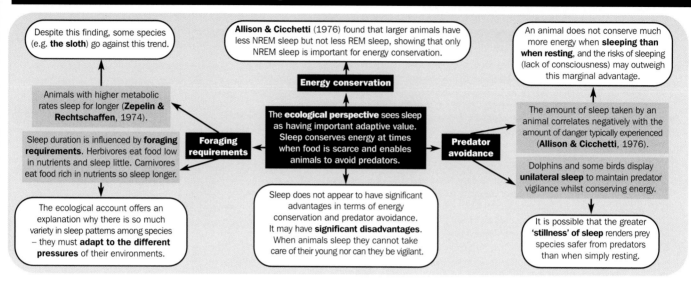

Despite this finding, some species (e.g. **the sloth**) go against this trend.

Animals with higher metabolic rates sleep for longer (**Zepelin & Rechtschaffen**, 1974).

Sleep duration is influenced by **foraging requirements**. Herbivores eat food low in nutrients and sleep little. Carnivores eat food rich in nutrients so sleep longer.

The ecological account offers an explanation why there is so much variety in sleep patterns among species – they must **adapt to the different pressures** of their environments.

Allison & Cicchetti (1976) found that larger animals have less NREM sleep but not less REM sleep, showing that only NREM sleep is important for energy conservation.

Energy conservation

Foraging requirements

The **ecological perspective** sees sleep as having important adaptive value. Sleep conserves energy at times when food is scarce and enables animals to avoid predators.

Predator avoidance

Sleep does not appear to have significant advantages in terms of energy conservation and predator avoidance. It may have **significant disadvantages**. When animals sleep they cannot take care of their young nor can they be vigilant.

An animal does not conserve much more energy when **sleeping than when resting**, and the risks of sleeping (lack of consciousness) may outweigh this marginal advantage.

The amount of sleep taken by an animal correlates negatively with the amount of danger typically experienced (**Allison & Cicchetti**, 1976).

Dolphins and some birds display **unilateral sleep** to maintain predator vigilance whilst conserving energy.

It is possible that the greater 'stillness' of sleep renders prey species safer from predators than when simply resting.

Topic 2: Function of sleep: Restoration accounts

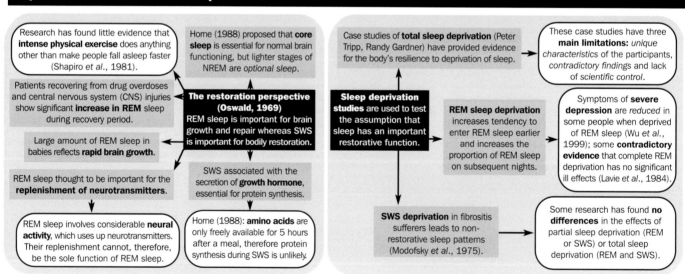

Research has found little evidence that **intense physical exercise** does anything other than make people fall asleep faster (Shapiro et al., 1981).

Patients recovering from drug overdoses and central nervous system (CNS) injuries show significant **increase in REM** sleep during recovery period.

Large amount of REM sleep in babies reflects **rapid brain growth**.

REM sleep thought to be important for the **replenishment of neurotransmitters**.

REM sleep involves considerable **neural activity**, which uses up neurotransmitters. Their replenishment cannot, therefore, be the sole function of REM sleep.

Horne (1988) proposed that **core sleep** is essential for normal brain functioning, but lighter stages of NREM are *optional sleep*.

The restoration perspective (Oswald, 1969)
REM sleep is important for brain growth and repair whereas SWS is important for bodily restoration.

SWS associated with the secretion of **growth hormone**, essential for protein synthesis.

Horne (1988): **amino acids** are only freely available for 5 hours after a meal, therefore protein synthesis during SWS is unlikely.

Case studies of **total sleep deprivation** (Peter Tripp, Randy Gardner) have provided evidence for the body's resilience to deprivation of sleep.

Sleep deprivation studies are used to test the assumption that sleep has an important restorative function.

REM sleep deprivation increases tendency to enter REM sleep earlier and increases the proportion of REM sleep on subsequent nights.

SWS deprivation in fibrositis sufferers leads to non-restorative sleep patterns (Modofsky et al., 1975).

These case studies have three **main limitations**: *unique characteristics* of the participants, *contradictory findings* and lack of *scientific control*.

Symptoms of **severe depression** are *reduced* in some people when deprived of REM sleep (Wu et al., 1999); some **contradictory evidence** that complete REM deprivation has no significant ill effects (Lavie et al., 1984).

Some research has found **no differences** in the effects of partial sleep deprivation (REM or SWS) or total sleep deprivation (REM and SWS).

Probable questions

1. Discuss **one or more** ecological theories of sleep. *(24 marks)*

2. (a) Outline the ecological account of sleep. *(6 marks)*

   (b) Discuss research studies relating to the ecological account of sleep. *(18 marks)*

Possible questions

3. (a) Describe the ecological account of sleep. *(12 marks)*

   (b) Evaluate the ecological account of sleep in terms of relevant research studies. *(12 marks)*

Questions on this topic are either related to the ecological theory or research studies related to such theories, or both, as you can see from these examples.

You might only need a 6 mark version of the theory (as in question 2) or a 12 mark version (as in question 1).

Research studies may form the AO1 part of a question (as in question 2 part b) or the AO2 part of a question (as in question 3 part b).

Take care how you *use* research studies in each case – describing a research study requires a different emphasis than when using such studies as evaluation.

Take care when a question part is worth 18 marks. This means that there is an unequal skill split. In the case of question 2b you are required to provide twice as much AO2 material.

Probable questions

1. Discuss **one or more** restoration theories of sleep. *(24 marks)*

2. (a) Outline the restoration account of sleep. *(6 marks)*

   (b) Discuss research studies relating to the restoration account of sleep. *(18 marks)*

Possible questions

3. (a) Describe the restoration account of sleep. *(12 marks)*

   (b) Evaluate the restoration account of sleep in terms of relevant research studies. *(12 marks)*

4. (a) Outline and evaluate **one** ecological account of the function of sleep. *(12 marks)*

   (b) Outline and evaluate **one** restoration account of the function of sleep. *(12 marks)*

The same questions appear here as for topic 1, with the exception of the last question, question 4. This is because the specification is exactly the same so the same questions will be set!

Note the different injunctions that have been used. 'Discuss' is an AO1 + AO2 term whereas 'outline' is an AO1 only term. It is used when there is a reduced amount of time – when you have 6 minutes instead of 12 minutes for AO1 you are not expected to provide the same amount of detail. Notice that the term 'outline' has been used in question 4 as well.

Question 4 is an example of a question that mixes both topics together but it only draws on the same knowledge that you will have prepared for the other questions in this division.

How many '12 mark chunks' do you need?

- 12 marks of ecological theory/theories
- 12 marks of ecological research studies (to use as AO1 or AO2)
- 12 marks of restoration theory/theories
- 12 marks of restoration research studies (to use as AO1 or AO2)

That's it for this division.

SAMPLE ESSAY PLAN

Question 1: Discuss **one or more** ecological theories of sleep. (24 marks)

ENERGY CONSERVATION (WEBB)	**15 MINUTES WORTH OF AO1** • Sleep is **adaptive**. • **Energy costs**: maintain body temperature, high metabolic rate (chemical processes in body), foraging, escaping from predators. • Sleep = **enforced inactivity** (like **hibernation**). • Amount of sleep **negatively correlated** to body size. • This relationship further modified by foraging needs and predator danger.	**15 MINUTES WORTH OF AO2** • Energy conserved in **NREM** not **REM** sleep. Supported by larger animals having less NREM sleep (**Allison and Cicchetti**, 1976). • **NREM sleep evolved first** (reptiles don't have REM sleep) for energy conservation. • **REM sleep evolved later** in animals with larger brains – to **exercise neural circuits**. • **But** energy conservation in sleep minimal (5–10%) and risks are large. Energy can be conserved by partial inactivity (e.g. **unilateral sleep**).
FORAGING REQUIREMENTS	• **Herbivores** need to spend time eating and therefore sleep less.	
PREDATOR AVOIDANCE (MEDDIS)	• Prey species **sleep less to be vigilant**. • But if they have to sleep then **best to do this when most vulnerable** e.g. at night. • Best to stay still (i.e. sleep) when there is **nothing better to do**.	• Sleep **seems more dangerous** than just being still. • **Loss of consciousness** may mean that prey animals remain more still. • Why hasn't **unilateral sleep** evolved in more animals (safer)? Maybe advantages not great enough.

Question 2: (a) Outline the ecological account of sleep. (6 marks)
(b) Discuss research studies relating to the ecological account of sleep. (18 marks).

ECOLOGICAL ACCOUNT	**(a) 7½ MINUTES WORTH OF AO1** • **Energy conservation**: maintain body temperature, high metabolic rate, foraging, etc. • Sleep = **enforced inactivity** (like **hibernation**). • **Predator avoidance**: Prey species **sleep less to be vigilant**. • But if they have to sleep then **best to do this when most vulnerable** e.g. at night. • Sleep **negatively correlated** to **size** and to predator danger.	
RESEARCH STUDIES	**(b) 7½ MINUTES WORTH OF AO1** • **Sleep length and energy conservation**: negative correlation between body size and sleep time e.g. elephant sleeps 4 hours, brown bat sleeps 20 hours (**Zepelin and Rechtschaffen**, 1974). • **Sleep length and predator avoidance**: negative correlation supported by research (**Allison and Cicchetti**, 1976). • **Unilateral sleep** e.g.in dolphins the two brain hemispheres swap every 2–3 hours (**Mukhametov**, 1987) and birds watching for predators keep one eye open and corresponding hemisphere active (**Rattenborg et al.**, 1999).	**15 MINUTES WORTH OF AO2** • Relationship between sleep and energy conservation **not true for all animals** e.g. sloths sleep 20 hours. • Correlation **doesn't demonstrate a cause**. • Research doesn't always separate NREM and REM sleep. Energy conserved in **NREM** not **REM** sleep. • **NREM sleep evolved first** (reptiles don't have REM sleep) for energy conservation. • Relationship between sleep and predator avoidance **not true for all animals** e.g. rabbits (high danger) sleep same as moles (low danger rating). • Being asleep **seems more dangerous** for prey species than just being still. • **Loss of consciousness** may mean that prey animals remain more still. • Why hasn't **unilateral sleep** evolved in more animals (safer)? Maybe advantages not great enough. • Data about animals' sleep patterns constantly being revised so evidence not totally reliable.

The central claim of the ecological account of sleep is that sleep serves an adaptive purpose. As a result of being able to sleep, animals are more likely to survive and reproduce, otherwise sleep would have disappeared from an animal's behavioural repertoire. Webb (1992) suggested that there were energy costs for animals when awake. These included having to maintain body temperature (particularly problematic for animals with a high metabolic rate), foraging and escaping from predators. Sleep, therefore, serves as a period of enforced inactivity, much like hibernation, as a way of conserving energy. Comparisons of sleep patterns in different species show that the percentage of time an animal spends sleeping varies according to its size and therefore its metabolic rate, with smaller animals having higher metabolic rates, and therefore spending more time asleep. The amount of sleep taken by an animal is further modified by other factors such as foraging demands and predator avoidance.

It is important to distinguish between NREM and REM sleep in terms of energy conservation, as energy is only conserved during NREM sleep, with the brain still active during REM sleep. This leads to the conclusion that only NREM sleep evolved for energy conservation. This conclusion is supported by studies which show that larger animals (with lower metabolic rates) have less NREM sleep rather than less REM sleep (Allison and Cicchetti, 1976). This view receives further support from the fact that 'primitive' animals, such as reptiles, have only NREM sleep. NREM sleep appears to have evolved first, for energy conservation, with REM sleep a relatively recent adaptation in species with larger brains, in order to maintain brain activity during sleep by exercising neural circuits.

However, this conclusion is challenged by the fact that energy conservation in sleep is minimal, reducing energy rates by only 5–10%. The risks associated with sleeping, such as lack of consciousness and therefore vulnerability to predators, are large and would appear to outweigh the marginal advantage of energy conservation. Energy can also be conserved by partial inactivity (e.g. unilateral sleep), suggesting that energy conservation cannot be the key adaptive feature of sleep.

An alternative view of the adaptive function of sleep claims that sleep is linked to an animal's foraging requirements. Because their food is relatively low in nutrients, herbivores need to spend time eating and therefore sleep less. Carnivores, on the other hand, eat food that is high in nutrients, therefore do not have to eat continuously and so can conserve energy by sleeping more. According to Meddis, sleep may have evolved simply as a way of staying still when other activities are impractical.

Meddis (1975) believes that the primary adaptive function of sleep is predator avoidance. Prey species sleep less in order to maintain vigilance, and so avoid predators. If sleep is vital, then animals should sleep when they are most vulnerable. For most species, adapted to a daylight environment, this is at night. For nocturnal species, that have evolved to hunt and forage during the hours of darkness, sleep is necessary during daylight hours.

The view that sleep has evolved as a way of avoiding predators might be challenged by the observation that waking inactivity would do a similar job and that lack of consciousness may be more dangerous than just being still, by making animals more rather than less vulnerable to predation. However, loss of consciousness ensures greater stillness than inactivity alone, and therefore offers greater protection from predators for prey species. During sleep, animals cannot take care of their young, and most cannot be vigilant. Some species have adapted to the need to both sleep and maintain vigilance through unilateral sleep, therefore we might ask why this hasn't evolved in more species. One explanation might be that the advantages are not great enough for this adaptation to become widespread.

Although there are many different ways to approach examination essay answers, an effective one is to place all your AO1 and AO2 material in separate paragraphs, thus making it easier to monitor what you are saying and how you are saying it. This is an entirely AO1 paragraph.

This is an entirely AO2 paragraph. Note the use of 'AO2 language' (e.g. 'This leads to the conclusion…' and 'This view receives further support from…').

When using alternative perspectives as AO2, you should ensure that you build them into your commentary rather than just *describing* them.

Many students, when answering a question such as this, are quite vague when describing the ecological account. It is important to make a series of clear descriptive points, and then expand them as here.

AO2 commentary can be gleaned from anywhere in your textbook, provided it is relevant to the question. Here, points made in the 'putting it all together' section of the *A2 Complete Companion* are used for this purpose.

Chapter 3

51

CHAPTER 3: BIOLOGICAL RHYTHMS, SLEEP AND DREAMS

TOPIC 2: FUNCTION OF SLEEP: RESTORATION ACCOUNTS

SAMPLE ESSAY PLAN

Question 1: Discuss **one or more** restoration theories of sleep. (24 marks)

REM SLEEP	**15 MINUTES WORTH OF A01**	**15 MINUTES WORTH OF A02**
	• **REM sleep** important for brain growth and repair, **SWS sleep** for bodily growth and repair. • Important for **brain recovery**. • Patients recovering from brain injury had more REM sleep (**Oswald**, 1969). • REM sleep in **babies** correlation with brain weight increase. • Way of conserving and replenishing **neurotransmitters** which are used up during the day.	• **Studies of REM deprivation**: show **REM rebound**, REM sleep 50% higher (**Empson**, 2002). • **Lack of REM sleep** has **positive consequences** for severe depression (**Wu et al.**, 1999). • **Lack of REM sleep** has no significant ill-effects e.g. brain injured patient who led normal life without REM sleep (**Lavie et al.**, 1984). • **REM negative effects unlikely** because REM sleep involves **neural activity** – neurotransmitters used not restored.
SWS	• Associated with secretion of **growth hormone**. • Growth hormone stimulates **protein synthesis** in children and enables protein synthesis in adults. • **Proteins need to be constantly restored** which relies on uninterrupted SWS.	• **Studies of SWS deprivation**: **fibrositis** patients experience tiredness and found that EEG patterns in SWS faster (SWS not restorative) (**Moldofsky et al.**, 1975). • Volunteers deprived of SWS sleep experienced symptoms of fibrositis (**Moldofsky et al.**, 1975). • **SWS effects unlikely** – protein synthesis uses **amino acids**, not available 5 hours after meal (**Horne**, 1988).
CORE SLEEP	• Core sleep = **REM + SWS** responsible for normal brain functioning (**Horne**, 1988). • **Optional sleep** for bodily restoration, takes place in some of NREM sleep and relaxed wakefulness.	• Does physical exercise lead to increased sleep? **Marathon runners** slept for an hour more (**Shapiro et al.**, 1981). • But Ps given **exhausting tasks** went to sleep faster but not longer (**Horne and Minard**, 1985). • **Runners in cold conditions** – SWS not increased. Link between SWS and temperature regulation?

Question 2: (a) Outline the restoration account of sleep. (6 marks)
(b) Discuss research studies relating to the restoration account of sleep. (18 marks).

RESTORATION ACCOUNT	**(a) 7½ MINUTES WORTH OF A01**	
	• **REM sleep** important for **brain recovery** and production of neurotransmitters. • Patients recovering from brain injury had more REM sleep (**Oswald**, 1969). • **SWS** associated with secretion of **growth hormone**.	• Growth hormone stimulates **protein synthesis**. • **Core sleep** = **REM + SWS** responsible for normal brain functioning (**Horne**, 1988). • **Optional sleep** for bodily restoration, takes place in some of NREM sleep and relaxed wakefulness.
RESEARCH STUDIES	**(b) 7½ MINUTES WORTH OF A01** • **Peter Tripp**: after 3 days abusive, after 5 days hallucinated and became paranoid, after 8 days brain waves like sleeping state. After 24 hours sleep was recovered. • **Randy Gardner**: after 11 days no abnormal symptoms. • **Studies of REM deprivation**: show **REM rebound**, REM sleep 50% higher (**Empson**, 2002). • **Studies of SWS deprivation**: **fibrositis** patients experience tiredness and found that EEG patterns in SWS faster (SWS not restorative) (**Moldofsky et al.**, 1975). • Volunteers deprived of SWS sleep experienced symptoms of fibrositis (**Moldofsky et al.**, 1975).	**15 MINUTES WORTH OF A02** • **Case studies** show no significant effects of sleep deprivation. • But individuals may be unique, there are contradictory findings, and not controlled studies. • **Lack of REM sleep** has **positive consequences** for severe depression (**Wu et al.**, 1999). • **Lack of REM sleep** has no significant ill-effects e.g. brain injured patient who led normal life without REM sleep (**Lavie et al.**, 1984). • **REM negative effects unlikely** because REM sleep involves **neural activity** – neurotransmitters used not restored. • **SWS effects unlikely** – protein synthesis uses **amino acids**, not available 5 hours after meal (**Horne**, 1988). • **Sleep deprivation studies contradictory** e.g. Ps deprived of REM or SWS or all sleep showed no differences in performance and subsequent time spent sleeping (**Johnson et al.**, 1974). • Rats deprived of sleep died (**Rechtshaffen et al.**, 1983) but may be due to stress.

The main assumption of the restoration account of sleep is that sleep is an important way of restoring energy used up during the day. Oswald (1983) claimed that REM sleep is important for brain growth and repair, while SWS is important for bodily growth and repair. From observations of patients recovering from brain injury, Oswald found that they had more REM sleep, suggesting that this was indicative of recovery processes going on in the brain.

Research has also shown that the quantity of REM sleep in babies correlates with brain weight increase, showing that the large amount of REM sleep in babies can be explained in terms of their rapid brain growth. Sleep also appears to be the time during which neurotransmitters are conserved and replenished. Over the course of a day, our neurotransmitter levels fall. During REM sleep, new neurotransmitters are synthesised by neurons, and these can then be released during waking.

Sleep deprivation studies are used to test the idea that sleep is essential for the restoration of bodily processes. This claim is supported by research on REM deprivation which show evidence of REM rebound, with REM sleep 50% higher (Empson, 2002) after deprivation. The idea that REM sleep contributes to brain restoration is contradicted by research on depression. Wu et al. (1999) found that lack of REM sleep has positive consequences for severe depression, with the symptoms of depression being reduced in some people deprived of REM sleep. Another problem for the claim that REM sleep is important for brain repair is the finding that lack of REM sleep had no significant ill-effects in a brain-injured patient who led a normal life without REM sleep (Lavie et al., 1984). A claim from this perspective is that neurotransmitters are restored during REM sleep, yet as REM sleep involves considerable neural activity, it is difficult to see how these neurotransmitters would be restored.

SWS sleep is associated with the secretion of growth hormone. This stimulates protein synthesis in the growing child and in adults. In adults, protein synthesis is vital in the restoration of body tissue as proteins must be constantly restored. For growth hormone to be secreted, uninterrupted SWS is vital. Without this, protein synthesis cannot take place, and the body's natural recovery process cannot function.

Studies of SWS deprivation are used to examine the restorative role of SWS. Fibrositis patients who experience disruption to their SWS experience tiredness the next day. Moldofsky et al. (1975) found that EEG patterns among fibrositis sufferers were faster in SWS compared to normal controls, explaining why fibrositis sufferers did not feel rested after sleep. Likewise normal controls who were deprived of SWS sleep showed many of the symptoms of fibrositis following deprivation. Both of these findings support the view that SWS has an important role in bodily restoration. Horne points out a problem for the protein synthesis explanation of SWS. Amino acids, the essential constituents of protein synthesis, are only freely available for about 5 hours after a meal, yet most people eat several hours before going to bed.

Horne (1988) extended Oswald's initial ideas with his claim that only core sleep, consisting of SWS and REM sleep, was essential for normal brain functioning in humans. The lighter stages (stages 1 and 2) were not essential, and could be referred to as 'optional sleep'. Horne believed that during core sleep the brain recovers and restores itself, whereas optional sleep is important for bodily restoration, and takes place in some of NREM sleep and in periods of relaxed wakefulness.

An implication of the restorative function of sleep is that increased physical exercise should lead to increased sleep in order to restore the extra energy used. This is supported by the finding that runners slept one hour a night more in the two nights following a marathon (Shapiro et al., 1981). SWS in particular increased, supporting the restorative role of SWS. This conclusion is challenged by the finding that if runners compete in cold conditions, they do not show subsequent increased levels of SWS. This suggests a possible link between SWS and temperature regulation. In general research has found that intense activity does little more than make people fall asleep more quickly rather than sleeping for longer (Horne and Minard, 1985).

It is easy to end up with a rag-bag of disconnected points in an essay such as this. Planning your answer will pay dividends. This answer begins with a general description of the restoration account, then moving on to a description of the restorative function of REM sleep.

When introducing research studies into your AO2 commentary, it is important to *use* this material to construct a critical argument. Ask yourself, 'What does this finding mean for this account of sleep?'

Don't get carried away with the biology, remember to relate this to sleep!

Although some of this material is actually AO1 description, it is being used as part of a critical commentary here and so would receive AO2 credit.

A useful way of turning material into AO2 is by saying 'this theory would claim that…' and 'this is supported by…' You can also earn valuable AO2 credit by drawing conclusions from a study or studies ('this suggests that…').

Topic 1: The nature of dreams

Who do we dream about?
Dreamer almost always personally involved. Kahn *et al.* (2000) found that half the characters in dreams were known to the dreamer, one-third were generic and less than one in six were unknown.

Problems conducting research on dreams
• Research must rely on *subjective* reports.
• Research carried out in *sleep laboratories*.
• Is recall equivalent to what was experienced?

Duration
The duration of dreams is thought to correspond to the duration of REM sleep.

Most dreams occur during REM sleep, which occurs every 90 minutes during sleep and lasts about 20 minutes. Dreams run 'in real time' and fade rapidly after waking.

Research (e.g. **Dement and Kleitman**, 1957) supports the direct relationship between REM activity and the duration of a dream.

What do we dream about?
Dreams frequently have a noticeable emotional content; they tend to be more negative than pleasurable. The dreamer takes the role of impartial observer.

Content
The content of dreams is hugely varied and almost certainly unpredictable.

Different kinds of dream
Most dreaming occurs in REM sleep but we also dream, albeit differently, in NREM sleep.

REM dreams. Dement and Kleitman (1957): when sleepers were woken during REM sleep they reported dreaming 80% of the time.

Only adults in a **laboratory setting**, so might not apply in other settings and other age groups.

Does the content mean anything?
Neurobiological theories: dreams are meaningless, the result of random neurological activity during REM sleep. *Psychological theories*: content of dream highly relevant.

Who dreams about what? Males dream about other males more than females dream about males (Martin, 2000). People undergoing life crises have dreams reflecting this (Cartwright *et al.*, 1997).

NREM dreams. Shorter, more mundane and more fragmentary than REM dreams and occur less often.

Distinction between REM and NREM dreams confirmed at a behavioural and neurobiological level (e.g. Antrobus, 1983).

Lucid dreams. Dreamer reports being fully aware of what they are dreaming, and can control events.

LaBerge et al. (1981) gave objective evidence of lucid dreaming, using eye movements during REM sleep.

Cultural background influences type of dreams, e.g. hunter-gatherer societies dream more of animals than do US students (Domhoff, 2002).

Hypnagogic dreams occur in the transitional state between wakefulness and sleep, **hypnopompic states** between sleep and wakefulness. Both are considered a 'reduced' version of normal dreaming.

Topic 2: Neurobiological theories of dreaming

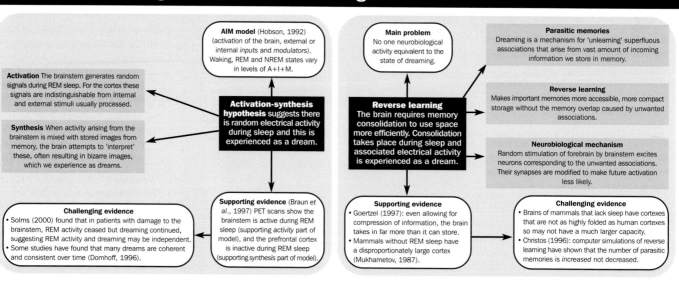

Activation The brainstem generates random signals during REM sleep. For the cortex these signals are indistinguishable from internal and external stimuli usually processed.

AIM model (Hobson, 1992) (*activation* of the brain, external or internal *inputs* and *modulators*). Waking, REM and NREM states vary in levels of A+I+M.

Main problem
No one neurobiological activity equivalent to the state of dreaming.

Parasitic memories
Dreaming is a mechanism for 'unlearning' superfluous associations that arise from vast amount of incoming information we store in memory.

Synthesis When activity arising from the brainstem is mixed with stored images from memory, the brain attempts to 'interpret' these, often resulting in bizarre images, which we experience as dreams.

Activation-synthesis hypothesis suggests there is random electrical activity during sleep and this is experienced as a dream.

Reverse learning
The brain requires memory consolidation to use space more efficiently. Consolidation takes place during sleep and associated electrical activity is experienced as a dream.

Reverse learning
Makes important memories more accessible, more compact storage without the memory overlap caused by unwanted associations.

Neurobiological mechanism
Random stimulation of forebrain by brainstem excites neurons corresponding to the unwanted associations. Their synapses are modified to make future activation less likely.

Challenging evidence
• Solms (2000) found that in patients with damage to the brainstem, REM activity ceased but dreaming continued, suggesting REM activity and dreaming may be independent.
• Some studies have found that many dreams are coherent and consistent over time (Domhoff, 1996).

Supporting evidence (Braun *et al.*, 1997) PET scans show the brainstem is active during REM sleep (supporting *activity* part of model), and the prefrontal cortex is inactive during REM sleep (supporting *synthesis* part of model).

Supporting evidence
• Goertzel (1997): even allowing for compression of information, the brain takes in far more than it can store.
• Mammals without REM sleep have a disproportionately large cortex (Mukhametov, 1987).

Challenging evidence
• Brains of mammals that lack sleep have cortexes that are not as highly folded as human cortexes so may not have a much larger capacity.
• Christos (1996): computer simulations of reverse learning have shown that the number of parasitic memories is *increased* not decreased.

Topic 3: Psychological theories of dreaming

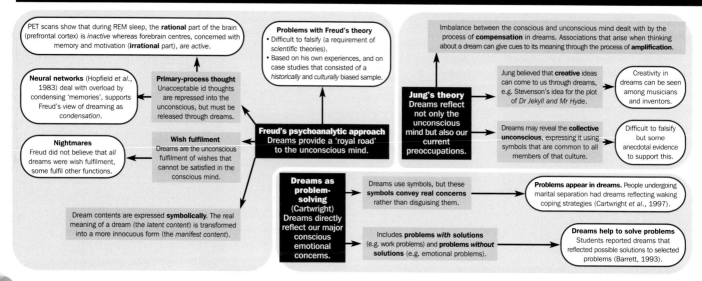

PET scans show that during REM sleep, the **rational** part of the brain (prefrontal cortex) is *inactive* whereas forebrain centres, concerned with memory and motivation (**irrational** part), are *active*.

Problems with Freud's theory
• Difficult to falsify (a requirement of *scientific* theories).
• Based on his own experiences, and on case studies that consisted of a *historically* and *culturally* biased sample.

Imbalance between the conscious and unconscious mind dealt with by the process of **compensation** in dreams. Associations that arise when thinking about a dream can give cues to its meaning through the process of **amplification**.

Neural networks (Hopfield *et al.*, 1983) deal with overload by condensing 'memories', supports Freud's view of dreaming as *condensation*.

Primary-process thought
Unacceptable id thoughts are repressed into the unconscious, but must be released through dreams.

Jung's theory
Dreams reflect not only the unconscious mind but also our current preoccupations.

Jung believed that **creative** ideas can come to us through dreams, e.g. Stevenson's idea for the plot of *Dr Jekyll and Mr Hyde*.

Creativity in dreams can be seen among musicians and inventors.

Nightmares
Freud did not believe that *all* dreams were wish fulfilment, some fulfil other functions.

Wish fulfilment
Dreams are the unconscious fulfilment of wishes that cannot be satisfied in the conscious mind.

Freud's psychoanalytic approach
Dreams provide a 'royal road' to the unconscious mind.

Dreams may reveal the **collective unconscious**, expressing it using symbols that are common to all members of that culture.

Difficult to falsify but some anecdotal evidence to support this.

Dreams as problem-solving (Cartwright) Dreams directly reflect our major conscious emotional concerns.

Dreams use symbols, but these **symbols convey real concerns** rather than disguising them.

Problems appear in dreams. People undergoing marital separation had dreams reflecting waking coping strategies (Cartwright *et al.*, 1997).

Dream contents are expressed **symbolically**. The real meaning of a dream (the *latent content*) is transformed into a more innocuous form (the *manifest content*).

Includes **problems with solutions** (e.g. work problems) and **problems without solutions** (e.g. emotional problems).

Dreams help to solve problems
Students reported dreams that reflected possible solutions to selected problems (Barrett, 1993).

research related to the nature of dreams (e.g. content, duration, relation with the stages of sleep)

Probable questions

1. Discuss research related to the nature of dreams. *(24 marks)*

Possible questions

2. Discuss research related to **two** aspects of the nature of dreams (e.g. content, duration, relation with the stages of sleep). *(24 marks)*

> You will note from these questions that there is essentially only one question that can be set on this topic. It is possible that you would be asked to discuss a specific number of aspects of the nature of dreams (as in question 2) but far more probable that you would be asked a 'catch-all' question about the nature of dreams.
>
> The specification provides three examples of research areas. These are sometimes given as pointers in the question (as in question 2). This doesn't mean you have to focus on these examples. The 'e.g.' is meant to help steer you in the right direction.

theories of the functions of dreaming, including neurobiological (e.g. Hobson and McCarley, Crick and Mitchison) accounts

Probable questions

1. Discuss **two or more** neurobiological theories of the functions of dreaming. *(24 marks)*

Possible questions

2. (a) Outline and evaluate research findings related to the nature of dreams. *(12 marks)*

   (b) Outline and evaluate **one** neurobiological theory of the functions of dreaming. *(12 marks)*

> You are not expected to have studied more than two neurobiological theories of dreaming but you may have done so, therefore the question allows for either possibility. If you do know about more than two theories it may not be the best idea to try to cover them all as it would mean you have less time for each theory and therefore are more limited in the time you have for writing detail (an AO1 criterion) and elaboration (an AO2 criterion).

> It is permissible to combine two topics as has been done here. In both parts of the question there are AO1 and AO2 marks which means 6 marks for describing research findings related to dreams and 6 marks evaluating these, 6 marks for outlining one neurobiological theory and 6 marks for evaluating this – this means that you have to organise yourself carefully to allow enough time for each component of your answer.

theories of the functions of dreaming, including (e.g. Freud, Webb and Cartwright) accounts

Probable questions

1. Discuss **two or more** psychological theories of the functions of dreaming. *(24 marks)*

2. (a) Outline and evaluate **one** neurobiological theory of the functions of dreaming. *(12 marks)*

   (b) Outline and evaluate **one** psychological theory of the functions of dreaming. *(12 marks)*

Possible questions

3. (a) Outline and evaluate research findings related to the nature of dreams. *(12 marks)*

   (b) Outline and evaluate **one** psychological theory of the functions of dreaming. *(12 marks)*

> The same range of questions are probable and possible here as for topic 2 with the addition of one question (question 2) which combines topics 2 and 3. Here again you have 4 chunks of 6 marks of material: outline and evaluate one neurobiological theory and outline and evaluate one psychological theory.
>
> When you are required to provide only one theory don't make the mistake of writing about two because only one will be credited (the best one) – *unless* you can group the theories together. For example you might write about 'the psychodynamic theory' and present both Freud and Jung's theories under this 'umbrella'.

> Remember that the injunction 'outline' does require less detail than when 'describe' is used, as appropriate for a question where there are only 6 AO1 marks instead of 12 AO1 marks.

SAMPLE ESSAY PLAN

Question 1: Discuss research related to the nature of dreams. (24 marks)

THE CONTENT OF DREAMS	**15 MINUTES WORTH OF AO1**	**15 MINUTES WORTH OF AO2**
	• Half of **people in dreams are known** to dreamer, less than 1 in 6 unknown (**Kahn et al., 2000**). • **Emotional** and often **negative content**. PET scans show emotional brain areas active (**Hobson et al., 2000**). • **Gender differences**: males dream more about males than females dream of males (**Martin, 2002**). • Dream content often **psychological** e.g. people with marital problems had dreams related to current problems (**Cartwright et al., 1984**).	• **Neurobiological theories** suggest that the content of dreams is meaningless e.g. **activation-synthesis**: dreams arise from random electrical signals and synthesis has no intrinsic meaning. • **Psychological theories** suggest the content is highly relevant to purpose e.g. **Freud's theory**: dreams permit unconscious fulfilment of wishes. • **Cultural differences**: Mexican-American dreams higher on emotion than Anglo-American, Dutch dreams lower on aggression than American (**Domhoff, 2002**).
THE DURATION OF DREAMS	• Some dreams **last over 1/2 hour** (**Horne**, 1999). • Last in **real time**. • **Fade rapidly** unless wake up soon after.	• Research often **assumes relationship between REM and dreams**. Relies on measuring REM activity and/or counting number of words to describe dream (**Dement and Kleitman, 1957**). • Impossible to measure length of NREM dreams except by subjective report.
DIFFERENT KINDS OF DREAM	• **REM activity**: 80% of time Ps report dreams (**Dement and Kleitman, 1957**). • **NREM activity**: 7% of time Ps report dreams (**Dement and Kleitman, 1957**). Tend to be shorter, more mundane and fragmentary (**Stickgold et al., 2001**). • **Hypnagogic/hypnopompic dreams**: between sleep and waking. 'Screen dreams' e.g. tetris images in Ps who played the game for several hours (**Stickgold et al., 2000**).	• **REM research**: all US adults, tested in sleep lab, subjective reports may not equal the experience. • **REM/NREM difference** confirmed: independent judges rated dreams for 'dreaminess', 93% correctly identified as REM or NREM (**Antrobus, 1983**). • **Brain scans** also show REM/NREM differences. • **Subjective nature** of dream research, and lacks realism because conducted in **sleep laboratories**.

Question 2: Discuss research related to **two** aspects of the nature of dreams (e.g. content, duration, relation with the stages of sleep). (24 marks)

THE CONTENT OF DREAMS	**7½ MINUTES WORTH OF AO1** Description as above for content of dreams, plus:	**7½ MINUTES WORTH OF AO2** Evaluation as above for content of dreams, plus:
	• The content of dreams was found to be biologically important; they enhance our ability to cope with life-threatening events (**Revonsuo, 2000**).	• This supports psychological theories of dreaming because they suggest dreams help to deal with anxiety.
DIFFERENT KINDS OF DREAM	**7½ MINUTES WORTH OF AO1** Description as above for different kinds of dreams, plus:	**7½ MINUTES WORTH OF AO2** Evaluation as above for different kinds of dreams, plus:
	• **Lucid dreams**: self-aware, pleasant and more straightforward; sex is a common theme.	• **Objective evidence of lucid dreams**: LaBerge trained himself to signal when he was having a lucid dream.

Research on the content of dreams has shown that about half of people in dreams are known to the dreamer, about a third were generic characters such as a policeman, and less than 1 in 6 unknown (Kahn *et al.*, 2000). Dreams frequently have a noticeable emotional content, which tends to be more negative than pleasurable. PET scans during REM sleep show that the brain areas most associated with emotion are very active during REM sleep, while those more associated with thinking and decision-making are less active (Hobson *et al.*, 2000). Evidence also suggests there are gender differences in dreams, with males dreaming about other males more than females dream about males (Martin, 2002). Dreams may also have a psychological core. Cartwright *et al.* (1984) found that people with marital problems had dreams related to their current problems, with the nature of the dream being strongly related to the way they were dealing with the crisis while awake.

Neurobiological theories suggest that the content of dreams is essentially meaningless, e.g. the activation-synthesis theory (Hobson and McCarley, 1977) claims that dreams arise from random electrical signals and the synthesis of these signals has no intrinsic meaning. Psychological theories, in contrast, suggest that the content of a dream is highly relevant to its purpose. Freud's theory proposes that dreams permit unconscious fulfilment of wishes. Research has also uncovered cultural differences in the content of dreams, with Mexican-American dreams higher on emotion than Anglo-American dreams, and Dutch dreams lower on aggression than American (Domhoff, 2002). Likewise, members of hunter-gatherer societies were found to dream more often of animals than did urban American or Japanese.

Research has shown that dreams mostly occur during REM sleep, a period that lasts for 20 minutes or so at a time. Dreams tend to run in 'real time', with some dreams lasting over ½ hour (Horne, 1999). Dreams fade rapidly (dream amnesia) unless the dreamer wakes and makes an effort to remember them.

It is only possible to establish the duration of dreams if we assume a relationship between REM activity and the length of the dream. Research that correlated the number of words used to describe a dream and the length of REM activity has tended to support the view that REM activity was directly related to the length of a dream (Dement and Kleitman, 1957). It is impossible to measure the length of NREM dreams except by subjective report, which makes any conclusions about this relationship tenuous.

REM sleep and dreaming tend to be synonymous. Dement and Kleitman (1957) found that if sleepers were awoken during REM activity, they tended to report dreaming 80% of the time. Dement and Kleitman also reported evidence of dreaming during NREM sleep, although only 7% of participants reported dreams during NREM sleep. NREM dreams also tend to be shorter, more mundane and fragmentary (Stickgold *et al.*, 2001). Types of dream also include hypnagogic (sleep onset) and hypnopompic (at waking) dream states. Many of the features of REM dreams are present in these dream states although there are fewer of them in any one dream, suggesting they are a 'reduced' version of normal dreaming. Research has also uncovered the phenomenon of 'screen dreams', e.g. participants who played the computer game 'Tetris' for several hours reported vivid dreams of Tetris screen imagery (Stickgold *et al.*, 2000).

The distinction between REM and NREM dreaming has been confirmed at a behavioural and neurobiological level. Antrobus (1983) found that 93% of those asked to judge correctly identified dream reports as REM or NREM. Brain scans and EEG recordings have also shown substantial differences between REM and NREM dreams at a neurobiological level. It is possible to obtain objective evidence for the existence of lucid dreams. A problem with conducting research in this area is that dream reports are inevitably subjective, and what is recalled is not necessarily what people experience. Also, much research is carried out in sleep laboratories where sleep and dreaming behaviour may be affected by the artificial surroundings.

In a question such as this, it is easy to make your answer sound 'non-psychological'. It is important, therefore, to try and include some research evidence to make your description more convincing – and the question requires that you base your answer on research findings.

The difference between AO1 description and AO2 commentary can be quite subtle. Here material is being used to consider the view that the content of dreams is important *and* whether dreams are universal or relative to cultural experience.

When constructing your AO2 commentary, ask yourself 'so what?' when making a point. This will ensure that you add something that puts the point in a more critical context.

There are about four separate points being made in this paragraph, each being elaborated just enough to give evidence of both depth (through technical detail) and breadth (through coverage) in the material.

By focusing on a smaller number of AO2 points one is able to provide sufficient elaboration to ensure that critical commentary is *effective*.

SAMPLE ESSAY PLAN

DIVISION C: DREAMING

Question 1: Discuss **two or more** neurobiological theories of the functions of dreaming. (24 marks)

ACTIVATION-SYNTHESIS HYPOTHESIS (HOBSON AND MCCARLEY, 1977)

7½ MINUTES WORTH OF AO1

- Neurobiological theories assume that **dreaming is the outcome of bodily states.**
- **Spontaneous electrical activity** from the **brainstem** occurs during REM sleep.
- The body is **paralysed** so no other sensory input or motor output.
- The **frontal cortex** tries to impose meaning on random signals in the same way as it does when awake.
- This experience is meaningful in the sense that nervous impulses are given **meaning derived from personal experiences.**
- But dreams have **no intrinsic meaning** – meaningfulness is not what drives the dream.

7½ MINUTES WORTH OF AO2

Support:
- **PET scans show brainstem** is active during REM (**Braun et al., 1997**) supporting activation.
- **Prefrontal cortex** (rational thought) on hold, supporting synthesis.

Challenge:
- Patients with **brainstem injuries** had no REM but still dreamt, or with **forebrain injuries** had REM but no dreams (**Solms**, 2000).
- Many dreams **not fragmentary**, they are coherent, consistent over time and related to past/present emotional concerns (**Domhoff**, 1996).
- **Dreaming absent in children age 3–5** but they do have REM (**Foulkes**, 1997). May remember less.

REVERSE LEARNING (CRICK AND MITCHISON, 1983)

7½ MINUTES WORTH OF AO1

- **Parasitic memories** are superfluous associations in memory arising from vast amount of information that is processing.
- Dreams allow **unlearning of parasitic memories** so that unwanted memories **don't clutter brain, especially pathological** memories (e.g. obsessions).
- Reverse learning makes important memories more accessible and allows more compact storage in **neural networks.**
- This is **adaptive** because can have a smaller, more efficient brain.
- **Neurological explanation**: random stimulation of forebrain stimulates neurons of unwanted memories, strength of synapses modified so less likely to be activated.

7½ MINUTES WORTH OF AO2

- Not easy to test.

Support:
- Brain takes in **much more information** (100 billion billion bits) than it can store (100 thousand billion) over a lifetime (**Goertzel**, 1997).
- **Negative correlation between body size and sleep length**, which suggests that brain size and REM are inversely related as would be predicted (**Siegel**, 1995).
- **Animals without REM sleep** (e.g. some dolphins) have larger neocortex – presumably to deal with unwanted connections (**Mukhametov**, 1987).

Challenge:
- But dolphin brain **less folded** than human brain so may not have larger capacity.
- **Computer simulation** didn't reduce parasitic associations (**Christos**, 1996).
- Presumed link between **dreaming and REM sleep** not exact: 80% of REM sleep has dreams, 7% of NREM (**Dement and Kleitman**, 1957).

Question 2: (a) Outline and evaluate research findings related to the nature of dreams. (12 marks)
(b) Outline and evaluate **one** neurobiological theory of the functions of dreaming. (12 marks)

(a) RESEARCH FINDINGS RELATED TO THE NATURE OF DREAMS

7½ MINUTES WORTH OF AO1

Select content of dreams or different kinds of dreams from page 56, or present a reduced version of each.

7½ MINUTES WORTH OF AO2

Evaluation from page 56.

(b) ONE NEUROBIOLOGICAL THEORY

7½ MINUTES WORTH OF AO1

Select either from above.

7½ MINUTES WORTH OF AO2

Evaluation of one theory, as above.

Neurobiological theories assume that dreaming is the outcome of bodily states with electrical activity in the brain creating the dream, and the experience of the dream being incidental. The activation-synthesis hypothesis (Hobson and McCarley, 1977) proposes that spontaneous electrical activity from the brainstem occurs during REM sleep. The body is paralysed so no other sensory input or motor output is possible. The cortex does not distinguish between the random stimuli coming from the brainstem and the stimuli it normally processes during wakefulness. The cortex tries to impose meaning on random signals in the same way as it does when awake. Hobson (1988) believed that dreams are nothing more than reactions to these random stimuli which the brain interprets as bizarre images and sensory hallucinations. The experience is meaningful in the sense that nervous impulses are given meaning derived from personal experiences, the often bizarre nature of dreams being due to the mixing of these electrical signals with stored images in the dreamer's memory. From this perspective, therefore, dreams have no intrinsic meaning – meaningfulness is not what drives the dream.

Support for the activation-synthesis hypothesis comes from PET scans which show that the brainstem is active during REM sleep (Braun et al., 1997), as are other brain areas responsible for mental functions such as emotion, hearing and vision. At the same time, areas in the prefrontal cortex responsible for rational thought appear to be on hold. This supports the synthesis part of the hypothesis.

Some research findings challenge the hypothesis. Solms (2000) found that patients with brainstem injuries had no REM sleep but still dreamt, and patients with forebrain injuries had REM sleep but did not dream. Although the activation-synthesis hypothesis claims that dreams lack meaning and are bizarre and inconsistent, many dreams are not fragmentary but are coherent, consistent over time and related to past or present emotional concerns (Domhoff, 1996). A final problem is the finding that young children dream very little if at all, yet have REM activity (Foulkes, 1997). Although it is possible that young children are less able to describe dreams coherently, giving the impression that they do not dream when they do.

In their reverse learning theory, Crick and Mitchison (1983) propose that we dream to forget. They suggest that dreaming could be a way of unlearning unwanted material from memory. Parasitic memories are superfluous associations in memory arising from the vast amount of information stored in memory during the day. Dreams allow unlearning of these associations so that unwanted memories don't clutter the brain. This is especially important in the case of pathological memories (such as obsessions or delusions) which might otherwise lead to pathological behaviour.

This makes important memories more accessible and allows more compact storage in neural networks, without the danger of memory overlap caused by unwanted associations in the brain. Such an arrangement is adaptive because it allows for a smaller, more efficient brain. Animals that do not dream (such as the spiny anteater) require a larger neural network to absorb these unwanted associations. The neurological explanation for this process is that random stimulation of the forebrain during dreaming excites the neurons of unwanted memories. As a result, the strength of these synapses is modified so they are less likely to be activated in the future.

A major problem for the reverse learning theory is that it is not easy to test. However, there is some research support for this theory. Goertzel (1997) claimed that the brain takes in far more information during the course of a day than it has the ability to store. This suggests that the brain needs to discard irrelevant information, which is consistent with the reverse learning theory. The theory would also predict a negative correlation between brain size and REM sleep. This is supported by the finding that larger animals (that have heavier brains) tend to sleep less (Siegel, 1995). Likewise, observational studies have also shown that mammals without REM sleep (e.g. some dolphins) require a larger neocortex to absorb unwanted information, again supporting the claim that dreaming is a way of removing unwanted connections (Mukhametov, 1987).

Despite this finding, the dolphin brain is less folded than the human brain so may not have larger capacity, making this conclusion invalid. A further problem is the finding that computer simulation of reverse learning showed that this didn't reduce parasitic associations, but actually increased them (Christos, 1996).

A final problem for neurobiological theories of dreaming is that the presumed link between dreaming and REM sleep is not exact, and no one neurobiological activity is equivalent to the state of dreaming.

Questions such as this are fairly predictable, so you should practise outlining each of the two main neurobiological theories in approx. 150–175 words. This outline is 179 words.

Note how this essay has split the AO2 material into *support* and *challenge*. This isn't vital, but is a good way of organising your evaluation.

Simply making the point that young children do not dream is not AO2 by itself, but adding a comment to put this in context makes it into AO2 commentary.

Many students point out that some animals do not dream, but don't really link this fact to the reverse learning theory. Note the way this fact is fitted into the outline of this theory here.

Although there are no extra marks for names and dates, it helps you to construct an effective commentary if you have specific research findings to draw upon.

TOPIC 3: PSYCHOLOGICAL THEORIES OF DREAMING

SAMPLE ESSAY PLAN

Question 1: Discuss two or more psychological theories of the functions of dreaming. (24 marks)

FREUD'S THEORY	**9 MINUTES WORTH OF AO1**	**9 MINUTES WORTH OF AO2**
	• **Primary-process thought** from the id is unacceptable to adult conscious mind, it is **repressed** to dreams.	• Freud's theory is **unfalsifiable** and based on restricted sample (neurotic Viennese women).
	• Dreams protect the sleeper. If we don't dream, the **energy associated with unconscious desires** builds up.	• **PET scans** show that rational part of brain (**prefrontal cortex** or the ego) is inactive, and emotional part (**forebrain** or the id) is active during REM sleep.
	• Dreams allow unconscious wishes to be fulfilled (**wish fulfilment**).	• But without rational part how is **manifest content turned into latent content**? (**Braun**, 1999).
	• Dream content expressed **symbolically**. Real meaning (**latent content**) disguised in more innocuous form (**manifest content**).	• **Computer simulations** show that overloaded memory is dealt with by **condensation** (**Hopfield et al.**, 1983).
	• For example, penis represented by a snake but **dream dictionaries** don't work because must interpret in terms of each individual's experience.	• **Nightmares** aren't wish fulfilments nor do they protect sleeper. Freud acknowledged that some dreams do not fit these categories.
PLUS EITHER... JUNG'S THEORY	**6 MINUTES WORTH OF AO1**	**6 MINUTES WORTH OF AO2**
	• Dreams more directly related to current issues.	• Emphasis on **social** rather than **sexual** influences.
	• Dreams provide solutions to problems (**compensation**) and reduce mental disorder.	• Many examples of creativity and dreams e.g. **Howe** invented sewing machine when dreamt of spears with holes in tips (**Martin**, 2002).
	• Meaning of dream discovered through associations dreamer makes when reporting dream (**amplification**).	• Difficult to **falsify**.
	• **Creative ideas** come through dreams.	• **Collective dreams**: artists dip into the **collective unconscious**, schizophrenic patients dreamed about things they couldn't know (**Jung**).
	• **Collective dreams** contain symbols common to cultural group.	
OR... PROBLEM-SOLVING THEORY (CARTWRIGHT, 1978)	**6 MINUTES WORTH OF AO1**	**6 MINUTES WORTH OF AO2**
	• Dreams directly reflect major **conscious emotional concerns**.	• Dreams related to waking coping strategies for **marital problems** (**Cartwright et al.**, 1984).
	• **Symbols** convey real concerns e.g. drowning incident reflects 'drowning under responsibilities' (**Wade and Tavris**, 1993).	• Dreams related to daytime activity playing **Tetris** (**Stickgold et al.**, 2000).
	• May lead to better **coping strategies** rather than problem-solving.	• Students selected personal problem and in a week 50% had dream that offered a solution (**Barrett**, 1993).

Question 2: (a) Outline and evaluate one neurobiological theory of the functions of dreaming. (12 marks)
(b) Outline and evaluate one psychological theory of the functions of dreaming. (12 marks)

ONE NEUROBIO-LOGICAL THEORY	**7½ MINUTES WORTH OF AO1**	**7½ MINUTES WORTH OF AO2**
	• Select one theory from page 58.	Evaluation from page 58.
ONE PSYCHOLOGICAL THEORY	**7½ MINUTES WORTH OF AO1**	**7½ MINUTES WORTH OF AO2**
	• Select Freud's theory from above.	Evaluation as above.

Freud believed that primary-process thought coming from the id is unacceptable to the adult conscious mind, therefore such thought is repressed to dreams. If we did not dream, the energy invested in these desires would build up to intolerable levels and threaten our sanity. According to Freud, all dreams are the unconscious fulfilment of wishes that cannot be satisfied in the conscious mind. Dreams therefore protect the sleeper from unacceptable thoughts, but allow some expression to these latent urges. Dreams represent unfulfilled wishes, but the content of dreams is expressed symbolically. The real meaning of a dream (its latent content) is disguised in more innocuous form (manifest content), which may be meaningless to anybody but a psychoanalyst trained in dream interpretation. For example, Freud believed that a penis may be represented by a snake although he claimed that dream dictionaries do not work because interpretation must be in terms of each individual's experience.

A major problem with this view of dreaming, as with all aspects of Freud's theory, is that it is unfalsifiable, and based on a restricted sample of neurotic, Victorian, Viennese women. This therefore reflects a historically and culturally biased sample that poses problems for the general validity of this theory. Although Freud's theory is generally criticised for lacking research support, the findings from research using PET scans show that the rational part of the brain (prefrontal cortex) is inactive and the emotional part (forebrain) is active during REM sleep. This might be seen as equivalent to the ego being suspended while the id is given free rein.

On the other hand, argues Braun (1999), if the rational, thinking part of the brain is not active during REM sleep, then it is difficult to explain the processing necessary to turn latent into manifest content. Freud's theory is given further support by research on neural networks. Computer simulations show that neural networks deal with an overloaded memory by condensing memories (Hopfield et al., 1983). This supports Freud's view that dreams are comprised of several different themes condensed into one symbol. A problem for Freud's theory is the issue of nightmares, which are not wish fulfilments nor do they protect the sleeper. Freud acknowledged that some dreams do not fit these categories.

Jung (1964) believed that dreams were more directly related to current issues in the person's life. He believed that through the process of compensation, dreams provide solutions to problems and prevent any mental disorder that might arise because of an imbalance between the conscious and unconscious mind. Jung claimed that the meaning of the dream can be discovered through associations the dreamer makes when reporting the dream (the process of amplification). Jung also believed that creative ideas come through dreams, giving the example of Stevenson's idea for Dr Jekyll and Mr Hyde coming to him in a dream. Collective dreams sometimes appear and contain symbolism that is relevant to a whole culture. These dreams arise from the collective unconscious, the storehouse of experiences from past generations, and may not be easily understood by the dreamer because they are impersonal in nature.

A strength of Jung's theory of dreams compared to the Freudian explanation is the shift away from sexual influences towards social influences. There are many examples of the link between creativity and dreams which would support Jung's claim that such a link exists. For example, Howe claimed that the idea for the sewing machine came to him in a dream of men carrying spears with holes in their tips (Martin, 2002). A problem with Jung's theory is that it is difficult to falsify, and almost impossible to provide objective evidence to support the theory's claims. Much of the supporting evidence, therefore, consists of subjective reports of dreams that fit the theory's main assumptions. As supporting evidence for his idea of collective dreams, Jung claimed that the ability of artists and scientists to dream up great works could only be explained by having dipped into the collective unconscious. Likewise, he referred to reports that schizophrenic patients frequently dreamed about things they could not possibly know unless they were drawing upon the collective unconscious.

In this essay, we have simply amplified the bullet points on page 60. It is useful for you to have a series of bullet points that detail a particular theory, and then amplify these in an essay response.

Students inevitably use Freud's sample as a criticism of his theory, but ask yourself 'so what?' and then explain *why* this poses a problem for the theory being evaluated.

Note that the introduction of this research is accompanied by commentary which makes it clear why this is important in the *evaluation* of this theory.

Because this is a fairly open-ended question, you could choose to include more than the two theories here, but if that were the case, you would need to shorten the Freud and Jung sections of this essay.

Much of the *language* used in this paragraph is explicitly AO2 in nature. This makes it obvious that the candidate is constructing a critical commentary rather than just describing points of interest.

Topic 1: Structure and function of the visual system

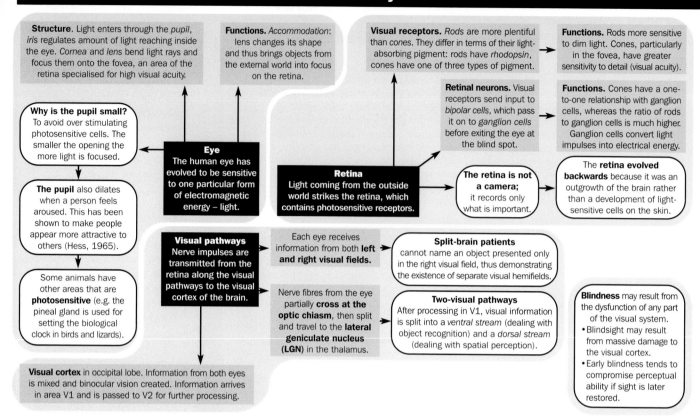

Structure. Light enters through the *pupil*, *iris* regulates amount of light reaching inside the eye. *Cornea* and *lens* bend light rays and focus them onto the fovea, an area of the retina specialised for high visual acuity.

Functions. *Accommodation*: lens changes its shape and thus brings objects from the external world into focus on the retina.

Visual receptors. *Rods* are more plentiful than *cones*. They differ in terms of their light-absorbing pigment: rods have *rhodopsin*, cones have one of three types of pigment.

Functions. Rods more sensitive to dim light. Cones, particularly in the fovea, have greater sensitivity to detail (visual acuity).

Why is the pupil small? To avoid over stimulating photosensitive cells. The smaller the opening the more light is focused.

Eye The human eye has evolved to be sensitive to one particular form of electromagnetic energy – light.

Retina Light coming from the outside world strikes the retina, which contains photosensitive receptors.

Retinal neurons. Visual receptors send input to *bipolar cells*, which pass it on to *ganglion cells* before exiting the eye at the blind spot.

Functions. Cones have a one-to-one relationship with ganglion cells, whereas the ratio of rods to ganglion cells is much higher. Ganglion cells convert light impulses into electrical energy.

The pupil also dilates when a person feels aroused. This has been shown to make people appear more attractive to others (Hess, 1965).

The retina is not a camera; it records only what is important.

The **retina evolved backwards** because it was an outgrowth of the brain rather than a development of light-sensitive cells on the skin.

Some animals have other areas that are **photosensitive** (e.g. the pineal gland is used for setting the biological clock in birds and lizards).

Visual pathways Nerve impulses are transmitted from the retina along the visual pathways to the visual cortex of the brain.

Each eye receives information from both **left and right visual fields.**

Split-brain patients cannot name an object presented only in the right visual field, thus demonstrating the existence of separate visual hemifields.

Nerve fibres from the eye partially **cross at the optic chiasm**, then split and travel to the **lateral geniculate nucleus (LGN)** in the thalamus.

Two-visual pathways After processing in V1, visual information is split into a *ventral stream* (dealing with object recognition) and a *dorsal stream* (dealing with spatial perception).

Blindness may result from the dysfunction of any part of the visual system.
• Blindsight may result from massive damage to the visual cortex.
• Early blindness tends to compromise perceptual ability if sight is later restored.

Visual cortex in occipital lobe. Information from both eyes is mixed and binocular vision created. Information arrives in area V1 and is passed to V2 for further processing.

Topic 2: The nature of visual information processing

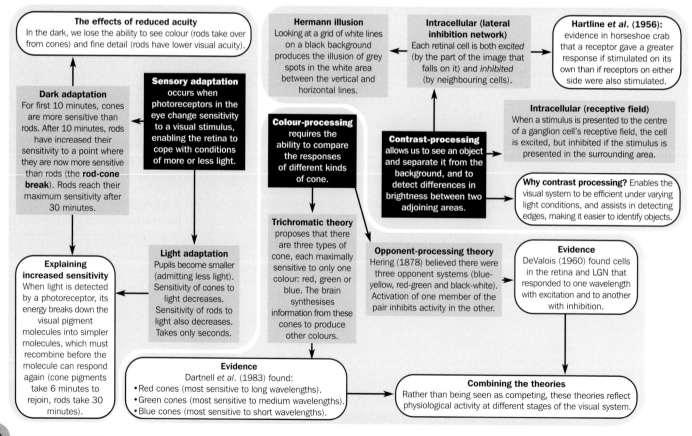

The effects of reduced acuity In the dark, we lose the ability to see colour (rods take over from cones) and fine detail (rods have lower visual acuity).

Hermann illusion Looking at a grid of white lines on a black background produces the illusion of grey spots in the white area between the vertical and horizontal lines.

Intracellular (lateral inhibition network) Each retinal cell is both *excited* (by the part of the image that falls on it) and *inhibited* (by neighbouring cells).

Hartline et al. (1956): evidence in horseshoe crab that a receptor gave a greater response if stimulated on its own than if receptors on either side were also stimulated.

Dark adaptation For first 10 minutes, cones are more sensitive than rods. After 10 minutes, rods have increased their sensitivity to a point where they are now more sensitive than rods (the **rod-cone break**). Rods reach their maximum sensitivity after 30 minutes.

Sensory adaptation occurs when photoreceptors in the eye change sensitivity to a visual stimulus, enabling the retina to cope with conditions of more or less light.

Colour-processing requires the ability to compare the responses of different kinds of cone.

Contrast-processing allows us to see an object and separate it from the background, and to detect differences in brightness between two adjoining areas.

Intracellular (receptive field) When a stimulus is presented to the centre of a ganglion cell's receptive field, the cell is excited, but inhibited if the stimulus is presented in the surrounding area.

Why contrast processing? Enables the visual system to be efficient under varying light conditions, and assists in detecting edges, making it easier to identify objects.

Explaining increased sensitivity When light is detected by a photoreceptor, its energy breaks down the visual pigment molecules into simpler molecules, which must recombine before the molecule can respond again (cone pigments take 6 minutes to rejoin, rods take 30 minutes).

Light adaptation Pupils become smaller (admitting less light). Sensitivity of cones to light decreases. Sensitivity of rods to light also decreases. Takes only seconds.

Trichromatic theory proposes that there are three types of cone, each maximally sensitive to only one colour: red, green or blue. The brain synthesises information from these cones to produce other colours.

Opponent-processing theory Hering (1878) believed there were three opponent systems (blue-yellow, red-green and black-white). Activation of one member of the pair inhibits activity in the other.

Evidence DeValois (1960) found cells in the retina and LGN that responded to one wavelength with excitation and to another with inhibition.

Evidence Dartnell *et al.* (1983) found:
• Red cones (most sensitive to long wavelengths).
• Green cones (most sensitive to medium wavelengths).
• Blue cones (most sensitive to short wavelengths).

Combining the theories Rather than being seen as competing, these theories reflect physiological activity at different stages of the visual system.

structure and functions of the visual system: the eye, retina and visual pathways.

Probable questions

1. Discuss the structure **and** functions of the visual system. *(24 marks)*

2. Discuss the functions of the visual system. *(24 marks)*

Possible questions

3. Discuss the structure **and** functions of the retina and visual pathways. *(24 marks)*

The difference between question 1 and 2 is obvious yet candidates often overlook such differences in an exam situation. Typically they write about structure and functions no matter what question is set. In question 2 material on structure would not be creditworthy – you do not need to discuss the structure of the retina in order to describe its function. In question 1 you must discuss structure **and** function, otherwise a partial performance penalty would be imposed (a maximum of 8 marks for AO1 instead of 12 marks, and the same for AO2 – in fact if you describe both structure and function but only evaluate structure or function then there would be a partial performance penalty on AO2).

Providing AO2 in this division of the specification is a challenging task but, once you get the hang of it, it is no more difficult than any other AO2. You can, for example, use research evidence as support or challenge, you can consider implications and/or applications of such knowledge, and you can also consider effects of system failure (e.g. blindness).

This less likely question limits the parts of the visual system that you should discuss. This is a permissible question because the specification lists three parts of the visual system (the eye, the retina and visual pathways). This means that a question may require you to discuss any one of these.

(e.g. sensory adaptation and the processing of contrast, colour and features)

Probable questions

1. Describe and evaluate research (theories **and/or** studies) into **two** forms of visual information processing. *(24 marks)*

2. Discuss the nature of visual information processing. *(24 marks)*

Possible questions

3. (a) Outline the structure of the eye. *(6 marks)*

   (b) Discuss research (theories **and/or** studies) into **one** form of visual information processing. *(12 marks)*

Despite the fact that these two questions look quite different, they could actually have fairly similar answers. In question 2 you are given the option of discussing more than two forms of visual information processing, or indeed discussing only one form of visual information processing (e.g. colour processing). In question 1, if you only discussed one form, you would be marked according to the partial performance penalty. If you wrote about more than two forms then credit would be given to the two best forms of visual information processing covered. Therefore, for both questions, you could write about two forms of visual information processing.

You are not required to provide the two forms in balance. You could gain full marks if one form is discussed in more detail because, according to the partial performance rule, you could get up to 16 marks for just one form of visual processing.

The open-ended nature of question 2 is a double-edged sword. Often candidates try to stuff as many different things as possible into their answer in order to impress the examiner. However this is likely to result in reduced depth (detail) and/or too much AO1 and too little AO2. It is important to be selective.

This question is an example of combined topics. Questions are always set on one sub-section of the specification (e.g. 'Perceptual processes and development') but within a sub-section topics may be combined because it is assumed that you have studied the whole sub-section. This means that it is vital, when revising, to revise the *whole* of the sub-section (including any nooks and crannies) and not just focus on your favourite topics.

TOPIC 1: STRUCTURE AND FUNCTION OF THE VISUAL SYSTEM

SAMPLE ESSAY PLAN

Question 1: Discuss the structure **and** functions of the visual system. (24 marks)

THE EYE

5 MINUTES WORTH OF AO1
- **Structure**: iris, pupil, cornea, lens, retina.
- The eye **focuses** light rays on the retina (light-sensitive cells).
- **Cornea** sharpens the image.
- **Lens** focuses light under changing conditions (**accommodation**).

5 MINUTES WORTH OF AO2
- **Pupil size** important too in sharpening image. **Pupil size** changes with increased/decreased light, also with arousal. People perceive a person with dilated pupils as more attractive (**Hess**, 1965).
- Possible to explain **headaches** in terms of dilation and contraction of the iris.
- Some animals have a **third eye** which just records levels of light and resets the **biological clock**.

THE RETINA

5 MINUTES WORTH OF AO1
- **Structure**: rod/cone layer, bipolar cells, ganglion cells; fovea, blind spot.
- **Photoreceptors** convert light energy into **neural impulses**.
- **Rods** function in dim lighting.
- **Cones** record colour and are less active in dim light; important for **visual acuity**.

5 MINUTES WORTH OF AO2
- The retina is not like a **camera**. Much data is redundant, which is why it is 'summarised' by ganglion cells.
- Eye/retina **evolved** to record most useful information.
- Rods are sensitive to **movement** because it is adaptive.
- The retina is **backwards** because it evolved as an outgrowth of the brain.

THE VISUAL PATHWAYS

5 MINUTES WORTH OF AO1
- **Structure**: right/left hemi-fields, optic nerve, optic chiasm, lateral geniculate nucleus, visual cortex.
- **Optic chiasm** enables fibres from right visual field of both eyes to pass to right visual cortex, and same for left visual field.
- **Visual cortex** mixes information from both eyes to create binocular vision.

5 MINUTES WORTH OF AO2
- **Split-brain** studies (**Sperry**, 1968) demonstrate the separation of signals from left and right hemi-fields. Split-brain patients cannot name an object visible only in the right visual field as language centres are in the left hemisphere.
- **Blindsight**, people with damaged visual cortex still can reach for objects due to input to **superior colliculus**.
- Visual cortex may be **permanently damaged** by lack of input, for example SB (**Gregory and Wallace**, 1963) who never 'saw' despite vision being restored late in life.

Question 2: Discuss the functions of the visual system. (24 marks)

THE EYE

5 MINUTES WORTH OF AO1
- The eye **focuses** light rays on the retina.
- **Iris** acts as aperture control, changing pupil size.
- **Cornea** sharpens the image.
- **Lens** focuses light under changing conditions.

5 MINUTES WORTH OF AO2
- The evaluation of theory 1 above.

THE RETINA

5 MINUTES WORTH OF AO1
- **Photoreceptors** convert light energy into **neural impulses**.
- **Rods** function in dim lighting.
- **Cones** record colour and are less active in dim light; important for **visual acuity**.
- **Bipolar** cells and **ganglion cells** summarise information collected by rods and cods. Ratio of rods to ganglion cells may be up to 200:1 whereas some cone to ganglion cells are 1:1.

5 MINUTES WORTH OF AO2
- The evaluation of theory 1 above.

THE VISUAL PATHWAYS

5 MINUTES WORTH OF AO1
- **Optic chiasm** enables fibres from right visual field of both eyes to pass to right visual cortex, and same for left visual field.
- **Visual cortex** mixes information from both eyes to create binocular vision.
- **Primary visual cortex** (area V1) does preliminary processing, then **secondary visual cortex** (area V2).

5 MINUTES WORTH OF AO2
- The evaluation of theory 1 above, plus:
- **V1** is split into **ventral** and **dorsal stream**, which deal with top-down and bottom-up respectively.

Light enters the eye through the pupil, with the iris regulating the amount of light reaching the inside of the eye. The small aperture causes an inverted image to be projected onto the retina, the light-sensitive cells at the back of the eye, and the brain later adjusts this information so we see objects as they really are. The cornea sharpens the image and brings it into focus on the retina, and then the image is sent along the optic nerve to the brain. To focus light under changing conditions, the lens is made either thicker or thinner through the process of accommodation.

As well as the cornea being responsible for sharpening the image on the retina, pupil size is also important in this process. Pupil size not only changes with increased or decreased light levels, but also with levels of arousal. Research studies on the relationship between pupil size and arousal have demonstrated that people tend to perceive a person with dilated pupils as being more attractive (Hess, 1965). It is also possible to explain headaches from watching television in a darkened room in terms of the constant dilation and contraction of the muscles of the iris. Photosensitivity may not be restricted to the eye, with some animals having a third eye which just records levels of light and resets the biological clock.

The retina contains two types of photosensitive receptors, rods and cones. There are many more rods than cones, although the area in and around the fovea contains mostly cones. Rods are more responsive to dim light, whereas cones are less active in dim light and are also important for the perception of colour. Because they are clustered around the fovea, cones are important for visual acuity. Rods and cones send their input to the bipolar cells, which in turn transmit their messages to the ganglion cells. The ganglion cells convert light impulses into electrical energy, and exit the eye at the blind spot.

Although the eye records information from the outside world, it is not like a camera. Much of the data reaching the retina is redundant, which is why it is 'summarised' by ganglion cells. The eye, and particularly the retina, has evolved to record the information that is most useful to an organism. In particular, the rods are sensitive to movement because this is important to our survival. The 'backwards' arrangement of the mammalian retina (where nerve impulses must pass back through the cells of the retina before leaving the eye) can be explained because the retina evolved as an outgrowth of the brain rather than a development of light-sensitive cells on the skin.

The image projected onto the retina can be divided into two. Each eye gets information from both the right and left hemi-field. Visual information leaves the eye via the optic nerve, with a partial crossing of these nerve fibres at the optic chiasm. From the optic chiasm, nerve fibres travel to the lateral geniculate nucleus in the thalamus, and from here on to the visual cortex. The optic chiasm enables fibres from the right visual field of both eyes to pass to the right visual cortex, and the same for the left visual field. The visual cortex mixes information from both eyes to create binocular vision.

Split-brain studies (Sperry, 1968) have provided support for the separation of signals from left and right hemi-fields. Sperry showed that a split-brain patient cannot name an object visible only in the right visual field because output from the right visual field of both eyes travels to the right hemisphere of the brain, but the language centres are in the left hemisphere. Some patients, despite damage to their visual cortex, can still reach for objects in their visual field (blindsight). This is because retinal ganglion cells still give some input to the superior colliculus. The visual cortex may be permanently damaged by lack of input, for example in the case of SB (Gregory and Wallace, 1963), who never 'saw' despite having his vision restored late in life.

This answer does not get too bogged down with the structural detail of the eye, but gives an overview of the structure and function of each component.

It is difficult to construct AO2 commentary for this topic, but making an *attempt* to think beyond just describing the eye will be met sympathetically by the examiners.

In this answer we have split the AO1 material into three paragraphs dealing with the eye, then specifically the retina (this paragraph) and the visual pathways (next AO1 paragraph).

Here two of the 'mysteries' of the eye are explained as part of the AO2 commentary – the *adaptive* nature of human vision, and the *backwards* arrangement of retinal cells.

You could also mention the primary and secondary visual cortex, but only if time allows within the overall context of your answer.

Showing the *consequences* of damage to normal visual processing provides commentary on the function of the visual pathways.

SAMPLE ESSAY PLAN

Question 1: Describe and evaluate research (theories **and/or** studies) into **two** forms of visual information processing. (24 marks)

SENSORY PROCESSING	**6 MINUTES WORTH OF AO1** • **Dark adaptation**: for first 10 minutes cones more sensitive than rods, therefore visual record largely from cones. At the **rod-cone break** the rods take over because they have become more sensitive. Maximum sensitivity after 30 minutes. • **Pupil also dilates** to let in more light. • **Light adaptation**: takes seconds, pupil contracts, sensitivity of rods and cones to light decreases.	**6 MINUTES WORTH OF AO2** • Increased sensitivity due to '**bleaching**' of pigments in the photoreceptors – light breaks down the pigment molecules which must rejoin before the photoreceptor can respond. **Cones** take 6 minutes to rejoin whereas **rods** take 30 minutes. • **Light adaptation is faster** than dark adaptation because in bright conditions fewer photoreceptors are needed. • In **dark** conditions there is reduced colour vision and reduced acuity because rods predominate, also visual responses slower. • This can explain difficulties when **driving in the dark**, and why bright lights cause problems.
COLOUR- PROCESSING	**9 MINUTES WORTH OF AO1** **Trichromatic theory** (Young and Von Helmholtz, 1802) • Any colour can be produced by a mixture of **red, green and blue**. • This led to proposed existence of **3 cones**, each maximally sensitive to only one colour. • The cones **respond to different degrees** when exposed to light e.g. yellow is produced when both green and red receptors are stimulated. **Opponent-processing theory** (Hering, 1878) • **Colour after-images**: if you stare at a blue circle then you'll see a yellow after-image. • **Three basic opponent systems**: blue-yellow, red-green, black-white. • **Activation** of one **inhibits** activity of the other.	**9 MINUTES WORTH OF AO2** • Physiological evidence for **trichromatic theory** (Dartnell *et al.*, 1983) found red, green, blue cones. • Most cones are red (64%) and fewest are blue (4%) which leads to a **warm colour bias**. • **Why 3 cones?** Because this is the minimum needed to respond to all colours. • Physiological evidence for **opponent-process** (DeValois, 1960) found cells in retina and LGN that respond to one wavelength with excitation and another with inhibition. • **Increases efficiency** of the system because it prevents redundant information being passed to the visual cortex. • The two theories are **not competing**, they reflect **physiological activity at different points** in the system: cone cells record wavelength, later opponent cells suppress redundant information.

Question 2: Discuss the nature of visual information processing. (24 marks)

SENSORY PROCESSING	**5 MINUTES WORTH OF AO1** • The description of theory 1 above.	**5 MINUTES WORTH OF AO2** • The evaluation of theory 1 above.
CONTRAST- PROCESSING	**5 MINUTES WORTH OF AO1** • **Lateral inhibition** enables one to see edges, and thus separate object and background. • **Intercellar lateral inhibition**: if a receptor cell is 'excited' then neighbouring cells are inhibited. • **Intracellar lateral inhibition**: if a stimulus is presented to the centre of a ganglion cell's **receptive field** it is excited, but if presented to the surround it is inhibited.	**5 MINUTES WORTH OF AO2** • Physiological evidence for **lateral inhibition** (Hartline *et al.*, 1956) from horseshoe crabs which have individual eyes. • Contrast-processing is an **adaptive feature** of visual processing because contrasts remain the same whatever the light conditions. • It also makes **object identification** easier because it 'sharpens' the edges.
COLOUR- PROCESSING	**5 MINUTES WORTH OF AO1** **Trichromatic theory** (Young, 1802, **von Helmhotz**, 1866) • Existence of **3 cones** (red, green, blue), each maximally sensitive to only one colour. • The cones **respond to different degrees** when exposed to light e.g. yellow is produced when both green and red receptors are stimulated. **Opponent-processing theory** (Hering, 1878) • **Colour after-images**: if you stare at a blue circle then you'll see a yellow after-image. • **Three basic opponent systems**: blue-yellow, red-green, black-white.	**5 MINUTES WORTH OF AO2** • Physiological evidence for **trichromatic theory** (Dartnell *et al.*, 1983) found red, green, blue cones. • **Why 3 cones?** Because this is the minimum needed to respond to all colours. • Physiological evidence for **opponent-process** (DeValois, 1960) found cells in retina and LGN that respond to one wavelength with excitation and another with inhibition. • The two theories are **not competing**, they reflect **physiological activity at different points** in the system: cone cells record wavelength, later opponent cells suppress redundant information.

Sensory adaptation takes place when photoreceptors in the eye change their sensitivity to a visual stimulus. In dark adaptation, for the first 10 minutes cones are more sensitive than rods, therefore what we see during this time comes largely from the cones. After about 10 minutes, the rods reach a point where they are more sensitive than the cones (the rod-cone break). Rods reach their maximum sensitivity after about 30 minutes. As part of the dark adaptation process, the pupil also dilates to let in more of the available light to stimulate the retina. The process of light adaptation takes only seconds, with the pupil contracting to let in less light and the sensitivity of the rods and cones to light decreases.

The increased sensitivity during dark adaptation is due to the 'bleaching' of pigments in the photoreceptors – light breaks down the pigment molecules which must rejoin before the photoreceptor can respond. Cones take 6 minutes to rejoin whereas rods take 30 minutes, thus explaining why rods reach their maximum sensitivity after 30 minutes. Light adaptation is faster than dark adaptation because in bright conditions fewer photoreceptors are needed to produce a visual image, so the recovery rate does not affect vision. As a consequence of sensory adaptation, in dark conditions there is reduced colour vision and reduced acuity because the rods predominate, and our visual responses are also slower. This can explain difficulties when driving in the dark (visual responses are slower), and why exposure to bright lights when driving reduces subsequent vision.

Trichromatic theory (Young, 1802) claimed that any colour can be produced by a mixture of red, green and blue light. This led to the proposal that the visual system perceives colour in a similar way. Because of this, there only needs to be three types of cone – red, green and blue – with each maximally sensitive to only one colour. The cones respond to different degrees when exposed to light, with the brain synthesising this information to produce all the other colours, e.g. yellow is produced when both green and red receptors are stimulated.

Opponent-processing theory (Hering, 1878) was able to explain why, when the eye had adapted to one colour stimulus, the removal of that stimulus leaves an after-image of a different colour. For example, if you stare at a blue circle then you'll see a yellow after-image. Hering claimed that there were three basic opponent systems: blue-yellow, red-green, black-white. Activation of one member of each pair inhibits activity of the other, which means that we cannot experience both colours at the same time (i.e. we cannot perceive visual stimuli as being 'reddish-green').

There is some physiological evidence for trichromatic theory. Dartnell et al. (1983) found evidence of red, green and blue cones, with red cones most sensitive to long wavelengths, green cones to medium wavelengths and blue cones to shorter wavelengths. It has also been discovered that in human vision, most cones are red (64%) and fewest are blue (4%) which creates a warm colour bias. The existence of three cones (rather than more or less) can be explained by the fact that this is the minimum needed to record all wavelengths and so recognise all colours in the visual spectrum.

Physiological evidence for the opponent-process theory comes from DeValois (1960), who found cells in the retina and the lateral geniculate nucleus that respond to one wavelength with excitation and another with inhibition. Opponent-processing performs an important function, increasing the efficiency of the system because it prevents redundant information being passed to the visual cortex. The two theories are not competing, but rather they reflect physiological activity at different points in the system, with cone cells recording wavelength, and later opponent cells suppressing redundant information.

The first 'form' of visual information processing is *sensory adaptation*, with dark and light adaptation being two aspects of it.

Here a practical application of sensory adaptation knowledge is used as AO2 commentary.

The AO1 material on colour processing is longer than for sensory adaptation because the decision was made to spend longer on colour processing than sensory adaptation. This is just as acceptable as giving each the same coverage *provided* each is sufficiently detailed.

There is a variety of different types of AO2 in these final paragraphs – research support, explanation for visual phenomena and comment on the relationship between the two theories.

Topic 1: Theories of visual perception – constructivist theories

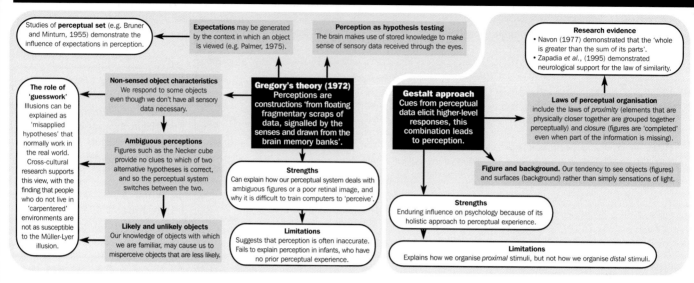

Studies of perceptual set (e.g. Bruner and Minturn, 1955) demonstrate the influence of expectations in perception.

Expectations may be generated by the context in which an object is viewed (e.g. Palmer, 1975).

Perception as hypothesis testing
The brain makes use of stored knowledge to make sense of sensory data received through the eyes.

Research evidence
- Navon (1977) demonstrated that the 'whole is greater than the sum of its parts'.
- Zapadia et al., (1995) demonstrated neurological support for the law of similarity.

The role of 'guesswork'
Illusions can be explained as 'misapplied hypotheses' that normally work in the real world. Cross-cultural research supports this view, with the finding that people who do not live in 'carpentered' environments are not as susceptible to the Müller-Lyer illusion.

Non-sensed object characteristics
We respond to some objects even though we don't have all sensory data necessary.

Gregory's theory (1972)
Perceptions are constructions 'from floating fragmentary scraps of data, signalled by the senses and drawn from the brain memory banks'.

Gestalt approach
Cues from perceptual data elicit higher-level responses, this combination leads to perception.

Laws of perceptual organisation
include the laws of *proximity* (elements that are physically closer together are grouped together perceptually) and *closure* (figures are 'completed' even when part of the information is missing).

Ambiguous perceptions
Figures such as the Necker cube provide no clues to which of two alternative hypotheses is correct, and so the perceptual system switches between the two.

Strengths
Can explain how our perceptual system deals with ambiguous figures or a poor retinal image, and why it is difficult to train computers to 'perceive'.

Figure and background. Our tendency to see objects (figures) and surfaces (background) rather than simply sensations of light.

Strengths
Enduring influence on psychology because of its holistic approach to perceptual experience.

Likely and unlikely objects
Our knowledge of objects with which we are familiar, may cause us to misperceive objects that are less likely.

Limitations
Suggests that perception is often inaccurate. Fails to explain perception in infants, who have no prior perceptual experience.

Limitations
Explains how we organise *proximal* stimuli, but not how we organise *distal* stimuli.

Topic 2: Theories of visual perception – direct theories

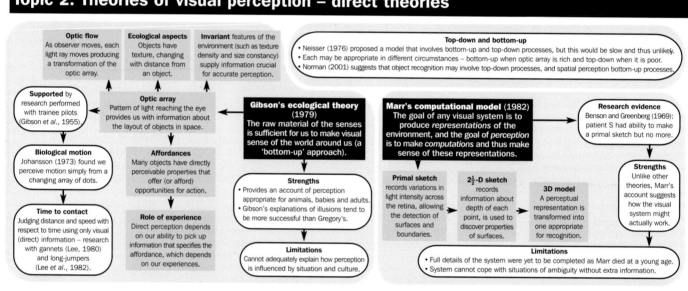

Optic flow
As observer moves, each light ray moves producing a transformation of the optic array.

Ecological aspects
Objects have texture, changing with distance from an object.

Invariant features of the environment (such as texture density and size constancy) supply information crucial for accurate perception.

Top-down and bottom-up
- Neisser (1976) proposed a model that involves bottom-up and top-down processes, but this would be slow and thus unlikely.
- Each may be appropriate in different circumstances – bottom-up when optic array is rich and top-down when it is poor.
- Norman (2001) suggests that object recognition may involve top-down processes, and spatial perception bottom-up processes.

Supported by research performed with trainee pilots (Gibson et al., 1955).

Optic array
Pattern of light reaching the eye provides us with information about the layout of objects in space.

Gibson's ecological theory (1979)
The raw material of the senses is sufficient for us to make visual sense of the world around us (a 'bottom-up' approach).

Marr's computational model (1982)
The goal of any visual system is to produce *representations* of the environment, and the goal of *perception* is to make *computations* and thus make sense of these representations.

Research evidence
Benson and Greenberg (1969): patient S had ability to make a primal sketch but no more.

Biological motion
Johansson (1973) found we perceive motion simply from a changing array of dots.

Affordances
Many objects have directly perceivable properties that offer (or afford) opportunities for action.

Strengths
- Provides an account of perception appropriate for animals, babies and adults.
- Gibson's explanations of illusions tend to be more successful than Gregory's.

Primal sketch
records variations in light intensity across the retina, allowing the detection of surfaces and boundaries.

$2\frac{1}{2}$-D sketch
records information about depth of each point, is used to discover properties of surfaces.

3D model
A perceptual representation is transformed into one appropriate for recognition.

Strengths
Unlike other theories, Marr's account suggests how the visual system might actually work.

Time to contact
Judging distance and speed with respect to time using only visual (direct) information – research with gannets (Lee, 1980) and long-jumpers (Lee et al., 1982).

Role of experience
Direct perception depends on our ability to pick up information that specifies the affordance, which depends on our experiences.

Limitations
Cannot adequately explain how perception is influenced by situation and culture.

Limitations
- Full details of the system were yet to be completed as Marr died at a young age.
- System cannot cope with situations of ambiguity without extra information.

Topic 3: Explanations of perceptual organisation

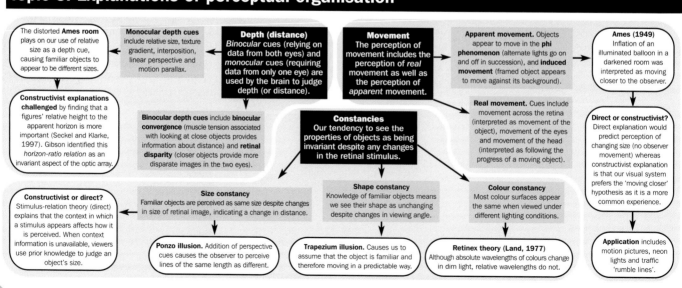

The distorted **Ames room** plays on our use of relative size as a depth cue, causing familiar objects to appear to be different sizes.

Monocular depth cues
include relative size, texture gradient, interposition, linear perspective and motion parallax.

Depth (distance)
Binocular cues (relying on data from both eyes) and *monocular* cues (requiring data from only one eye) are used by the brain to judge depth (or distance).

Movement
The perception of movement includes the perception of *real* movement as well as the perception of *apparent* movement.

Apparent movement. Objects appear to move in the **phi phenomenon** (alternate lights go on and off in succession), and **induced movement** (framed object appears to move against its background).

Ames (1949)
Inflation of an illuminated balloon in a darkened room was interpreted as moving closer to the observer.

Constructivist explanations challenged by finding that a figures' relative height to the apparent horizon is more important (Seckel and Klarke, 1997). Gibson identified this *horizon-ratio relation* as an invariant aspect of the optic array.

Binocular depth cues include **binocular convergence** (muscle tension associated with looking at close objects provides information about distance) and **retinal disparity** (closer objects provide more disparate images in the two eyes).

Constancies
Our tendency to see the properties of objects as being invariant despite any changes in the retinal stimulus.

Real movement. Cues include movement across the retina (interpreted as movement of the object), movement of the eyes and movement of the head (interpreted as following the progress of a moving object).

Direct or constructivist?
Direct explanation would predict perception of changing size (no observer movement) whereas constructivist explanation is that our visual system prefers the 'moving closer' hypothesis as it is a more common experience.

Constructivist or direct?
Stimulus-relation theory (direct) explains that the context in which a stimulus appears affects how it is perceived. When context information is unavailable, viewers use prior knowledge to judge an object's size.

Size constancy
Familiar objects are perceived as same size despite changes in size of retinal image, indicating a change in distance.

Shape constancy
Knowledge of familiar objects means we see their shape as unchanging despite changes in viewing angle.

Colour constancy
Most colour surfaces appear the same when viewed under different lighting conditions.

Application includes motion pictures, neon lights and traffic 'rumble lines'.

Ponzo illusion. Addition of perspective cues causes the observer to perceive lines of the same length as different.

Trapezium illusion. Causes us to assume that the object is familiar and therefore moving in a predictable way.

Retinex theory (Land, 1977)
Although absolute wavelengths of colours change in dim light, relative wavelengths do not.

theories of visual perception, including constructivist theories (e.g. Gregory)

Probable questions

1. Describe and evaluate **one** constructivist theory of visual perception. *(24 marks)*

2. Describe and evaluate **one or more** constructivist theories of visual perception. *(24 marks)*

Possible questions

3. Outline and evaluate **two** constructivist theories of visual perception. *(24 marks)*

4. (a) Outline and evaluate **one** constructivist theory of visual perception. *(12 marks)*

   (b) Outline and evaluate **one** direct theory of visual perception. *(12 marks)*

theories of visual perception, including direct theories (e.g. Gibson)

Probable questions

1. Describe and evaluate **one** direct theory of visual perception. *(24 marks)*

2. Describe and evaluate **one or more** direct theories of visual perception. *(24 marks)*

Possible questions

3. Outline and evaluate **two** direct theories of visual perception. *(24 marks)*

4. Describe and evaluate **one or more** theories of visual perception. *(24 marks)*

explanations of perceptual organisation (e.g. depth, movement, constancies and illusions)

Probable questions

1. Outline and evaluate **two or more** explanations of perceptual organisation. *(24 marks)*

2. Critically consider explanations of **two or more** types of perceptual organisation (e.g. depth, movement, constancies, illusions). *(24 marks)*

Possible questions

3. Outline and evaluate **one or more** explanations of perceptual organisation. *(24 marks)*

You may be asked questions about theories of visual perception but are more likely to be asked specifically about constructivist or direct theories of visual perception as these are named in the specification. You would not be asked a question about Gregory's theory because his name is given only as an *example* of a constructivist theory in the specification. Since the specification refers to theories you can be asked to discuss more than one theory but it would be more probable (as indicated here) that you are just asked about one theory, or given the option of 'one or more'. Most candidates will know one theory in sufficient detail for a 30 minute answer and may well find they have *too* much when asked to write about two theories. Asking for 'one or more' is a nice compromise – but don't count on it. You should be ready for a question about one theory or two theories.

Note that here the injunction is 'outline' whereas above it was 'describe' to reflect the fact that the same amount of detail is not required when two theories are asked for.

Question 4 is unusual in two ways. First, both parts of the question are AO1+AO2 as indicated by the fact that they each start 'outline and evaluate'. This means there are 6 AO1 marks for outlining one constructivist theory and 6 AO2 marks for evaluating it. You have 7 1/2 minutes for each and therefore need to be selective about what you include or else you will lose marks on other questions because you have reduced the time available for your other answers.

The second unusual feature of question 4 is that it combines two topics which is perfectly legitimate. It is important, when revising, not to leave topics out in case a combined question appears.

The specification entry for direct theories is the same as that for constructivist theories, therefore the questions will follow the same format.

The phrase 'one or more' is used to indicate that you can get full marks for just considering one theory. Don't forget you can always use another theory as a form of commentary as long as you do *use it effectively*. You will not gain AO2 credit if you just say 'In contrast there is another theory' and then you describe the other theory.

One extra question has been included here which is possible but unlikely – question 4 permits you to write about any theory of visual perception and any number of theories.

There is an important distinction between questions 1 and 2 which is obvious, however the end result may not be that different. You *could* answer question 1 by looking at the Gestalt explanation of perceptual organisation, plus one other explanation, *or* you could take the view that explanations of depth, movement, constancies, illusions relate to perceptual organisation. In question 1 you therefore could outline explanations of depth, movement, constancies or illusions. In question 2 you would do the same.

It pays to organise your essay along the lines set out in the question just to make sure you *are* answering the question. So, for question 1, you should state 'The first explanation I will discuss is ...', 'The second explanation is ...'.

In question 2, state explicitly 'One type of perceptual organisation is ...', 'A second type of perceptual organisation is ...'.

Questions 1 and 3 are almost identical except that in question 1 there would be a partial performance penalty if you only outlined one explanation (maximum of 8 marks AO1 and 8 marks AO2). In question 3 you are given the option of only discussing one explanation.

In question 1 you do not have to provide both explanations in the same depth. Since one explanation could attract a maximum of 16 out of 24 marks, the second explanation can be '8 marks worth' (4 marks AO1 and 4 marks AO2).

SAMPLE ESSAY PLAN

Question 1: Describe and evaluate **one** constructivist theory of visual perception. (24 marks)

GREGORY'S THEORY (1972)

15 MINUTES WORTH OF AO1

- *Gregory* (1972): light signals give rise to neural impulses, which interact with stored knowledge in the brain to create perception.
- **Hypothesis testing**: hypotheses are generated to make sense of incoming data.
- **This is necessary** because physical data is often incomplete.
- **Interaction**: neural impulses interact with stored knowledge to produce psychological data.
- **The role of expectation**: expectations generated by **context**, for example in kitchen setting a mailbox 'seen' as a loaf but not true for a drum (unexpected object) (**Palmer**, 1975).
- **Erroneous hypotheses lead to perceptual errors**, for example:
- **Non-sensed object characteristics** – we respond to some objects even though we do not have all necessary sensory data.
- **Ambiguous perceptions** such as the Necker cube which has no 'right' answer and therefore perception changes back and forth.
- **Likely objects** such as the hollow face illusion, brain's prior assumptions override physical data.

15 MINUTES WORTH OF AO2

- **Empirical support** e.g. 13 perceived as number or letter depending on context (**Bruner and Minturn**, 1955), false playing cards misperceived e.g. red clubs seen as purple (**Bruner et al.**, 1951), hungry participants perceived food pictures as brighter (**Gilchrist and Nesburg**, 1952). All show the role of expectations.
- **Visual illusions** demonstrate **misapplied hypotheses** e.g. Müller–Lyer effect due to expectation about corners of buildings and rooms, gives illusion of shorter/longer.
- Constructivist explanation of illusions **supported by cross-cultural studies** that Müller–Lyer not perceived by people who don't live in carpentered environments.
- **Not supported** by fact that if fins replaced by circles illusion persists, and no effect if Ps walk around a 3D model (**Wraga et al.**, 2000).
- **Strengths**: explains ambiguous situations and when retinal image poor, and why it's so difficult to programme computers.
- **Limitations**: can't explain accurate perceptions (**direct theory** can), supporting evidence relates to an artificial class of perceptions (ambiguous, incomplete data) whereas direct theory more 'real world'.

Question 3: Outline and evaluate **two** constructivist theories of visual perception. (24 marks)

THEORY 1: GREGORY'S THEORY (1972)

10 MINUTES WORTH OF AO1

- **Hypothesis testing**: hypotheses are generated to make sense of incoming data.
- **The role of expectation**: expectations generated by **context**, for example in kitchen setting a mailbox 'seen' as a loaf (**Palmer**, 1975).
- **Erroneous hypotheses lead to perceptual errors**, for example:
- **Non-sensed object characteristics** – we respond to some objects even though we do not have all necessary sensory data.
- **Ambiguous perceptions** such as the Necker cube which has no 'right' answer and therefore perception changes back and forth.
- **Likely objects** such as the hollow face illusion, brain's prior assumptions override physical data.

10 MINUTES WORTH OF AO2

- **Visual illusions** demonstrate **misapplied hypotheses** e.g. Müller-Lyer effect due to expectation about corners of buildings and rooms, gives illusion of shorter/longer.
- Constructivist explanation of illusions **supported by cross-cultural studies** that Müller–Lyer not perceived by people who don't live in carpentered environments.
- **Not supported** by fact that if fins replaced by circles illusion persists, and no effect if Ps walk around a 3D model (**Wraga et al.**, 2000); supports direct perception.
- **Strengths**: explains ambiguous situations and when retinal image poor, and why it's so difficult to programme computers.
- **Limitations**: can't explain accurate perceptions, supporting evidence relates to an artificial class of perceptions (ambiguous, incomplete data), rather than real-world perception.

THEORY 2: GESTALT THEORY

5 MINUTES WORTH OF AO1

- The **whole** is greater that the **sum of its parts**.
- **Laws of perceptual organisation** e.g. law of proximity or closure, explain how visual arrays are perceived as more than individual parts, i.e. perception is not direct.
- **Figure-ground** e.g Rubin vase, is interpreted differently under different conditions.

5 MINUTES WORTH OF AO2

- **Experimental** support from **Navon** (1977), large letter perceived rather than smaller constituent letters.
- **Neurological** support: neurons respond more strongly when nearby lines have similar orientation (**Zapadia et al.**, 1995).
- **Strengths**: enduring influence of Gestalt movement, explains common experiences.
- **Limitations**: only explains proximal stimuli, based on study of static 2D images.

Gregory (1972) believed that light signals received by the eye give rise to neural impulses, which in turn interact with stored knowledge in the brain to create the final perception. A key assumption of this theory is that the individual must generate hypotheses to make sense of incoming data because physical data provided by the senses is often incomplete. Gregory also emphasised the role of expectation in the perceptual process. Expectations may be generated by the context in which an object is viewed. In a study by Palmer (1975) a mailbox, when viewed in a kitchen setting, was 'seen' as a loaf, because for that setting participants expected to see a loaf rather than a mailbox. When the stimulus conflicted with the context (e.g. a drum in a kitchen) there was no such perceptual error, with a correct perception being made.

A feature of this explanation of perception is that perceptual errors will occur when stored knowledge leads to erroneous hypotheses about the object being viewed. Another feature of this explanation is that we respond to non-sensed object characteristics, we respond to some objects even though we do not have all the sensory data necessary for a full identification. For example, an individual may perceive a table when only some of its features are visible. Ambiguous perceptions such as the Necker cube also illustrate the process of hypothesis testing in perception. In this illusion, there is no 'right' answer, with either of two alternative hypotheses being possible. As a result, the perception of this figure changes back and forth with the perceptual system settling first on one hypothesis and then the other. We are sometimes misled by our expectations of the world, and so we misperceive objects in it. In the hollow face illusion, the likely interpretation, based on the brain's prior assumptions, of the face being convex overrides the physical data of it being hollow.

Research studies have provided empirical support for the role of expectation in perception (perceptual set). In a study by Bruner and Minturn (1955), the number 13 was perceived as a number or letter depending on context. Evidence for perceptual set has also been found in a study where false playing cards were misperceived, e.g. red clubs seen as purple (Bruner et al., 1951), and where hungry participants perceived food pictures as brighter (Gilchrist and Nesburg, 1952). All these studies show the important role played by expectations in perception. Visual illusions in perception demonstrate misapplied hypotheses that normally work in the real world. For example, the fact that the Müller-Lyer effect is found in laboratory studies can be explained as the consequence of expectations about corners of buildings and rooms, which give the illusion of lines being shorter or longer than they actually are.

The constructivist explanation of illusions is supported by cross-cultural studies (e.g. Segall et al., 1963) that the Müller-Lyer illusion is only perceived by people who live in carpentered environments, and not by those who have little experience of an environment comprised of straight lines and corners. However, this explanation of perception is not supported by the fact that if fins are replaced by circles in the Müller-Lyer illusion, the illusion persists, despite removing the main cues. Furthermore, Wraga et al. (2000) found no effect when participants were presented with a three-dimensional model of the illusion. The strengths of this theory are that it can explain how we still are able to perceive in ambiguous situations and when the retinal image is poor, and why it's so difficult to programme computers to simulate human perception. The limitations are that Gregory's theory can't explain why perceptions are usually accurate (unlike Gibson's direct theory which can explain this), when the theory would suggest that they would often be inaccurate. Supporting evidence tends to relate to an artificial class of perceptions (i.e. ambiguous and incomplete data) rather than explaining real-world perception.

This first paragraph focuses on the role of expectation. Notice how the assumption is first explained and then illustrated by a description of a research study.

Illusions are an important part of Gregory's theory, but you should do more than just *describe* these illusions. You should try to use them to illustrate the nature of hypothesis testing in perception.

It is important to do more than just *describe* supporting studies. You should indicate how they support or challenge the assumptions of the theory.

There are a number of critical points being made here, some negative, but some positive. Each critical point should be elaborated to make sure it is being used *effectively*.

SAMPLE ESSAY PLAN

Question 1: Describe and evaluate **one** direct theory of visual perception. (24 marks)

GIBSON'S THEORY (1979)

15 MINUTES WORTH OF AO1

- **Gibson** (1979) suggested the optic array enables us to judge the layout of objects in space.
- **Optic array** (pattern of light that reaches the eye) contains sufficient information combined with:
- Our **movement** through the environment provides about displacement.
- **Optic flow:** objects to side appear to move towards us but those directly ahead stay fixed. The further away, the faster the apparent movement.
- **Texture gradient:** closer objects have coarser texture, helps judge distance.
- **Invariants** (things that don't change as we move), perception is based on changes relative to invariants.
- **For example,** texture and distance changes: if change in size and texture, object is getting closer. If not, then the object must still be the same distance away but is getting bigger.
- **Affordances:** many objects have directly perceivable properties that describe their potential for action e.g. a flat stone of a particular height is a seat.
- **Role of experience:** we learn to discriminate the information available in order to perceive directly, as described by **differentiation theory** (Gibson and Gibson, 1955).

15 MINUTES WORTH OF AO2

- **Optic array in pilot's** use of texture, apparent movement etc. to land a plane (**Gibson et al.,** 1955).
- **Biological motion** (innate ability to recover movement information) demonstrated by showing films of array of dots (**Johansson,** 1973). Even babies (**Fox and McDaniel,** 1982) and animals (**Blake,** 1993) respond appropriately to such sequences.
- **Time to contact** (judging distance using direct information) demonstrated in long jumpers (**Lee et al.,** 1982) and gannets (**Lee,** 1980).
- **Other innate abilities** shown in research with infants, depth perception (**Gibson and Walk,** 1960), use of shadows (**Yonas et al.,** 2001), shape constancy (**Bower,** 1966).
- Can explain **visual illusions** e.g. **Wraga et al.** (2000) found movement overcame Müller-Lyer, must be because of unambiguous sensory information.
- **Strengths:** accounts for perception in many instances and especially for animals and babies.
- **Limitations:** can't explain influence of expectations in perception.
- **Affordances** inevitably involve top-down processes.
- **Neisser** (1976) proposed a top-down/bottom-up system.

Question 3: Outline and evaluate **two** direct theories of visual perception. (24 marks)

THEORY 1: GIBSON'S THEORY (1979)

10 MINUTES WORTH OF AO1

- **Optic array** (pattern of light that reaches the eye) contains sufficient information combined with:
- Our **movement** through the environment provides about displacement.
- **Optic flow:** objects to side appear to move towards us but those directly ahead stay fixed. The further away, the faster the apparent movement.
- **Texture gradient:** closer objects have coarser texture, helps judge distance.
- **Affordances:** many objects have directly perceivable properties e.g. a flat stone of a particular height is a seat.
- **Role of experience:** we learn to discriminate the information available in order to perceive directly, as described by **differentiation theory** (Gibson and Gibson, 1955).

10 MINUTES WORTH OF AO2

- **Optic array in pilot's** use of texture, apparent movement etc. to land a plane (**Gibson et al.,** 1955).
- **Biological motion** (innate ability to recover movement information) demonstrated by showing films of array of dots (**Johansson,** 1973). Even babies (**Fox and McDaniel,** 1982) and animals (**Blake,** 1993) respond appropriately to such sequences.
- **Other innate abilities** shown in research with infants, depth perception (**Gibson and Walk,** 1960) – though such studies **may lack reliability.**
- **Strengths:** accounts for perception in many instances and especially for animals and babies.
- **Limitations:** can't explanation influence of expectations in perception.
- **Affordances** inevitably involve top-down processes.

THEORY 2: MARR'S COMPUTATIONAL MODEL OF PERCEPTION (1982)

5 MINUTES WORTH OF AO1

- Developed **algorithms** to explain transformation of 2D retinal image to 3D.
- Stage 1 of analysis: **primal sketch**, retinal image is like a line drawing.
- Stage 2 of analysis: **2½-D sketch**, surface details filled in using depth cues.
- Stage 3 of analysis: **3D model**

5 MINUTES WORTH OF AO2

- Patients found who lack these representations e.g. S could 'see' the primal sketch but couldn't copy simple figures (**Benson and Greenberg,** 1969).
- **Strengths:** suggests how the visual system might work, unlike other theories.
- **Limitations:** details rather vague; can't cope with ambiguous information, can't assume the visual information works the same just because output the same.

Gibson (1979) suggested that the pattern of light that reaches the eye (the optic array) contains sufficient unambiguous information to enable us to judge the layout of objects in space. Gibson claimed that our movement through the environment produces a change in the pattern of light rays and so provides us with information about our displacement (e.g. forwards, sideways, etc.) in the environment. As the observer moves, this produces a change in the optic array that Gibson referred to as the optic flow. As we move towards a point in our visual environment, objects to the side of us appear to move towards us but those directly ahead appear to stay fixed. The further away something is from that fixed point in the visual environment, the faster the apparent movement toward us. Gibson stated that most objects in our visual world have texture, and that the grain of this texture appears finer as we move further away from an object. This texture gradient, with closer objects having coarser texture, helps us to judge distance.

> Although it is relatively easy to illustrate this theory through examples, you should also make sure that you are making definite statements about the assumptions of the theory.

It is a characteristic of perception that some aspects of the environment change as the observer moves around, while others do not. One such invariant is that changes in texture are associated with changes in distance. The observer can, for example, use this information to understand why a small object is getting bigger. If the change in size is also accompanied by a change in texture, then the object is getting closer. If it is not, then the object must still be the same distance away but is getting bigger. Gibson used the term 'affordance' to refer to the fact that many objects have directly perceivable properties that describe their potential for action, e.g. a flat stone of a particular height affords the opportunity for sitting on it. Direct perception depends on our ability to pick up the information that specifies a particular affordance, and this, therefore, depends on our experiences. Through experience, we learn to discriminate the information available in our visual world so we are able to perceive directly.

> The concept of invariants in perception is a complicated one. Make sure *you* understand it before using it in your essay.

Gibson's views on the direct nature of perception can be traced back to perceptual problems in real-world settings, in particular the perceptual problems faced by pilots. Evidence for the optic array can be seen in a pilot's use of texture, apparent movement and other cues to land a plane (Gibson et al., 1955). Biological motion (the innate ability to recover movement information) has been demonstrated in a study by Johansson (1973) who showed that we perceive motion simply from a changing array of light dots. Even babies (Fox and McDaniel, 1982) and animals (Blake, 1993) have been shown to respond appropriately to such sequences, suggesting that this is innate and universal. Time to contact (judging distance using direct information) has been demonstrated in long jumpers (Lee et al., 1982) and in gannets (Lee, 1980), suggesting that this ability is also innate. Other innate abilities have been shown in research with infants, e.g. depth perception (Gibson and Walk, 1960), use of shadows (Yonas et al., 2001) and shape constancy (Bower, 1966), providing further evidence of the importance of direct sensory information in perception.

> Note the frequent use of AO2 'language' such as 'evidence for…', 'suggesting that…', 'has been demonstrated in…' This turns mere description into effective commentary.

A strength of Gibson's theory is that it can explain visual illusions, e.g. research by Wraga et al. (2000) found that movement overcame the Müller-Lyer illusion as movement provides important and unambiguous sensory information. An additional strength of the theory is that it is able to account for perception in many real-world instances and especially for animals and babies. Limitations include the fact that, unlike constructivist theories, it cannot explain the influence of expectations in perception whereas constructivist theory can. Although the theory may explain perception from the general perspective of a species, it does not acknowledge the inevitable top-down processes that are present in affordances. The debate over whether perception is top-down (Gregory) or bottom-up (Gibson) may be redundant, as Neisser (1976) has proposed a combined top-down/bottom-up system, although in practice such a model would be slow and therefore unlikely.

> Strengths and limitations should not just be listed, but should be elaborated to gain higher marks. **Think**: identify a critical point and then elaborate it.

SAMPLE ESSAY PLAN

Question 2: Critically consider explanations of **two or more** types of perceptual organisation (e.g. depth, movement, constancies, illusions). (24 marks)

DEPTH

5 MINUTES WORTH OF AO1

Monocular depth cues, range of cues:
- **Relative size:** smaller is further.
- **Texture gradient:** less detail is further.
- **Interposition:** objects in front are closer.

Binocular depth cues:
- **Binocular convergence:** the more turned in the eyes, the closer the object.
- **Retinal disparity:** the closer the object, the more disparate the image.

5 MINUTES WORTH OF AO2
- Monocular cues can explain different interpretations of sensory data (**visual illusions**) e.g. **Ames Room** depth cues (relative size) triumph over size constancy.
- However, illusion still seen with no depth cues. Can be explained by the **horizon-ratio relation** (a **direct** explanation): proportion of an object above and below the horizon is unchanging despite changes in distance.

MOVEMENT

5 MINUTES WORTH OF AO1

Real movement:
- **Movement across retina:** photoreceptors respond sequentially.
- **Movement of eyes:** eyes follow moving object so retinal image still but brain interprets this as movement because of feedback from eyes.
- **Movement of head** is also interpreted by brain.

Apparent movement:
- **Phi phenomenon:** brain fills in missing data because time delay same as normal when perceiving moving object.

5 MINUTES WORTH OF AO2
- **Visual illusion:** balloon inflated in dark room appears to move closer (**Ames**, 1949).
- **Direct theory** would predict that this would not happen because no sensation of movement.
- **Constructivist theory** explains that more common experience is 'preferred' hypothesis.

CONSTANCIES

5 MINUTES WORTH OF AO1
- The **perception of constancy** is the tendency to see the properties of objects as being invariant despite any changes in the retinal stimulus.
- **Size constancy:** familiar objects maintain size even if retinal image smaller.
- **Shape constancy:** when door is a trapezoid shape still perceived as a rectangle e.g. a door.
- **Colour constancy:** red shirt still looks red in changed lighting but not monochromatic lighting.

5 MINUTES WORTH OF AO2
- **Size constancy** explains **Ponzo illusion**, we have learned that the same image in the distance represents a larger object.
- Size constancy can be explained by **stimulus-relation theory**, where apparent size of an object is affected by another object of known size e.g. the **moon illusion**.
- **Shape constancy** explains illusory effect of rotating trapezoid that looks like a window, appears to go back and forth.
- **Colour constancy** explained by **retinex theory** (**Land et al.**, 1983), relative wavelengths remain constant so colour perceived.

Question 1: Outline and evaluate **two or more** explanations of perceptual organisation. (24 marks)

EXPLANATION 1: DEPTH PERCEPTION

7½ MINUTES WORTH OF AO1

The description of theory 1 above, plus:
- **Linear perspective:** convergence in distance.
- **Horizontal plane:** closer objects lower in field of vision.
- **Motion parallax:** closer objects move more quickly.

7½ MINUTES WORTH OF AO2

The evaluation of theory 1 above, plus:
- Constructivist explanation appropriate when certain cues available, in **absence of such cues** depth perceived directly using innate cues.

EXPLANATION 2: MOVEMENT PERCEPTION

7½ MINUTES WORTH OF AO1

The description of theory 1 above, plus:
- **Induced movement:** framed object appears to move while frame remains stationary.

7½ MINUTES WORTH OF AO2

The evaluation of theory 1 above, plus:
- **Applications:** phi phenomenon used to make films; rumble lines give illusion of faster movement, used to calm traffic.
- **Perceptual organisation** can be explained by both constructivist (**top-down**) and direct (**bottom-up**) theories.

The perception of depth is possible with a range of monocular depth cues. These include relative size, where objects that are smaller are assumed to be further away. In the cue of texture gradient, the closer we are to an object, the more detail we see in its surface density. Less detail is indicative of an object that is further away. In the cue of interposition, objects that are occluded are perceived as being further away, whereas objects in front are perceived as being closer. Binocular depth cues, which rely on data from both eyes, include binocular convergence, where the more turned in the eyes, the closer the object is perceived as being. As each eye has a slightly different perspective of an object, the closer the object, the more disparate the image. Thus retinal disparity is used as a binocular depth cue.

Monocular cues are able to explain how we can have different interpretations of the same sensory data (visual illusions). For example, in the Ames room illusion, the available depth cue of relative size is more influential in the resulting perceptual judgement than is size constancy. However, a problem for this example is that the illusion can still be seen even with no depth cues. This phenomenon can be explained by the horizon-ratio relation (a direct explanation), an invariant part of the optic array. This states that the proportion of an object above and below the horizon is unchanging despite changes in distance, therefore in the absence of other information about depth, in the Ames room one object must be larger than the other.

Movement can be perceived as either real movement or apparent movement. The progressive stimulation of the retina is interpreted by the brain as movement of an object in the visual field. The eyes also follow a moving object with the result that the retinal image is still but the brain interprets this as movement because of feedback from the eyes. Movement of the head, where the object remains stable on the retina, is also interpreted by the brain as indicating the object's movement. Movement may be perceived even though the object in question is not moving. In the phi phenomenon, the brain perceives a single light moving back and forth. The brain fills in any missing data because the time delay between the events is the same as normal when perceiving a moving object.

A demonstration of how the brain perceives movement can be seen in a study by Ames (1949). In another visual illusion, an illuminated balloon was inflated in an otherwise dark room. Rather than being seen as growing larger, most observers reported that the inflating balloon was actually moving closer. This presents a problem for Gibson's direct theory of perception which, in the absence of any sensation of movement, would predict that this would not happen. However, Gregory's constructivist theory would explain the tendency to see the balloon as moving closer as being a more common experience and therefore the 'preferred' hypothesis.

The perception of constancy is the tendency to see the properties of objects as being invariant despite any changes in the retinal stimulus. In size constancy, familiar objects maintain their perceived size even if the retinal image is actually smaller as a result of varying distances from the eye. In shape constancy, we see an object's shape as the same despite changes in the viewing angle. For example, when a door is a trapezoid shape on the retina, it is still perceived as a rectangle. In colour constancy, most colour surfaces appear the same even when viewed in different lighting conditions. However, this is only approximate as surfaces do not retain their daylight colours under fluorescent and monochromatic lighting.

Size constancy is able to explain the Ponzo illusion, where perspective cues give the impression that one line is longer than another simply because it is on top. We have learned that the same image in the distance represents a larger object. Size constancy can be explained by stimulus-relation theory, where the apparent size of an object may be affected by the presentation next to it of another object of known size, e.g. the moon illusion. Shape constancy explains the illusory effect of a rotating trapezoid that looks like a window, therefore appears to go back and forth as a window might. Colour constancy can be explained by retinex theory (Land et al., 1983). Under normal lighting conditions we perceive colour in terms of its absolute wavelength. In sub-optimum lighting conditions, it is the relative wavelengths that remain constant so colour is still perceived.

In this essay, *three* types of perceptual organisation are explained. This necessitates very tight (yet sufficiently detailed) outlines of each type.

Showing how a perceptual phenomenon can be explained counts as AO2 commentary.

You do not have to distinguish between real and apparent movement, just explain them.

It is easy to get carried away when describing illusions, but you should remember to *use* these descriptions only to illustrate an explanation. Remember what you are getting marks for in this question.

What counts as AO1 and what counts as AO2 is often dependent on the context of your discussion. Although these are still explanations, they are presented in the context of commentary and so count as AO2.

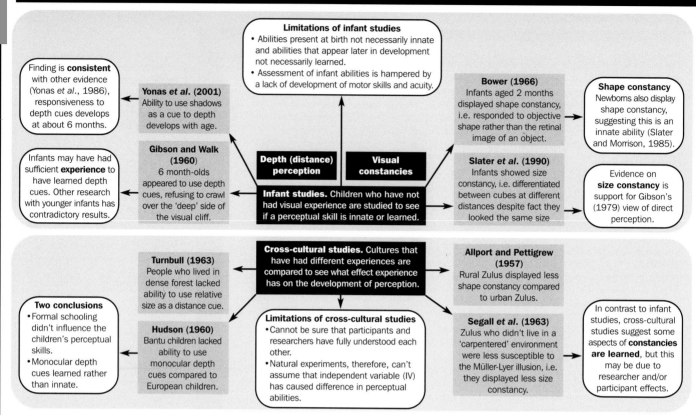

Limitations of infant studies
- Abilities present at birth not necessarily innate and abilities that appear later in development not necessarily learned.
- Assessment of infant abilities is hampered by a lack of development of motor skills and acuity.

Finding is consistent with other evidence (Yonas et al., 1986), responsiveness to depth cues develops at about 6 months.

Yonas et al. (2001) Ability to use shadows as a cue to depth develops with age.

Infants may have had sufficient **experience** to have learned depth cues. Other research with younger infants has contradictory results.

Gibson and Walk (1960) 6 month-olds appeared to use depth cues, refusing to crawl over the 'deep' side of the visual cliff.

Depth (distance) perception

Visual constancies

Infant studies. Children who have not had visual experience are studied to see if a perceptual skill is innate or learned.

Bower (1966) Infants aged 2 months displayed shape constancy, i.e. responded to objective shape rather than the retinal image of an object.

Shape constancy Newborns also display shape constancy, suggesting this is an innate ability (Slater and Morrison, 1985).

Slater et al. (1990) Infants showed size constancy, i.e. differentiated between cubes at different distances despite fact they looked the same size

Evidence on **size constancy** is support for Gibson's (1979) view of direct perception.

Cross-cultural studies. Cultures that have had different experiences are compared to see what effect experience has on the development of perception.

Turnbull (1963) People who lived in dense forest lacked ability to use relative size as a distance cue.

Allport and Pettigrew (1957) Rural Zulus displayed less shape constancy compared to urban Zulus.

Two conclusions
- Formal schooling didn't influence the children's perceptual skills.
- Monocular depth cues learned rather than innate.

Hudson (1960) Bantu children lacked ability to use monocular depth cues compared to European children.

Limitations of cross-cultural studies
- Cannot be sure that participants and researchers have fully understood each other.
- Natural experiments, therefore, can't assume that independent variable (IV) has caused difference in perceptual abilities.

Segall et al. (1963) Zulus who didn't live in a 'carpentered' environment were less susceptible to the Müller-Lyer illusion, i.e. they displayed less size constancy.

In contrast to infant studies, cross-cultural studies suggest some aspects of **constancies are learned**, but this may be due to researcher and/or participant effects.

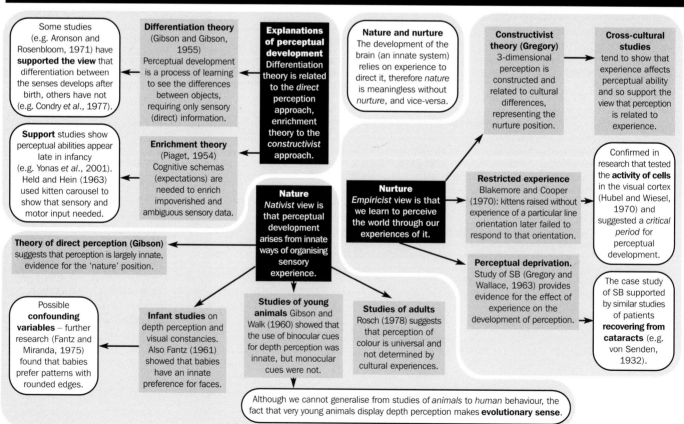

Some studies (e.g. Aronson and Rosenbloom, 1971) have **supported the view** that differentiation between the senses develops after birth, others have not (e.g. Condry et al., 1977).

Differentiation theory (Gibson and Gibson, 1955) Perceptual development is a process of learning to see the differences between objects, requiring only sensory (direct) information.

Explanations of perceptual development Differentiation theory is related to the *direct* perception approach, enrichment theory to the *constructivist* approach.

Nature and nurture The development of the brain (an innate system) relies on experience to direct it, therefore *nature* is meaningless without *nurture*, and vice-versa.

Constructivist theory (Gregory) 3-dimensional perception is constructed and related to cultural differences, representing the nurture position.

Cross-cultural studies tend to show that experience affects perceptual ability and so support the view that perception is related to experience.

Support studies show perceptual abilities appear late in infancy (e.g. Yonas et al., 2001). Held and Hein (1963) used kitten carousel to show that sensory and motor input needed.

Enrichment theory (Piaget, 1954) Cognitive schemas (expectations) are needed to enrich impoverished and ambiguous sensory data.

Nurture *Empiricist* view is that we learn to perceive the world through our experiences of it.

Restricted experience Blakemore and Cooper (1970): kittens raised without experience of a particular line orientation later failed to respond to that orientation.

Confirmed in research that tested the **activity of cells** in the visual cortex (Hubel and Wiesel, 1970) and suggested a *critical period* for perceptual development.

Theory of direct perception (Gibson) suggests that perception is largely innate, evidence for the 'nature' position.

Nature *Nativist* view is that perceptual development arises from innate ways of organising sensory experience.

Perceptual deprivation. Study of SB (Gregory and Wallace, 1963) provides evidence for the effect of experience on the development of perception.

The case study of SB supported by similar studies of patients **recovering from cataracts** (e.g. von Senden, 1932).

Possible **confounding variables** – further research (Fantz and Miranda, 1975) found that babies prefer patterns with rounded edges.

Infant studies on depth perception and visual constancies. Also Fantz (1961) showed that babies have an innate preference for faces.

Studies of young animals Gibson and Walk (1960) showed that the use of binocular cues for depth perception was innate, but monocular cues were not.

Studies of adults Rosch (1978) suggests that perception of colour is universal and not determined by cultural experiences.

Although we cannot generalise from studies of *animals* to *human* behaviour, the fact that very young animals display depth perception makes **evolutionary sense**.

Probable questions

1. Describe and evaluate studies of the development of perceptual abilities. *(24 marks)*

2. (a) Outline and evaluate **one or more** infant studies of the development of perceptual abilities. *(12 marks)*

   (b) Outline and evaluate **one or more** cross-cultural studies of the development of perceptual abilities. *(12 marks)*

Possible questions

3. Outline and evaluate **either** infant **or** cross-cultural studies of the development of perceptual abilities. *(24 marks)*

This division of the specification focuses on the development of perceptual abilities – the focus of question 1. Since the specification also includes reference to infant and cross-cultural studies, exam questions may specifically require you to base your answer on one or both of these, as is the case in question 2.

In both questions the number of studies you cover is left up to you (though in question 1 there is a minimum of two studies). There is always a danger that this leads candidates into an 'overwriting' trap – you know about lots of studies and wish to impress the examiner so try to stuff them all in. There has got to be a cost for this – usually less time for AO2 and/or less time for other questions on the paper. Structure all answers carefully and give yourself enough time for detailed AO1 (depth and not just breadth), and elaborated AO2 (not just a shopping list of AO2 points).

It is possible that you could be asked to discuss infant or cross-cultural studies, as is the case here. This means that you need enough material on each of these topics for a 30 minute essay.

If you write about *both* infant and cross-cultural studies then credit will only be given to the group of studies that would attract the higher mark.

Probable questions

1. Outline and evaluate **two or more** explanations of perceptual development. *(24 marks)*

2. Discuss the nature-nurture debate in perception. *(24 marks)*

Possible questions

3. (a) Outline **two or more** studies of the development of perceptual abilities. *(12 marks)*

   (b) To what extent do these studies contribute to the nature-nurture debate in perception? *(12 marks)*

This topic area generates two obvious questions: one on explanations and one on the nature-nurture debate. Your answers to both of these may include material from the previous topic (infant or cross-cultural studies) as support for explanations or evidence of nature and/or nurture.

In question 1 your answer must be *driven* by explanations. In question 2 your answer must be structured around the nature–nurture debate. Take care not to assume what is AO1 or AO2. If you describe arguments for nurture then you might *use* arguments for nature as commentary (AO2) or you might use arguments for nature as AO1 and then use arguments for nurture as AO2. You can clearly indicate AO1 and AO2 through the lead-in phrases you use and the structure of your answer.

Question 2 restricts you to discussing the nature-nurture debate in perception (not surprisingly because this sub-section is on perception) – don't introduce general material on nature-nurture unless you make this relevant.

Part (a) of this question is straightforward though you must resist the temptation to include any evaluation of the studies because these would not attract credit in part (a) (because part (a) is pure AO1) and is unlikely to be exported for the purpose of awarding marks to part (b).

In part (b) you may introduce studies not mentioned in part (a) but should resist the temptation to describe them beyond the bare minimum to make sense. Your task is to *use* this material to construct a sustained critical argument about whether perceptual development can be explained in terms of nature or nurture.

TOPIC 1: STUDIES OF THE DEVELOPMENT OF PERCEPTUAL ABILITIES

SAMPLE ESSAY PLAN

Question 2: (a) Outline and evaluate one or more infant studies of the development of perceptual abilities. (12 marks)
(b) Outline and evaluate one or more cross-cultural studies of the development of perceptual abilities. (12 marks)

INFANT STUDIES	7½ MINUTES WORTH OF AO1	7½ MINUTES WORTH OF AO2
	Depth perception:	• **Gibson and Walk** (1960). Infants may have developed depth perception but other studies (e.g. **Bower et al.**, 1970) show very early depth perception.
	• *Gibson and Walk* (1960). Procedures: used the **visual cliff**. Findings: infants 6–14 months refused to crawl over 'cliff'. Shows innate depth perception.	• Younger infants showed no **wariness** in visual cliff (**Scarr and Salapek**, 1970) so it may be wariness not depth perception that develops.
	Visual constancies:	• **Bower** (1966). Findings may be due to experience though **Slater and Morison** (1985) found shape constancy in newborns.
	• **Bower** (1966). Procedures: infants (50–60 days) conditioned to a rectangle slanted at 45°, then varied objective shape, retinal image and slant of the object. Findings: responded to objective shape rather than same retinal image. Shows innate shape constancy.	• **Limitations:** some perceptual learning in the womb, lack of motor skills and poor acuity confounds conclusions, infants susceptible to experimenter bias.
	• **Slater et al.** (1990). Procedures: familiarise infants with small or large cube and use preferential looking. Findings: Newborn infants gazed longer at cube they weren't familiarised with, indicating they perceived it as a novel stimulus. Shows size constancy is innate.	

CROSS-CULTURAL STUDIES	7½ MINUTES WORTH OF AO1	7½ MINUTES WORTH OF AO2
	Depth perception:	• **Turnbull** (1963). Anecdotal but supported by physiological evidence (e.g. **Blakemore and Cooper**, 1970) some perceptual capacities disappear if not used.
	• **Turnbull** (1963). BaMbuti pygmies misperceived distant objects (buffaloes 'seen' as ants) presumably due to lack of experience. Shows depth perception learned.	• **Hudson** (1960). Difficulties may be because Ps not used to interpreting pictures.
	• **Hudson** (1960). Bantu children unable to correctly interpret depth cues (e.g. linear perspective and interposition). Shows monocular cues learned.	• **Limitations:** tends to be poorly controlled, anecdotal, relies on interpreters, Ps may not fully understand the task(s), natural experiments which may not demonstrate a cause because of confounding variables.
	Visual constancies:	• In contrast with **infant** studies, **cross-cultural** studies support the view that **perceptual abilities are learned**.
	• **Allport and Pettigrew** (1957). Rural Zulu people didn't perceive trapezoid window illusion whereas urban Zulus did. Shows shape constancy learned.	

Question 3: Outline and evaluate either infant or cross-cultural studies of the development of perceptual abilities. (24 marks)

INFANT STUDIES	15 MINUTES WORTH OF AO1	15 MINUTES WORTH OF AO2
	The description of theory 1 above, plus:	The evaluation of theory 1 above, plus:
	Depth perception	• **Yonas et al.** (2001). Infants may lack grasping ability though van Hoftsten (1984) found that 21-week infants were capable of grasping.
	• **Bower et al.** (1970). Procedures: different sized cubes moved towards an infant. Findings: infants aged 4–20 days were more upset by smaller closer ones. Shows innate depth perception.	• **Fantz** (1961). Study involved confounding variables (symmetricality), **Fantz and Miranda** (1975) found infants preferred rounded outer edges which might explain original findings. **However**, innate facial preference makes **evolutionary** sense.
	• **Yonas et al.** (2001). Procedures: one toy appeared to be closer due to use of shadow, one eye covered (binocular vision). Findings: infants aged 30 weeks reached for apparently closer toy but not 21 weeks. Shows use of shadows develops with age.	• **Infant studies** supported by **cross-cultural studies** (e.g. **Hudson** found cultural/ learned differences in interpretation of monocular cues for depth perception) and **animal studies** (e.g. **Gibson and Walk** found that perception of binocular cues were innate).
	Face perception	• Also supports **differentiation theory** (Gibson and Gibson, 1955) – perceptual abilities develop through differentiation not learning expectations.
	• **Fantz** (1961). Procedures: 4-day-old babies shown various patterns. Findings: preference for a schematic face rather than jumbled up face or complex pattern. Shows that face preference is innate.	

Gibson and Walk (1960) studied the development of depth perception in infants using a 'visual cliff' that gave visual cues which suggested that one side was shallow and the other deep. They found that although all the infants readily crossed the 'shallow' side, most (aged 6–14 months) refused to crawl over 'cliff' onto the 'deep' side. The findings suggest that the infants had innate depth perception. Bower (1966) studied the development of visual constancies in infants aged 50–60 days. He conditioned these infants so that they would respond to a rectangle slanted at 45° (giving a trapezoidal shape), and then presented different conditions that varied the objective shape, retinal image and slant of the object. He found that infants responded to the objective shape rather than same retinal image, which shows they possessed innate shape constancy. Slater et al. (1990) used preferential looking to study size constancy, familiarising infants with either a small or large cube. They found that newborn infants gazed longer at the cube they weren't familiar with, indicating they perceived it as a novel stimulus, and also suggesting that size constancy is innate.

In Gibson and Walk's study, it is possible that, because of their age, infants may already have developed depth perception. However, other studies (e.g. Bower et al., 1970) have shown very early depth perception in children as young as 50 days old. In another study of depth perception, younger infants showed no wariness when wheeled across the visual cliff (Scarr and Salapek, 1970) which suggests that it may be wariness about depth rather than the perception of depth that develops with age. Although the infants used in the Bower (1966) study were very young, this does rule out the possibility that the findings obtained may be due to experience. However, later research by Slater and Morison (1985) found evidence of shape constancy in newborns. The limitations of infant studies such as this are that there is some perceptual learning in the womb, and the lack of motor skills and poor visual acuity in infants confounds the conclusions that might be drawn. Infants are also susceptible to experimenter bias, and may respond to inadvertent cues from the experimenter.

Turnbull (1963) provided evidence of depth perception in BaMbuti pygmies, who misperceived distant objects (buffaloes 'seen' as ants) presumably due to lack of experience. This suggests that depth perception might be learned, as the pygmies, who live in dense forest, had no experience of making adjustments for distance when judging size. Hudson (1960) also studied depth perception, showing that, compared to European children, Bantu children were unable to correctly interpret depth cues (e.g. linear perspective and interposition) by the end of primary school. This suggests that monocular cues are learned, and that the Bantu children had less experience of two-dimensional representations of depth in books. Allport and Pettigrew (1957) studied the development of visual constancies, showing that rural Zulu people did not perceive the trapezoid window illusion whereas urban Zulus (who had greater experience of windows) did. This suggests that shape constancy is learned, with urban Zulus responding like Europeans.

Although anecdotal, the findings of Turnbull's study are supported by physiological evidence. Blakemore and Cooper (1970) found that the development of the brain depends on visual experience, and that some perceptual capacities disappear if not used. In the Hudson study, the difficulties encountered by the non-European children may be attributed more to the fact that they are not used to interpreting pictures, than to the fact that they cannot perceive depth using monocular cues. Limitations of cross-cultural studies include the fact that they tend to be poorly controlled, sometimes anecdotal, and may rely on interpreters to give instructions and translate responses. This may introduce bias and make any conclusions invalid. Similarly, participants may not fully understand the task(s), and most cross-cultural studies, being natural experiments, are unable to demonstrate a cause-effect relationship because the IV has not been directly manipulated and there may be extraneous variables. In contrast with infant studies, cross-cultural studies support the view that perceptual abilities are learned.

Unless you feel confident that you have enough material to describe and evaluate just one study, feel free to use more than one. Don't go overboard when describing the procedures, as the findings are also important.

There is a mix here of *specific* criticisms of individual studies, and *general* criticisms of infant studies of perception.

It is easy to get carried away with the description of an individual study (particularly if it has captured your imagination in some way), but heed the advice in the first point above.

This comparative point is a fairly simple one to make, but is appropriate nonetheless, and will earn valuable AO2 marks. It is a good example of something that is a conclusion rather than a summary.

TOPIC 2: PERCEPTUAL DEVELOPMENT: NATURE VERSUS NURTURE

SAMPLE ESSAY PLAN

Question 2: Discuss the nature-nurture debate in perception. (24 marks)

EVIDENCE FOR NATURE	7½ MINUTES WORTH OF AO1	7½ MINUTES WORTH OF AO2
	• **Direct theory** (**Gibson**, 1979) suggests perception is largely innate as demonstrated by evidence such as **biological motion** (**Johansson**, 1973) even in babies (**Fox and McDaniel**, 1982). • **Infant studies** such as study of shape constancy (**Bower**, 1966) suggest that many perceptual abilities are innate. • **Fantz** (1961) preference for a schematic face rather than jumbled up face or complex pattern. Shows that face preference is innate. • **Studies of adults** e.g. **Rosch** (1978) have suggested that the perception of colour is universal and not determined by cultural experiences. **Animal studies** e.g. **Gibson and Walk** (1960) found that binocular cues in perception were also innate.	• **Direct theory**: can't explain the influence of expectations in perception. • **Affordances** inevitably involve top-down processes. • **Infant studies, limitations**: some perceptual learning in the womb, lack of motor skills and poor acuity confounds conclusions, infants susceptible to experimenter bias. • **Fantz** (1961). Study involved confounding variables (symmetricality). • **Fantz and Miranda** (1975) found infants preferred rounded outer edges which might explain original findings. • **However**, innate facial preference makes **evolutionary** sense as facial contact important for communication and attachment.
EVIDENCE FOR NURTURE	7½ MINUTES WORTH OF AO1	7½ MINUTES WORTH OF AO2
	• **Constructivist theory** (**Gregory**, 1972) suggests that sensory data is enriched by expectations. • **Cross-cultural studies** tend to show that learning does affect perception e.g. **Hudson** (1960) found cultural/ learned differences in interpretation of monocular cues for depth perception. • **Animal studies**: kittens raised in restricted world (horizontal or vertical stripes) were blind to lines of opposite orientation (**Blakemore and Cooper**, 1970). • **Human restricted experience**: **squint eyesight** leads to permanent damage (**Banks et al.**, 1975).	• **Constructivist theory**: can't explain accurate perceptions, supporting evidence relates to an artificial class of perceptions (ambiguous, incomplete data). • **Cross-cultural studies, limitations**: poorly controlled, anecdotal, natural experiments which may not demonstrate a cause because of confounding variables. • **Physiological effects of restricted experience**: in kittens' visual cortex cells of certain orientations were absent (**Hubel and Wiesel**, 1970). • **Nature and nurture**: development of brain (an innate system) depends on experience to direct it, an **adaptive process**.

Question 1: Outline and evaluate **two or more** explanations of perceptual development. (24 marks)

EXPLANATION 1: DIFFERENTIATION THEORY (GIBSON AND GIBSON, 1955)	7½ MINUTES WORTH OF AO1	7½ MINUTES WORTH OF AO2
	• This is a **bottom-up** theory. • Perceptual development occurs through **differentiation** i.e. learning to make distinctions between objects. • This happens through **experience** but doesn't require additional input to interpret sensory data. • Like **direct theory** (**Gibson**, 1979) suggests that sensory information is all we need.	• Infants are born **amodal**, e.g. infants distressed when saw mother but voice in a different place (**Aronson and Rosenbloom**, 1971). • **Infant studies** such as study of shape constancy (**Bower**, 1966) suggest that many perceptual abilities are innate. **Fantz** (1961): face preference is innate. • **However**, some cross-cultural research suggests aspects of depth perception are learned, e.g. **Hudson** (1960) found cultural/ learned differences in interpretation of monocular cues for depth perception.
EXPLANATION 2: ENRICHMENT THEORY (PIAGET, 1954)	7½ MINUTES WORTH OF AO1	7½ MINUTES WORTH OF AO2
	• This is a **top-down** theory. • Like **constructivist theory** (**Gregory**, 1972) suggests that sensory data is often impoverished. • We draw on expectations (**schemas**) to enrich the data. • Schemas develop through **experience**, particularly the coordination of motor and sensory schemas.	• **Yonas et al.** (2001): use of shadows for depth perception develops with age. • **Held and Hein** (1963): the **kitten carousel** showed that perceptual experience on its own not enough. Sensory and motor experience necessary. • **Constructivist theory** research supports the role of expectations which must be learned, e.g. **Palmer** (1975) in kitchen setting a mailbox 'seen' as a loaf. • However both **enrichment and constructivist theories** relate to impoverished input – some sensory data is complete and doesn't need expectations.

Gibson's direct theory (Gibson, 1979) suggests that perception is largely innate. Evidence for this theory, such as Johansson's demonstration that people perceive motion (biological motion) simply from a changing array of dots, and Fox and McDaniel's finding that even babies and young children respond appropriately in the same circumstances, provides important evidence for the innate nature of perception. Infant studies such as Bower's study of shape constancy (Bower, 1966) suggest that many perceptual abilities are innate. This is not restricted to aspects of perceptual organisation such as constancies, but is also evident in face preferences. Fantz (1961) demonstrated that babies appear to have an innate preference for a schematic face rather than a jumbled up face or similarly complex pattern. Studies of adults, e.g. Rosch (1978) have suggested that the perception of colour is universal and not determined by cultural experiences. Similarly, studies using very young animals to overcome some of the methodological problems of infant studies (e.g. Gibson and Walk, 1960) have found that binocular cues in perception were also innate.

> In this opening paragraph, the *nature* side of the debate is put forward through description of studies that have demonstrated some of the innate aspects of perception.

A problem for the direct theory, and the implication that perception must be largely innate, is that (unlike constructivist theories) it cannot explain the influence of expectations in perception. Likewise, the notion of affordances that is a key part of Gibson's direct theory inevitably involves top-down processes that are based on experience. Using infant studies to support the nature argument in perception also presents problems. There is some perceptual learning in the womb, and the lack of motor skills and poor visual acuity in infants confounds the conclusions that might be drawn. Infants are also susceptible to experimenter bias, and may respond to inadvertent cues from the experimenter. In the Fantz (1961) study, there were a number of confounding variables (e.g. schematic face was more symmetrical than the jumbled face), which might explain why the original face was preferred. Further research by Fantz and Miranda (1975) found infants preferred rounded outer edges which might explain the original findings. However, an innate preference for faces makes sound evolutionary sense, as facial contact is important for communication and attachment.

> Instead of simply presenting an alternative side to the debate as commentary, the nature arguments themselves are evaluated here. This is an effective form of AO2 commentary.

An alternative to the direct theory view that perception is innate is the constructivist theory view (e.g. Gregory, 1972) which suggests that sensory data is enriched by expectations, and is therefore a product of nurture. For example, cross-cultural studies tend to show that learning does affect perception. In one study of depth perception (Hudson, 1960) Hudson found that, compared to European children, Bantu children were unable to correctly interpret depth cues (e.g. linear perspective and interposition) by the end of primary school. This suggests that monocular cues were learned, and that the Bantu children had less experience of two-dimensional representations of depth in books. Animal studies also show the importance of learning in perception. Blakemore and Cooper (1970) found that kittens raised in a restricted perceptual world (either horizontal or vertical stripes) later appeared not to perceive lines of opposite orientation. In studies of restricted experience in humans, children born with squint eyesight could not develop binocular eyesight and had impaired depth perception (Banks et al., 1975).

> There is a great deal of relevant information in the previous spread, and its associated essay, that could be used in the construction of both sides of this debate.

The limitations of the constructivist position, and therefore the idea that perception is largely a product of learning, is that it can't explain why perceptions are usually accurate (unlike Gibson's direct theory), when the theory would suggest that they would often be inaccurate. Supporting evidence also tends to relate to an artificial class of perceptions (i.e. ambiguous and incomplete data) rather than explaining real-world perception. Cross-cultural studies are of limited value in this debate because they tend to be poorly controlled, sometimes anecdotal, and may rely on interpreters to give instructions and translate responses. This may introduce bias and make any conclusions invalid. Similarly, participants may not fully understand the task(s), and most cross-cultural studies, being natural experiments, are unable to demonstrate a cause-effect relationship because the IV has not been directly manipulated and there may be confounding variables. The effects of restricted experience in animals can be demonstrated physiologically. Hubel and Wiesel (1970) found that in kittens' visual cortex cells of certain orientations were absent if they were visually deprived before the age of 8 weeks. In conclusion, perception is a matter of both nature and nurture. The development of the brain (an innate system) depends on experience to direct it. This is an adaptive process which requires both nature and nurture.

> As with the previous paragraph, you can get extra usage out of material previously used in the infant and cross-cultural studies answer. However, you must *use* this information slightly differently here in order to inform the nature–nurture debate.

Topic 1: Piaget's theory of cognitive development

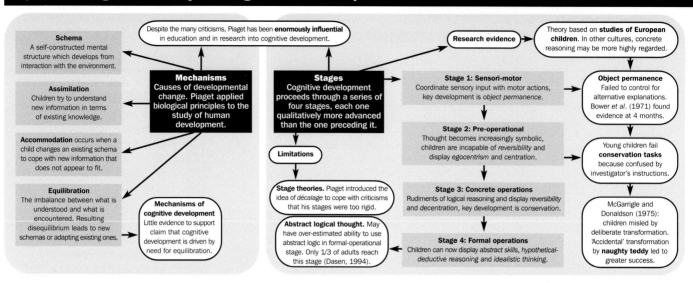

Schema
A self-constructed mental structure which develops from interaction with the environment.

Assimilation
Children try to understand new information in terms of existing knowledge.

Accommodation occurs when a child changes an existing schema to cope with new information that does not appear to fit.

Equilibration
The imbalance between what is understood and what is encountered. Resulting disequilibrium leads to new schemas or adapting existing ones.

Despite the many criticisms, Piaget has been **enormously influential** in education and in research into cognitive development.

Mechanisms
Causes of developmental change. Piaget applied biological principles to the study of human development.

Mechanisms of cognitive development
Little evidence to support claim that cognitive development is driven by need for equilibrium.

Stages
Cognitive development proceeds through a series of four stages, each one qualitatively more advanced than the one preceding it.

Limitations

Stage theories. Piaget introduced the idea of *décalage* to cope with criticisms that his stages were too rigid.

Abstract logical thought. May have over-estimated ability to use abstract logic in formal-operational stage. Only 1/3 of adults reach this stage (Dasen, 1994).

Research evidence

Theory based on **studies of European children**. In other cultures, concrete reasoning may be more highly regarded.

Stage 1: Sensori-motor
Coordinate sensory input with motor actions, key development is *object permanence*.

Stage 2: Pre-operational
Thought becomes increasingly symbolic, children are incapable of *reversibility* and display *egocentrism* and *centration*.

Stage 3: Concrete operations
Rudiments of logical reasoning and display *reversibility* and *decentration*, key development is *conservation*.

Stage 4: Formal operations
Children can now display *abstract skills*, *hypothetical-deductive reasoning* and *idealistic thinking*.

Object permanence
Failed to control for alternative explanations. Bower *et al*. (1971) found evidence at 4 months.

Young children fail **conservation tasks** because confused by investigator's instructions.

McGarrigle and Donaldson (1975): children misled by deliberate transformation. 'Accidental' transformation by **naughty teddy** led to greater success.

Topic 2: Vygotsky's theory of cognitive development

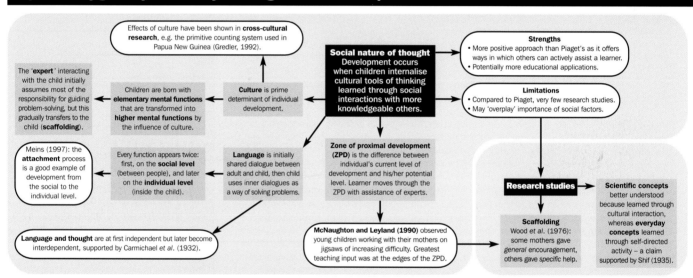

Effects of culture have been shown in **cross-cultural research**, e.g. the primitive counting system used in Papua New Guinea (Gredler, 1992).

The **'expert'** interacting with the child initially assumes most of the responsibility for guiding problem-solving, but this gradually transfers to the child (**scaffolding**).

Meins (1997): the **attachment** process is a good example of development from the social to the individual level.

Children are born with **elementary mental functions** that are transformed into **higher mental functions** by the influence of culture.

Culture is prime determinant of individual development.

Every function appears twice: first, on the **social level** (between people), and later on the **individual level** (inside the child).

Language is initially shared dialogue between adult and child, then child uses inner dialogues as a way of solving problems.

Language and thought are at first independent but later become interdependent, supported by Carmichael *et al*. (1932).

Social nature of thought
Development occurs when children internalise cultural tools of thinking learned through social interactions with more knowledgeable others.

Zone of proximal development (ZPD) is the difference between individual's current level of development and his/her potential level. Learner moves through the ZPD with assistance of experts.

McNaughton and Leyland (1990) observed young children working with their mothers on jigsaws of increasing difficulty. Greatest teaching input was at the edges of the ZPD.

Strengths
• More positive approach than Piaget's as it offers ways in which others can actively assist a learner.
• Potentially more educational applications.

Limitations
• Compared to Piaget, very few research studies.
• May 'overplay' importance of social factors.

Research studies

Scaffolding
Wood *et al*. (1976): some mothers gave *general* encouragement, others gave *specific* help.

Scientific concepts better understood because learned through cultural interaction, whereas **everyday concepts** learned through self-directed activity – a claim supported by Shif (1935).

Topic 3: Applications of theories of cognitive development

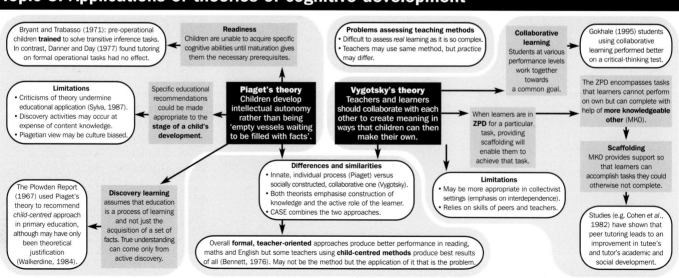

Bryant and Trabasso (1971): pre-operational children **trained** to solve transitive inference tasks. In contrast, Danner and Day (1977) found tutoring on formal operational tasks had no effect.

Readiness
Children are unable to acquire specific cognitive abilities until maturation gives them the necessary prerequisites.

Problems assessing teaching methods
• Difficult to assess *real* learning as it is so complex.
• Teachers may use same method, but *practice* may differ.

Collaborative learning
Students at various performance levels work together towards a common goal.

Gokhale (1995) students using collaborative learning performed better on a critical-thinking test.

Limitations
• Criticisms of theory undermine educational application (Sylva, 1987).
• Discovery activities may occur at expense of content knowledge.
• Piagetian view may be culture biased.

Specific educational recommendations could be made appropriate to the **stage of a child's development**.

Piaget's theory
Children develop intellectual autonomy rather than being 'empty vessels waiting to be filled with facts'.

Vygotsky's theory
Teachers and learners should collaborate with each other to create meaning in ways that children can then make their own.

When learners are in **ZPD** for a particular task, providing scaffolding will enable them to achieve that task.

The ZPD encompasses tasks that learners cannot perform on own but can complete with help of **more knowledgeable other** (MKO).

The Plowden Report (1967) used Piaget's theory to recommend *child-centred* approach in primary education, although may have only been theoretical justification (Walkerdine, 1984).

Discovery learning assumes that education is a process of learning and not just the acquisition of a set of facts. True understanding can come only from active discovery.

Differences and similarities
• Innate, individual process (Piaget) versus socially constructed, collaborative one (Vygotsky).
• Both theorists emphasise construction of knowledge and the active role of the learner.
• CASE combines the two approaches.

Limitations
• May be more appropriate in collectivist settings (emphasis on interdependence).
• Relies on skills of peers and teachers.

Scaffolding
MKO provides support so that learners can accomplish tasks they could otherwise not complete.

Studies (e.g. Cohen *et al*., 1982) have shown that peer tutoring leads to an improvement in tutee's and tutor's academic and social development.

Overall **formal, teacher-oriented** approaches produce better performance in reading, maths and English but some teachers using **child-centred methods** produce best results of all (Bennett, 1976). May not be the method but the application of it that is the problem.

Probable questions

1. Describe and evaluate Piaget's theory of cognitive development. (*24 marks*)

2. Outline and evaluate **two** theories of cognitive development. (*24 marks*)

Possible questions

3. (a) Describe Piaget's theory of cognitive development. (*12 marks*)

   (b) To what extent can theories such as Piaget's be successfully applied (e.g. to education)? (*12 marks*)

This is the only area of the specification where theories are named. So it is the only area where you can be asked to discuss one specified theory, as in question 1. It is possible (as you can see from question 2) that you would be asked to discuss two theories, in which case you must be careful to reduce the content covered for each theory, otherwise you'll end up with a 60 minute answer!

You can use your knowledge of one theory to evaluate the other theory, as long as this material is used as part of a sustained critical commentary (any description of the alternative theory would receive no credit).

A less likely question would use the AO2 injunction 'To what extent' for the AO2 part of the question. This means that you must avoid any evaluation in part (a). It would not gain credit in part (a) and would not be exported to part (b) because it is not likely to be relevant. Part (b) is concerned with the third topic in this division – applications. As this is all AO2 you must restrain yourself from providing descriptions of applications and instead focus on whether the applications are valuable or not. Inevitably this will require *some* description but keep it minimal.

Note that part (a) is about Piaget's theory whereas part (b) can be related to any theory/theories.

Probable questions

1. Describe and evaluate Vygotsky's theory of cognitive development. (*24 marks*)

2. (a) Outline **one** theory of cognitive development. (*6 marks*)

   (b) Outline and evaluate applications of theories of cognitive development (e.g. to education). (*18 marks*)

Possible questions

3. Compare and contrast Piaget's and Vygotsky's theories of cognitive development. (*24 marks*)

The same range of questions can be set for Topic 1 and 2, but here a different sample is shown. Question 1 is the same as question 1 on Piaget.

Question 2 involves an unusual mark split. There are only 6 marks for part (a) which means you must use your reduced version of Vygotsky. You must also not include any evaluation of Vygotsky's theory as it would not be creditworthy in part (a) and is unlikely to be creditworthy in part (b) – though an evaluation of Vygotsky's theory *might* be creditworthy in part (b) if it is used as an *effective* commentary on an application of the theory; 'straight' evaluation would not be creditworthy.

In part (b) you must take care to write twice as much AO2 as AO1 because the 18 marks consist of 6 AO1 marks and 12 AO2 marks.

It is extremely unusual to be asked a 'compare and contrast' question in Unit 4 but it is possible. The simplest way to answer this is, for AO1, to outline the two theories (using your two 'reduced' versions) and then, for AO2, consider how the two theories are similar and different. You must consider both similarities *and* differences (or you will incur a partial performance penalty for the AO2 mark – maximum of 8 out of 12 marks). A 'consideration' of similarities and differences essentially means describing the similarities and differences, and providing evidence to support your points.

Probable questions

1. Discuss applications of **two or more** theories of cognitive development (e.g. to education). (*24 marks*)

2. Discuss applications of **one** theory of cognitive development. (*24 marks*)

Possible questions

3. (a) Outline **two** theories of cognitive development. (*12 marks*)

   (b) To what extent have these theories been successfully applied (e.g. to education)? (*12 marks*)

The third topic in this division is linked to the previous two but focuses on the applications of these theories. There is no credit in these questions for descriptions (or evaluations) of Piaget and Vygotsky's theories – though, as we have already pointed out, you could use an evaluation of the theory as a means of evaluating the application – if the theory has flaws then the application based on the theory is flawed. However you must be careful to use such evidence *effectively* as an evaluation of the application.

Questions 1 and 2 either require you to consider the application of two (or more) theories or just one theory. You do not have to restrict yourself to education but it is given as an example in the specification.

This is a mixed question – mixing all three topics of this division. It is similar to question 3 for topic 1 but this time you must consider two theories in both part (a) and part (b). In part (b) you are directed to consider whether the application of the theories has been successful – you can divide your AO2 answer into 4 sections: (1) Piaget's theory has been successfully applied, (2) it has not been successfully applied, (3) Vygotsky's theory has been successfully applied, (4) it has not been successfully applied. Each time use evidence to support your arguments.

SAMPLE ESSAY PLAN

Question 1: Describe and evaluate Piaget's theory of cognitive development. (24 marks)

15 MINUTES WORTH OF AO1

Mechanisms of cognitive development:
- Development due to **maturation** and **experience**.
- **Schema**: innate schema (e.g. sucking) develop through interaction with environment. Schema are behavioural or cognitive.
- **Assimilation**: new knowledge understood in terms of existing schema.
- **Accommodation**: existing schema changed to understand new information.
- Development driven by **equilibration** – when existing schemas and new information are imbalanced this creates disequilibrium.

Stages in cognitive development:
- **Stage 1: sensori-motor**: sensory input co-ordinated with motor actions through **circular reactions**. Child develops **object permanence** in this stage.
- **Stage 2: pre-operational**: between 2–7 years thought becomes increasingly symbolic, but not capable of reversibility as illustrated by **egocentrism** and **centration**.
- **Stage 3: concrete operational**: rudiments of logical operations but not abstract e.g. **conservation** and **seriation**.
- **Stage 4: formal operational**: from age 11 develop abstract skills, **hypothetic-deductive** reasoning and **idealistic** thinking.

15 MINUTES WORTH OF AO2

Research evidence:
- **Methods of investigation**: ingenious investigations but Ps were children of intelligent European families.
- Often didn't exclude other explanations e.g. lack of **object permanence** in infants may be due to lack of ability to uncover object; when tested using surprise found that infants aged 4 months did show object permanence (**Bower et al., 1971**).
- Tasks were confusing e.g. **conservation** failures due to use of two questions; when **one question** asked younger children did better (**Samuel and Bryant, 1984**).
- Tasks not realistic e.g. **three mountains** easier when given same task with a **policeman** (Hughes, 1975).
- **Demand characteristics** e.g. **naughty teddy** used and then younger children not misled by deliberate transformation (**McGarrigle and Donaldson, 1974**).

Limitations of theory:
- Piaget **overestimated ability** to use abstract logic in **Stage 4**: only ⅓ of adults reach this stage (**Dasen, 1994**).
- **Equilibration** not supported, children may learn better in situations of mild conflict (**Inhelder et al., 1974**).
- **Stage theories** too rigid though **horizontal décalage** may explain this.

Strengths:
- Remains highly influential theory and has had major effect on education in UK.

Question 3: (a) Describe Piaget's theory of cognitive development. (12 marks)
(b) To what extent can theories such as Piaget's be successfully applied (e.g. to education)? (12 marks)

(a) 15 MINUTES WORTH OF AO1
- The description of theory 1 above.

(b) 15 MINUTES WORTH OF AO2
- Piaget's theory implied that teachers should wait until a child is **ready**, and that practice doesn't matter.
- However, research has shown that training can have an effect e.g. successful training on transitive inference tasks (**Bryant and Trebasso**, 1971) and formal tasks (**Danner and Day**, 1977).
- But Piaget argued that children may be able to do it but their **understanding** is incomplete.
- Piaget's theory promoted **discovery learning**, implemented through the **Plowden Report** – though these ideas stem back to the Greeks.
- Discovery learning may occur at the expense of content knowledge, and may lead to backwardness (**Modgil** et al., 1983).
- **Culture-biased** (**individualist**) approach. Vygotskian approach more appropriate for collectivist societies.
- Can be **combined with Vygotskian** approach e.g. CASE, improvements in science, Maths and English (**Adey and Shayer**, 1993).
- **Research hampered** by problems with **assessment** (what counts as success) and individual variations in **teaching style** (not the method but the application which is problematic).

Piaget believed that there were a number of mechanisms involved in cognitive development, with development due to a combination of maturation and experience. During development, the child develops mental structures known as schema. Schema can be either behavioural or cognitive, with cognitive schema helping children to solve problems and classify objects. Some schema are innate (e.g. sucking), whereas other develop through interaction with the environment. Children are born with very few schema, but these develop gradually through the processes of assimilation and accommodation, which together help the child adapt to his or her environment. Assimilation is the mechanism used when a child tries to understand new information in terms of existing schema. In some situations, a child must change an existing schema to understand new information. Piaget called this mechanism accommodation. A child's cognitive development is driven by equilibration; when existing schemas and new information are imbalanced this creates disequilibrium. The child is motivated to reduce this by developing new schemas or adapting old ones until equilibrium is restored.

In the first stage of cognitive development, the sensori-motor stage, sensory input is co-ordinated with motor actions through circular reactions, where children repeat the same action over and over to test sensori-motor relationships. One development of this stage is object permanence, the recognition that objects continue to exist even when out of sight. In stage 2, the pre-operational stage, which develops between 2 and 7 years, thought becomes increasingly symbolic as they begin to represent their world in words and images. The child is not yet capable of reversibility of thought, which results in the child's tendency towards egocentrism, a failure to understand that what the child sees is relative to his or her own perspective. The child is also guilty of centration, a tendency to focus attention on one aspect of a situation and not take other details into account. In stage 3, the concrete operational stage, the child develops the rudiments of logical operations such as conservation and seriation, although he or she cannot solve such problems when in abstract form. In the final stage, the formal operational stage, from age 11 onwards, the child develops abstract skills such as hypothetic-deductive reasoning and idealistic thinking.

Piaget's theory is based on studies of intelligent European children. However, research carried out in other cultures has shown that concrete reasoning may be more highly regarded, which may explain why children in those cultures often do not display formal operational reasoning. A problem with some of the earlier research on this theory is that it often failed to consider other explanations for the findings. For example, the lack of object permanence in infants may be due to the lack of an ability to uncover the object. Research that has used surprise to test object permanence has found that infants aged 4 months showed this ability (Bower et al., 1971). In many of the studies, the tasks used were confusing, e.g. conservation failures may have been due to the use of two questions, as when one question was asked younger children did better (Samuel and Bryant, 1984). Many of the tasks were unrealistic, e.g. the three mountains used to test for egocentricity. This problem was easier when children were given a more realistic test (i.e. the policeman and the naughty boy – Hughes, 1975). Children may also have displayed demand characteristics. McGarrigle and Donaldson (1974) found that when transformation in conservation tasks was accidental (using naughty teddy) children were more successful than when the transformation was deliberate.

Limitations of theory include the fact that Piaget may have overestimated the ability to use abstract logic in the formal operational stage. Dasen (1994) found that only one third of adults reach this stage. There is little empirical support for the concept of equilibration, in fact some research has shown that children may learn better in situations of mild conflict (Inhelder et al., 1974). Stage theories such as Piaget's are seen by many psychologists as being too rigid. Piaget introduced the idea of horizontal décalage, the fact that certain cognitive abilities are shown in some circumstances but not others, to deal with this criticism. Despite this, a strength of Piaget's theory is that it has been highly influential and has had a major effect on education in the UK.

Describing a theory such as this is an exercise in writing discipline. There is a massive amount of information that *could* be included, so your editing skills will be tested as well as your psychology skills.

In approximately 150 words, you would only have the chance to summarise each of the stages. You should practise doing just that, and then practise halving that (for a question that asks for an *outline* of this theory).

Remember to do more than just *describe* these studies – you should point out how they impact on Piaget's theory. That is, do they support its claims, or do they pose problems for it?

You will also have studied applications of this theory. The fact that they exist does not constitute AO2 commentary, but the fact that they have been *successful* does.

TOPIC 2: VYGOTSKY'S THEORY OF COGNITIVE DEVELOPMENT

SAMPLE ESSAY PLAN

Question 1: Describe and evaluate Vygotsky's theory of cognitive development. (24 marks)

<u>15 MINUTES WORTH OF AO1</u>
- Development mainly due to social interactions.

Role of culture:
- Transforms **elementary** (e.g. perception – innate and involuntary) to **higher mental functions** (e.g. logical memory – voluntary and controlled).
- Children acquire **content** (what to think) and **processes** (how to think).
- **Experts** transfer problem-solving skills to child (**scaffolding**).

Role of language:
- Culture transmitted through language.
- Starts as shared dialogue (**pre-intellectual speech**) then used for problem-solving (**egocentric** and then **inner speech**).
- Learning starts on **social plane** and then language enables this to move to **individual plane**.

Zone of proximal development:
- Learning **precedes** development.
- Distance between **current** and **potential** level.
- Learner moves through ZPD **assisted by experts**.

<u>15 MINUTES WORTH OF AO2</u>
Research evidence:
- **The role of culture**: can limit cognitive development e.g. counting in Papua New Guinea (**Gredler**, 1992) or enhance e.g. teaching apes to use human language through acculturation (**Savage-Rumbaugh**, 1991).
- **Role of language**: words affect recall (e.g. **Carmichael et al.**, 1932) but **Sinclair-de-Zwart** (1969) could not improve conservation skills with language.
- **ZPD**: children reached higher level of difficulty (on puzzles) when working with mother than on own (**McNaughton and Leyland**, 1990).
- **Scaffolding** observed in children and mothers working on puzzles (**Wood et al.**, 1976).
- LIMITATIONS: overplayed importance of social environment, lacking research support.
- STRENGTHS: provides a bridge between social and cognitive domains, a positive approach.
- **Contrast with Piaget** who suggested learning was solitary (not social) and due to maturation. However **Glassman** (1999) suggests the two theories aren't that different – may reflect different kinds of learner (e.g. introvert vs extrovert (**Miller**, 1994).

Question 2: (a) Outline **one** theory of cognitive development. (6 marks)
(b) Outline and evaluate applications of theories of cognitive development (e.g. to education). (18 marks)

(a)

<u>7½ MINUTES WORTH OF AO1</u>
- Development mainly due to social interactions.

The role of culture:
- Transforms **elementary** (e.g. perception – innate and involuntary) to **higher mental functions** (e.g. logical memory – voluntary and controlled).
- **Experts** transfer problem-solving skills to child (**scaffolding**).

The role of language:
- Culture transmitted through language.
- Starts as shared dialogue (**pre-intellectual speech**) then used for problem-solving (**egocentric** and then **inner speech** about age 7).

The zone of proximal development:
- Distance between **current** and **potential** level.

(b)

<u>7½ MINUTES WORTH OF AO1</u>
Piaget:
- **Readiness**: operations can't be taught until child has matured sufficiently.
- **Discovery learning**: understanding incomplete unless child can discover things for themselves. Learning is a process not just acquiring facts.
- **Teacher** creates **curiosity** (questions/materials).

Vygotsky:
- **Collaborative learning**: learners at different levels work together towards common goal, promotes exchange of ideas and critical thinking.
- **Scaffolding**: experts help learner through ZPD with appropriate assistance.
- **More knowledgeable others** (MKOs) may act as experts = **peer tutoring**.

<u>15 MINUTES WORTH OF AO2</u>
- **Readiness**. Training can have an effect e.g. on transitive inference tasks (**Bryant and Trebasso**, 1971) and formal tasks (**Danner and Day**, 1977). But Piaget argued that **understanding** is incomplete.
- **Discovery learning** may occur at the expense of content knowledge, and may lead to backwardness (**Modgil** et al., 1983).
- **Culture-biased** (**individualist**) approach. Vygotskian approach more appropriate for collectivist societies.
- **Collaborative learning**: improved performance on critical thinking test (**Gokhale**, 1995); small groups best (**Mulyran**, 1992).
- **Scaffolding** observed in children and mothers working on puzzles (**Wood et al.**, 1976), specific vs. general help.
- **Peer tutoring**: most effective for peer tutors (Cloward, 1967).
- **Combined approach** e.g. CASE, improvements in science, Maths and English (**Adey and Shayer**, 1993).
- **Research hampered** by problems with **assessment** (what counts as success) and individual variations in **teaching style** (it's the application which is problematic).

Vygotsky believed that social interaction plays a fundamental role in the child's cognitive development. The child is born with elementary mental functions such as perception and memory. These lower mental functions are innate and involuntary. These are transformed into higher mental functions (such as selective attention and logical memory) through the influence of culture. These are voluntary, controlled by the individual and social in origin. Culture influences the child's cognitive development in two ways. First, children acquire the content of their thinking (it shows them what to think). Second, the surrounding culture provides them with the processes of their thinking (i.e. it shows them how to think). Vygotsky believed that experts (e.g. parents and teachers and even more knowledgeable peers) in the child's environment transfer problem-solving skills to the child through the process of scaffolding. In scaffolding, the expert initially assumes most of the responsibility for guiding problem solving, but this responsibility gradually transfers to the child.

Vygotsky claimed that language is the most important way in which adults transmit cultural knowledge to the child. This starts as shared dialogue between the adult and child (pre-intellectual speech), but as children develop the skill of mental representation they begin to communicate with themselves. Language is later used to solve problems (egocentric speech), which then gives way to inner speech at the age of 7. According to Vygotsky, learning starts on a social plane (through interactions with experts) and then language enables this to move to the individual plane (i.e. the development of higher mental functions). Vygotsky believed that learning precedes development. The difference between a child's current level of development and their potential level is his or her zone of proximal development. A zone in between these two levels is the optimum zone for learning. The learner moves through the ZPD with the assistance of experts, i.e. those with greater knowledge.

Research evidence for this theory has supported the important role that culture plays in cognitive development. Gredler (1992) showed how culture can limit cognitive development, using the primitive counting system in Papua New Guinea as an example. Culture can also enhance cognitive development, for example studies that have taught apes to use human language through acculturation (e.g. Savage-Rumbaugh, 1991). Research has also supported the role of language. Vygotsky's belief that the acquisition of a new word was the beginning of a concept was supported in a study by Carmichael et al. (1932) which showed that words affect recall. However, Sinclair-de-Zwart (1969) tried to use language to teach children who could not conserve, but found little improvement in their conservation skills. Evidence for the ZPD has shown that children reached a higher level of difficulty (on jigsaw puzzles) when working with their mothers than on their own (McNaughton and Leyland, 1990). Similarly, scaffolding has been observed in children and mothers when jointly working on puzzles (Wood et al., 1976).

Among the limitations of Vygotsky's theory is the claim that he overplayed the importance of social environment. If social influence were all that were needed for cognitive development, learning would be a lot faster than it is. Compared to the vast amount of supporting evidence for Piaget's theory, there are relatively few empirical studies that support the main claims of Vygotsky's theory. A strength of this theory is that it provides a bridge between the social and cognitive domains of learning, and reflects a more positive approach to cognitive development than Piaget's theory because it demonstrates ways in which others can be actively involved in assisting a learner. This contrasts markedly with Piaget who suggested that learning was solitary (i.e. not social) and mainly due to maturation. However Glassman (1999) suggests the two theories are not that different, and may reflect different kinds of learner. Miller (1994) believed that Piaget's child is very much an introvert, whereas Vygotsky's child is more extroverted in the way he or she approaches learning.

In theories where a number of the assumptions appear unfamiliar to you, it pays to structure your description as a series of points (as we have done here). This makes the description far more systematic.

It is okay to use abbreviations such as ZPD in an answer, but you should use the full version at least once before switching to the abbreviated version.

Using research evidence as AO2 commentary can be very effective, but don't forget to link it to the descriptive content of your essay rather than leaving it to the examiner to make the link.

Showing how this theory contrasts with Piaget's theory is a useful form of AO2 commentary, but note that Piaget's theory has not been *described* at all.

SAMPLE ESSAY PLAN

Question 1: Discuss applications of **two or more** theories of cognitive development (e.g. to education). (24 marks)

THEORY 1: PIAGET

7½ MINUTES WORTH OF AO1

- **Readiness**: operations can't be taught until child has matured sufficiently.
- Tasks should be appropriate to **stages of development** e.g. stimulating environment in stage 1 and use of concrete objects in stage 3.
- **Discovery learning**: understanding incomplete unless child can discover things for themselves. Learning is a process not just acquiring facts.
- **Teacher** creates **curiosity** by providing the setting and appropriate materials.

7½ MINUTES WORTH OF AO2

- **Readiness**. Training can have an effect e.g. on transitive inference tasks (**Bryant and Trebasso**, 1971) and formal tasks (**Danner and Day**, 1977). But Piaget argued that **understanding** is incomplete.
- **Discovery learning** may occur at the expense of content knowledge, and may lead to backwardness (**Modgil et al.**, 1983).
- **Culture-biased** (**individualist** rather than collectivist) approach.

THEORY 2: VYGOTSKY

7½ MINUTES WORTH OF AO1

- **Collaborative learning**: learners at different levels work together towards common goal, promotes exchange of ideas and critical thinking.
- **Scaffolding**: experts help learner through ZPD with appropriate assistance – ranging from specific instructions to general guidance.
- Eventually **scaffolding removed** and child is able to complete the task on their own.
- **MKOs** may act as experts = **peer tutoring**.

7½ MINUTES WORTH OF AO2

- **Collaborative learning**: improved performance on critical thinking test (**Gokhale**, 1995); small groups best (**Mulyran**, 1992).
- **Scaffolding** observed in children and mothers working on puzzles (**Wood et al.**, 1976).
- **Peer tutoring**: most effective for peer tutors (**Cloward**, 1967).
- **Combined approach** e.g. CASE, improvements in science, Maths and English (**Adey and Shayer**, 1993).
- **Research hampered** by problems with **assessment** (what counts as success) and individual variations in **teaching style** (it's the application which is problematic).

Question 2: Discuss applications of **one** theory of cognitive development. (24 marks)

THEORY 1: PIAGET

15 MINUTES WORTH OF AO1

- **Readiness**: operations can't be taught until child has matured sufficiently.
- Activities should involve **appropriate level of mental operation** for a child of given age.
- Tasks should be appropriate to **stages of development** e.g. stimulating environment in stage 1 and use of concrete objects in stage 3.
- **Discovery learning**: to allow children to experience assimilation and accommodation.
- **Understanding incomplete** unless child can discover things for themselves. Learning is a process not just acquiring facts.
- **Teacher** creates **curiosity** by using appropriate materials and asking questions.
- Teacher **does not simply transmit knowledge** (as in more formal, teacher-oriented teaching styles).
- **Peers** may take a similar role.

15 MINUTES WORTH OF AO2

- **Readiness**. Training can have an effect e.g. on transitive inference tasks (**Bryant and Trebasso**, 1971) and formal tasks (**Danner and Day**, 1977). But Piaget argued that **understanding** is incomplete.
- **Discovery learning** may occur at the expense of content knowledge, and may lead to backwardness (**Modgil** et al., 1983).
- Piaget's theory promoted **discovery learning**, implemented through the **Plowden Report** – though these ideas stem back to the Greeks.
- **Underlying theory flawed** e.g. ages for stages may be wrong because children perform better when tasks less confusing (**Samuel and Bryant**, 1984) or more realistic (**Hughes**, 1975).
- **Culture-biased** (**individualist**) approach. Vygotskian approach more appropriate for collectivist societies.
- **Combined approach** e.g. CASE, improvements in science, Maths and English (**Adey and Shayer**, 1993).
- **Research hampered** by problems with **assessment** and individual variations in **teaching style**.

A key concept in the application of Piagetian theory to education is the concept of readiness, i.e. the belief that children are unable to acquire specific cognitive abilities (or operations) until they have matured sufficiently. Piaget believed that because cognitive development is characterised by qualitative differences in how children think about the world, educational tasks should be appropriate to the child's stage of development, e.g. providing a stimulating environment in the sensori-motor stage and making use of concrete objects to help learning in the concrete-operational stage. Piaget believed in the use of discovery learning, with activities planned to allow learners to discover knowledge for themselves rather than having it delivered. He argued that understanding was incomplete unless children can discover things for themselves, as learning is a process not just the acquisition of facts. Piaget claimed that a teacher's job is to provide the setting and materials that will help naturally curious children gain the satisfaction of discovery, and bring about true understanding.

A common error is for students to describe Piaget's *theory* rather than its applications. Such an approach would get very few marks.

There is research evidence for and against the concept of readiness. Bryant and Trebasso (1971) showed that pre-operational children could be trained on transitive inference tasks, arguing that failure was due to memory restriction rather than lack of operational thinking. This suggests that children could successfully complete tasks before they were maturationally ready according to Piaget's theory. In contrast, Danner and Day (1977) found no evidence of improvement in students aged 10–13 who were tutored in formal operational tasks. Piaget was able to explain why some children appear to have learned something before they are 'ready', arguing that despite having learned a task, their understanding was incomplete. Piaget's ideas have had a major influence on education, particularly his child-centred approach that was represented by discovery learning. However, discovery learning may occur at the expense of content knowledge, and may lead to backwardness in reading and writing (Modgil et al., 1983). Piaget's approach may also be criticised as being culture-biased, with the idea that children are the agents of their own learning being more characteristic of an individualist rather than a collectivist approach.

It is possible to get some marks for an evaluation of Piaget's theory (an application is only as good as the underlying theory), but it is better to focus on the applications themselves.

Vygotsky believed that learning was a collaborative activity, as learners construct knowledge in interaction with their social environment. Collaborative learning is a method of learning where learners at different levels work together towards a common goal, with each child being responsible for their own and each other's learning. Vygotsky believed that this promotes an exchange of ideas and critical thinking. When learners are in the zone of proximal development (ZPD) for a particular task, others can provide appropriate assistance (scaffolding), which helps the learner through the ZPD. This assistance ranges from specific instructions to general guidance. Eventually the scaffolding is removed and the child is able to complete the task on their own. The more knowledgeable other (MKO) helps the child with tasks that they cannot perform on their own, but can perform with the help of someone who has a better understanding of that task than the learner. Although the MKO is usually an adult, a child's peers can also take this role in what Vygotsky referred to as peer tutoring.

There is a considerable overlap between the applications of Vygotky's theory and the theory itself as, unlike Piaget, Vygotsky focused on the process of education in his theory. His theory of cognitive development, therefore, reads like a series of applications.

Research has supported the value of collaborative learning. Gokhale (1995) found that students who participated in collaborative learning improved their performance on a critical thinking test compared to those who studied individually. Mulyran (1992) investigated the most effective group conditions for collaborative learning, discovering that small groups work more efficiently than large groups. Evidence for the effectiveness of scaffolding has been shown in studies of children and mothers when jointly working on puzzles (Wood et al., 1976). Research has also shown that peer tutoring leads to an improvement in both tutee's and tutor's development, although it is consistently most effective for the peer tutors rather than the tutees (Cloward, 1967). Some approaches have drawn on the best of both approaches, with the CASE scheme, which draws on Piaget's notion of cognitive conflict and Vygotsky's ideas of social construction producing significant improvements in science, maths and English (Adey and Shayer, 1993). A problem with research in this area is that it is hampered by problems with assessment (i.e. what counts as 'success') as well as individual variations in teaching style which make comparison between approaches difficult.

The CASE approach is included here to show that the most effective approach may be a combination of both Piagetian *and* Vygotskian approaches.

Topic 1: The role of genetics in the development of measured intelligence

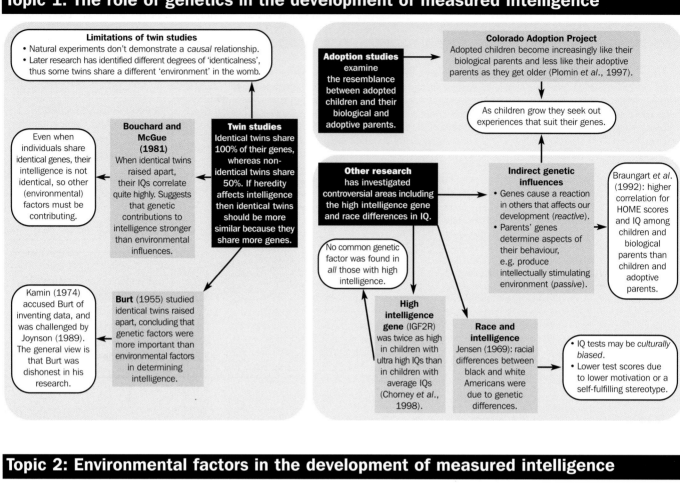

Limitations of twin studies
- Natural experiments don't demonstrate a *causal* relationship.
- Later research has identified different degrees of 'identicalness', thus some twins share a different 'environment' in the womb.

Bouchard and McGue (1981)
When identical twins raised apart, their IQs correlate quite highly. Suggests that genetic contributions to intelligence stronger than environmental influences.

Twin studies
Identical twins share 100% of their genes, whereas non-identical twins share 50%. If heredity affects intelligence then identical twins should be more similar because they share more genes.

Even when individuals share identical genes, their intelligence is not identical, so other (environmental) factors must be contributing.

Kamin (1974) accused Burt of inventing data, and was challenged by Joynson (1989). The general view is that Burt was dishonest in his research.

Burt (1955) studied identical twins raised apart, concluding that genetic factors were more important than environmental factors in determining intelligence.

Adoption studies
examine the resemblance between adopted children and their biological and adoptive parents.

Colorado Adoption Project
Adopted children become increasingly like their biological parents and less like their adoptive parents (Plomin *et al.*, 1997).

As children grow they seek out experiences that suit their genes.

Other research
has investigated controversial areas including the high intelligence gene and race differences in IQ.

No common genetic factor was found in *all* those with high intelligence.

Indirect genetic influences
- Genes cause a reaction in others that affects our development (*reactive*).
- Parents' genes determine aspects of their behaviour, e.g. produce intellectually stimulating environment (*passive*).

Braungart *et al.* (1992): higher correlation for HOME scores and IQ among children and biological parents than children and adoptive parents.

High intelligence gene (IGF2R)
was twice as high in children with ultra high IQs than in children with average IQs (Chorney *et al.*, 1998).

Race and intelligence
Jensen (1969): racial differences between black and white Americans were due to genetic differences.

- IQ tests may be *culturally biased*.
- Lower test scores due to lower motivation or a self-fulfilling stereotype.

Topic 2: Environmental factors in the development of measured intelligence

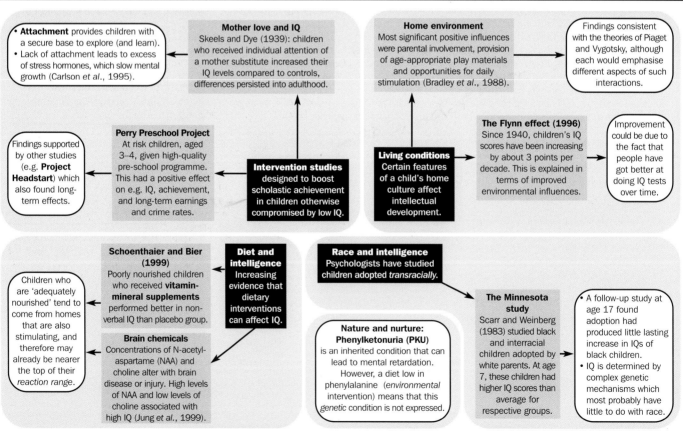

- **Attachment** provides children with a secure base to explore (and learn).
- Lack of attachment leads to excess of stress hormones, which slow mental growth (Carlson *et al.*, 1995).

Mother love and IQ
Skeels and Dye (1939): children who received individual attention of a mother substitute increased their IQ levels compared to controls, differences persisted into adulthood.

Home environment
Most significant positive influences were parental involvement, provision of age-appropriate play materials and opportunities for daily stimulation (Bradley *et al.*, 1988).

Findings consistent with the theories of Piaget and Vygotsky, although each would emphasise different aspects of such interactions.

Findings supported by other studies (e.g. **Project Headstart**) which also found long-term effects.

Perry Preschool Project
At risk children, aged 3–4, given high-quality pre-school programme. This had a positive effect on e.g. IQ, achievement, and long-term earnings and crime rates.

Intervention studies
designed to boost scholastic achievement in children otherwise compromised by low IQ.

Living conditions
Certain features of a child's home culture affect intellectual development.

The Flynn effect (1996)
Since 1940, children's IQ scores have been increasing by about 3 points per decade. This is explained in terms of improved environmental influences.

Improvement could be due to the fact that people have got better at doing IQ tests over time.

Children who are 'adequately nourished' tend to come from homes that are also stimulating, and therefore may already be nearer the top of their *reaction range*.

Schoenthaler and Bier (1999)
Poorly nourished children who received **vitamin-mineral supplements** performed better in non-verbal IQ than placebo group.

Brain chemicals
Concentrations of N-acetyl-aspartame (NAA) and choline alter with brain disease or injury. High levels of NAA and low levels of choline associated with high IQ (Jung *et al.*, 1999).

Diet and intelligence
Increasing evidence that dietary interventions can affect IQ.

Race and intelligence
Psychologists have studied children adopted *transracially*.

Nature and nurture: Phenylketonuria (PKU)
is an inherited condition that can lead to mental retardation. However, a diet low in phenylalanine (*environmental intervention*) means that this *genetic* condition is not expressed.

The Minnesota study
Scarr and Weinberg (1983) studied black and interracial children adopted by white parents. At age 7, these children had higher IQ scores than average for respective groups.

- A follow-up study at age 17 found adoption had produced little lasting increase in IQs of black children.
- IQ is determined by complex genetic mechanisms which most probably have little to do with race.

Probable questions

1. Discuss research (theories **and/or** studies) into the role of genetics in the development of measured intelligence. (*24 marks*)

2. Discuss research (theories **and/or** studies) into the development of measured intelligence. (*24 marks*)

Possible questions

3. (a) Outline and evaluate research (theories **and/or** studies) into the role of genetics in the development of measured intelligence. (*12 marks*)

   (b) Outline and evaluate research (theories **and/or** studies) into the role of environmental factors in the development of measured intelligence. (*12 marks*)

The specification for this division only uses the term 'research' therefore questions cannot be asked specifically about theories or studies – the choice is left to you.

Question 1 focuses on the role of genetics. This means that the AO1 content of your essay should outline research evidence (theories and/or studies) that demonstrates the role of genetics. The simplest way to do this is to describe research that shows genetics does play a role and, for AO2, criticise the methodology of such research or use research that suggests genetics actually plays a minimal role. For AO2 you can also use research that shows the role of environmental factors.

Question 2 permits you to use any material as AO1 (research related to genetics or environment). This means that you must clearly indicate what material is intended as AO2 because a description of a study that supports genetics followed by a study that supports environment could be seen as AO1 + AO1, or AO1 + AO2 depending on how the second study was *used*.

Like question 2 you are now invited to present research on genetics and environmental factors as AO1. In question 2 this was an option (you could write the same essay for question 2 as for question 1). In question 3 you must clearly separate the two essays. In essence this question 3 is a combination of question 1 from topic 1 and question 1 from topic 2, so take care not to end up writing a 60-minute answer. Select your material for each part of the answer and time yourself carefully (7½ minutes for each of AO1, AO2, AO1, and AO2). You could use the same material in both parts, for example using a study that indicates the importance of environmental factors as AO2 in part (a) and describing the same study as AO1 for part (b) – however the important difference is that in one case you will *use* it as commentary and in the other you will *describe* it.

Probable questions

1. Discuss research (theories **and/or** studies) into the role of environmental factors in the development of measured intelligence. (*24 marks*)

2. Critically consider the role of genetics and environmental factors in the development of measured intelligence. (*24 marks*)

Possible questions

3. Describe and evaluate research into **two or more** environmental factors associated with the development of measured intelligence. (*24 marks*)

In answering question 1 for Topic 2 you could use the same material that you used in answering question 1 for Topic 1, except the material would obviously need to be organised in a different way. What was AO2 now becomes AO1 and vice versa. Nothing is intrinsically AO1 or AO2; it's all about how you use it. This is especially important in this division of the specification because Topic 2 forms some of the commentary for Topic 1 (and vice versa). There are, of course, other forms of commentary. For example you can criticise the methodology used in any study or you could consider applications of this knowledge.

Question 2, like question 2 above, permits genetics and environmental factors to be AO1 – though here you must do both, or else you will incur a partial performance penalty. This means a maximum of 8 marks for AO1 if you only describe genetics or environmental factors, and also a maximum of 8 marks for AO2 if you only evaluate one of these.

It is probable that your answer to this question would be the same as your answer to question 1 – though this time you must ensure that you have both described and evaluated at least two environmental factors. It would pay to organise your essay clearly along these lines – saying 'The first environmental factor is …', and then later 'The second environmental factor is …'.

Chapter 5

TOPIC 1: THE ROLE OF GENETICS IN THE DEVELOPMENT OF MEASURED INTELLIGENCE

SAMPLE ESSAY PLAN

Question 1: Discuss research (theories **and/or** studies) into the role of genetics in the development of measured intelligence. (24 marks)

15 MINUTES WORTH OF A01

- **Twin studies**: identical twins (100% share of genes) should be more similar than fraternal twins (50%).
- **Bouchard and McGue** (1981) analysed 66 studies, mean correlation for IQ of 0.86 for identical twins reared together, 0.72 reared apart and 0.62 for fraternal twins.
- **Burt** (1955): 42 identical twins reared apart closer IQ than fraternal twins reared together.
- **Adoption studies**: look at IQ similarity between adopted children and biological/adopted parents.
- **Colorado Adoption Project** (Plomin *et al.*, 1997): ongoing study of 245 adopted children who have become increasingly more similar to biological parents as they get older, and less similar to adopted parents.
- **Intelligence gene**: variant of the IGF2R gene twice as common in highly intelligent children compared to those with average IQs (**Chorney** *et al.*, 1998).
- **Race and IQ**: Jensen (1969) provided evidence that black Americans had mean IQ of 85 (compared to white average of 100 points), due to genetic factors.
- **Indirect influences**: **reactive** effects (e.g. genes affect people's reactions and thus change the environment) and **passive** effects (e.g. genes affect home environment).

15 MINUTES WORTH OF A02

- **Twin studies** are natural experiments, can't show a causal relationship. Effect could be direct or indirect.
- Identical twins may **not be that similar** e.g. womb environment alters them (**Kaufman**, 1999) nor easily identified.
- **Bouchard and McGue** data shows contribution of environment.
- **Adoption** data supported by zero correlation between children and adopted siblings by age 18 (0.26 at 8 years) (**Texas Adoption Project**, Loehlin *et al.*, 1989).
- **Zero correlation** can be explained by **active** effects (with increasing age children seek out their own environments which suit their genes).
- **Intelligence gene** not found in all high IQ children.
- Conclusion about **race** flawed because low IQ in black children may be due to lower **motivation**, negative **self-image** which affects performance, lower SES (when making cross-environmental comparisons, environmental factors account for variation).
- **Jensen's** view that IQ was unchangeable is challenged by the success of **intervention programmes** such as the Perry Preschool Project.

Question 3: (a) Outline and evaluate research (theories **and/or** studies) into the role of genetics in the development of measured intelligence. (12 marks)
(b) Outline and evaluate research (theories **and/or** studies) into the role of environmental factors in the development of measured intelligence. (12 marks)

(a)
GENETIC FACTORS

7½ MINUTES WORTH OF A01

- **Twin studies**: identical twins (100% share of genes) should be more similar than fraternal twins (50%).
- **Bouchard and McGue** (1981) analysed 66 studies, mean correlation for IQ of 0.86 for identical twins reared together, 0.72 reared apart and 0.62 for fraternal twins.
- **Adoption studies**: look at IQ similarity between adopted children and biological/adopted parents.
- **Colorado Adoption Project** (Plomin *et al.*, 1997): ongoing study of 245 adopted children who have become increasingly more similar to biological parents as they get older, and less similar to adopted parents.
- **Intelligence gene**: variant of the IGF2R gene twice as common in highly intelligent children compared to those with average IQs. (**Chorney** *et al.*, 1998).

7½ MINUTES WORTH OF A02

- **Twin studies** are natural experiments, can't show a causal relationship. Effect could be direct or indirect.
- Identical twins may **not be that similar** e.g. womb environment alters them (**Kaufman**, 1999) nor easily identified.
- **Bouchard and McGue** data shows contribution of environment. Also twins reared together may be similar because of similar **unshared environment**.
- **Zero correlation** can be explained by **active** effects (with increasing age children seek out their own environments which suit their genes = **niche-picking**).
- **Intelligence gene** not found in all high IQ children.

(b)
ENVIRONMENTAL FACTORS

7½ MINUTES WORTH OF A01

- **A01** for environmental factors on page 94.

7½ MINUTES WORTH OF A02

- **A02** for environmental factors on page 94.

Identical twins share 100% of their genes whereas fraternal twins share just 50%. If intelligence is inherited, then identical twins should be more similar than fraternal twins because they share more of their genes. Bouchard and McGue (1981) analysed 66 studies, and discovered that even when identical twins are reared apart, their IQs still correlate quite highly. They found a mean correlation for IQ of 0.86 for identical twins reared together, 0.72 reared apart and 0.62 for fraternal twins. An earlier study by Burt (1955) had studied 42 pairs of identical twins who had been reared apart. He found that they were closer in terms of their IQ scores than fraternal twins reared together. Adoption studies examine the resemblance in IQ between adopted children and their biological and adoptive parents. The Colorado Adoption Project (Plomin et al., 1997), in an ongoing study of 245 adopted children, found that they have become increasingly similar to their biological parents as they get older, and less like their adopted parents.

> You don't have to worry about remembering numbers of children studied or the exact correlations obtained. Using terms like 'high, moderate, low or zero' when describing a correlation, is usually sufficient.

Researchers have also tried to isolate the genes that affect general cognitive ability. Chorney et al. (1998) studied highly intelligent children in the US and discovered that a particular variant of the IGF2R gene was twice as common in these children compared to those with average IQs. Jensen (1969) provided evidence that black Americans had a mean IQ score of 85 (compared to the white average of 100 points), and argued that this difference was due to genetic factors, and was therefore not changeable. Genes can also affect intelligence indirectly. They can have reactive effects, in that certain genetic factors create a microenvironment which then promotes development of high IQ. For example, some genetically inherited characteristics lead others to respond more or less favourably to the child, which then influences the child's IQ. Genes may also have passive effects, in that parental genes influence aspects of the parents' behaviour. For example, parents with a high IQ create a more intellectually stimulating environment for the child, which in turn raises their IQ.

> This is a case where the abbreviation is fine or you could even simply call it 'the high intelligence gene'.

> Examples help here, but don't indulge yourself in overly long examples at the expense of your description elsewhere.

A problem with twin studies is that they are natural experiments, which means that they can't show a causal relationship between genes and IQ. Any observed relationship between genes and IQ may be a direct effect or an indirect effect, and therefore cannot be used to claim that intelligence itself is genetically inherited. An additional problem with twin studies is that identical twins may not be that similar. Recent research has shown that some identical twins develop using separate placentas in their mother's womb, which could have a major influence on their development (Kaufman, 1999). The Bouchard and McGue study also provides support for environmental factors. Even though identical twins share the same genes, their intelligence levels are not identical, with any difference therefore due to environmental factors. The finding that there is little correlation between parents and their adopted children when the children reach adulthood suggests a stronger influence for genetic factors over environmental factors in the determination of intelligence. This conclusion is supported by the Texas Adoption Project (Loehlin et al., 1989), which showed that the IQ correlation between adopted children and their adopted siblings was 0.26 at aged 8 years, but zero at age 18. This zero correlation can be explained by active genetic effects, i.e. with increasing age children seek out their own environments which suit their genes, and therefore change their intelligence levels accordingly.

> The introduction of the direct/indirect possibility is an elaboration of the first sentence, which by itself would not constitute *effective* commentary. You have to explain why this is a criticism.

The 'intelligence gene' is not found in all children with high IQ. In Chorney et al.'s research, 46% of the high IQ children had allele 5 of the IGF2R gene, but 54% did not. Jensen's conclusion about race and intelligence is flawed because low IQ in black children may be due to lower motivation and a negative self-image which leads to a self-fulfilling stereotype. Many black American children, particularly at the time of Jensen's research, come from lower socio-economic backgrounds, which means that when making cross-environmental comparisons, environmental factors must account for any subsequent developmental variation. Jensen's claim that variation in IQ was almost entirely genetic and therefore unchangeable, is challenged by the success of intervention programmes such as the Perry Preschool Project.

> Although you may find many of Jensen's claims objectionable, any rejection should be based on reasoned argument rather than personal opinion.

SAMPLE ESSAY PLAN

Question 1: Discuss research (theories and/or studies) into the role of environmental factors in the development of measured intelligence. (24 marks)

15 MINUTES WORTH OF AO1

- **Intervention studies**: orphanage children showed increased IQ with improved emotional care (**Skeels and Dye**, 1939), effects apparent 27 years later (**Skeels**, 1966).
- **Perry Preschool Project**: African American children who received high quality programme for 2 years had higher IQ at age 5 and higher achievement scores at age 15 than those with no preschool programme (**Schweinhart et al**, 1993).
- **Living conditions**: IQ of children with low HOME score decreased by 10–20 points from age 1–3 whereas opposite true for high HOME score (**Bradley et al.**, 1989).
- **Flynn effect**: IQ of children in rural community increased as living conditions improved (**Wheeler**, 1942).
- Children given **vitamin-mineral supplements** had higher IQs than placebo group; also standard deviation greatest which suggests that most poorly nourished showed largest improvement (**Schoenthaler and Bier**, 1999).
- High levels of NAA and choline associated with higher IQ (**Jung et al.**, 1999).
- At age 7 **black/interracial children** had higher IQs than controls when adopted by white families – due to better environment (**Minnesota transracial adoption study**, **Scarr and Weinberg**, 1983).

15 MINUTES WORTH OF AO2

- **Lack of attachment** in orphanage children may affect IQ because reduces exploration and increases stress.
- **Perry Project** supported by e.g. **Headstart** – initial IQ gains disappeared but persistent effects e.g. high rate of high school diplomas (**Zigler and Styfco**, 1993).
- **Theories of cognitive development** support the view that home interventions matter to create curiosity (Piaget) or for scaffolding (Vygotsky).
- Effects of **better living conditions** could be due to enriched experience: rats raised in enriched environment had more connections between neurons in the brain (**Greenough et al.**, 1987).
- **Flynn effect**: an alternative explanation is that people have got better at taking IQ tests.
- **Effects of diet** can be explained by **reaction range** (**Gottesman**, 1963).
- **Minnesota study** follow-up (**Weinberg et al.**, 1993) found black adoptees at age 17 had same IQs as those raised by biological parents i.e. environment had no lasting effect.
- **Race studies** flawed because race only affects simple genetic mechanisms e.g. skin colour; no consistent difference between racial groups (**Olsen**, 2001).

Question 2: Critically consider the role of genetics and environmental factors in the development of measured intelligence. (24 marks)

GENETIC FACTORS

7½ MINUTES WORTH OF AO1

- AO1 for genetic factors on page 92.

7½ MINUTES WORTH OF AO2

- AO2 for genetic factors on page 92.

ENVIRONMENTAL FACTORS

7½ MINUTES WORTH OF AO1

- **Intervention studies**: orphanage children showed increased IQ with improved emotional care (**Skeels and Dye**, 1939), effects apparent 27 years later (**Skeels**, 1966).
- **Perry Preschool Project**: African American children who received high quality programme for 2 years had higher IQ age 5, higher achievement score age 15, less likely to commit crime or receive welfare than those with no preschool programme (**Schweinhart et al**, 1993).
- **Flynn effect**: IQ of children in rural community increased as living conditions improved (**Wheeler**, 1942).
- Children given **vitamin-mineral supplements** had higher IQs than placebo group; also standard deviation greatest which suggests that most poorly nourished showed largest improvement (**Schoenthaler and Bier**, 1999).

7½ MINUTES WORTH OF AO2

- **Lack of attachment** in orphanage children may affect IQ because reduces exploration and increases stress.
- **Perry Project** supported by e.g. **Headstart** – initial IQ gains disappeared but persistent effects e.g. high rate of high school diplomas (**Zigler and Styfco**, 1993).
- **Theories of cognitive development** support the view that home interventions matter to create curiosity (piaget) or for scaffolding (Vygotsky).
- Effects of **better living conditions** could be due to enriched experience: rats raised in enriched environment had more connections between neurons in the brain.
- **Effects of diet** can be explained by **reaction range** (**Gottesman**, 1963).

A belief in the importance of environmental factors for human intelligence has led to the development of intervention programmes to boost the achievement levels of children with low IQ levels. In one such study (Skeels and Dye, 1939), orphanage children showed an increased IQ (32 points over 4 years) with improved emotional care from a mother substitute figure. These effects were still apparent 27 years later (Skeels, 1966). The Perry Preschool Project studied children who were at high risk of failing at school. These children received a high quality pre-school programme over a period of two years. Compared to a control group, these children had higher IQ at age 5 and higher achievement scores at age 15 (Schweinhart et al., 1993). Using the HOME inventory, which measures the influence of home factors on intelligence, Bradley et al. (1989) found that the IQ of children with low HOME scores decreased by 10–20 points from age 1–3 whereas the opposite was true for children with high HOME scores. Wheeler (1942) found that the IQ of children in a rural community increased as living conditions improved, something that is evident worldwide, and is known as the Flynn effect.

Other environmental influences on IQ include diet, particularly the effect of vitamins and minerals. Schoenthaler and Bier (1999) found that children who were given vitamin-mineral supplements had higher non-verbal IQs than a placebo group. They also found that the standard deviation was greatest for the vitamin-mineral group, which suggests that most of the poorly nourished showed the largest improvement as a result of the supplements. Jung et al. (1999) claim that levels of NAA and choline account for much of the variation in IQ. NAA levels drop after a serious brain injury and the damaged cells then release more choline. This shift is associated with a loss of thinking ability. In the Minnesota transracial adoption study, Scarr and Weinberg (1983) found that at age 7, black/interracial children had higher IQs than controls when adopted by white families, which the researchers attributed to growing up in a 'good' home.

Skeels and Dye's finding can be explained in terms of the fact that lack of attachment reduces exploration and increases stress, and so providing an attachment figure would increase the former and decrease the latter, leading to developmental progress. The findings of the Perry Preschool Project have been supported by other intervention studies such as Operation Headstart. In this study, although the initial IQ gains of 10 points disappeared, there were persistent positive effects, e.g. a high rate of high school diplomas among children who had experienced the intervention programme (Zigler and Styfco, 1993). For Piaget, the increased stimulation from home interventions would be necessary to create conflict, leading children to reassess current schemas. For Vygotsky, intervention from a more knowledgeable other would provide the child with the appropriate scaffolding to lead them through their zone of proximal development. The Flynn effect can be explained in terms of enriched experience. Greenough et al. (1987) found evidence that rats reared in enriched environments had larger brains and more connections than control rats. This indicates that an increase in living conditions causes physiological changes which result in higher levels of intelligence. The Flynn effect could alternatively be explained by the fact that people may have got better at taking IQ tests.

The beneficial effects of diet on intelligence can be explained by the concept of reaction range (Gottesman, 1963). Children who are well-nourished are likely to come from higher socioeconomic status homes, which are more stimulating. As a result, they would already be near the top of their reaction range, so further supplements would have little effect. In a follow-up to the Minnesota study, Weinberg et al. (1993) found that black adoptees at age 17 had the same IQs as those raised by their biological parents, showing that a changed environment had no lasting effect on the IQs of black children in the study. Studies of race and IQ tend to be flawed because race only affects simple genetic mechanisms such as skin colour. Intelligence, on the other hand, is determined by complex genetic mechanisms, with the general view that there are no consistent differences between racial groups (Olsen, 2001).

It is difficult to cram everything you know into a relatively short paragraph. The answer is DON'T! Be selective, and only cover enough research that you can do justice to in such a confined space.

Why does this material on NAA and choline count as 'environmental factors'? Two reasons – brain injuries are part of our *experiences* rather than our genetics, and these chemicals constitute the environment for our brain.

Making a point across different areas of the specification can be effective commentary. Here a link is made with Piaget and Vygotsky's views of intellectual development.

Rather than just stating this finding, ask yourself 'so what', i.e. what does this show, or how does it challenge a previous finding or belief?

Topic 1: Theories of the development of moral understanding/pro-social reasoning

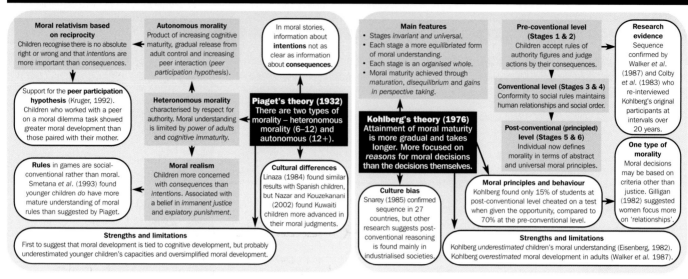

Moral relativism based on reciprocity
Children recognise there is no absolute right or wrong and that *intentions* are more important than *consequences*.

Support for the peer participation hypothesis (Kruger, 1992). Children who worked with a peer on a moral dilemma task showed greater moral development than those paired with their mother.

Rules in games are social-conventional rather than moral. Smetana *et al.* (1993) found younger children *do* have more mature understanding of moral rules than suggested by Piaget.

Autonomous morality
Product of increasing cognitive maturity, gradual release from adult control and increasing peer interaction (*peer participation hypothesis*).

Heteronomous morality characterised by respect for authority. Moral understanding is limited by *power of adults* and *cognitive immaturity*.

Moral realism
Children more concerned with *consequences* than *intentions*. Associated with a belief in *immanent justice* and *expiatory punishment*.

In moral stories, information about **intentions** not as clear as information about **consequences**.

Piaget's theory (1932)
There are two types of morality – heteronomous morality (6–12) and autonomous (12+).

Cultural differences
Linaza (1984) found similar results with Spanish children, but Nazar and Kouzekanani (2002) found Kuwaiti children more advanced in their moral judgments.

Main features
- Stages *invariant and universal*.
- Each stage a more *equilibrated* form of moral understanding.
- Each stage an *organised whole*.
- Moral maturity achieved through *maturation, disequilibrium and gains in perspective taking*.

Kohlberg's theory (1976)
Attainment of moral maturity is more gradual and takes longer. More focused on *reasons* for moral decisions than the decisions themselves.

Culture bias
Snarey (1985) confirmed sequence in 27 countries, but other research suggests post-conventional reasoning is found mainly in industrialised societies.

Pre-conventional level (Stages 1 & 2)
Children accept rules of authority figures and judge actions by their consequences.

Conventional level (Stages 3 & 4)
Conformity to social rules maintains human relationships and social order.

Post-conventional (principled) level (Stages 5 & 6)
Individual now defines morality in terms of abstract and universal moral principles.

Moral principles and behaviour
Kohlberg found only 15% of students at post-conventional level cheated on a test when given the opportunity, compared to 70% at the pre-conventional level.

Research evidence
Sequence confirmed by Walker *et al.* (1987) and Colby *et al.* (1983) who re-interviewed Kohlberg's original participants at intervals over 20 years.

One type of morality
Moral decisions may be based on criteria other than justice. Gilligan (1982) suggested women focus more on 'relationships'.

Strengths and limitations
First to suggest that moral development is tied to cognitive development, but probably underestimated younger children's capacities and oversimplified moral development.

Strengths and limitations
Kohlberg *underestimated* children's moral understanding (Eisenberg, 1982). Kohlberg *overestimated* moral development in adults (Walker *et al.* 1987).

Topic 2: Gender and cultural differences in moral understanding/pro-social reasoning

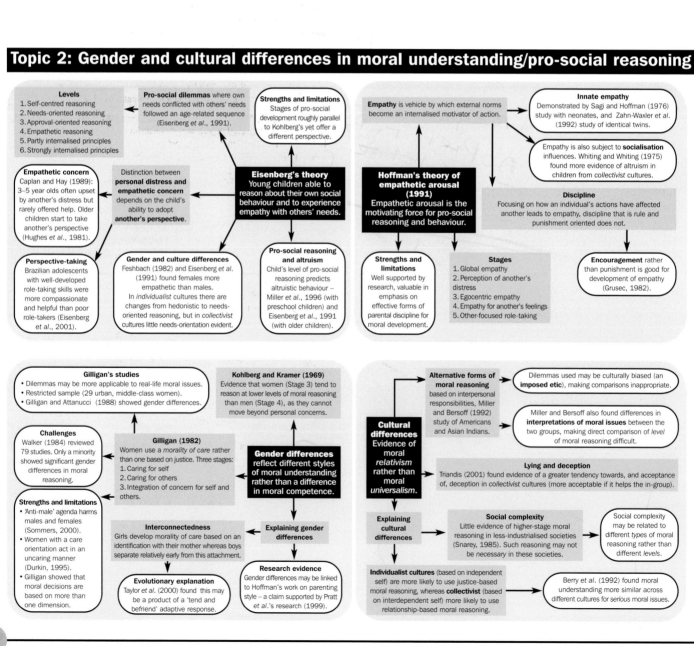

Levels
1. Self-centred reasoning
2. Needs-oriented reasoning
3. Approval-oriented reasoning
4. Empathetic reasoning
5. Partly internalised principles
6. Strongly internalised principles

Pro-social dilemmas where own needs conflicted with others' needs followed an age-related sequence (Eisenberg *et al.*, 1991).

Strengths and limitations
Stages of pro-social development roughly parallel to Kohlberg's yet offer a different perspective.

Empathetic concern
Caplan and Hay (1989): 3–5 year olds often upset by another's distress but rarely offered help. Older children start to take another's perspective (Hughes *et al.*, 1981).

Distinction between **personal distress and empathetic concern** depends on the child's ability to adopt **another's perspective**.

Eisenberg's theory
Young children able to reason about their own social behaviour and to experience empathy with others' needs.

Perspective-taking
Brazilian adolescents with well-developed role-taking skills were more compassionate and helpful than poor role-takers (Eisenberg *et al.*, 2001).

Gender and culture differences
Feshbach (1982) and Eisenberg *et al.* (1991) found females more empathetic than males. In *individualist* cultures there are changes from hedonistic to needs-oriented reasoning, but in *collectivist* cultures little needs-orientation evident.

Pro-social reasoning and altruism
Child's level of pro-social reasoning predicts altruistic behaviour – Miller *et al.*, 1996 (with preschool children) and Eisenberg *et al.*, 1991 (with older children).

Empathy is vehicle by which external norms become an internalised motivator of action.

Hoffman's theory of empathetic arousal (1991)
Empathetic arousal is the motivating force for pro-social reasoning and behaviour.

Strengths and limitations
Well supported by research, valuable in emphasis on effective forms of parental discipline for moral development.

Stages
1. Global empathy
2. Perception of another's distress
3. Egocentric empathy
4. Empathy for another's feelings
5. Other-focused role-taking

Innate empathy
Demonstrated by Sagi and Hoffman (1976) study with neonates, and Zahn-Waxler *et al.* (1992) study of identical twins.

Empathy is also subject to **socialisation** influences. Whiting and Whiting (1975) found more evidence of altruism in children from *collectivist* cultures.

Discipline
Focusing on how an individual's actions have affected another leads to empathy, discipline that is rule and punishment oriented does not.

Encouragement rather than punishment is good for development of empathy (Grusec, 1982).

Gilligan's studies
- Dilemmas may be more applicable to real-life moral issues.
- Restricted sample (29 urban, middle-class women).
- Gilligan and Attanucci (1988) showed gender differences.

Challenges
Walker (1984) reviewed 79 studies. Only a minority showed significant gender differences in moral reasoning.

Strengths and limitations
- 'Anti-male' agenda harms males and females (Sommers, 2000).
- Women with a care orientation act in an uncaring manner (Durkin, 1995).
- Gilligan showed that moral decisions are based on more than one dimension.

Kohlberg and Kramer (1969)
Evidence that women (Stage 3) tend to reason at lower levels of moral reasoning than men (Stage 4), as they cannot move beyond personal concerns.

Gilligan (1982)
Women use a *morality of care* rather than one based on justice. Three stages:
1. Caring for self
2. Caring for others
3. Integration of concern for self and others.

Gender differences
reflect different styles of moral understanding rather than a difference in moral competence.

Interconnectedness
Girls develop morality of care based on an identification with their mother whereas boys separate relatively early from this attachment.

Evolutionary explanation
Taylor *et al.* (2000) found this may be a product of a 'tend and befriend' adaptive response.

Explaining gender differences

Research evidence
Gender differences may be linked to Hoffman's work on parenting style – a claim supported by Pratt *et al.*'s research (1999).

Alternative forms of moral reasoning
based on interpersonal responsibilities, Miller and Bersoff (1992) study of Americans and Asian Indians.

Cultural differences
Evidence of moral *relativism* rather than moral *universalism*.

Explaining cultural differences

Dilemmas used may be culturally biased (an **imposed etic**), making comparisons inappropriate.

Miller and Bersoff also found differences in **interpretations of moral issues** between the two groups, making direct comparison of *level* of moral reasoning difficult.

Lying and deception
Triandis (2001) found evidence of a greater tendency towards, and acceptance of, deception in *collectivist* cultures (more acceptable if it helps the in-group).

Social complexity
Little evidence of higher-stage moral reasoning in less-industrialised societies (Snarey, 1985). Such reasoning may not be *necessary* in these societies.

Social complexity may be related to different *types* of moral reasoning rather than different *levels*.

Individualist cultures (based on independent self) are more likely to use justice-based moral reasoning, whereas **collectivist** (based on interdependent self) more likely to use relationship-based moral reasoning.

Berry *et al.* (1992) found moral understanding more similar across different cultures for *serious* moral issues.

Probable questions

1. Describe and evaluate **one** theory of moral understanding/pro-social reasoning.
(*24 marks*)

2. Outline and evaluate **two** theories of moral understanding/pro-social reasoning.
(*24 marks*)

Possible questions

3. (a) Outline **two** theories of moral understanding/pro-social reasoning. (*12 marks*)

(b) Evaluate **one** of the theories of moral understanding/pro-social reasoning that you outlined in part (a). (*12 marks*)

The specification does not distinguish between the development of moral understanding and theories of the development of pro-social reasoning. The two most likely examples are given in the specification – Kohlberg and Eisenberg. Other examples would be equally creditworthy, such as Piaget's theory of moral development.

Questions may be asked about one theory (as in question 1) or two theories (as in question 2). This means you must be prepared to discuss one theory for 30 minutes, and also to produce a cut-down version of this theory when asked for two theories. It also means that you only need a cut down version of your second theory. *And* you might use your second theory as commentary for theory 1 – as long as it is *effectively* used.

Note that there is a distinction between 'outline' (for two theories) and 'describe' (for one theory). 'Outline' indicates that less detail is expected whereas the use of 'describe' means that both depth and breadth are required.

Question 3 is a variation of questions 1 and 2. The main point (which candidates in an exam could well overlook) is that you are only required to evaluate one of the theories. If you did evaluate both theories, credit would only be given to the better evaluation *unless* you shaped your answer so that both evaluations were applied to just one theory. Remember that it is what you *do* with your knowledge which determines whether it gets credit or not.

Probable questions

1. Critically consider the influence of gender and/or cultural variations on moral understanding/pro-social reasoning.
(*24 marks*)

2. Critically consider the influence of gender and cultural variations on moral understanding/pro-social reasoning.
(*24 marks*)

Possible questions

3. Discuss the influence of gender on moral understanding/pro-social reasoning.
(*24 marks*)

4. Discuss the influence of cultural variations on moral understanding/pro-social reasoning. (*24 marks*)

The injunction 'critically consider' is used less often than 'discuss' but it has the same meaning, i.e. 'describe and evaluate'.

The difference between these questions lies in the word 'or'. In question 1 you can write the whole essay about the influence of gender or the whole essay about cultural variations or present a combination of both (describe and evaluate gender and just describe culture, describe gender and describe and evaluate culture, or describe and evaluate both). In question 2 you must choose one or the other. If you do both then credit will only be given to one of them – whichever attracts more marks (examiners have some heart).

In both essays you do not have to identify what is gender and what is culture, but it is always best to make this clear to help the examiner make sense of your answer. You could argue that gender-related behaviour is a form of culture because men and women are socialised to behave differently – but this argument must be explicit for gender material to be credited as culture.

Questions 3 and 4 use a slightly different wording but are essentially the same as those above *except* you have no choice about which route to take. You are directed to answer only on gender or only on culture. If you choose to present your argument that gender = culture you would need to sustain this throughout your answer. It would not be creditworthy to say at the outset that gender is an example of culture and then proceed to present your 'gender essay'. At best this would be a limited answer because it limits the answer to only one kind of cultural variation – that of gender.

SAMPLE ESSAY PLAN

Question 1: Describe and evaluate **one** theory of moral understanding/pro-social reasoning. (24 marks)

15 MINUTES WORTH OF AO1

As below plus:

- **Stages** are **invariant** and **universal**.
- Based on **cognitive-developmental** perspective.
- Each stage is a more **equilibrated** form of more understanding, more **logically consistent**.
- Each stage is an **organised whole**.
- Change due to **maturation, disequilibrium**, and gains in **perspective-taking**.

15 MINUTES WORTH OF AO2

As below plus:

- **Empirical support:**
- **Walker et al.** (1980) tested 40 boys and 40 girls, confirmed invariant sequence; 2 years later 22% had moved up a stage.
- **Moral principles linked to behaviour:** 15% of students at post-conventional level **cheated on test** but 70% of pre-conventional ones did (**Kohlberg**, 1976).
- But **Burton** (1976) found people consistent only on some behaviours e.g. cheating, and other factors (e.g. likelihood of punishment) affect moral behaviour.
- A restricted view, **Eisenberg's theory of pro-social development** is wider.

Question 2: Outline and evaluate **two** theories of moral understanding/pro-social reasoning. (24 marks)

THEORY 1: KOHLBERG

7½ MINUTES WORTH OF AO1

- Developed **stage theory** from **clinical interviews** conducted with boys aged 10–16 using **moral dilemmas** e.g. Heinz.
- Three **levels**:
- **Pre-conventional**: (1) punishment and obedience (heteronomous), (2) **instrumental purpose orientation** (satisfy own needs).
- **Conventional level**: (3) **interpersonal cooperation** ('right' defined by role expectations), (4) **social order-maintaining** ('right' defined by social norms).
- **Post-conventional (principled)**: (5) **social-contract orientation** (laws can be changed), (6) **universal ethical principles** (self-chosen abstract principles).

7½ MINUTES WORTH OF AO2

- **Empirical support:**
- **Colby et al.** (1983) re-interviewed Kohlberg's participants over 20 years and confirmed sequence of development.
- **Gender-bias**: dilemmas based on **morality of justice**, women focus more on 'caring' (**Gilligan**, 1982).
- **Culture bias**: Kohlberg (1987) and **Snarey** (1985) found same sequence of development in over 30 countries. But post-conventional understanding may only be true in industrialised societies perhaps because they pose conflicts (disequilibrium) (**Snarey and Keljo**, 1991).
- **Limitations**: most adults may not go beyond stage 4 (**Walker et al.**, 1987) but support is compelling (**Bee**, 1995).

THEORY 2: EISENBERG

7½ MINUTES WORTH OF AO1

- Pro-social behaviour stems from experiencing **empathy**, which occurs when a child feels **another's distress** and feels **concern**.
- Children reason from **several different levels**, so reasoning not that predictable.
- Eisenberg used **simpler pro-social dilemmas** where child's needs conflict with another.
- **Produced 6 levels**: self-centred (hedonistic), needs-oriented, approval-oriented, empathetic, partly internalised principles (adolescents), strongly internalised.

7½ MINUTES WORTH OF AO2

- **Empirical support:**
- Importance of **empathetic concern**: 3–5 year olds upset by another's distress but don't offer help (**Caplan and Hey**, 1989).
- **Perspective-taking**: Brazilian adolescents with role-taking skills more helpful than poor role-takers (**Eisenberg et al.**, 2001).
- **Gender differences**: females more empathetic than males (**Feshbach**, 1982).
- **Cultural differences**: kibbutz-reared children more focused on communal values than needs-oriented as found in **individualist** cultures (**Eisenberg**, 1986).

Kohlberg (1987) developed a stage theory of moral reasoning, based on clinical interviews conducted with boys aged 10–16. Using moral dilemmas such as the Heinz dilemma, Kohlberg studied the reasons underlying participants' moral choices rather than their final judgements. He discovered that there are three distinct levels of moral reasoning. The first of these is the pre-conventional level, where children accept the rules of authority figures and judge actions by their consequences. This level is divided into two stages, the first focuses on the need to obey authority and avoid punishment, and the second, the 'instrumental purpose orientation' stage, based on a desire to satisfy one's own needs. In the second level, the conventional level, the individual is motivated by the importance of social order. This level is further divided into the interpersonal cooperation stage, where what is 'right' is defined by interpersonal role expectations, and the social order-maintaining stage, where what is right is 'right' defined by social norms. In the first part of the post-conventional level, the social-contract orientation, laws are seen as relative and flexible. In the final, universal ethical principles stage, the individual defines morality in terms of self-chosen absolute moral principles.

It is difficult to get the whole theory into one short paragraph. This account is 197 words. Can you edit this down to 150–160 words without losing too much detail?

Empirical support for this theory comes from Colby et al. (1983), who re-interviewed Kohlberg's participants at intervals over a 20-year period, and confirmed the sequence of development. A criticism of this theory is that it is gender-biased, with Kohlberg's classification based on a morality of justice rather than the morality of caring that is more typical of female responses (Gilligan, 1982). There is also evidence of a culture bias in Kohlberg's theory, although Kohlberg (1987) and Snarey (1985) found the same sequence of development in over 30 countries. However, other research (e.g. Snarer and Keljo, 1991) found that post-conventional understanding occurs mainly in industrialised societies rather than in rural communities. Industrialisation may be the cause because more diverse societies pose more conflicts which may promote moral development because of the increased questioning of moral standards. Limitations include the claim that Kohlberg may have overestimated moral development, in that most adults may not go beyond stage 4 (Walker et al., 1987). Despite this, Bee (1995) concludes that research support for Kohlberg's theory is compelling.

Note that each criticism is *identified*, and then *elaborated* in order to make each point effective (and so earn more AO2 credit).

Eisenberg (1982) claimed that young children are able to reason about their own pro-social behaviour, and to experience empathy with others' needs. Pro-social behaviour stems from experiencing empathy, which occurs when a child feels another's distress and feels concern. Based on cross-sectional and longitudinal research, Eisenberg found that children's pro-social reasoning was not always predictable, as they could reason from several different levels rather than using one at a time. Eisenberg used simpler pro-social dilemmas than did Kohlberg, using situations where the child's own needs conflicted with another person's needs. From responses to these dilemmas, she found that there was an age-related sequence of pro-social reasoning, as the child moved from self-centred (pursuing their own needs and considering only consequences to themselves), through needs-oriented, approval-oriented, empathetic, partly internalised principles, and finally to strongly internalised principles, where justifications for action are based on strongly felt internalised values.

When outlining *two* theories, one theory can be covered in slightly less detail than the other. Note how just two of Eisenberg's levels are elaborated here to give a flavour of how children progress through the sequence.

Eisenberg's theory has received considerable empirical support. Caplan and Hey (1989) showed the importance of empathetic concern, finding that 3–5 year olds were frequently upset by another's distress but did not offer help. Older children were more likely to help because they were able to take the other person's perspective (Hughes et al. 1981). The importance of perspective-taking was demonstrated in a study by Eisenberg et al. (2001), which showed that Brazilian adolescents with role-taking skills were more helpful than poor role-takers. Feshbach (1982) found evidence of gender differences in pro-social reasoning, reporting that females are more empathetic than males, although Eisenberg claims that this may be due to the fact that girls mature earlier than boys, and that by adolescence these gender differences had disappeared. Eisenberg did, however, find evidence of cultural differences in pro-social reasoning, with kibbutz-reared children being focused on communal values and showing little evidence of the needs-oriented reasoning found in Germany, Italy and other individualist cultures (Eisenberg, 1986).

Here empirical support has been used effectively as commentary on Eisenberg's theory. Gender and cultural differences are both identified and elaborated for maximum effect.

SAMPLE ESSAY PLAN

Question 1: Critically consider the influence of gender and/or cultural variations on moral understanding/pro-social reasoning. (24 marks)

INFLUENCE OF GENDER

15 MINUTES WORTH OF AO1

- **Kohlberg's research** based on male participants, gender biased.
- **Found that** females generally respond at stage 3 (interpersonal cooperation) (**Kohlberg and Kramer,** 1969).
- **Males** more likely to be at **stage 4**, a higher level of moral development.
- **Females 'held back'** because they can't move beyond personal concerns.
- An **androcentric bias** to Kohlberg's theory.
- Women's concerns are a **morality of care**, women focus on care more than justice (**Gilligan,** 1982).
- **3 stages** in the development of female morality (their 'different voice'):
    (1) **Caring for self** similar to pre-conventional.
    (2) **Caring for others**, may involve sacrificing one's own needs.
    (3) **Integration of concern** for self and others.
- **Explanation:** women develop a different morality because of greater **interconnectedness**, stems from identity with mothers (**Gilligan et al.,** 1990).
- **Male focus on justice** because early separation from mother to form separate masculine identity, heightens awareness of inequality.

15 MINUTES WORTH OF AO2

- Gilligan's research involved **real-life** dilemmas rather than hypothetical dilemmas.
- **Criticism** (**Sommers,** 2000): it was anecdotal research, never replicated. Only 29 US middle-class urban women.
- **Further support:** **Gilligan and Attanucci** (1988) found women more care focused and men more justice focused, though 35% showed mixed focus.
- Same findings by **Garmon et al.** (1996) testing over 500 Ps.
- **Gilligan's sample** restricted to urban women and never replicated (**Somers,** 2000).
- **Contradictory evidence:** Walker (1984) reviewed 79 studies, only 20 showed gender differences and these were not consistent.
- **Sommers** (2000) argues that promoting an anti-male agenda harms both sexes.
- **Interconnectedness:** higher level of moral understanding in children with more responsive mothers and fathers (**Pratt et al.,** 1999).
- **Alternatively** women may be more caring because they evolved a **tend and befriend** response to stress (**Taylor et al.,** 2000).
- **Limitation:** Gilligan's theory doesn't explain why women with a care orientation still act in an uncaring manner (**Durkin,** 1995).
- **Strengths:** suggests that moral decisions based on more than one dimension, 'different voice' may explain other individual.

Question 2: Critically consider the influence of gender and cultural variations on moral understanding/pro-social reasoning. (24 marks)

INFLUENCE OF CULTURAL VARIATIONS

15 MINUTES WORTH OF AO1

- **Kohlberg's theory** based on **justice**, but an alternative is a morality based on **interpersonal reasoning**.
- **Indians** are more likely to resolve moral dilemmas in terms of interpersonal relations than justice, whereas opposite true of **Americans** (**Miller and Bershoff,** 1992).
- **Deception** more acceptable in collectivist cultures if it helps the group (**Triandis,** 2001).
- In **individualist** societies regard authenticity as more important (because a strong sense of self) (**Trilling,** 1972). Tradition more important in collectivist societies.
- **Individualist** cultures more concerned with **justice** because focus on independence. Fits Kohlberg's abstract, justice-based system.
- **Collectivist** societies develop **relationship-based** morality because of interdependence.
- People in **less industrialised** societies less likely to be at higher stages in Kohlberg's scale (**Snarey,** 1985), stages 1–4 universal but not 5 and 6.
- Individuals in **complex societies** have more need for moral rules to keep order.

15 MINUTES WORTH OF AO2

- Using **Kohlberg's dilemmas** cross-culturally is an **imposed ethic** – the dilemmas describe situations that are culturally-specific and therefore findings may be meaningless.
- **Miller and Bershoff** also found cultural differences in **interpretation** e.g. Americans regard losing best friend's wedding ring as an interpersonal matter, Indians see it as a moral matter.
- Since morals are learned through **socialisation** makes sense that they differ cross-culturally.
- **Berry et al.** (1992) greater cultural similarity when Ps asked to consider serious moral issues.
- **Social complexity and morality:** assumes that stages 5 and 6 are 'higher'.
- Moral rules necessary in more **industrialised societies** because they have to **think more** about such issues.
- **Moral universalism** (both Kohlberg and Gilligan's approach) or **moral relativism** – the view that morals only make sense in relation to cultural context.
- Many pro-social behaviours are related to the meaning of the act rather than the act itself (**Feldman,** 1986).

Kohlberg's original research on moral reasoning was based on male participants, therefore offering a gender-biased perspective on moral development. He claimed that females generally respond at stage 3 (the morality of interpersonal cooperation) whereas males are more likely to be at stage 4 (the social-order maintaining orientation), a higher level of moral development (Kohlberg and Kramer, 1969). Kohlberg claimed that females tend not to attain higher levels of moral development because they can't move beyond personal concerns. Gilligan offered a different perspective on moral understanding that overcame the androcentric nature of Kohlberg's theory. Gilligan believed that men and women reason differently about moral issues. She claimed that women's concerns are part of a morality of care, with women focusing more on interpersonal relationships and care than on abstract ideas of justice (Gilligan, 1982). Gilligan's theory emphasises the difference between men and women, which she suggests arises during early development.

Gilligan proposed three stages in the development of what she called the 'different voice' of female morality. The first of these was caring for the self, which is similar to Kohlberg's pre-conventional level. In this stage, morality is defined by the personal consequences of a person's actions. The second stage, caring for others, may involve sacrificing one's own needs to meet the needs of others. In the third stage, there is an integration of concern for self and others, with individuals able to balance their own and others' needs. Gilligan et al. (1990) claimed that women develop a different morality because of their greater interconnectness, which stems from their early identity formation with their mothers. Males, on the other hand, focus on justice because early separation from the mother causes them to form a separate masculine identity. This makes them aware of the power differences between themselves and adults, and makes them more concerned with inequality than are girls, whose continued attachment to their mother makes them less concerned with issues of fairness and justice.

Gilligan's research has the advantage of using real-life dilemmas rather than the hypothetical dilemmas used by Kohlberg in his research. Further support for Gilligan's theory comes from Gilligan and Attanucci (1988), who interviewed 46 men and 36 women on real-life moral conflicts. Consistent with the predictions of the theory, they found that women were more care focused and men more justice focused, although 35% of those interviewed showed a mixed focus in their moral decisions. This was further supported by Garmon et al. (1996) who tested over 500 participants and found females more likely to refer to care issues in their moral decisions. However, there were criticisms of Gilligan's research sample, in that only 29 middle-class women from an urban area of the US were used. Sommers (2000) also claims that Gilligan's original research was anecdotal, and was never replicated. Further challenge to Gilligan's theory comes from Walker (1984), who reviewed 79 research studies that had looked for gender differences in moral understanding. Only 20 of these showed gender differences and these were not consistent.

Sommers (2000) argues that promoting an anti-male agenda harms both sexes, particularly as research suggests that gender differences in moral reasoning are not that clear. The idea that greater interconnectedness comes from relationships with a warm, uncritical parent is supported in research by Pratt et al. (1999), who found a higher level of moral understanding in children with more responsive mothers and fathers. An alternative explanation for why women might be more caring focuses more on evolutionary pressure than family relationships. Taylor et al. (2000) argued that women have evolved a 'tend and befriend' response to stress that leads to increased concern for the safety of others in times of stress. A limitation of Gilligan's theory is that it doesn't explain why women with a care orientation still act in an uncaring manner (Durkin, 1995). A strength of this approach to moral reasoning is that it suggests that moral decisions are based on more than one dimension, and even if the 'different voice' is not restricted to gender, it may also apply to some other individual difference.

The question gives you the choice or writing about one or both of these types of variations. If you choose both, make sure you can offer a detailed account of each, otherwise stick to just the one (as here).

Rather than just describing the two theories, you should accentuate how each of these theories deals with the issue of gender variation in moral development.

There is no requirement to restrict yourself to research studies in this answer, so explanations can also receive AO1 credit.

Although you do not have to present a balanced criticism when evaluating a theory, it is good practice to look at the good points and bad points of a theory, as it opens up a greater range of possibilities.

Gilligan later claimed that the 'different voice' may not only apply to gender, but may be a product of other types of division within society.

Topic 1: Psychodynamic explanations of personality development

Two basic drives motivate all our thoughts and behaviours – *eros* (life instinct) and *thanatos* (death instinct).

Freud's psychoanalytic theory
Psychodynamic theories emphasise the constant change and development of the individual.

Psychosexual stages
At any given time the child's libido is focused on the primary erogenous zone for that stage. Frustration and overindulgence may result in *fixation*.

Oral stage (0-18 months)
The mouth is the primary focus of libidinal energy. Frustration may result in an 'oral aggressive' character, and overindulgence in 'oral receptive' character.

Oral personality
Some researchers (Blum and Miller, 1952; Goldberg and Lewis, 1978) have linked oral fixation and oral personalities, but others (Fisher and Greenberg, 1996) claim no such link exists.

Structure of the personality
The dynamic interaction between *id*, *ego* and *superego* determines personality.

Levels of consciousness
Everything we are aware of is stored in our **conscious** mind. Underlying impulses and emotions are stored at an **unconscious** level.

Freud's research
- Theory based on a restricted sample of mainly Viennese women.
- Other equally valid explanations exist for Freud's case studies.
- Theory lacks *falsifiability*.
- The sexual repression of Freud's time may explain the nature of his theory.

Anal stage (18 months-3 years)
Focus of pleasure is on eliminating and retaining bodily wastes – represents a conflict between id and ego. Resolution may lead to an 'anal expulsive' or 'anal retentive' character.

Tripartite personality
- *Id* allows us to get our basic needs met and operates on the pleasure principle.
- *Ego*'s job is to meet the needs of the id within the constraints of reality.
- *Superego* develops as a result of the moral restraints placed on us by our parents.

Ego defence mechanisms
Repression pushes unacceptable id impulses into the unconscious. *Projection* involves externalisation of unacceptable wishes onto others.

Freud recorded only a few of his **case histories**, such as the Wolf Man. Some, despite being persuaded at the time, later rejected Freud's interpretations.

Phallic stage (3-6 years)
Boys identify with their father to escape punishment as a result of their *Oedipus complex*. Girls must resolve their *Electra complex*.

Little Hans
Confirmation of the phallic stage, but does not show us whether the Oedipus complex is universal.

Research support
Solms (2000): using PET scans has provided support for the concepts of the id and ego.

Research support
Evidence of *repression*: Williams (1994) study of sexually abused women. Evidence of *reaction formation*: Adams *et al.* (1996) study of homophobics.

Latency stage (6 years-puberty)
Period where sexual desires and erogenous impulses are repressed and so become less dominant.

Neo-Freudian approaches
Others (such as Jung and Erikson) have adapted Freud's ideas, largely because of his failure to incorporate social and cultural influences.

Genital stage
Sexual urges are re-awakened. Interest turns to heterosexual relationships.

Topic 2: Social learning explanations of personality development

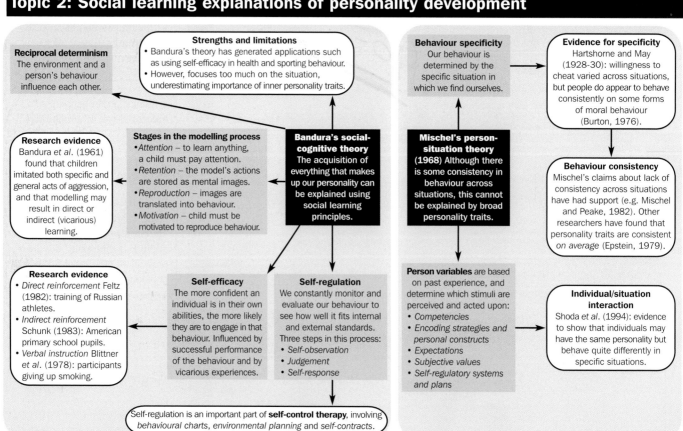

Reciprocal determinism
The environment and a person's behaviour influence each other.

Strengths and limitations
- Bandura's theory has generated applications such as using self-efficacy in health and sporting behaviour.
- However, focuses too much on the situation, underestimating importance of inner personality traits.

Behaviour specificity
Our behaviour is determined by the specific situation in which we find ourselves.

Evidence for specificity
Hartshorne and May (1928-30): willingness to cheat varied across situations, but people do appear to behave consistently on some forms of moral behaviour (Burton, 1976).

Research evidence
Bandura *et al.* (1961) found that children imitated both specific and general acts of aggression, and that modelling may result in direct or indirect (vicarious) learning.

Stages in the modelling process
- *Attention* – to learn anything, a child must pay attention.
- *Retention* – the model's actions are stored as mental images.
- *Reproduction* – images are translated into behaviour.
- *Motivation* – child must be motivated to reproduce behaviour.

Bandura's social-cognitive theory
The acquisition of everything that makes up our personality can be explained using social learning principles.

Mischel's person-situation theory (1968) Although there is some consistency in behaviour across situations, this cannot be explained by broad personality traits.

Behaviour consistency
Mischel's claims about lack of consistency across situations have had support (e.g. Mischel and Peake, 1982). Other researchers have found that personality traits are consistent *on average* (Epstein, 1979).

Research evidence
- *Direct reinforcement* Feltz (1982): training of Russian athletes.
- *Indirect reinforcement* Schunk (1983): American primary school pupils.
- *Verbal instruction* Blittner *et al.* (1978): participants giving up smoking.

Self-efficacy
The more confident an individual is in their own abilities, the more likely they are to engage in that behaviour. Influenced by successful performance of the behaviour and by vicarious experiences.

Self-regulation
We constantly monitor and evaluate our behaviour to see how well it fits internal and external standards. Three steps in this process:
- *Self-observation*
- *Judgement*
- *Self-response*

Person variables are based on past experience, and determine which stimuli are perceived and acted upon:
- *Competencies*
- *Encoding strategies and personal constructs*
- *Expectations*
- *Subjective values*
- *Self-regulatory systems and plans*

Individual/situation interaction
Shoda *et al.* (1994): evidence to show that individuals may have the same personality but behave quite differently in specific situations.

Self-regulation is an important part of **self-control therapy**, involving *behavioural charts*, *environmental planning* and *self-contracts*.

Probable questions

1. Discuss **one or more** psychodynamic explanation(s) of personality development. *(24 marks)*

2. Discuss **two** explanations of personality development. *(24 marks)*

Possible questions

3. Outline and evaluate **two** psychodynamic explanations of personality development. *(24 marks)*

Questions 1 and 2 offer you different options. You could write the same answer for both – a description and evaluation of two psychodynamic explanations. In question 1 you have the option of focusing on one explanation theory. Most students know Freud's theory extremely well and therefore have more than enough to write in 30 minutes and do not need to go beyond this theory. If you stick just to Freud you would not incur the partial performance penalty (maximum of 8 marks out of 12 for AO1, and the same for AO2).

In question 2, however, you must cover two explanations. They do not have to be psychodynamic explanations. In order to attract full marks it is not enough to do your 'Freud' essay and a little bit of something else. If you did Freud alone you might be given the full 16 marks possible for partial performance, then you need to do half as much again for your second theory.

The question on two theories (question 2 above) may be restricted to psychodynamic explanations alone, as in the case of question 3. A question of this nature means that you must know two psychodynamic explanations, though you only need to know the second one in half as much detail.

Note that there is a distinction between 'outline' (for two explanations) and 'describe' (for one explanation). 'Outline' indicates that less detail is expected whereas the use of 'describe' means that both depth and breadth are required.

Probable questions

1. Discuss **one or more** social learning explanations of personality development. *(24 marks)*

2. Outline and evaluate the social learning **and** psychodynamic approaches to personality development. *(24 marks)*

Possible questions

3. Discuss **two or more** social learning explanations of personality. *(24 marks)*

4. Compare and contrast the social learning **and** psychodynamic explanations of personality development. *(24 marks)*

Since the specification for both topics 1 and 2 is the same, the same range of questions is probable and possible. The questions given for topic 2 show the other combinations that are possible. In question 2 you are required to give one explanation from each perspective. The danger here is that you have two 30-minute essays (one probably on Freud and the other possibly on social learning theory) and must combine these in one essay. If you try to write a 60-minute answer you will lose marks on other questions. It therefore pays to prepare a shortened version of each theory just to be ready for a question such as this. It is not a good idea to leave making selections to the exam – making decisions about what to put in and what to leave out inevitably wastes precious time.

The injunction 'compare and contrast' is possible on Unit 4 but not very common. The simplest way to answer such questions is to provide a *description* of the social learning and psychodynamic explanations as the AO1 content of your essay. For AO2 credit you must consider *similarities and differences* between these two groups of explanations. If you only look at similarities or differences then you will incur a partial performance penalty. Your 'consideration' may involve evaluation but is more likely to consist of descriptions of differences/similarities (which is what makes it AO2) and evidence to support your statements (which is a form of evaluation).

TOPIC 1: PSYCHODYNAMIC EXPLANATIONS OF PERSONALITY DEVELOPMENT

SAMPLE ESSAY PLAN

Question 1: Discuss **one or more** psychodynamic explanation(s) of personality development. (24 marks)

15 MINUTES WORTH OF AO1

As description for Freud below, plus:

- Two basic **drives**: eros (the life instinct, sex) and **thanatos** (death instinct, aggression).
- Source of psychic energy from eros: **libido**.
- **Ego defence mechanisms** (e.g. repression, projection) deal with anxiety created for the ego by unacceptable id impulses.
- Part of our personality is **unconsciously motivated**, underlying emotions and impulses are buried.

15 MINUTES WORTH OF AO2

As evaluation for Freud below, plus:

- **Repression**: about 1/3 of women sexually abused as children had no recollection (**Williams**, 1994).
- **Reaction formation**: 80% of homophobics aroused by videos of male homosexual sex (**Adams et al.**, 1996).
- However, **review** of studies on oral and anal personality concluded that there is no evidence that these types are linked to early experience (**Fisher and Greenberg**, 1996).

Question 3: Outline and evaluate **two** psychodynamic explanations of personality development. (24 marks)

EXPLANATION 1: FREUD

10 MINUTES WORTH OF AO1

- **Dynamic interaction** between id, ego and superego determines our personality.
- **Tripartite personality**: **id** (pleasure principle, immediate satisfaction), **ego** (reality principle, constrains impulsive id), **superego** (moral restraint).
- At certain **stages** libido is focused on different erogenous zones. **Frustration and overindulgence** both lead to **fixations** and libido permanently locked in that stage.
- **Oral stage**, frustration may lead to **oral aggressive character** (pessimistic, envious), overindulgence to **oral receptive character** (optimistic, gullible).
- **Anal stage**, overindulgence may lead to **anal expulsive character** (disorganised, defiant), frustration to **anal retentive character** (neat, stingy).
- **Phallic stage**, Oedipus complex or Electra complex leads to identification with same sex parent and gender-appropriate traits, moral character.
- **Final stages**: Latent and genital, the fewer the unresolved conflicts the more that normal adult development can take place.

10 MINUTES WORTH OF AO2

- **Culture and gender bias** (alpha biased): Theory largely based on interviews with neurotic, middle-class Viennese women.
- Theory of normal development based on observations of **abnormal development**.
- **Case histories** could be explained differently e.g. Little Hans explained using classical conditioning.
- The theory is **unfalsifiable**, therefore fails to meet the main criterion of a scientific theory.
- Sexual nature of interpretations may be because Freud was a Victorian (**historical bias**).
- However, more **recent research** has shown support.
- **Tripartite personality** supported by brain scans showing rational part inactive during REM sleep (dreaming) but memory and motivation (id) is active (**Solms**, 2000).
- **Oral personality**: children with high orality rating more likely to have abnormal interest in food (**Blum and Miller**, 1952).

EXPLANATION 2: ERIKSON

5 MINUTES WORTH OF AO1

- **Neo-Freudian theory**, more focus on social influences.
- Personality is a **lifelong** development.
- Individuals have to resolve 8 different **psychosocial crises** at specific points in life.
- For example, during first year: **trust versus mistrust**. Positive outcome is to be trusting. **Adolescence** is a time of identity crisis.
- Everyone has a **mixture of good and bad traits** attained at each stage.

5 MINUTES WORTH OF AO2

- Theory again based on research with **abnormal individuals**, stemming from his work as a psychoanalyst.
- **Trust in infancy** supported by attachment research e.g. the love quiz which showed that early experiences of secure attachment related to trusting adult relationships (**Hazan and Shaver**, 1987).
- **Adolescence**: evidence that need not be a time of crisis if key issues are spread out (**Coleman and Hendry**, 1990).

Freud believed that two basic drives motivate all our thought and behaviours: eros (the life instinct, motivated primarily by sex) and thanatos (the death instinct, motivated primarily by aggression). The course of our development is determined by our psychic energy or libido. The structure of our personality is determined by the dynamic interaction between the three parts of the personality. The id, which operates on the pleasure principle, motivates us to meet our basic needs and is concerned with immediate satisfaction. The ego, which is governed by the reality principle, constrains the impulsive id, while at the same time allowing the id to meet its needs without the constraints of reality. The superego develops during the phallic stage as a result of the moral restraints placed on us by parents. A strong superego inhibits the id whereas a weak superego allows the id more expression. The ego must make use of ego defence mechanisms (e.g. repression and projection) to deal with the anxiety created for the ego by unacceptable id impulses. Freud believed that part of our personality is unconsciously motivated, in that many emotions and impulses are unavailable to the conscious mind.

At certain stages of development libido is focused on different erogenous zones. The child has certain needs that must be met during that stage, otherwise frustration occurs. Both frustration and overindulgence lead to fixations and some of the libido is permanently locked in that stage. In the oral stage, frustration may lead to the development of an oral aggressive character (pessimistic and envious), whereas overindulgence may lead to development of an oral receptive character (optimistic and gullible). In the anal stage, overindulgence may lead to development of an anal expulsive character (disorganised and defiant), whereas frustration may lead to development of an anal retentive character (neat and stingy). In the phallic stage, the boy experiences the Oedipus conflict, and the girl the Electra conflict. Each of these leads to identification with same-sex parent and the development of gender-appropriate traits and moral character. In the final stages, the latent and genital stages, the less energy the child has invested in unresolved conflicts the more that normal adult development can take place.

Freud's view of personality development shows a cultural bias in that his theory was largely based on interviews with neurotic, middle-class Viennese women. It is also claimed to be gender biased, in that it devalues women as being morally inferior to men, thus it displays an alpha bias. Freud's theory is also criticised for being a theory of normal development based on observations of abnormal development. Freud relied heavily on case studies as evidence for his theory, but each of these could be explained differently. For example, the case of Little Hans could be explained using classical conditioning rather than the Freudian explanation of castration anxiety. An important limitation with this theory is that it is unfalsifiable, and therefore fails to meet the main criterion of a scientific theory. The sexual nature of Freud's interpretations may be because he lived in a time of great sexual repression, therefore the theory shows an historical bias.

Despite these limitations, more recent research has shown support for many of the claims of this theory. The idea of the tripartite personality is supported by brain scans showing the rational part of the brain (equivalent to the ego) is inactive during REM sleep (dreaming) but areas of the brain involved in memory and motivation (equivalent to the id) are active (Solms, 2000). Research has also provided evidence for the oral personality, in that children with a high orality rating were more likely to have abnormal interest in food (Blum and Miller, 1952). A study of repression (Williams, 1994) found that about one-third of women who had been sexually abused as children had no recollection of the abuse, supporting the notion of ego defence mechanisms. Likewise, in a demonstration of reaction formation, Adams et al. (1996) found that 80% of homophobics were aroused by videos of male homosexual sex. However, a review of studies on oral and anal personality concluded that there is no evidence that these types are linked to early experience (Fisher and Greenberg, 1996).

Although you may feel confident enough to discuss more than one theory in detail, Freud's theory will probably be the only one you attempt for this question.

Although Freud's theory is fundamentally a theory of personality development, it may be valuable to *stress* how different personality types *develop* as this question is about personality development.

Don't go into too much detail about the Oedipal and Electra conflicts, otherwise you will quickly run out of time.

It is easy to just list these criticisms, but you should try to do more than this. Elaboration of each point helps push your AO2 marks up.

Remember the golden rule – don't just *describe* studies when using them as AO2, but *use* them to provide commentary on the theory.

SAMPLE ESSAY PLAN

Question 1: Discuss **one or more** social learning explanations of personality development. (24 marks)

15 MINUTES WORTH OF AO1

As description for Bandura below, plus:

- **Self-regulation**: each individual actively monitors behaviour.
- **Process of self-regulation** (1) self-observation, (2) judgement, (3) self-response (self-reward or self-punishment, leads to high or low **self-esteem**).
- **Self-efficacy**: an individual's perception of their own abilities (expectations) influences the likelihood of success.
- **Self-efficacy** can be **increased** directly or vicariously.

15 MINUTES WORTH OF AO2

As evaluation for Bandura below, plus:

- **Self-regulation** important in self-control therapy, make behavioural charts, change environment and self-contracts to change habits (e.g. smoking, studying).
- **Direct** reinforcement on **self-efficacy**: Russian athletes' performance improved when shown edited videos of their performance (**Feltz**, 1982).
- **Indirect reinforcement** on **self-efficacy**: children who were told that classmates had done well on a test did better themselves (**Schunk**, 1983).
- **Self-efficacy** can also be achieved through direct verbal instruction: Ps who were told they scored high on a test of willpower did better at giving up smoking (**Blittner et al.**, 1978).

Question 2: Discuss **two or more** social learning explanations of personality development. (24 marks)

EXPLANATION 1: BANDURA

7½ MINUTES WORTH OF AO1

- Social learning theory (**Bandura**) can be applied to personality.
- **Reciprocal determinism**: people change their environment and the environment shapes behaviour.
- People acquire new behaviours through **observational learning** (indirect reinforcement) and **modelling**.
- **Stages** in the modelling process: attention, retention, reproduction, motivation.
- **Motivation**: behaviour may be learned but will only continue to be reproduced if **directly reinforced**.

7½ MINUTES WORTH OF AO2

- Research on aggression (Bobo studies) (**Bandura et al.**, 1963) demonstrated observational learning in children, both specific acts and general aggressiveness.
- Bobo studies showed difference between **learning and performance**, modelling occurs when model is rewarded and when P is directly rewarded.
- **Strengths**: testable hypotheses, generated useful applications such as self-control therapy.
- **Limitations**: focuses too much on the situation though recognised interaction between person and situation; lack of unity in some of the concepts.

EXPLANATION 2: MISCHEL

7½ MINUTES WORTH OF AO1

- Traditional theories of personality overlook the **importance of context/situation**.
- **Mischel** (1968) found correlation between behaviours across different situations = .30.
- **Behaviour specificity** – people behave the same way in the same situations because of similar goals/consequences. We 'hedge' our behaviour.
- Behaviour also determined by **person variables** based on experience:
- **High competency** leads to greater task persistence.
- **Subjective values**: individual differences in values attached to behaviours.

7½ MINUTES WORTH OF AO2

- **Behaviour specificity**: people not consistent e.g. cheat in one situation and not another (**Hartshorne and May**, 1928).
- **Behaviour consistency**: same behaviour in same situations consistent across time (.65) but not across situations (.13).
- **Criticism**: correlation bound to be low when correlating two events (e.g. mood on day 5 and 17); if you correlate average ratings for two events (e.g. mood on odd and even days) then correlation increases (from .20 to .80) (**Epstein**, 1979).
- **Compromise**: apparent paradox between inconsistency and sense of one's own consistency due to having a consistent way of responding to different situations (**Mischel and Shoda**, 1998).

Although Bandura did not have a theory of personality as such, the principles of social learning theory can be applied to explain the development of everything that makes up an individual's behaviour, and therefore their personality. In his principle of reciprocal determinism, Bandura believed that people are active in that they influence their environment which in turn subsequently shapes their behaviour. People acquire new behaviours through observational learning (vicarious reinforcement) and through the process of modelling. Bandura saw four stages in the modelling process: attention to the model, retention of the model's actions in terms of mental images, reproduction into actual behaviour and finally motivation to reproduce the model's actions. Motivation is important because behaviour may be learned but will only continue to be reproduced if there is an expectation of reinforcement.

Bandura believes that individuals constantly monitor and evaluate their behaviour to judge how well it fits internal and external standards. Bandura suggests three steps in this process of self-regulation. The first is self-observation, where we monitor our behaviour and the reaction of others to the way we act. The second stage is judgement, when we judge our actions according to our own internal standards or to traditional external standards (such as politeness). Finally, in the self-response stage, if the self-comparison has been favourable, we self-reward (e.g. feeling proud) but if it is unfavourable we engage in self-punishment (e.g. feeling ashamed). If self-monitoring mostly leads to self-reward, the individual will develop a positive self-concept, whereas consistent self-punishment leads to a more negative self-concept.

Bandura stressed the importance of self-efficacy in personality development, in that an individual's perception of their own abilities (expectations) influences the likelihood of success in a behaviour, and therefore the likelihood that they will adopt it. Self-efficacy can be increased directly (through our own behaviour) or vicariously (through observing others). Observing someone of equal competence fail at a behaviour may lower our own feelings of self-efficacy.

Bandura's early work on the development of aggressive behaviour (Bandura et al., 1963) demonstrated the importance of observational learning in children, both in terms of specific acts and in general aggressiveness. These Bobo doll studies showed an important difference between learning and performance. Modelling of a behaviour only occurs when the model is rewarded for the behaviour (vicarious reinforcement) and when the individual is directly rewarded for the same behaviour. Evidence of the effect of direct reinforcement on self-efficacy has been demonstrated in the training of Russian athletes who are shown edited videos of their performance, which makes them appear better than they actually are (Feltz, 1982). Evidence for the effect of indirect reinforcement was shown in a study of children who, when they were told that classmates had done well on a test, did better themselves (Schunk, 1983). Self-efficacy has also been shown to develop through direct verbal instruction. Participants who were told they had scored high on a test of personal control and willpower later did better at giving up smoking compared to a control group (Blittner et al., 1978). Self-regulation is an important component of self-control therapy. By making behavioural charts, changing the environment and developing self-contracts, this form of therapy has been found to be effective in dealing with habit problems such as smoking and studying.

The strengths of Bandura's theory include the fact that it lends itself to empirical research, with clearly defined terms and testable hypotheses, and it has generated useful applications, such as using self-efficacy to improve health behaviour and sporting performance. Limitations include the fact that the theory focuses too much on the situation, largely ignoring the role of inner personality traits. However, unlike Freud, who overemphasised person variables in personality development, Bandura recognised that there was an interaction between the person and the situation. Critics claim there is a lack of unity in some of the concepts, in that although observational learning and self-efficacy are well-researched, there is little explanation of the relationship between them.

Don't get tempted to describe the Bobo doll studies here, but use the principles of SLT to explain how an individual develops their personality.

Self-efficacy is a measure of the effectiveness of a person to bring about desired ends. We do not incorporate everything we observe into our own makeup.

The fact that research studies have been shown to support the assumptions of the theory counts as AO2 commentary. However, you need to make this explicit rather than relying on the examiner to make the link.

Making a point of contrast between this theory and Freud's theory is a useful form of AO2, particularly if you're running out of things to say!

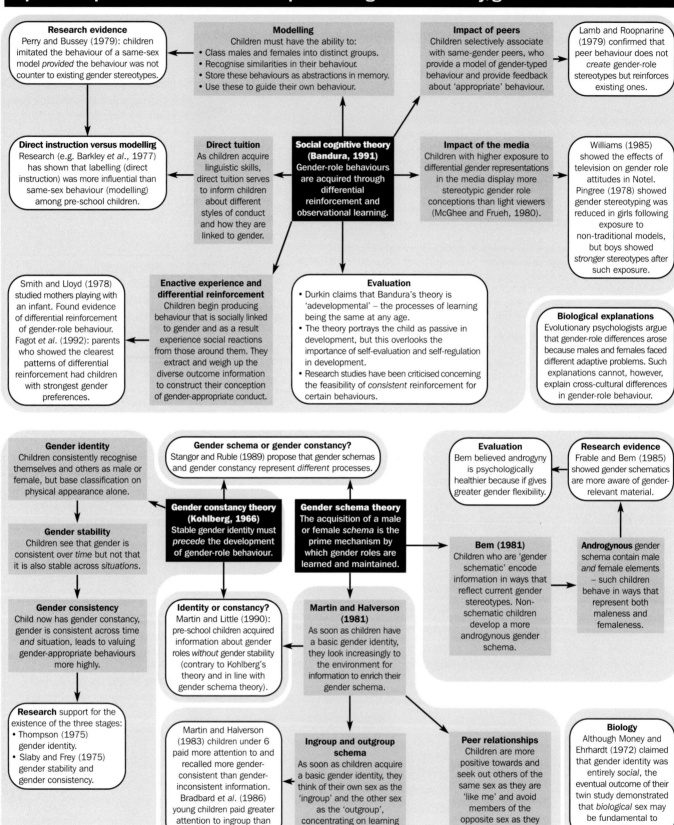

Research evidence
Perry and Bussey (1979): children imitated the behaviour of a same-sex model *provided* the behaviour was not counter to existing gender stereotypes.

Modelling
Children must have the ability to:
• Class males and females into distinct groups.
• Recognise similarities in their behaviour.
• Store these behaviours as abstractions in memory.
• Use these to guide their own behaviour.

Impact of peers
Children selectively associate with same-gender peers, who provide a model of gender-typed behaviour and provide feedback about 'appropriate' behaviour.

Lamb and Roopnarine (1979) confirmed that peer behaviour does not *create* gender-role stereotypes but reinforces existing ones.

Direct instruction versus modelling
Research (e.g. Barkley *et al.*, 1977) has shown that labelling (direct instruction) was more influential than same-sex behaviour (modelling) among pre-school children.

Direct tuition
As children acquire linguistic skills, direct tuition serves to inform children about different styles of conduct and how they are linked to gender.

Social cognitive theory (Bandura, 1991)
Gender-role behaviours are acquired through differential reinforcement and observational learning.

Impact of the media
Children with higher exposure to differential gender representations in the media display more stereotypic gender role conceptions than light viewers (McGhee and Frueh, 1980).

Williams (1985) showed the effects of television on gender role attitudes in Notel. Pingree (1978) showed gender stereotyping was reduced in girls following exposure to non-traditional models, but boys showed *stronger* stereotypes after such exposure.

Smith and Lloyd (1978) studied mothers playing with an infant. Found evidence of differential reinforcement of gender-role behaviour. Fagot *et al.* (1992): parents who showed the clearest patterns of differential reinforcement had children with strongest gender preferences.

Enactive experience and differential reinforcement
Children begin producing behaviour that is socially linked to gender and as a result experience social reactions from those around them. They extract and weigh up the diverse outcome information to construct their conception of gender-appropriate conduct.

Evaluation
• Durkin claims that Bandura's theory is 'adevelopmental' – the processes of learning being the same at any age.
• The theory portrays the child as passive in development, but this overlooks the importance of self-evaluation and self-regulation in development.
• Research studies have been criticised concerning the feasibility of *consistent* reinforcement for certain behaviours.

Biological explanations
Evolutionary psychologists argue that gender-role differences arose because males and females faced different adaptive problems. Such explanations cannot, however, explain cross-cultural differences in gender-role behaviour.

Gender identity
Children consistently recognise themselves and others as male or female, but base classification on physical appearance alone.

Gender schema or gender constancy?
Stangor and Ruble (1989) propose that gender schemas and gender constancy represent *different* processes.

Evaluation
Bem believed androgyny is psychologically healthier because if gives greater gender flexibility.

Research evidence
Frable and Bem (1985) showed gender schematics are more aware of gender-relevant material.

Gender stability
Children see that gender is consistent over *time* but not that it is also stable across *situations*.

Gender constancy theory (Kohlberg, 1966)
Stable gender identity must *precede* the development of gender-role behaviour.

Gender schema theory
The acquisition of a male or female *schema* is the prime mechanism by which gender roles are learned and maintained.

Bem (1981)
Children who are 'gender schematic' encode information in ways that reflect current gender stereotypes. Non-schematic children develop a more androgynous gender schema.

Androgynous gender schema contain male *and* female elements – such children behave in ways that represent both maleness and femaleness.

Gender consistency
Child now has gender constancy, gender is consistent across time *and* situation, leads to valuing gender-appropriate behaviours more highly.

Identity or constancy?
Martin and Little (1990): pre-school children acquired information about gender roles *without* gender stability (contrary to Kohlberg's theory and in line with gender schema theory).

Martin and Halverson (1981)
As soon as children have a basic gender identity, they look increasingly to the environment for information to enrich their gender schema.

Research support for the existence of the three stages:
• Thompson (1975) gender identity.
• Slaby and Frey (1975) gender stability and gender consistency.

Martin and Halverson (1983) children under 6 paid more attention to and recalled more gender-consistent than gender-inconsistent information. Bradbard *et al.* (1986) young children paid greater attention to ingroup than outgroup schemas.

Ingroup and outgroup schema
As soon as children acquire a basic gender identity, they think of their own sex as the 'ingroup' and the other sex as the 'outgroup', concentrating on learning activities on ingroup.

Peer relationships
Children are more positive towards and seek out others of the same sex as they are 'like me' and avoid members of the opposite sex as they are 'not like me'.

Biology
Although Money and Ehrhardt (1972) claimed that gender identity was entirely *social*, the eventual outcome of their twin study demonstrated that *biological* sex may be fundamental to gender identity.

explanations of the development of gender roles (e.g. social learning theories, cognitive-developmental theories)

Probable questions

1. Describe and evaluate **one** explanation of the development of gender identity/gender roles. *(24 marks)*

2. Outline and evaluate **two** explanations of the development of gender identity/gender roles. *(24 marks)*

Possible questions

3. (a) Describe **one** explanation of the development of gender identity/gender roles. *(12 marks)*

   (b) To what extent is the explanation of the development of gender identity/gender roles you described in (a) supported by research studies? *(12 marks)*

The specification does not distinguish between gender identity and gender roles as they are overlapping concepts. Your gender identity affects the gender roles you adopt so it is difficult, in practice, to separate these concepts.

You may be asked to discuss one theory (as in question 1) or to discuss two theories (as in question 2). This means that you need to have one 30-minute explanation (for example social learning theory). This would enable you to answer question 1. For question 2 you can use a reduced 15-minute version of this theory plus a second explanation. You only need a 15-minute version of the second theory (7½ minutes worth of AO1 and 7½ minutes worth of AO2).

You are not required to present both theories in balance but it is best to try to do this because, if you present a very abbreviated version of explanation 2, then you are unlikely to provide sufficient detail/elaboration.

In the case of both questions it would be permissible to include several theories under the heading of 'the social learning explanation' or 'the cognitive-developmental explanation'.

If you wish to use an alternative theory/explanation as a form of commentary this is acceptable but you must recognise that it is not sufficient to simply write 'An alternative theory is …' and then provide a description of the alternative theory. This is not evaluation (AO2). For AO2 credit you must use aspects of the alternative theory to make critical comments about the first theory.

Part (a) is a straightforward AO1 question. Part (b) is more challenging. It is all AO2 which means that descriptions of research studies would gain little, if any, credit. You must cut out such descriptions and focus on what the research study tells us. Does it provide support for the explanation? If so, how does it support the explanation? Does it challenge the explanation? You can gain further AO2 credit by considering the methodological flaws or strengths of the studies – is the validity of the study challenged? You can also contrast one study with another study.

SAMPLE ESSAY PLAN

Question 2: Outline and evaluate **two** explanations of the development of gender identity/gender roles. (24 marks)

EXPLANATION 1: SOCIAL COGNITIVE THEORY (BANDURA, 1991)

7½ MINUTES WORTH OF AO1

- *Gender identity/roles acquired through 3 major* **modes of influence:**
- *(1)* **Modelling:** *notice behaviour of males/females, store abstractions which are then used as models for own behaviour.*
- *(2)* **Enactive experience:** *as child becomes mobile behaviours enacted and child receives* **direct, differential** *reinforcement.*
- *Boys and girls are* **reinforced quite differently** *e.g. fathers react more negatively to sons' feminine behaviours than mothers* (**Idle et al.**, 1993).
- *(3)* **Direct tuition:** *when language skills acquired children* **told** *how to behave, though the effect is weakened when models say one thing and do another* (**Hildebrandt et al.**, 1973).

7½ MINUTES WORTH OF AO2

- *Evidence for modelling comes from studies on aggression* (**Bandura et al.**, 1961) *and on gender* (**Perry and Bussey**, 1979). *The effects of modelling are limited by existing* **stereotypes.**
- **Direct instruction** *may override modelling: boys played with toys labelled 'boys toys' even after seeing girls playing with them* (**Martin et al.**, 1995).
- *Evidence for* **differential reinforcement** *e.g. mothers selected gender-appropriate toys when playing with a child 'labelled' as girl or boy* (**Smith and Lloyd**, 1978).
- **Criticisms:** *lacks the developmental sequence of cognitive-developmental theories – though there is a sequence.*

EXPLANATION 2: COGNITIVE-DEVELOPMENTAL (KOHLBERG, 1966)

7½ MINUTES WORTH OF AO1

- **Stable gender identity** *precedes gender-role behaviour.*
- **Cognitive maturation** *governs development e.g. conservation skills, which lead to gender constancy, the belief that gender is fixed and irreversible.*
- **Stage (1):** *gender identity (age 2–3) – gender identity based on physical appearance alone.*
- **Stage (2):** *gender stability (age 4) – gender is consistent across time but not situations.*
- **Stage (3):** *gender consistency (age 6–7) – gender is consistent over time and situation.*
- *With gender consistency, higher value given to* **gender-appropriate** *behaviours, lower value to gender-inappropriate behaviours.*

7½ MINUTES WORTH OF AO2

- *Evidence that* **conservation** *abilities appear after age 7* (**Piaget**).
- *Evidence for stages: 2-year olds were 76% correct in their identification of sex, whereas 3-year olds were 90% correct* (**Thompson**, 1975).
- *Evidence for gender stability: children age 3–4 don't recognise sex-related traits consistent over time e.g. asked 'when you grow up will you be a mummy or daddy?'* (**Slaby and Frey**, 1975).
- *Children high in gender constancy showed the greatest interest in same-sex models* (**Slaby and Frey**, 1975).
- **Strengths:** *sets out an invariant developmental sequence for gender-role development.*
- **Limitations:** *gender-schema research suggests gender constancy not necessary for gender-role development* (**Martin and Little**, 1990), *children start collecting information about gender-appropriate stereotypes as soon as they are aware of their gender identity.*

Question 1: Describe and evaluate **one** explanation of the development of gender identity/gender roles. (24 marks)

SOCIAL COGNITIVE THEORY (BANDURA, 1991)

15 MINUTES WORTH OF AO1

As description for social cognitive theory above, plus:

- **Peers** *act as models and reinforcers, rewarding gender-appropriate behaviour and punishing gender-inappropriate behaviour* (**Lamb et al.**, 1980).
- **Boys** *more likely to be criticised for feminine behaviour than girls for masculine behaviour* (**Fagot**, 1985).
- **Media** *(TV, ads) portrays men and women differently (e.g. independent, directive versus dependent, emotional)* (**Bussey and Bandura**, 1999).
- **Media models** *create sense of* **self-efficacy:** *increases boys' sense of control and girls' sense of being controlled* (**Hodges et al.**, 1981).

15 MINUTES WORTH OF AO2

As evaluation for social cognitive theory above, plus:

- **Peers** *may be the prime socialising agent* (**Maccoby**, 1998) *though it may simply reinforce existing stereotypes – when male-typed behaviour was reinforced in girls it continued for a shorter time than when reinforced in boys* (**Lamb and Roopnarine**, 1979).
- *Introduction of* **TV** *in a Canadian town led to more stereotyped gender roles* (**Williams**, 1985).
- *Showing girls* **ads** *of women in non-traditional roles led to reduced stereotyping* (**Pingree**, 1978).
- *Children's* **books** *have changed in the way they portray men and women* (**Crabb and Bielawski**, 1994).

Criticisms

- *Child is mainly* **passive** *– though there is a shift from external reinforcement to self-regulation.*
- *Some of the research support is* **short-term and contrived.**

In Bandura's social cognitive theory, gender roles are acquired through 3 major modes of influence. The first of these is modelling. For modelling to influence gender-role development, children must have the ability to classify males and females into two distinct groups and to recognise similarities in their behaviour. Children notice the behaviours that are performed frequently by their own sex and infrequently by the opposite sex. They must then store these in their memory in order to guide their own behaviour. The second mode of influence occurs as the child becomes mobile, they become capable of acting directly on their environment and so receive differential reinforcement for their gender-role behaviours (enactive experience). Boys and girls are reinforced quite differently, e.g. fathers react more negatively to their sons' feminine behaviours than do mothers (Idle et al., 1993). Children may also learn aspects of their gender role through direct tuition. The third mode of influence occurs when language skills are acquired: children are told how to behave, although the effect is weakened when models say one thing and do another (Hildebrandt et al., 1973).

> The use of the term 'social cognitive theory' rather than 'social learning theory' simply reflects Bandura's development of SLT to include the notion of mental abstractions in social learning.

Evidence for the influence of modelling comes from Bandura's early work on aggression (Bandura et al., 1961) and on gender, where children were found to imitate behaviour of same-sex model unless the model portrayed a gender-inappropriate behaviour (Perry and Bussey, 1979). This shows that the effects of modelling are limited by existing stereotypes. Martin et al. (1995) showed that pre-school boys played with toys labelled 'boys toys' even after seeing girls playing with them but did not play with toys labelled 'girls toys' after seeing boys play with them. This demonstrates that in this age group, direct instruction may be more important than same-sex modelling. There is also evidence for the influence of differential reinforcement. Smith and Lloyd (1978) found that mothers selected gender-appropriate toys when playing with a child 'labelled' as girl or boy and responded more when the children showed gender-appropriate behaviour. Despite this evidence, the theory can be criticised for lacking the developmental sequence of cognitive-developmental theories, and for portraying the child as relatively passive in his or her development.

> When introducing a study as AO2, it is important to say what it contributes to your commentary. Note the use of the words 'This demonstrates that…'

Kohlberg (1966) believed that a stable gender identity must precede gender-role behaviour. In his theory of gender constancy, he claimed that cognitive maturation governs the development of gender identity and gender role. Particularly important in this process are conservation skills. When children have developed these, they acquire gender constancy, the belief that their own gender is fixed and irreversible. Children gradually move through three stages of gender-role development. First they acquire gender identity (age 2–3), where they recognise themselves and others as either male or female, but base this on physical appearance alone, and so gender identity changes with appearance. At around the age of 4, they develop gender stability, where gender is seen as consistent across time, but not across situations. Boys may still turn into girls if they engage in feminine activities. At about 6, children believe that gender is consistent across time and situation. Higher value is now given to gender-appropriate behaviours, and lower value to gender-inappropriate behaviours.

> The inclusion of the ages in this sequence is not absolutely necessary, but it helps in this case because AO2 commentary later focuses on the age/stage relationship.

Research evidence supporting the emergence of conservation skills at approximately age 6–7 (Piaget) are consistent with Kohlberg's claim that gender constancy develops at about the same age. Evidence for the age basis of gender identity comes from Thompson (1975), who found that 2-year-olds were 76% correct in their identification of sex, whereas 3-year-olds were 90% correct. Evidence for gender stability comes from Slaby and Frey (1975), who found that children did not recognise that sex-related traits were consistent over time until 3–4 years old, as Kohlberg had predicted. Slaby and Frey also found, again as predicted by Kohlberg, that children high in gender constancy showed the greatest interest in same-sex models. Strengths of this theory include the fact that it sets out an invariant developmental sequence for gender-role development, but Kohlberg's claim that gender constancy is necessary for gender-role development to begin is challenged by gender schema research (e.g. Martin and Little, 1990), which has found that children start collecting information about gender-appropriate stereotypes as soon as they are aware of their gender identity.

> The introduction of an alternative perspective (gender schema theory) is used explicitly here to highlight a limitation of Kohlberg's theory.

Topic 1: Social development in adolescence

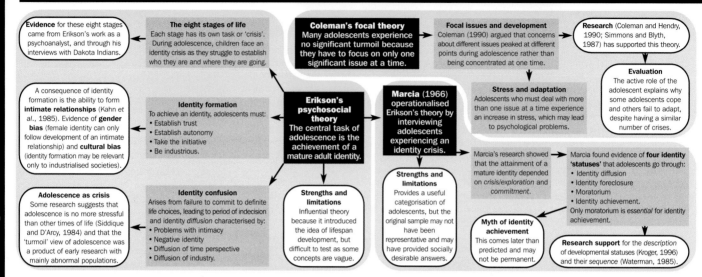

Evidence for these eight stages came from Erikson's work as a psychoanalyst, and through his interviews with Dakota Indians.

The eight stages of life
Each stage has its own task or 'crisis'. During adolescence, children face an identity crisis as they struggle to establish who they are and where they are going.

Coleman's focal theory
Many adolescents experience no significant turmoil because they have to focus on only one significant issue at a time.

Focal issues and development
Coleman (1990) argued that concerns about different issues peaked at different points during adolescence rather than being concentrated at one time.

Research (Coleman and Hendry, 1990; Simmons and Blyth, 1987) has supported this theory.

A consequence of identity formation is the ability to form **intimate relationships** (Kahn et al., 1985). Evidence of **gender bias** (female identity can only follow development of an intimate relationship) and **cultural bias** (identity formation may be relevant only to industrialised societies).

Identity formation
To achieve an identity, adolescents must:
• Establish trust
• Establish autonomy
• Take the initiative
• Be industrious.

Erikson's psychosocial theory
The central task of adolescence is the achievement of a mature adult identity.

Marcia (1966) operationalised Erikson's theory by interviewing adolescents experiencing an identity crisis.

Stress and adaptation
Adolescents who must deal with more than one issue at a time experience an increase in stress, which may lead to psychological problems.

Evaluation
The active role of the adolescent explains why some adolescents cope and others fail to adapt, despite having a similar number of crises.

Adolescence as crisis
Some research suggests that adolescence is no more stressful than other times of life (Siddique and D'Arcy, 1984) and that the 'turmoil' view of adolescence was a product of early research with mainly abnormal populations.

Identity confusion
Arises from failure to commit to definite life choices, leading to period of indecision and identity *diffusion* characterised by:
• Problems with intimacy
• Negative identity
• Diffusion of time perspective
• Diffusion of industry.

Strengths and limitations
Influential theory because it introduced the idea of lifespan development, but difficult to test as some concepts are vague.

Strengths and limitations
Provides a useful categorisation of adolescents, but the original sample may not have been representative and may have provided socially desirable answers.

Marcia's research showed that the attainment of a mature identity depended on *crisis/exploration* and *commitment*.

Marcia found evidence of **four identity 'statuses'** that adolescents go through:
• Identity diffusion
• Identity foreclosure
• Moratorium
• Identity achievement.
Only moratorium is *essential* for identity achievement.

Myth of identity achievement
This comes later than predicted and may not be permanent.

Research support for the *description* of developmental statuses (Kroger, 1996) and their *sequence* (Waterman, 1985).

Topic 2: Relationships with parents and peers during adolescence

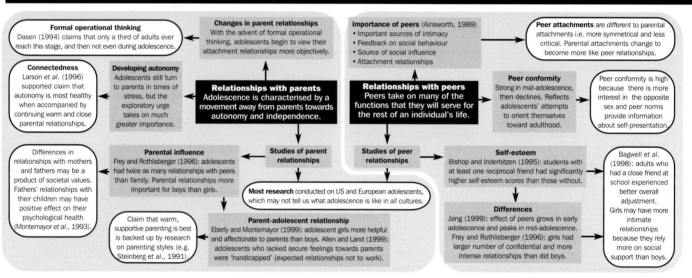

Formal operational thinking
Dasen (1994) claims that only a third of adults ever reach this stage, and then not even during adolescence.

Changes in parent relationships
With the advent of formal operational thinking, adolescents begin to view their attachment relationships more objectively.

Importance of peers (Ainsworth, 1989)
• Important sources of intimacy
• Feedback on social behaviour
• Source of social influence
• Attachment relationships

Peer attachments are *different* to parental attachments i.e. more symmetrical and less critical. Parental attachments change to become more like peer relationships.

Connectedness
Larson et al. (1996) supported claim that autonomy is most healthy when accompanied by continuing warm and close parental relationships.

Developing autonomy
Adolescents still turn to parents in times of stress, but the exploratory urge takes on much greater importance.

Relationships with parents
Adolescence is characterised by a movement away from parents towards autonomy and independence.

Relationships with peers
Peers take on many of the functions that they will serve for the rest of an individual's life.

Peer conformity
Strong in mid-adolescence, then declines. Reflects adolescents' attempts to orient themselves toward adulthood.

Peer conformity is high because there is more interest in the opposite sex and peer norms provide information about self-presentation.

Differences in relationships with mothers and fathers may be a product of societal values. Fathers' relationships with their children have positive effect on their psychological health (Montemayor et al., 1993).

Parental influence
Frey and Rothlisberger (1996): adolescents had twice as many relationships with peers than family. Parental relationships more important for boys than girls.

Studies of parent relationships

Studies of peer relationships

Self-esteem
Bishop and Inderbitzen (1995): students with at least one reciprocal friend had significantly higher self-esteem scores than those without.

Bagwell et al. (1998): adults who had a close friend at school experienced better overall adjustment. Girls may have more intimate relationships because they rely more on social support than boys.

Claim that warm, supportive parenting is best is backed up by research on parenting styles (e.g. Steinberg et al., 1991).

Most research conducted on US and European adolescents, which may not tell us what adolescence is like in *all* cultures.

Parent-adolescent relationship
Eberly and Montemayor (1999): adolescent girls more helpful and affectionate to parents than boys. Allen and Land (1999): adolescents who lacked secure feelings towards parents were 'handicapped' (expected relationships not to work).

Differences
Jang (1999): effect of peers grows in early adolescence and peaks in mid-adolescence. Frey and Rothlisberger (1996): girls had larger number of confidential and more intense relationships than did boys.

Topic 3: Cultural differences in adolescent behaviour

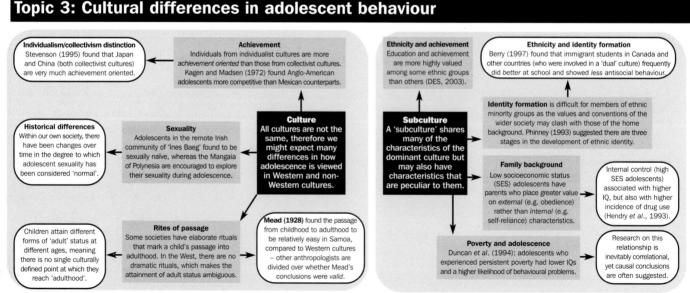

Individualism/collectivism distinction
Stevenson (1995) found that Japan and China (both collectivist cultures) are very much achievement oriented.

Achievement
Individuals from individualist cultures are more *achievement oriented* than those from collectivist cultures. Kagen and Madsen (1972) found Anglo-American adolescents more competitive than Mexican counterparts.

Ethnicity and achievement
Education and achievement are more highly valued among some ethnic groups than others (DES, 2003).

Ethnicity and identity formation
Berry (1997) found that immigrant students in Canada and other countries (who were involved in a 'dual' culture) frequently did *better* at school and showed *less* antisocial behaviour.

Identity formation is difficult for members of ethnic minority groups as the values and conventions of the wider society may clash with those of the home background. Phinney (1993) suggested there are three stages in the development of ethnic identity.

Historical differences
Within our own society, there have been changes over time in the degree to which adolescent sexuality has been considered 'normal'.

Sexuality
Adolescents in the remote Irish community of 'Ines Baeg' found to be sexually naïve, whereas the Mangaia of Polynesia are encouraged to explore their sexuality during adolescence.

Culture
All cultures are not the same, therefore we might expect many differences in how adolescence is viewed in Western and non-Western cultures.

Subculture
A 'subculture' shares many of the characteristics of the dominant culture but may also have characteristics that are peculiar to them.

Family background
Low socioeconomic status (SES) adolescents have parents who place greater value on *external* (e.g. obedience) rather than *internal* (e.g. self-reliance) characteristics.

Internal control (high SES adolescents) associated with higher IQ, but also with higher incidence of drug use (Hendry et al., 1993).

Children attain different forms of 'adult' status at different ages, meaning there is no single culturally defined point at which they reach 'adulthood'.

Rites of passage
Some societies have elaborate rituals that mark a child's passage into adulthood. In the West, there are no dramatic rituals, which makes the attainment of adult status ambiguous.

Mead (1928) found the passage from childhood to adulthood to be relatively easy in Samoa, compared to Western cultures – other anthropologists are divided over whether Mead's conclusions were *valid*.

Poverty and adolescence
Duncan et al. (1994): adolescents who experienced persistent poverty had lower IQs and a higher likelihood of behavioural problems.

Research on this relationship is inevitably correlational, yet causal conclusions are often suggested.

research into social development in adolescence, including the formation of identity (e.g. Marcia)

Probable questions

1. Discuss research (theories **and/or** studies) into social development in adolescence. *(24 marks)*

2. Discuss research (theories **and/or** studies) into the formation of identity in adolescence. *(24 marks)*

Possible questions

3 (a) Outline research into social development in adolescence. *(12 marks)*

(b) To what extent do relationships with parents **and/or** peers influence this process? *(12 marks)*

These two questions follow the specification closely – the specification identifies the general area of study (social development in adolescence) and then narrows this down to one particular area (formation of identity). You could use your answer for question 2 to answer, though it might be viewed as 'slightly limited' because of the exclusive focus on identity.

In both cases it is likely that the AO1 content will be a description of appropriate theories and studies. Such studies could alternatively be used as evaluation as long as the focus is on using such studies rather than describing them.

Although unlikely, it *is* possible that the two topics in this division might be combined in one question. The first part of the question is straightforward, but the second asks you to judge whether social development is influenced by relationships with parents and/or peers. This calls for more than just description, it calls for a considered appraisal of whether it is or it isn't. In other words, you are in AO2 territory for part (b), so you need to make sure that's what you are doing rather than just treating it as an excuse for more AO1.

---

research into relationships with parents and peers during adolescence

Probable questions

1. Critically consider research (theories **and/or** studies) into relationships with parents **and/or** peers during adolescence. *(24 marks)*

2. (a) Describe research (theories **and/or** studies) into social development in adolescence. *(12 marks)*

(b) To what extent do relationships with parents **and/or** peers influence this development? *(12 marks)*

Possible questions

3. Discuss research (theories **and/or** studies) into relationships with parents during adolescence. *(24 marks)*

4. Discuss research (theories **and/or** studies) into relationships with peers during adolescence. *(24 marks)*

The injunction 'critically consider' means the same as 'discuss', i.e. you should describe and evaluate what follows.

In both questions 1 and 2 you are permitted to focus on parents and/or peers (both or one). The danger with such essays is that you have too much to write and this results in either too much AO1 and too little AO2 (because of lack of time), or too little time for other questions on the paper. It is vital that you are selective in what you use in an exam essay. You can't always include all you know. It is more important to provide detail/elaboration for a few studies than briefly mentioning a lot of studies (about five or six studies would be about right – leaving time to include sufficient detail).

Part (b) of question 2 is the slightly more challenging 'to what extent?'. It is more challenging because you have to be careful not to describe the research but instead you must focus on whether development has been affected, and *use* your knowledge of research to answer this question rather than *describing* it.

It is less probable that you would be asked a question about relationships with parents *or* peers only but since this is possible you do need to be prepared with a 30-minute essay for each.

---

research into cultural differences in adolescent behaviour

Probable questions

1. Discuss research (theories **and/or** studies) into cultural differences in adolescent behaviour. *(24 marks)*

2. (a) Describe research (theories **and/or** studies) into social development in adolescence. *(12 marks)*

(b) To what extent are there cultural differences in adolescent behaviour? *(12 marks)*

Possible questions

3. (a) Discuss research (theories **and/or** studies) into relationships with parents during adolescence. *(12 marks)*

(b) Discuss research (theories **and/or** studies) into cultural differences in adolescent behaviour. *(12 marks)*

You can see that question 1 is directly lifted from the specification. You may use theories or studies, or both, as the AO1 content of your answer. The same advice applies here as given earlier – studies could also be used as evaluation as long as they are used in this way.

Question 2 combines two topics from this division, a perfectly legitimate way to set a question (in fact it is legitimate to combine topics from two different divisions within one sub-section). Your answer to part (a) of question 2 would be the same as for question 2 (a) in topic 2. Your answer for part (b) will draw on the same material that you would use in answer to question 1 in topic 3 – except this time you must omit the AO1 description and focus on what the research tells us about cultural differences. Any plus or minus points about the research could be used as part of your answer because a 'bad' piece of research doesn't tell us much.

It is possible that two topics from the division could be combined in this way. Such a question would mean that you have (hopefully) lots to write, but take care not to be fooled by this. You still have only 30 minutes so you must be selective. You won't gain extra marks by writing a longer answer.

TOPIC 1: SOCIAL DEVELOPMENT IN ADOLESCENCE

SAMPLE ESSAY PLAN

Question 1: Discuss research (theories and/or studies) into social development in adolescence. (24 marks)

IDENTITY DEVELOPMENT

10 MINUTES WORTH OF AO1

- **Erikson** (1968) formulated 8 stages of life, at each stage a **psychosocial crisis** needs to be resolved.
- **Stage 5 is adolescence**, the crisis is **identity**, unsuccessful resolution leads to **identity confusion**.
- To achieve **successful identity** need to establish trust, autonomy, initiative, and be industrious.
- The **negative outcome** (confusion) occurs when an individual can't commit to life choices.
- Leads to **unhealthy identity diffusion**: problems with intimacy, negative identity, diffusion of time perspective (lack of interest in planning for the future), and diffusion of industry.
- **Marcia** (1966) **operationalised** Erikson's theory through interviews with adolescents.
- **Key variables** in attaining mature identity: crisis/exploration (questions parental values and searches for alternatives) and commitment.
- **Four identity statuses**: identity diffusion (crisis not yet experienced), foreclosure, moratorium, achievement (crisis resolved).

10 MINUTES WORTH OF AO2

- **Erikson's** theory largely derived from experience as psychoanalyst therefore **grounded in abnormal behaviour** which may lead to view of adolescence as crisis.
- Adolescence **not more stressful** than any other stage: 2/3 of adolescents interviewed reported no or mild distress (**Siddique and D'Arcy**, 1984).
- But **Smith and Crawford** (1986) found 60% of adolescents think about suicide.
- Students low in identity development less successful in **intimate relationships** (**Kahn et al.**, 1985).
- **Support for identity statuses**: increase of achievement and decrease of diffusion with age (**Waterman**, 1985).
- But **Meilman** (1979) found only 50% of men interviewed reached achievement by 24.
- **Marcia** (1976) found some who had achieved identity returned later to foreclosure or diffusion.

OTHER SOCIAL DEVELOPMENT

5 MINUTES WORTH OF AO1

- **Coleman's focal theory** (1974) proposed that adolescents deal with a number of issues.
- **Certain (focal) issues** peak at particular stages of development e.g. physical changes of puberty, fear of peer group rejection, conflict with parents.
- **Stress** occurs when a number of issues occur at same time.

5 MINUTES WORTH OF AO2

- **Empirical support**: 800 children aged 11–17, different issues peaked at particular ages e.g. peer group rejection age 15, anxiety about romantic relationships age 17 (**Coleman and Hendry**, 1990).
- Further supported by **Simmons and Blyth** (1987): self-esteem and school performance lowered when adolescents coping with 3 or more transitions.
- Is this just a theory of **life events** applied to adolescence? But adolescent plays an active role – a **person-context** approach.

Question 2: Discuss research (theories and/or studies) into the formation of identity in adolescence. (24 marks)

15 MINUTES WORTH OF AO1

As description of identity development above, plus:

- **Erikson**: identity established by trying out different identities.
- Identity is **multi-dimensional**: sexual, religious, political, ideological, occupational.
- **Marcia**: one status is not a prerequisite for the next though moratorium appears to be a prerequisite for identity achievement.

15 MINUTES WORTH OF AO2

As evaluation of identity development above, plus:

- **Gender bias**: Erikson suggested that male intimacy comes after identity, female intimacy comes before, but this may no longer be the case.
- **Culture bias**: choices only available in industrialised societies so identity formation may not be relevant (**Kroger**, 1996).
- **Identity-achievers** function well under stress, whereas those in moratorium more anxious and avoided intimate relationships (**Kroger**, 1996).

Erikson (1968) suggested there were eight stages of life, with each stage associated with a different psychosocial crisis. The fifth of these stages is adolescence, and the associated crisis is the formation of an identity. In order to achieve a successful identity, the adolescent must establish trust in others, and establish autonomy by breaking away from parental control. They must take the initiative in terms of future goals and plans, and be industrious in working towards the achievement of these. An individual who does not navigate this process successfully is left with identity confusion. This state is characterised by uncertainty, and occurs when adolescents are unable to commit to life choices. Erikson believed this becomes unhealthy if the individual cannot move out of this period of indecision called identity diffusion. This state of identity diffusion is characterised by problems with intimacy, negative identity, diffusion of time perspective, and diffusion of industry, where the adolescent lacks the ability to concentrate on current responsibilities. Marcia (1966) operationalised Erikson's theory through interviews with adolescents and found evidence for two key variables in the attainment of a mature identity – (1) crisis/exploration, where the adolescent questions parental goals and values and searches for personal alternatives, and (2) commitment, where they commit to their own goals and values. Marcia found there were four distinct stages in this process, from identity diffusion, where the individual has yet to experience an identity crisis, through foreclosure, moratorium, and finally achievement, where they have experienced an identity crisis and resolved it in their own way.

Erikson's theory was largely derived from his experience as psychoanalyst and therefore was grounded in the study of abnormal individuals, which may have led him to view adolescence as a time of crisis. Some research has shown that, contrary to Erikson's claims, adolescence is no more stressful than any other stage of life. In one study, two-thirds of adolescents interviewed reported no stress or just mild psychological distress (Siddique and D'Arcy, 1984). In defence of the view of adolescence as a state of turmoil, Smith and Crawford (1986) found that 60% of adolescents reported at least one instance of suicidal thinking. Erikson's claim that a consequence of identity formation was the ability to form intimate relationships was supported in a study by Kahn et al. (1985), which showed that students assessed as low in identity development were less successful in developing intimate relationships later on. There is also support for Marcia's claim that there are four identity stages (or statuses). Waterman (1985) found an increase in identity achievement and a decrease in diffusion status with age. However, research from Meilman (1979) suggested that identity achievement may not actually be a part of adolescence, in that only 50% of the men interviewed in this study had reached identity achievement by the age of 24. Marcia (1976) also found that some people who had achieved identity returned later to foreclosure or diffusion.

Coleman's focal theory (1974) proposed that concerns about different issues peaked at different points during adolescence. For example, issues such as fear of peer group rejection and conflict with parents tend to come into focus at different stages of development. When the individual has finished with one problem, they are then ready to cope with another. Because adaptation to the changing demands of adolescence is spread over a relatively long period, the stresses of adolescence are rarely concentrated at any one time. However, adolescents who have to deal with more than one issue at a time are more at risk than those for whom these issues are more spaced out. This may lead to an increase in stress, which may lead to psychological problems.

Support for Coleman's theory comes from a study of children aged 11–17, which found that different issues peaked at particular ages, e.g. fear of peer group rejection peaked at age 15, and anxiety about romantic relationships peaked at age 17 (Coleman and Hendry, 1990). Further support comes from Simmons and Blyth (1987), who found that self-esteem and school performance were unaffected when adolescents were dealing with just one crisis, but dropped significantly in adolescents coping with 3 or more life transitions. Critics claim that Coleman's theory is just a theory of life events that has been applied to adolescence, but Coleman claims that the value of this approach is that it explains why some adolescents cope and others fail to adapt despite having the same number of crises.

Don't make the mistake of describing all eight stages, only the one that is relevant to adolescence.

It is not essential to include Marcia's research, although it does complement Erikson's theory well. In another context, Marcia's research could have been used as *commentary* on Erikson's theory.

Note that several times there is a 'reminder' of an assumption of the theory followed by a research finding that supports (or challenges) this assumption. This is a good way to organise your commentary to make it effective.

Although Coleman's theory has not been given the same number of 'column inches' as Erikson's theory, it is still important for the description to be detailed. You are not required to give equal time to both theories but detail is required for high marks.

This final point emphasises the important interaction of the individual adolescent and the context of their development.

SAMPLE ESSAY PLAN

Question 1: Critically consider research (theories **and/or** studies) into relationships with parents **and/or** peers during adolescence. (24 marks)

RELATIONSHIPS WITH PARENTS

7½ MINUTES WORTH OF AO1

- **Formal operational thinking** leads to objective and idealistic look at relationships. May lead adolescent to think that parental relationship is deficient in meeting their attachment needs.
- The **development of autonomy** is recognised as one of the most important tasks of adolescence. Adolescents turn to parents despite increasing autonomy (**Sternberg**, 1990).
- In adolescence **urge to explore** is greater than in infancy, important for major tasks of adolescence.
- **Parental influence:** as many *important* relationships with parents as with peers (though *more* peer relationships) (**Frey and Rothlisberger**, 1996).
- **Frey and Rothlisberger** also found that parents give **day-to-day** not crisis support. **Mothers** more receptive to emotional needs, **fathers** more instrumental help.

7½ MINUTES WORTH OF AO2

- Evidence that not all adolescents have **formal operational thinking**, only 1/3 of adults do (**Dasen**, 1994).
- **Autonomy** most effective when accompanied by close relationship with parents (**connectedness**) (**Coleman and Hendry**, 1999).
- **Supported** by study which showed that time adolescents spent with family decreased from 11–18 but time spent with each parent individually stayed constant (**Larson et al.**, 1996).
- Research often concerns **US populations** and may not generalise to other cultures. Research that does involve other cultures (e.g. **Frey and Rothlisberger** was Swiss) may not apply to us.

RELATIONSHIPS WITH PEERS

7½ MINUTES WORTH OF AO1

- **Peers** can be **attachment figures** (**Ainsworth**, 1989) – offer intimacy, feedback, social influence, relationships.
- Pressure to **peer conformity** is strong especially mid-adolescence. Decline in late adolescence as more pressure to orient towards **adult norms** (**Jessop and Jessop**, 1977).
- **Peer influence** peaks in mid-adolescence and declines towards end of adolescence (**Jang**, 1999).
- Adolescent **self-esteem** related to friendships (**Bishop and Inderbitzen**, 1995).
- Girls have more confidential friendships, **boys** have as many but less intense (**Frey and Rothlisberger**, 1996).

7½ MINUTES WORTH OF AO2

- Peers are not alternative to parents, they offer **different relationships**. During adolescence parent relationships become more like peer relationships (more symmetrical and less critical).
- In early adolescence, stronger focus on physical appearance and an increasing interest in opposite sex.
- In later adolescence this gives way to greater sense of individual identity, which means a **decline in peer norms**.
- Adolescents who do have a close friend are more likely to be **better adjusted** at school and later have **higher self-worth** (**Bagwell et al.**, 1998).
- **Males** have less intimate friends – explained by fact that males use confrontational coping strategies to deal with stress, **females** rely more on social support (**Frydenberg and Lewis**, 1993).

Question 3: Discuss research (theories **and/or** studies) into relationships with parents during adolescence. (24 marks)

15 MINUTES WORTH OF AO1

As description of relationships with parents above, plus:

- **Parent-adolescent relationship:** girls more helpful and affectionate, both showed less affection as they got older (**Eberly and Montemayor**, 1999).
- Also found that parents who were viewed as **warm and supportive** received more affection.
- **Secure parental relationships** important as a 'launching pad' for new relationships.
- Adolescents with **secure parental relationships** had greater confidence in themselves and expected relationships to work (**Allen and Land**, 1999).

15 MINUTES WORTH OF AO2

As evaluation of relationships with parents above, plus:

- **Mother/father differences** related to society's values not because mothers have special qualities (**Coleman and Hendry**, 1999).
- **Fathers' involvement** is good for them – mid-life stress in fathers negatively correlated with involvement with adolescent children (**Montemayor et al.**, 1993).
- **Parent-adolescent relationship:** Children raised in **authoritative** families (warmth, structure, autonomy) have higher self-esteem, lower risk-taking (**Steinberg et al.**, 1991). Authoritative parents are high in demandingness and high in responsiveness.

As adolescents develop formal operational thinking it leads to an objective and idealistic look at their attachment relationships. This may lead the adolescent to think that one or both parents are deficient in meeting the adolescent's current attachment needs. The development of autonomy is recognised as one of the most important tasks of adolescence, yet adolescents still turn to their parents in times of stress despite this increasing independence (Sternberg, 1990). Frey and Rothlisberger (1996) found that although adolescents had twice as many relationships with peers as with family, the number of important relationships within each group was about the same. They also found that peers primarily provided support with day-to-day matters, but were of little help in crisis situations whereas the opposite was true for parents (they provide crisis rather than day-to-day support). Mothers were found to be more receptive to the emotional needs of their adolescents, whereas fathers were a greater source of instrumental help.

A reliance on the development of formal operational thinking for the development of objective thinking about parental relationships may be misplaced, as research suggests that not all adolescents have formal operational thinking, and only one-third of adults do (Dasen, 1994). Although autonomy is important in adolescence, recent research suggests that it is most healthy when accompanied by a continuing close relationship with parents (i.e. connectedness) (Coleman and Hendry, 1999). This is supported by a study by Larson et al. (1996), which showed that the amount of time that adolescents spent with their family decreased from 11–18 but the time spent with each parent individually stayed constant, showing that both autonomy and connectedness occur. A criticism of research in this area is that it often concerns US populations and may not generalise to other cultures. Similarly, research that does involve other cultures (e.g. Frey and Rothlisberger were Swiss) may not apply to adolescents in the UK.

During adolescence, peers may take on the function of attachment figures. Ainsworth claims that peers serve four important functions. They provide importance sources of intimacy, feedback on social behaviour, they are an important source of social influence and information, and provide attachment relationships. The pressure to conform to peers is especially strong in mid-adolescence, and declines in late adolescence as there is more pressure to orient towards adult norms (Jessop and Jessop, 1977). Jang (1999) tracked over 1700 children for 5 years, and found that peer influence peaked in mid-adolescence and then slowly declined. Bishop and Inderbitzen (1995) found that adolescent self-esteem scores were significantly related to friendships; adolescents with at least one reciprocal friend had higher self-esteem scores than those without any. Frey and Rothlisberger (1996) found that girls have a larger number of confidential friendships that provided emotional support, whereas boys have as many relationships, but these are less intense.

Peer attachments do not simply replace parental attachments, but offer a different type of relationship for the adolescent. During adolescence parental relationships also change, and become more like peer relationships, being more symmetrical and less critical. The rise and fall of peer conformity can be explained by the fact that in early and mid-adolescence, there is a stronger focus on physical appearance because of body changes and an increasing interest in the opposite sex. In later adolescence this gives way to romantic relationships and a greater sense of individual identity, which means a decline in peer norms. The effect of close friends in adolescence was demonstrated in a study by Bagwell et al. (1998), which showed that adolescents who do have a close friend are more likely to be better adjusted at school and later have higher self-worth. The fact that boys have fewer intimate relationships may be explained by the fact that males tend to use confrontational coping strategies to deal with stress, whereas females rely more on social support (Frydenberg and Lewis, 1993).

The question allows for either *both* parents and peers in your answer or just one of these. There is no one best way of answering the question. If you feel you have enough to just write about parental relationships (or peer relationships) then fine. If not, then write about both. In this answer both parents and peers relationships are discussed.

Note the constant use of 'AO2-speak' e.g. '…as research suggests', 'This is supported by…', 'A criticism of research in this area…'.

Don't worry too much about numbers of children and time periods over which the study took place. It is sufficient to describe the main findings of the study.

There is a mix of AO2 commentary here, including research support, explanations and consequences of having friends in adolescence.

SAMPLE ESSAY PLAN

Question 1: Discuss research (theories and/or studies) into cultural differences in adolescent behaviour. (24 marks)

15 MINUTES WORTH OF AO1

- **Individualist** cultures – adolescents achievement-oriented and independent.
- **Collectivist** societies – more value placed on obedience and responsibility (**Bacon et al.**, 1963).
- American culture may be **too achievement-oriented and competitive**, may not be good for mental health (**Elkind**, 1981).
- **Variations in sexuality**: adolescent experience is non-existent (e.g. 'Ines Beag', **Messinger**, 1971) or encouraged (e.g. Mangaia of Polynesia, **Santrock**, 2002).
- **Rites of passage** mark transition from child to adulthood, and help emerging adults to see themselves as separate from existing family.
- In the West, **no equivalent rites**, although Jewish faith marks it with Bar Mitzvah for boys.
- **Subculture: identity formation** difficult for **ethnic minority groups** because of gulf between values of own and host culture.
- **Stages in development of ethnic identity**: unexamined, searchers, resolution (**Phinney**, 1993).
- **Subculture: SES status** related to different values e.g. low SES parents value obedience, high SES value self-reliance and internal control.

15 MINUTES WORTH OF AO2

- **Some collectivist cultures** (e.g. Japanese and American-Asians) are achievement-oriented. In US 86% of Asian Americans go on to higher ed. compared to 64% white Americans (**Stevenson**, 1995).
- **Cooperation** may be better than competition e.g. **collaborative learning** encourages critical thinking (**Gokhale**, 1995).
- **Variations in sexuality** in our own culture: between 1964 and 1991 intercourse before the age of 16 has doubled (**Coleman and Hendry**, 1999).
- **For most Westerners adolescence** is a time of mixed child/adult status. Some use other achievements e.g. learning to drive as a 'rite'.
- **Ethnic identity** oversimplified by Phinney, **Berry** (1997) proposed 4 resolutions: integration, assimilation, separation, marginalisation (each is high or low in retention of cultural values and relationships with wider society).
- Ethnic adolescents who do both (= integration) do better at school and less anti-social behaviour (**Berry**, 1997).
- High internal control related to higher IQ (**Shoda et al.**, 1990).
- Some undesirable behaviours more common in high SES families e.g. drug use (**Hendry et al.**, 1993).
- Most research in this area is **correlational**, SES an indirect rather than direct cause of differences.

Question 2: (a) Describe research (theories and/or studies) into social development in adolescence. (12 marks)
(b) To what extent are there cultural differences in adolescent behaviour? (12 marks)

(a) 15 MINUTES WORTH OF AO1
Same as for essay on page 114.

(b) 15 MINUTES WORTH OF AO2

- **Individualist-collectivist differences**, value placed on achievement and competitiveness or obedience and responsibility respectively.
- But **some collectivist cultures** (e.g. Japanese and American-Asians) are achievement-oriented. In US 86% of Asian Americans go on to higher ed. compared to 64% white Americans (**Stevenson**, 1995).
- **Variations in sexuality**: adolescent experience is non-existent (e.g. 'Ines Beag', **Messinger**, 1971) or encouraged (e.g. Mangaia of Polynesia, **Santrock**, 2002).
- **Variations in sexuality** in our own culture: between 1964 and 1991 intercourse before the age of 16 has doubled (**Coleman and Hendry**, 1999).
- **Rites of passage** in some cultures e.g. Jewish faith marks it with Bar Mitzvah for boys, in some African societies **genital mutilation** is a rite of passage.
- **For most Westerners adolescence** is a time of mixed child/adult status. Some use other achievements e.g. learning to drive as a 'rite'.
- **Identity formation** difficult for **ethnic minority groups** because of gulf between values of own and host culture.
- **Ethnic adolescents** who both retain cultural values and have relationships with wider society (= integration) do better at school and less anti-social behaviour (**Berry**, 1997).
- **SES status** related to different values e.g. low SES parents value obedience whereas high SES value self-reliance and internal control.
- Some undesirable behaviours more common in high SES families e.g. drug use (**Hendry et al.**, 1993).

Research on cultural differences in achievement has shown that in individualist cultures such as the UK, parents socialise adolescents to be achievement-oriented and independent, whereas in collectivist societies such as Mexico, parents place more value on obedience and responsibility (Bacon et al., 1963). This has led some to suggest that American culture may be too achievement-oriented and competitive for rearing mentally healthy adolescents (Elkind, 1981). Research has also shown considerable cultural variations in attitudes to sexuality among adolescents. In some cultures (e.g. 'Ines Beag' studied by Messinger, 1971), adolescent knowledge of sex or any form of adolescent sexual experience was virtually non-existent. In other cultures, such as the Mangaia of Polynesia, adolescent sexual experience is seen as extremely important for both sexes, and adolescents are encouraged to have many sexual experiences before marriage (Santrock, 2002).

Some cultures have elaborate ceremonies to mark the transition from child to adulthood. This helps the emerging adults to see themselves as separate from their existing family and ready to take on their adult role. In the West, there are no equivalent dramatic rites of passage. Some religions retain a symbolic passage from child to adult, e.g. the Jewish faith marks this passage with a Bar Mitzvah for boys, but for most Western adolescents, the lack of a clear-cut rite of passage makes the attainment of adult status ambiguous. Differences in adolescent experience and behaviour are also evident among different subcultures. Identity formation is difficult for members of ethnic minority groups because of the gulf between the values of the host culture and their own. Phinney (1993) suggests there are three stages in development of ethnic identity. For some, the question of ethnic identity is as yet unexamined, others may be classified as searchers, because as a result of experiences such as racial harassment they have begun to consider their ethnicity, and finally, others have reached resolution. Socioeconomic status (SES) is also related to different experiences in adolescence e.g. low SES parents place greater value on obedience, whereas high SES parents place greater value on self-reliance and internal control.

The claim that there are clear differences between the adolescent experience in individualist and collectivist cultures is challenged by the findings of research. Contrary to the claim that achievement is more highly valued in individualist cultures, some collectivist cultures (e.g. Japanese and American-Asians) are also achievement-oriented. In the US 86% of Asian Americans go on to higher education, compared to only 64% of white Americans (Stevenson, 1995). Research has also suggested that cooperation may actually be better than competition for learning e.g. collaborative learning encourages critical thinking in adolescents (Gokhale, 1995). Variations in sexuality are not just between cultures, but historical differences also exist in our own culture. Between 1964 and 1991, sexual intercourse before the age of 16 has doubled (Coleman and Hendry, 1999). For most members of Western cultures, adolescence is a time of mixed child/adult status, with young people being given adult status at varying ages. Some use the age of consent, whereas others use other achievements such as learning to drive as a 'rite' of passage into adulthood. However, there is no one, culturally defined moment where the adolescent becomes an adult.

The stage model of ethnic identity may have been oversimplified by Phinney. In contrast, Berry (1997) proposed four possible resolutions – integration, assimilation, separation and marginalisation. Each of these is either high or low in terms of the retention of cultural values and relationships with wider society. Berry's own research has shown that in Canada, and many other countries, immigrant adolescents who were involved in both their heritage culture and that of the larger society (i.e. showed integration) did better at school and showed less evidence of anti-social behaviour. In relation to SES differences, a consequence of internal control in adolescents (valued in high SES families) may be increased IQ performance (Shoda et al., 1990). However, Hendry et al. (1993) found that some undesirable behaviours (e.g. drug use) are more common in adolescents from high SES families. Most research in this area is correlational, with SES being an indirect cause of differences in adolescent behaviour rather than a direct cause.

This first paragraph focuses on a description of cross-cultural differences in attitudes to achievement and attitudes towards sexuality.

Despite their fascination, try to resist going into too much detail describing specific rites of passage.

Subcultural differences (e.g. ethnicity and socioeconomic status) are also relevant in this context.

This demonstrates that the differences between AO1 and AO2 material is more to do with how it is used, rather than any other definable property of the material itself. AO2 should be built into a *commentary* on the material.

This final point is commentary on the *conclusions* drawn from much of the research on subcultural differences, i.e. adolescents from different SES backgrounds also experience differences in health, living conditions, educational background of parents, etc.

Topic 1: The relationship between sexual selection and human reproductive behaviour

Research support
for these predictions comes from a study of 37 cultures (Buss, 1989) and from a study of women seeking sperm donors for impregnation (Scheib, 1994).

Cultural factors
Although males value attractiveness in potential mates, the specific details are predictable from cultural norms and change across historical time.

This view of sexual attraction cannot explain attraction in partners who have **no interest in reproductive potential** (e.g. homosexual relationships).

Gender-specific criteria
Human females make a greater investment in their offspring (gestation and infant care) so are choosy when selecting a partner. Males must therefore compete with each other to be chosen.

Nature of sexual selection
Darwin believed that female choice created a selective pressure among males in order to guarantee their reproductive success.

Origins of mate preferences
Current mate preferences exist as evolved psychological mechanisms that originally solved the problem of mate choice in the environment of evolutionary adaptation (EEA). These bias mating in favour of individuals with the preferred characteristics

The idea that human behaviour can be explained in terms of the selective pressures operating in the **EEA** is not universally accepted, as it ignores the importance of *cultural* evolution since that time.

Commentary on the evolutionary approach
Dawkins (1976) believes that humans, with their large brains and intelligence, are in a position to depart from the dictates of their evolutionary past, rather than having their behaviour *determined* by pressures that are no longer relevant.

Human beings are perceptually pre-programmed to attend to displays of important physical and behavioural **indicators** (relevant to 'good genes' and 'good parenting') and are more willing to mate with those who possess them.

Indicators represent good genetic quality but can be faked. Facial symmetry is an honest signal because it is physiologically difficult to achieve and (virtually) impossible to fake.

Forms
Sexual selection may influence the development of physical and behavioural *indicators* of desirable traits, and characteristics that are a response to *sperm competition*.

Sperm competition
Research on comparative testicle size in primate species (Baker and Bellis, 1995), suggests ancestral human females in the EEA must have had multiple partners.

The idea that humans are by nature promiscuous is **supported by** research (e.g. Betzig, 1993 and Baker and Bellis, 1995).

Consequences
The selective pressures on males and females have led to different physical and behavioural consequences for each sex.

Physical characteristics
In species where females must choose males, this is likely to bring about *sexual dimorphism*, as males compete to be selected.
Facial characteristics such as *neotony* (in females) and *facial symmetry* are important indicators of reproductive capacity and/or quality.

Human mental evolution
Mate choices in the EEA may have led to the evolution of *neophilia* (the love of novelty and creativity) and *language*, which would help in the selection of a suitable mate.

Topic 2: Evolutionary explanations of parental investment

Smith (1984): 80% of cultures are **polygynous**, consistent with the claim that men have more to gain from this mating arrangement. However, reproduction rate in Western cultures is *lowest* among the wealthiest people.

Parental investment theory (Trivers, 1972)
Female investment is greater because eggs are more costly than sperm. Males compete for *quantity* of females, and females select for *quality* of males and their resources.

Trivers (1974)
• Parents and offspring will be in conflict over when weaning should finish.
• Parents should encourage children to value siblings.
• Parents will punish conflict and reward cooperation between siblings.

Sibling rivalry
This may develop as individual offspring try to maximise their own fitness by taking more than their 'fair share' of parental resources.

An alternative strategy
Lalumière *et al*. (1996) suggest that parents tend to steer siblings along *different* developmental paths, thus reducing competition for the same resources.

Male choosiness
In some cases (e.g. among the Ache Indians), a surplus of women has led to greater competition among women and increased promiscuity among married women.

Parental investment
Parents invest in their offspring in many different ways, including the provision of resources, and instructing and protecting the young.

Parent-offspring conflict
Resource allocations that would maximise *parental* fitness are not identical to those which would maximise *offspring* fitness – this results in conflict.

Conflict before birth
High blood pressure during pregnancy is caused by the foetus secreting hormones when it perceives the need for more nutrition.

Research has found that mothers with higher blood pressure have larger babies and fewer spontaneous abortions (Haig, 1993).

Shared care
Because of the high cost of childrearing, human males tend to restrict their reproductive opportunities and invest more in each individual offspring. This results in greater selectivity in males (e.g. for attractive females).

Maternal investment
Human mothers make a greater *prenatal* contribution of resources (through pregnancy) and a greater *postnatal* contribution (through breastfeeding). As a result, the costs of random mating would be high for human females.

• Infant dependency means that females want male providers.
• The expense of childrearing means that females want to ensure good-quality offspring and thus a good-quality mate.

Paternal investment
Males expend a large part of their reproductive effort on courtship and mating, and relatively little on parental care.

Sexual jealousy
This may have evolved as a solution to the problems of *cuckoldry* (for males) and *loss of resources* (for females).

Research support
• Buss *et al*. (1992) found male students indicated more concern about sexual infidelity and females about emotional infidelity.
• Many cultures have social practices that are aimed at reducing the chance of female infidelity.

Conflict after birth
Conflict with a current child is most intense at the stage where parents attempt to maximise their own fitness by transferring resources to a younger offspring.

Salmon and Daly (1998) suggest that younger children do not compete, but instead form alliances to gain access to resources.

Probable questions

1. Discuss the relationship between sexual selection and human reproductive behaviour. *(24 marks)*

2. Discuss evolutionary explanations of human reproductive behaviour. *(24 marks)*

Possible questions

3. Discuss the relationship between sexual selection and **two** areas of human reproductive behaviour. *(24 marks)*

The two probable questions are lifted directly from the specification. The wording of the two questions is different but, in essence, your answer to them both could be the same. Clearly in question 2 you are not required to describe and evaluate the relationship between sexual selection and human reproductive behaviour but that would be one way to answer the question. In question 1 you are not required to present evolutionary explanations but it is likely that this will be the route that you take.

In both questions then you could describe evolutionary explanations of the relationship between sexual selection and human reproductive behaviour. You also need to evaluate these explanations which can be done using research evidence and/or examples. Note that research evidence and/or examples *could* also be credited as AO1 if they have been used as illustrations of your explanation. For AO2 credit you need to use this material as part of a sustained critical commentary. Further AO2 credit might be gained by offering criticisms of any research evidence, contrasting evolutionary explanations with other explanations (such as learning theory), considering flaws in evolutionary explanations, etc.

Your answer to question 2 need not be concerned with sexual selection only. It would be perfectly creditworthy to include material from topic 2 on parental investment as well – but take care to avoid the danger of having too much to write and sacrificing depth for breadth (the depth-breadth trade-off is discussed on page ix).

It is possible that the question set would require you to focus on two *areas* of human reproductive behaviour. The difficulty here is that, if you simply write your 'prepared' answer for question 1, you may actually write about more than two reproductive behaviours or write about only one. If you had to answer a question like this you must clearly identify your two areas of human reproductive behaviour. Examples of areas of human reproductive behaviour include mate choice, mate competition, jealousy, body size, gender differences, cultural differences and so on.

Probable questions

1. Critically consider evolutionary explanations of parental investment. *(24 marks)*

2. Discuss the relationship between sexual selection and parental investment. *(24 marks)*

Possible questions

3. (a) Outline and evaluate the relationship between sexual selection and human reproductive behaviour. *(12 marks)*

   (b) Outline and evaluate evolutionary explanations of parental investment. *(12 marks)*

Question 1 is the only question that can be asked on this topic area but question 2 serves to remind you that topics 1 and 2 can be combined. Again it would be creditworthy to present very similar answers to questions 1 and 2 – however in question 2 you need to ensure that the descriptions of parental investment are related to sexual selection rather than just being a description of parental investment alone.

In question 1 the use of the injunction 'critically consider' does not require anything different to 'discuss' – they both require you to describe and evaluate in equal measure. In questions such as these (which are rather discursive) it is easy to overlook the AO2 requirement and therefore it pays to follow the plan suggested in most of this book – to clearly separate your answer into AO1 and AO2 components (about 300–350 words of each).

It is possible that a question might combine the topics in this division, as is the case with question 3. One thing to pay attention to in such 'combined' questions is time management. You should have enough material for both parts (a) and (b) to write for 60 minutes (because you should have a 30-minute answer for question (a) and a have a 30-minute answer for question (b)). You must carefully select what to include for AO1 and AO2 in each part otherwise you could end up with an answer that is more AO1 than AO2, or end up leaving yourself insufficient time to do justice to the other questions on the paper. In part (a) you should only write about 150 words of AO1 and 150 words of AO2, and do the same for part (b). The examiner can't give you any more than 6 marks for each AO1 and AO2 component.

Chapter 7

SAMPLE ESSAY PLAN

Question 1: Discuss the relationship between sexual selection and human reproductive behaviour. (24 marks)

15 MINUTES WORTH OF AO1

- **Sexual selection** – any trait that increases the reproductive success of an individual becomes exaggerated over evolutionary time.
- **Nature of sexual selection** – **Darwin** believed that female choice created a selective pressure among males in order to guarantee their reproductive success.
- **Females** have greater investment, therefore are more choosy to ensure best genetic quality in mate.
- **Males** have to compete to be chosen.
- **Current mate preferences** evolved in the **EEA**, adaptive in mobile hunter-gather tribes of Africa.
- These preferences now exist as neural circuits that bias preferences.
- **Physical/behavioural indicators** of 'good genes' or 'good parenting'.
- **Polygyny** indicated: males have medium-sized testicles by primate standards (**Baker and Bellis**, 1995), also moderate size difference (**sexual dimorphism**).
- **Physical characteristics**: sexual dimorphism (due to male competition), **neotony** (in females), **facial symmetry**.
- **Mental evolution**: **neophilia** (the love of novelty) and **language** (to select suitable mate).

15 MINUTES WORTH OF AO2

- **Gender-specific criteria**: shown in study of 37 cultures (**Buss**, 1989) and study of women seeking sperm donors for impregnation (**Scheib**, 1994).
- **Cultural factors**: although males value attractiveness in potential mates, the specific details are predictable from cultural norms and change across historical time.
- Recent studies show that females now advertise for men who are family-oriented as well as financially sound (**Bereczkei et al.**, 1997).
- Can't explain attraction in partners who have **no interest in reproductive potential** (e.g. homosexual relationships).
- However **Dunbar** (1995) – study of gay personal ads: lesbians less likely than heterosexual women to seek resources, gay males less likely to offer them.
- **Origins in the EEA** not universally accepted, as it ignores influence of **cultural** evolution since that time.
- **Indicators** can be **faked**. **Facial symmetry** is an honest signal because it is physiologically difficult to achieve and to fake.
- **Human promiscuity** indicated by 9% rate of 'misattributed' fatherhood (**Baker and Bellis**, 1995).
- **Evolutionary approach**, **Dawkins** (1976) believes that intelligent humans can depart from the dictates of their evolutionary past, rather than having their behaviour **determined** by pressures that are no longer relevant.

Question 3: Discuss the relationship between sexual selection and **two** areas of human reproductive behaviour. (24 marks)

MATE CHOICE

7½ MINUTES WORTH OF AO1

- Males and females face different adaptive problems when selecting a mate.
- **Females** have greater investment through gestation and infant care, therefore are choosier to ensure best genetic quality in mate.
- Females who choose mates unable or unwilling to invest **resources** in them and their offspring enjoy lower reproductive success than those who choose higher quality males (**Buss**, 1995).
- **Current mate preferences** evolved in the **EEA**, adaptive in mobile hunter-gatherer tribes of African savannah.
- **Forms of sexual selection**: physical/behavioural **indicators** of 'good genes' or 'good parenting'.
- **Consequences of sexual selection**: neotony (in females), **facial symmetry**.

7½ MINUTES WORTH OF AO2

- **Gender-specific criteria**: shown in study of 37 cultures (**Buss**, 1989) and study of women seeking sperm donors for impregnation (**Scheib**, 1994).
- Recent studies show that females now advertise for men who are family-oriented as well as financially sound (**Bereczkei et al.**, 1997).
- Can't explain attraction in partners who have **no interest in reproductive potential** (e.g. homosexual relationships).
- **Dunbar** (1995) – study of gay personal ads: lesbians less likely than heterosexual women to seek resources, gay males less likely to offer them.
- **Indicators** can be faked. **Facial symmetry** is an honest signal because it is physiologically difficult to achieve and to fake.

MATE COMPETITION

7½ MINUTES WORTH OF AO1

- **Darwin** believed that female choice created a selective pressure among males in order to guarantee their reproductive success.
- **Males** have to compete to be chosen.
- **Sperm competition** necessary for male success, comparative testicle size in primate species (**Baker and Bellis**, 1995) suggests ancestral human females had multiple partners.
- **Consequences of sexual selection**: sexual dimorphism (due to male competition).

7½ MINUTES WORTH OF AO2

- **Cultural factors**: Although males value attractiveness in potential mates, the specific details are predictable from cultural norms and change across historical time.
- **Human promiscuity** indicated by 9% rate of 'misattributed' fatherhood (**Baker and Bellis**, 1995).
- **Evolutionary approach**, **Dawkins** (1976) believes that intelligent humans can depart from the dictates of their evolutionary past, rather than having their behaviour **determined** by pressures that are no longer relevant.

The basic principle of sexual selection is that any trait that increases the reproductive success of an individual will become more and more exaggerated over evolutionary time. Darwin believed that female choice created a selective pressure among males in order to guarantee their reproductive success. If a particular characteristic becomes established as a universal preference among females, males possessing the best examples of this characteristic are more likely to be chosen as mates. Because females make a greater investment in offspring, they are choosier in order to ensure the best genetic quality in their mate. As a result of this female choosiness, males must compete to be chosen. Current mate preferences among human males and females evolved in the EEA, and were adaptive in mobile hunter-gatherer tribes of African savannah. The preferences that were adaptive then now exist as neural circuits that bias mating in favour of those individuals that possess the desired characteristics.

Physical and behavioural indicators reveal genetic characteristics that could be passed on to offspring (selection for 'good genes'), or indicate the likelihood of the mate surviving to protect and support the offspring (selection for 'good parenting'). Human beings are 'pre-programmed' to attend to displays of these indicators, which in turn increases their willingness to mate with an individual who possesses them. A study of comparative testicle size in primate species (Baker and Bellis, 1995) showed that human males have medium-sized testicles by primate standards. This fact, together with the moderate size differences between human males and females (sexual dimorphism) suggests that our species evolved under a polygynous mating system, with more intense competition among males than females. Research has shown that both sexes are attracted to faces that are symmetrical. Facial symmetry is indicative of reproductive capacity as it is associated with robust genes and the absence of harmful mutations. Sexual selection may also affect mental evolution as neophilia (the love of novelty and creativity) influences mate choice in many species, with mate choice in the EEA favouring creative courtship displays.

Support for the universal nature of mate choice comes from a study of mate preferences in 37 cultures (Buss, 1989). Buss found that men value potential female partners in terms of ability to produce children, expressed as a preference for youth and physical attractiveness. Support also comes from a study of women seeking sperm donors for impregnation (Scheib, 1994). Women based their choice on the same qualities predicted by evolutionary theory. However, although males value attractiveness in potential mates, the specific details are predictable from cultural norms and change across time. Bereczkei et al. (1997) found that females now advertise for men who are family-oriented. This suggests that they are concerned less with resources and more about a partner who will help care for offspring but this too could be predicted from evolutionary theory. Sexual selection cannot explain attraction in partners who have no interest in reproductive potential (e.g. homosexual relationships). However, in line with the predictions of evolutionary theory, Dunbar (1995) found that lesbians were far less likely than heterosexual women to seek resources, and gay males were less likely than heterosexual males to offer them in gay personal ads.

A problem of relying on physical and behavioural indicators in human reproductive behaviour is that these indicators can be faked. If an indicator is not costly, it can be easily faked, and the offspring would not have increased fitness. Facial symmetry, on the other hand, is an honest signal because it is physiologically difficult to achieve and difficult to fake. Support for the claim that humans are more naturally promiscuous than monogamous comes from a study which suggested a worldwide rate of 9% for 'misattributed' fatherhood, where the presumed father turns out not to be genetically related to his child (Baker and Bellis, 1995). Although human mate choice may be affected by sexual selection, Dawkins (1976) believes that intelligent humans can depart from the dictates of their evolutionary past, rather than having their behaviour determined by pressures that are no longer relevant.

It is easy to get carried away when describing the mechanisms of sexual selection. Remember the question at all times (which is about human behaviour). When you find yourself talking about peacocks, you know you're doomed!

There is no 'essential list' of topics that must be included in an answer to this question, so sample the available material to construct your own answer.

Some research supports the predictions from evolutionary theory, whereas other research appears to challenge them. It is up to you to make this explicit in your commentary.

This final sentence makes the important point that *despite* the influence of evolutionary forces in our reproductive behaviour, we are not prisoners of our biology.

TOPIC 2: EVOLUTIONARY EXPLANATIONS OF PARENTAL INVESTMENT

SAMPLE ESSAY PLAN

Question 1: Critically consider evolutionary explanations of parental investment. (24 marks)

15 MINUTES WORTH OF AO1

As description of explanations of parental investment below for part (b), plus:

- **Parent-offspring conflict**: Resource allocations maximising **parental fitness** are not same as those maximising **offspring fitness**.
- This results in **conflict** for example **sibling rivalry**.
- **Conflict before birth**: pre-eclapsia caused by the foetus secreting hormones when it perceives the need for more nutrition (**Haig**, 1998).
- Parent-offspring conflict most intense when parents **transfer investment** from older child to more vulnerable younger children.

15 MINUTES WORTH OF AO2

As evaluation of explanations of parantal investment below for part (b), plus:

- **Parent-offspring conflict**: **Lalumière et al.** (1996) suggest that parents tend to steer siblings along different developmental paths, thus reducing competition for the same resources.
- An alternative explanation is that siblings turn out differently because **peer socialisation** has a greater effect than parental care (**Harris**, 1999).
- Research has found that mothers with higher **blood pressure** have larger babies and fewer spontaneous abortions (**Haig**, 1993).
- Humans adopt **many different strategies** depending on the prevailing conditions in the social and physical world.

Question 3: (a) Outline and evaluate the relationship between sexual selection and human reproductive behaviour. (12 marks)
(b) Outline and evaluate evolutionary explanations of parental investment. (12 marks)

(a) SEXUAL SELECTION AND HUMAN REPRODUCTIVE BEHAVIOUR

7½ MINUTES WORTH OF AO1

- **Sexual selection**: traits solely concerned with reproduction success are naturally selected.
- **Females** have greater investment, therefore are more choosy to ensure best genetic quality in mate.
- **Males** have to compete to be chosen.
- **Current mate preferences** evolved in the **EEA**, adaptive in mobile hunter-gatherer tribes of African savannah.

Consequences of sexual selection:

- **Physical characteristics: sexual dimorphism** (due to male competition), **neotony** (in females), **facial symmetry**.
- **Mental evolution: neophilia** (the love of novelty and creativity) and **language** (helps select suitable mate).

7½ MINUTES WORTH OF AO2

- **Gender-specific criteria**: shown in study of 37 cultures (**Buss**, 1989) and study of women seeking sperm donors for impregnation (**Scheib**, 1994).
- **Cultural factors**: Although males value attractiveness in potential mates, the specific details are predictable from cultural norms and change across historical time.
- Recent studies show that females now advertise for men who are family-oriented as well as financially sound (**Bereczkei et al.**, 1997).
- Can't explain attraction in partners who have **no interest in reproductive potential** (e.g. homosexual relationships).
- **Origins in the EEA** not universally accepted, as it ignores influence of **cultural** evolution since that time.

(b) EVOLUTIONARY EXPLANATIONS OF PARENTAL INVESTMENT

7½ MINUTES WORTH OF AO1

- **Parental investment theory** (**Trivers**, 1972): female investment is greater because eggs are more costly than sperm.
- Males compete for **quantity** of females, females select for **quality** of males and their resources.
- **Maternal investment**: human mothers make a greater **prenatal** contribution (pregnancy) and a greater **postnatal** contribution (breastfeeding).
- As a result, the **costs of random mating** would be high for human females.
- **Paternal investment**: males expend a large part of their reproductive effort on courtship and mating, and relatively little on parental care.
- **Sexual jealousy**: this may have evolved as a solution to the problems of **cuckoldry** (for males) and **loss of resources** (for females).

7½ MINUTES WORTH OF AO2

- **Consequence of differential parental investment**: men stand to gain from polygyny and women from monogamy.
- **Smith** (1984): 80% of cultures are **polygynous**. However, reproduction rate in Western cultures is **lowest** among the wealthiest people.
- **Males are sometimes selectors** e.g. a surplus of women has led to greater competition among women and increased promiscuity among married women.
- **Maternal investment**: high cost means that females want male providers to ensure good-quality offspring and thus a good-quality mate.
- **Sexual jealousy: Buss et al.** (1992) found that male students indicated more concern about sexual infidelity and females about emotional infidelity.

Trivers (1972) states that female investment is greater because eggs are less numerous and more costly than sperm. A female can have only a limited number of offspring, whereas males can have a virtually unlimited number of offspring. As a result, males compete for quantity of females, whereas females select for quality of males and their resources. Human mothers make a greater prenatal contribution (pregnancy) and a greater postnatal contribution (breastfeeding). The costs of childcare are higher for females than males, and so the costs of random mating would be high for human females. Males, however, expend a large part of their reproductive effort on courtship and mating, and relatively little on parental care. The possibility of sexual infidelity posed different adaptive problems for males and females. A man whose mate was unfaithful risked investing in offspring that were not his own (cuckoldry), whereas a woman whose mate was unfaithful risked the diversion of resources away from her and the family. Sexual jealousy may have evolved as a solution to the problems.

> Although there are similarities with an answer on sexual selection, it is important to focus on parental investment explicitly in response to this question.

A consequence of differential parental investment by males and females is that men stand to gain from polygyny and women have more to gain from monogamy. Smith (1984) showed that 80% of cultures are polygynous, thus supporting the predictions made by parental investment theory. However, despite the predicted relationship between resources and mating success, reproduction rate in Western cultures is lowest among the wealthiest people. Contrary to the predictions of parental investment theory, males do not always compete, and females do not always select, e.g. in some cultures, a relative decrease in the number of men has led to greater competition among women and increased promiscuity among married women. A consequence of the high cost of maternal investment is that females want good male providers, and they want to ensure good-quality offspring so that they do not waste their reproductive efforts. In line with the predictions about differential jealousy, Buss et al. (1992) found that male students indicated more concern about sexual infidelity and females indicated more concern about emotional infidelity.

> Notice the variety of AO2 opportunities in this paragraph, including consequences, contradictions, research support, research challenge, etc.

Parents must allocate resources in a way that maximises their reproductive fitness, whereas offspring compete for resources in order to maximise their share of these limited resources. Parent-offspring conflict occurs because resource allocations that maximise parental fitness are not the same as those maximising offspring fitness, which results in conflict such as sibling rivalry. Parent-offspring conflict begins before birth. High blood pressure in pregnancy, which may lead to pre-eclampsia, is caused by the foetus secreting hormones when it perceives the need for more nutrition (Haig, 1998). This mechanism benefits the foetus at the expense of the mother. Parent-offspring conflict is most intense at the stage at which parents transfer their investment from the relatively mature older child to the more vulnerable younger children. Older children thus attempt to prolong the parents' primary focus on them for as long as possible.

> Parent-offspring conflict is related to parental investment because offspring are able to influence the amount of investment that parents make in them.

Lalumière et al. (1996) suggest that parents cope with sibling rivalry by steering siblings along different developmental paths, thus reducing competition for the same resources. This might explain why siblings turn out to be so different. An alternative explanation comes from Harris (1999) who suggests that siblings turn out differently because peer socialisation has a greater effect than parental care. Research has found that mothers with higher blood pressure tend to have larger babies and fewer spontaneous abortions (Haig, 1993). This suggests that high blood pressure is associated with healthier foetuses and so is an adaptive strategy. Humans thus adopt many different strategies depending on the prevailing conditions in the social and physical world. This is an adaptive strategy because it maximises reproductive success in relation to a changing environment.

> It is acceptable to throw in an alternative explanation (in this case from developmental psychology) for a prediction from evolutionary theory.

Topic 1: Evolutionary explanations of depression

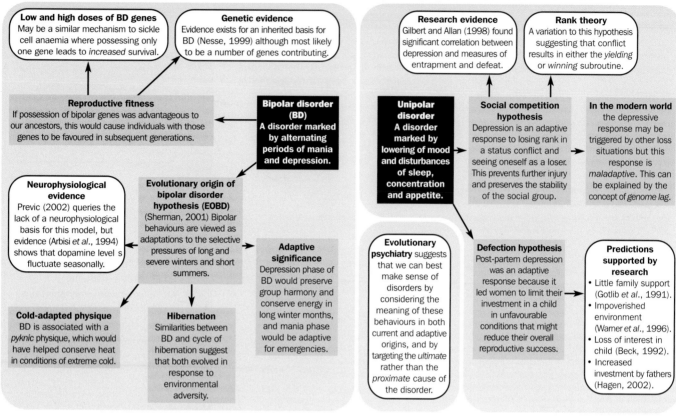

Low and high doses of BD genes
May be a similar mechanism to sickle cell anaemia where possessing only one gene leads to *increased* survival.

Genetic evidence
Evidence exists for an inherited basis for BD (Nesse, 1999) although most likely to be a number of genes contributing.

Reproductive fitness
If possession of bipolar genes was advantageous to our ancestors, this would cause individuals with those genes to be favoured in subsequent generations.

Bipolar disorder (BD)
A disorder marked by alternating periods of mania and depression.

Neurophysiological evidence
Previc (2002) queries the lack of a neurophysiological basis for this model, but evidence (Arbisi *et al.*, 1994) shows that dopamine level s fluctuate seasonally.

Evolutionary origin of bipolar disorder hypothesis (EOBD)
(Sherman, 2001) Bipolar behaviours are viewed as adaptations to the selective pressures of long and severe winters and short summers.

Adaptive significance
Depression phase of BD would preserve group harmony and conserve energy in long winter months, and mania phase would be adaptive for emergencies.

Cold-adapted physique
BD is associated with a *pyknic* physique, which would have helped conserve heat in conditions of extreme cold.

Hibernation
Similarities between BD and cycle of hibernation suggest that both evolved in response to environmental adversity.

Research evidence
Gilbert and Allan (1998) found significant correlation between depression and measures of entrapment and defeat.

Rank theory
A variation to this hypothesis suggesting that conflict results in either the *yielding* or *winning* subroutine.

Unipolar disorder
A disorder marked by lowering of mood and disturbances of sleep, concentration and appetite.

Social competition hypothesis
Depression is an adaptive response to losing rank in a status conflict and seeing oneself as a loser. This prevents further injury and preserves the stability of the social group.

In the modern world
the depressive response may be triggered by other loss situations but this response is *maladaptive*. This can be explained by the concept of *genome lag*.

Evolutionary psychiatry suggests that we can best make sense of disorders by considering the meaning of these behaviours in both current and adaptive origins, and by targeting the *ultimate* rather than the *proximate* cause of the disorder.

Defection hypothesis
Post-partem depression was an adaptive response because it led women to limit their investment in a child in unfavourable conditions that might reduce their overall reproductive success.

Predictions supported by research
- Little family support (Gotlib *et al.*, 1991).
- Impoverished environment (Warner *et al.*, 1996).
- Loss of interest in child (Beck, 1992).
- Increased investment by fathers (Hagen, 2002).

Topic 2: Evolutionary explanations of anxiety disorders

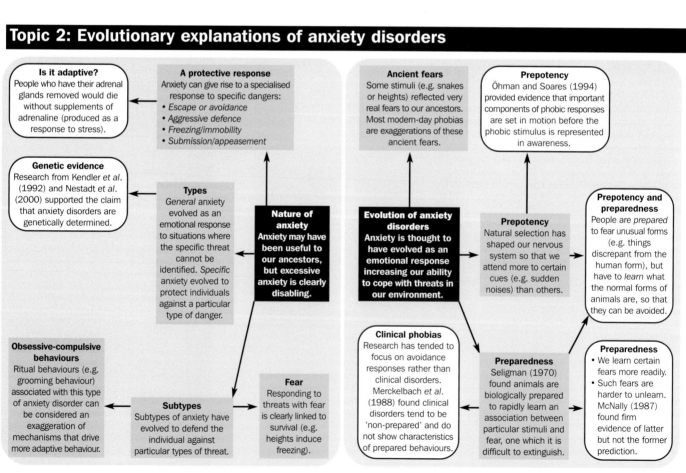

Is it adaptive?
People who have their adrenal glands removed would die without supplements of adrenaline (produced as a response to stress).

A protective response
Anxiety can give rise to a specialised response to specific dangers:
- *Escape or avoidance*
- *Aggressive defence*
- *Freezing/immobility*
- *Submission/appeasement*

Ancient fears
Some stimuli (e.g. snakes or heights) reflected very real fears to our ancestors. Most modern-day phobias are exaggerations of these ancient fears.

Prepotency
Öhman and Soares (1994) provided evidence that important components of phobic responses are set in motion before the phobic stimulus is represented in awareness.

Genetic evidence
Research from Kendler *et al.* (1992) and Nestadt *et al.* (2000) supported the claim that anxiety disorders are genetically determined.

Types
General anxiety evolved as an emotional response to situations where the specific threat cannot be identified. *Specific* anxiety evolved to protect individuals against a particular type of danger.

Nature of anxiety
Anxiety may have been useful to our ancestors, but excessive anxiety is clearly disabling.

Evolution of anxiety disorders
Anxiety is thought to have evolved as an emotional response increasing our ability to cope with threats in our environment.

Prepotency
Natural selection has shaped our nervous system so that we attend more to certain cues (e.g. sudden noises) than others.

Prepotency and preparedness
People are *prepared* to fear unusual forms (e.g. things discrepant from the human form), but have to *learn* what the normal forms of animals are, so that they can be avoided.

Obsessive-compulsive behaviours
Ritual behaviours (e.g. grooming behaviour) associated with this type of anxiety disorder can be considered an exaggeration of mechanisms that drive more adaptive behaviour.

Subtypes
Subtypes of anxiety have evolved to defend the individual against particular types of threat.

Fear
Responding to threats with fear is clearly linked to survival (e.g. heights induce freezing).

Clinical phobias
Research has tended to focus on avoidance responses rather than clinical disorders. Merckelbach *et al.* (1988) found clinical disorders tend to be 'non-prepared' and do not show characteristics of prepared behaviours.

Preparedness
Seligman (1970) found animals are biologically prepared to rapidly learn an association between particular stimuli and fear, one which it is difficult to extinguish.

Preparedness
- We learn certain fears more readily.
- Such fears are harder to unlearn. McNally (1987) found firm evidence of latter but not the former prediction.

Probable questions

1. Critically consider **one or more** explanations of depression from an evolutionary perspective. *(24 marks)*

2. Critically consider explanations of **two** types of mental disorder from an evolutionary perspective. *(24 marks)*

Possible questions

3. Describe and evaluate **one** explanation of depression from an evolutionary perspective. *(24 marks)*

The specification requires that you know more than one evolutionary explanation (because the word 'explanations' is in the plural). Question 1 gives you the option of whether you focus on one explanation only or more than one. It is possible that you would not be able to write 600 words (AO1 and AO2) on one explanation so you will gain more marks by writing about more than one. However, be careful about trying to cover too many explanations because the more you include (greater breadth) the less time you have for details (depth). This depth-breadth trade-off is critical in terms of attracting high marks. Unless you include details you cannot clearly demonstrate your knowledge and understanding. So if you know lots of explanations don't feel pressed to include them all just because you know them – be selective.

You may answer question 2 by looking at unipolar and bipolar depression, or you could look at depression and anxiety disorders, or at two types of anxiety disorder (e.g. phobias and obsessive-compulsive disorder). It always helps to make it clear to the examiner what your two types of mental disorder are: state 'The first disorder is …' and 'The second disorder is …'.

One of the ways to provide evaluation is to contrast evolutionary explanations of depression with other explanations – you may know a lot of these if you have studied the psychopathology section for Unit 5. Take care to *use* alternative explanations as sustained critical commentary rather than simply presenting additional (and uncreditworthy) descriptions.

Question 3 is the same as question 1 except that you are not given the choice of including more than one explanation. If you do present more than one explanation they will all be read and marks awarded to the best explanation. You possibly could have put your other explanations to valuable use as a form of commentary *but* only if they were used as a sustained critical commentary.

Probable questions

1. Critically consider **one or more** explanations of anxiety disorders from an evolutionary perspective. *(24 marks)*

2. (a) Outline and evaluate **one or more** explanations of anxiety disorders from an evolutionary perspective. *(12 marks)*

   (b) Outline and evaluate **one or more** explanations of depression from an evolutionary perspective. *(12 marks)*

Possible questions

3. Discuss the explanation of **two** types of anxiety disorder from an evolutionary perspective. *(24 marks)*

Questions on this topic are likely to be similar to those on depression as the specification entries are similar. Again you are required to be familiar with more than one explanation. In question 1 you have the option of describing and evaluating just one explanation or more than one explanation. Remember the depth-breadth trade-off.

Question 2 combines the two topics in this division. You are required to provide 6 marks of description (AO1) for one or more anxiety disorders. You could opt for the 'or more' but would have to cram a lot into your 6 marks-worth – you have 7½ minutes to write about 150 words. The same limitations apply to evaluation of the one or more anxiety disorders and the description and evaluation of the one or more explanations of depression. This is a question that requires you to be very selective in what you choose to include if you are going to get top marks.

You can be asked to explain two different types of anxiety disorder because the specification mentions 'anxiety disorders'. Question 3 is less likely to be set but it is possible so you must make sure that you can explain more than one anxiety disorder. The specification offers two examples, but these are examples only – it would be perfectly acceptable to write about, for example, post-traumatic stress disorder or generalised anxiety disorder. You could also present two different phobias e.g. zoophobia (fear of animals) and agoraphobia (fear of public places) as your two types of anxiety disorder.

Chapter 7

TOPIC 1: EVOLUTIONARY EXPLANATIONS OF DEPRESSION

SAMPLE ESSAY PLAN

Question 1: Critically consider **one or more** explanations of depression from an evolutionary perspective. (24 marks)

EXPLANATION 1: REPRODUCTIVE FITNESS	**5 MINUTES WORTH OF AO1** • Genes that contribute to survival and reproduction are **naturally selected**. • If **genes for bipolar disorder** (BD) were advantageous to ancestors that would increase the reproductive fitness of individuals with such genes. • **Sherman** (2001) EOBD: bipolar behaviours adaptive for severe winters and short summers. • **Winter**: lack of interest in food, sex etc. would preserve group harmony, **mania** important for emergencies and other physical challenges. • Possible that in **small doses** such genes would be favourable but large doses decrease fitness.	**5 MINUTES WORTH OF AO2** • Evidence of **genetic basis** for BD e.g. **Nesse** (1999) found concordance of 68%. • A number of genes contribute to BD supporting low/high dose concept (**Hyman**, 1999). • Small doses might lead to increases in creativity and high motivation, large doses leads to racing thoughts and inability to focus. • **Previc** (2002) – Sherman's EOBD model is **unproven**, and lacks a neurophysiological foundation.
EXPLANATION 2: SOCIAL COMPETITION HYPOTHESIS (PRICE ET AL., 1994)	**5 MINUTES WORTH OF AO1** • An evolved response to **loss of rank** in a status conflict in a dominance hierarchy. • Seeing oneself as **the loser** and experiencing **lowered mood, energy and confidence** prevents injury and preserves stability of social group. • Same **mental module** triggered by other kinds of loss (e.g. ending of a relationship) and may be **maladaptive** in modern setting (**genome lag**).	**5 MINUTES WORTH OF AO2** • **Research evidence**: significant correlation between depression and measures of entrapment and defeat (**Gilbert and Allan**, 1998). • **Variation: Rank theory** (**Price and Sloman**, 1987) proposes that conflict results in both a **winning or losing** (yielding) subroutine. • Winning is akin to mania and makes it clear to loser that any comeback will be successfully resisted.
EXPLANATION 3: DEFECTION HYPOTHESIS (HAGEN, 1999)	**5 MINUTES WORTH OF AO1** • In the EEA post-partum depression (**PPD**) was an **adaptive response** which led women to **limit their investment** in a child. • This was more likely to happen when conditions were unfavourable e.g. conditions which would reduce their overall reproductive success. • Can be **generalised to all forms of depression** as an adaptive response to an event that has an evolutionarily significant cost (**Hagen**, 2002).	**5 MINUTES WORTH OF AO2** • **Predictions supported by research**, e.g. PPD more likely when: • Low marital satisfaction (**Gotlib et al.**, 1991). • Unemployment of mother or father (**Warner et al.**, 1996). • Loss of interest in child (**Beck**, 1992). • PPD led to increased investment by fathers and other relatives (**Hagen**, 2002).

Question 2: Critically consider explanations of **two** types of mental disorder from an evolutionary perspective. (24 marks)

BIPOLAR DISORDER	**7½ MINUTES WORTH OF AO1** Description of **reproductive fitness** as above, plus: • EOBD: Similarities between BD and **cycle of hibernation** suggest that both evolved in response to environmental adversity. • **Pyknic type** (thick compact physique) associated with BD and also associated with cold adaptation (**Kretschmer**, 1970). • This adaptation not necessary after clothing worn, indicates that BD was an **early adaptation**.	**7½ MINUTES WORTH OF AO2** Evaluation of **reproductive fitness** as above, plus: • Lack of neurophysiological basis for this model (**Previc**, 2002). • However **dopamine** levels (linked to depression) do vary seasonally (**Arbisi et al.**, 1994).
UNIPOLAR DISORDER	**7½ MINUTES WORTH OF AO1** Description of **social competition hypothesis** as above, plus: • **Defection hypothesis** (Hagen, 1999). • In the EEA post-partum depression (**PPD**) was an **adaptive response** which led women to **limit their investment** in a child • This was more likely to happen when conditions were unfavourable e.g. conditions which would reduce their overall reproductive success.	**7½ MINUTES WORTH OF AO2** Evaluation of **social competition hypothesis** as above, plus: • **Defection hypothesis, predictions supported by research**, e.g. PPD more likely when: • Low marital satisfaction (**Gotlib et al.**, 1991). • Unemployment of mother or father (**Warner et al.**, 1996). • Loss of interest in child (**Beck**, 1992).

Genes that contribute to survival and reproduction are preserved because more individuals with these genes would survive to reproduce, i.e. they are naturally selected. If possession of genes for bipolar disorder (BD) was advantageous to our ancestors, that would increase the reproductive fitness of individuals with such genes. Sherman's EOBD model (2001) states that bipolar behaviours were adaptations to the pressure of long, severe winters and short summers. In the winter months, a lack of interest in food, sex and other activities would preserve group harmony, and mania would have adaptive importance for emergencies and other physical challenges. It is possible that in small doses such genes would be favourable but large doses would decrease fitness. At this extreme, the individual would have too many symptoms and so would be unable to function adequately.

There is evidence for an inherited basis for BD, with concordance rates of 68% for identical twins reared together, compared to just 13% for non-identical twins (Nesse, 1999). Further support for the reproductive fitness argument comes from research which has shown there are a number of genes involved in BD, thus supporting the low/high dose concept (Hyman, 1999). This concept makes sense, as small doses might lead to increased creativity and high motivation, whereas large doses may lead to racing thoughts and inability to focus, both characteristics of individuals with BD. Previc (2002) claims that Sherman's EOBD model is as yet unproven, and questions the neurophysiological foundation for this explanation.

The social competition theory (Price et al., 1994) is based on the idea that depression is an evolved response to loss of rank in a status conflict. Such a response is adaptive because it helps individuals adjust to the fact that they must now adopt a subordinate position in the dominance hierarchy. Seeing oneself as the loser and experiencing lowered mood, energy and confidence (characteristics of depression) prevents further injury and preserves the stability of the social group. In the modern world, the same mental module that was originally adaptive in the EEA is now triggered by other kinds of loss (e.g. ending of a relationship) and may be maladaptive in a modern setting (genome lag).

Although the social competition hypothesis is difficult to test, research evidence has shown a significant correlation between depression and measures of entrapment and defeat, as predicted by this hypothesis (Gilbert and Allan, 1998). Price and Sloman (1987) proposed a variation on this hypothesis, claiming in their 'rank theory' that conflict results in two adaptive responses. The first is a losing subroutine, which ensures that the loser truly yields, and does not attempt to make a comeback. The second is a winning subroutine, akin to mania, which makes it clear to the loser that any comeback will be successfully resisted.

The defection hypothesis (Hagen, 1999) proposes that, in the EEA, post-partum depression (PPD) was an adaptive response. This led women to limit their investment in a child when conditions were unfavourable, e.g. conditions which would reduce their overall reproductive success. Conditions that might have triggered sharply reduced maternal investment included problems with the pregnancy or birth, lack of support and environmental factors such as a harsh winter or famine conditions. Hagen believes that this explanation can be generalised to all forms of depression in that depression is an adaptive response to an event that has an evolutionarily significant cost.

The predictions that arise from this hypothesis are supported by research. For example, Gotlib et al. (1991) found that when marital satisfaction was low during pregnancy, PPD was more likely. Warner et al. (1996) also found evidence that the unemployment of either mother or father was a significant risk factor for PPD, which supports the claim that PPD would be more likely when support was low, and where there might be food shortages. Beck (1992) confirmed the prediction that PPD should result in a loss of interest in the child. In order to maintain their reproductive fitness, PPD in the mother should result in increased investment from fathers and other relatives. Hagen (2002) found that this was exactly what tended to happen.

You could base your entire answer on bipolar disorder, but in this answer, where both bipolar and unipolar disorder are covered, there is only room for a very brief outline.

Be careful when making statements such as 'This concept makes sense…'. This example is backed up with evidence and argument, so is okay.

Genome lag – human culture changes more rapidly than can the human genome through evolution, therefore there is always a lag. We have 'stone-age minds in modern skulls'.

Although this alternative explanation is only being described here, the adaptive advantages of these subroutines are made clear, therefore this counts as commentary.

You might also mention that under extreme conditions, this may have driven the mother to infanticide.

Rather than simply list these pieces of support, you should aim to put each of them in context, as here. It is very clear what these studies show us about the defection hypothesis.

TOPIC 2: EVOLUTIONARY EXPLANATIONS OF ANXIETY DISORDERS

SAMPLE ESSAY PLAN

Question 1: Critically consider **one or more** explanations of anxiety disorders from an evolutionary perspective. (24 marks)

15 MINUTES WORTH OF AO1

- Anxiety probably **evolved** as an emotional response **increasing our ability to cope** with threats in our environment particularly situations that threatened a loss of reproductive resources.
- **Explanation 1: Ancient fears**: some stimuli (e.g. snakes, heights) represented very real dangers to our ancestors, but not stones and leaves.
- Most **modern-day phobias** are exaggerations of these ancient fears (**Marks and Nesse**, 1994).
- **Explanation 2: Prepotency**: an advantage in responding appropriately to 'ancient' threats, rather than learning afterwards.
- Natural selection has shaped our nervous system so that we **attend more to certain cues** (e.g. sudden noises, snake-like stimuli) than others.
- **Explanation 3: Preparedness**: animals are biologically prepared to rapidly learn an association between particular stimuli and fear (**Seligman**, 1970).
- Once learned such associations are **difficult to extinguish**.
- What is inherited is the predisposition to form certain associations rather than a fear of certain things (e.g. towards things that your mother shows a fear response to) (**Marks**, 1987).

15 MINUTES WORTH OF AO2

- Ancient fears explain **uneven distribution** of phobias.
- Modern things which are **dangerous** (e.g. cars, guns) rarely develop into phobias.
- **Prepotency**: Öhman and Soares (1994) provided evidence that important components of phobic responses are set in motion before the phobic stimulus is represented in awareness.
- Humans express greatest fear of animals whose form is most **discrepant** from human form e.g. skin texture, number of limbs (**Bennett-Levy and Marteau**, 1984).
- It is **strangeness** rather than discrepancy from the human form which explains why phobias increase through childhood and then decline (**Agras et al.**, 1969).
- **Preparedness**: a review of evidence by **McNally** (1987) concluded that there is evidence that ancient fears are harder to unlearn but not that they are learned more readily.
- **Alternative explanation: expectancy bias** (**Davey**, 1995) – an expectation that fear-relevant stimuli will produce negative consequences. No reference to evolutionary past needed. Can explain modern fears (e.g. hypodermic needles).
- **Clinical phobias** tend to be 'non-prepared' and do not show characteristics of prepared behaviours (**Merckelbach et al.**, 1988).

Question 3: Discuss the explanation of **two** types of anxiety disorder from an evolutionary perspective. (24 marks)

OBSESSIVE-COMPULSIVE BEHAVIOURS

7½ MINUTES WORTH OF AO1

- **Ritual behaviours** associated with OCD can be considered an exaggeration of the mechanisms that drive more adaptive behaviour (**Marks and Nesse**, 1994), for example:
- **Grooming behaviour** valuable to reduce parasites and smooth social interaction; washing and grooming are characteristic of OCD.
- **Concern for others** helps avoid ostracism from the group; excessive fear of harming others characteristic of OCD.
- **Hoarding** guards against future shortages; grossly exaggerated in some obsessive-compulsives.

7½ MINUTES WORTH OF AO2

- **Genetic basis** for OCD found by e.g. **Nestadt et al.** (2000), people with a first degree relative with OCD were five times more likely to also have OCD at some point in their lives.
- **Alternative explanations**: OCD learned e.g. behavioural explanation – thoughts become associated with a traumatic event (classical conditioning), and the resulting anxiety can be reduced by compulsive behaviours (operant conditioning). Behavioural therapies have some success.
- **Evolutionary arguments** are **post hoc**, we are only speculating about what behaviours might have been adaptive in the EEA.

PHOBIAS (FEAR)

7½ MINUTES WORTH OF AO1

- **Ancient fears**: some stimuli (e.g. snakes, heights) reflected very real fears to our ancestors.
- Most **modern-day phobias** are exaggerations of these ancient fears (**Marks and Nesse**, 1994).
- Modern things which are **dangerous** (e.g. cars, guns) rarely develop into phobias.
- **Preparedness**: animals are biologically prepared to rapidly learn an association between particular stimuli and fear (**Seligman**, 1970).
- Once learned such associations are **difficult to extinguish**.

7½ MINUTES WORTH OF AO2

- Ancient fears explain **uneven distribution** of phobias.
- **Genetic basis** for phobias e.g. **Kendler** (2001) concluded that there is a common genetic factor in all phobias as well as unique genetic factors for specific phobias.
- **Preparedness**: a review of evidence by **McNally** (1987) concluded that there is evidence that ancient fears are harder to unlearn but they are learned more readily.
- However **clinical phobias** tend to be 'non-prepared' and do not show characteristics of prepared behaviours (**Merckelbach et al.**, 1988).
- **Alternative explanations**: behavioural therapies successful with phobias which supports the learned component.

Anxiety probably evolved as an emotional response increasing our ability to cope with threats in our environment, particularly situations that threatened a loss of life, health, relationships, status, etc. Some stimuli are more likely to be feared than others. These 'ancient fears' represented very real dangers to our ancestors, and included snakes, heights and leaving the home range, whereas other stimuli that were also around in the ancestral environment (such as stones and leaves) posed no significant danger and so were rarely feared. Most modern-day phobias are exaggerations of these ancient fears (Marks and Nesse, 1994).

> The fear that many of us have of dentists may have grown out of the ancient fears of pain, injury and infection.

The main value of an ancient fear explanation of the evolution of anxiety disorders is that it explains the uneven distribution of phobias, i.e. that some fears are more common than others. It also explains why things which are dangerous in modern times (e.g. cars, guns) rarely develop into phobias because they have not been around for long enough to influence our adaptive selection.

Anxiety is only useful if it is regulated, and if it gives us an adaptive advantage. Experiencing anxiety after a loss would not be adaptive, so human beings have evolved to respond to potential threats (prepotency). Those individuals who could respond appropriately to the 'ancient fears' would be more likely to survive and pass on their genes. Natural selection has shaped our nervous system so that we attend more to certain cues (e.g. sudden noises, snake-like stimuli) than others. For example, fear of spiders and snakes provided survival advantages to early humans, and present-day phobias are linked to the remnants of these fears.

> Prepotency leads to a non-random distribution of fears – most of which would be classified as 'ancient fears'.

Support for prepotency theory comes from Öhman and Soares (1994), who provided evidence that important components of phobic responses are set in motion before the phobic stimulus is represented in awareness. Humans express the greatest fear of animals whose form is most discrepant from human form, e.g. skin texture, number of limbs (Bennett-Levy and Marteau, 1984), which suggests an innate readiness to fear certain objects and characteristics that might represent danger to the individual. Agras et al. (1969) claim that it is strangeness rather than discrepancy from the human form, which explains why phobias increase through childhood and then decline, i.e. we must learn what the normal forms of animals are.

> We tend to fear things that are *unpredictable*, and therefore more potentially dangerous.

It is more flexible to have an innate readiness to learn about dangerous situations rather than to inherit rigid behavioural responses to specific situations. The concept of preparedness (Seligman, 1970) accounts for this. Seligman claims that animals are biologically prepared to rapidly learn an association between particular stimuli and fear. Once learned, such associations are difficult to extinguish. For example, an infant may observe fear of strangers in the mother, which then produces an equivalent fear response in the child. What is inherited, therefore, is the predisposition to learn this fear through observation rather than having an innate fear of strangers.

> Examples help to illustrate a point, but are more effective if embedded into the description as here.

A review of laboratory studies of preparedness concluded that there is evidence that ancient fears are harder to unlearn but not that they are learned more readily (McNally, 1987). Davey (1995) therefore proposed a simpler explanation – expectancy bias. This is the expectation that fear-relevant stimuli (such as dangerous situations) will produce negative consequences in the future. Davey claims that no reference to evolutionary past history is needed. This explains the existence of some modern phobias (e.g. of hypodermic needles). Most studies of preparedness have focused on avoidance responses rather than on clinical disorders. Studies of individuals suffering from clinical anxiety disorders do not support the concept of preparedness. For example, in Merckelbach et al.'s study (1988) most of the clinical phobias in the sample studied were rated as unprepared rather than prepared.

> It is important that alternative explanations are not just offered as more description, but that they are part of a critical commentary.

Chapter 7

Topic 1: Evolutionary factors in the development of human intelligence

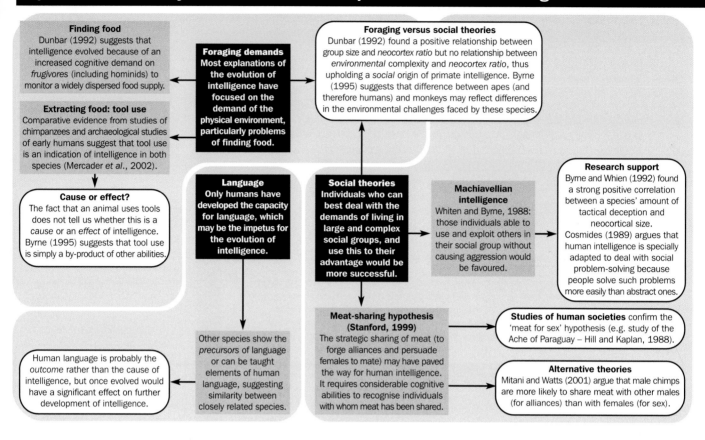

Finding food
Dunbar (1992) suggests that intelligence evolved because of an increased cognitive demand on *frugivores* (including hominids) to monitor a widely dispersed food supply.

Extracting food: tool use
Comparative evidence from studies of chimpanzees and archaeological studies of early humans suggest that tool use is an indication of intelligence in both species (Mercader *et al.*, 2002).

Cause or effect?
The fact that an animal uses tools does not tell us whether this is a *cause* or an *effect* of intelligence. Byrne (1995) suggests that tool use is simply a by-product of other abilities.

Foraging demands
Most explanations of the evolution of intelligence have focused on the demand of the physical environment, particularly problems of finding food.

Language
Only humans have developed the capacity for language, which may be the impetus for the evolution of intelligence.

Foraging versus social theories
Dunbar (1992) found a positive relationship between group size and *neocortex ratio* but no relationship between *environmental* complexity and *neocortex ratio*, thus upholding a *social* origin of primate intelligence. Byrne (1995) suggests that difference between apes (and therefore humans) and monkeys may reflect differences in the environmental challenges faced by these species.

Social theories
Individuals who can best deal with the demands of living in large and complex social groups, and use this to their advantage would be more successful.

Machiavellian intelligence
Whiten and Byrne, 1988: those individuals able to use and exploit others in their social group without causing aggression would be favoured.

Research support
Byrne and Whien (1992) found a strong positive correlation between a species' amount of tactical deception and neocortical size.
Cosmides (1989) argues that human intelligence is specially adapted to deal with social problem-solving because people solve such problems more easily than abstract ones.

Human language is probably the *outcome* rather than the cause of intelligence, but once evolved would have a significant effect on further development of intelligence.

Other species show the *precursors* of language or can be taught elements of human language, suggesting similarity between closely related species.

Meat-sharing hypothesis (Stanford, 1999)
The strategic sharing of meat (to forge alliances and persuade females to mate) may have paved the way for human intelligence. It requires considerable cognitive abilities to recognise individuals with whom meat has been shared.

Studies of human societies confirm the 'meat for sex' hypothesis (e.g. study of the Ache of Paraguay – Hill and Kaplan, 1988).

Alternative theories
Mitani and Watts (2001) argue that male chimps are more likely to share meat with other males (for alliances) than with females (for sex).

Topic 2: The relationship between brain size and intelligence

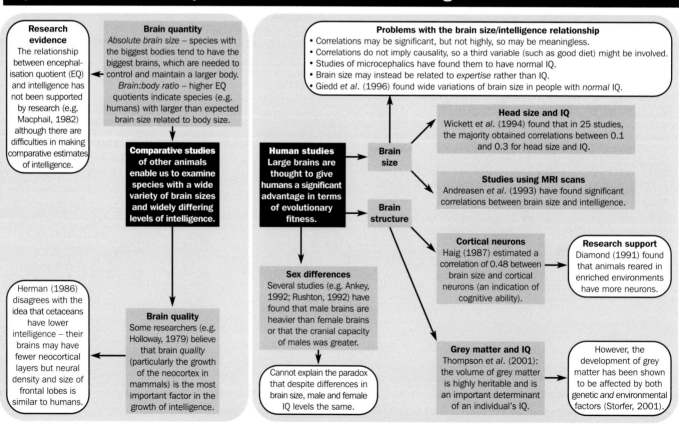

Research evidence
The relationship between encephalisation quotient (EQ) and intelligence has not been supported by research (e.g. Macphail, 1982) although there are difficulties in making comparative estimates of intelligence.

Brain quantity
Absolute brain size – species with the biggest bodies tend to have the biggest brains, which are needed to control and maintain a larger body.
Brain:body ratio – higher EQ quotients indicate species (e.g. humans) with larger than expected brain size related to body size.

Problems with the brain size/intelligence relationship
- Correlations may be significant, but not highly, so may be meaningless.
- Correlations do not imply causality, so a third variable (such as good diet) might be involved.
- Studies of microcephalics have found them to have normal IQ.
- Brain size may instead be related to *expertise* rather than IQ.
- Giedd *et al.* (1996) found wide variations of brain size in people with *normal* IQ.

Comparative studies of other animals enable us to examine species with a wide variety of brain sizes and widely differing levels of intelligence.

Human studies
Large brains are thought to give humans a significant advantage in terms of evolutionary fitness.

Brain size

Brain structure

Head size and IQ
Wickett *et al.* (1994) found that in 25 studies, the majority obtained correlations between 0.1 and 0.3 for head size and IQ.

Studies using MRI scans
Andreasen *et al.* (1993) have found significant correlations between brain size and intelligence.

Herman (1986) disagrees with the idea that cetaceans have lower intelligence – their brains may have fewer neocortical layers but neural density and size of frontal lobes is similar to humans.

Brain quality
Some researchers (e.g. Holloway, 1979) believe that brain *quality* (particularly the growth of the neocortex in mammals) is the most important factor in the growth of intelligence.

Sex differences
Several studies (e.g. Ankey, 1992; Rushton, 1992) have found that male brains are heavier than female brains or that the cranial capacity of males was greater.

Cannot explain the paradox that despite differences in brain size, male and female IQ levels the same.

Cortical neurons
Haig (1987) estimated a correlation of 0.48 between brain size and cortical neurons (an indication of cognitive ability).

Research support
Diamond (1991) found that animals reared in enriched environments have more neurons.

Grey matter and IQ
Thompson *et al.* (2001): the volume of grey matter is highly heritable and is an important determinant of an individual's IQ.

However, the development of grey matter has been shown to be affected by both genetic *and* environmental factors (Storfer, 2001).

Probable questions

1. Critically consider evolutionary factors in the development of human intelligence. *(24 marks)*

2. Discuss **two** evolutionary factors in the development of human intelligence. *(24 marks)*

Possible questions

3. Discuss the evolution of human intelligence. *(24 marks)*

You do have to take care to read any question carefully because the wording of each question requires you to shape your knowledge in different ways. Question 1 is worded in the most likely way as it follows the specification directly, so you may have a 'prepared' answer ready. Question 2 uses a less predictable wording and requires you to shape your 'prepared' answer to fit the demands of the question.

In both questions 1 and 2 you could present an answer that described and evaluated two evolutionary factors in the development of human intelligence. In both answers you would receive a partial performance penalty if you discussed only one factor (maximum of 8 marks for AO1 and maximum of 8 marks for AO2). However in question 2 you would not get credit for discussing more than two factors. All your work would be read by the examiner and marks awarded to the best two factors.

Possible 'factors' would be foraging demands, social complexity or language. In question 2 there is no requirement for the two factors to be described and evaluated in equal measure (i.e. balanced). This is because if you described one factor only you could receive a maximum of 16 marks; therefore you could still get full marks if the second factor was covered in half as much time (less breadth but similar detail).

It is possible that you could be asked a more open question about the evolution of human intelligence. Essentially you could present the same answer here as you would for question 1 but the 'openness' of this question means that you could shift the emphasis of your answer and, instead of considering evolutionary factors in the development of human intelligence, you could describe the stages in the evolution of intelligence and offer commentary by using research evidence. You could also launch a general attack on the theory of evolution (e.g. that there is no actual evidence for it and in some instances it is difficult to see how certain characteristics would be selected).

In all three of these essays you could incorporate material related to topic 2, on the relationship between brain size and intelligence. However, it is important to ensure that you use evidence relating to brain size to explain how intelligence has evolved rather than simply describing the relationship between brain size and intelligence. Just stating that there is a relationship between brain size and intelligence doesn't tell us anything about how intelligence evolved.

Probable questions

1. Discuss the relationship between brain size and intelligence. *(24 marks)*

2. Describe and evaluate research (theories **and/or** studies) of the relationship between brain size and intelligence. *(24 marks)*

Possible questions

3. (a) Outline evolutionary factors in the development of human intelligence. *(12 marks)*

   (b) To what extent has research supported the claim that there is a relationship between brain size and intelligence? *(12 marks)*

Again questions 1 and 2 are simply different ways of saying the same thing. Even though question 2 includes the term 'research' this is an umbrella term including theories/explanations/studies. It would be hard to see how you would answer question 1 without describing research.

If you do wish to use studies as AO2 this must be clear in terms of the way you use such material, otherwise they would be seen as part of the AO1 content of your answer.

Question 3 is less likely but still a question possibility. The part (a) is all AO1. The use of the term 'outline' indicates that breadth is important in this particular question – the question acknowledges that if you describe many factors then you may well sacrifice depth for breadth. So here you are encouraged to go more for breadth.

Part (b) uses the AO2 injunction 'to what extent?'. Candidates often find it difficult to avoid including AO1 material in their answers to such questions but, if you do, such AO1 material would receive a maximum of 4 marks. The key is to *use* your knowledge to present an answer to the question – is brain size related to intelligence? You might look at arguments that suggest brain size is related to intelligence and arguments that suggest brain size is not related to intelligence. You do not have to present a conclusion but can if it seems appropriate. Don't confuse a summary with a conclusion. A summary is a brief resumé of the points covered whereas a conclusion is a generalisation based on the facts examined.

Chapter 7

TOPIC 1: EVOLUTIONARY FACTORS IN THE DEVELOPMENT OF HUMAN INTELLIGENCE

SAMPLE ESSAY PLAN

Question 1: Critically consider evolutionary factors in the development of human intelligence. (24 marks)

FORAGING DEMANDS

5 MINUTES WORTH OF AO1
- **Frugivores** deal with spatially and temporally dispersed food supply leading to increased cognitive demand (**Dunbar**, 1992).
- **Foliovores** have smaller home ranges.
- **Early hominids** were frugivores.
- **More successful species use tools** e.g. chimpanzees, early humans and successful hunter-gatherers (e.g. !Kung San) (**Mercader et al.**, 2002).

5 MINUTES WORTH OF AO2
- Foraging skills may be a **cause or effect**.
- **Dunbar** (1992) found no relationship between neocortex ratio and environmental complexity.
- Tool use may be a **cause or effect**, only chimpanzees use them in the wild and so they may be a by-product of other abilities (**Byrne**, 1995).
- Many animals who use tools acquire such skills through **trial-and-error** learning not intelligence (**Visalberghi and Trinca**, 1987).

SOCIAL COMPLEXITY

5 MINUTES WORTH OF AO1
- **Social factors** are more complex than physical factors (**Humphrey**, 1976).
- Individuals who exploit others without causing aggression display **Machiavellian intelligence**.
- Individuals who cope best with **social situations** have an adaptive advantage.
- Such manipulative behaviour **appears cooperative** but is ultimately selfish.
- Only catarrhine primates (baboons, apes, humans) **cultivate alliances** based on an individual's future help (**Harcourt**, 1992).
- Only great apes can **plan** manipulative tricks e.g. divert attention or create an image (**Byrne**, 1995).

5 MINUTES WORTH OF AO2
- Strong positive correlation between mean group size and neocortex ratio (as measure of intelligence) (**Dunbar**, 1992).
- **Polygamous primates** have larger neocortex ratio, as polygamy involves more complex social relations.
- Strong positive correlation between species' amount of tactical deception and neocortex size (**Byrne and Whiten**, 1992).
- People **solve social problems** more easily and solve social problems involving cheating best of all (**Cosmides and Tooby**, 1992).
- **Byrne** (1995) suggests apes and monkeys different because of environmental challenges.

LANGUAGE

5 MINUTES WORTH OF AO1
- **Language** only found in humans, may be impetus for development of intelligence.
- Some animals have **precursors of language** (e.g. understanding others' intentions) suggesting similarity between related species.
- Can also teach some animals **sign language**, this would then lead to increased intelligence.

5 MINUTES WORTH OF AO2
- Human language may be the **outcome of intelligence** rather than cause.
- Once it developed would **further affect intelligence**.
- Language makes **cultural transmission** of knowledge possible.

Question 2: Discuss **two** evolutionary factors in the development of human intelligence. (24 marks)

FORAGING DEMANDS

5 MINUTES WORTH OF AO1
- The description of theory 1, above.

5 MINUTES WORTH OF AO2
- The evaluation of theory 1, above.

LANGUAGE

10 MINUTES WORTH OF AO1
The description of theory 1 above, plus:
- **Meat-sharing hypothesis** (**Stanford**, 1999): shared meat involved forging alliances and used to persuade females to mate.
- Stanford in the **Gombe** observed male chimpanzees **using meat** to entice females, and **hunting more** when females in season.
- Considerable cognitive abilities needed to **recognise individuals** with whom meat has been shared.

10 MINUTES WORTH OF AO2
The evaluation of theory 1 above, plus:
- Studies of human societies confirm 'meat for sex', e.g. the Ache of Paraguay (**Hill and Kaplan**, 1988).
- Other studies in the Gombe (e.g. **Gilby**, 2001) found alpha males sharing meat in and out of oestrus – perhaps meat for sex only needed by lower males.
- **Mitani and Watts** (2001) argue that meat is for alliances not sex.

Dunbar (1992) suggests that intelligence evolved because of an increased cognitive demand on frugivores to monitor a food supply that was both spatially and temporally dispersed. Foliovores, on the other hand, have smaller home ranges and can therefore monitor food availability more easily. As a result, there was less pressure for the development of complex cognitive abilities. It is likely that early hominids were frugivores, and therefore faced the foraging pressures that would lead to the evolution of intelligence. More successful species such as chimpanzees, early humans and successful hunter-gatherers (e.g. the !Kung San) developed tool use (Mercader et al., 2002). Tool use is therefore regarded as an indication of intelligence in both human and non-human species.

> In this first explanation, intelligence is seen as a response to the demands of the *physical* environment.

Foraging skills may be a cause or an effect of intelligence. Dunbar (1992) assessed environmental complexity for primate species, and found no relationship between neocortex ratio (an indicator of intelligence) and environmental complexity as might be predicted by this explanation. The fact that an animal uses tools does not tell us whether tool use is a cause or an effect of intelligence. Of all the great apes, only chimpanzees make use of tools in the wild, which led Byrne (1995) to suggest that tool use may be a by-product of other abilities, i.e. an effect rather than a cause. Many animals who use tools acquire such skills through trial-and-error learning rather than through intelligence (Visalberghi and Trinca, 1987).

> You might also use the archaeological evidence (about tool use) from Mercader *et al.* (2000) as supporting evidence for the importance of tool use in the evolution of intelligence.

Humphrey (1976) argues that members of the same species present a different type of complexity to the relatively stable world of the physical environment. Individuals who can use and exploit others without causing aggression display Machiavellian intelligence (Byrne and Whiten, 1988). This hypothesis proposes that much of the intelligent behaviour of primates is primarily an adaptation to the complexities of their social lives. Such manipulative behaviour may appear cooperative but is ultimately selfish. Power in complex social groups is often determined by having the right allies, but only catarrhine primates (baboons, apes, humans) cultivate alliances based on an individual's potential future help (Harcourt, 1992). Among social-living animals, individuals can use behavioural tactics to manipulate others into unwitting help. The ability to understand and plan deception (e.g. diverting attention or creating an image) appears to be restricted to the great apes (Byrne, 1995).

> In an essay such as this you don't need to explain *why* this is called Machiavellian intelligence.

Research evidence for the social origin of intelligence comes from studies which show a strong positive correlation between mean group size and neocortex ratio (Dunbar, 1992). Dunbar also reported that polygamous primates had a larger neocortex ratio than monogamous primates, as polygamy would involve more complex social relations. Further support comes from a study which found a strong positive correlation between species' amount of tactical deception and neocortex size (Byrne and Whiten, 1992). Research by Cosmides and Tooby (1992) showed that humans solve social problems more easily than abstract ones, and solve social problems involving cheating best of all. This illustrates the importance of social intelligence in human evolution. Group size alone does not explain why apes are more intelligent than monkeys. Byrne (1995) suggests apes and monkeys are different because of their different environmental challenges.

> Some challenges (such as hunting) involve both physical and social skills, so it may be impossible to disentangle their respective influences.

True language is only found in humans, and so may have been the impetus for the development of intelligence. Some animals have precursors of language (e.g. understanding others' intentions), and research has also shown that primates can be taught to express thoughts and emotions through sign language. This suggests that there is some similarity between related species, and a relatively narrow gap between human cognitive skills and those of other primates.

> This mention of the role of language in the evolution of human intelligence is brief but just about sufficiently detailed to have an impact on the overall mark for the essay.

Human language may be the outcome of intelligence rather than its cause, although once language evolved, it had a significant effect on the future development of intelligence. In any generation, learning is enhanced by a cultural transmission of knowledge, which is made possible by language.

TOPIC 2: THE RELATIONSHIP BETWEEN BRAIN SIZE AND INTELLIGENCE

SAMPLE ESSAY PLAN

Question 1: Discuss the relationship between brain size and intelligence. (24 marks)

15 MINUTES WORTH OF AO1

Brain quantity and quality:

- **Absolute brain size**: animals with biggest bodies have biggest brains to control body.
- **Brain–body ratio**: higher EQ indicates species with larger than expected brains, suggesting higher levels of intelligence (**Jerison**, 1978).
- **Brain quality**: e.g. mammals have six layers of neocortex but cetaceans have only five (**Holloway**, 1979).

Human brain size:

- **Human head size** and IQ correlations between 0.1 & 0.3 (**Wickett et al.**, 1994).
- **Human brain size** and IQ significantly correlated in studies using MRI scans (**Andreasen et al.**, 1993).

Human brain structure:

- **Cortical neurons** (indication of cognitive ability) significantly correlated (.48) with brain size (**Haig**, 1987).
- **Grey matter** is highly heritable, demonstrated in studies of twins (**Thompson et al.**, 2001), accounts for 15% variation in IQ.
- **Sex differences**: male brains heavier than female brains (e.g. **Ankey**, 1992), males have more cortical brain cells (**Pakkenberg and Gunderson**, 1997).

15 MINUTES WORTH OF AO2

- Relationship between EQ and intelligence not supported, **Macphail** (1982) found that rats and squirrels performed as well but squirrels had higher EQ.
- But **difficult to compare intelligence** in different species because depends on how it is tested (**Davis**, 1996) e.g. rats do poorly when tested visually but not if smell is used.
- **Cetaceans** have **less neocortex** but still outperform chimpanzees (**Herman**, 1986).
- **Brain size and intelligence: correlations fairly low** and may be meaningless e.g. highest correlation between cerebrospinal fluid volume and IQ (**Egan et al.**, 1994).
- People with small brains (**microcephalics**) have normal IQ (**Sassaman and Zartler**, 1982).
- Brain size may be related to **expertise** rather than IQ, a critical skill for survival which is not measured by IQ tests (**Skoyles**, 1999).
- **Wide variation** in people with normal IQ suggests no simple relationship between brain size and IQ (**Giedd et al.**, 1996).
- **Cortical neurons**: animals raised in enriched environments have more neurons (**Diamond**, 1991), therefore an effect not a cause.
- Development of **grey matter** is affected by genetic and environmental factors (e.g. diet) (**Storfer**, 2001).
- **Sex differences** in brain can't explain **paradox** that women and men have same IQ scores (**Peters**, 1993).

Question 3: (a) Outline evolutionary factors in the development of human intelligence. (12 marks)
(b) To what extent has research supported the claim that there is a relationship between brain size and intelligence? (12 marks)

(A) 15 MINUTES WORTH OF AO1

- As AO1 for question 1 on page 134.

(B) 15 MINUTES WORTH OF AO2

- Higher EQ indicates species with higher than expected intelligence (**Jerison**, 1978).
- But contradictory evidence e.g **Macphail** (1982) found rats and squirrels (higher EQ) performed as well.
- **Difficult to compare intelligence** in different species because different abilities.
- Growth of neocortex in humans may explain intelligence (**Holloway**, 1979).
- But **cetaceans** have **less neocortex** but still outperform chimpanzees (**Herman**, 1986).
- **Correlations** found between **human head size** and IQ (**Wickett et al.**, 1994), **human brain size** and IQ using MRI scans (**Andreasen et al.**, 1993), human brain size and **cortical neurons** (cognitive ability) (**Haig**, 1987).
- But **cause and effect** not demonstrated, e.g. **diet** may be an intervening variable.
- People with small brains (**microcephalics**) have normal IQ (**Sassaman and Zartler**, 1982).
- **Cortical neurons**: animals raised in enriched environments have more neurons (**Diamond**, 1991), therefore an effect not a cause.
- **Wide variation** in people with normal IQ suggests no simple relationship between brain size and IQ (**Giedd et al.**, 1996).
- **Sex differences** in brain can't explain **paradox** that women and men have same IQ scores (**Peters**, 1993).

If intelligence were determined by absolute brain size, the most intelligent species would be the sperm whale. However, animals with the biggest bodies have the biggest brains to control and maintain their large bodies. Jerison (1978) developed the encephalisation quotient (EQ) as a way of judging the intelligence of different species by comparing actual brain size to expected brain size for that body size. A higher EQ indicates species with larger than expected brains, suggesting higher levels of intelligence. Using this approach, human beings have the highest EQ of any animal. Some researchers believe that brain quality is the most important factor in the development of intelligence. In particular, Holloway (1979) suggests that the growth of the neocortex in mammals is responsible for the evolution of intelligence. In mammals, the neocortex has six layers, whereas in cetaceans such as whales and dolphins, there are only five, which may account for the development of greater intelligence in humans compared to cetaceans.

Research into the relationship between head size (as an indicator of brain size) and IQ has shown correlations between 0.1 & 0.3 (Wickett et al., 1994). Andreasen et al. (1993) found a significant correlation between human brain size and IQ using MRI scans. Other studies have focused more on human brain structure. Haig (1987) estimated a correlation of 0.48 between brain size and number of cortical neurons (and indicator of cognitive ability and therefore IQ), with smaller brains having considerably less cortical neurons than larger brains. Thompson et al. (2001) found that the volume of grey matter (important for cognition) was highly heritable, and an important determinant of an individual's IQ, accounting for up to 15% of the variation in intelligence. Ankey (1992) found that male brains were heavier than female brains, and research using stereological techniques has shown that males also have more cortical brain cells (Pakkenberg and Gunderson, 1997).

The relationship between EQ and intelligence claimed by Jerison has not been supported in research, for example Macphail (1982) found that rats and squirrels performed at about the same level on learning tasks, but squirrels had higher EQ. A further problem is trying to make a comparison in intelligence across different species. A species' intelligence may be underestimated because of the circumstances used in testing (Davis, 1996). For example, rats have typically been given a low intelligence rating because they were unable to complete a visual discrimination task. However, when given the same discrimination task, but with a different sensory modality (smell), they performed well. The claim that cetaceans have lower levels of intelligence because they have less neocortex has been challenged by the finding that dolphins have the ability to perform complex tasks beyond the level of chimpanzees (Herman, 1986).

Many of the correlations obtained for brain size and IQ have been fairly low and may be meaningless. For example Egan et al. (1994) found that the highest correlation was not between brain matter and IQ, but cerebrospinal fluid volume and IQ. A further problem for the claim that large brains are associated with high IQ is the finding that people with very small brains (microcephalics) still have normal IQ (Sassaman and Zartler, 1982). Brain size may be related to expertise rather than IQ, a critical skill for survival which is not measured by IQ tests (Skoyles, 1999). Giedd et al. (1996) found a wide variation in people with normal IQ levels, suggesting there is no simple relationship between brain size and IQ. The number of cortical neurons may not be the cause of high IQ, but an effect, as animals raised in enriched environments develop more cortical neurons (Diamond, 1991). Likewise, Storfer (2001) showed that the development of grey matter is not only affected by genetic factors, but also by environmental factors such as improved diet. Finally, research showing differences in brain size between males and females cannot explain the paradox that women and men tend to score the same on IQ tests (Peters, 1993).

You may be tempted to give lots of *examples* (of different species) in this paragraph. This would limit the scope of your description, so any such examples should be restricted to enough to make your point.

But do these sex differences in brain size correlate with IQ differences? The AO2 commentary will answer this question.

It would be insufficient to make the claim that dolphins are clever because they can do tricks. It is necessary to provide research evidence to substantiate your claim.

An alternative explanation is that men and women excel at different intellectual abilities, with male abilities requiring extra capacity.

Topic 1: Clinical characteristics

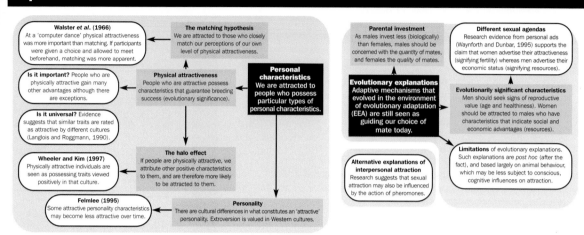

Walster et al. (1966)
At a 'computer dance' physical attractiveness was more important than matching. If participants were given a choice and allowed to meet beforehand, matching was more apparent.

The matching hypothesis
We are attracted to those who closely match our perceptions of our own level of physical attractiveness.

Personal characteristics
We are attracted to people who possess particular types of personal characteristics.

Is it important? People who are physically attractive gain many other advantages although there are exceptions.

Physical attractiveness
People who are attractive possess characteristics that guarantee breeding success (evolutionary significance).

Is it universal? Evidence suggests that similar traits are rated as attractive by different cultures (Langlois and Roggmann, 1990).

Wheeler and Kim (1997)
Physically attractive individuals are seen as possessing traits viewed positively in that culture.

The halo effect
If people are physically attractive, we attribute other positive characteristics to them, and are therefore more likely to be attracted to them.

Felmlee (1995)
Some attractive personality characteristics may become less attractive over time.

Personality
There are cultural differences in what constitutes an 'attractive' personality. Extroversion is valued in Western cultures.

Parental investment
As males invest less (biologically) than females, males should be concerned with the *quantity* of mates, and females the *quality* of mates.

Different sexual agendas
Research evidence from personal ads (Waynforth and Dunbar, 1995) supports the claim that women advertise their attractiveness (signifying fertility) whereas men advertise their economic status (signifying resources).

Evolutionary explanations
Adaptive mechanisms that evolved in the environment of evolutionary adaptation (EEA) are still seen as guiding our choice of mate today.

Evolutionarily significant characteristics
Men should seek signs of reproductive value (age and healthiness). Women should be attracted to males who have characteristics that indicate social and economic advantages (resources).

Alternative explanations of interpersonal attraction
Research suggests that sexual attraction may also be influenced by the action of pheromones.

Limitations of evolutionary explanations. Such explanations are *post hoc* (after the fact), and based largely on animal behaviour, which may be less subject to conscious, cognitive influences on attraction.

Topic 2: Biological explanations of schizophrenia

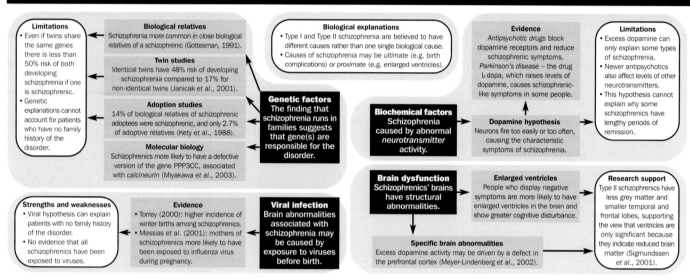

Limitations
• Even if twins share the same genes there is less than 50% risk of *both* developing schizophrenia if one is schizophrenic.
• Genetic explanations cannot account for patients who have no family history of the disorder.

Biological relatives
Schizophrenia more common in close biological relatives of a schizophrenic (Gottesman, 1991).

Twin studies
Identical twins have 48% risk of developing schizophrenia compared to 17% for non-identical twins (Janicak et al., 2001).

Adoption studies
14% of biological relatives of schizophrenic adoptees were schizophrenic, and only 2.7% of adoptive relatives (Kety et al., 1988).

Molecular biology
Schizophrenics more likely to have a defective version of the gene PPP3CC, associated with *calcineurin* (Miyakawa et al., 2003).

Genetic factors
The finding that schizophrenia runs in families suggests that gene(s) are responsible for the disorder.

Biological explanations
• Type I and Type II schizophrenia are believed to have different causes rather than one single biological cause.
• Causes of schizophrenia may be *ultimate* (e.g. birth complications) or *proximate* (e.g. enlarged ventricles).

Evidence
Antipsychotic drugs block dopamine receptors and reduce schizophrenic symptoms. *Parkinson's disease* – the drug L-dopa, which raises levels of dopamine, causes schizophrenic-like symptoms in some people.

Limitations
• Excess dopamine can only explain *some* types of schizophrenia.
• Newer antipsychotics also affect levels of other neurotransmitters.
• This hypothesis cannot explain why some schizophrenics have lengthy periods of remission.

Biochemical factors
Schizophrenia caused by abnormal *neurotransmitter* activity.

Dopamine hypothesis
Neurons fire too easily or too often, causing the characteristic symptoms of schizophrenia.

Strengths and weaknesses
• Viral hypothesis can explain patients with no family history of the disorder.
• No evidence that all schizophrenics have been exposed to viruses.

Evidence
• Torrey (2000): higher incidence of winter births among schizophrenics.
• Messias et al. (2001): mothers of schizophrenics more likely to have been exposed to influenza virus during pregnancy.

Viral infection
Brain abnormalities associated with schizophrenia may be caused by exposure to viruses before birth.

Brain dysfunction
Schizophrenics' brains have structural abnormalities.

Enlarged ventricles
People who display negative symptoms are more likely to have enlarged ventricles in the brain and show greater cognitive disturbance.

Research support
Type II schizophrenics have less grey matter and smaller temporal and frontal lobes, supporting the view that ventricles are only significant because they indicate reduced brain matter (Sigmundssen et al., 2001).

Specific brain abnormalities
Excess dopamine activity may be driven by a defect in the prefrontal cortex (Meyer-Lindenberg et al., 2002).

Topic 2: Psychological explanations of schizophrenia

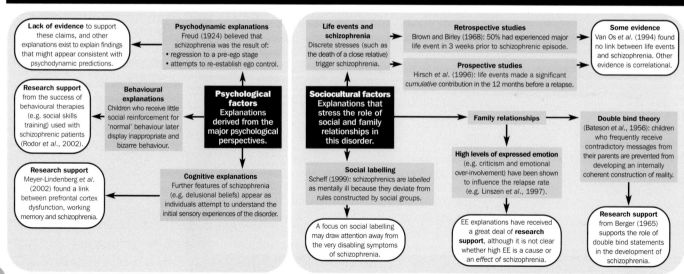

Lack of evidence to support these claims, and other explanations exist to explain findings that might appear consistent with psychodynamic predictions.

Psychodynamic explanations
Freud (1924) believed that schizophrenia was the result of:
• regression to a pre-ego stage
• attempts to re-establish ego control.

Life events and schizophrenia
Discrete stresses (such as the death of a close relative) trigger schizophrenia.

Retrospective studies
Brown and Birley (1968): 50% had experienced major life event in 3 weeks prior to schizophrenic episode.

Some evidence
Van Os et al. (1994) found no link between life events and schizophrenia. Other evidence is correlational.

Prospective studies
Hirsch et al. (1996): life events made a significant *cumulative* contribution in the 12 months before a relapse.

Research support from the success of behavioural therapies (e.g. social skills training) used with schizophrenic patients (Rodor et al., 2002).

Behavioural explanations
Children who receive little social reinforcement for 'normal' behaviour later display inappropriate and bizarre behaviour.

Psychological factors
Explanations derived from the major psychological perspectives.

Sociocultural factors
Explanations that stress the role of social and family relationships in this disorder.

Family relationships

Double bind theory
(Bateson et al., 1956): children who frequently receive contradictory messages from their parents are prevented from developing an internally coherent construction of reality.

Research support
Meyer-Lindenberg et al. (2002) found a link between prefrontal cortex dysfunction, working memory and schizophrenia.

Cognitive explanations
Further features of schizophrenia (e.g. delusional beliefs) appear as individuals attempt to understand the initial sensory experiences of the disorder.

Social labelling
Scheff (1999): schizophrenics are *labelled* as mentally ill because they deviate from rules constructed by social groups.

High levels of expressed emotion
(e.g. criticism and emotional over-involvement) have been shown to influence the relapse rate (e.g. Linszen et al., 1997).

A focus on social labelling may draw attention away from the very disabling symptoms of schizophrenia.

EE explanations have received a great deal of **research support**, although it is not clear whether high EE is a *cause* or an *effect* of schizophrenia.

Research support from Berger (1965) supports the role of double bind statements in the development of schizophrenia.

Probable questions

1. Critically consider **two or more** biological explanations of schizophrenia. *(30 marks)*

2. (a) Outline **two or more** clinical characteristics of schizophrenia. *(5 marks)*

   (b) Discuss **two or more** biological explanations of schizophrenia. *(25 marks)*

3. (a) Outline **two** biological explanations of schizophrenia. *(15 marks)*

   (b) To what extent are the **two** biological explanations of schizophrenia outlined in part (a) supported by research evidence? *(15 marks)*

Possible questions

4. (a) Describe **one** biological explanation of schizophrenia. *(10 marks)*

   (b) Outline and evaluate evidence on which the explanation of schizophrenia you described in part (a) is based. *(20 marks)*

Probable questions

1. Critically consider **two or more** psychological explanations of schizophrenia. *(30 marks)*

2. Outline and evaluate **one** psychological explanation of schizophrenia and **one** biological explanation of schizophrenia. *(30 marks)*

3. Critically consider **two or more** explanations of schizophrenia. *(30 marks)*

Possible questions

4. Describe and evaluate evidence on which **two or more** explanations of schizophrenia are based. *(30 marks)*

There is one important fact to recognise through the whole of this subsection – each division entry is exactly the same – the word 'schizophrenia' is replaced by 'depression' or any **one** anxiety disorder. This means that the same questions can be set in any division. In addition each division is subdivided into biological and psychological explanations – the same questions can be set on biological or psychological explanations as shown in topics 1 and 2 on this page. Or a question could be set combining biological and psychological explanations or, indeed, combining explanations of schizophrenia and explanations of depression.

In question 2 you have been asked to outline at least two clinical characteristics (if you provided only one clinical characteristic then there would be a partial performance penalty of maximum 3 marks). Note that this is the only time you should write about the clinical characteristics. In any essay on explanations of schizophrenia a description of the clinical characteristics would receive *no* marks even as an introduction. If you are not asked for them do not include them or in fact any definition of schizophrenia. Go straight into explanations.

Question 3 differs from question 1 in two ways. First, you will not gain credit for more than two explanations so you must restrict yourself to your best two. Second, you cannot simply present your prepared evaluations of the two explanations. In this question the AO2 component has been specified in part (b). Credit will be awarded only through the use of research evidence. This probably means that you need to avoid the use of research evidence in part (a) (as part of the explanation) and save it for part (b). However, in part (b) you must take care not to *describe* the evidence but to use it to consider the validity of the two explanations.

Question 4 contains an unusual mark split. Part (a) is all AO1 and means that you need to be able to write about 250–300 words describing one biological explanation. This means that you need to know one explanation in considerable detail. (Note that, in order to answer questions such as those above, you need about one or two explanations in less detail.)

Part (b) is a combination of 5 AO1 marks and 15 AO2 marks. This means that there will be some credit for descriptions of evidence (unlike question 3 (b)) but don't go overboard because you should have 3 times as much AO2 as AO1.

As suggested above the same questions could be set for psychological explanations as for biological explanations. We have shown a slightly different selection here just to indicate the range of possibilities.

Question 2 combines both topics in this division. You are required to give one example of each type of explanation. There is no credit for extra explanations. You are not, however, required to give both explanations in balance. If you only described and evaluated one explanation (psychological or biological) then the partial performance penalty states that the maximum mark would be 18 out of 30. So 'notionally' there are 18 marks for one explanation and 12 for the other.

In question 3 the choice of psychological or biological is yours – you can even do both, but again take care to remain selective and write appropriately detailed AO1 and elaborated AO2 rather than trying to briefly list everything you know.

Question 4 displays another question variety which just requires you to discuss the evidence for either psychological or biological explanations (or both). There will be no credit for describing the explanations themselves.

Chapter 8

SAMPLE ESSAY PLAN

Question 2: (a) Outline **two or more** clinical characteristics of schizophrenia. (5 marks)
(b) Discuss **two or more** biological explanations of schizophrenia. (25 marks)

(a)

6½ MINUTES WORTH OF AO1
- **Positive symptoms:** distortion of normal function.
- **Includes** delusions, sense of being controlled, auditory hallucinations, disordered thinking.
- **Negative symptoms** reflect a loss of normal function.
- **Includes** affective flattening, alogia (poverty of speech), avolition.
- **Diagnosis** based on at least a one-month duration of two or more positive symptoms.
- Negative symptoms persist during periods of few positive symptoms.

(b) EXPLANATION 1: GENETIC FACTORS

6½ MINUTES WORTH OF AO1
- **Family studies:** schizophrenia more common in closer biological relatives of a schizophrenic (**Gottesman**, 1991).
- **Twin studies:** identical twins have 48% risk of developing schizophrenia compared to 17% for non-identical twins (**Janicak et al.**, 2001).
- **Adoption studies:** 14% of biological relatives of schizophrenic adoptees were schizophrenic, and only 2.7% of adoptive relatives (**Kety et al.**, 1988).
- **Molecular biology:** Miyakawa *et al.* (2003). Schizophrenics more likely to have a defective version of the gene PPP3CC, associated with **calcineurin**.

6½ MINUTES WORTH OF AO2
- **Environmental component:** Even if twins share the same genes there is less than 50% risk of *both* developing schizophrenia if one is schizophrenic.
- **Diathesis-stress** model proposes that individuals may be genetically predisposed to become schizophrenic but the actual disorder depends on experience/stressors.
- Genetic explanations cannot account for patients who have **no family history** of the disorder (**Stirling and Hellewell**, 1999).
- If schizophrenia caused by **large number of genes**, then individuals with only a few of these genes would not develop schizophrenia.

(b) EXPLANATION 2: BIOCHEMICAL FACTORS

6½ MINUTES WORTH OF AO1
- **Dopamine hypothesis:** neurons fire too easily or too often, causing the characteristic symptoms of schizophrenia.
- **Dopamine neurons** important in **attention** which may explain problems of attention and thought that are common in schizophrenics (**Cromer**, 2003).
- **Evidence: antipsychotic drugs** block dopamine receptors and reduce schizophrenic symptoms.
- **Evidence: Parkinson's disease** – the drug L-dopa, which raises levels of dopamine, causes schizophrenic-like symptoms in some people (**Grilly**, 2002)

13½ MINUTES WORTH OF AO2
- Excess dopamine can only explain **some types** of schizophrenia.
- **Newer atypical antipsychotics** also affect levels of other neurotransmitters (e.g. **serotonin**) so doesn't point to dopamine exclusively (**Kasper et al.**, 1999).
- This hypothesis cannot explain why some schizophrenics have lengthy periods of **remission**.
- Could be explained by **variation in dopamine**, but there is no suggestion why this might occur.
- **Biological explanations in general:** Type I and Type II schizophrenia are believed to have different causes rather than one single biological cause.
- **Psychological explanations** offer a contrast e.g. EE and relapse (**Linszen et al.**, 1997).

Question 1: Critically consider **two or more** biological explanations of schizophrenia. (30 marks)

20 MINUTES WORTH OF AO1
The description of theory 1 above for part (b), plus:
- **Brain dysfunction:** structural abnormalities.
- People who display negative symptoms are more likely to have **enlarged ventricles** in the brain and show greater cognitive disturbance.
- Excess dopamine activity may be driven by a defect in the **prefrontal cortex** (**Meyer-Lindenberg et al.**, 2002).
- Brain abnormalities associated with schizophrenia may be caused by **exposure to viruses** before birth.
- Higher incidence of winter births among schizophrenics (**Torrey**, 2000).

20 MINUTES WORTH OF AO2
The evaluation of theory 1 above for part (b).

(a)

The symptoms of schizophrenia are divided into positive and negative. Positive symptoms reflect a distortion of normal function, and include delusions (bizarre beliefs that appear real but are not), a sense of being controlled (e.g. by an alien force), auditory hallucinations (e.g. hearing voices), and disordered thinking (e.g. the belief that thoughts are being broadcast to others). Negative symptoms reflect a lessening or loss of normal function, and include affective flattening (a reduction in the range and intensity of emotional expression), alogia (poverty of speech) and avolition (the inability to initiate and persist in goal-directed behaviour). A diagnosis of schizophrenia requires at least a one-month duration of two or more positive symptoms. Negative symptoms often persist during periods of few positive symptoms.

> The 'two or more' instruction is satisfied here by the distinction between positive and negative symptoms. These count as 'clinical characteristics' in the context of this question.

(b)

Family studies have found that schizophrenia is more common in the biological relatives of a schizophrenic, and the closer the degree of genetic relatedness, the greater the risk (Gottesman, 1991). Twin studies have shown that identical twins have a 48% risk of developing schizophrenia if their twin has the disorder compared to 17% for non-identical twins (Janicak et al., 2001). Adoption studies have shown that 14% of the biological relatives of adoptees with schizophrenia were classified as schizophrenic, compared to only 2.7% of their adoptive relatives (Kety et al., 1988). Research in molecular biology has found that schizophrenics are more likely to have a defective version of the gene PPP3CC, associated with the production of calcineurin, an enzyme that regulates the immune system (Miyakawa et al., 2003).

> There is sometimes a fine line between a research study and an explanation. You should stress the explanatory nature of research studies if they are used in lieu of explanations.

Evidence from genetic studies indicates that even when two individuals share the same genes (i.e. identical twins), there is less than 50% risk of both developing schizophrenia if one is schizophrenic, thus showing a significant environmental contribution to the disorder. The diathesis-stress model proposes that individuals may be genetically predisposed to become schizophrenic but the actual disorder depends on exposure to significant life stressors. A further problem for genetic explanations is that they cannot account for patients who have no family history of the disorder, which is the case for about two-thirds of schizophrenic patients (Stirling and Hellewell, 1999). However, if schizophrenia is caused by a large number of genes, then individuals who possess only a few of these genes would not develop schizophrenia. Schizophrenia would only develop when a large number of these genes are present.

> The diathesis-stress model does not deny a role for genetics, but proposes that the environment also plays an important 'triggering' role in schizophrenia.

The dopamine hypothesis emphasises the role of excess dopamine activity in schizophrenia. In schizophrenics dopamine neurons fire too easily or too often, leading to the characteristic symptoms of the disorder. Dopamine neurons play a key role in guiding attention, so disturbances in this process may lead to the problems of attention and thought that are common in people with schizophrenia (Cromer, 2003). The importance of dopamine in schizophrenia was demonstrated by the effect of antipsychotic drugs, which bind to the D2 dopamine receptors, blocking the transmission of nerve impulses and consequently reducing schizophrenic symptoms. Low levels of dopamine activity are found in sufferers of Parkinson's disease, and the drug L-dopa, which raises levels of dopamine, causes schizophrenic-type symptoms in some people (Grilly, 2002).

> As the specification includes reference to the evidence on which explanations are based, here evidence is being used *descriptively*. In another context it might be used as part of an AO2 commentary.

A problem with the dopamine hypothesis is that because antipsychotic drugs are effective only for the positive symptoms, this means that excess dopamine can only explain some types of schizophrenia. Newer atypical antipsychotics also affect levels of other neurotransmitters (e.g. serotonin) which suggests that dopamine is not the only biochemical factor involved in schizophrenia (Kasper et al., 1999). Also, this hypothesis cannot explain why some schizophrenics have lengthy periods of remission, where they are relatively free from the symptoms of the disorder. This could be explained by a variation in dopamine levels over time, but there is no suggestion why this might occur.

Attempts to explain schizophrenia simply in terms of one biological cause are challenged by the fact that there are different types of schizophrenia. Type I schizophrenia (characterised by positive symptoms) and Type II schizophrenia (characterised by negative symptoms) are believed to have different causes rather than one single biological cause. Explaining schizophrenia from a purely biological perspective is further challenged by research which shows an important role for environmental influences in the development and maintenance of the disorder. Research by Linszen et al. (1997), for example, found that patients returning to a family with high levels of expressed emotion (EE) were four times more likely to relapse than those in families with low levels of EE.

> As ever, alternative explanations must be handled carefully, i.e. built into your commentary rather than simply offered as alternative description.

SAMPLE ESSAY PLAN

Question 1: Critically consider **two or more** psychological explanations of schizophrenia. (30 marks)

PSYCHOLOGICAL FACTORS

10 MINUTES WORTH OF AO1

Psychodynamic explanations: Freud (1924) believed that schizophrenia was the result of:

- **Regression** to a pre-ego (infantile) stage; shown in some symptoms (e.g. delusions of grandeur).
- Attempts to re-establish **ego control**, some symptoms reflect this (e.g. delusions of grandeur).
- **Behavioural explanations:** faulty learning.
- Child receives **little social reinforcement** for 'normal' behaviour then displays inappropriate and bizarre behaviour.
- People ignore or respond erratically, thus reinforcing bizarre behaviour.
- **Cognitive explanations:** features of schizophrenia appear as individuals attempt to understand the initial **sensory experiences** of the disorder.
- Not confirmed by others which leads to **delusional beliefs** that others are hiding the truth.

10 MINUTES WORTH OF AO2

- There is **no research evidence** to support Freud's claims about the origins of schizophrenia.
- **Psychodynamic explanations:** schizophrenogenic mothers (rejecting, overprotective, dominant) (**Fromm-Reichmann,** 1948), parents of schizophrenics do behave differently but could be a consequence as well as cause (**Oltmanns et al.,** 1999).
- **Behavioural explanations: research supports** from the success of behavioural therapies (e.g. social skills training) used with schizophrenic patients (**Rodor et al.,** 2002).
- **Cognitive explanations: research supports** link between prefrontal cortex dysfunction, working memory and schizophrenia (**Meyer-Lindenberg et al.,** 2002).
- **Schielke et al.** (2000) found an abscess in the dorsal pons of a patient with auditory hallucinations.

SOCIOCULTURAL FACTORS

10 MINUTES WORTH OF AO1

- **Life events:** discrete stresses (such as the death of a close relative) trigger schizophrenia.
- **Retrospective studies:** 50% had experienced major life event in 3 weeks prior to schizophrenic episode (**Brown and Birley,** 1968).
- **Prospective studies:** life events made a significant cumulative contribution in the 12 months before a relapse (**Hirsch et al.,** 1996).

Family relationships:

- **Double bind theory** (**Bateson et al.,** 1956). Children who receive **contradictory messages** from their parents are prevented from developing an internally coherent construction of reality.
- Leads to **delusions** and **incoherent thought patterns.**
- **High levels of expressed emotion** (e.g. criticism and emotional over-involvement) have been shown to increase relapse rate (4 times greater) (**Linszen et al.,** 1997).

10 MINUTES WORTH OF AO2

- **Life events: van Os et al.** (1994) found no link between life events and schizophrenia. Other evidence is correlational.
- **Family relationships:** adopted children with biological schizophrenic parent developed illness if adopted family was 'disturbed' (**Tienari et al.,** 1994).
- **Double bind theory: Berger** (1965). Schizophrenics reported more double bind statements by mothers (but evidence from patients may not be reliable).
- **Liem** (1974) found **no difference** in parental communication in schizophrenic and normal families.
- **EE explanations** have received a great deal of **research support,** although it is not clear whether high EE is a **cause or an effect** of schizophrenia.
- **Diathesis-stress** model proposes that individuals may be genetically predisposed to become schizophrenic but the actual disorder depends on experience/stressors.

Question 4: Describe and evaluate evidence on which **two or more** explanations of schizophrenia are based. (30 marks)

EVIDENCE FOR PSYCHOLOGICAL FACTORS

10 MINUTES WORTH OF AO1

- **Twin studies** (e.g. **Janicak et al.,** 2001) **show** significant environmental component.
- Fromm-Reichmann (1948)
- Oltmanns et al. (1999)
- Rodor et al. (2002)
- Meyer-Lindenberg et al. (2002)

10 MINUTES WORTH OF AO2

- **Psychodynamic evidence:** could be consequence rather than cause.
- **Behavioural research** leads to successful therapies.
- **Meyer-Lindenberg et al.** (2002) study supports cognitive-biological link.
- Could produce 'virtual' therapy (**Yellowlees et al.,** 2002).

EVIDENCE FOR SOCIOCULTURAL FACTORS

10 MINUTES WORTH OF AO1

- Brown and Birley (1968)
- Hirsch et al. (1996)
- Tienari et al. (1994)
- Bateson et al. (1956)
- Berger (1965)
- Linszen et al. (1997)

10 MINUTES WORTH OF AO2

- **Life events** evidence is correlational.
- Contradicted by **van Os et al.** (1994).
- **Berger** study may be flawed and contradicted by **Liem** (1974).
- **EE** is a **cause or an effect** of schizophrenia.
- Psychological evidence contradicted by **biological evidence** e.g. success of drug therapies.
- **Diathesis-stress** explanation most likely.

Freud (1924) believed that schizophrenia was the result of regression to a pre-ego stage, and attempts to re-establish ego control. Freud believed that schizophrenia was an infantile state, with some symptoms (e.g. delusions of grandeur) reflecting this state, and others (e.g. auditory hallucinations) reflecting their attempt to re-establish ego control. Behavioural explanations of schizophrenia see the disorder as a consequence of faulty learning. Children who receive little social reinforcement for displaying 'normal' behaviour will begin to attend to inappropriate and irrelevant environmental cues. As a result, they will later display inappropriate and bizarre behaviour. Those who observe this bizarre behaviour either avoid it or respond erratically, thus reinforcing this behaviour which eventually deteriorates into a psychotic state. Cognitive explanations claim that the features of schizophrenia appear as individuals attempt to understand the initial sensory experiences of the disorder. When they first experience voices and other sensory disturbances, they turn to friends and family to confirm the validity of what they are experiencing. Others fail to confirm the reality of these experiences, so the schizophrenic develops delusional beliefs that other people are hiding the truth and are manipulating and persecuting them.

> There is a minimum of two explanations necessary for this question. If you include more than two (as we have here), you must ensure that there is sufficient detail in each.

There is no research evidence to support Freud's claims about the origins of schizophrenia, although other psychodynamic theorists have agreed that disordered family patterns are the cause of this disorder. For example, Fromm-Reichmann claimed that schizophrenogenic families, which were rejecting, overprotective and dominant were important contributors to the development of schizophrenia. Oltmanns et al. (1999) provided evidence that the parents of schizophrenics do behave differently in the presence of the disturbed schizophrenic, although this could be a consequence of their disorder as well as a cause. The validity of behavioural explanations of schizophrenia is supported by the success of behavioural therapies (e.g. social skills training) used with schizophrenic patients (Rodor et al., 2002). The success of such programmes in reintegrating schizophrenics into the community suggests that these are skills schizophrenics failed to learn in the first place. Cognitive explanations have some physiological evidence to support them. Meyer-Lindenberg et al. (2002) found a link between poor working memory (typical of schizophrenics) and reduced activity in the prefrontal cortex. Similarly, Schielke et al. (2000) found evidence of an abscess in the dorsal pons of a patient who developed continuous auditory hallucinations. Both studies suggest that initial sensory disturbances may lead to schizophrenia.

> The fact that certain therapies *help* schizophrenics can give us an insight into what caused their condition in the first place.

A major stress factor that has been associated with a higher risk of schizophrenic episodes is the occurrence of stressful life events. These are discrete stresses (such as the death of a close relative) that in some way trigger schizophrenia. In retrospective studies of life events and the onset of schizophrenia, 50% of schizophrenics had experienced a major life event in the three weeks prior to a schizophrenic episode (Brown and Birley, 1968). In studies that have monitored the presence or absence of life events prospectively, life events have been shown to make a significant *cumulative* contribution in the 12 months before a relapse rather than having a more concentrated effect in the period just before an episode (Hirsch et al., 1996). Bateson et al.'s double bind theory suggests that children who receive contradictory messages from their parents are prevented from developing an internally coherent construction of reality, as one message effectively invalidates the other. In the long term, this manifests itself in typically schizophrenic symptoms such as delusions and incoherent thought patterns. In families where there are high levels of expressed emotion (EE) (e.g. criticism and emotional over-involvement), this has been shown to significantly influence relapse rate, with schizophrenics returning to families with high EE being four times as likely to relapse as those in low EE families (Linszen et al., 1997).

> Note that the question does not specify the *initial* causes of schizophrenia, therefore discussion of the conditions affecting relapse rates are also relevant.

Not all evidence supports the role of life events in the development of schizophrenia. For example, van Os et al. (1994) found no link between life events and schizophrenia. Other evidence is correlational, with the possibility that the beginnings of the disorder (e.g. erratic behaviour) were the cause of the life events rather than the effect. The importance of family relationships in schizophrenia was demonstrated in a study by Tienari et al. (1994) which showed that adopted children with a biological schizophrenic parent developed the disorder only if the adopted family was 'disturbed'. Berger (1965) found evidence for the double bind theory in that schizophrenics reported more double bind statements by mothers than did non-schizophrenics, although this may not be reliable as these patients' recall may be affected by their disorder. However, Liem (1974) found no difference in parental communication in schizophrenic and normal families. EE explanations have received a great deal of research support, although it is not clear whether high EE is a cause or an effect of schizophrenia. In an attempt to resolve the debate over whether schizophrenia is caused by biological or psychological factors, the diathesis-stress model proposes that individuals may be genetically predisposed to become schizophrenic but the development of the disorder depends on specific experiences or stressors in their life.

> Rather than just state that studies were correlational, it is necessary to present the consequences of that fact for full AO2 credit.

Topic 1: Biological explanations of depression (unipolar disorder)

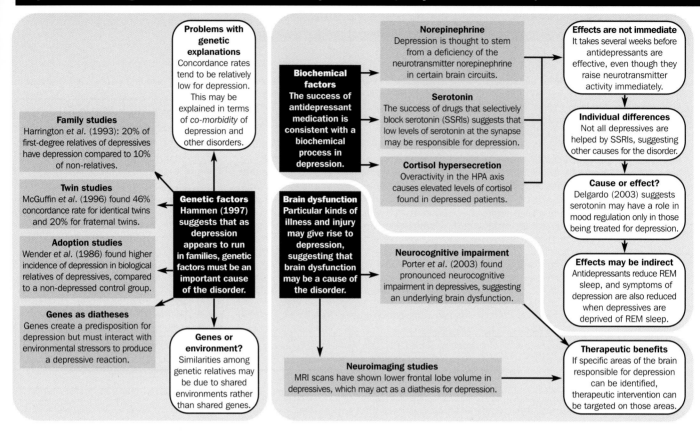

Problems with genetic explanations
Concordance rates tend to be relatively low for depression. This may be explained in terms of *co-morbidity* of depression and other disorders.

Family studies
Harrington *et al.* (1993): 20% of first-degree relatives of depressives have depression compared to 10% of non-relatives.

Twin studies
McGuffin *et al.* (1996) found 46% concordance rate for identical twins and 20% for fraternal twins.

Adoption studies
Wender *et al.* (1986) found higher incidence of depression in biological relatives of depressives, compared to a non-depressed control group.

Genes as diatheses
Genes create a predisposition for depression but must interact with environmental stressors to produce a depressive reaction.

Genetic factors
Hammen (1997) suggests that as depression appears to run in families, genetic factors must be an important cause of the disorder.

Genes or environment?
Similarities among genetic relatives may be due to shared environments rather than shared genes.

Biochemical factors
The success of antidepressant medication is consistent with a biochemical process in depression.

Brain dysfunction
Particular kinds of illness and injury may give rise to depression, suggesting that brain dysfunction may be a cause of the disorder.

Norepinephrine
Depression is thought to stem from a deficiency of the neurotransmitter norepinephrine in certain brain circuits.

Serotonin
The success of drugs that selectively block serotonin (SSRIs) suggests that low levels of serotonin at the synapse may be responsible for depression.

Cortisol hypersecretion
Overactivity in the HPA axis causes elevated levels of cortisol found in depressed patients.

Neurocognitive impairment
Porter *et al.* (2003) found pronounced neurocognitive impairment in depressives, suggesting an underlying brain dysfunction.

Neuroimaging studies
MRI scans have shown lower frontal lobe volume in depressives, which may act as a diathesis for depression.

Effects are not immediate
It takes several weeks before antidepressants are effective, even though they raise neurotransmitter activity immediately.

Individual differences
Not all depressives are helped by SSRIs, suggesting other causes for the disorder.

Cause or effect?
Delgardo (2003) suggests serotonin may have a role in mood regulation only in those being treated for depression.

Effects may be indirect
Antidepressants reduce REM sleep, and symptoms of depression are also reduced when depressives are deprived of REM sleep.

Therapeutic benefits
If specific areas of the brain responsible for depression can be identified, therapeutic intervention can be targeted on those areas.

Topic 2: Psychological explanations of depression (unipolar disorder)

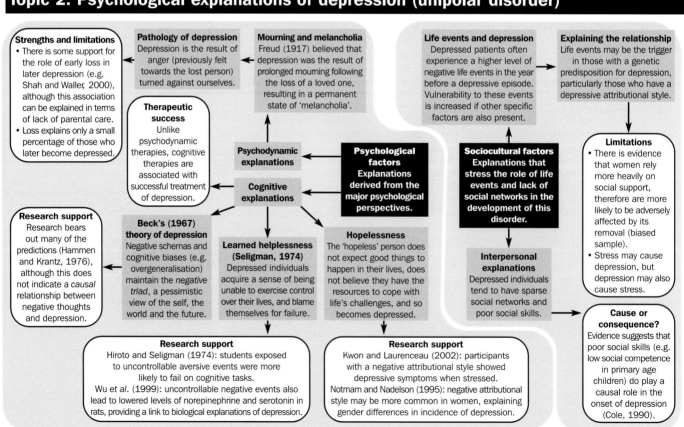

Strengths and limitations
• There is some support for the role of early loss in later depression (e.g. Shah and Waller, 2000), although this association can be explained in terms of lack of parental care.
• Loss explains only a small percentage of those who later become depressed.

Pathology of depression
Depression is the result of anger (previously felt towards the lost person) turned against ourselves.

Mourning and melancholia
Freud (1917) believed that depression was the result of prolonged mourning following the loss of a loved one, resulting in a permanent state of 'melancholia'.

Life events and depression
Depressed patients often experience a higher level of negative life events in the year before a depressive episode. Vulnerability to these events is increased if other specific factors are also present.

Explaining the relationship
Life events may be the trigger in those with a genetic predisposition for depression, particularly those who have a depressive attributional style.

Therapeutic success
Unlike psychodynamic therapies, cognitive therapies are associated with successful treatment of depression.

Psychodynamic explanations

Cognitive explanations

Psychological factors
Explanations derived from the major psychological perspectives.

Sociocultural factors
Explanations that stress the role of life events and lack of social networks in the development of this disorder.

Limitations
• There is evidence that women rely more heavily on social support, therefore are more likely to be adversely affected by its removal (biased sample).
• Stress may cause depression, but depression may also cause stress.

Research support
Research bears out many of the predictions (Hammen and Krantz, 1976), although this does not indicate a *causal* relationship between negative thoughts and depression.

Beck's (1967) theory of depression
Negative schemas and cognitive biases (e.g. overgeneralisation) maintain the *negative triad*, a pessimistic view of the self, the world and the future.

Learned helplessness (Seligman, 1974)
Depressed individuals acquire a sense of being unable to exercise control over their lives, and blame themselves for failure.

Hopelessness
The 'hopeless' person does not expect good things to happen in their lives, does not believe they have the resources to cope with life's challenges, and so becomes depressed.

Interpersonal explanations
Depressed individuals tend to have sparse social networks and poor social skills.

Cause or consequence?
Evidence suggests that poor social skills (e.g. low social competence in primary age children) do play a causal role in the onset of depression (Cole, 1990).

Research support
Hiroto and Seligman (1974): students exposed to uncontrollable aversive events were more likely to fail on cognitive tasks.
Wu *et al.* (1999): uncontrollable negative events also lead to lowered levels of norepinephrine and serotonin in rats, providing a link to biological explanations of depression.

Research support
Kwon and Laurenceau (2002): participants with a negative attributional style showed depressive symptoms when stressed.
Notmam and Nadelson (1995): negative attributional style may be more common in women, explaining gender differences in incidence of depression.

Probable questions

1. Critically consider **two or more** biological explanations of depression. *(30 marks)*

2. (a) Outline **two or more** clinical characteristics of depression. *(5 marks)*

   (b) Discuss **two or more** biological explanations of depression. *(25 marks)*

3. (a) Outline **two** biological explanations of depression. *(15 marks)*

   (b) To what extent are the **two** biological explanations of depression outlined in part (a) supported by research evidence? *(15 marks)*

Possible questions

4. Compare and contrast biological and psychological explanations of depression. *(30 marks)*

If you look back to page 139 you will see that the questions for Division B are almost exactly the same as the ones for schizophrenia (except of course 'depression' has been substituted for 'schizophrenia'). This is because the specification entries are identical. You need to prepare for questions on one biological explanation only, or one psychological explanation only, or two or more biological or psychological explanations. You also need to prepare to use the evidence on which these explanations are based as commentary on the explanations *or* to be able to describe and evaluate these explanations. Finally you need 5 marks worth of clinical characteristics.

In question 3, part (b), as before, you must take care not to *describe* evidence but to use this as part of a sustained critical commentary. One of the ways to do this is to use phrases such as 'This shows that …' or 'The findings demonstrate that …'. Don't forget that there is AO2 credit for contradictory evidence ('On the other hand.') and criticisms (positive and/or negative) of the methodology used in studies cited.

This question 4 is different to the one for schizophrenia. The injunction 'compare and contrast' has been used. This is a form of question which students find challenging, but there is no need for this. You can divide your answer into four components: description of biological explanations (one or more), description of psychological explanations (one or more), consideration of similarities, consideration of differences. These 'considerations' (AO2 content) may simply involve identifying similarities and differences, but for full AO2 credit you need to provide supporting evidence for the similarities/differences.

Probable questions

1. Critically consider **two or more** psychological explanations of depression. *(30 marks)*

2. Outline and evaluate **one** psychological explanation of depression and **one** biological explanation of depression. *(30 marks)*

3. Critically consider **two or more** explanations of depression. *(30 marks)*

Possible questions

4. Describe and evaluate evidence on which **two or more** explanations of depression are based. *(30 marks)*

Questions 1, 2 and 3 are the same as for Division A: either psychological explanations alone (question 1) or psychological and biological explanations (question 2) or psychological and/or biological explanations (question 3). Don't forget the inherent danger in 'large' questions such as question 3. There are marks for detail (AO1) and elaboration (AO2) so if you try to cover too many explanations you will fail to get full marks because you will have to sacrifice the detail/elaboration for breadth.

In all of these questions you are not required to give all the explanations in equal balance. However, if one of them is very detailed but the second is treated very superficially this would lower your mark. All explanations must be detailed.

This question is less likely but possible. You could be asked a question solely about the evidence on which biological or psychological explanations are based. Note that your evidence must be related to at least two explanations – but it is difficult to see how you could present evidence for only one explanation, such as genetic factors.

Chapter 8

TOPIC 1: BIOLOGICAL EXPLANATIONS OF DEPRESSION

SAMPLE ESSAY PLAN

Question 4: Compare and contrast biological and psychological explanations of depression. (30 marks)

BIOLOGICAL EXPLANATIONS	<u>10 MINUTES WORTH OF AO1</u> • Some of points below.
PSYCHOLOGICAL EXPLANATIONS	<u>10 MINUTES WORTH OF AO1</u> • Some of points on next spread.
SIMILARITIES	<u>10 MINUTES WORTH OF AO2</u> • **Determinist.** • **Quality of research evidence**: examine examples. • **Success of therapies**: both successful. • **Cause or effect?** Both could be either.
DIFFERENCES	<u>10 MINUTES WORTH OF AO2</u> • **Reductionist**: psychological explanations less reductionist. • **Individual differences**: psychological explanations account for these.

Question 2: (a) Outline two or more clinical characteristics of depression. (5 marks)
(b) Discuss two or more biological explanations of depression. (25 marks)

(a)	**6½ MINUTES WORTH OF AO1** • **Sad depressed mood** – indicated by subjective report (feeling sad) or others' observations. • **DSM (Diagnostic and Statistical Manual)** requires the first plus 4 other criteria. • For example, **loss of interest** in usual activities, **difficulty sleeping, loss of energy**, recurrent thoughts of **death or suicide.**	
(b) EXPLANATION 1: GENETIC FACTORS	**6½ MINUTES WORTH OF AO1** • Depression appears to run in families, therefore implicates a genetic cause (**Hammen**, 1997). • **Family studies:** 20% of first-degree relatives of depressives have depression compared to 10% of non-relatives (**Harrington et al.**, 1993). • **Twin studies:** 46% concordance rate for MZ (Monozygotic) and 20% for DZ (Dizygotic) twins (**McGuffin et al.**, 1996). • **Adoption studies**: more depression in biological relatives (**Wender et al.**, 1986). • Genes create a **predisposition** for depression but must interact with environmental stressors.	**6½ MINUTES WORTH OF AO2** • **Concordance rates** relatively low for depression. • This may be explained in terms of **co-morbidity** of depression and other disorders. • Supported by **Kendler et al.** (1992) found higher incidence when looking at depression and generalised anxiety disorder. • Similarities among genetic relatives may be due to **shared environments** rather than shared genes.
(b) EXPLANATION 2: BIOCHEMICAL FACTORS	**6½ MINUTES WORTH OF AO1** • Success of **antidepressant medication** is consistent with a biochemical explanation. • **Norepinephrine** deficient in certain brain circuits; markers of norepinephrine low in depressives' urine (**Bunney and Davis**, 1965). • **Serotonin**: success of SSRIs (block reuptake of serotonin) suggests low levels of serotonin at the synapse. • Serotonin by-products low in **cerebrospinal fluid** (**McNeal and Cimbolic**, 1986). • **Cortisol hypersecretion**: overactivity in the Hypothalamus Pituitary Axis (HPA) causes elevated levels of cortisol.	**13½ MINUTES WORTH OF AO2** • Effects of drugs on depression **not immediate** even though they raise neurotransmitter activity immediately. • **Individual differences**: not all depressives are helped by SSRIs, suggesting other causes. • **Cause or effect?** Serotonin may simply regulate mood in depressives (**Delgardo**, 2003). • **Effects may be indirect** e.g. anti-depressants reduce REM sleep which itself is associated with depression. • Causes of depression may be **ultimate** (e.g. ancestral loss of rank in status conflict) or **proximate** (e.g. serotonin deficiency). • Biological explanations are **determinist**, lead to **drug therapies** for good or bad. • **Psychological explanations** offer a contrast e.g. negative triad (**Beck**, 1967).

Depression appears to run in families, and so suggests a genetic cause for the disorder. This has been demonstrated in family studies which show that 20% of first-degree relatives of depressives have depression compared to 10% of non-relatives (Harrington *et al.*, 1993). Twin studies have shown that depression has a large inherited component, with a 46% concordance rate for identical twins and 20% for non-identical twins (McGuffin *et al.*, 1996). Adoption studies have also shown more depression in biological relatives of a depressed person than in their adoptive relatives (Wender *et al.*, 1986). The diathesis-stress model suggests that genes create a predisposition for depression but must interact with environmental stressors for the disorder to develop. Success of antidepressant medication is consistent with a biochemical explanation for the disorder. It has been proposed that depression arises from a deficiency of norepinephrine in some brain circuits. This is demonstrated by the finding that the byproducts of norepinephrine tend to be low in depressives' urine (Bunney and Davis, 1965). The success of SSRIs, which block the re-uptake of serotonin at the synapse, suggests low levels of serotonin are responsible for depression.

According to the psychodynamic explanation of depression (Freud, 1917), depression is the consequence of mourning following the loss of a loved one (through bereavement or withdrawal of affection), resulting in a permanent state of 'melancholia'. Or it is the consequence of anger that was previously felt towards the lost person which becomes turned against the individual themselves. Cognitive explanations include Beck's concept of the negative triad, Seligman's concept of learned helplessness and Abrahamson *et al.*'s concept of hopelessness. Beck (1967) believed that depressed individuals feel as they do because their thinking is biased towards negative interpretations of the world. Negative schemas and cognitive biases maintain the negative triad, a pessimistic view of the self, the world and the future. Seligman (1974) believed that depressives develop learned helplessness, a sense of being unable to exercise control over their lives, blaming themselves for failure (a depressive attributional style). In their hopelessness theory, Abrahamson *et al.* (1989) argue that the 'hopeless' person does not expect good things to happen in their lives, does not believe they have the resources to cope with life's challenges, and so becomes depressed. Sociocultural factors may also explain depression. For example, depressed patients typically experience a higher level of negative life events in the year before a depressive episode. These may be the trigger in those with a genetic predisposition for depression, particularly those who have a depressive attributional style.

A similarity between biological and psychological explanations is that both tend to be determinist. Biological explanations emphasise the role of genetic and biochemical factors over which the individual has no control, and psychological explanations stress aspects of experience or cognition that predispose the individual to depression. The diathesis-stress model combines elements of each form of determinism, with genetics providing a biological vulnerability, and psychological experiences providing the trigger for the disorder. Both biological and behavioural explanations have mixed research support, with some aspects of the biological explanation having clear and unambiguous research support (e.g. the success of SSRIs indicating the influence of serotonin) and others being less clear-cut (e.g. the genetic basis of depression). Some psychological explanations of depression have a great deal of research support (e.g. learned helplessness), whereas others have very little (e.g. Freud's explanation of depression). Both biological and behavioural explanations have led to the establishment of successful therapies for depression, particularly in the case of antidepressant drugs and cognitive therapy, thereby validating their particular views on the causes of this disorder. A problem for both explanations is that the existence of a link between neurochemical imbalance and depression, or negative thoughts and depression, does not mean that the former has caused the latter.

A difference between the two types of explanation is that psychological explanations are *less reductionist*. Biological explanations explain depression in terms of inherited factors or biochemical deficiencies. Psychological explanations stress a much more involved route to the onset of the disorder. For example, in Beck's theory of depression, the acquisition of a negative schema may be caused by a variety of factors, including parental rejection, criticism from others or parents' depressive attitudes. The diathesis-stress model does attempt to reconcile these different perspectives. For example, Kendler *et al.* (1995) found that the highest levels of depression were found in those who were exposed to significant negative life events and the most genetically at risk for depression. A further problem for biological explanations of depression is a relative inability to account for individual differences. It is unclear, for example, why some people become depressed when their serotonin or norepinephrine levels are low, whereas others remain depression free. Psychological explanations are generally able to account for such individual differences, in that different individuals have different experiences, which may or may not lead to the onset of a depressive episode.

In response to this question, the AO1 component is an outline of biological and psychological explanations. You need to be selective in what you choose to illustrate these explanations given the time limitations, remembering to include sufficient detail for each point.

This second paragraph contains the outline of the second perspective (psychological) on depression. Again it is important to be selective in your choice of material to illustrate this perspective.

Although there is no set way to answer a question such as this, you must include both the 'compare' and the 'contrast' elements in your answer. This paragraph is showing similarities between the two perspectives, therefore accounts for the 'compare' component. Note that elaboration has been provided for each similarity – referring to research evidence (theories and studies) to support the claims made.

And in this paragraph, the points of *dissimilarity* (i.e. the 'contrast' component) are covered. Again each point of contrast is well-elaborated for good AO2 marks.

TOPIC 2: PSYCHOLOGICAL EXPLANATIONS OF DEPRESSION (UNIPOLAR DISORDER)

SAMPLE ESSAY PLAN

Question 1: Critically consider **two or more** psychological explanations of depression. (30 marks)

PSYCHOLOGICAL FACTORS	**10 MINUTES WORTH OF AO1**	**10 MINUTES WORTH OF AO2**
	Psychodynamic (**Freud**, 1917) depression due to: • **Mourning** following the loss of a loved one, resulting in a permanent state of '**melancholia**'. • **Anger** (previously felt towards the lost person) turned against ourselves. **Cognitive:** • **Beck** (1967): negative schemas and cognitive biases maintain the **negative triad**, a pessimistic view of the self, the world and the future. • **Learned helplessness** (**Seligman**, 1974): sense of being unable to exercise control over their lives, and blame themselves for failure (depressive **attributional style**). • **Hopelessness** (**Abrahamson et al.**, 1989): 'hopeless' person doesn't expect good things to happen, doesn't believe they have the resources to cope, and so becomes depressed.	• Some support for the role of **early loss**, e.g. parents described as affectionless (**Shah and Waller**, 2000), children whose mothers died in childhood prone to depression (**Bifulco et al.**, 1992). • Link can be explained as **lack of parental care**. • **Loss** explains only 10% of depressives (**Paykel and Cooper**, 1992). • **Cognitive explanations** are associated with successful therapies for depression. • **Beck**: depressed women made more errors on task (**Hammen and Krantz**, 1976), doesn't show a **causal** relationship between negative thoughts and depression. • **Learned helplessness**: students exposed to uncontrollable aversive events more likely to fail on cognitive tasks (**Hiroto and Seligman**, 1974). • **Hopelessness**: Ps with negative attributional style had depressed symptoms when stressed (**Kwon and Laurenceau**, 2002).
SOCIOCULTURAL FACTORS	**10 MINUTES WORTH OF AO1** • Depressives experience negative **life events** e.g. **Brown and Harris** (1978) housewives. • **Vulnerability** to these events is increased if other factors are also present (e.g. no close friends). • Life events may be **trigger** when there's a **genetic predisposition**, particularly those with a **depressive attributional style**. • **Interpersonal explanations**: depressives have sparse social networks (**Billings et al.**, 1983). • Poor social skills are more likely to elicit **rejection** from others (**Joiner et al.**, 1992).	**10 MINUTES WORTH OF AO2** Limitations. • There is evidence that **women** rely more heavily on social support, therefore are more likely to be adversely affected by its removal (biased sample). • Stress may cause depression, or vice versa. • **Cause or consequence?** Evidence suggests that poor social skills (e.g. low social competence in primary age children) do play a causal role in the onset of depression (**Cole**, 1990). • Poor interpersonal problem-solving skills related to depression among adolescents (**Davila et al.** 1995).

Question 4: Describe and evaluate evidence on which **two or more** explanations of depression are based. (30 marks)

EVIDENCE FOR PSYCHOLOGICAL EXPLANATIONS	**10 MINUTES WORTH OF AO1**	**10 MINUTES WORTH OF AO2**
	• Role of **early loss**, e.g. parents described as affectionless (**Shah and Waller**, 2000), maternal death in childhood (**Bifulco et al.**, 1992). • **Negative thoughts**: depressed women made more errors on task (**Hammen and Krantz**, 1976), • **Learned helplessness**: students exposed to uncontrollable aversive events more likely to fail on cognitive tasks (**Hiroto and Seligman**, 1974). • **Hopelessness**: Ps with a negative attributional style showed depressive symptoms when stressed (**Kwon and Laurenceau**, 2002). • Depressives often experience negative life events e.g. **Brown and Harris** (1978) housewives.	• Link between loss and depression can be explained in terms of **lack of parental care**. • **Loss** explains only 10% of depressives (**Paykel and Cooper**, 1992). • **Negative thoughts**: this does not indicate a **causal** relationship between negative thoughts and depression. • **Learned helplessness** – link to biological explanation: **uncontrollable negative events** led to lower levels of norepinephrine and serotonin in rats (**Wu et al.**, 1999). • **Negative attributional style** may be more common in **women**, explaining gender differences in incidence of depression (**Notman and Nadelson**, 1995).
EVIDENCE FOR BIOLOGICAL EXPLANATIONS	**10 MINUTES WORTH OF AO1** • **Family studies**: 20% of first-degree relatives of depressives have depression compared to 10% of non-relatives (**Harrington et al.**, 1993). • **Twin studies**: 46% concordance rate for MZ and 20% for DZ twins (**McGuffin et al.**, 1996). • **Adoption studies**: more depression in biological relatives (**Wender et al.**, 1986). • **Norepinephrine** low in depressives' urine (**Bunney and Davis**, 1965). • **Serotonin** by-products low in cerebrospinal fluid (**McNeal and Cimbolic**, 1986).	**10 MINUTES WORTH OF AO2** • **Concordance rates** relatively low for depression. • This may be explained in terms of **co-morbidity** of depression and other disorders. • Similarities among genetic relatives may be due to **shared environments** rather than shared genes. • Effects of drugs on depression **not immediate** even though they raise neurotransmitter activity immediately. • **Cause or effect?** Serotonin may simply regulate mood in depressives (**Delgardo**, 2003). • **Effects may be indirect** e.g. anti-depressants reduce REM sleep which itself is associated with depression.

According to the psychodynamic explanation of depression (Freud, 1917), depression is the consequence of mourning following the loss of a loved one (through bereavement or withdrawal of affection), resulting in a permanent state of 'melancholia'. As a consequence, anger that was previously felt towards the lost person becomes turned against the individual themselves. Cognitive explanations include Beck's concept of the negative triad, Seligman's concept of learned helplessness and Abrahamson et al.'s concept of hopelessness. Beck (1967) believed that depressed individuals feel as they do because their thinking is biased towards negative interpretations of the world. Negative schemas and cognitive biases maintain the negative triad, a pessimistic view of the self, the world and the future. Seligman (1974) believed that depressives develop learned helplessness, a sense of being unable to exercise control over their lives, blaming themselves for failure (a depressive attributional style). In their hopelessness theory, Abrahamson et al. (1989) argue that 'hopeless' people do not expect good things to happen in their lives, do not believe they have the resources to cope with life's challenges, and so become depressed.

The *synoptic* nature of Unit 5 questions means that you will frequently be offered the chance to write about 'two or more' explanations. There are a number of explanations in this answer, but you could restrict yourself to just two.

There is some support for the role of early loss in later depression. Shah and Waller (2000) found that many people who have suffered depression described their parents as 'affectionless' thus supporting Freud's concept of loss through withdrawal of affection. Similarly, children whose mothers died in childhood have also been found to be prone to depression (Bifulco et al., 1992). However, this association can be explained entirely in terms of lack of parental care following the loss rather than by the loss itself. Loss explains only a small percentage of cases of depression. Paykel and Cooper (1992) found that only 10% of those who experience early loss later go on to become depressed. In contrast, cognitive explanations are associated with successful therapies for depression. Beck's explanation of depression as negative thinking is supported by a study that showed depressed women made more errors of logic than non-depressed women when asked to interpret written material (Hammen and Krantz, 1976). However, the existence of a link between negative thoughts and depression does not mean that the former has caused the latter. Seligman's learned helplessness explanation is supported by research which found that students exposed to uncontrollable aversive events were later more likely to fail on cognitive tasks (Hiroto and Seligman, 1974). Kwon and Laurenceau (2002) provided evidence to support the hopelessness model, showing that participants with a more negative attributional style showed more of the symptoms associated with depression when stressed.

Notice the use of 'AO2 language' such as '…thus supporting…', 'However…', 'In contrast…', '…provided evidence to support…'. This makes your commentary more effective and more obvious to an examiner.

Sociocultural factors may also be important. For example, depressed patients typically experience a higher level of negative life events in the year before a depressive episode. Brown and Harris (1978) found that the presence of long-term difficulties (such as being in a difficult relationship) and the presence of vulnerability factors (such as the lack of a close confiding relationship) increased women's vulnerability to life events, and therefore the likelihood of them developing depression. Life events may be the trigger in those with a genetic predisposition for depression, particularly those who have a depressive attributional style. The presence of a depressive attributional style acts as a diathesis that predisposes an individual to interpret a significant life event and its consequences in ways that are more likely to bring about depression. Interpersonal explanations of depression stress the fact that depressives tend to report having sparse social networks which makes them less able to handle negative life events (Billings et al., 1983). The behaviour of depressives also includes poor social skills which are more likely to elicit rejection from others (Joiner et al., 1992).

The cognitive model is used here to interpret *why* life events have such an impact for some people.

Limitations of the life events and depression link comes from evidence that women rely more heavily on social support, therefore are more likely to be adversely affected by its removal (Frydenberg and Lewis, 1993). This means that Brown and Harris' study contained a biased sample, with the implication that men may not be affected in quite the same way by these vulnerability factors. Research has shown that life stressors may cause depression, but depression may also cause stress, which leads to a spiralling in an individual's depressive state. Although social skills deficits could be a consequence of depression, evidence suggests that these play a causal role in depression. Cole (1990) found that low social competence predicted the onset of depression in primary age children, and poor interpersonal problem-solving skills have been found to predict increases in depression among adolescents (Davila et al., 1995). Psychological explanations are generally more able than biological explanations to account for individual differences, in that different individuals have different experiences, which may or may not lead to the onset of a depressive episode. The diathesis-stress model combines the strengths of both psychological and biological explanations suggesting the genetic predisposition on one hand and the importance of life experiences on the other.

It isn't sufficient to just *identify* a critical point (a biased sample) – you should make this effective through elaboration.

Chapter 8

Topic 1: Biological explanations of an anxiety disorder (obsessive-compulsive disorder)

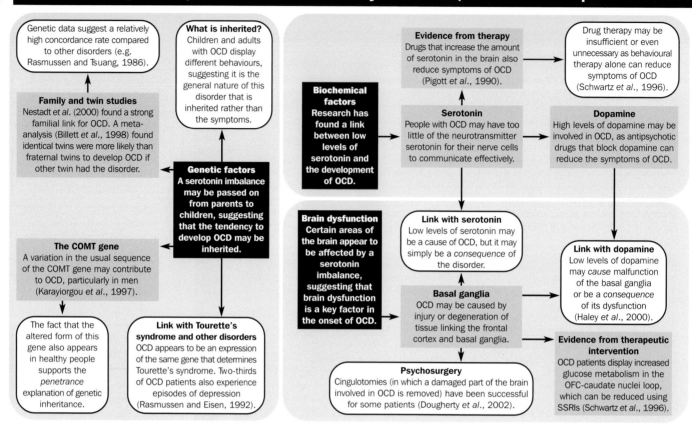

Genetic data suggest a relatively high concordance rate compared to other disorders (e.g. Rasmussen and Tsuang, 1986).

What is inherited?
Children and adults with OCD display different behaviours, suggesting it is the general nature of this disorder that is inherited rather than the symptoms.

Family and twin studies
Nestadt et al. (2000) found a strong familial link for OCD. A meta-analysis (Billett et al., 1998) found identical twins were more likely than fraternal twins to develop OCD if other twin had the disorder.

Genetic factors
A serotonin imbalance may be passed on from parents to children, suggesting that the tendency to develop OCD may be inherited.

The COMT gene
A variation in the usual sequence of the COMT gene may contribute to OCD, particularly in men (Karayiorgou et al., 1997).

The fact that the altered form of this gene also appears in healthy people supports the *penetrance* explanation of genetic inheritance.

Link with Tourette's syndrome and other disorders
OCD appears to be an expression of the same gene that determines Tourette's syndrome. Two-thirds of OCD patients also experience episodes of depression (Rasmussen and Eisen, 1992).

Biochemical factors
Research has found a link between low levels of serotonin and the development of OCD.

Evidence from therapy
Drugs that increase the amount of serotonin in the brain also reduce symptoms of OCD (Pigott et al., 1990).

Drug therapy may be insufficient or even unnecessary as behavioural therapy alone can reduce symptoms of OCD (Schwartz et al., 1996).

Serotonin
People with OCD may have too little of the neurotransmitter serotonin for their nerve cells to communicate effectively.

Dopamine
High levels of dopamine may be involved in OCD, as antipsychotic drugs that block dopamine can reduce the symptoms of OCD.

Brain dysfunction
Certain areas of the brain appear to be affected by a serotonin imbalance, suggesting that brain dysfunction is a key factor in the onset of OCD.

Link with serotonin
Low levels of serotonin may be a cause of OCD, but it may simply be a *consequence* of the disorder.

Link with dopamine
Low levels of dopamine may *cause* malfunction of the basal ganglia or be a *consequence* of its dysfunction (Haley et al., 2000).

Basal ganglia
OCD may be caused by injury or degeneration of tissue linking the frontal cortex and basal ganglia.

Psychosurgery
Cingulotomies (in which a damaged part of the brain involved in OCD is removed) have been successful for some patients (Dougherty et al., 2002).

Evidence from therapeutic intervention
OCD patients display increased glucose metabolism in the OFC-caudate nuclei loop, which can be reduced using SSRIs (Schwartz et al., 1996).

Topic 2: Psychological explanations of an anxiety disorder (obsessive-compulsive disorder)

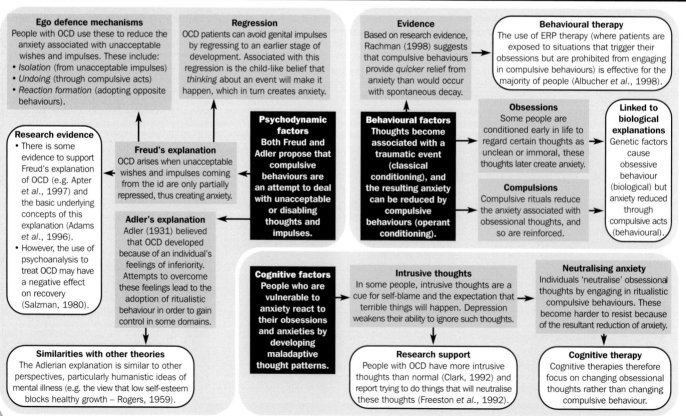

Ego defence mechanisms
People with OCD use these to reduce the anxiety associated with unacceptable wishes and impulses. These include:
• *Isolation* (from unacceptable impulses)
• *Undoing* (through compulsive acts)
• *Reaction formation* (adopting opposite behaviours).

Regression
OCD patients can avoid genital impulses by regressing to an earlier stage of development. Associated with this regression is the child-like belief that *thinking* about an event will make it happen, which in turn creates anxiety.

Evidence
Based on research evidence, Rachman (1998) suggests that compulsive behaviours provide *quicker* relief from anxiety than would occur with spontaneous decay.

Behavioural therapy
The use of ERP therapy (where patients are exposed to situations that trigger their obsessions but are prohibited from engaging in compulsive behaviours) is effective for the majority of people (Albucher et al., 1998).

Research evidence
• There is some evidence to support Freud's explanation of OCD (e.g. Apter et al., 1997) and the basic underlying concepts of this explanation (Adams et al., 1996).
• However, the use of psychoanalysis to treat OCD may have a negative effect on recovery (Salzman, 1980).

Freud's explanation
OCD arises when unacceptable wishes and impulses coming from the id are only partially repressed, thus creating anxiety.

Psychodynamic factors
Both Freud and Adler propose that compulsive behaviours are an attempt to deal with unacceptable or disabling thoughts and impulses.

Adler's explanation
Adler (1931) believed that OCD developed because of an individual's feelings of inferiority. Attempts to overcome these feelings lead to the adoption of ritualistic behaviour in order to gain control in some domains.

Behavioural factors
Thoughts become associated with a traumatic event (classical conditioning), and the resulting anxiety can be reduced by compulsive behaviours (operant conditioning).

Obsessions
Some people are conditioned early in life to regard certain thoughts as unclean or immoral, these thoughts later create anxiety.

Compulsions
Compulsive rituals reduce the anxiety associated with obsessional thoughts, and so are reinforced.

Linked to biological explanations
Genetic factors cause obsessive behaviour (biological) but anxiety reduced through compulsive acts (behavioural).

Similarities with other theories
The Adlerian explanation is similar to other perspectives, particularly humanistic ideas of mental illness (e.g. the view that low self-esteem blocks healthy growth – Rogers, 1959).

Cognitive factors
People who are vulnerable to anxiety react to their obsessions and anxieties by developing maladaptive thought patterns.

Intrusive thoughts
In some people, intrusive thoughts are a cue for self-blame and the expectation that terrible things will happen. Depression weakens their ability to ignore such thoughts.

Neutralising anxiety
Individuals 'neutralise' obsessional thoughts by engaging in ritualistic compulsive behaviours. These become harder to resist because of the resultant reduction of anxiety.

Research support
People with OCD have more intrusive thoughts than normal (Clark, 1992) and report trying to do things that will neutralise these thoughts (Freeston et al., 1992).

Cognitive therapy
Cognitive therapies therefore focus on changing obsessional thoughts rather than changing compulsive behaviour.

Probable questions

1. Critically consider **two or more** biological explanations of any **one** anxiety disorder. *(30 marks)*

2. (a) Outline **two or more** clinical characteristics of any **one** anxiety disorder. *(5 marks)*

   (b) Discuss **two or more** biological explanations of any **one** anxiety disorder. *(25 marks)*

3. (a) Outline **two** biological explanations of any **one** anxiety disorder. *(15 marks)*

   (b) To what extent are the **two** biological explanations of the **one** anxiety disorder outlined in part (a) supported by research evidence? *(15 marks)*

Possible questions

4. (a) Describe **one** biological explanation of any **one** anxiety disorder. *(10 marks)*

   (b) Outline and evaluate evidence on which the explanation of the **one** anxiety disorder you described in part (a) is based. *(20 marks)*

Probable questions

1. Critically consider **two or more** psychological explanations of any **one** anxiety disorder. *(30 marks)*

2. Outline and evaluate **one** psychological explanation of **one** anxiety disorder and **one** biological explanation of **one** anxiety disorder. *(30 marks)*

3. Critically consider **two or more** explanations of any **one** anxiety disorder. *(30 marks)*

Possible questions

4. Describe and evaluate evidence on which **two or more** explanations of any **one** anxiety disorder are based. *(30 marks)*

There are many different kinds of anxiety disorder – those that are listed in the specification (post-traumatic stress disorder, phobic disorder(s), obsessive-compulsive disorder) plus others, such as generalised anxiety disorder and panic disorder with agoraphobia. You are not restricted about which anxiety disorder you choose (the list in the specification is of examples only). Questions will also ask for 'one anxiety disorder'. This does mean that, in any answer in this division, you must focus on one anxiety disorder exclusively. If you do write about more than one anxiety disorder then the examiner will read both accounts and credit the one that attracts the highest mark (this is called 'positive marking').

The questions here are the same as those in the previous divisions. Remember that clinical characteristics (see question 2) should only be included when they have specifically been asked for in a question. General introductions that explain what an anxiety disorder is and/or list some of the clinical characteristics would only gain credit if that is what is required in the question.

It may be worth mentioning here that the same advice applies to conclusions as to introductions. These are not required in any essay. They can be included *if* they add relevant material to your answer but frequently conclusions are nothing more than a summary of points already made. A *true* conclusion is a kind of synthesis of already-examined material.

This less probable question is an amalgamation of the questions above, requiring a more detailed description of one biological explanation plus a discussion of the evidence for the explanation in part (a). This means you do have to restrict the evidence examined to be relevant only to the explanation in part (a).

In part (b) you must be careful to present the AO1 and AO2 in appropriate measure – *three* times as much AO2 which means very little description of the evidence.

The injunction 'critically consider' is an AO1+AO2 injunction which means the same as 'discuss' – it is sometimes used as an alternative because it sounds better! It suggests the idea of 'sustained critical commentary' which is so important for high AO2 marks. Often, when evaluating explanations of mental disorders, you need to use research evidence and the difficulty is that candidates end up *describing* these studies rather than focusing more on what they tell us about the explanation. *Critically* consider the explanations *using* research evidence plus other arguments.

Note again the restrictions in question 2, but remember that you can get full marks even if one explanation is more comprehensive than the other – you are not expected to provide both explanations in equal amount.

In an exam some candidates may well misread this question and think they have been asked to discuss explanations of any one anxiety disorder. If this were to happen your answer might include some of the evidence related to the explanation (which would receive credit) but a description of the explanation would receive no credit and any evaluation that was not related to evidence would also not be credited. Always read exam questions carefully.

Chapter 8

SAMPLE ESSAY PLAN

Question 2: (a) Outline two or more clinical characteristics of any one anxiety disorder. (5 marks)
(b) Discuss two or more biological explanations of any one anxiety disorder. (25 marks)

(a)

6½ MINUTES WORTH OF A01

- Characterised by excessive, intrusive and inappropriate obsessions or compulsions.
- **Obsessions**: recurrent, intrusive thoughts or impulses that produce anxiety.
- **Compulsions**: repetitive behaviours (e.g. hand-washing) or mental acts that reduce anxiety (e.g. counting).
- Individual recognises these are unreasonable, but they prevent disaster, this creates **further anxiety**.

GENETIC FACTORS

6½ MINUTES WORTH OF A01

- A **serotonin** imbalance (levels too low) which prevents nerve cells communicating effectively.
- Other studies (focused on drug therapies) suggest the role of **dopamine** in OCD.
- Neurotransmitter **imbalances** may be inherited.
- **Family studies**: people with first-degree relative with OCD five times greater risk than normal population (**Nestadt et al.**, 2000).
- **Twin studies**: MZ twins twice as likely to develop OCD if their twin had OCD than DZ twins (meta-analysis by **Billett et al.**, 1998).
- Variation in usual sequence of the **COMT gene** may contribute to OCD because it normally produces an enzyme which helps terminate dopamine action (**Karayiorgou et al.**, 1997).

10 MINUTES WORTH OF A02

- Role of **serotonin** supported by use of SSRIs to reduce symptoms of OCD (**Piggott et al.**, 1990); antidepressants which don't inhibit the re-uptake of serotonin are less effective (**Jenicke**, 1992).
- **PET scans** of OCD sufferers after SSRI treatment look like normal brains.
- **Concordance rate** for OCD higher than for depression (**Rasmussen and Tsuang**, 1986).
- OCD appears to be an expression of the same gene that determines **Tourette's syndrome**.
- Also two-thirds of OCD patients experience episodes of **depression** (**Rasmussen and Eisen**, 1992).
- This **challenges the value** of classification systems that see OCD as a distinct disorder.
- Genetic alteration sometimes present in healthy people, supports **penetrance** explanation.

BRAIN DYSFUNCTION

6½ MINUTES WORTH OF A01

- Injury or degeneration of tissue linking the **frontal cortex and basal ganglia**.
- Positron Emission Tomography (PET) scans of OCD patients with symptoms show activity in **orbitofrontal cortex** (OFC), which gives rise to obsessional thinking
- Compulsive symptoms can be caused by injury to **caudate nuclei** (in basal ganglia, filters messages from OFC).
- OCD patients display increased glucose metabolism in the OFC-caudate nuclei loop, reduced using SSRIs (**Schwartz et al.**, 1996).

10 MINUTES WORTH OF A02

- Low levels of serotonin may be a **cause or effect** of brain dysfunction. **Comer** (1998) suggests it is a cause.
- But damage to other areas (e.g. brainstem nuclei) may cause low serotonin (**Hollander et al.**, 1990).
- **Cingulotomies** (part of brain removed) have been successful in half of cases (**Dougherty et al.**, 2002).
- However such psychosurgery may **affect behaviour generally** (**Sachdev and Hay**, 1995).
- Lack of success with **drug therapies** undermines the biochemical explanation.

Question 1: Critically consider two or more biological explanations of any one anxiety disorder. (30 marks)

BIOCHEMICAL FACTORS

20 MINUTES WORTH OF A01

The description of theory 1 above, plus:

- **Serotonin**: PET scans show lower levels in OCD patients.
- After treatment with **SSRIs** PET scans look normal.
- **Dopamine**: high levels may be involved in OCD, as drugs that block dopamine in animals can reduce compulsive behaviours (**Szechtman et al.**, 1998).
- **Tourette's patients** have dopamine dysfunction.
- Antipsychotic drugs reduce dopamine and reduce OCD symptoms in patients resistant to SSRIs.

20 MINUTES WORTH OF A02

The evaluation of theory 1 above.

(a)

Obsessive-compulsive disorder (OCD) is characterised by excessive, intrusive and inappropriate obsessions or compulsions. A diagnosis of OCD is given if a person experiences persistent and intrusive thoughts or impulses. These obsessional thoughts are perceived as inappropriate or forbidden, and produce anxiety. The individual with OCD also displays repetitive behaviours or mental acts that he or she feels driven to perform in response to the obsession. These are called 'compulsions'. Compulsions include both overt behaviours, such as hand-washing, and mental acts such as counting. These compulsions reduce the anxiety that accompanies an obsession. Most people with OCD recognise that their compulsions are unreasonable, but also believe that something terrible will happen if they do not perform that behaviour or mental act. This creates further anxiety.

> Only one type of anxiety disorder can be covered here. The three diagnostic criteria (together with appropriate elaboration) are included in response to the 'two or more' instruction in the question.

(b)

OCD has been associated with a low level of serotonin in the brain, which prevents the nerve cells communicating effectively. Other studies suggest the role of dopamine in OCD, in that antipsychotic drugs that reduce dopamine activity in the brain reduce the severity of symptoms in some OCD patients. Neurotransmitter imbalances may be inherited. Family studies have shown that people with a first-degree relative with OCD have a five times greater risk than the normal population of developing the disorder (Nestadt et al., 2000). In a meta-analysis of twin studies, Billett et al. (1998) found that, compared to non-identical twins, identical twins are twice as likely to develop OCD if their twin also had OCD. A variation in the usual sequence of the COMT gene may contribute to OCD (Karayiorgou et al., 1997). This variation reduces the production of COMT, an enzyme which helps to terminate the action of dopamine in the brain.

> *Studies* of OCD can be used to elaborate an explanation. Here, the underlying proposal is that a biochemical imbalance is passed on genetically.

The role of serotonin in OCD is supported by the use of SSRIs to reduce its symptoms (Piggott et al., 1990), whereas antidepressants which do not inhibit the re-uptake of serotonin are less effective (Jenicke, 1992). PET scans of the brains of OCD sufferers look more like the brains of normal people after treatment with SSRIs than with other treatments. Support for the genetic basis of OCD comes from studies that show that the genetic concordance rate is significantly higher for OCD than for other disorders (Rasmussen and Tsuang, 1986). It is possible, however, that OCD is the expression of the same gene that determines other disorders, such as Tourette's syndrome, with Tourette's patients showing typically obsessional behaviour. Two-thirds of OCD patients experience episodes of depression (Rasmussen and Eisen, 1992), which challenges the value of classification systems that see OCD as a distinct disorder with its own distinct causes. The fact that genetic alteration sometimes appears in healthy people supports the penetrance explanation of genetic inheritance, that single 'defective' genes do not cause any disorder, which only arises when a sufficient number of these defective genes are present.

> It is important to remember the AO1/AO2 division in this part of your answer. There are 10 marks available for AO1 in part (b) and 15 for AO2, so your AO2 paragraphs will be *longer*.

There is evidence of abnormal brain structure and activity in patients with OCD. This abnormality appears to lie in the pathway linking the frontal cortex and basal ganglia. PET scans of patients with active symptoms of OCD show heightened activity in the orbitofrontal cortex (OFC) which gives rise to obsessional thinking, and compulsive symptoms can also be caused by injury or degeneration of neural tissue in the caudate nuclei, an area in the basal ganglia that filters messages from the OFC. The caudate nuclei appear to perform this function poorly in people with OCD. PET scans have also shown that, compared to controls, OCD patients display increased glucose metabolism in the OFC-caudate nuclei loop, which can be reduced using SSRIs (Schwartz et al., 1996). This increased metabolism is also correlated with the severity of OCD.

> Explanations of the role of brain dysfunction in OCD are elaborated with insights from research. This is an acceptable way of providing AO1 material.

Although low levels of serotonin may be a cause or an effect of brain dysfunction, Comer (1998) suggests that because serotonin plays a key role in the operation of the OFC and caudate nuclei, it is likely that low levels of serotonin *cause* these areas to function poorly. However, Hollander et al. (1990) propose that damage in other brain areas (e.g. the brainstem nuclei) may be the cause of low serotonin levels. Evidence from psychosurgery has supported the view that OCD is a consequence of brain dysfunction. In a cingulotomy, the part of the brain involved in OCD is removed. Such operations have been reasonably successful in the alleviation of OCD symptoms for some people. In one study (Dougherty et al., 2002), nearly half of patients who had previously been unresponsive to treatment improved after cingulotomy. However, it is possible that such psychosurgery may affect behaviour generally by reducing motivation and energy, which may explain the reduced symptoms (Sachdev and Hay, 1995). Drug therapies have had only partial success in the treatment of OCD, with patients tending to relapse within a few weeks if medication is stopped (Maina et al., 2001). This undermines biochemical explanations of OCD.

> The success of therapies in the treatment of mental disorders is a valuable insight into what may have caused the disorder in the first place.

TOPIC 2: PSYCHOLOGICAL EXPLANATIONS OF AN ANXIETY DISORDER

SAMPLE ESSAY PLAN

Question 1: Critically consider **two or more** psychological explanations of any **one** anxiety disorder. (30 marks)

PSYCHODYNAMIC FACTORS	**6½ MINUTES WORTH OF AO1** • **Freud's explanation**: unacceptable **id** impulses are only partially repressed, thus creating anxiety. • **Ego defence mechanisms** reduce anxiety, e.g. • **Isolation** (from unacceptable impulses). • **Undoing** (through compulsive acts). • **Reaction formation** (adopting opposite behaviours e.g. compulsive kindness). • **Regression**: avoid genital impulses by regressing to an earlier stage of development. • Regression reactivates **child-like belief** that **thinking** about an event will make it happen, which in turn creates anxiety.	**6½ MINUTES WORTH OF AO2** • **Supporting evidence** e.g. suicidal OCD patients scored higher on regression and other ego defences (**Apter et al.**, 1997). • **General support for Freud's theory** e.g. men who were most aroused by gay videos were most homophobic, shows reaction formation (**Adams et al.**, 1996). • The use of psychoanalysis to treat OCD may have a **negative effect** on recovery (**Salzman**, 1980). • Can use **short-term therapy** instead which reduces OCD tendency to 'think too much'. • Presence of **specific neural abnormalities** in OCD sufferers makes psychoanalytic explanation implausible.
BEHAVIOURAL FACTORS	**6½ MINUTES WORTH OF AO1** • Situations that create anxiety are avoided through **classical conditioning** (**Mowrer**, 1960). • **Obsessions**: thoughts become associated with a traumatic event (**classical conditioning**). • The resulting anxiety can be reduced by compulsive behaviours (**operant conditioning**). • **Compulsive rituals** developed to neutralise anxiety and regain control. • Such ritualistic behaviours are thus **reinforced**. • **Rachman and Hodgson** (1980): patients asked to delay compulsions, anxiety level persisted and then declined i.e. compulsions give quicker relief.	**6½ MINUTES WORTH OF AO2** • Linked to **biological explanations**: genetic factors cause obsessive behaviour (biological) but anxiety reduced through compulsive acts (behavioural). • Leads to **ERP therapy** (Exposure and Response Prevention) – patients exposed to situations that trigger their obsessions but are prohibited from engaging in compulsive behaviours. • Effective for the majority of people (**Albucher et al.**, 1998). • But not true for all patients, therefore behavioural explanations alone are not sufficient.
COGNITIVE FACTORS	**6½ MINUTES WORTH OF AO1** • Everyone has intrusive thoughts but some people are vulnerable to anxiety and 'over-react'. • **Intrusive thoughts** are a cue for self-blame and expectation that terrible things will happen. • **Depression** weakens ability to ignore such thoughts. • Obsessional thoughts **neutralised** by engaging in **ritualistic compulsive behaviours**. • These become harder to resist because of the resultant reduction of anxiety. • Over time become convinced that intrusive thoughts are dangerous, and fear increases.	**6½ MINUTES WORTH OF AO2** • People with OCD have **more intrusive thoughts** than normal (**Clark**, 1992). • They report trying to do things that will **neutralise** these thoughts (**Freeston et al.**, 1992). • **Cognitive therapies** focus on changing obsessional thoughts rather than changing compulsive behaviour. • Cognitive behaviour therapies have been demonstrated to be as effective as drug treatment for OCD (e.g. **Hembree et al.**, 2003). • **Piacentini et al.** (2002) successfully treated children with OCD although a poorer outcome for those with severe obsessions suggesting that OCD **can't be explained solely** in terms of disordered thinking.

Question 2: Outline and evaluate **one** psychological explanation of **one** anxiety disorder and **one** biological explanation of **one** anxiety disorder. (30 marks)

PSYCHOLOGICAL EXPLANATION: PSYCHODYNAMIC EXPLANATION	**10 MINUTES WORTH OF AO1** The description of theory 1 above, plus: • **Adler** (1931): OCD due to sense of inferiority. • **Inferiority complex** may develop if parents too domineering or pampering. • Ritualistic behaviour used to gain control in some domains.	**10 MINUTES WORTH OF AO2** The evaluation of theory 1 above, plus: • Adlerian explanation is **similar to other perspectives**, particularly humanistic ideas of mental illness (e.g. the view that low self-esteem blocks healthy growth – **Rogers**, 1959). • **Adlerian therapy** similar to behaviour therapy, aims to increase self-confidence.
BIOLOGICAL EXPLANATION: BRAIN DYSFUNCTION	**10 MINUTES WORTH OF AO1** As on page 152 (add more details on serotonin and dopamine).	**10 MINUTES WORTH OF AO2** As on page 152.

154

Freud believed OCD arises when unacceptable wishes and impulses coming from the id are only partially repressed, thus creating anxiety. People with OCD use ego defence mechanisms to reduce this anxiety. These include isolation, as people attempt to disown themselves from these unacceptable impulses. When the id is dominant, these impulses intrude as obsessional thoughts. Undoing is a secondary defence of producing compulsive acts if isolation fails. Undoing involves the production of compulsive acts and takes place if isolation fails. A third ego defence, reaction formation, involves adopting behaviours that are the exact opposite of the unacceptable impulses. Freud believed that regression was an important mechanism in the formation of OCD symptoms. OCD patients can avoid anxiety associated with genital impulses by regressing to an earlier stage of development. Regression can reactivate the childhood belief that merely thinking about an event will cause it to happen, which creates further anxiety.

> There is always a temptation (to be avoided here) to begin describing Freud's theory of personality rather than his explanation of OCD.

Apter et al. (1997) assessed suicidal adolescents for evidence of regression and found that they scored higher on the use of defence mechanisms than non-suicidal adolescents. The concepts underlying Freud's explanation of reaction formation were supported by Adams et al. (1996), who found that men who were most aroused by gay videos were also most homophobic. This explanation is undermined by two factors. The first is the failure of psychoanalytic therapy to provide significant improvement in the symptoms of OCD. Salzman (1980) suggests that the use of psychoanalysis to treat OCD may even have a negative effect on recovery. An alternative is to use short-term therapy which reduces the OCD tendency to 'think too much'. The second factor is the identification of specific neural abnormalities in OCD sufferers, which effectively renders an unfalsifiable psychoanalytic explanation as implausible.

> If psychoanalytic therapy reduces OCD symptoms, that would strengthen the psychoanalytic explanation. If it doesn't, then this would weaken the psychoanalytic explanation.

Behavioural explanations of anxiety disorders claim that anxiety is a learned behaviour that can also be unlearned. People who feel uncomfortable in a given situation or near a certain object will avoid it. Mowrer (1960) claimed that stimuli acquire their aversive properties through classical conditioning. In OCD, obsessional thoughts become associated with a traumatic event, and so when such thoughts recur, they become a source of conditioned anxiety. Compulsive rituals develop as a way of avoiding these fear-associated obsessions, reducing the anxiety and re-establishing control over the obsessions. As a result, ritualistic behaviour is reinforced, as individuals link whatever act they have performed with changing the fearful situation. Rachman and Hodgson (1980) found that compulsive behaviours serve an important function because they provide quicker relief from anxiety that would occur if patients relied on spontaneous decay.

> Effectiveness can also be measured in terms of the *speed* of relief from anxiety.

Behavioural explanations for OCD can be linked to underlying biological explanations. Genetic factors may cause obsessive behaviour but the resulting anxiety can be reduced through compulsive acts which are rewarding and so will be repeated. A consequence of the behavioural explanation is the establishment of a behavioural therapy to treat OCD. In ERP therapy, patients are exposed to situations that trigger their obsessions but are prohibited from engaging in compulsive behaviours. Albucher et al. (1998) reported that the majority of adults improved considerably using this technique, supporting the view that their compulsive rituals had been learned in the first place. However, not all patients are helped by this therapy, therefore behavioural explanations alone cannot account for all cases of OCD.

> If a behavioural therapy *cures* OCD, this supports a behavioural explanation of the disorder.

Cognitive-behavioural explanations of OCD stress that everybody has intrusive thoughts, but in some people, these obsessional thoughts are a cue for self-blame and the expectation that terrible things will happen as a result. Anxious people cannot stop these thoughts easily as depression weakens their ability to ignore such thoughts. Obsessional thoughts can be neutralised by engaging in ritualistic compulsive behaviours. Every time a neutralising thought or action is repeated it becomes harder to resist because of its consequent reduction of anxiety, and eventually these actions turn into compulsions. Over time, people become convinced that intrusive thoughts are dangerous, and so their fear of them increases. These thoughts turn into obsessions, and the need to reduce the anxiety associated with them becomes even more acute.

> Because of the emphasis on compulsive acts reducing anxiety (i.e. being reinforcing), cognitive explanations are referred to as cognitive-*behavioural*.

Supporting the cognitive explanation of OCD, Clark (1992) found that people with OCD have more intrusive thoughts than normal people, and report trying to do things that will neutralise these thoughts (Freeston et al., 1992). Cognitive therapies focus on changing obsessional thoughts rather than changing compulsive behaviour, therefore if cognitive therapies are at least as successful as behavioural therapies in reducing the symptoms of OCD, this would support a cognitive explanation of this disorder rather than a behavioural one. Cognitive behaviour therapies have been demonstrated to be as effective than drug treatment for OCD (e.g. Hembree et al., 2003). Piacentini et al. (2002) used cognitive-behavioural therapy with children suffering from OCD. There was a significant positive response to this form of treatment, although a poorer outcome was associated with more severe obsessions prior to treatment, suggesting that OCD cannot be explained solely in terms of disordered thinking.

> Remember that to make a study into effective commentary, you should comment on its implications for this explanation.

Topic 1: Chemotherapy

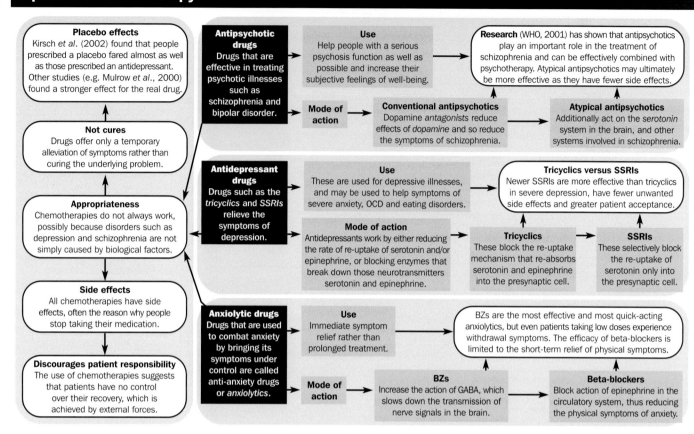

Placebo effects
Kirsch et al. (2002) found that people prescribed a placebo fared almost as well as those prescribed an antidepressant. Other studies (e.g. Mulrow et al., 2000) found a stronger effect for the real drug.

Not cures
Drugs offer only a temporary alleviation of symptoms rather than curing the underlying problem.

Appropriateness
Chemotherapies do not always work, possibly because disorders such as depression and schizophrenia are not simply caused by biological factors.

Side effects
All chemotherapies have side effects, often the reason why people stop taking their medication.

Discourages patient responsibility
The use of chemotherapies suggests that patients have no control over their recovery, which is achieved by external forces.

Antipsychotic drugs
Drugs that are effective in treating psychotic illnesses such as schizophrenia and bipolar disorder.

Use
Help people with a serious psychosis function as well as possible and increase their subjective feelings of well-being.

Research (WHO, 2001) has shown that antipsychotics play an important role in the treatment of schizophrenia and can be effectively combined with psychotherapy. Atypical antipsychotics may ultimately be more effective as they have fewer side effects.

Mode of action

Conventional antipsychotics
Dopamine antagonists reduce effects of dopamine and so reduce the symptoms of schizophrenia.

Atypical antipsychotics
Additionally act on the serotonin system in the brain, and other systems involved in schizophrenia.

Antidepressant drugs
Drugs such as the tricyclics and SSRIs relieve the symptoms of depression.

Use
These are used for depressive illnesses, and may be used to help symptoms of severe anxiety, OCD and eating disorders.

Tricyclics versus SSRIs
Newer SSRIs are more effective than tricyclics in severe depression, have fewer unwanted side effects and greater patient acceptance.

Mode of action
Antidepressants work by either reducing the rate of re-uptake of serotonin and/or epinephrine, or blocking enzymes that break down those neurotransmitters serotonin and epinephrine.

Tricyclics
These block the re-uptake mechanism that re-absorbs serotonin and epinephrine into the presynaptic cell.

SSRIs
These selectively block the re-uptake of serotonin only into the presynaptic cell.

Anxiolytic drugs
Drugs that are used to combat anxiety by bringing its symptoms under control are called anti-anxiety drugs or anxiolytics.

Use
Immediate symptom relief rather than prolonged treatment.

BZs are the most effective and most quick-acting anxiolytics, but even patients taking low doses experience withdrawal symptoms. The efficacy of beta-blockers is limited to the short-term relief of physical symptoms.

Mode of action

BZs
Increase the action of GABA, which slows down the transmission of nerve signals in the brain.

Beta-blockers
Block action of epinephrine in the circulatory system, thus reducing the physical symptoms of anxiety.

Topic 2: ECT and psychosurgery

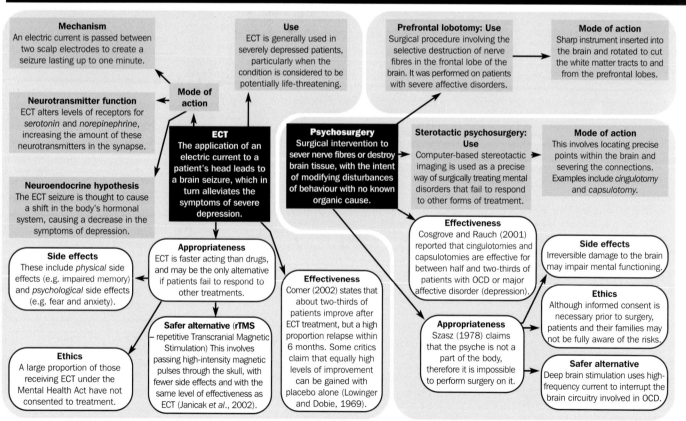

Mechanism
An electric current is passed between two scalp electrodes to create a seizure lasting up to one minute.

Use
ECT is generally used in severely depressed patients, particularly when the condition is considered to be potentially life-threatening.

Prefrontal lobotomy: Use
Surgical procedure involving the selective destruction of nerve fibres in the frontal lobe of the brain. It was performed on patients with severe affective disorders.

Mode of action
Sharp instrument inserted into the brain and rotated to cut the white matter tracts to and from the prefrontal lobes.

Neurotransmitter function
ECT alters levels of receptors for serotonin and norepinephrine, increasing the amount of these neurotransmitters in the synapse.

Mode of action

ECT
The application of an electric current to a patient's head leads to a brain seizure, which in turn alleviates the symptoms of severe depression.

Psychosurgery
Surgical intervention to sever nerve fibres or destroy brain tissue, with the intent of modifying disturbances of behaviour with no known organic cause.

Sterotactic psychosurgery: Use
Computer-based stereotactic imaging is used as a precise way of surgically treating mental disorders that fail to respond to other forms of treatment.

Mode of action
This involves locating precise points within the brain and severing the connections. Examples include cingulotomy and capsulotomy.

Neuroendocrine hypothesis
The ECT seizure is thought to cause a shift in the body's hormonal system, causing a decrease in the symptoms of depression.

Side effects
These include physical side effects (e.g. impaired memory) and psychological side effects (e.g. fear and anxiety).

Appropriateness
ECT is faster acting than drugs, and may be the only alternative if patients fail to respond to other treatments.

Effectiveness
Cosgrove and Rauch (2001) reported that cingulotomies and capsulotomies are effective for between half and two-thirds of patients with OCD or major affective disorder (depression).

Side effects
Irreversible damage to the brain may impair mental functioning.

Ethics
A large proportion of those receiving ECT under the Mental Health Act have not consented to treatment.

Safer alternative (rTMS
– repetitive Transcranial Magnetic Stimulation) This involves passing high-intensity magnetic pulses through the skull, with fewer side effects and with the same level of effectiveness as ECT (Janicak et al., 2002).

Effectiveness
Comer (2002) states that about two-thirds of patients improve after ECT treatment, but a high proportion relapse within 6 months. Some critics claim that equally high levels of improvement can be gained with placebo alone (Lowinger and Dobie, 1969).

Appropriateness
Szasz (1978) claims that the psyche is not a part of the body, therefore it is impossible to perform surgery on it.

Ethics
Although informed consent is necessary prior to surgery, patients and their families may not be fully aware of the risks.

Safer alternative
Deep brain stimulation uses high-frequency current to interrupt the brain circuitry involved in OCD.

Probable questions

1. Outline and evaluate **two or more** biological therapies. *(30 marks)*

2. (a) Outline **two** biological therapies. *(15 marks)*

   (b) Evaluate the **two** biological therapies you outlined in (a) with reference to issues surrounding their use (e.g. appropriateness and effectiveness). *(15 marks)*

Possible questions

3. (a) Describe chemotherapy as a form of biological therapy. *(15 marks)*

   (b) Evaluate the use of chemotherapy with reference to issues surrounding its use (e.g. appropriateness and effectiveness). *(15 marks)*

4. Discuss issues surrounding the use of biological therapies. *(30 marks)*

The specification for this division identifies three forms of biological therapy: chemotherapy, ECT and psychosurgery. This means that questions may be set specifically on any one of these therapies or a combination of them or set generally on biological therapies. Question 1 is an example of the more general question. As 'therapies' is in the plural this means you must write about at least two therapies. If you only describe one therapy then your AO1 mark would be limited to a maximum of 9 (partial performance penalty – remember on Unit 5 AO1 marks are a maximum of 15). If you described two therapies but only evaluated one then your AO2 mark would also be marked out of a total of 9 marks. You can, of course, discuss more than one form of therapy, though if you choose to do this take care to be selective – you only have 20 minutes for the AO1 component and if you spend more time on AO1 you will restrict what you can include in AO2.

It is possible that you would be asked a question about chemotherapy alone and thus should have a 40-minute answer prepared, but it is more likely that you will be asked to discuss more than one biological therapy so you need a 'cut-down' version as well.

Question 4 is taken directly from the specification. This shows that, in addition to being expected to describe and evaluate the individual therapies, you need to be able to describe and evaluate issues surrounding their use. This knowledge can be used to provide evaluation of treatments – questions 2b and 3b require you to do this. In question 4 you need to focus on the issues alone – and describe and evaluate them.

Probable questions

1. Outline and evaluate ECT and psychosurgery as biological therapies. *(30 marks)*

2. (a) Outline ECT and psychosurgery as biological therapies. *(15 marks)*

   (b) Evaluate ECT and psychosurgery with reference to issues surrounding their use (e.g. appropriateness and effectiveness). *(15 marks)*

Possible questions

3. (a) Describe ECT as a form of biological therapy. *(15 marks)*

   (b) Evaluate the use of ECT with reference to issues surrounding its use (e.g. appropriateness and effectiveness). *(15 marks)*

4. (a) Describe psychosurgery as a form of biological therapy. *(15 marks)*

   (b) Evaluate the use of psychosurgery with reference to issues surrounding its use (e.g. appropriateness and effectiveness). *(15 marks)*

Question 1 limits you to two therapies and names the particular therapies. You would receive no credit for mentioning chemotherapy *unless* you can use it as a form of contrast, for example suggesting why chemotherapy might be preferable to ECT/psychosurgery. However, there would still not be any credit for a *description* of chemotherapy.

Question 2 differs from question 1 because the AO2 component has been specified. You can't evaluate the therapies in whatever way you choose but must refer to the issues surrounding their use. In reality your evaluation is likely to be largely, if not entirely, focused on issues and therefore your answer to questions 1 and 2 would be the same.

In question 4 for topic 1 there was credit for description and evaluation of the issues but in question 2 for topic 1 and topic 2 you must use evidence related to the issues as commentary. The two examples given (appropriateness and effectiveness) are examples only. You do not have to refer to these and can refer to other issues (such as ethics).

Questions 3 and 4 serve to remind you that you could be asked a question solely on ECT or psychosurgery which again means that you need to prepare a 40-minute essay for each, as well as 'cut-down' versions.

In both questions 3 and 4, part (a) is pure AO1 and part (b) is pure AO2. If you mentioned research evidence as a means of evaluation this would be creditworthy as long as it was related to an issue such as effectiveness. In these questions you have not simply been asked to evaluate the treatments – but to do this in terms of issues. It is preferable to make the issues explicit to the examiner rather than just presenting your 'prepared' evaluation in the hope that the examiner regards it as creditworthy.

SAMPLE ESSAY PLAN

Question 1: Outline and evaluate **two or more** biological therapies. (30 marks)

CHEMOTHERAPY

10 MINUTES WORTH OF AO1

- **Antipsychotics** (e.g. for schizophrenia, BD):
- To improve **functioning** and **subjective feelings** of well-being.
- **Conventional antipsychotics** for **positive** symptoms: **dopamine antagonists** reduce effects of dopamine.
- May also reduce **negative** symptoms.
- **Atypical antipsychotics** act on the **serotonin** and other systems involved in schizophrenia.
- **Antidepressants** (depression, severe anxiety, OCD and eating disorders):
- **Tricyclics**: **block re-uptake** mechanism that re-absorbs **serotonin** and **epinephrine** into the presynaptic cell.
- **SSRIs** selectively block the **re-uptake of serotonin** into the presynaptic cell.

10 MINUTES WORTH OF AO2

- **Antipsychotics** play an important role in the treatment of schizophrenia (relapse rate twice as high for **placebos**).
- Can be effectively combined with **psychotherapy** (WHO, 2001).
- **Atypical antipsychotics** may ultimately be more effective as they have fewer side effects (**Lewis et al.**, 2001).
- Newer **SSRIs** are more effective than **tricyclics** in severe depression, have fewer unwanted side effects and greater patient acceptance (**WHO**, 2001).
- **Appropriateness**: chemotherapies do not always work, possibly because disorders such as depression and schizophrenia are not simply caused by biological factors.
- **Placebo** effectiveness suggests that patient belief may cause beneficial effects.
- **Not cures**: drugs offer only a temporary alleviation of symptoms rather than curing the underlying problem.
- **Discourages patient responsibility**: recovery achieved by external forces.

ECT OR PSYCHOSURGERY

10 MINUTES WORTH OF AO1
See page 160.

10 MINUTES WORTH OF AO2
See page 160.

Question 3(a) Describe chemotherapy as a form of biological therapy. (15 marks)
(b) Evaluate the use of chemotherapy with reference to issues surrounding its use (e.g. appropriateness and effectiveness). (15 marks)

20 MINUTES WORTH OF AO1

The description of theory 1 above plus:

- **Atypical antipsychotics**: temporarily occupy D2 receptors allowing normal dopamine transmission.
- **Antidepressants**: aim to increase amounts of serotonin and epinephrine which are low in depressives.
- **Anxiolytics**: combat anxiety by bringing its symptoms under control.
- **BZs** depress **RAS** (Reticular Activating System) that regulates how active the brain is.
- **BZs** increase the action of **GABA**, which slows down the transmission of nerve signals in the brain.
- **GABA** also reduces **serotonin** activity.
- **Beta-blockers** block action of **epinephrine** in the circulatory system, thus reducing the physical symptoms of anxiety.

20 MINUTES WORTH OF AO2

The evaluation of theory 1 above plus:

- **BZs** are the most effective and most quick-acting anxiolytics, but even patients taking low doses experience **withdrawal** symptoms.
- The efficacy of **beta-blockers** is limited to the **short-term relief** of physical symptoms.
- **Placebo effects**: Kirsch et al. (2002) found people prescribed a placebo fared almost as well as those prescribed with an antedepressant.
- Other studies (e.g. **Mulrow et al.**, 2000) found a stronger effect for the real drug.
- **Side effects**: all chemotherapies have side effects, often the reason why people stop taking their medication.

Antipsychotic drugs are used in the treatment of the most disturbing forms of psychotic illness, such as schizophrenia and bipolar disorder. Antipsychotic medication helps patients to function as well as possible, and increases their subjective feelings of well-being. Conventional antipsychotics such as chlorpromazine are used to combat the positive symptoms of schizophrenia, acting as dopamine antagonists to reduce the effects of dopamine. As well as combating positive symptoms, atypical antipsychotics are claimed to have some beneficial effects on the negative symptoms of schizophrenia. As well as acting on the dopamine system, they additionally act on the serotonin system and other systems involved in schizophrenia. Antidepressants are drugs that relieve the symptoms of moderate to severe depression and are also used in the treatment of severe anxiety, OCD and eating disorders. Depression is thought to be due to insufficient amounts of serotonin and epinephrine available at the synapse. Tricyclics block the re-uptake mechanism that re-absorbs serotonin and epinephrine into the presynaptic cell. SSRIs selectively block the re-uptake of serotonin into the presynaptic cell. As a result, more of these neurotransmitters are available to excite neighbouring brain cells, thus reducing the effects of depression.

> It isn't necessary to go too deeply into the underlying physiology of drug action. This amount of detail would be fine.

The World Health Organisation (2001) reports that antipsychotics play an important role in the treatment of schizophrenia. This conclusion is a result of evidence that shows that relapse rates for schizophrenics are twice as high with the use of placebos than for antipsychotics, but this rate is even lower when combined with psychotherapy. However, Lewis et al. (2001) claim that atypical antipsychotics may ultimately be more effective in the treatment of schizophrenia as they have fewer side effects. Although tricyclics are as effective as the SSRIs in the treatment of depression (WHO, 2001), the newer SSRIs are more effective in severe depression, have fewer unwanted side effects and so have greater patient acceptance. However, chemotherapies do not always work without psychotherapy, possibly because disorders such as depression and schizophrenia are not simply caused by biological factors alone. Some studies have found that patients fared as well with placebos as they did with the actual drug, suggesting that it is patient belief that causes the beneficial effect rather than any chemical action of the drug. Drugs offer only a temporary alleviation of symptoms rather than curing the underlying problem; when the patient stops taking them their effectiveness ceases. Biological treatments also discourage patient responsibility as recovery is achieved by external forces (i.e. the drugs) that are beyond the patient's control.

> 'Drugs only treat the symptoms and not the causes' is a commonly used point of evaluation, but one that needs some form of elaboration to be effective.

ECT is generally used in severely depressed patients, particularly when the condition is considered to be potentially life-threatening. A small amount of electric current is applied to a patient's head in order to initiate a brain seizure. The patient is first injected with short-acting barbiturate and nerve-blocking agent to prevent the muscles from contracting during the seizures. The current passes between two scalp electrodes for about half a second to create a seizure lasting up to one minute. A patient usually requires between 3 and 15 treatments. One possible explanation for the mechanism of ECT is that the seizure alters levels of receptors for serotonin and norepinephrine, so that the presynaptic neuron produces more of these neurotransmitters, thus alleviating many of the symptoms of depression (Sapolsky, 2000). The neuroendocrine hypothesis states that ECT seizures cause a shift in the body's hormonal system, leading to a decrease in the symptoms of depression. The ECT seizure causes the hypothalamus to release chemicals that cause changes in areas of the brain that regulate mood.

> You can get too much into the mechanics of ECT and the underlying biology. Try to strike a balance between the two in any description of how and why it works.

ECT has been shown to be effective in the treatment of depression, with about 66% showing improvement after ECT treatment (Comer, 2002). However, a high proportion of these relapse within 6 months (Sackheim et al., 2001), and some critics claim that equally high levels of improvement can be gained with placebo alone (Lowinger and Dobie, 1969). ECT is faster acting than drugs, and may be the only alternative if patients fail to respond to other treatments. Critics claim that ECT has a number of side effects, including impaired memory, with at least one-third of patients complaining of persistent memory loss after ECT (Rose et al., 2003). There are also a number of psychological side effects, with some patients reporting that their ECT treatment had resulted in permanent fear and anxiety (DOH, 1999). The DOH report also found that over half of the patients given ECT in the UK had not consented to treatment, which creates an ethical problem concerning the lack of informed consent. More recent developments have provided a safer alternative to traditional ECT. In rTMS, high-intensity magnetic pulses are passed through the skull, with fewer side effects and with the same level of effectiveness as ECT.

> There are a number of commentary points used here. Rather than just being identified, each has been *elaborated* for maximum effectiveness.

SAMPLE ESSAY PLAN

Question 3: a) Describe ECT as a form of biological therapy. (15 marks)
(b) Evaluate the use of ECT with reference to issues surrounding its use (e.g. appropriateness and effectiveness). (15 marks)

(A) 20 MINUTES WORTH OF A01

The description of theory 1 below plus:

- Electric current approximately **0.6 amps**.
- Usually given **3 times a week**.
- **Unilateral** ECT: one electrode on non-dominant side and the other in the middle of the forehead.
- **Bilateral** ECT: electrode on each temple.
- **Neurotransmitter function:** ECT **decreases norepinephrine** autoreceptors, so neuron is tricked into producing more because it senses less.
- **Serotonin receptors** in post-synaptic neurons are sensitised by repeated ECT, which produces an anti-depressant effect.
- **Neuroendocrine hypothesis:** seizure causes **hypothalamus** to release **neuropeptides** that regulate mood.

(B) 20 MINUTES WORTH OF A02

The evaluation of theory 1 below plus:

- **Effectiveness: subjective reports:** 27% reported it unhelpful, 36% said it was helpful (**DOH**, 1999).
- Success of **low-dose bilateral therapy** was 65% successful compared with 43% for **high-dose unilateral** and 17% for low-dose unilateral (**Sackheim et al.**, 1993).
- **Coffey et al.** (1991) used brain imaging techniques and found no evidence of changes in brain anatomy after ECT.
- **Why does it work?** Abrams (1997) concluded we are no nearer understanding why it works.
- It is like arguing that if you thump the TV and get a picture this is a recommendation to keep doing it.
- **Youssef and Youssef** (1999) argue that ECT was acceptable when there were no alternatives but not now.

Question 1: Outline and evaluate ECT and psychosurgery as biological therapies. (30 marks)

ECT

10 MINUTES WORTH OF A01

- ECT used in **severely depressed** patients, particularly when the condition is considered to be potentially life-threatening.
- An **electric current** is applied to a patient's head causing a **brain seizure**.
- Patient injected with short-acting **barbiturate** and **nerve-blocking** agent.
- Current passes between two **scalp electrodes** to create a seizure lasting up to one minute.
- Usually need **3–15 treatments**.
- **Neurotransmitter function:** alters levels of receptors for **serotonin** and **norepinephrine**, presynaptic neuron produces more of these neurotransmitters (**Sapolsky,** 2000).
- **Neuroendocrine hypothesis:** seizure is thought to cause a shift in the body's hormonal system, causing a decrease in the symptoms of depression.
- **Hypothalamus** releases chemicals that cause changes in areas of the brain that regulate mood.

10 MINUTES WORTH OF A02

- **Effectiveness:** about 66% improve after ECT treatment (**Comer,** 2002) but a high proportion relapse within 6 months (**Sackheim et al.,** 2001).
- Some critics claim that equally high levels of improvement can be gained with **placebo** alone (**Lowinger and Dobie,** 1969).
- **Appropriateness:** faster acting than drugs, and may be the only alternative if patients fail to respond to other treatments.
- **Side effects: physical** (e.g. impaired memory in 33% of patients, **Rose et al.,** 2003) and **psychological** side effects (e.g. fear and anxiety in 30%, **DOH,** 1999).
- **Ethics:** large proportion of those receiving ECT under the Mental Health Act have not consented to treatment (**DOH,** 1999).
- **Safer alternative (rTMS):** high-intensity magnetic pulses passed through the skull, with fewer side effects and with the same level of effectiveness as ECT.

PSYCHOSURGERY

10 MINUTES WORTH OF A01

- **Brain surgery** aimed to modify disturbances of behaviour with no known organic cause.
- **Prefrontal lobotomy:** severe affective disorders.
- **Mode of action:** sharp instrument inserted into the brain and rotated to cut the white matter tracts to and from the **prefrontal lobes**.
- **Stereotactic psychosurgery:** mental disorders that fail to respond to other forms of treatment.
- **Mode of action:** computer-based stereotactic imaging, involves locating precise points within the brain and severing the connections.
- Examples include **cingulotomy** (cut link between orbitofrontal cortex and deeper structures to treat OCD) and **capsulotomy** (link between the capsule and cortex).

10 MINUTES WORTH OF A02

- **Effectiveness:** cingulotomies and capsulotomies are effective for 50–66% of patients with OCD or depression (**Cosgrove and Rauch,** 2001).
- **Appropriateness:** Szasz (1978) claims that the psyche is not a part of the body, therefore impossible to perform surgery on it.
- **Side effects:** may impair mental functioning.
- **Ethics:** informed consent necessary but patients and their families may not be fully aware of the risks e.g. case of **Mary Lou Zimmerman**.
- **Safer alternative: deep brain stimulation** uses high-frequency current to interrupt the brain circuitry involved in OCD.
- **Successful** with 3 out of 4 OCD patients (**Gabriels et al.,** 2003).

ECT is generally used in severely depressed patients, particularly when the condition is considered to be potentially life-threatening, and when other forms of treatment (such as medication and psychotherapy) have proved to be ineffective. It can also be used with patients suffering from schizophrenia or with those experiencing severe manic episodes. ECT is used when there is a risk of suicide because it tends to give quicker results than antidepressants. A small amount of electric current (approximately 0.6 amps) is applied to a patient's head in order to initiate a brain seizure. The patient is first injected with short-acting barbiturate and nerve-blocking agent to prevent the muscles from contracting during the seizures. In unilateral ECT, one electrode is placed above the non-dominant side of the brain, and the other in the middle of the forehead, but usually bilateral ECT is given, with an electrode placed above each temple. The current passes between two scalp electrodes for about half a second to create a seizure lasting up to one minute. ECT is usually given three times a week, with a patient usually requiring between 3 and 15 treatments.

> The AO1 description is an expanded version of the outline in the previous question, therefore there is a good deal more detail in the description of what goes on in ECT.

Research has highlighted the role of neurotransmitter deficiencies in depression, and it is believed that ECT alters levels of available neurotransmitters, thus reducing the low mood associated with depression. One possible explanation for the mechanism of ECT is that the seizure alters levels of receptors for serotonin and norepinephrine. ECT decreases norepinephrine autoreceptors, so the neuron is tricked into producing more norepinephrine because it senses there is too low a level of this neurotransmitter. Serotonin receptors in post-synaptic neurons are sensitised by repeated ECT. It is this change in sensitivity that is thought to account for the anti-depressant effect of ECT. Because more neurotransmitters involved in mood regulation are produced, this has the direct effect of alleviating many of the symptoms of depression. The neuroendocrine hypothesis states that ECT seizures cause a shift in the body's hormonal system, leading to a decrease in the symptoms of depression. Like neurotransmitters, some hormones also affect emotion. The ECT seizure causes the hypothalamus to release neuropeptides that cause changes in areas of the brain that regulate mood.

> As with the previous paragraph, there is a good deal of biological detail in this paragraph. To be confident in reproducing this amount of detail, it is a good idea to use the internet to research the underlying biology of ECT action.

ECT has been shown to be effective in the treatment of depression, with about 66% showing improvement after ECT treatment (Comer, 2002). However, these beneficial effects do not appear to last, with a high proportion of depressives treated with ECT relapsing within 6 months (Sackheim et al., 2001). Some critics claim that equally high levels of improvement can be gained with placebo alone, with improvement rates as high as 80% being found in one study (Lowinger and Dobie, 1969). In a Department of Health report (DOH, 1999) 27% of those who had received ECT reported it unhelpful, whereas only a slightly higher figure (36%) said it was helpful. The effectiveness of different types of ECT has shown that the success rate for low-dose bilateral therapy was 65% compared with 43% for high-dose unilateral and 17% for low-dose unilateral ECT (Sackheim et al., 1993). ECT is faster acting than drugs, and may be the only alternative if patients fail to respond to other treatments.

> Does it work? This is where research is vital in providing commentary on ECT's *effectiveness*. This is not a simple yes or no answer, as can be seen by the material used.

Critics claim that ECT has a number of side effects, including impaired memory and cardiovascular changes, with at least one-third of patients complaining of persistent memory loss after ECT (Rose et al., 2003). However, Coffey et al. (1991) used imaging techniques to obtain very sensitive brain scans, and found no evidence of changes in brain anatomy after ECT. There are also a number of psychological side effects, with some patients reporting that their ECT treatment had resulted in permanent fear and anxiety (DOH, 1999). The DOH report also found that over half of the patients given ECT in the UK had not consented to treatment, which creates an ethical problem concerning the lack of informed consent. Abrams (1997) concluded we are no nearer understanding why ECT works, and claims that it is rather like arguing that if you thump the TV to get a picture this is an acceptable recommendation to keep doing it. Youssef and Youssef (1999) argue that ECT was acceptable when there were no alternatives but not now, because more recent developments have provided a safer alternative to traditional ECT. In rTMS, high-intensity magnetic pulses are passed through the skull, with fewer side effects and with the same level of effectiveness as ECT.

> The image of thumping a TV set is one that students always tend to remember, but can you place this effectively within the context of a critical commentary?

Topic 1: Behavioural therapies based on classical conditioning

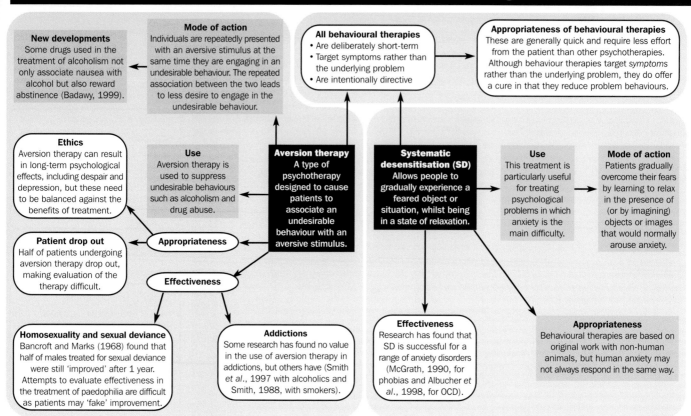

New developments
Some drugs used in the treatment of alcoholism not only associate nausea with alcohol but also reward abstinence (Badawy, 1999).

Mode of action
Individuals are repeatedly presented with an aversive stimulus at the same time they are engaging in an undesirable behaviour. The repeated association between the two leads to less desire to engage in the undesirable behaviour.

All behavioural therapies
• Are deliberately short-term
• Target symptoms rather than the underlying problem
• Are intentionally directive

Appropriateness of behavioural therapies
These are generally quick and require less effort from the patient than other psychotherapies. Although behaviour therapies target *symptoms* rather than the underlying problem, they do offer a cure in that they reduce problem behaviours.

Ethics
Aversion therapy can result in long-term psychological effects, including despair and depression, but these need to be balanced against the benefits of treatment.

Use
Aversion therapy is used to suppress undesirable behaviours such as alcoholism and drug abuse.

Aversion therapy
A type of psychotherapy designed to cause patients to associate an undesirable behaviour with an aversive stimulus.

Systematic desensitisation (SD)
Allows people to gradually experience a feared object or situation, whilst being in a state of relaxation.

Use
This treatment is particularly useful for treating psychological problems in which anxiety is the main difficulty.

Mode of action
Patients gradually overcome their fears by learning to relax in the presence of (or by imagining) objects or images that would normally arouse anxiety.

Appropriateness

Patient drop out
Half of patients undergoing aversion therapy drop out, making evaluation of the therapy difficult.

Effectiveness

Effectiveness
Research has found that SD is successful for a range of anxiety disorders (McGrath, 1990, for phobias and Albucher et al., 1998, for OCD).

Appropriateness
Behavioural therapies are based on original work with non-human animals, but human anxiety may not always respond in the same way.

Homosexuality and sexual deviance
Bancroft and Marks (1968) found that half of males treated for sexual deviance were still 'improved' after 1 year. Attempts to evaluate effectiveness in the treatment of paedophilia are difficult as patients may 'fake' improvement.

Addictions
Some research has found no value in the use of aversion therapy in addictions, but others have (Smith et al., 1997 with alcoholics and Smith, 1988, with smokers).

Topic 2: Behavioural therapies based on operant conditioning

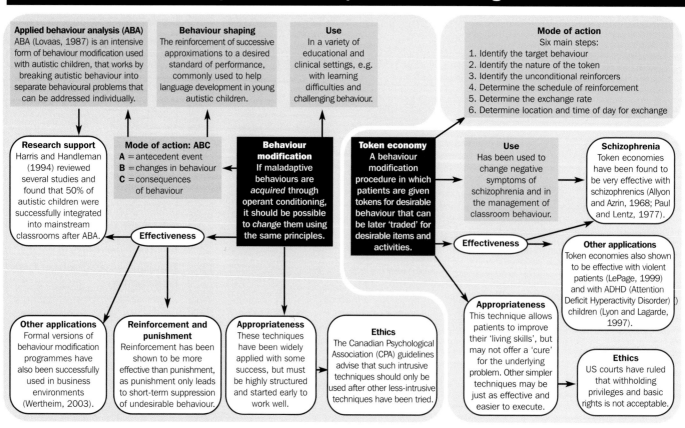

Applied behaviour analysis (ABA)
ABA (Lovaas, 1987) is an intensive form of behaviour modification used with autistic children, that works by breaking autistic behaviour into separate behavioural problems that can be addressed individually.

Behaviour shaping
The reinforcement of successive approximations to a desired standard of performance, commonly used to help language development in young autistic children.

Use
In a variety of educational and clinical settings, e.g. with learning difficulties and challenging behaviour.

Mode of action
Six main steps:
1. Identify the target behaviour
2. Identify the nature of the token
3. Identify the unconditional reinforcers
4. Determine the schedule of reinforcement
5. Determine the exchange rate
6. Determine location and time of day for exchange

Research support
Harris and Handleman (1994) reviewed several studies and found that 50% of autistic children were successfully integrated into mainstream classrooms after ABA.

Mode of action: ABC
A = antecedent event
B = changes in behaviour
C = consequences of behaviour

Behaviour modification
If maladaptive behaviours are *acquired* through operant conditioning, it should be possible to *change* them using the same principles.

Token economy
A behaviour modification procedure in which patients are given tokens for desirable behaviour that can be later 'traded' for desirable items and activities.

Use
Has been used to change negative symptoms of schizophrenia and in the management of classroom behaviour.

Schizophrenia
Token economies have been found to be very effective with schizophrenics (Allyon and Azrin, 1968; Paul and Lentz, 1977).

Effectiveness

Effectiveness

Other applications
Token economies also shown to be effective with violent patients (LePage, 1999) and with ADHD (Attention Deficit Hyperactivity Disorder) children (Lyon and Lagarde, 1997).

Other applications
Formal versions of behaviour modification programmes have also been successfully used in business environments (Wertheim, 2003).

Reinforcement and punishment
Reinforcement has been shown to be more effective than punishment, as punishment only leads to short-term suppression of undesirable behaviour.

Appropriateness
These techniques have been widely applied with some success, but must be highly structured and started early to work well.

Ethics
The Canadian Psychological Association (CPA) guidelines advise that such intrusive techniques should only be used after other less-intrusive techniques have been tried.

Appropriateness
This technique allows patients to improve their 'living skills', but may not offer a 'cure' for the underlying problem. Other simpler techniques may be just as effective and easier to execute.

Ethics
US courts have ruled that withholding privileges and basic rights is not acceptable.

Probable questions

1. Outline and evaluate **two or more** behavioural therapies. *(30 marks)*

2. (a) Outline **two** behavioural therapies based on classical conditioning. *(15 marks)*

   (b) Evaluate the **two** behavioural therapies based on classical conditioning outlined in (a) with reference to issues surrounding their use (e.g. appropriateness and effectiveness). *(15 marks)*

Possible questions

3. Discuss issues surrounding the use of behavioural therapies based on classical conditioning. *(30 marks)*

The questions for division B are similar to those for division A, which is not surprising because the specification entries are fairly similar. The main difference is that here no specific therapies are named whereas they were for biological therapies. In division B a distinction has been made, however, between therapies based on classical and operant conditioning which means that questions may specify classical or operant conditioning (as in question 2) or may simply ask for behavioural therapies (as in question 1).

The term 'outline' has been used in question 1 in recognition of the fact that a discussion of two or more therapies may entail more breadth than depth. In fact 'detail' is not included in the marking allocation for 'outline' questions whereas it is for 'describe' questions. Breadth is more important.

As previously pointed out, questions 1 and 2 would elicit the same answer since any evaluation used for question 1 is likely to be related to issues of effectiveness, appropriateness, ethics and so on.

Question 3 entails both describing and evaluating issues relating to the use of behavioural therapies and is limited to those based on classical conditioning alone. No examples have been included in the question because it would make it unreadable. It is likely that you would address effectiveness and appropriateness and might also include ethical issues. The challenging part of this question is providing description and evaluation. In question 2 (b) you only need to use 'issues' for evaluation. What's the difference? Think of a research study you might use to illustrate effectiveness. For AO1 you could describe this study. For AO2 you might consider what the study shows us and could also consider methodological flaws, applications, implications and so on. In question 2 (b) you must focus on AO2 only.

Probable questions

1. Outline and evaluate **two or more** behavioural therapies based on operant conditioning. *(30 marks)*

2. (a) Outline **two** behavioural therapies based on operant conditioning. *(15 marks)*

   (b) Evaluate the **two** behavioural therapies based on operant conditioning outlined in (a) with reference to issues surrounding their use (e.g. appropriateness and effectiveness). *(15 marks)*

3. Compare and contrast biological and behavioural therapies. *(30 marks)*

Possible questions

4. Discuss issues surrounding the use of behavioural therapies based on operant conditioning. *(30 marks)*

The questions here are similar to those for topic 1 except they now refer to therapies based on operant conditioning. The specification provides one example (token economies) but you can see from questions 1 and 2 that you need to know at least two therapies based on operant conditioning (the same advice applies for therapies based on classical conditioning).

Question 3 uses an unusual 'injunction' – 'compare and contrast'. The simplest way to answer such questions is to describe the therapies named (in this case at least one biological therapy and at least one behavioural therapy). This is the AO1 component of your answer. For AO2 credit you must consider similarities and differences. You can divide your answer into four components: description of biological therapies (one or more), description of behavioural therapies (one or more), consideration of similarities, consideration of differences. These 'considerations' (AO2 content) may simply involve identifying similarities and differences, but for full AO2 credit you need to provide supporting evidence for the similarities/differences.

Question 3 combines material from division A and division B, which is legitimate. A question might also legitimately combine topics.

Question 4 is the same as question 4 for topic 1. You may struggle to have 40 minutes of material for such questions that focus solely on issues surrounding the use of therapies but don't fill time by describing the therapies themselves as this would gain no credit. You are better spending your time by adding just one or two relevant sentences than adding several paragraphs of irrelevant material.

SAMPLE ESSAY PLAN

Question 2: (a) Outline **two** behavioural therapies based on classical conditioning. (15 marks)
(b) Evaluate the **two** behavioural therapies based on classical conditioning outlined in (a) with reference to issues surrounding their use (e.g. appropriateness and effectiveness). (15 marks)

THERAPY 1: AVERSION THERAPY	**10 MINUTES WORTH OF AO1**	**10 MINUTES WORTH OF AO2**
	• Patients taught to associate an **undesirable behaviour** with an **aversive stimulus**.	• **Miller** (1978) found no difference between aversion therapy and counselling together or alone.
	• Used for undesirable behaviours such as **alcoholism** and **drug abuse, homosexuality**.	• Treating **addictions**: success with alcoholics (**Smith et al.**, 1997) and with smokers – 52% abstaining after one year (**Smith**, 1988).
	• Based on **classical conditioning**: individuals repeatedly presented with an unconditioned stimulus (UCS) when engaging in undesirable behaviour.	• **Bancroft and Marks** (1968): 50% of males treated for **sexual deviance** still 'improved' after one year.
	• The **repeated association** leads to less desire to engage in the undesirable behaviour (conditioned stimulus, CS).	• However, **McConaghy** (1999): treatment of homosexuals and paedophiles no better than placebo.
	• **Covert sensitisation** involves imagining aversive stimuli e.g. repulsive scenes.	• Evaluating effectiveness when treating **paedophilia** difficult as patients may 'fake' improvement.
	• **New developments**: drugs used to treat alcoholism not only associate nausea with alcohol but also reward abstinence (**Badawy**, 1999).	• **Patient drop out** makes evaluation difficult.
		• **Ethics: long-term effects**, including despair and depression (**Harris**, 1988), but be balanced against the **benefits** of treatment (**Lang and Melamed**, 1969).
THERAPY 2: SYSTEMATIC DESENSITISATION (SD)	**10 MINUTES WORTH OF AO1**	**10 MINUTES WORTH OF AO2**
	• Developed by **Wolpe** (1950s), particularly useful for treating **anxiety-related** problems.	• **Effectiveness**: 75% patients with phobias respond to SD (**McGrath**, 1990), 80–90% of OCD patients respond (**Albucher et al.**, 1998).
	• Feared object not so fearful if could be **re-experienced**, blocked by anxiety.	• However **spontaneous recovery** from phobias as high as 50–60% (**McMorran et al.**, 2001).
	• People **gradually experience** a feared object or situation, whilst being in a state of **relaxation**.	• **Appropriateness**: based animal research, but human anxiety may not be the same.
	• **Mode of action**: patients taught how to relax.	• **All behavioural therapies**: deliberately short-term, target symptoms rather than underlying problem, are intentionally directive.
	• Therapist and patient construct a **desensitisation hierarchy**.	• **Appropriateness of behavioural therapies**: quick and require less effort from the patient than other psychotherapies.
	• Patient gradually works through each while relaxing (relaxed state **incompatible** with anxiety).	
	• Eventually fear is **dispelled**.	

Question 3: Discuss issues surrounding the use of behavioural therapies based on classical conditioning. (30 marks)

20 MINUTES WORTH OF AO1	**20 MINUTES WORTH OF AO2**
Issue 1: Effectiveness	• **Miller** (1978) compared **aversion therapy**, aversion therapy + counselling and counselling alone and found same recovery in all groups.
• Aversion therapy used with **addictions**, success with alcoholics (**Smith et al.**, 1997) and smokers (**Smith**, 1988).	• May be some other factor (**dodo bird effect**).
• Used with homosexuality (**Bancroft and Marks**, 1968) with 50% success after 1 year and paedophiles (**Cautela**, 1967).	• **McConaghy** (1999): treatment of homosexuals and paedophiles no better than placebo.
• SD is successful for many anxiety disorders, e.g. phobias (**McGrath**, 1990) and OCD (**Albucher et al.**, 1998).	• **Apparent effectiveness** due to faking to prevent further treatment.
Issue 2: Appropriateness	• Studies often involve very **small samples**.
• **Patient drop out** by 50% of aversion therapy patients, making evaluation difficult.	• SD: **spontaneous recovery** from phobias as high as 50–60% (**McMorran et al.**, 2001).
• **Ethics: long-term psychological effects**, including despair and depression (**Harris**, 1988).	• Evaluating effectiveness when treating **paedophilia** difficult as patients may 'fake' improvement.
• **Based** on research with non-human animals.	• **Ethical costs** balanced against the **benefits** of treatment e.g. for paedophiles (**Melamed**, 1969).
• **Generally** quick and require less effort from the patient than other psychotherapies.	• Some patients want **quick cure** and lack of effort.
• Targets **symptoms** rather than problem.	• At least they **reduce problem behaviours**.
• **Directive** – who decides what is desirable?	• May be appropriate for a narrow range of behaviours.

In aversion therapy, patients are taught to associate an undesirable behaviour with an aversive stimulus, thus leading to suppression of the undesirable behaviour. It has been used for undesirable behaviours such as alcoholism and drug abuse, although the technique has also been more controversially used in the treatment of homosexuality and aggressive behaviour. Aversion therapy is based on the principles of classical conditioning, with individuals being repeatedly presented with an aversive stimulus (such a drug that makes them feel nauseous) at the same time they are engaging in an undesirable behaviour. The aversive stimulus acts as an unconditioned stimulus (UCS) and already leads to an avoidance response (the UCR). The repeated association between the aversive stimulus (UCS) and the undesirable behaviour (now a CS) leads to the same avoidance response, i.e. less desire to engage in the undesirable behaviour. In a variation of this technique used in the treatment of alcoholism (covert sensitisation), patients are required to imagine upsetting, repulsive or frightening scenes while they are drinking. New developments in the treatment of alcoholism using aversion therapy techniques use drugs that make users feel sick if mixed with alcohol, but reward abstinence with feelings of tranquillity and well-being (Badawy, 1999).

> Although a brief explanation of classical conditioning is necessary to explain how aversion therapy works, this should be in the context of aversion therapy rather than just a general description.

Miller (1978) compared the effectiveness of aversion therapy, counselling plus aversion therapy, or counselling alone in the treatment of alcoholics. After one year, the recovery rate was the same for all three conditions, indicating that aversion therapy offered no benefit above counselling alone. In contrast, however, Smith et al. (1997) found that alcoholics treated with aversion therapy had a higher abstinence rate after one year than those treated with counselling alone. Smith (1988) also reported the same success in the treatment of smokers, with 52% treated with aversion therapy still abstaining from smoking one year after treatment. When used as a treatment for sexual behaviour, aversion therapy has also been shown to be effective. Bancroft and Marks (1968) found that 50% of males treated for sexual deviance still showed evidence of 'improvement' after 1 year. However, McConaghy (1999) found that attempts to change paedophilic behaviour using aversion therapy was no more effective than a placebo treatment. There are, however, difficulties in evaluating the effectiveness of aversion therapy when treating this type of behaviour as patients may 'fake' improvement to prevent further therapy. A further problem is that a large proportion of patients drop out of treatment programmes, making accurate evaluation difficult. There are also ethical problems with this form of treatment, as it can result in long-term psychological effects, including despair and depression (Harris, 1988). However, Lang and Melamed (1969) argue that these must be balanced against the benefits of treatment.

> It is often assumed that effective evaluation of therapies is fairly straightforward. This is not the case, as explained here.

Systematic desensitisation (SD) was developed by Wolpe in the 1950s, and is particularly useful for treating anxiety-related problems. SD is based on the idea that a feared stimulus would not be so fearful if it could be re-experienced, but the anxiety it creates blocks such recovery. It enables individuals to overcome their anxieties by learning to relax in the presence of stimuli (such as spiders) that once made them nervous and afraid. This is done by introducing the feared stimulus or situation gradually, whilst the individual is in a state of relaxation. Patients are first taught how to relax their muscles completely. Then the therapist and patient construct a desensitisation hierarchy, a series of imagined scenes, each causing slightly more anxiety than the previous one. The patient gradually works through the desensitisation hierarchy, visualising each anxiety-provoking event, whilst at the same time engaging in a competing relaxation response. Because relaxation and fear are incompatible responses, the person feels less fearful when imagining the feared object or situation. Once patients have mastered one step in the hierarchy, they are ready to move on to the next, and eventually the fear is dispelled.

> The main description of SD will inevitably involve the different steps involved, but these are part of an overall description of the technique.

Research has found that SD is effective in the treatment of a range of anxiety disorders. For example, McGrath (1990) found that about 75% of patients with phobias respond positively to SD, and Albucher et al. (1998) found that 80–90% of patients with OCD improve considerably when using this technique. However, spontaneous recovery from phobias without treatment can be as high as 50–60% (McMorran et al., 2001), suggesting that SD may actually contribute little to recovery. Behavioural therapies such as SD are based on non-human animal research, but human anxiety may not always respond in the same way. Behavioural therapies may not always be the most appropriate course of treatment, as they are deliberately short-term, target symptoms rather than the underlying problem, and are intentionally directive, with the therapist tending to set the goals of desirable behaviour. However, such therapies are quick in bringing about desired behavioural change, and require less effort from the patient than other psychotherapies.

> These final points apply to all behavioural therapies rather than just SD.

SAMPLE ESSAY PLAN

Question 1: Outline and evaluate **two or more** behavioural therapies based on operant conditioning. (30 marks)

BEHAVIOUR MODIFICATION

10 MINUTES WORTH OF AO1

- If maladaptive behaviours are acquired through **operant conditioning**, it should be possible to change them using the same principles.
- **Used** in educational and clinical settings, e.g. learning difficulties and challenging behaviour.
- Teach **appropriate** behaviours, eliminate **inappropriate** ones.
- ABC: **A** = antecedent event, **B** = changes in behaviour, **C** = consequences of behaviour.
- **Behaviour shaping**: reinforcement of successive approximations to a desired standard.
- **Applied behaviour analysis (ABA)** (**Lovaas**, 1987) for autistic children, works by breaking autistic behaviour into separate behavioural problems.

10 MINUTES WORTH OF AO2

- Behaviour modification programmes successfully used in **business environments** (**Wertheim**, 2003).
- ABA: 50% of autistic children successfully integrated into mainstream classrooms (**Harris and Handleman**, 1994) though support still needed.
- **Reinforcement** more effective than **punishment**, as punishment only leads to short-term suppression of undesirable behaviour (**Hall**, 1996).
- **To be effective** techniques need to be highly structured and started early.
- **Ethics:** CPA guidelines advise that such intrusive techniques should only be used after other less-intrusive techniques have been tried.

TOKEN ECONOMY

10 MINUTES WORTH OF AO1

- A form of **behaviour modification**.
- Aim to **increase desirable behaviours** and decrease undesirable ones.
- Patients **given tokens** for desirable behaviour, later be 'traded' for desirable items and activities.
- **Used** to change negative symptoms of schizophrenia and managing classroom behaviour.

Six main steps:

- Identify the target behaviour.
- Identify the nature of the token.
- Identify the unconditioned reinforcers.
- Determine the schedule of reinforcement.
- Determine the exchange rate.
- Determine location and time of day for exchange.

10 MINUTES WORTH OF AO2

- Very effective with **schizophrenics** (**Allyon and Azrin**, 1968; **Paul and Lentz**, 1977).
- Effective with **violent patients** (**LePage**, 1999), ADHD children (**Lyon and Lagarde**, 1997).
- Allows patients to improve their '**living skills**', but may not offer a '**cure**' for the underlying problem.
- **Simpler techniques** may be just as effective and easier to execute.
- **Ethics:** US courts ruled that withholding privileges and basic rights is not acceptable.

Question 4: Discuss issues surrounding the use of behavioural therapies based on operant conditioning. (30 marks)

20 MINUTES WORTH OF AO1

Effectiveness:

- Behaviour modification programmes successfully used in **business environments** (**Wertheim**, 2003).
- ABA: 50% of autistic children were successfully integrated into mainstream classrooms (**Harris and Handleman**, 1994).
- TE very effective with **schizophrenics** (**Allyon and Azrin**, 1968). **Paul and Lentz** (1977) found 98% of patients released after 4 years compared to 71% using other programmes.
- TE effective with **violent patients** (**LePage**, 1999), ADHD (**Lyon and Lagarde**, 1997), **classroom management** (**O'Leary et al.**, 1969).
- **Ethics:** CPA guidelines advise that such intrusive techniques should only be used after other less-intrusive techniques have been tried.
- **Ethics:** US courts ruled that withholding privileges and basic rights in TE is not acceptable.
- **All behavioural therapies:** short-term, directive.
- **Appropriateness of behavioural therapies:** quick, less effort for patient than other therapies.
- Can therapies be investigated **scientifically**?

20 MINUTES WORTH OF AO2

- **To be effective** techniques need to be highly structured and started early.
- Best in **institutional settings** though may be used at home (**Barkley**, 2002).
- **Simpler techniques** may be just as effective and easier to execute e.g. ADHD children improved more **using drugs** than behaviour modification programme (**Jensen**, 1999).
- **Reinforcement** more effective than **punishment**, as punishment only leads to short-term suppression.
- Parents often don't realise that they **reinforce undesirable behaviours** e.g. with attention.
- Allows patients to improve their '**living skills**', but may not offer a '**cure**' for the underlying problem.
- **TE success** with schizophrenia questioned because we don't know how long effects maintained once treatment stopped (**McMonagle and Sultana**, 2001).
- Learning in one setting **may not generalise** to other settings.
- **Ethically less objectionable** than therapies based on classical conditioning.
- Trying to evaluate therapies is difficult e.g. **dodo bird** effect, only some findings published, individual differences, **hello-goodbye effect**.

If maladaptive behaviours are acquired through operant conditioning, it should be possible to change them using the same principles. Behaviour modification programmes are used in a variety of educational and clinical settings, particularly with people with learning difficulties or challenging behaviour. The aim of behaviour modification is to teach appropriate behaviours while eliminating inappropriate ones. Simple behaviour modification is explained in terms of the ABC model, where A is the antecedent event, B the subsequent changes in behaviour and C the consequences of behaviour. Behaviour can be changed by manipulating either the conditions preceding the behaviour or the consequences following it. Behaviour that is reinforced will occur more often, while behaviour that is not reinforced, or is punished, will occur less frequently. Behaviour shaping involves reinforcement of successive approximations to a desired standard of performance, with an individual being first reinforced for a behaviour that only remotely approximates to the desired behaviour and then performing closer and closer to the end behaviour to achieve the same reinforcement. Applied behaviour analysis (ABA) is a form of intensive behaviour modification used with autistic children. ABA works by breaking autistic behaviour into separate behavioural problems that can be addressed individually, using techniques such as shaping, modelling and reinforcement.

> The ABC model applies to all aspects of operant conditioning, but here is being applied to the acquisition of maladaptive behaviours, which follow the same learning sequence.

Behaviour modification programmes have been successfully used in a variety of settings, including business environments (Wertheim, 2003), and in the treatment of autistic children. Harris and Handleman (1994) reviewed the results of several studies, showing that more than half of autistic children who participated in ABA programmes were later integrated into mainstream classrooms. However, using this as a measure of the success of ABA programmes is problematic, as some children will still need extensive support in mainstream classrooms, whereas others will need none at all. Behaviour modification programmes have been shown to be more effective when reinforcement rather than punishment is used, and only when positive behaviours are reinforced. The use of punishment may only lead to short-term suppression of undesirable behaviour (Hall, 1996). Although behaviour modification programmes have been successfully applied in a variety of clinical and educational settings, they must be highly structured to be effective. It is also evident that in the treatment of autistic behaviour, effectiveness is reduced unless treatment is started early. In Canada, CPA guidelines advise that behavioural interventions should be considered the most invasive of behavioural procedures, and should only be used after other less-intrusive techniques have been tried.

> The ethical issues surrounding therapies are also important and make for useful evaluation. Don't just make claims that a particular form of therapy is unethical without elaborating this claim.

The token economy is a form of behaviour modification in which patients are given tokens for desirable behaviour, these being withheld when undesirable behaviours are exhibited. The aim of the programme is to increase the frequency of a patient's desirable behaviours and decrease the frequency of undesirable behaviours. Tokens can later be 'traded' for desirable items and activities (e.g. spending time away from the ward). Although originally developed as a behavioural management system for schizophrenics, where it was used to change the negative symptoms of the disorder, token economies are also used to manage classroom behaviour. There are six main steps. First the target behaviour is identified so that reinforcement can be assigned to that behaviour. Next the nature of the token is identified, as are the unconditioned reinforcers for exchange. Finally, the schedule of reinforcement (initially continuous but then partial), the exchange rate for tokens and rewards, and the location and time of day for exchange are determined.

> In an outline answer, you don't have the time to detail all of the different steps, so just outline the main point in each step.

Research has shown that token economies are very effective with schizophrenics (Allyon and Azrin, 1968), although tokens were most effective when associated with behaviours already in the patient's repertoire. Subsequent research has supported the initial success in the treatment of schizophrenia. Paul and Lentz (1977) found that 98% of patients who participated in a token economy programme were subsequently released from their institutions, compared to 71% who did not participate. LePage (1999) found that when used with violent patients, a token economy programme led to a significant reduction in the number of negative incidents in an acute psychiatric unit. Similarly, Lyon and Lagarde (1997) have successfully used tokens when teaching ADHD children. Critics argue that although token economy programmes allow patients to improve their 'living skills', they may not offer a 'cure' for the underlying problem (Comer, 2002). Simpler behaviour modification techniques may be just as effective and easier to execute. Token economies have also been accused of being manipulative, and US courts have ruled that withholding privileges and basic rights is not acceptable.

> This final point is an issue of human rights, and therefore allied to the ethical issues discussed in the previous essay.

Chapter 9: Treating mental disorders

Topic 1: Psychodynamic therapies

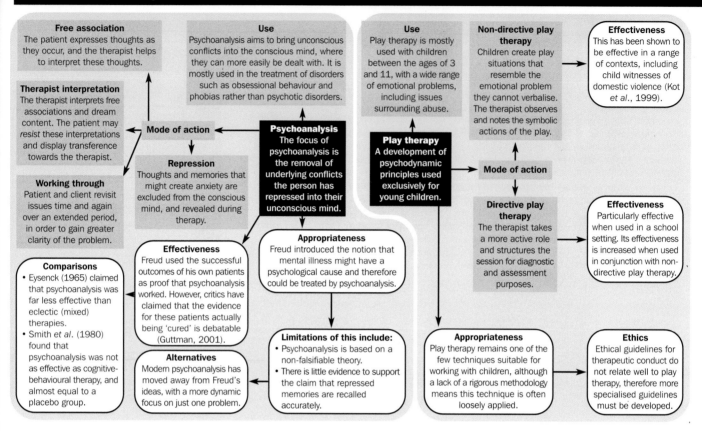

Free association
The patient expresses thoughts as they occur, and the therapist helps to interpret these thoughts.

Therapist interpretation
The therapist interprets free associations and dream content. The patient may *resist* these interpretations and display transference towards the therapist.

Working through
Patient and client revisit issues time and again over an extended period, in order to gain greater clarity of the problem.

Comparisons
• Eysenck (1965) claimed that psychoanalysis was far less effective than eclectic (mixed) therapies.
• Smith et al. (1980) found that psychoanalysis was not as effective as cognitive-behavioural therapy, and almost equal to a placebo group.

Mode of action

Repression
Thoughts and memories that might create anxiety are excluded from the conscious mind, and revealed during therapy.

Psychoanalysis
The focus of psychoanalysis is the removal of underlying conflicts the person has repressed into their unconscious mind.

Use
Psychoanalysis aims to bring unconscious conflicts into the conscious mind, where they can more easily be dealt with. It is mostly used in the treatment of disorders such as obsessional behaviour and phobias rather than psychotic disorders.

Effectiveness
Freud used the successful outcomes of his own patients as proof that psychoanalysis worked. However, critics have claimed that the evidence for these patients actually being 'cured' is debatable (Guttman, 2001).

Alternatives
Modern psychoanalysis has moved away from Freud's ideas, with a more dynamic focus on just one problem.

Appropriateness
Freud introduced the notion that mental illness might have a psychological cause and therefore could be treated by psychoanalysis.

Limitations of this include:
• Psychoanalysis is based on a non-falsifiable theory.
• There is little evidence to support the claim that repressed memories are recalled accurately.

Use
Play therapy is mostly used with children between the ages of 3 and 11, with a wide range of emotional problems, including issues surrounding abuse.

Play therapy
A development of psychodynamic principles used exclusively for young children.

Non-directive play therapy
Children create play situations that resemble the emotional problem they cannot verbalise. The therapist observes and notes the symbolic actions of the play.

Mode of action

Directive play therapy
The therapist takes a more active role and structures the session for diagnostic and assessment purposes.

Effectiveness
This has been shown to be effective in a range of contexts, including child witnesses of domestic violence (Kot et al., 1999).

Effectiveness
Particularly effective when used in a school setting. Its effectiveness is increased when used in conjunction with non-directive play therapy.

Appropriateness
Play therapy remains one of the few techniques suitable for working with children, although a lack of a rigorous methodology means this technique is often loosely applied.

Ethics
Ethical guidelines for therapeutic conduct do not relate well to play therapy, therefore more specialised guidelines must be developed.

Topic 2: Cognitive-behavioural therapies

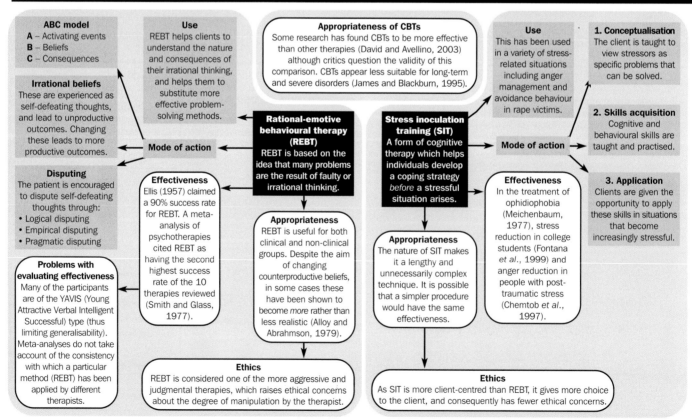

ABC model
A – Activating events
B – Beliefs
C – Consequences

Irrational beliefs
These are experienced as self-defeating thoughts, and lead to unproductive outcomes. Changing these leads to more productive outcomes.

Disputing
The patient is encouraged to dispute self-defeating thoughts through:
• Logical disputing
• Empirical disputing
• Pragmatic disputing

Problems with evaluating effectiveness
Many of the participants are of the YAVIS (Young Attractive Verbal Intelligent Successful) type (thus limiting generalisability). Meta-analyses do not take account of the consistency with which a particular method (REBT) has been applied by different therapists.

Use
REBT helps clients to understand the nature and consequences of their irrational thinking, and helps them to substitute more effective problem-solving methods.

Mode of action

Rational-emotive behavioural therapy (REBT)
REBT is based on the idea that many problems are the result of faulty or irrational thinking.

Effectiveness
Ellis (1957) claimed a 90% success rate for REBT. A meta-analysis of psychotherapies cited REBT as having the second highest success rate of the 10 therapies reviewed (Smith and Glass, 1977).

Appropriateness
REBT is useful for both clinical and non-clinical groups. Despite the aim of changing counterproductive beliefs, in some cases these have been shown to become *more* rather than less realistic (Alloy and Abrahmson, 1979).

Ethics
REBT is considered one of the more aggressive and judgmental therapies, which raises ethical concerns about the degree of manipulation by the therapist.

Appropriateness of CBTs
Some research has found CBTs to be more effective than other therapies (David and Avellino, 2003) although critics question the validity of this comparison. CBTs appear less suitable for long-term and severe disorders (James and Blackburn, 1995).

Stress inoculation training (SIT)
A form of cognitive therapy which helps individuals develop a coping strategy *before* a stressful situation arises.

Appropriateness
The nature of SIT makes it a lengthy and unnecessarily complex technique. It is possible that a simpler procedure would have the same effectiveness.

Use
This has been used in a variety of stress-related situations including anger management and avoidance behaviour in rape victims.

Mode of action

1. Conceptualisation
The client is taught to view stressors as specific problems that can be solved.

2. Skills acquisition
Cognitive and behavioural skills are taught and practised.

3. Application
Clients are given the opportunity to apply these skills in situations that become increasingly stressful.

Effectiveness
In the treatment of ophidiophobia (Meichenbaum, 1977), stress reduction in college students (Fontana et al., 1999) and anger reduction in people with post-traumatic stress (Chemtob et al., 1997).

Ethics
As SIT is more client-centred than REBT, it gives more choice to the client, and consequently has fewer ethical concerns.

Probable questions

1. Outline and evaluate **two or more** therapies derived from *either* the psychodynamic *or* cognitive-behavioural models of abnormality. *(30 marks)*

2. (a) Outline **two** therapies derived from *either* the psychodynamic *or* cognitive-behavioural models of abnormality. *(15 marks)*

   (b) Evaluate the **two** therapies derived from *either* the psychodynamic *or* cognitive-behavioural models of abnormality outlined in (a) with reference to issues surrounding their use (e.g. appropriateness and effectiveness). *(15 marks)*

Possible questions

3. Discuss issues surrounding the use of therapies derived from *either* the psychodynamic *or* cognitive-behavioural models of abnormality. *(30 marks)*

4. Compare and contrast biological therapies and therapies derived from *either* the psychodynamic *or* cognitive-behavioural models of abnormality *(30 marks)*

The final division of this subsection offers you a choice – you can either study therapies derived from the psychodynamic model of abnormality or from the cognitive-behavioural model of abnormality. This means that the questions set in this division end up being worded in a rather clumsy way. They must always offer candidates the choice of '*either* the psychodynamic *or* cognitive-behavioural models of abnormality'. It also means that we have given the same questions for both topics of this division. If you have studied therapies derived from the psychodynamic model then you need only be concerned with topic 1.

In the division on biological therapies three therapies were named, so all three can be used in exam questions. In the division on behavioural therapies two kinds of therapy were named (those based on classical and operant conditioning). You need to know two of each of these, therefore a minimum of four behavioural therapies in all. In this division you just need to know two psychodynamic therapies. In question 1 you do have the option of including other psychodynamic therapies.

One thing to note about question 1 and 2 is that you are not required to provide both therapies in balance. You may get up to 9 AO1 marks for one therapy alone (partial performance). A second or third therapy should be described in the same amount of detail but not necessarily in the same breadth.

Question 4 is possible though unlikely because it is so clumsy. However, it is a valuable exercise to prepare an answer for such a question because it makes you think about the comparative strengths and limitations of each kind of therapy – which should improve your ability to evaluate the therapy.

Probable questions

1. Outline and evaluate **two or more** therapies derived from *either* the psychodynamic *or* cognitive-behavioural models of abnormality. *(30 marks)*

2. (a) Outline **two** therapies derived from *either* the psychodynamic *or* cognitive-behavioural models of abnormality. *(15 marks)*

   (b) Evaluate the **two** therapies derived from *either* the psychodynamic *or* cognitive-behavioural models of abnormality outlined in (a) with reference to issues surrounding their use (e.g. appropriateness and effectiveness). *(15 marks)*

Possible questions

3. Discuss issues surrounding the use of therapies derived from *either* the psychodynamic *or* cognitive-behavioural models of abnormality. *(30 marks)*

4. Compare and contrast behavioural therapies and therapies derived from *either* the psychodynamic *or* cognitive-behavioural models of abnormality. *(30 marks)*

If you have studied therapies derived from the cognitive-behavioural model then you need only be concerned with topic 2. However the same advice applies here as for topic 1. You need to be able to describe and evaluate a minimum of two cognitive-behavioural therapies. In question 2 part (b) your evaluation of the therapies must refer to issues surrounding their use, such as effectiveness, appropriateness and ethics. The trick here is to *use* the issues as part of a sustained critical commentary rather than just describing them.

As with all other topics in this subdivision you could be asked a question on the issues surrounding the use of the therapies as distinct from being about the therapies themselves. In this case there is no credit for description of therapies; AO1 credit is for a description of the issues. AO2 credit is for an evaluation of/commentary on these issues.

Chapter 9

TOPIC 1: PSYCHODYNAMIC THERAPIES

SAMPLE ESSAY PLAN

Question 2: (a) Outline two therapies derived from *either* the psychodynamic *or* cognitive-behavioural models of abnormality. (15 marks)
(b) Evaluate the two therapies derived from *either* the psychodynamic *or* cognitive-behavioural models of abnormality outlined in (a) with reference to issues surrounding their use (e.g. appropriateness and effectiveness). (15 marks)

PSYCHOANALYSIS

13 MINUTES WORTH OF AO1

- Focus on the removal of **underlying conflicts** the person has repressed into their unconscious.
- **Repression**: anxiety-producing thoughts and memories are revealed in dreams/behaviour.
- Aims to make the **unconscious conscious**, where it can more easily be dealt with.
- Used e.g. with **obsessional behaviour** and **phobias** rather than psychotic disorders.
- **Free association**: patient expresses thoughts as they occur, to reveal areas of conflict.
- **Therapist interpretation** of free associations and dream content to make them conscious.
- The patient may **resist** these interpretations or display **transference** towards the therapist.
- **Working through**: patient and client revisit issues over an extended period, to gain clarity.

13 MINUTES WORTH OF AO2

- **Freud** used case histories (e.g. **Anna O.**) of his patients to demonstrate effectiveness.
- However, evidence for these patients actually being 'cured' is debatable (**Guttman**, 2001).
- **Eysenck** (1965) claimed that psychoanalysis was far less effective than eclectic (mixed) therapies.
- Re-evaluated by **Bergin** (1971) and found support for psychoanalysis.
- **Smith et al.** (1980): psychoanalysis not as effective as **cognitive-behavioural therapy**, equal to **placebo**.
- **Freud** introduced the notion that mental illness might have a psychological cause.
- **Limitations** include:
- Appropriate for certain **mental illnesses** and certain groups of **people** (YAVIS).
- There is little evidence to support the claim that **repressed memories** are recalled accurately.
- **Alternative**: short-forms, more dynamic focus on just one problem.

PLAY THERAPY

7 MINUTES WORTH OF AO1

- Mostly used with **children** aged 3–11.
- For a wide range of **emotional problems**, e.g. depression, child abuse.
- **Non-directive**: children create play situations like emotional problem they can't verbalise.
- Therapist notes the symbolic actions.
- **Axline** (1947) believed children can solve own problems.
- **Directive play therapy**: therapist takes a more active role; for diagnostic/ assessment purposes.
- **Post-traumatic play** enables mastery over event.

7 MINUTES WORTH OF AO2

- Effective in a range of contexts, including children with **diabetes** (**Jones and Landreth**, 2002), **child witnesses** of domestic violence (**Kot et al.**, 1999).
- 80% success (**Phillips and Landreth**, 1998).
- Particularly effective when used in a **school setting**.
- Effectiveness increased when used in conjunction with **non-directive play therapy**.
- Lack of a rigorous **methodology** means this technique is often loosely applied.
- One of the few techniques **suitable for children**.
- **Ethical guidelines** for therapeutic conduct do not relate well to play therapy.

Question 3: Discuss issues surrounding the use of therapies derived from *either* the psychodynamic *or* cognitive-behavioural models of abnormality. (30 marks)

EFFECTIVENESS

10 MINUTES WORTH OF AO1

- **Freud** used case histories (e.g. **Anna O.**).
- **Play therapy**: effective with children with **diabetes** (**Jones and Landreth**, 2002), **child witnesses** of domestic violence (**Kot et al.**, 1999).
- Particularly effective in a **school setting**.
- Effectiveness increased when used in conjunction with **non-directive play therapy**.

10 MINUTES WORTH OF AO2

- However, evidence for these patients actually being 'cured' is debatable (**Guttman**, 2001).
- **Eysenck** (1965) claimed that psychoanalysis was far less effective than eclectic (mixed) therapies.
- **Smith et al.** (1980) found that psychoanalysis was not as effective as cognitive-behavioural therapy, and almost equal to a placebo group.

APPROPRIATENESS

10 MINUTES WORTH OF AO1

- **Freud** introduced the notion that mental illness might have a psychological cause.
- **Alternative**: short-forms, more dynamic focus on just one problem.
- **Play therapy**: one of the few techniques **suitable for working with children**.
- **Ethical guidelines** for therapeutic conduct do not relate well to play therapy.
- Can therapies be investigated **scientifically**?

10 MINUTES WORTH OF AO2

- Appropriate for certain **mental illnesses** and certain groups of **people** (YAVIS).
- There is little evidence to support the claim that **repressed memories** are recalled accurately.
- **Play therapy**: lack of a rigorous **methodology** means this technique is often loosely applied.
- More specialised guidelines must be developed.
- Trying to evaluate therapies is difficult e.g. **dodo bird** effect, only some findings published, individual differences, **hello-goodbye effect**.

The focus of psychoanalysis is not necessarily the treatment of the 'presenting problem', but the removal of underlying conflicts the person has repressed into their unconscious mind, leading to the symptoms that caused them to seek help. Freud believed that thoughts and memories that might cause anxiety were repressed from the conscious mind. Repressed memories may continue to influence a person's behaviour through their dreams or in their neurotic behaviour. The aim of psychoanalytic therapy is to bring these unconscious conflicts into the conscious mind where they can more easily be dealt with. It is mostly used in the treatment of disorders such as obsessional behaviour and phobias rather than psychotic disorders. It is believed that patients with severe psychopathological problems such as schizophrenia do not have the mental resources necessary for the analytic process. Psychoanalysis uses the technique of free association, where the patient expresses thoughts exactly as they occur. This is designed to reveal areas of conflict and bring them into consciousness. The therapist then interprets these, with help from the patient. The therapist's interpretation of free associations and of dream content is a key part of the analytic process. The patient may resist these interpretations or display transference towards the therapist, when they recreate feelings and conflicts and transfer these towards the therapist. The therapist and patient work through issues time and time again over an extended period in order to gain greater clarity concerning the causes of the patient's neurotic behaviour.

> It is important to remember that this is a question about *therapy* rather than the Freudian model of abnormality or even the theory of personality. You need to maintain this focus at all times.

Freud used case histories of his own patients (e.g. Anna O.) and their successful outcomes to demonstrate the effectiveness of psychoanalysis. However, evidence for these patients actually being 'cured' is debatable (Guttman, 2001), with Anna O. never fully recovering and later spending time in institutions. Eysenck (1965) examined a large number of patient histories, and claimed that psychoanalysis was far less effective than eclectic (mixed) therapies. However, Bergin (1971) re-evaluated Eysenck's data using different judgements about what constituted 'improved' and found modest support for the therapeutic value of psychoanalysis. Smith et al. (1980) carried out a meta-analysis of 475 studies of therapy, and concluded that psychoanalysis was not as effective as cognitive-behavioural therapy and about equal to a placebo treatment. On the positive side, Freud introduced the notion that mental illness might have a psychological cause, and therefore treatment should also be psychological. Limitations of psychoanalysis include the claim that it is appropriate only for certain mental illnesses and for certain groups of people (e.g. young, attractive, verbal, etc.). There is little evidence to support the claim that repressed memories are recalled accurately during therapy, with some claims that therapists unwittingly plant false memories of childhood sexual abuse. Some of these limitations have been addressed by alternative developments in psychoanalysis, particularly in the newer shorter forms of psychoanalysis, where there is a more dynamic focus on just one problem.

> It is fine to say 'a large number' or simply not specify any number rather than getting anxious about the actual number of case histories (10,000) used in this study.

Play therapy is mostly used with children aged 3–11 with a wide range of emotional problems, such as depression, adjustments to life events and issues surrounding abuse. In non-directive play therapy, children create play situations that resemble the emotional problem they are struggling with internally that cannot be expressed verbally. The therapist's role is to listen, observe and note the symbolic actions of the child's play. Axline (1947) believed that children possess the ability to solve their own problems and play therapy allows the child to develop this independence. In directive play therapy, the therapist takes a more active role and structures the session for diagnostic and assessment purposes. In post-traumatic play, a scene may be played out again and again until the child attains a degree of mastery over the event.

> This second form of psychodynamic therapy is given far less space than psychoanalysis, therefore there isn't the chance (or the need) to go into as much descriptive breadth but detail is still important.

Non-directive play therapy has been shown to be effective in a range of contexts, including children with diabetes (Jones and Landreth, 2002) and child witnesses of domestic violence (Kot et al., 1999). Phillips and Landreth (1998) concluded that this form of therapy was successful with 80% of children treated. Directive play therapy has been shown to be particularly effective when used in a school setting, although its effectiveness is increased when used in conjunction with non-directive play therapy. The lack of a rigorous methodology means this technique is often loosely applied, but it is one of the few techniques suitable for working with children. Ethical guidelines for therapeutic conduct do not relate well to play therapy, therefore more specialised guidelines must be developed.

> Part of the 'success' of this technique has been due to its widespread application in a field with few alternatives.

COGNITIVE-BEHAVIOURAL THERAPIES

SAMPLE ESSAY PLAN

Question 1: Outline and evaluate **two or more** therapies derived from *either* the psychodynamic *or* cognitive-behavioural models of abnormality. (30 marks)

RATIONAL-EMOTIVE BEHAVIOURAL THERAPY (REBT)

10 MINUTES WORTH OF AO1

- CBT based on the fact that how we feel is dependent on how we think about events.
- Treatment involves identifying **maladaptive thinking** and developing **coping strategies**.
- Many problems are the result of **faulty or irrational thinking** (Ellis, 1957).
- REBT helps clients to understand **consequences** of their irrational thinking, and helps them to **substitute** effective problem-solving methods.
- ABC model: A – Activating events, B – Beliefs, C – Consequences.
- **Irrational beliefs**: experienced as self-defeating thoughts, and lead to unproductive outcomes.
- **Disputing**: patient is encouraged to dispute self-defeating thoughts through: logical disputing, empirical disputing and pragmatic disputing.

10 MINUTES WORTH OF AO2

- **Effectiveness**: Ellis (1957) 90% success rate.
- A **meta-analysis** of psychotherapies cited REBT as having the **second highest success rate** of the 10 therapies reviewed (**Smith and Glass**, 1977).
- **REBT plus medication** is more effective than medication alone (**Macaskill and Macaskill**, 1996).
- REBT for OCD as effective as most behavioural treatments (**Emmelkamp and Beens**, 1991).
- **Appropriateness**: useful for both clinical and non-clinical groups (**Muran and Motta**, 1993).
- Counterproductive beliefs sometimes *more* rather than *less* realistic e.g. when **estimating disasters** depressed people more accurate (**Alloy and Abrahmson**, 1979).
- Half of REBT therapists use more **indirect methods**, makes meta-analyses of effectiveness less valid.
- **Ethics**: considered one of the more aggressive and **judgmental** therapies, which raises ethical concerns about the degree of **manipulation** by the therapist.

STRESS INOCULATION TRAINING (SIT)

10 MINUTES WORTH OF AO1

- Aims to help develop a **coping strategy** before a stressful situation arises.
- Used in **stress-related situations** including anger management and avoidance behaviour in rape victims.
- To **avoid anger** when inappropriate.
- Meichenbaum (1985) proposed three phases:
- 1 **Conceptualisation**: stressors seen as specific problems that can be solved, broken down into specific components.
- 2 **Skills acquisition**: cognitive and behavioural skills (e.g. positive thinking, relaxation, time management) are taught and practised.
- 3 **Application** of these skills in situations that become increasingly stressful, using modelling and role-playing.

10 MINUTES WORTH OF AO2

- **Effectiveness**: SIT equivalent to SD for snake phobia but generalised to other phobias (**Meichenbaum**, 1977).
- **Effective** in stress reduction in college students (**Fontana et al.**, 1999), Ps had lower heart-rate and anxiety levels, maintained over a 6 month period.
- **Effective** in anger reduction in Ps with post-traumatic stress (**Chemtob et al.**, 1997) maintained at 18 months.
- **Appropriateness**: skills learned can be generalised.
- Lengthy therefore only suits **determined clients**.
- Unnecessarily **complex** technique; a simpler procedure may have same effectiveness.
- **Ethics**: As SIT is more client-centred than REBT, it gives more choice to the client, and consequently has fewer ethical concerns.
- CBTs appear less suitable for long-term and severe disorders (**James and Blackburn**, 1995).

Question 4: Compare and contrast behavioural therapies and therapies derived from *either* the psychodynamic *or* cognitive-behavioural models of abnormality. (30 marks)

20 MINUTES WORTH OF AO1

Issue 1: Effectiveness:
- Ellis (1957) 90% success rate for REBT.
- **Meta-analysis** cited REBT as having the **second highest success rate** (**Smith and Glass**, 1977).
- SIT equivalent to SD for snake phobia, but generalised to other phobias (**Meichenbaum**, 1977).
- SIT successful stress reduction in students (**Fontana et al.**, 1999), anger reduction in Ps with post-traumatic stress (**Chemtob et al.**, 1997).

Issue 2: Appropriateness:
- REBT useful for both clinical and non-clinical.
- **Appropriateness**: skills can be generalised.
- **Appropriateness of CBTs**: CBTs most effective (**David and Avellino**, 2003).

Issue 3: Ethics:
- REBT considered one of the more aggressive and **judgmental** therapies.

20 MINUTES WORTH OF AO2

Issue 1: Effectiveness:
- **REBT** used with medication more effective than medication alone (**Macaskill and Macaskill**, 1996).
- **REBT** has similar effectiveness to behavioural therapies for OCD (**Emmelkamp and Beens**, 1991).

Issue 2: Appropriateness:
- **REBT**, counterproductive beliefs sometimes *more* rather than *less* realistic (**Alloy and Abrahmson**, 1979).
- **SIT**: Lengthy therefore only suits **determined clients**.
- Unnecessarily **complex** technique.
- **CBTs** appear less suitable for long-term and severe disorders (**James and Blackburn**, 1995).

Issue 3: Ethics:
- As SIT is more client-centred than REBT, it gives more choice to the client.
- **Judgemental** nature of REBT raises ethical concerns about the degree of **manipulation** by the therapist.

Cognitive-behavioural therapy is based on the fact that how we feel is partly dependent on how we think about events. Treatment involves identifying maladaptive thinking and developing coping strategies. In rational-emotive behavioural therapy (REBT), problems are believed to be the result of faulty or irrational thinking, particularly the unrealistic beliefs that people have about themselves and their behaviours (Ellis, 1957). REBT helps clients to understand the consequences of their irrational thinking, and helps them to substitute effective problem-solving methods. REBT operates on the ABC model, where A refers to the activating events (i.e. things that happen in a person's life), B the beliefs or explanations for these events; and C the consequences. Irrational beliefs are experienced as self-defeating thoughts, and lead to unproductive outcomes. Some people effectively talk themselves into emotional traumas yet still believe it is the events rather than their thoughts that are upsetting them. REBT focuses on these self-defeating beliefs and the patient is encouraged to dispute them through logical disputing (i.e. that self-defeating beliefs do not follow logically from the information available), empirical disputing (they may not be consistent with reality) and pragmatic disputing (self-defeating beliefs are not useful to the individual).

> You could use examples to illustrate the ABC model, but these should not be replacements for effective description of REBT.

Ellis (1957) claimed a 90% success rate for REBT. A meta-analysis of psychotherapies cited REBT as having the second highest success rate of the ten therapies reviewed (Smith and Glass, 1977). Other research has suggested that in the treatment of depression, REBT in conjunction with medication is more effective than medication alone (Macaskill and Macaskill, 1996). Emmelkamp and Beens (1991) found that REBT is as effective in the treatment of OCD as most behavioural treatments. REBT has been shown to be useful for both clinical and non-clinical groups. For example, high levels of irrational beliefs have been associated with anxiety and depression in both college students and clinical samples (Muran and Motta, 1993). Despite the success of REBT, it is possible that many counterproductive beliefs are more rather than less realistic. For example, Alloy and Abrahmson (1979) found that depressed people gave more accurate estimates of the likelihood of a disaster than non-depressed controls. A problem with the evaluation of REBT is that about half of REBT therapists do not use 'disputing' to challenge irrational beliefs, but use more indirect methods, which makes meta-analyses of the effectiveness of REBT less valid. REBT is considered one of the more aggressive and judgmental therapies, which raises ethical concerns about the degree of manipulation by the therapist.

> Although names and dates are widely used in this paragraph, they are not absolutely necessary. It is the study and its implications for REBT that is more important than the name(s) of the researchers concerned.

Stress-inoculation training (SIT) aims to help develop a coping strategy before a stressful situation arises. SIT is used in stress-related situations including anger management and avoidance behaviour in rape victims. In anger management programmes, the aim of SIT is to prevent anger in situations where it would be inappropriate, and to regulate the arousal and expression of anger in these situations. Meichenbaum (1985) proposed three phases in SIT. In conceptualisation, the client is taught to view stressors as specific problems that can be solved, and to break stressors down into specific components that can be dealt with. In the skills acquisition phase, cognitive and behavioural skills are taught and practised, first in the clinic and then gradually rehearsed in real life. These skills include positive thinking, relaxation and time management. In the final application phase, clients are given the opportunity to apply these skills in situations that become increasingly stressful. Techniques used include watching someone else cope with stressors and then imitating this behaviour (modelling) and role-playing (acting out scenes involving stressors).

> Again, you could illustrate SIT by using examples of coping self-statements, but don't go overboard with these.

SIT has been shown to be as effective as systematic desensitisation when treating fear of snakes, but SIT was demonstrated to be superior because it inoculated against other phobias (Meichenbaum, 1977). SIT was also shown to be effective in stress reduction in college students, where participants showed lower heart-rate and anxiety levels than controls and maintained this over a six-month period (Fontana et al., 1999). When used as a therapy for anger reduction in people with post-traumatic stress, a SIT group showed significant differences in anger control compared to a control group, which was maintained at an 18-month follow-up (Chemtob et al., 1997). SIT is appropriate for a range of stressful situations as the skills learned in response to one situation can be generalised to others. However, SIT is a lengthy therapy, therefore only suits determined clients. Critics claim that SIT is an unnecessarily complex technique, and that a simpler procedure with a reduced range of activities may have the same effectiveness. As SIT is more client-centred than REBT, it gives more choice to the client, and consequently has fewer ethical concerns. Although CBTs such as REBT and SIT have been shown to be effective for some disorders, they appear less suitable for long-term and severe disorders (James and Blackburn, 1995).

> This final point of commentary concerns all CBTs. Other research suggests that CBT can be used effectively with some severe disorders – critical commentary is never-ending!

Topic 1: Gender bias in psychological theory and research

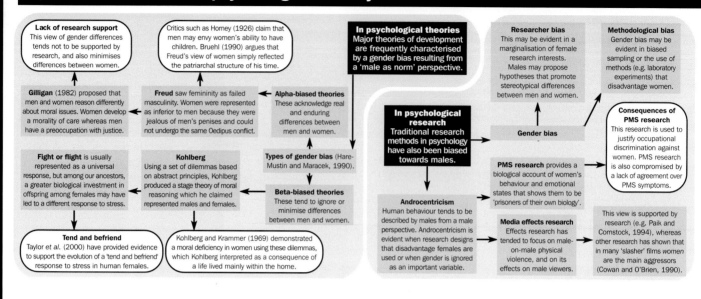

Lack of research support
This view of gender differences tends not to be supported by research, and also minimises differences between women.

Critics such as Horney (1926) claim that men may envy women's ability to have children. Bruehl (1990) argues that Freud's view of women simply reflected the patriarchal structure of his time.

In psychological theories
Major theories of development are frequently characterised by a gender bias resulting from a 'male as norm' perspective.

Researcher bias
This may be evident in a marginalisation of female research interests. Males may propose hypotheses that promote stereotypical differences between men and women.

Methodological bias
Gender bias may be evident in biased sampling or the use of methods (e.g. laboratory experiments) that disadvantage women.

Gilligan (1982) proposed that men and women reason differently about moral issues. Women develop a morality of care whereas men have a preoccupation with justice.

Freud saw femininity as failed masculinity. Women were represented as inferior to men because they were jealous of men's penises and could not undergo the same Oedipus conflict.

Alpha-biased theories
These acknowledge real and enduring differences between men and women.

In psychological research
Traditional research methods in psychology have also been biased towards males.

Gender bias

Consequences of PMS research
This research is used to justify occupational discrimination against women. PMS research is also compromised by a lack of agreement over PMS symptoms.

Fight or flight is usually represented as a universal response, but among our ancestors, a greater biological investment in offspring among females may have led to a different response to stress.

Kohlberg
Using a set of dilemmas based on abstract principles, Kohlberg produced a stage theory of moral reasoning which he claimed represented males and females.

Types of gender bias (Hare-Mustin and Maracek, 1990).

Beta-biased theories
These tend to ignore or minimise differences between men and women.

Androcentrism
Human behaviour tends to be described by males from a male perspective. Androcentrism is evident when research designs that disadvantage females are used or when gender is ignored as an important variable.

PMS research provides a biological account of women's behaviour and emotional states that shows them to be 'prisoners of their own biology'.

Media effects research
Effects research has tended to focus on male-on-male physical violence, and on its effects on male viewers.

This view is supported by research (e.g. Paik and Comstock, 1994), whereas other research has shown that in many 'slasher' films *women* are the main aggressors (Cowan and O'Brien, 1990).

Tend and befriend
Taylor et al. (2000) have provided evidence to support the evolution of a 'tend and befriend' response to stress in human females.

Kohlberg and Krammer (1969) demonstrated a moral deficiency in women using these dilemmas, which Kohlberg interpreted as a consequence of a life lived mainly within the home.

Topic 2: Cultural bias in psychological theory and research

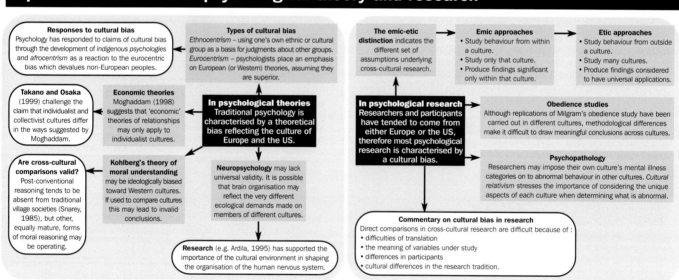

Responses to cultural bias
Psychology has responded to claims of cultural bias through the development of *indigenous psychologies* and *afrocentrism* as a reaction to the eurocentric bias which devalues non-European peoples.

Types of cultural bias
Ethnocentrism – using one's own ethnic or cultural group as a basis for judgments about other groups.
Eurocentrism – psychologists place an emphasis on European (or Western) theories, assuming they are superior.

The emic-etic distinction indicates the different set of assumptions underlying cross-cultural research.

Emic approaches
• Study behaviour from within a culture.
• Study only that culture.
• Produce findings significant only within that culture.

Etic approaches
• Study behaviour from outside a culture.
• Study many cultures.
• Produce findings considered to have universal applications.

Takano and Osaka (1999) challenge the claim that individualist and collectivist cultures differ in the ways suggested by Moghaddam.

Economic theories
Moghaddam (1998) suggests that 'economic' theories of relationships may only apply to individualist cultures.

In psychological theories
Traditional psychology is characterised by a theoretical bias reflecting the culture of Europe and the US.

In psychological research
Researchers and participants have tended to come from either Europe or the US, therefore most psychological research is characterised by a cultural bias.

Obedience studies
Although replications of Milgram's obedience study have been carried out in different cultures, methodological differences make it difficult to draw meaningful conclusions across cultures.

Are cross-cultural comparisons valid?
Post-conventional reasoning tends to be absent from traditional village societies (Snarey, 1985), but other, equally mature, forms of moral reasoning may be operating.

Kohlberg's theory of moral understanding may be ideologically biased toward Western cultures. If used to compare cultures this may lead to invalid conclusions.

Neuropsychology may lack universal validity. It is possible that brain organisation may reflect the very different ecological demands made on members of different cultures.

Psychopathology
Researchers may impose their own culture's mental illness categories on to abnormal behaviour in other cultures. *Cultural relativism* stresses the importance of considering the unique aspects of each culture when determining what is abnormal.

Research (e.g. Ardila, 1995) has supported the importance of the cultural environment in shaping the organisation of the human nervous system.

Commentary on cultural bias in research
Direct comparisons in cross-cultural research are difficult because of :
• difficulties of translation
• the meaning of variables under study
• differences in participants
• cultural differences in the research tradition.

Probable questions

1. Discuss gender bias in psychological research (theories **and/or** studies). *(30 marks)*

2. (a) Outline **two** types of gender bias in psychology. *(5 marks)*

   (b) Discuss gender bias in psychological research (theories **and/or** studies). *(25 marks)*

3. 'Psychology has represented male behaviour as the norm, and consequently has ignored female behaviour and experience.'

   Discuss gender bias in **two or more** psychological theories, with reference to issues such as those raised in the quotation above. (30 marks)

Possible questions

4. Discuss gender bias in **two** psychological theories. *(30 marks)*

5. 'Psychologists have sometimes ignored gender differences, and at other times represented female experience as abnormal or deficient. This has undervalued the usefulness of theories of *human* behaviour.'

   With reference to the issues raised in the quotation above, discuss gender bias in **two or more** psychological theories. *(30 marks)*

The specification entry for gender bias is brief but the same cannot be said for the question possibilities, as shown on the right. You may be asked to write about gender bias in research (question 1). The term 'research' encompasses both theories and/or studies. The major mistake made by candidates is to describe (and evaluate) particular theories/studies that are gender biased – but that is not what the question requires. Your focus must be on the gender bias in such research rather than the research itself.

The other main problem is that candidates describe gender bias rather generally making little or no reference to theories/studies. Again this is not the question and little credit would be awarded.

In question 2, five AO1 marks have been isolated in part (a). Part (b) is the same as question 1 but you have 5 less AO1 marks so should write more AO2 than AO1. In part (a) there is credit for a brief (about 100 words) outline of two types of gender bias (such as alpha and beta bias).

Question 3 is different again in two ways. First there is a quotation and second the question is different to questions 1 and 2. The quotation is there as a kind of 'inspiration' – you are not required to address it in your answer (because the question says issues 'such as' those in the quotation). The question itself directs you to focus on theories only.

Question 4 is similar to question 3 except there is no quotation and, more importantly, you are required to discuss only two theories rather than 'two or more'.

In Question 5 you are required to address the quotation. This does not mean just making reference to the quotation at the start of the essay and then writing your usual answer. You must engage with the quotation throughout the essay. It is best to identify issues raised in the quotation and use these to organise your answer.

Probable questions

1. Discuss cultural bias in psychological research (theories **and/or** studies). *(30 marks)*

2. (a) Outline **two** types of cultural bias in psychology. *(5 marks)*

   (b) Discuss cultural bias in psychological research (theories **and/or** studies). *(25 marks)*

3. 'Psychological research is focused almost exclusively on Western cultures. This invalidates any claim that we may have a universal understanding of human behaviour.'

   Discuss cultural bias in **two or more** theories of psychology, with reference to issues such as those raised in the quotation above. *(30 marks)*

Possible questions

4. Discuss cultural bias in **two** psychological theories. *(30 marks)*

5. 'The cultural bias of psychological theories means that they offer only a partial understanding of human behaviour.'

   With reference to the issues raised in the quotation above, discuss cultural bias in **two or more** psychological theories. *(30 marks)*

The questions for cultural bias are similar to those for gender bias (not surprising since the specification entries for both of these topics is almost the same). Again questions may be set on theories and/or studies (question 1), theories alone (questions 3, 4 and 5) and might include a separate AO1 part requiring you to describe types of cultural bias (as question 2). If you have studied more than two types of cultural bias don't make the mistake of listing all of these in your answer when asked for only two. If you do provide more than two the examiner will read your whole answer and award marks to the best two types.

You can use the quotation in question 3 as a useful starting point in your essay. It may help you to avoid the dangers mentioned earlier – discussing the theories or discussing cultural bias rather than discussing the culture bias in the theories.

Note your answer to question 3 would do for question 1 – so you don't actually need to prepare material on studies because no question will specify studies alone.

Question 4 is again limited to only two theories – choose carefully so you have plenty to describe and evaluate. If you run out of steam don't try to describe the theory itself or offer general evaluations of the theory. This would simply be a waste of time.

The quotation in question 5 must be addressed. You might identify the points in the quotation: to what extent are psychological theories culturally biased? (Examine examples that show they are biased or are not biased.) Does this mean that they are only partial explanations (can we generalise from culturally biased theories?). If you do not show evidence of addressing the quotation your AO2 mark will be limited to 9 out of 15 marks.

TOPIC 1: GENDER BIAS IN PSYCHOLOGICAL THEORY AND RESEARCH

SAMPLE ESSAY PLAN

Question 2: (a) Outline **two** types of gender bias in psychology. (5 marks)
(b) Discuss gender bias in psychological research (theories **and/or** studies). (25 marks)

(a)

6½ MINUTES WORTH OF AO1

- **Alpha-bias** is an emphasis on real and enduring differences between men and women.
- This may **heighten or devalue** women.
- **Beta-bias** occurs when a theory tends to ignore or minimise differences between men and women.
- This approach assumes that insights derived from **studies of men** will apply equally well to women.
- Because of the **androcentric bias** in psychology, most psychological theories tend to be beta biased.

(b)

13½ MINUTES WORTH OF AO1

Alpha-biased theories:

- **Devaluing females:** Freud saw femininity as failed masculinity.
- Women were inferior to men because they were jealous of men's penises (**penis envy**).
- Women could not undergo the same Oedipus conflict thus leading to weaker **moral development**.
- **Heightening the value of women:** Gilligan (1982) men and women reason differently about moral issues because of 'interconnectedness'.
- Girls develop a **morality of care** whereas men have a preoccupation with justice (**Gilligan et al.**, 1990).

Beta-biased theories:

- **Kohlberg** produced a theory of moral reasoning which he claimed represented males and females.
- His research used **male-oriented dilemmas** involving justice, developed from studies with boys.
- **Stress response** is represented as **fight or flight** but may be a male response.
- In our **evolutionary past**, a greater biological investment in offspring among females may have led to a different response to stress.

20 MINUTES WORTH OF AO2

- **Freud** overlooked certain things e.g. men may envy women's ability to have children (**Horney**, 1926).
- Freud's view of women simply reflected the patriarchal structure of **his time** (**Bruehl**, 1990).
- **Gilligan:** lack of support e.g. **meta-analysis** only 8/108 studies found gender differences (**Walker**, 1984).
- **Promotes female qualities** that otherwise seen as inferior but minimises differences between women (**Hare-Mustin and Maracek**, 1988).
- **Kohlberg's research** showed women to be morally inferior (**Kohlberg and Kramer**, 1969).
- Kohlberg suggested that female moral **deficiency due to** a life lived mainly within the home.
- Kohlberg's theory also **alpha-biased** because it ultimately exaggerates the difference between men and women.
- This is an inevitable **consequence of beta bias** because such theories categorise women as inferior.
- **Taylor et al.** (2000) related gender differences to evolution. Biological mechanisms should evolve that inhibit fight/ flight response in **females** and shift their attention to **tending** (attachment behaviour) and **befriending** (forming defensive networks).
- **Taylor et al.** (2000) found evidence that male and female **sex hormones** activate behaviours that conform to these gender-related differences in stress reaction.
- Gender bias in these theories detracts from their overall value as **universal theories** of human behaviour.
- **Feminist psychology** aims to increase awareness of and to compensate for that bias in research.

Question 1: Discuss gender bias in psychological research (theories **and/or** studies). (30 marks)

20 MINUTES WORTH OF AO1

The description of theory 1 above plus:

- **Researcher bias:** males may propose hypotheses that promote stereotypical differences between men and women.
- **Methodological bias:** biased sampling or the use of methods (e.g. laboratory experiments) that disadvantage women.
- **PMS research** shows women to be 'prisoners of their own biology'.
- **Media effects research** focuses on male-on-male physical violence, and effects on male viewers.

20 MINUTES WORTH OF AO2

- The evaluation of theory 1 above.

(a)

Alpha-biased theories emphasise real and enduring differences between men and women. Some theories heighten the value of one sex over the other or may be used to devalue one sex (e.g. Freud's theory devalues women) compared to the other. Beta-bias occurs when a theory tends to ignore or minimise differences between men and women. This approach either ignores questions about women's lives or assumes that insights derived from studies of men will apply equally well to women. Because of the androcentric bias in psychology, most psychological theories tend to be beta-biased. This has resulted in a 'male as norm' perspective within theory and research, with traditional research methods being biased towards males.

(b)

Some alpha-biased theories have devalued women. Freud saw femininity as a form of failed masculinity. Freud believed that women were inferior to men because they were jealous of men's penises (penis envy), and therefore could not undergo the same Oedipus conflict. As a result, Freud believed that this would lead to weaker moral development in women. Some alpha-biased theories have heightened the value of women. Gilligan (1982) developed her theory of moral development as a response to Kohlberg's findings that women were morally inferior to men. She proposed instead that men and women reason differently about moral issues, with girls developing a morality of care arising from their greater 'interconnectedness'. Males, on the other hand, tend to have a preoccupation with justice, which would explain why they score higher in abstract moral dilemmas.

An example of a beta-biased theory is Kohlberg's theory of moral reasoning, which he claimed represented males and females. Kohlberg developed a set of moral dilemmas that were used to assess why people made particular moral decisions. These dilemmas were based on male-oriented abstract principles of justice, developed from studies with boys. As a result he produced a theory that ignored the difference between genders. Most research on stress has emphasised the fight or flight response as a universal reaction to stressful situations. It is possible that this may be predominantly a male response that is essential to male survival. However in our evolutionary past, different considerations would apply to females, with a greater biological investment in offspring leading to a different response to stress, i.e. the tend and befriend response.

Horney (1926) believed that it did not make sense to assume that a woman is mentally affected by a wish for male attributes. In particular, Horney believed that Freud overlooked the possibility that men may envy women's ability to have children. Bruehl (1990) suggests that Freud's view of women simply reflected the patriarchal structure of his time. Gilligan's view of gender difference in moral reasoning has not, in general, been supported by research. In one meta-analysis of studies of moral behaviour, Walker (1984) found that only 8 out of 108 studies showed gender differences. Hare-Mustin and Maracek (1988) suggest that Gilligan's approach has the advantage of having promoted feminine qualities, which can now be seen as different rather than inferior. However, this approach to moral reasoning also minimises the possible differences that exist between different women, and so leads to a misrepresentation of individuals.

Kohlberg's research has suggested that women are morally inferior (Kohlberg and Kramer, 1969), with most females typically responding to abstract moral dilemmas with Stage 3 responses that are focused on interpersonal issues. Kohlberg believed that female moral deficiency was due to a life lived mainly within the home, which denied women the opportunity for the social interaction that would foster moral development at the higher stages of moral reasoning. In a sense, Kohlberg's theory is also alpha-biased because it exaggerates the difference between men and women. This is an inevitable consequence of beta-biased theories. By using male participants and then claiming that this is a universal explanation of behaviour, such theories inevitably categorise women as inferior.

Taylor et al. (2000) supported the idea that gender differences in the reaction to stress might be rooted in our evolutionary history. Contrary to early research, they believed that biological mechanisms should evolve to inhibit the fight or flight response in females and shift their attention to tending (attachment behaviour) and befriending (forming defensive networks of females). Taylor et al. found evidence that sex hormones activate behaviours conforming to these predicted gender-related stress reactions. The gender bias in these theories detracts from their value as universal theories of human behaviour. Feminist psychology has made an effort to increase awareness of gender bias in psychological theories and research and to compensate for that bias in feminist research methods.

Because the two parts of this question are essentially separate, it would be creditworthy to refer to specific theories or research studies to elaborate your outline of the two types of gender bias even though you may repeat this in part (b).

It is important that you describe the gender bias in these theories rather than just offering a general description of the theory itself.

This may seem to be an unusual claim and so you need to qualify it, i.e. why would we expect such a gender difference to have evolved?

Some theories also demonstrate a bias because they minimise the possible differences within the different genders.

This is a consequence of any theory that claims to be universal, but then utilises methods of inquiry that inevitably disadvantage one gender.

How do we deal with gender bias? The idea that feminist research can compensate for male-centred psychology is a point of commentary.

SAMPLE ESSAY PLAN

Question 2: (a) Outline two types of cultural bias in psychology. (5 marks)
(b) Discuss cultural bias in psychological research (theories and/or studies). (25 marks)

(a)

6½ MINUTES WORTH OF AO1

- **Ethnocentrism** – using one's ethnic or cultural group as a basis for judgments about other groups.
- We view the beliefs, customs and behaviours of our own group as '**normal**' and even **superior**, whereas others are 'strange' or deviant.
- The opposite of ethnocentrism in psychology is **cultural relativism**.
- **Eurocentrism** – psychologists place an emphasis on European (or Western) theories, assuming they are superior.
- Western research is then applied to other cultures to create a **universal** view of human behaviour.

(b)

3½ MINUTES WORTH OF AO1

- **Economic theories** of relationships (e.g. social exchange theory) may only apply to individualist cultures (**Moghaddam**,1998).
- In **collectivist** societies group members are more concerned with the success of their groups rather than individual profit and loss.
- Also relevant to **short-term relationships** among individuals with **high mobility** (e.g. students).
- **Kohlberg's theory** of moral understanding claimed to be universal but ideologically biased toward Western democratic cultures.
- Other cultures have different moral values, thus using Kohlberg's stages to compare cultures may lead to **invalid conclusions**.
- **Neuropsychological theories** (brain function) may lack universal validity (**Matthews**, 1992).
- Brain organisation reflects different **ecological demands** on members of different cultures.

20 MINUTES WORTH OF AO2

- **Individualist-collectivist** distinction may not be true – **Takano and Osaka** (1999) looked at studies comparing US and Japan and 14/15 didn't support the distinction.
- Apparent distinction may be due to the **fundamental attribution error** (over-estimating the influence of personal characteristics, under-estimating situational factors).
- **Kohlberg: Snarey** (1985) found that stages 1–4 appear to be universal, but stages 5 and 6 don't always appear in less industrialised cultures.
- **Other, equally mature, forms** of moral reasoning may be operating.
- **Effects of ecological and cultural factors** evident in neuropsychological assessments (**Ardila**, 1995).
- Bias in **research process** as well which contributes to bias in theories, e.g. most psychologists are trained in the West, and most participants from Western cultures.
- **Responses to cultural bias**: development of **indigenous psychologies** (e.g. psychologists in Asia and South Africa producing their own theories of human behaviour).
- Development of **Afrocentrism** to counter idea of universally appropriate theories of human behaviour.

Question 1: Discuss cultural bias in psychological research (theories and/or studies). (30 marks)

20 MINUTES WORTH OF AO1

The description of theory 1 above, plus:

- **Emic-etic distinction** indicates the different set of assumptions underlying cross-cultural research.
- **Emic approaches** study behaviour from within a culture and produce findings significant only within that culture.
- **Etic approaches** study behaviour from outside a culture, study many cultures, produce findings considered to have universal applications.
- **Imposed etic**: researchers use Western tests/methods to study non-Western populations resulting in culture bias e.g. studies of **mental illness**.

20 MINUTES WORTH OF AO2

- The evaluation of theory 1 above.

(a)

Ethnocentrism is a type of bias resulting from using one's own ethnic or cultural group as a basis for judgments about other groups. We tend to view the beliefs, customs and behaviours of our own group as 'normal' and even superior, whereas others are 'strange' or deviant. The opposite of ethnocentrism in psychology is cultural relativism – the idea that all cultures are worthy of respect – and in studying another culture, we must try to understand how that culture sees the world. Eurocentrism is a type of bias whereby psychologists place an emphasis on European (or Western) theories and ideas at the expense of those from other cultures. Implicit in this type of bias is the assumption that Western ideas are superior to those of other cultures. Western research is then applied to other cultures to create a universal view of human behaviour.

> The inclusion of cultural relativism acts as elaboration of ethnocentrism rather than a bias in its own right. Although eurocentrism is a form of ethnocentrism, it counts as the second form of bias in this answer.

(b)

Moghaddam (1998) claims that 'economic' theories of relationships (e.g. social exchange theory) may only apply to individualist cultures, and only to short-term relationships among individuals who have high mobility (e.g. students). Such theories reflect only the characteristics of individualist societies, where people are mostly concerned with their own success (i.e. their profit and loss in relationships). In collectivist societies group members are more concerned with the success of their groups and so 'equity' and 'profit and loss' in personal relationships are less important.

> Economic theories of relationships are used to illustrate cultural bias, so don't spend unnecessary time describing the theories themselves – focus on the bias in the theory.

Kohlberg's theory of moral understanding is claimed to be a universal theory of moral understanding, with members of all cultures going through the same stages in the same order. Kohlberg's description of the sequence of moral development may be ideologically biased toward Western democratic cultures. Other cultures have different moral values, thus using Kohlberg's stages to compare cultures may lead to invalid conclusions. Although there is a general acceptance that brain structure and function are universal, our understanding of cultural differences in neuropsychology is extremely limited, and the claim for universality in neuropsychology has been questioned. Matthews (1992) claimed that a very limited kind of neuropsychology that is appropriate to only a fraction of the world's population is represented as applying to the whole of the human species. Matthews argues that there is a strong possibility that different patterns of brain organisation may appear over time owing to different ecological demands faced by members of different cultures.

Many of the claims for cultural differences in psychology are related to the distinction between individualist and collectivist societies, yet this distinction may not be valid. Takano and Osaka (1999) looked at studies comparing US and Japan in terms of individualist and collectivist characteristics. They found that 14 of the 15 studies did not support this distinction. This apparent distinction may be a product of the fundamental attribution error, the tendency to overestimate the influence of personal characteristics on behaviour. As a result, this may have led to the under-estimation of situational factors when interpreting the collectivist behaviour of the Japanese, commonly presumed to be a collectivist culture.

> The view of cultural bias in neuropsychology is still controversial, but is a point worth making in this context.

Kohlberg's theory does not easily lend itself to cross-cultural comparison. Snarey (1985) found that although stages 1–4 appear to be universal, stages 5 and 6 don't always appear in less industrialised cultures. Snarey found that moral judgements in some cultures did not fit into Kohlberg's stages, suggesting that other, equally mature, forms of moral reasoning may be operating, and are missing from Kohlberg's model.

Recent neuroscience research has supported the importance of the cultural environment in shaping the organisation of the human nervous system. In a review of neuropsychological studies, Ardila (1995) found that the outcomes of neuropsychological assessments are significantly influenced by ecological and cultural factors. The ecological conditions of our day-to-day lives appear to generate adaptive processes at both biological and cultural levels simultaneously. Bias in the research process itself also contributes to bias in theories, particularly as most psychologists are trained in the West, and most participants are from Western cultures. However, psychology as practised in other parts of the world has created the need for an alternative view of human behaviour that is based on indigenous (i.e. native) cultures. This has resulted in the development of indigenous psychologies (e.g. psychologists in Asia and South Africa producing their own theories of human behaviour) as a response to the cultural bias inherent in Western theories and research studies. The Afrocentrism movement disputes the view that European values are universally appropriate descriptions of human behaviour that apply to Europeans and non-Europeans alike. It argues that these values at worst devalue non-European peoples and are at best irrelevant to the life and culture of Africans and people of African descent.

> Here the fundamental attribution error is used to explain this particular form of cultural bias.

> Afrocentrism is offered as critical commentary on Eurocentrism, and cultural bias in psychology generally.

Chapter 10

Topic 3: Ethical issues in psychological investigations

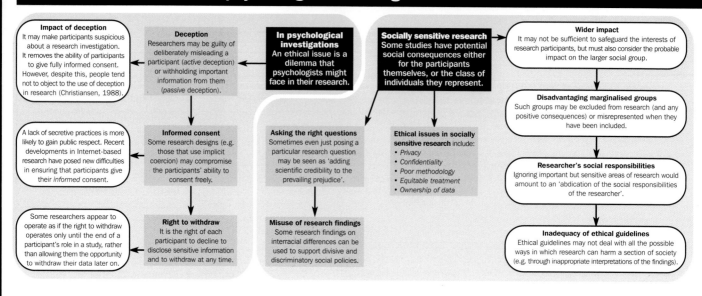

Impact of deception
It may make participants suspicious about a research investigation. It removes the ability of participants to give fully informed consent. However, despite this, people tend not to object to the use of deception in research (Christiansen, 1988).

Deception
Researchers may be guilty of deliberately misleading a participant (*active* deception) or withholding important information from them (*passive* deception).

In psychological investigations
An ethical issue is a dilemma that psychologists might face in their research.

Socially sensitive research
Some studies have potential social consequences either for the participants themselves, or the class of individuals they represent.

Wider impact
It may not be sufficient to safeguard the interests of research participants, but must also consider the probable impact on the larger social group.

A lack of secretive practices is more likely to gain public respect. Recent developments in Internet-based research have posed new difficulties in ensuring that participants give their *informed* consent.

Informed consent
Some research designs (e.g. those that use implicit coercion) may compromise the participants' ability to consent freely.

Asking the right questions
Sometimes even just posing a particular research question may be seen as 'adding scientific credibility to the prevailing prejudice'.

Ethical issues in socially sensitive research include:
• Privacy
• Confidentiality
• Poor methodology
• Equitable treatment
• Ownership of data

Disadvantaging marginalised groups
Such groups may be excluded from research (and any positive consequences) or misrepresented when they have been included.

Some researchers appear to operate as if the right to withdraw operates only until the end of a participant's role in a study, rather than allowing them the opportunity to withdraw their data later on.

Right to withdraw
It is the right of each participant to decline to disclose sensitive information and to withdraw at any time.

Misuse of research findings
Some research findings on interracial differences can be used to support divisive and discriminatory social policies.

Researcher's social responsibilities
Ignoring important but sensitive areas of research would amount to an 'abdication of the social responsibilities of the researcher'.

Inadequacy of ethical guidelines
Ethical guidelines may not deal with all the possible ways in which research can harm a section of society (e.g. through inappropriate interpretations of the findings).

Topic 4: The use of non-human animals in psychological investigations

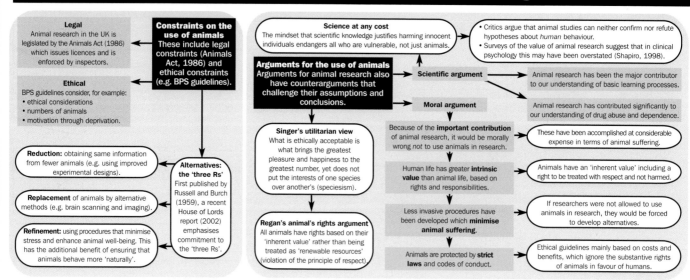

Legal
Animal research in the UK is legislated by the Animals Act (1986) which issues licences and is enforced by inspectors.

Constraints on the use of animals
These include legal constraints (Animals Act, 1986) and ethical constraints (e.g. BPS guidelines).

Science at any cost
The mindset that scientific knowledge justifies harming innocent individuals endangers all who are vulnerable, not just animals.

• Critics argue that animal studies can neither confirm nor refute hypotheses about *human* behaviour.
• Surveys of the value of animal research suggest that in clinical psychology this may have been overstated (Shapiro, 1998).

Ethical
BPS guidelines consider, for example:
• ethical considerations
• numbers of animals
• motivation through deprivation.

Arguments for the use of animals
Arguments for animal research also have counterarguments that challenge their assumptions and conclusions.

Scientific argument

Animal research has been the major contributor to our understanding of basic learning processes.

Moral argument

Animal research has contributed significantly to our understanding of drug abuse and dependence.

Reduction: obtaining same information from fewer animals (e.g. using improved experimental designs).

Alternatives: the 'three Rs'
First published by Russell and Burch (1959), a recent House of Lords report (2002) emphasises commitment to the 'three Rs'.

Singer's utilitarian view
What is ethically acceptable is what brings the greatest pleasure and happiness to the greatest number, yet does not put the interests of one species over another's (speciesism).

Because of the **important contribution** of animal research, it would be morally wrong *not* to use animals in research.

These have been accomplished at considerable expense in terms of animal suffering.

Replacement of animals by alternative methods (e.g. brain scanning and imaging).

Human life has greater **intrinsic value** than animal life, based on rights and responsibilities.

Animals have an 'inherent value' including a right to be treated with respect and not harmed.

Refinement: using procedures that minimise stress and enhance animal well-being. This has the additional benefit of ensuring that animals behave more 'naturally'.

Regan's animal's rights argument
All animals have rights based on their 'inherent value' rather than being treated as 'renewable resources' (violation of the principle of respect).

Less invasive procedures have been developed which **minimise animal suffering**.

If researchers were not allowed to use animals in research, they would be forced to develop alternatives.

Animals are protected by **strict laws** and codes of conduct.

Ethical guidelines mainly based on costs and benefits, which ignore the substantive rights of animals in favour of humans.

Probable questions

1. With reference to **two or more** psychological investigations, discuss ethical issues in research with human participants. *(30 marks)*

2. Discuss the ethics of socially sensitive research. *(30 marks)*

Possible questions

3. (a) Outline **two or more** ethical issues involved in psychological investigations using human participants. *(15 marks)*

   (b) To what extent does socially sensitive research pose special ethical problems for the researcher? *(15 marks)*

4. 'The rights of research participants to be treated openly, honestly and with dignity, must take precedence over all other aspects of the research process.'

   With reference to issues such as those in the quotation above, discuss ethical issues in psychological investigations using human participants. *(30 marks)*

Probable questions

1. Discuss the use of non-human animals in psychological research. *(30 marks)*

2. Discuss arguments (both ethical **and** scientific) **for** the use of non-human animals in psychological investigations. *(30 marks)*

3. Discuss arguments (both ethical **and** scientific) **against** the use of non-human animals in psychological investigations. *(30 marks)*

Possible questions

4. Critically consider constraints on the use of non-human animals in psychological investigations. *(30 marks)*

5. 'Psychologists have a special responsibility to protect the rights and welfare of non-human animals in research.'

   Discuss the use of non-human animals in psychological research, with reference to the issues in the quotation above. *(30 marks)*

This topic is split into two possible questions: ones on ethical issues (such as question 1) and those on socially sensitive research (question 2). If you are writing an answer on ethical issues you may include the ethics of socially sensitive research but the reverse is not true – the ethics of socially sensitive research is a special area and general ethical considerations are not relevant.

In question 1 you are required to discuss ethical issues in the context of at least two psychological investigations. You must avoid describing the investigations themselves (the procedures may be relevant to ethical issues but the findings are unlikely to be relevant). You must also avoid evaluating the investigations, except in terms of ethical issues.

Question 3 is similar to question 1 except that the AO2 component has been separated from the AO1 part of the question and uses the less common AO2 injunction 'to what extent?'. When composing an answer to this question you should note first of all that you are restricted to socially sensitive research and secondly you must avoid, as far as possible, falling into the 'description trap'. There is no credit in part (b) for a description of research. You must *use* your knowledge to compose an effective answer to the question. So you might, for example, take the stance that socially sensitive research does pose problems. You would give examples of this and consider the problems posed and possible resolutions. You could take the opposite stance, that socially sensitive research does not pose problems, and provide evidence for this view. But *don't* describe the research – it will not gain marks.

Question 4 is a 'quote discuss' question where you are not required to refer to the quotation in your answer. The number of investigations has not been specified but you must consider more than one as 'investigations' is in the plural. If you were to focus exclusively on Milgram's study then your answer would be marked according to the partial performance rule – maximum of 9 out of 15 marks for AO1 and the same for AO2.

There are two main pieces of advice for this topic area. First, all questions refer to *psychological* research. There is no credit for reference to cosmetic or medical research unless you have clearly linked this to psychology (e.g. treatment of Alzheimer's patients because this is a mental/psychological condition). Second, you must not allow your emotions to dominate your arguments. Good answers will be balanced and well-informed.

If you are asked about the 'use of non-human animals' it would be creditworthy to focus on investigations where animals are used. This might not be the case in questions 2 and 3, unless you use investigations as support for your arguments.

In questions 2 and 3 you must consider both ethical and scientific arguments, or incur a partial performance penalty. In both questions you may present the same material but the way you *use* it will be different. In question 2 you would describe arguments 'for' the use of non-human animals, expanding this description using examples of research. This is the AO1 content of your essay. You could present arguments 'against' their use as AO2. However if you simply describe all the arguments 'for' and then describe all the arguments 'against', then the 'against' arguments would not have been used *effectively* and would gain minimal credit.

In question 3 you would reverse this process – describe arguments 'against' with examples, and then use arguments 'for' as counterpoints.

The specification also makes reference to 'constraints on the use of non-human animals'. You can simply re-use your knowledge for the answers to the questions above but must *shape* this knowledge appropriately. For example, what constrains the use of non-human animals? Ethical issues such as physical harm and scientific issues such as being able to generalise to human behaviour.

Question 5 is an example of a quote-discuss question where you would need to address the quotation (the phrase 'such as' has not been included). If you don't then the maximum mark for AO2 would be 9 rather than 15 – that is the penalty.

SAMPLE ESSAY PLAN

Question 2: Discuss the ethics of socially sensitive research. (30 marks)

20 MINUTES WORTH OF A01

- Studies with potential social consequences for Ps or class of individuals they represent (**Sieber and Stanley,** 1988).
- For example, **IQ, race, homosexuality**.
- **Posing certain questions** adds scientific credibility to prevailing prejudice e.g. 'Is homosexuality inherited?'.
- **Misuse of findings** e.g. **Scarr and Weinberg** (1983) adopted black children didn't improve, suggesting inherited black inferiority, may support divisive social policies. **Herrnstein and Murray** (1994) wasteful to educate disadvantaged groups.

Important ethical issues:

- **Privacy**: unwitting information provided.
- May lead to invasive social policies.
- **Confidentiality**: if not respected future participation may be compromised.
- **Poor methodology** may be overlooked by media who publicise findings.
- **Equitable treatment** of Ps and of individuals they represent.
- **Ownership of data**: sponsorship may prejudice eventual use.
- Researchers should **think in advance** about use of data (**Kelman**, 1965).

20 MINUTES WORTH OF A02

- Some issues same as for **other research** but also different.
- Potential for **indirect impact** e.g. families, co-workers, groups which are represented.
- Not sufficient to safeguard the interests of Ps, but also impact on **larger social group**.
- Impact is **subtle** and wide-ranging but may be **beneficial**.
- **Marginalised groups** may be excluded from research, research process becomes **biased**.
- Also means that such groups may miss out on any **positive consequences**.
- **Lack of ethical guidelines** for dealing with socially sensitive research.
- Guidelines may protect **immediate needs** of Ps.
- But don't deal with all the **possible ways** in which research can harm a section of society (e.g. through inappropriate interpretations of the findings).
- For example, **Mandel** (1999) obedience alibi provided an excuse for destructive obedience.
- **Social responsibilities**: ignoring sensitive areas of research would amount to an 'abdication of the social responsibilities of the researcher' (**Sieber and Stanley,** 1988).
- But need to avoid giving 'scientific creditability to **prevailing prejudice**' (**Sieber and Stanley**, 1988).

Question 1: With reference to **two or more** psychological investigations, discuss ethical issues in research with human participants. (30 marks)

20 MINUTES WORTH OF A01

Deception:

- Deliberately misleading a participant (**active** deception) e.g. **Milgram** (1974) Ps deceived about purpose of study and their role in it.
- Withholding important information (**passive**) e.g. **Zimbardo et al.** (1973) Ps didn't know about arrest, **Hofling et al.** (1966) a field experiment.

Informed consent:

- Should be given **comprehensive information** e.g. Milgram or **Tizard and Hodges**.
- Use of **implicit coercion** e.g. money (e.g. Milgram) or course credits.
- The **greater the risk** the more meticulous researchers should be (**Homans**, 1991).

Right to withdraw:

- Informed consent doesn't cancel right to withdraw at any time.
- Nor right to decline to disclose sensitive information (**Stark**, 1998).

Socially sensitive research:

- Studies with potential social consequences either for the participants themselves, or the class of individuals they represent.
- For example, studies on IQ and race (**Scarr and Weinberg,** 1983).
- May involve misuse of findings, privacy, confidentiality.

20 MINUTES WORTH OF A02

Deception:

- Ps become suspicious about research investigations.
- Removes ability to give fully informed consent.
- However, people tend not to object to the use of deception in research (**Christiansen**, 1988).

Informed consent:

- Secretive practices lose public respect.
- **Internet-based research** poses new difficulties in ensuring that participants give their informed consent, 'I agree' button isn't adequate.

Right to withdraw:

- Some researchers act as if right to withdraw ends with end of Ps' role in a study, rather than allowing them the opportunity to withdraw their data later on.
- **Ethical guidelines** introduced to cope with issues, but may not resolve them e.g. create more dilemmas, close off discussions, absolve researchers of responsibility.
- **Socially sensitive research**: ignoring sensitive areas of research would amount to an 'abdication of the social responsibilities of the researcher'.
- **Lack of ethical guidelines** for dealing with socially sensitive research.
- Guidelines may protect **immediate needs** of Ps.
- But don't deal with all the **possible ways** in which research can harm a section of society (e.g. through inappropriate interpretations of the findings).

Socially sensitive research refers to studies that have potential social consequences for the participants, or for the class of individuals they represent (Sieber and Stanley, 1983). Examples of socially sensitive research include research into race differences in IQ, and research into different sexual orientations. Simply posing certain questions (e.g. whether homosexuality is inherited) may disadvantage members of that group because the research may be seen as adding scientific credibility to the prevailing prejudice against the group in question. In some cases, it is the misuse of research findings that creates an ethical issue. An example of such misuse of research has been the consideration of interracial differences in IQ. Scarr and Weinberg (1983) studied underprivileged black children placed with white adoptive families to see whether this boosted their IQ. Although such research may stimulate a search for the causes and remedies of such disadvantage, it might also be interpreted as supporting the idea of an inherited black inferiority. This may in turn support divisive social policies. As a result of research such as this, Herrnstein and Murray (1994) argued that it is a waste to put resources into improving the educational opportunities of disadvantaged groups because they are genetically destined to be low achievers.

> It is acceptable to use examples of research to elaborate a descriptive point.

Ethical issues that are especially important in socially sensitive research include privacy, as during a research study, an investigator may extract more information from participants than they intended to give. Some research may lead to social policies that are an invasion of people's private lives (e.g. research into behaviours consistent with the spread of AIDS may lead to compulsory antibody testing). Questions may also reveal information of a sensitive nature, and so confidentiality becomes paramount. If this is not respected then future participation may be compromised. Some of the controversies that arise from socially sensitive research can be attributed to poor methodology or inappropriate interpretation of the findings. This may be overlooked by the media who publicise these findings, to the detriment of the groups represented by the research. An important issue in any psychological research, but one that is particularly important in socially sensitive research, is the need for all participants to be treated in an equitable manner. For example, ideas that lead to prejudicial treatment of one sector of society (such as Freud's view of women as 'deficient') would be seen as unfair and therefore unacceptable. A major concern in socially sensitive research is ownership of data, as sponsorship (e.g. by a commercial organisation) may lead to the research findings being used for reasons other that those originally intended. Kelman (1965) suggests it is the responsibility of all researchers to think in advance about how their research might be used.

> Instead of simply listing a series of ethical issues relevant to socially sensitive research, you should make it clear why each one is such an important issue in such research.

In socially sensitive research there is the potential for a more indirect impact on participants' families, co-workers, or even the groups they represent (e.g. women or the elderly). It is not sufficient, therefore, merely to safeguard the interests of the individual in research – there must also be consideration of the probable impact of the research on the larger group of which the participant is a member. The negative impact of research may be potentially subtle and wide-ranging. However, much of the research that takes place in socially sensitive areas has important and potentially beneficial effects for certain sections of society. Some social groups have already suffered from being misrepresented in research (e.g. the elderly and some minority groups), but the failure to represent and research such groups may lead to them being further marginalised and missing out on any potential benefits from such research. As a result, our understanding of human behaviour is lessened by our failure to carry out meaningful research on such groups, and so the research process becomes biased.

> Not all criticisms are negative. Here the point is made that research may have positive benefits for groups, and so not studying them places them at a disadvantage compared to other groups.

A problem for psychologists carrying out socially sensitive research is the lack of ethical guidelines that protect participants from the specific issues of this type of research. Ethical guidelines such as those provided by the BPS may protect the immediate needs of participants, but may not deal with all the possible ways that a research study can harm a particular section of society (e.g. through inappropriate interpretations of the findings). For example, Mandel (1999) has criticised the interpretation of Milgram's conclusion that people would obey even the most destructive of orders when confronted by a figure of authority. Mandel claimed that this merely offered an 'obedience alibi' to Nazi war criminals, and therefore was an insult to all those who were part of or affected by the Holocaust. Research in socially sensitive areas inevitably raises difficult ethical issues, yet ignoring sensitive areas of research would amount to an 'abdication of the social responsibilities of the researcher' (i.e. their duty to society to study important areas of behaviour). Psychologists must guard against the possibility of abuse and discrimination as a result of their research, and must be careful that their research does not add 'scientific credibility to the prevailing prejudice' (Sieber and Stanley, 1988).

> Milgram's research is used to make a specific point about socially sensitive research. Whatever example you use, you must make it relevant. Milgram's research is actually a difficult study to fit into a socially sensitive question response.

SAMPLE ESSAY PLAN

Question 2: Discuss arguments (both ethical and scientific) **for the use of non-human animals in psychological investigations. (30 marks)**

ETHICAL ARGUMENTS

10 MINUTES WORTH OF AO1
- **Important contribution** of animal research, morally wrong *not* to use animals in research.
- Human life has greater **intrinsic value** than animal life, based on rights and responsibilities.
- Animals have no **responsibilities** and therefore **no rights**.
- Less invasive procedures have been developed which **minimise animal suffering**, thus morally justified.
- Animals are protected by **Animals (1986) Act**.
- Animal research conforms to **BPS ethical guidelines** (e.g. numbers of animals, motivation through deprivation).

10 MINUTES WORTH OF AO2
- **Important contribution** but accomplished at considerable expense in terms of animal **suffering**.

- Animals too have **intrinsic value** because they are **sentient** beings (**Regan**, 1984).
- This gives animals **rights** including a right to be treated with respect and not harmed.
- If we fail to recognise rights of other animals we are violating the **principle of respect**.
- **Regan** (1984): animals are not **renewable resources**.
- Suffering may be minimised, but researchers should be **forced to develop alternatives**.
- **Animals Act** prevents severe abuses. Needs updating to accommodate **three Rs** (**House of Lords**, 2002).
- **Ethical guidelines** mainly based on costs and benefits, which ignore the substantive rights of animals in favour of humans.
- **Three Rs** don't go far enough. **Singer** (1990) – to put the interests of one species over another's is **speciesism**.

SCIENTIFIC ARGUMENTS

10 MINUTES WORTH OF AO1
Animal research has helped to understand:
- **Basic learning processes** e.g. **Skinner's** research with pigeons applied to therapeutic work.
- **Stress and disease** e.g. **Selye.**
- **Drug abuse and dependence.**
- **Drug use** e.g. for treating mental disorders and Alzheimer's disease.
- The **basic physiology** of the brain and nervous systems of all mammals is the same.

10 MINUTES WORTH OF AO2
- Animal studies can neither confirm nor refute hypotheses about **human behaviour**.
- Usefulness in clinical psychology may have been **overstated** (**Shapiro**, 1998).
- '**Science at any cost**' mindset that scientific knowledge justifies harming innocent individuals endangers all who are vulnerable, not just animals.
- Has led to the **Tuskegee experiment** and unethical medical experiments during the **Holocaust** (**Lifton**, 1986).

Question 4: Critically consider constraints on the use of non-human animals in psychological investigations. (30 marks)

20 MINUTES WORTH OF AO1
Animals are protected by Animals (1986) Act:
- Must take place in labs which are **licensed** and as part of a licensed research project.

Licences are only granted if:
- Potential results are **important** enough.
- The research **can't be done** using non-animals.
- The **minimum** number of animals will be used.
- Any **discomfort or suffering** kept to a minimum.
- Researchers have the **necessary training**, skills and experience.
- Act is **enforced** by a team of inspectors who visit each establishment an average of 8 times a year.
- Use also constrained by **BPS ethical guidelines**, e.g.:
- **Ethical considerations** – experimenter must be sure that the ends justify the means.
- **Numbers of animals** – minimum number of animals used to maximum effect.
- **Statisticians** may be able to advise on techniques of analysis which can give meaningful results from the fewest number of subjects.
- **Motivation** – animals shouldn't be motivated to behave by being deprived of food.
- **Needs** of individual species should be understood, e.g. a short period of deprivation for one species could be intolerable to another.

20 MINUTES WORTH OF AO2
- **Animals Act** prevents severe abuses. Needs updating to accommodate **three Rs** (**House of Lords**, 2002).
- **Three Rs** (**Russell and Burch** (1959):
1 **Reduction** – using methods that obtain the same amount of information from fewer animals, or more information from the same number of animals.
2 **Replacement** e.g. use of brain imaging and scanning procedures (such as MRI and PET scans) in humans.
- Use of **computer simulations** and mathematical models of human behaviour.
- **Lord Dowding Fund** for Humane Research funds methods which replace the use of animals.
3 **Refinement** – using procedures that minimise stress and enhance animal well-being.
- For example, **testing animals** in their own time and in the security of their own pens.
- Produces more **reliable and natural** results than if the animals are stressed.
- **Ethical guidelines** mainly based on costs and benefits, which ignore the substantive rights of animals in favour of humans.

Bateson's model (1986) assesses research on 3 criteria:
- The **quality** of the research.
- The degree of animal **suffering.**
- The certainty of **benefit.**
- This model provides a **clear indication** of when animal research may be tolerated and when it cannot.

The ethical arguments for animal research include the fact that it has made an important contribution to advances in clinical psychology that have brought about major improvements to the health and well-being of human beings. Because of this, it would be morally wrong not to use animals in research. A second ethical argument is that human life has a greater intrinsic value than animal life. Human rights arise because of the implicit contracts between members of society, and this implies duties and responsibilities. Because animals have no responsibilities, it is argued, they cannot have rights. Animal research is also defended on the basis that less invasive procedures have been developed which minimise animal suffering, and so provide moral justification for animal research. Most animal research carried out in the UK is by definition 'ethical' because it conforms both to the 1986 'Use of Animals Act' which protects animals from cruelty or mistreatment. Animals are also protected by the ethical guidelines given out by the BPS, which gives specific advice on the numbers of animals to be used in a study and other issues that are likely to arise in animal research (such as studies which involve deprivation).

Scientific arguments for animal research include the claim that animal research has contributed to our understanding of basic learning processes, e.g. Skinner's research with pigeons. Conditioning techniques derived from work on animals are now in regular use within therapeutic contexts. Animal research has also informed us about important connections between stress and disease (e.g. Selye's work on stress and disease). Such research has suggested psychological interventions for coping with stress more effectively. Research with animals has also contributed significantly to our understanding of drug abuse and physical dependence. Psychologists use animals to develop new drugs used in the treatment of mental disorders such as anxiety, schizophrenia and depression. Animal research is also important in our current attempts to develop effective drug treatment for the cognitive deficits of ageing and Alzheimer's disease. Animal research would be less relevant to human behaviour if there were significant differences between the physiology of humans and other mammals. The basic physiology of the brain and nervous systems of all mammals is, however, essentially the same. Although the human brain might be more highly developed, its similarity to the brains of non-human mammals is far greater than critics of this approach would have us believe.

The ethical arguments for animal research have their counterpoints. Animal research has made an important contribution to human welfare, but this has been accomplished at considerable expense in terms of animal suffering. By adopting a cost-benefit approach to animal research, it is assumed that both of these can be accurately predicted prior to the study, yet this is often not the case. Regan (1984) argues that animals too have intrinsic rights by virtue of the fact that they have 'inherent value' because they are sentient beings. Any animal that is motivated to avoid suffering is assumed to be sentient. These rights include the right to be treated with respect and not harmed. Regan argues that if we fail to recognise the rights of other animals we are violating the principle of respect. Regan also argues that animals are not, and should not be seen as, renewable resources. Although suffering may be minimised in the procedures used in modern research, those against animal research believe that researchers should be forced to develop alternatives. The Animals Act prevents severe abuses but a House of Lords committee (2002) concluded that it needs updating to accommodate the three Rs (i.e. reduction, replacement and refinement of animal research). Ethical guidelines such as those published by the BPS are mainly based on the costs and benefits of animal research, which ignore the substantive rights of animals in favour of humans. Singer (1990) claims that the Three Rs don't go far enough, as putting the interests of one species over another's amounts to speciesism.

Although animal research has contributed to our knowledge in a number of different areas of human behaviour, animal studies can neither confirm nor refute hypotheses about human behaviour. At best animal experiments can suggest new hypotheses that might be relevant to humans. Shapiro (1998) claims that the usefulness of animal research to clinical psychology may have been overstated. Although animal models have been developed, the more successful treatments do not derive from such models. There is a danger to the 'science at any cost' mindset that scientific knowledge justifies harming innocent individuals. This attitude endangers all who are vulnerable, not just animals, and was the mentality that led to the infamous Tuskegee experiment and some of the crimes committed under the guise of medical research in the Holocaust (Lifton, 1986).

This first paragraph is all AO1 and is confined to the ethical arguments for animal research. You could, however, divide your essay up differently, but approximately one quarter should be AO1 ethical arguments as these are requirements of the question.

This is usually used as an argument *against* animal research (i.e. that animals and humans are different), but it has been turned around here to be an argument *for* animal research.

The three R's are mentioned briefly here, but the context of this question does not allow for an extensive discussion of these proposals.

Although this point strays from animal research, it is an appropriate point to make. This mindset that science is more important than the subjects of research is a dangerous attitude that underlies much of animal research.

Topic 1: Free will and determinism

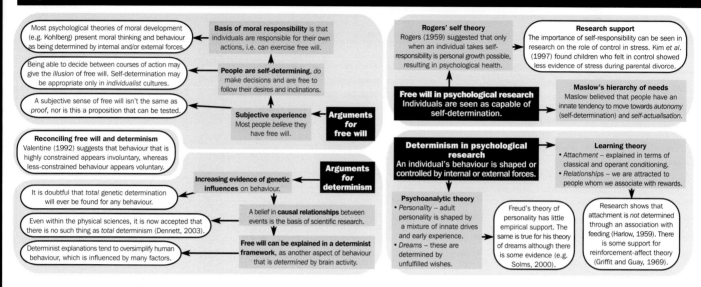

Most psychological theories of moral development (e.g. Kohlberg) present moral thinking and behaviour as being determined by internal and/or external forces.

Basis of moral responsibility is that individuals are responsible for their own actions, i.e. can exercise free will.

Being able to decide between courses of action may give the *illusion* of free will. Self-determination may be appropriate only in *individualist* cultures.

People are self-determining, do make decisions and are free to follow their desires and inclinations.

A subjective sense of free will isn't the same as *proof*, nor is this a proposition that can be tested.

Subjective experience Most people *believe* they have free will.

Arguments for free will

Reconciling free will and determinism Valentine (1992) suggests that behaviour that is highly constrained appears involuntary, whereas less-constrained behaviour appears voluntary.

Increasing evidence of genetic influences on behaviour.

Arguments for determinism

It is doubtful that *total* genetic determination will ever be found for any behaviour.

A belief in **causal relationships** between events is the basis of scientific research.

Even within the physical sciences, it is now accepted that there is no such thing as *total* determinism (Dennett, 2003).

Determinist explanations tend to oversimplify human behaviour, which is influenced by many factors.

Free will can be explained in a determinist framework, as another aspect of behaviour that is *determined* by brain activity.

Rogers' self theory Rogers (1959) suggested that only when an individual takes self-responsibility is personal growth possible, resulting in psychological health.

Research support The importance of self-responsibility can be seen in research on the role of control in stress. Kim *et al.* (1997) found children who felt in control showed less evidence of stress during parental divorce.

Free will in psychological research Individuals are seen as capable of self-determination.

Maslow's hierarchy of needs Maslow believed that people have an innate tendency to move towards *autonomy* (self-determination) and *self-actualisation*.

Determinism in psychological research An individual's behaviour is shaped or controlled by internal or external forces.

Learning theory
• *Attachment* – explained in terms of classical and operant conditioning.
• *Relationships* – we are attracted to people whom we associate with rewards.

Psychoanalytic theory
• *Personality* – adult personality is shaped by a mixture of innate drives and early experience.
• *Dreams* – these are determined by unfulfilled wishes.

Freud's theory of personality has little empirical support. The same is true for his theory of dreams although there is *some* evidence (e.g. Solms, 2000).

Research shows that attachment is *not* determined through an association with feeding (Harlow, 1959). There is some support for reinforcement-affect theory (Griffit and Guay, 1969).

Topic 2: Reductionism

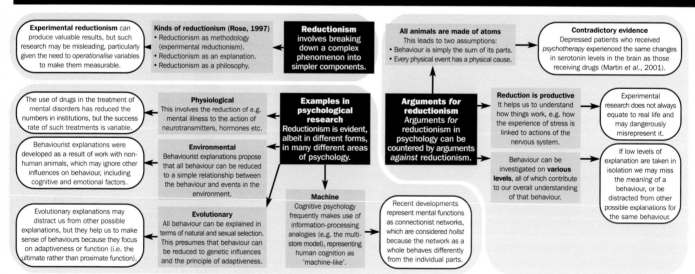

Experimental reductionism can produce valuable results, but such research may be misleading, particularly given the need to *operationalise* variables to make them measurable.

Kinds of reductionism (Rose, 1997)
• Reductionism as methodology (experimental reductionism).
• Reductionism as an explanation.
• Reductionism as a philosophy.

Reductionism involves breaking down a complex phenomenon into simpler components.

All animals are made of atoms This leads to two assumptions:
• Behaviour is simply the sum of its parts.
• Every physical event has a physical cause.

Contradictory evidence Depressed patients who received *psychotherapy* experienced the same changes in serotonin levels in the brain as those receiving drugs (Martin *et al.*, 2001).

The use of drugs in the treatment of mental disorders has reduced the numbers in institutions, but the success rate of such treatments is variable.

Physiological This involves the reduction of e.g. mental illness to the action of neurotransmitters, hormones etc.

Examples in psychological research Reductionism is evident, albeit in different forms, in many different areas of psychology.

Arguments *for* reductionism Arguments *for* reductionism in psychology can be countered by arguments *against* reductionism.

Reduction is productive It helps us to understand how things work, e.g. how the experience of stress is linked to actions of the nervous system.

Experimental research does not always equate to real life and may dangerously misrepresent it.

Behaviourist explanations were developed as a result of work with non-human animals, which may ignore other influences on behaviour, including cognitive and emotional factors.

Environmental Behaviourist explanations propose that all behaviour can be reduced to a simple relationship between the behaviour and events in the environment.

Behaviour can be investigated on **various levels**, all of which contribute to our overall understanding of that behaviour.

If low levels of explanation are taken in isolation we may miss the *meaning* of a behaviour, or be distracted from other possible explanations for the same behaviour.

Evolutionary explanations may distract us from other possible explanations, but they help us to make sense of behaviours because they focus on adaptiveness or function (i.e. the ultimate rather than proximate function).

Evolutionary All behaviour can be explained in terms of natural and sexual selection. This presumes that behaviour can be reduced to genetic influences and the principle of adaptiveness.

Machine Cognitive psychology frequently makes use of information-processing analogies (e.g. the multi-store model), representing human cognition as 'machine-like'.

Recent developments represent mental functions as connectionist networks, which are considered *holist* because the network as a whole behaves differently from the individual parts.

Probable questions

1. Discuss the free will versus determinism debate with reference to **two or more** psychological theories. *(30 marks)*

2. (a) Explain what is meant by the terms 'free will' and 'determinism'. *(5 marks)*

   (b) With reference to **two or more** psychological theories, discuss the free will versus determinism debate. *(25 marks)*

Possible questions

3. 'The suggestion that human beings have free will is an illusion, we actually have very little control over our own behaviour.'

   With reference to issues such as those in the quotation above, discuss arguments for and against free will. *(30 marks)*

4. Critically consider arguments **for** determinism in psychology. *(30 marks)*

Both questions 1 and 2 require you to discuss the free will/determinism debate in psychological theories. Both questions make it clear that you must discuss at least two theories. You can of course discuss more than two theories but don't forget that a detailed discussion of each theory (depth) is as important as the number of theories (breadth).

The important difference between questions 1 and 2 is that in question 2 the question is parted, requiring you to describe the concepts of free will/determinism for 5 AO1 marks. This means that there are fewer AO1 marks for the description of the theories in part (b) than in question 1. In question 1 you have 15 marks (20 minutes writing time) to describe the theories. In question 2 part (b) you have 10 marks (about 13 minutes writing time) to describe the theories.

In both questions the most common way that marks are lost is that candidates describe and evaluate their chosen theories. That may well *appear* to be what is required – but it isn't. You are required to describe free will/determinism in your chosen theories and evaluate the theories in terms of consequences, implications, etc., of free will/determinism in these theories.

Question 3 begins with a quotation. You are not required to use this quotation in your answer (because the question contains the phrase 'such as' which means you can refer to other issues). The quotation may provide you with a good starting point for your answer. The AO1 content should be a description of arguments both 'for' and 'against' free will. This means that you are able to use your arguments 'for' and 'against' determinism as AO2. However these will only be creditworthy as AO2 if you use them as counterpoints for the AO1 arguments.

Question 4 concerns arguments 'for' determinism but again the other arguments (those 'against' determinism, and those 'for' and/or 'against' free will) can be used as AO2 if they are presented as effective counterarguments.

Probable questions

1. 'By adopting a reductionist approach, we may overlook the real causes of human behaviour.'

   With reference to issues such as those in the quotation above, discuss the value of a reductionist approach to psychological theory **and/or** research. *(30 marks)*

2. (a) Explain what is meant by 'reductionism' in psychology. *(5 marks)*

   (b) With reference to **two or more** areas of psychology, discuss different examples of reductionism. *(25 marks)*

Possible questions

3. Describe and evaluate arguments **for** reductionist explanations in psychology. *(30 marks)*

4. Describe and evaluate arguments **against** reductionist explanations in psychology. *(30 marks)*

In question 1 of this topic the 'quote-discuss' has been included in the 'probable' questions because it helps to direct you in answering the question. You might otherwise wonder what was required to answer this question about the value of a reductionist approach (really just another way to ask for arguments 'for' the reductionist approach). The quotation makes a negative statement about reductionism – you should try to think of the arguments against this position.

Question 2 is a two-parter that begins with a definition in part (a). As this part is worth 5 marks you need to aim to write about 100 words explaining reductionism. You might use examples as a means of amplifying your explanation though you may want to reserve some of these for part (b). In part (b) there are only 10 AO1 marks compared to 15 AO2 marks, so more of your answer should evaluate the examples than describe them. A general discussion of arguments for/against reductionism is unlikely to gain much credit. You need to identify examples in psychological research (such as certain explanations of mental illness) and describe how each example is reductionist and the strengths/limitations of this example.

Questions 3 and 4 are on arguments 'for' and 'against' reductionism. In both essays you can use the same material but *how* you use it will be crucial. In question 3 arguments 'for' reductionist explanations in psychology would count as AO1. The arguments 'against' would count as AO2 but only if they are used as effective counterpoints to the AO1 arguments. If you described all the arguments 'for' and then said 'on the other hand' and then described all the arguments against you would only receive AO1 credit for the 'for' arguments.

In question 4 the same advice applies but obviously the arguments 'against' are now AO1 and arguments 'for' must be phrased in such a way that they provide effective counterarguments.

Chapter 10

TOPIC 1: FREE WILL AND DETERMINISM

SAMPLE ESSAY PLAN

Question 2: (a) Explain what is meant by the terms 'free will' and 'determinism'. (5 marks)
(b) With reference to two or more psychological theories, discuss the free will versus determinism debate. (25 marks)

(a)
6½ MINUTES WORTH OF AO1
- **Free will**: *we are capable of self-determination.*
- Accords with **subjective experience**: *most people believe they have free will.*
- People do make **decisions**.
- **Determinism**: *an individual's behaviour is shaped or controlled by internal or external forces.*
- The basis of the **scientific approach**.
- If free will is the **product of our brains** *then can be explained in a determinist framework.*

(b)
13½ MINUTES WORTH OF AO1
Free will in psychological theories:
- **Humanistic theory (Maslow**, 1950s): *an innate tendency towards* **autonomy** *(self-determination) and* **self-actualisation** *(sought after basic needs satisfied).*
- **Rogers' self theory** (1959): **self-development** *related to free will and self-actualisation, which leads to psychological health; those controlled by others cannot change their own behaviour.*

Determinism in psychological theories:
- **Psychoanalytic theory** *proposes that adult* **personality** *is shaped by a mixture of innate drives and early experience.*
- *Behaviour driven by the* **libido**, *frustration/indulgence during stages of development leads to* **fixation** *and* **shapes adult personality.**
- **Dreams** *determined by* **unfulfilled wishes**, *id-driven though* **repressed**.
- **Learning theory: attachment** *determined by* **classical** *(mother associated with food) and* **operant** *conditioning (mother is secondary reinforcer).*
- **Relationships (Byrne and Clore**, 1970): *reinforcement-affect model, relationships determined by rewards.*
- **Cognitive model of abnormality**: *mental disorder determined by maladaptive thinking.*

20 MINUTES WORTH OF AO2
- **Humanistic psychology**: *important third force, counterpoint to determinism.*
- Effects of control on healthy development: **Rogers**: *children who felt in control showed less stress during parental divorce (***Kim** *et al.*, 1997).
- **Freud's** *theory of personality has little empirical support, at best shows correlation but not that early experience* **causes** *adult personality.*
- Some support for Freud's theory of **dreams**, *for example* **Solms** (2000) *irrational part of brain is active during dreaming.*
- Alternative **neurobiological theories** *also determinist.*
- **Lucid dreaming** – *dreaming controlled by dreamer.*
- **Attachment** *is not determined through association with feeding e.g.* **Harlow** (1959) *research with monkeys.*
- **Reinforcement-affect theory** *e.g.* **Griffit and Guay** (1969) *Ps rated experimenter highest when given positive evaluations.*
- Such research tends to **oversimplify** *real life.*
- **Cognitive therapies** *involve free will, clients encouraged to control their thoughts.*
- Most theories **tend towards determinism** – *the scientific approach relies on it.*
- Determinism isn't **fatalism**, *individuals free to choose behaviour from limited repertoire (***soft determinism**).

Question 4: Critically consider arguments for determinism in psychology. (30 marks)

20 MINUTES WORTH OF AO1
Some examples from above, plus:
- Increasing evidence of **genetic influences**.
- Belief in **causal relationships** *between events is the basis of scientific research.*
- If free will is the **product of our brains** *then can be explained in a determinist framework.*
- Theories of **moral development** *(e.g.* **Kohlberg**) *present moral thinking and behaviour as determined by internal and/or external forces.*
- *Being able to decide between courses of action may give the* **illusion of free will**.
- *Self-determination may be appropriate only in* **individualist** *cultures.*
- *A subjective sense of free will isn't the same as* **proof**, *nor is this a proposition that can be tested.*

20 MINUTES WORTH OF AO2
Some evaluation from above, plus:
- *It is doubtful that* **total** *genetic determination will ever be found for any behaviour.*
- *Even within the physical sciences, it is now accepted that there is no such thing as* **total determinism** (**Dennett**, 2003).
- *Determinist explanations tend to* **oversimplify** *human behaviour, which is influenced by many factors.*
- **Basis of moral responsibility** *is that individuals are responsible for their own actions, i.e. can exercise free will.*
- **People are self-determining**, *they do make decisions.*
- Accords with **subjective experience**: *most people believe they have free will.*
- Determinism isn't **fatalism**, *individuals free to choose behaviour from limited repertoire (***soft determinism**).

(a)

The term 'free will' means that we are capable of self-determination. We act in accordance with our subjective experience rather than in response to any external or internal (i.e. biological) pressures. Free will is the product of subjective experience in that most people believe they have free will, and are aware of making conscious decisions. The term 'determinism' refers to the belief that an individual's behaviour is shaped or controlled by internal or external forces and is the basis of the scientific approach in psychology. If free will is the product of conscious thought and decision making, and we can explain this activity in terms of brain processes, then free will can be explained within a determinist framework.

(b)

Humanistic theory is characterised by the belief that individuals have the capacity to be self-determining and responsible for their actions. Maslow (1954) believed that humans had an innate tendency towards autonomy (self-determination) and self-actualisation. Maslow proposed that individuals are first motivated to satisfy fundamental needs such as food and warmth, and then needs such as seeking love. If these are satisfied the person is motivated by more personal needs such as self-actualisation. Rogers (1959) proposed a theory of self development based upon the concept of free will. He believed that taking responsibility for our own behaviour is the route to healthy self-development. Those who are controlled by others cannot take responsibility for their behaviour and so cannot begin to change it.

Freud's theory proposes that adult personality is shaped by a mixture of innate drives and early experience. Behaviour is driven by the libido, and if the child is frustrated or overindulged at any stage during development the child remains fixated on the erogenous zone for that stage and its associated method of obtaining satisfaction. This in turn shapes the adult personality. Freud also believed that dreams were determined by unfulfilled wishes – unacceptable, id-driven thought is repressed from conscious thought and re-emerges in dreams. Behaviourists believe that all behaviour is determined by experience. The learning theory view of attachment is that attachment is determined by classical (mother associated with food) and operant conditioning (mother is a secondary reinforcer). Behaviourist principles have also been applied to the formation of relationships. Byrne and Clore's reinforcement-affect model claims that relationships form because some people are associated with rewards. The cognitive model of abnormality sees many mental disorders as being determined by maladaptive thinking, which is a product of previous experiences which create expectations in the mind of the person concerned.

Humanistic psychology has been influential as a 'third force' in psychology, and offers a counterpoint to more determinist theories of personality. Humanistic views on behaviour are supported by research evidence on the experience of stress. The harmful effects of stress are reduced if a person feels more in control of events around them. For example, Kim et al. (1997) found that children who felt in control showed fewer signs of stress when their parents divorced.

Freud's determinist theory of personality has little empirical support; at best research shows a correlation between early experience and later adult personality, but not that early experience causes adult personality. Freud's view that dreams are caused by the re-emergence of repressed wishes considered unacceptable for conscious thought is partially supported by research by Solms (2000). Solms found that the irrational areas of the brain remain active during dreaming but the rational areas do not. Alternative neurobiological theories of dreaming are also determinist, seeing dreams as being determined by neural activity, although in lucid dreaming, dreaming is controlled by dreamer, and so could be seen as evidence of free will.

Research does not tend to support the claim that attachment is determined through association with feeding, e.g. Harlow's research with monkeys found that contact comfort is more important, although this merely replaces one determinant of attachment with another. On the other hand, research supports other behaviourist theories such as reinforcement-affect theory. For example, in research by Griffit and Guay (1969) participants rated the experimenter highest when they received positive evaluations (i.e. their feelings toward the experimenter were determined by association with a rewarding experience). However such research tends to be conducted in artificial situations and tends to oversimplify the factors involved in real-life relationship formation. Despite the claim that abnormal behaviour is determined by prior experiences, this does not mean that there is no place for free will in this model. Cognitive therapies involve free will, as clients are encouraged to take control of their thoughts. Most psychological theories tend towards determinism, particularly as the scientific approach relies on a belief in the determination of behaviour. Individuals are essentially free to choose their behaviour from a limited repertoire of available alternatives (soft determinism).

This final point helps to integrate the two terms and deal with the apparent paradox – how can our behaviour be both the product of free will and determinism?

When describing Maslow's theory, take care not to give too much information about the theory itself, but just enough to emphasise its place in the free will versus determinism debate.

As many, if not most, of the psychological theories you will be aware of emphasise the determination of behaviour, you could choose your own example. This theory is taken from social psychology.

Always aim to elaborate any AO2 point. Here this has been done by using an example from your AS studies of stress.

It isn't sufficient to just describe an alternative perspective, as it needs to be used within the context of a critical commentary. Here the word 'although' indicates that not all theories of dreaming are determinist.

You could make more of the idea of 'soft determinism', although be careful to work this into an AO2 commentary rather than just describing this alternative view.

SAMPLE ESSAY PLAN

Question 2: (a) Explain what is meant by 'reductionism' in psychology. (5 marks)
(b) With reference to **two or more** areas of psychology, discuss different examples of reductionism. (25 marks)

(a)

6½ MINUTES WORTH OF AO1
- **Reductionism** involves breaking down a complex phenomenon into simpler components.

Kinds of reductionism (Rose, 1997):
- As **methodology** (experimental reductionism), operationalising variables for cause-and-effect.
- As an **explanation**: parsimony, *Occam's razor*.
- As a **philosophy**, unity with all science.

(b)

13½ MINUTES WORTH OF AO1
- **Physiological psychology**: reduction of behaviour to the action of neurotransmitters, etc.
- For example, explaining **schizophrenia** as excessive activity of dopamine.
- **Behaviourist** explanations reduce all behaviour to simple stimulus-response units.
- For example, **attachment** is reduced **classical** (mother associated with food) and **operant** conditioning (mother is secondary reinforcer).
- **Evolutionary psychology** (e.g. natural and sexual selection), presumes that behaviour can be reduced to genetic influences and adaptiveness.
- For example, **schizophrenia** was adaptive in the EEA (**Crow, 1995**).
- **Cognitive psychology**: machine reductionism: cognitive psychology represents human cognition as 'machine-like'.
- For example, **multi-store model** describes memory as input, process, output.

20 MINUTES WORTH OF AO2
- Use of **drug therapies** for mental disorders has reduced the numbers in institutions, however **success rate** is variable and there are **side effects**.
- **Behaviourist** explanations were developed as a result of work with **non-human animals**.
- Even in animals there are **other influences** on behaviour, including cognitive and emotional factors.
- Evolutionary explanations **distract** from other possible explanations, however they increase understanding because they focus on **ultimate** function.
- Memory described using **connectionist networks**, which are considered **holist** because the network as a whole behaves differently from the individual parts.
- Reductionist theories have produced **valuable results** but can be misleading because they **oversimplify** reality.
- May **distract** us from other explanations for the same behaviour e.g. using Ritalin to treat hyperactivity.
- Rose (1992): differing levels should be separate and non-competing but lower levels may still be distracting.
- Reality is probably best served by acknowledging all **levels of explanation**.

Question 3: Describe and evaluate arguments **for** reductionist explanations in psychology. (30 marks)

20 MINUTES WORTH OF AO1
Kinds of reductionism (Rose, 1997):
- As **methodology** (experimental reductionism), operationalising variables for cause-and-effect.
- As an **explanation**: parsimony, *Occam's razor*.
- **As a** philosophy, **unity with all science.**
- All animals are made of atoms, which leads to two assumptions:
- Behaviour is simply the **sum of its parts**.
- Every physical event has a **physical cause**.
- Reduction is **productive** (reduction as methodology).
- **Necessary part** of understanding how things work.
- For example, to understand **human stress** need to understand the actions of the nervous system.
- Laboratory (reductionist) research on leading questions (**Loftus and Palmer**, 1974).
- Various **levels of explanation**, all contribute to overall understanding.
- For example, analyse **signature** at a high and low level: social meaning and muscular activity.

20 MINUTES WORTH OF AO2
- All animals are made of atoms.
- **Is the 'mind' physical?** Mind-body problem.
- **Dualists** believe the physical and mental are separate but interacting e.g. psychotherapy affects levels of neurotransmitters (**Martin et al.**, 2001).
- A link between physical and mental events doesn't mean that one **causes** the other (**Bell**, 2000).
- Reduction is productive, may be true for **simple systems**.
- Experimental research does not always equate to real life and may dangerously misrepresent it.
- **Real-life research** on leading questions produced different results (**Yuille and Cutshall**, 1986).
- Various levels, may miss the **meaning** of a behaviour e.g. **Wolpe's** (1973) misinterpretation of a woman's fear of insects.
- May **distract** us from other explanations for the same behaviour e.g. using Ritalin to treat hyperactivity.
- Rose (1992) regard different levels as non-competing – different 'universes of discourse'.
- **Correspondence between levels** has been found e.g. perception of lines and simple cells in visual cortex.

(a)

Reductionism involves breaking down a complex phenomenon into simpler components. Rose (1997) identified three kinds of reductionism. Experimental reductionism reduces complex behaviours to operationalised variables that can be manipulated to determine cause and effect relationships. Reductionism is also an approach to explanation in psychology, as the best explanations are those with the fewest sets of laws or principles. The principle of parsimony, or Occam's razor, states that of two competing theories, all other things being equal, the simpler one is to be preferred. Reductionism also serves as a philosophy that underlies psychology and science in general. If all science is unitary we should be able to reduce all explanations of behaviour to physical laws.

> The most obvious way to explain the nature of reductionism is to define it in general terms and then offer an explanation of different types of reductionism that operate in psychology.

(b)

Physiological psychology involves the reduction of behaviour to the action of neurotransmitters, hormones, etc. One way to explain mental illness is in terms of such units. For example, schizophrenia can be explained as excessive activity of dopamine in the brain. Behaviourist explanations suggest that all behaviour can be reduced to simple stimulus-response units, which are formed through the relationship between the behaviour and events in the environment. For example, attachment can be reduced to a set of probabilities that determine the likelihood of an attachment bond forming between the child and an individual with whom the child comes into contact. The mother is likely to provide food, which reduces discomfort. Hence she becomes a rewarding part of the child's environment (operant conditioning) and an attachment bond is more likely to form with her than with other individuals.

> Two examples of reductionist explanations are described here, but it is important to remember why you are describing these (i.e. the context) and so not get carried away with your descriptions.

Evolutionary psychology explains all behaviour in terms of the principles of natural and sexual selection. Such explanations are reductionist because they presume that all behaviour can be reduced to genetic influences and the principle of adaptiveness. Since there is well-established evidence that schizophrenia has a strong inherited component, the genes that cause it must have been adaptive in some way for our ancestors (Crow, 1995). Therefore, according to the principle of natural selection, only genes that cause adaptive characteristics or behaviours are perpetuated. Reductionism is also evident in much of cognitive psychology, which represents much of human cognition in the same way as a machine functions (machine reductionism). For example, the multi-store model of memory represents memory as a series of inputs, outputs and processes.

> Schizophrenia may well have been adaptive in some form to our ancestors – this is reductionist because it represents a complex disorder as being passed on through the genes simply because it once served some adaptive function and ignoring other possible explanations.

Physiological explanations of mental illness have led to drug treatments. The use of drug therapies for mental disorders has reduced the numbers in institutions. However the success rate of such treatments is variable and there are side effects. Reducing mental illness to the physiological level ignores the context and function of such behaviour. Behaviourist explanations were developed as a result of work with non-human animals. Such explanations may not be appropriate for more complex human behaviour. Even in non-human animals, reductionist explanations ignore other possible influences on behaviour, including cognitive and emotional factors. Evolutionary explanations may be undesirable because they distract us from other possible explanations and oversimplify reality. However they increase understanding because they help us to make sense of behaviours that otherwise would not make sense because they focus on adaptiveness and function, i.e. they focus on the ultimate cause of behaviour rather than its proximate function. For example, an ultimate explanation of depression might emphasise its adaptive significance in conflict situations, where the loser's depressed mood state would influence their survival by inhibiting further challenges against the victor.

> All evolutionary explanations focus on conditions that were operating in the ancestral environment (the EEA), hence behaviours can be reduced to their adaptive significance then rather than now.

The multi-store model of memory was a linear representation of memory, but more recent developments in cognitive psychology have described mental functions in terms of connectionist networks. Such networks are considered holist because the network as a whole behaves differently from the individual parts, whereas linear models such as the multi-store model assume that the sum of the parts equals the whole. Reductionist theories have produced valuable results but they oversimplify reality. If lower levels (e.g. physiological or behavioural explanations) are viewed in isolation, the meaning of behaviour may be overlooked, which can lead to errors in understanding. The danger of lower-level explanations is that they may distract us from a more appropriate level of explanation. For example, the administration of the drug Ritalin to hyperactive children may miss the real causes of a child's hyperactive behaviour (e.g. family or emotional problems). Rose (1992) suggests that the problem of different levels can be resolved if the levels are regarded as separate and non-competing. Reality is probably best served by acknowledging all levels of explanation and not allowing lower levels to dominate explanations.

> This final AO2 paragraph is a more general commentary on reductionism in psychology, although reference is still made to specific examples of psychological research or practice.

Topic 3: Is psychology a science?

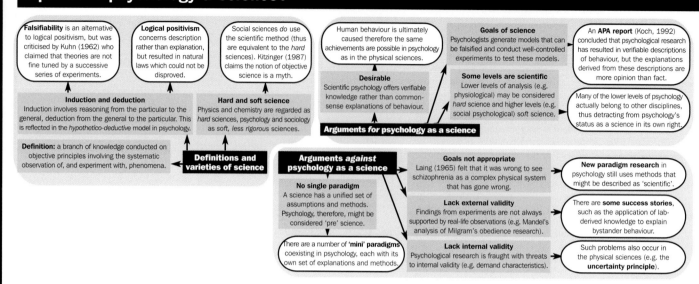

Falsifiability is an alternative to logical positivism, but was criticised by Kuhn (1962) who claimed that theories are not fine tuned by a successive series of experiments.

Logical positivism concerns description rather than explanation, but resulted in natural laws which could not be disproved.

Social sciences *do* use the scientific method (thus are equivalent to the *hard* sciences). Kitzinger (1987) claims the notion of objective science is a myth.

Human behaviour is ultimately caused therefore the same achievements are possible in psychology as in the physical sciences.

Goals of science
Psychologists generate models that can be falsified and conduct well-controlled experiments to test these models.

An **APA report** (Koch, 1992) concluded that psychological research has resulted in verifiable descriptions of behaviour, but the explanations derived from these descriptions are more opinion than fact.

Induction and deduction
Induction involves reasoning from the particular to the general, deduction from the general to the particular. This is reflected in the *hypothetico-deductive* model in psychology.

Hard and soft science
Physics and chemistry are regarded as *hard* sciences, psychology and sociology as *soft, less rigorous* sciences.

Desirable
Scientific psychology offers verifiable knowledge rather than common-sense explanations of behaviour.

Some levels are scientific
Lower levels of analysis (e.g. physiological) may be considered *hard* science and higher levels (e.g. social psychological) *soft* science.

Many of the lower levels of psychology actually belong to other disciplines, thus detracting from psychology's status as a science in its own right.

Definition: a branch of knowledge conducted on objective principles involving the systematic observation of, and experiment with, phenomena.

Definitions and varieties of science

Arguments *for* psychology as a science

Arguments *against* psychology as a science

Goals not appropriate
Laing (1965) felt that it was wrong to see schizophrenia as a complex physical system that has gone wrong.

New paradigm research in psychology still uses methods that might be described as 'scientific'.

No single paradigm
A science has a unified set of assumptions and methods. Psychology, therefore, might be considered 'pre' science.

Lack external validity
Findings from experiments are not always supported by real-life observations (e.g. Mandel's analysis of Milgram's obedience research).

There are **some success stories**, such as the application of lab-derived knowledge to explain bystander behaviour.

There are a number of **'mini' paradigms** coexisting in psychology, each with its own set of explanations and methods.

Lack internal validity
Psychological research is fraught with threats to internal validity (e.g. demand characteristics).

Such problems also occur in the physical sciences (e.g. the **uncertainty principle**).

Topic 4: Nature–nurture

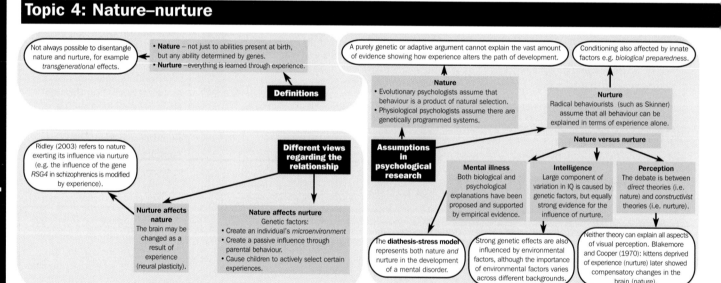

Not always possible to disentangle nature and nurture, for example *transgenerational* effects.

• **Nature** – not just to abilities present at birth, but any ability determined by genes.
• **Nurture** –everything is learned through experience.

A purely genetic or adaptive argument cannot explain the vast amount of evidence showing how experience alters the path of development.

Conditioning also affected by innate factors e.g. *biological preparedness*.

Definitions

Nature
• Evolutionary psychologists assume that behaviour is a product of natural selection.
• Physiological psychologists assume there are genetically programmed systems.

Nurture
Radical behaviourists (such as Skinner) assume that all behaviour can be explained in terms of experience alone.

Ridley (2003) refers to nature exerting its influence via nurture (e.g. the influence of the gene *RSG4* in schizophrenics is modified by experience).

Different views regarding the relationship

Assumptions in psychological research

Nature versus nurture

Nurture affects nature
The brain may be changed as a result of experience (neural plasticity).

Nature affects nurture
Genetic factors:
• Create an individual's *microenvironment*
• Create a passive influence through parental behaviour.
• Cause children to actively select certain experiences.

Mental illness
Both biological and psychological explanations have been proposed and supported by empirical evidence.

Intelligence
Large component of variation in IQ is caused by genetic factors, but equally strong evidence for the influence of nurture.

Perception
The debate is between *direct* theories (i.e. nature) and *constructivist* theories (i.e. nurture).

The **diathesis-stress model** represents both nature *and* nurture in the development of a mental disorder.

Strong genetic effects are also influenced by environmental factors, although the importance of environmental factors varies across different backgrounds.

Neither theory can explain all aspects of visual perception. Blakemore and Cooper (1970): kittens deprived of experience (nurture) later showed compensatory changes in the brain (nature).

Probable questions

1. Critically consider the view that psychology is a science. *(30 marks)*

2. (a) Outline what is meant by 'science' in the context of psychological research. *(5 marks)*

   (b) Outline and evaluate arguments **for** the claim that psychology is a science. *(25 marks)*

Possible questions

3. Critically consider arguments **for** the claim that psychology is a science. *(30 marks)*

4. Critically consider arguments **against** the claim that psychology is a science. *(30 marks)*

The injunction 'critically consider' is the same as 'discuss' (an AO1 + AO2 injunction). It is sometimes used because it emphasises the 'critical' nature of the required discussion. This first question is lifted from the specification and permits you to organise your answer in any way you choose: you can just describe arguments 'for' and then evaluate these, just describe arguments 'against' and evaluate these, or describe arguments 'for' and 'against' and evaluate these. It may also be appropriate to consider what is meant by a 'science' in order to decide whether psychology is one – but just defining the term is not likely to be creditworthy.

Question 2 is more restricted. You must first of all write about 100 words explaining the concept of science. This must be set in the context of psychological research in order to attract full marks. Part (b) has a reduced number of AO1 marks (10 rather than 15) and restricts you to describing the arguments 'for' psychology as a science. As before, the arguments 'against' may be used as AO2 as long as they are presented as effective counterpoints to individual AO1 arguments.

Question 3 is almost the same as question 2 except there is no part (a) which means more AO1 is required for the description of the arguments 'for'.

In question 4 you may use the same arguments as those presented in question 3 but you need to shape the arguments to suit the question.

Probable questions

1. Discuss the nature–nurture debate with reference to **two or more** psychological theories **and/or** studies. *(30 marks)*

2. (a) Explain what is meant by the terms 'nature' and 'nurture'. *(5 marks)*

   (b) With reference to **two or more** psychological theories, discuss assumptions made about nature and nurture. *(25 marks)*

Possible questions

3. 'We are essentially a product of our genetic heritage, yet the environment plays an important role in determining how this heritage is manifested.'

   With reference to the issues in the quotation above, discuss the nature–nurture debate in psychology. *(30 marks)*

4. Discuss different views regarding the relationship between nature and nurture. *(30 marks)*

The two probable questions given here mirror those given for the other three debates. You may get a parted question (as in question 2) where part (a) requires an explanation of the key term(s). This is always worth 5 marks (about 100 words). The part (b) of such a parted question is likely to be similar to the other kinds of question set on this topic area.

In both question 1 and 2(b) you must discuss the debate in the context of at least two theories. As always it is critical that you do not describe and evaluate the theories themselves but, in order to gain marks, you must describe the nature–nurture elements in the theories and evaluate the nature–nurture aspects of the theories (in terms of, for example, implications, applications, alternative explanations).

In question 2(b) the wording is different to question 1. In both cases you are required to discuss nature–nurture in the context of psychological theories but in question 2 your attention is particularly drawn to the 'assumptions' made by the theories. Top marks will be given to candidates who specifically address the assumptions of the theory – i.e. the basic 'beliefs' of the theory.

One final point – in question 1 it actually says 'theories and/or studies' even though 'studies' are not mentioned in the specification. Since the specification does mention 'research' (which is theories and/or studies) it is reasonable to presume that some candidates will be ready and willing to discuss studies as well as theories, and this question gives them the opportunity to do this if they wish.

The 'quote-discuss' question given here is an example of one where you do have to address the quotation – or else incur a penalty. The penalty is that your AO2 marks are restricted to a maximum of 9 out of 15 marks. It is not sufficient to simply start your essay making reference to the quotation. 'Addressing the quotation' requires a sustained effort to wrap your response around the quotation. In order to satisfy this criterion, each paragraph should make some allusion to the quotation.

The final question for this topic is taken directly from the specification but is a less likely choice because it restricts what can be included in your answer. You are not required to discuss the debate here but instead must describe how nature and nurture may interact.

Chapter 10

TOPIC 3: IS PSYCHOLOGY A SCIENCE?

SAMPLE ESSAY PLAN

Question 1: Critically consider the view that psychology is a science. (30 marks)

15 MINUTES WORTH OF AO1

Arguments 'for' psychology as a science:

- **Desirable:** scientific psychology offers verifiable knowledge rather than common-sense explanations of behaviour.
- **Goals of science** shared by psychology: generate models that can be falsified and conduct well-controlled experiments to test these models.
- **Some levels of psychology are scientific:** lower levels of analysis (e.g. physiological) may be considered **hard science** and higher levels (e.g. social psychological) **soft science**.
- **Hard science:** precise conditions, replication.

Arguments 'against' psychology as a science:

- **No single paradigm:** a science has a unified set of assumptions and methods.
- Psychology might be considered **'pre' science**.
- **Experiments lack external validity:** findings from experiments are not always supported by real-life observations (e.g. Mandel's analysis of Milgram's obedience research).
- **Experiments lack internal validity:** experimenter bias and demand characteristics mean that observed effects may not be due to IV.
- **Goals not appropriate:** Laing (1965) wrong to see schizophrenia as a physical-chemical system that has gone wrong.
- **Modest success of psychotherapy** suggests that goals of science not appropriate.

15 MINUTES WORTH OF AO2

Response to arguments 'for':

- **Desirability:** human behaviour is determined by outside forces, therefore the **same achievements** are possible in psychology as in the physical sciences.
- Some psychological theories (e.g. **Freud**) can't be **falsified** and thus aren't scientific.
- Some areas of psychological research concern feelings/emotions **not objective measurement**.
- Using scientific methods doesn't make psychology a science, maybe it is a **'pseudo-science'** (Miller, 1983).
- **APA (American Psychological Association) report** (Koch, 1992) psychological research has resulted in verifiable descriptions of behaviour, but derived explanations are more opinion than fact.
- Lower levels belong to other disciplines, detracts from psychology's status as a **science in its own right**.

Response to arguments 'against':

- A number of **'mini' paradigms** in psychology, each with its own set of explanations and methods.
- **Lab research** has been successful e.g. application of lab-derived knowledge to explain bystander behaviour.
- Problems similar to experimenter bias also occur in the **physical sciences** (e.g. Heisenberg's **uncertainty principle**).
- **Alternatives:** new paradigm research in psychology uses methods that might be described as 'scientific'.
- Findings using different techniques (e.g. interviews, discourse analysis) **triangulated** to achieve objectivity.

Question 2: (a) Outline what is meant by 'science' in the context of psychological research. (5 marks)
(b) Outline and evaluate arguments **for** the claim that psychology is a science. (25 marks)

(a)

6½ MINUTES WORTH OF AO1

- **Science:** objective principles involving systematic observation of, and experiment with, phenomena.
- **Many examples** where IV varied to observe effects on DV e.g. effects of stress on immune system, effects of retention interval on recall.
- Physics and chemistry are **hard sciences**, psychology and sociology are **soft**, less rigorous.
- **Scientific method:** the **hypothetico-deductive** model used in psychology e.g. testing normative social influence in Asch studies.
- Social sciences do use the scientific method (thus are **equivalent to the hard sciences**).

(b)

13½ MINUTES WORTH OF AO1

Use arguments 'for' as above, plus:

- **'Mini' paradigms** in psychology.
- **Lab research** has been successful.
- Problems similar to experimenter bias also occur in the **physical sciences**.
- **Goals are appropriate** e.g. research on aggression.
- **Alternatives:** new paradigm research in psychology still uses methods that might be described as 'scientific'.

20 MINUTES WORTH OF AO2

Use responses to arguments 'for' as above, plus:

- **No single paradigm** unlike true science.
- Psychology might be considered **'pre'** science.
- Experiments lack **external validity**.
- Experiments lack **internal validity**.
- **Goals not appropriate:** Laing (1965) wrong to see schizophrenia as a complex physical system gone wrong.
- **Only modest success of psychotherapy** suggests that goals of science not appropriate.
- Findings using different techniques (e.g. interviews, discourse analysis) **triangulated** to achieve objectivity.

Arguments 'for' psychology as a science include the claim that scientific research is desirable, and scientific psychology offers verifiable knowledge rather than common-sense explanations of behaviour. Psychology is a science insofar as it shares the goals of science and uses the scientific method. Indeed, the laboratory experiment has become the dominant mode of investigation in psychology, and therefore offers opportunities for control and prediction that are absent in less 'scientific' methods. Psychologists generate models that can be falsified and conduct well-controlled experiments to test these models. Some levels of psychology are clearly scientific. The lower levels of analysis (e.g. physiological, genetic and behavioural) may be considered hard science and higher levels (e.g. social psychological) may be considered soft science. The distinction between hard and soft science is the ability to falsify theories and reproduce experiments. Soft science deals with conditions where it is often impractical to replicate particular experimental conditions or to test particular theories, so results tend not to be as precise as they might be in areas such as cognitive and physiological psychology, where experiments can be precisely repeated over and over again.

Arguments 'against' psychology as a science include the fact that psychology has no single paradigm. Science tends to have a unified set of assumptions and methods, which psychology does not, therefore psychology might be considered 'pre-science'. Psychological experiments frequently lack external validity, i.e. findings from experiments are not always supported by real-life observations. For example, Mandel's analysis of obedience research showed that Milgram's findings did not explain obedience in the Nazi death camps. Psychological experiments may also lack internal validity in that the observed effects may result from variables other than the experimental manipulation. Psychological research has problems that are not usually found in the physical sciences, particularly experimenter bias and demand characteristics. The goals of science may not be appropriate for psychology. For example, Laing (1965) claimed that it was inappropriate to see schizophrenia as a physical-chemical system that has simply gone wrong. The modest success of psychotherapy in the treatment of mental disorders suggests that the goals of science are not appropriate for all areas of psychology.

It is desirable to be objective, but this may not be possible in psychological research. However, human behaviour is determined by outside forces, therefore the same achievements are possible in psychology as in the physical sciences. Not all theories in psychology are falsifiable. If a theory cannot be falsified, it is not scientific. Freud's theory of psychoanalysis cannot be falsified and so cannot be considered scientific. Only some psychologists are willing to restrict their field of study to objective measurements. Other areas of psychology concern feelings/emotions which do not lend themselves to objective measurement. A further problem is that the use of scientific methods does not necessarily make psychology a science. Miller (1983) suggests that psychology is at best a 'pseudo-science', with the consequence that psychologists who believe that they are scientists occasionally claim their discoveries to be fact. The most damning criticism comes from an APA report (Koch, 1992) which claims that although psychological research has resulted in verifiable descriptions of behaviour, the explanations derived from this research are more opinion than fact. Many of the lower levels of psychological explanation that might be considered 'scientific' actually belong to other disciplines, which detracts from psychology's status as a science in its own right.

Although there is no one single defining paradigm in psychology, there are a number of 'mini' paradigms (such as behaviourist and the cognitive perspectives), each with its own set of explanations and methods of data collection. There are also many examples where laboratory research has been successfully applied to the explanation of real-life behaviour. Research on helping behaviour in the laboratory (Darley and Latané, 1968) has led to a better understanding of bystander behaviour. Problems similar to experimenter bias also occur in the physical sciences. Heisenberg's uncertainty principle asserts that the very process of observation invariably changes the observed object. Even alternative approaches in psychology (new paradigm research) use methods that might be described as 'scientific', insofar as they aim to be objective. Data can be collected using different techniques (e.g. interviews, discourse analysis) which can then be triangulated to achieve objectivity.

In this paragraph, arguments for psychology being a science are used as AO1 description.

Similarly, in this second paragraph, description of arguments against psychology as science constitutes the second half of the AO1 component of the answer.

In this question arguments for and against may be used for AO1.

For this AO2 paragraph, commentary on the points made in the first paragraph must match the material there. You are commenting on those points rather than introducing a fresh set of arguments.

Finally, the second half of the AO2 component addresses the AO1 points made in paragraph 2. Note that each of these commentary paragraphs takes issue with the position that psychology is or is not scientific. It is the way that you use material in this context that makes it either AO1 or AO2.

SAMPLE ESSAY PLAN

Question 2: (a) Explain what is meant by the terms 'nature' and 'nurture'. (5 marks)
(b) With reference to two or more psychological theories, discuss assumptions made about nature and nurture. (25 marks)

(a)

6½ MINUTES WORTH OF AO1
- **Nature** – not just the abilities present at birth, but any ability determined by genes.
- Early psychologists influenced by Darwinism and the importance of **innate tendencies**.
- **Nurture** – everything learned through experience.
- We are born like a '**blank slate**' (**Locke**), view taken by the **behaviourists**.
- Not always possible to **disentangle** nature and nurture, for example **transgenerational** effects.

(b)

13½ MINUTES WORTH OF AO1

Nature:
- **Evolutionary theories** assume that behaviour is due to **natural selection** in the EEA (e.g. altruism).
- Also **sexual selection** (e.g. explaining interpersonal attraction).
- **Physiological theories** assume there are genetically programmed systems (e.g. stress).

Nurture:
- **Radical behaviourists** (such as **Skinner**) assume that all behaviour can be explained in terms of experience alone e.g. language acquisition.
- **Non-behaviourist** explanations assume experience is important e.g. double bind theory of schizophrenia (**Bateson et al.**, 1956).

Nature versus nurture:
- **Perception: direct** theories (i.e. nature) e.g. **Gibson** (1979).
- Or **constructivist** theories (i.e. nurture) e.g. **Gregory** (1972).
- **Intelligence:** large component of variation in IQ is caused by genetic factors (e.g. gene-mapping study **Chorney et al.**, 1998).
- Equally strong evidence for the influence of nurture (e.g. Flynn effect: **Flynn**, 1987).

20 MINUTES WORTH OF AO2

Nature:
- Cannot explain the vast amount of evidence showing how **experience** alters the path of development e.g. Bandura's SLT explanation of aggression.
- Evolutionary theories criticised as **speculative**.

Nurture:
- Conditioning also affected by **innate factors** e.g. biological preparedness (e.g. **Mineka et al.**, 1985).
- Evolutionary theory suggests that **learning is adaptive**.
- Even the capacity to learn is innate e.g. mutant fruit flies can't be conditioned (**Quinn et al.**, 1979).

Nature versus nurture:
- **Perception:** Gibson's theory can't explain perceptual set, Gregory's theory appropriate mainly for ambiguous data. Neither is sufficient.
- **Perception:** kittens' innate visual system affected by experience (**Blakemore and Cooper**, 1970).
- **Intelligence:** research indicates a strong genetic component but environmental contribution minimised because most studies concern **affluent children**.
- **Turkheimer et al.** (2003): importance of environmental factors varies across different backgrounds.
- **Mental illness: diathesis-stress model** represents both nature and nurture.

Question 4: Discuss different views regarding the relationship between nature and nurture. (30 marks)

20 MINUTES WORTH OF AO1

Nature affects nurture, genes have direct or indirect effects, they create:
- An individual's **microenvironment**, a **reactive** gene-environment interaction (**Plomin et al.**, 1977).
- **Passive influence** through parental behaviour.
- **Active influence:** select certain experiences (**niche-picking**), explains why genetic influence increases with age.
- **Shared versus unshared** environment.

Nurture affects nature:
- Brain may be changed as a result of experience (**neural plasticity**).
- For example, studies by **Blakemore and Cooper** (1970) on visual deprivation and **Pascual-Leone et al.** 1995) on piano exercise or imagined exercise, and brain growth.

20 MINUTES WORTH OF AO2
- **Views on nature alone**, e.g.
- Evolutionary theories.
- Physiological theories.
- **Views on nurture alone**, e.g.
- Behaviourist explanations.
- Other theories based on effects of experience.
- Most behaviour is **best explained** by a combination of nature and nurture, e.g.
- Perception.
- Intelligence.
- Mental illness.
- **Ridley** (2003) refers to nature exerting its influence via nurture (e.g. the influence of the gene RSG4 in schizophrenics is modified by experience).

(a)

Nature refers not just to abilities present at birth, but also to any ability determined by genes, including those appearing through maturation. Early psychologists were influenced by Darwinism and the importance of innate tendencies. The nature perspective sees most behaviour, including abstract traits such as intelligence, personality and aggression, as being encoded in an individual's DNA. While not discounting that genetic tendencies may exist, supporters of the nurture view believe that they ultimately don't matter – that our characteristics and behaviour originate only from environmental influences in our upbringing, i.e. through experience. According to Locke, we are born like a blank slate, on which experience is written. It is not always possible to disentangle nature and nurture, for example transgenerational effects are passed on from parent to offspring (and therefore inherited) but are not produced by genetic inheritance.

> Whilst it is not essential to include mention of transgenerational effects, it is handy if you run out of material for your definition.

(b)

Evolutionary psychologists assume that behaviours are a product of natural selection in the EEA. For example, altruism can be traced back to behaviours that had adaptive value for our ancestors. Likewise, interpersonal attraction can be explained in terms of sexual selection. Physiological psychology is also based on the assumption that behaviour can be explained in terms of genetically programmed systems, e.g. the stress response.

> The 'theories' referred to here are natural and sexual selection, and the physiology of stress.

Radical behaviourists (such as Skinner) assume that all behaviour can be explained in terms of experience alone. For example, Skinner (1957) proposed that a child's acquisition of language could be explained entirely in terms of rewards and shaping. Non-behaviourist explanations also assume that experience is important. For example, the double bind theory of schizophrenia (Bateson et al., 1956) suggests that this develops in children who frequently receive contradictory messages from their parents.

> Nurture is not just about behaviourism, but any perspective that emphasises the role of experience in development.

Direct theories of perception (e.g. Gibson, 1979) represent the nature perspective. Gibson argued that perception is entirely innate whereas constructivist theories (e.g. Gregory, 1972) emphasise the ambiguous nature of most sensory input, which must rely on expectations to complete the perceptual process. Twin and adoption studies suggest that a large component of the variation in IQ is caused by genetic factors, for example gene-mapping studies (Chorney et al., 1998) have identified individual genes associated with high IQ. There is also strong evidence for the influence of nurture, for example the fact that IQs all over the world have increased by as much as 20 points over the last 30 years (the Flynn effect).

A purely genetic perspective cannot explain the vast amount of evidence showing how experience alters the path of development (e.g. Bandura's studies on the social learning of aggression). Evolutionary psychology has also been challenged concerning adaptiveness in the EEA. There is little hard evidence to support such claims, and some critics claim that the evolutionary approach simply generates 'after the fact' explanations.

> Don't get carried away describing these theories – they are simply being used to make a point.

Conditioning is also affected by innate factors, e.g. Mineka et al. (1985) found that monkeys more easily acquired a fear of snakes than they did fear of a flower. This is explained by the principle of biological preparedness. Through biological preparedness an organism is innately predisposed to form associations between certain stimuli and responses. Learning is a very sophisticated ability that would be impossible without specialised adaptations that have evolved over time. Even the capacity to learn is innate, as demonstrated by studies using mutant fruit flies. The changes made to their genes meant that it was no longer possible to condition them (Quinn et al., 1979).

> This point is continued in the next paragraph. Does the existence of learning preclude evolved adaptations?

Gibson's theory cannnot explain perceptual set because our tendency to distort ambiguous images relies on expectations. Gregory's theory is criticised as being appropriate mainly for ambiguous data, which are unrepresentative of all sensory data. Neither is sufficient on its own. Research on visual deprivation has provided compelling evidence for the role of visual experience on perceptual development. Blakemore and Cooper (1970) found that kittens' innate visual system was affected by experience. Kittens deprived of horizontal or vertical visual experience for five months could no longer see lines of that orientation. Research on intelligence indicates a strong genetic component but environmental contribution is minimised because most studies concern affluent children. A poor environment on the other hand would permit small variations to have a larger influence on behaviour. Turkheimer et al. (2003) supported this claim showing that the importance of environmental factors varies across different backgrounds. Almost all the variability in the IQ of children from poor backgrounds was accounted for by their shared environment, whereas the opposite was true for children from richer families. The diathesis-stress model of mental illness represents both nature and nurture. Individuals who have a genetic vulnerability to a disorder may develop it under certain environmental conditions.

> Nature or nurture? This suggests that the tendency to study children from relatively affluent families has biased the results of intelligence research.

Exam question

This part of the Unit 5 paper will be assessed through a stimulus material question. While the stimulus material will change from examination to examination, the basic form of the questions will remain the same.

They will be as follows:

(a) Describe how the subject presented in the stimulus material might be explained by two different approaches.

(6 marks + 6 marks) AO1

(b) Assess **one** of these explanations of the subject presented in the stimulus material in terms of its strengths and limitations.

(6 marks) AO2

(c) How might the subject presented in the stimulus material be investigated by one of these approaches?

(6 marks) AO2

(d) Evaluate the use of this method of investigating the subject material presented in the stimulus material.

(6 marks) AO2

The stimulus material comes in two varieties: either a description of an individual's behaviour or a description of a more general form of behaviour. This 'behaviour' constitutes the 'subject of the stimulus material'.

The kind of behaviour identified in the stimulus material has to be something that is not a topic in the A2 specification. Why is this? If, for example, pro-social behaviour were described, then candidates who had studied this subsection of the specification would have an advantage over those who had not.

In part (a) marks are awarded for the extent to which you engage with the material. (See mark scheme on page viii.) This 'engagement' applies to all parts of the question.

In part (b) you can use either approach from part (a) but must consider strengths and limitations.

In part (c) you do not have to refer to the same approach as used in part (b). Your investigation must be plausible.

In part (d) there is no requirement to consider both strengths and limitations.

Realistically you will probably have time to write about 150–200 words for every 6 marks of this question.

The behavioural approach: Key concepts

Classical conditioning	Operant conditioning	Social learning theory	Methodology
association	reinforcement	observation	laboratory experiment
stimulus	rewards	indirect learning	generate research aims
reflex response	punishments	role models	experimental hypothesis
unconditioned stimulus (UCS)	aversive consequences	identification	IV and DV operationalised
neutral stimulus (NS)	reinforcers	consequences	design decisions:
unconditioned reflex (UCR)	negative reinforcers	vicarious reinforcement	• What design would be
conditioned response (CR)	positive reinforcers	expectancies of future outcomes	suitable?
conditioned stimulus (CS)	primary reinforcers	internal mental representations	• How should participants be
forward conditioning	shaping	performance	selected?
generalised	reinforcement schedule	skills	• Control extraneous variables.
discrimination	continuous reinforcement	direct reinforcement	• Ethical issues?
one trial learning	extinguished	value of the behaviour	• ABAB design.
	avoidance learning	self-efficacy	

Strengths

- Operationalised concepts.
- Falsifiable, empirical approach.
- Importance of rewards supported by research (e.g. Lepper et al., 1973, children respond to rewards).
- Individual differences..
- Selective reinforcement.
- Context dependent learning.

Limitations

- Non-human animal evidence.
- At best a partial account.
- Emotion, expectations, higher level motivation not included.
- Reductionist, prevents investigating other explanations, doesn't explain all behaviour.
- Determinist, encourages lack of personal responsibility.

Strengths

- Effects of direct and indirect reinforcement.
- Cognitive factors.
- Social influences (e.g. parents, media).
- Gender and cultural differences.

Limitations

- Other factors, e.g. genetic influences.
- Reinforcements not sufficiently consistent.

Strengths

- Causal relationships.
- Controlled.
- Internal validity.
- Replication shows reliability and validity.
- Demonstrate underlying mechanisms.

Limitations

- Artificial.
- Operationalisation reduces the meaningfulness.
- Low external validity.
- Experimenter bias and demand characteristics reduce the internal validity.
- Ethical issues.

The psychodynamic approach: Key concepts

Effects of early experience on personality development	Adult personalities	Factors that motivate behaviour	Methodology
psychosexual stages body parts sexual (physical) stimulation libido (psychic energy) mouth oral stage 0–18 months anus anal stage 18 months–3 years genital region phallic stage 3–6 years frustration or overindulgence may result in fixation identification with one's same-sex parent Oedipus conflict penis envy	• Oral aggressive character characterised by pessimism, envy, and suspicion. • Oral receptive character is optimistic, gullible, and full of admiration for others. • Anal retentive character is neat, stingy, and obstinate. • Anal expulsive character is disorganised, reckless, and defiant.	id, ego and superego pleasure principle reality principle conscious rational part ego defence mechanisms (repression, displacement, reaction formation, intellectualisation) unconscious sublimation dynamics of behaviours mental disorders	case studies psychoanalysis free association dream interpretation manifest content latent content experiments

Strengths

- Importance of unconscious factors, complexity of behaviour.
- Support for ego defences, e.g. Williams' (1994) study of repression.
- Support for phallic stage e.g., gender development theory (Martin and Halverson, 1981).
- Support for rational vs irrational thinking e.g., Solms (2000) REM sleep.

Limitations

- Difficult to falsify explanations.
- Determinist.
- Reductionist.
- Gender-biased.
- Culture biased because:
  - Too much emphasis on biological factors.
  - Too little emphasis on social influences.

Strengths

- Rich details.
- Not reductionist.
- Relates to real life.
- Idiographic approach.
- Collect case studies together to generalise.

Limitations

- Unconscious not accessible.
- Unreliable.
- Researcher bias.
- Subjective interpretation.
- Difficult to generalise.
- Not replicable.
- Time-consuming and expensive.

The evolutionary approach: Key concepts

Natural selection	Kin selection	Methodology
selective pressure fitness adapted environmental niche survival reproduction genes, genetically-transmitted	the selfish gene inclusive fitness gene pool **The modular mind** ultimate proximate environment of evolutionary adaptation (EEA) selection pressures mental modules	Range of methods: • Naturalistic observations. • Experiments, mainly with non-human animals. • Surveys/interviews. • Cross-cultural studies.

Sexual selection

exaggerated characteristics
males compete
females select
strategy
sexiest traits

Strengths

- Fits with genetic explanations, genes create vulnerabilities (i.e. predispose us to certain behaviours).
- Not reductionist.
- Ultimate functions.

Limitations

- Reductionist.
- Determinist.
- Ignore cultural influences.
- Speculative arguments.

OStrengths

- Naturalistic observations: unbiased data, realistic, starting point for a theory.
- Experiments: see behavioural approach.
- Surveys: collect large quantities of data relatively easily.
- Cross-cultural studies provide a less culturally biased view of human behaviour, more likely to discover universals of behaviour.

Limitations

- Naturalistic observation: not cause and effect relationships, affected by observer bias, ethical issues.
- Experiments: see behavioural approach.
- Surveys: interviewer bias, social desirability bias.
- Cross-cultural studies: may be unrepresentative, imposed etics.

It is a fundamental desire for many people, particularly males, to be creative, either through music, art, literature or poetry. People will spend a great deal of their time learning to play a musical instrument, produce a work of art or write something that others acknowledge as a masterpiece.

(a) Describe how the desire to be creative might be explained by the behavioural approach.

- Vicarious reinforcement, watching, learning, rewards.
- Direct reinforcement, primary reinforcers (e.g. praise), secondary reinforcers (e.g. money).
- Operant conditioning increases probability.
- Increased feelings of self-efficacy, increases probability.
- Strength: falsifiable, empirical, good research support.
- Limitations: partial account, reductionist, doesn't explain all behaviour.
- Laboratory experiment, aim, experimental hypothesis, independent variable, dependent variable, operationalised, matched participants design.
- Strengths: causal relationships, demonstrate underlying mechanism, controlled, can be replicated.
- Limitation: operationalisation reduces the meaningfulness.

(b) Assess the behavioural explanation of the desire to be creative in terms of its strengths and limitations.

- Strengths: falsifiable, empirical, good research support.
- Limitations: partial account, reductionist, doesn't explain all behaviour.

(c) How might the desire to be creative be investigated by the behavioural approach?

- Laboratory experiment, aim, experimental hypothesis, independent variable, dependent variable, operationalised, matched participants design.

(d) Evaluate the use of this method of investigating the desire to be creative.

- Strengths: causal relationships, demonstrate underlying mechanism, controlled, can be replicated.
- Limitation: operationalisation reduces the meaningfulness.

(a) Describe how the desire to be creative might be explained by the behavioural approach.

A person's need to become creative might be explained in terms of vicarious reinforcement. Through watching the adulation afforded to celebrity pop stars and artists, they would have learned that creativity was a valued characteristic, and one that brought rewards from other people. Once they have acquired their own creative skill, they would have received direct reinforcement from others, perhaps in the form of primary reinforcers such as praise and adulation, or in the form of secondary reinforcers such as money (from the sale of their work), which could then be used to satisfy their material needs. Through the process of operant conditioning, therefore, they would be more likely to produce creative artefacts in the future. As they became more successful, they would develop a greater confidence that their work would be appreciated by others, which would give them increased feelings of self-efficacy, which in turn would increase the likelihood that their creative behaviour would be repeated in the future.

(b) Assess the behavioural explanation of the desire to be creative in terms of its strengths and limitations. (6 marks)

A strength of a behaviourist explanation for the need to be creative is that it is falsifiable. By manipulating the consequences of a person's creative behaviour, for example, it should be possible to alter the future probability of it occurring, thus demonstrating empirically the contingent relationship between creative behaviour and reinforcement. This explanation is also supported by considerable research evidence showing that rewards (the praise and adulation of others toward the creative person) are an important determinant of human behaviour.

A limitation of this explanation is that it is at best a partial account of the acquisition of creative behaviour. As such, behaviourist explanations are reductionist, in that they prevent psychologists investigating the potential role played by other factors, such as the expression of the person's own inner feelings. Many creative people persevere with their work despite the lack of appreciation from others. Operant conditioning theory would claim that such lack of reward should decrease creative behaviour in such situations, but it clearly does not.

(c) How might the desire to be creative be investigated by the behavioural approach? (6 marks)

A laboratory experiment could be conducted with the aim of investigating whether vicariously observing positive reinforcement from others (the independent variable) increases the likelihood that individuals will be influenced by that role model. The experimental hypothesis would be that children who see a model rewarded for their creative behaviour display a higher desire to be like that model than those who see a more neutral reaction to the same behaviour. Using a matched participants design, male children could be allocated to one of two groups, matched for age and personality. They would be shown one of two specially prepared films. In one condition, an adult male would be shown demonstrating creative behaviour (e.g. reading a poem or painting) and receiving praise from those around him. In the other condition, the same model's creative behaviour would be followed by a more neutral reaction from those around him. The dependent variable is operationalised as the rating (on a scale of 1 to 10) of how much they would like to be like the person on the film.

(d) Evaluate the use of this method of investigating the desire to be creative. (6 marks)

This method would allow researchers to investigate the causes of people's desire to be creative, particularly as variables that might confound this relationship (such as age and personality) can be controlled through matching. By using the same model and behaviour in each condition, the possibility of extraneous variables in the characteristics or behaviour of the model can be eliminated. This would also mean that the study could be more accurately replicated. A limitation of this method is that by operationalising variables into simple measurable events, it reduces the meaningfulness of this research. This may only demonstrate one aspect of people's desire to be creative. For example, it only demonstrates that people are drawn to behaviour that is reinforced rather than being attracted to creative behaviour itself. However, by reducing a complex motivation (the desire to be creative) down to simple testable relationships (i.e. the relationship between reinforcement and creative behaviour), it is possible to demonstrate the underlying mechanisms for that behaviour.

In the exam you are required to provide two explanations to part (a) (6 + 6 marks). We have only given one explanation here because your second one would be drawn from a different approach.

It is possible to combine concepts from social learning theory (such as self-efficacy) with concepts from conditioning theory under the umbrella of 'behaviourism'.

Although you may think the view of the penniless artist is not relevant in an evaluation of a behavioural explanation, it quite clearly demonstrates that such behaviours can be acquired even in the absence of obvious reinforcers such as praise and financial reward.

This experimental design, where observers see a model displaying the behaviour in question, can be used in many 'approaches' questions when using the behavioural approach, but you must take care to contextualise your description.

Although both strengths and limitations are included here, they are not necessary for maximum marks. However, having good and bad things to say about your chosen method does give you more to say!

It is a fundamental desire for many people, particularly males, to be creative, either through music, art, literature or poetry. People will spend a great deal of their time learning to play a musical instrument, produce a work of art or write something that others acknowledge as a masterpiece.

(a) Describe how the desire to be creative might be explained by the psychodynamic approach.

- Identify with same-sex parent, psychosexual development, fixation, anal stage.
- Anal retentive adult personality is neatness, anal expulsive character is recklessness.
- Ego defence mechanisms, sublimation, reaction formation.
- Dynamics, conscious/unconscious factors.

(b) Assess the behavioural explanation of the desire to be creative in terms of its strengths and limitations.

- Strengths: importance of unconscious factors, complexity of behaviour, ego defences supported by research (e.g. Williams, 1994, repression).
- Limitations: difficult to falsify, reductionist.

(c) How might the desire to be creative be investigated by the psychodynamic approach?

- Case study, psychoanalysis, free association, dream interpretation, latent and manifest content.

(d) Evaluate the use of this method of investigating the desire to be creative.

- Limitations: unconscious not accessible, subjective interpretation, difficult to generalise (idiographic), unreliable.
- Strength: collect case studies together to generalise.

(a) Describe how the desire to be creative might be explained by the psychodynamic approach.

There are a number of ways in which a psychoanalytic theorist might explain a person's need to be creative. It is possible that the person identifies with the same-sex parent in an attempt to avoid punishment. Many creative children have creative same-sex parents. During their psychosexual development, they may become fixated in one particular stage. Over- or under-indulgence in the anal stage may produce an adult personality whose creativity is characterised by neatness (e.g. minimalist interior design) or one whose creativity is characterised by recklessness or defiance (e.g. 'punk' music). Some creative behaviour might be explained in terms of ego defence mechanisms, for example sexual humour might be considered an example of sublimated sexual desire, or through reaction formation, a way of dealing with sexual inadequacy. These defences are unconscious and explain the dynamics of creative behaviours that might otherwise be a mystery when explained in terms of conscious factors.

> The particular psychodynamic approach chosen here is Freud's psychoanalytic theory. Inevitably there is a fair amount of speculation in a psychoanalytic explanation, so a number of possible reasons why people may desire to be creative are offered under the umbrella of the psychoanalytic approach.

(b) Assess the psychodynamic explanation of the desire to be creative in terms of its strengths and limitations. (6 marks)

A strength of the psychoanalytic explanation of the desire to be creative is that it recognises the importance of unconscious factors. The underlying reasons for a person's drive to be creative may be far more complex than is claimed by the behavioural approach. A number of the concepts in this explanation, such as the importance of ego defence mechanisms in the development of behaviour, are supported by research studies (e.g. Williams' study of repression). This gives more credibility to the claim that the dynamics of creative behaviours are essentially unconscious.

> It is essential that you don't get carried away when evaluating psychoanalytic explanations. It is relatively easy to drift into more general criticisms of Freud's theory rather than concentrating on the explanation of the behaviour in question.

Limitations of this explanation include the fact that it is difficult to falsify. It is difficult to generate testable hypotheses that could demonstrate the relationship between the desire to be creative and unconscious factors such as fixation or identification with the same-sex parent. This explanation is also reductionist in that it reduces a culturally valued behaviour (creativity) to aspects of development such as fixation in the anal stage, and ignores all other possible explanations such as financial gain and public acclaim.

(c) How might the desire to be creative be investigated by the psychodynamic approach? (6 marks)

In order to study the underlying reasons for a person's desire to be creative, the research team might employ a psychoanalyst to conduct case studies of certain people. The psychoanalyst would interview creative individuals and collect detailed information, including their personal history, family background and education. During the process of psychoanalysis, the analyst might also use free association where the person expresses thoughts exactly as they occur. In psychoanalysis, the analyst attempts to discover whether the initial event or emotion that gave rise to the person's desire to be creative (e.g. the need to avoid punishment from a creative yet domineering father) has been repressed into the unconscious. Through methods such as free association and dream interpretation, the analyst attempts to make the unconscious conscious and thus gain insight into the underlying reasons for the individual's creativity. The psychoanalyst seeks to understand the latent content of the dream by examining its manifest content.

> Most psychoanalytic methods need to be handled carefully when fitting them into an investigation. It would be insufficient, for example, to simply say 'the researcher would see if they dream about being creative'. You must also focus on saying what you would do and not explaining why. Most importantly you must focus on investigating the behaviour and not the patient.

(d) Evaluate the use of this method of investigating the desire to be creative. (6 marks)

Although free association has been used extensively in psychoanalytic case studies, analysts often find that some memories are completely repressed, and essentially not accessible to the conscious mind. This means that the true reasons for a person's desire for creativity may not be discovered during psychoanalysis, and that the individual may instead accept a subjective interpretation from the analyst that is not the real reason for the behaviour. An additional problem with the use of the case study method in this context is that it involves a single, unique case (i.e. they are idiographic) rather than explaining why people in general desire to be creative. As such they may be considered unreliable in this context. The value of this method also depends on the accuracy of the individual's own memory and the accuracy of the analyst's interpretations. However, case studies do have their value, as several collected together enables a researcher to extract common themes and experiences that would allow them to generalise their explanation to other creative individuals.

> Case studies are inevitably about just one person. This isn't really a problem for the psychoanalyst as they are attempting to understand just that one individual, but it creates problems when we are trying to discover more general causes of behaviour.

It is a fundamental desire for many people, particularly males, to be creative, either through music, art, literature or poetry. People will spend a great deal of their time learning to play a musical instrument, produce a work of art or write something that others acknowledge as a masterpiece.

(a) Describe how the desire to be creative might be explained by the evolutionary approach.

- Trait, sexual selection, EEA.
- Males compete, females select on basis of sexy traits.
- An ultimate explanation, selection pressures lead to mental modules.

(b) Assess the evolutionary explanation of the desire to be creative in terms of its strengths and limitations.

- Strengths: fits with genetic explanations, an ultimate explanation.
- Limitations: reductionist, determinist.

(c) How might the desire to be creative be investigated by the evolutionary approach?

- Experiment, hypothesis, repeated measures design, independent variable, opportunity sample, operationalise, dependent variable.

(d) Evaluate the use of this method of investigating the desire to be creative.

- Strengths: control.
- Limitations: artificial, other variables.

(a) Describe how the desire to be creative might be explained by the evolutionary approach.

An evolutionary explanation of why people need to be creative might be that creativity is a trait that has been shaped by sexual selection. In the environment of evolutionary adaptation (EEA), males would have competed for females so they could pass on their genes. Although much of this competition would have been in terms of resources, it is also possible that males who had the ability to amuse or entertain would have been more likely to have been selected as mates by females. Creativity, therefore, would be seen as a sexy trait. Female choice for creative males would lead to the evolution of exaggerated characteristics, in much the same way as the peacock's tail has evolved to be extremely large and colourful. This is an example of an ultimate explanation, in that selection pressures in the EEA have led to the development of mental modules that lead males to seek creativity as a way of attracting members of the opposite sex.

> Note that it would not be sufficient to just describe evolutionary concepts; these must be neatly integrated with the stimulus material – in this case, concerned with creativity.

(b) Assess the evolutionary explanation of the desire to be creative in terms of its strengths and limitations. (6 marks)

A strength of this explanation of creativity is that it fits our understanding of how genes predispose us to particular behaviours, in this case how something that would have had adaptive significance in the EEA (i.e. attracting females through creative courtship displays) has become more widespread in the gene pool. Such explanations have the advantage of showing how behaviour that appears nowadays (e.g. writing a modern novel) can be explained in terms of the mate selection pressures that were operating in the time of our ancestors (i.e. its ultimate function). A problem with evolutionary explanations such as this is that they are inevitably reductionist, stressing the role of inherited factors rather than any more contemporary factors (such as financial rewards for creativity, etc.). Such explanations can also be criticised for being determinist, in that they remove the possibility of free will. People may choose to become creative (e.g. becoming penniless artists or poets) despite the social isolation of their work.

> When making claims about an explanation being reductionist or determinist, you must remember to make it clear why that is a problem for this particular explanation.

(c) How might the desire to be creative be investigated by the evolutionary approach? (6 marks)

It would be possible to test this explanation by doing an experiment. The hypothesis would be that women rate men who are creative more highly than men who are not creative. You could test this by taking photographs of men and use a repeated measures design. Each photograph would be accompanied by a short description of the man, giving an indication of his education, resources and occupation. The independent variable is creativity. The descriptions of half of the men would include an occupation consistent with creativity (e.g. artist, author, musician) and the other half (the non-creative condition) would be given more neutral occupations (e.g. teacher, accountant). Education and resources would be varied equally across the two conditions (creative and non-creative). Female participants would be found using an opportunity sample and asked to rate the photographs (on a ten point scale) in terms of their potential as long-term partners. This would be the operationalised dependent variable. Finally the ratings given to those photographs in the creative condition could be compared with photographs in the non-creative condition in terms of ratings.

> What works best in this part of the question is to start with a hypothesis and then design your experiment around this, describing the key design decisions.

(d) Evaluate the use of this method of investigating the desire to be creative. (6 marks)

The use of this method can test the evolutionary explanation that women will rate creative men as more attractive with a reasonable amount of control over other variables that might influence women's decisions in choosing potential partners. For example, the photographs across the two conditions can be matched in terms of variables that have been shown to affect female choice (e.g. education and resources). A problem with this method is that it assumes that women are able to make an effective choice from photographs alone (an artificial form of partner choice) and that selections are not actually being made on the basis of other variables (e.g. facial symmetry or feminine features) that have been shown to influence mate choice. The experiment requires the women to make their decision on the basis of long-term partner choice, whereas sexual selection theory might expect women to make their choice based on short-term partner choice as this is more likely to result in offspring that possess the desirable creative traits.

> Remember you are not evaluating the method itself (i.e. the experimental method) but its application in the context of testing the evolutionary explanation given in part (a).

CHAPTER 1 RELATIONSHIPS

Division	Topics	Revision areas		Basic Under-standing	Good Grasp	Complete Mastery
Division A : Issues						
		Topic 1: Explanations relating to interpersonal attraction				
		One explanation relating to interpersonal attraction	AO1			
			AO2			
		Two explanations relating to interpersonal attraction	Outline AO1			
			Outline AO2			
		Topic 2 : Explanations relating to the formation/maintenance of relationships				
		One explanation relating to the formation/maintenance of relationships	AO1			
			AO2			
		Two explanations relating to the formation/maintenance of relationships	Outline AO1			
			Outline AO2			
		Topic 3 : Research studies relating to interpersonal attraction				
		Research studies relating to interpersonal attraction	Outline AO1			
			Outline AO2			
Division B : Debates						
		Topic 1 : Psychological explanations of love				
		One psychological explanation of love	AO1			
			AO2			
		Two psychological explanations of love	Outline AO1			
			Outline AO2			
		Topic 2 : The breakdown of relationships				
		One theory of the breakdown of relationships	AO1			
			AO2			
		Two theories of the breakdown of relationships	Outline AO1			
			Outline AO2			
		Research studies related to the breakdown of relationships	Outline AO1			
			Outline AO2			
Division B : Debates						
		Topic 1 : The nature of relationships in different cultures				
		One explanation relating to the nature of relationships in different cultures	Outline AO1			
			Outline AO2			
		Two explanations relating to the nature of relationships in different cultures	Outline AO1			
			Outline AO2			
		Research studies relating to the nature of relationships in different cultures	Outline AO1			
			Outline AO2			
		Topic 4 : Understudied relationships				
		Research into **one** type of understudied relationship	AO1			
		(e.g. gay, lesbian or mediated)	AO2			
		Research into **two** types of understudied relationship	Outline AO1			

CHAPTER 2 PRO- AND ANTI-SOCIAL BEHAVIOUR

Division	Topics	Revision areas		Basic Under-standing	Good Grasp	Complete Mastery
Division A : Nature and causes of aggression						
	Topic 1 : Social psychological theories of aggression					
		One social psychological theory of aggression	AO1			
			AO2			
		Two social psychological theories of aggression	Outline AO1			
			Outline AO2			
	Topic 2 : Effects of environmental stressors on aggressive behaviour bystander behaviour					
		Research into effects of **two** environmental stressors	Outline AO1			
			Outline AO2			
Division B : Altruism and bystander behaviour						
	Topic 1 : Human altruism and					
		One explanation of human altruism/bystander behaviour	AO1			
			AO2			
		Two explanations of human altruism/bystander behaviour	Outline AO1			
			Outline AO2			
		Two or more research studies relating to human altruism/bystander behaviour	Outline AO1			
			Outline AO2			
	Topic 2 : Cultural differences in pro-social behaviour					
		Research (theories and/or studies) relating to cultural differences in pro-social behaviour	AO1			
			AO2			
Division C : Media influences						
	Topic 1 : Media influences in pro-social behaviour					
		Two or more explanations relating to media influences on pro-social behaviour	Outline AO1			
			Outline AO2			
		Research studies relating to media influences on pro-social behaviour	Outline AO1			
			Outline AO2			
	Topic 2 : Media influences in anti-social behaviour					
		Two or more explanations relating to media influences on anti-social behaviour	Outline AO1			
			Outline AO2			
		Research studies relating to media influences on anti-social behaviour	Outline AO1			
			Outline AO2			

Division	Topics	Revision areas		Basic Under-standing	Good Grasp	Complete Mastery
Division A : Biological rhythms						
	Topic 1 : Circadian, infradian and ultradian rhythms					
		Research into circadian rhythms	AO1			
			AO2			
		Research into infradian rhythms	AO1			
			AO2			
		Research into ultradian rhythms	AO1			
			AO2			
		Research into **two** or more rhythms	Outline AO1			
			Outline AO2			
	Topic 2 : The role of endogenous pacemakers and exogenous zeitgebers					
		Role of endogenous pacemakers	AO1			
			AO2			
		Role of exogenous zeitgebers	AO1			
			AO2			
	Topic 3 : Consequences of disrupting rhythms (e.g. shift work, jet lag)					
		Consequences of disrupting biological rhythms	Outline AO1			
			Outline AO2			
Division B : Sleep						
	Topic 1 : Function of sleep: Ecological accounts					
		One ecological theory of sleep	AO1			
			AO2			
		Two ecological theories of sleep	Outline AO1			
			Outline AO2			
		Research studies relating to the ecological account of sleep	Outline AO1			
			Outline AO2			
	Topic 2 : Function of sleep: Restoration accounts					
		One restoration theory of sleep	AO1			
			AO2			
		Two restoration theories of sleep	Outline AO1			
			Outline AO2			
		Research studies relating to the restoration account of sleep	Outline AO1			
			Outline AO2			
Division C : Dreaming						
	Topic 1 : The nature of dreams					
		Research related to the nature of dreams	Outline AO1			
			Outline AO2			
	Topic 2 : Neurobiological theories of dreaming					
		One neurobiological theory of dreaming	AO1			
			AO2			
		Two neurobiological theories of dreaming	Outline AO1			
			Outline AO2			
	Topic 3 : Psychological theories of dreaming					
		One psychological theory of dreaming	AO1			
			AO2			
		Two psychological theories of dreaming	Outline AO1			
			Outline AO2			

CHAPTER 4 PERCEPTUAL PROCESS AND DEVELOPMENT

Division	Topics	Revision areas		Basic Under-standing	Good Grasp	Complete Mastery
Division A : The visual system						
	Topic 1 : Structure and function of the visual system					
		Structure of the visual system (eye, retina, visual pathways)	Outline AO1			
			Outline AO2			
		Functions of the visual system (eye, retina, visual pathways)	Outline AO1			
			Outline AO2			
	Topic 2 : The nature of visual information processing					
		Research into **one** form of visual information processing	AO1			
			AO2			
		Research into **two** forms of visual information processing	Outline AO1			
		(e.g. sensory adaptation and the processing of contrast, colour and features)	Outline AO2			
Division B : Perceptual organisation						
	Topic 1 : Theories of visual perception – constructivist theories					
		One constructivist theory of visual perception	AO1			
			AO2			
		Two constructivist theories of visual perception	Outline AO1			
			Outline AO2			
	Topic 2 : Theories of visual perception – direct theories					
		One direct theory of visual perception	AO1			
			AO2			
		Two direct theories of visual perception	Outline AO1			
			Outline AO2			
	Topic 3 : Explanations of perceptual organisation					
		One explanation of perceptual organisation	AO1			
			AO2			
		Two explanations of perceptual organisation	Outline AO1			
			Outline AO2			
Division C : Perceptual development						
	Topic 1 : Studies of the development of perceptual abilities (infant and cross-cultural studies)					
		Infant studies of the development of perceptual abilities	Outline AO1			
			Outline AO2			
		Cross-cultural studies of the development of perceptual abilities	Outline AO1			
			Outline AO2			
	Topic 2 : Nature versus nurture					
		Two explanations of perceptual development	Outline AO1			
			Outline AO2			
		Nature–nurture debate in perception	Outline AO1			
			Outline AO2			

Division	Topics	Revision areas		Basic Under-standing	Good Grasp	Complete Mastery

Division A : Development of thinking

Topic 1 : Piaget's theory of cognitive development

Piaget's theory of cognitive development	AO1	
	AO2	
Piaget's theory of cognitive development (6 mark version)	Outline AO1	
	Outline AO2	

Topic 2 : Vygotsky's theory of cognitive development

Vygotsky's theory of cognitive development	AO1	
	AO2	
Vygotsky's theory of cognitive development (6 mark version)	Outline AO1	
	Outline AO2	

Topic 3 : Applications of theories of cognitive development

Application of **one** theory of cognitive development (e.g. to education)	AO1	
	AO2	
Application of **two** theories of cognitive development (e.g. to education)	Outline AO1	
	Outline AO2	

Division B : Development of measured intelligence

Topic 1 : The role of genetics in the development of measured intelligence

Research (theories and/or studies) into the role of genetics in the development of measured intelligence	Outline AO1	
	Outline AO2	

Topic 2 : Environmental factors in the development of measured intelligence

Research (theories and/or studies) into the role of environmental factors in the development of measured intelligence	Outline AO1	
	Outline AO2	

Division C : Development of moral understanding

Topic 1 : Theories of the development of moral understanding/pro-social reasoning

One theory of moral understanding/pro-social reasoning	AO1	
	AO2	
Two theories of moral understanding/pro-social reasoning	Outline AO1	
	Outline AO2	

Topic 2 : Gender and cultural differences in moral understanding/pro-social reasoning

Influence of gender differences on moral understanding/pro-social reasoning	AO1	
	AO2	
Influence of cultural differences on moral understanding/pro-social reasoning	AO1	
	AO2	

CHAPTER 6 SOCIAL AND PERSONALITY DEVELOPMENT

Division	Topics	Revision areas		Basic Under-standing	Good Grasp	Complete Mastery
Division A : Personality development						
	Topic 1 : Psychodynamic explanations of personality development					
		One psychodynamic explanation of personality development	AO1			
			AO2			
		Two psychodynamic explanations of personalitydevelopment	Outline AO1			
			Outline AO2			
	Topic 2 : Social learning explanations of personality development					
		One social learning explanation of personality development	AO1			
			AO2			
		Two social learning explanations of personality development	Outline AO1			
			Outline AO2			
Division B : Gender development						
	Topic 1 : Explanations of the development of gender identity/gender roles					
		Two explanation of the development of gender identity/gender roles	AO1			
			AO2			
		Two explanations of the development of gender identity/gender roles	Outline AO1			
			Outline AO2			
Division C : Adolescence						
	Topic 1 : Social development in adolescence					
		Research (theories and/or studies) into socia ldevelopment in adolescence	Outline AO1			
			Outline AO2			
		Research (theories and/or studies) into the formation of identity in adolescence	Outline AO1			
			Outline AO2			
	Topic 2 : Relationships with parents and peers during adolescence					
		Research (theories and/or studies) into relationships with parents during adolescence	Outline AO1			
			Outline AO2			
		Research (theories and/or studies) into relationships with parents during adolescence	Outline AO1			
			Outline AO2			

CHAPTER 7 EVOLUTIONARY EXPLANATIONS OF HUMAN BEHAVIOUR

Division	Topics	Revision areas		Basic Under-standing	Good Grasp	Complete Mastery
Division A : Human reproductive behaviour						
	Topic 1 : The relationship between sexual selection and human reproductive behaviour					
		Relationship between sexual selection and human reproductive behaviour	Outline AO1			
			Outline AO2			
		Two evolutionary explanations of human reproductive behaviour	Outline AO1			
			Outline AO2			
	Topic 2 : Evolutionary explanations of parental investment					
		Relationship between sexual selection and parental investment	Outline AO1			
			Outline AO2			
		Two evolutionary explanations of parental investment	Outline AO1			
			Outline AO2			
Division B: Evolutionary explanations of mental disorders						
	Topic 1 : Evolutionary explanations of depression					
		One explanation of depression from an evolutionary perspective	AO1			
			AO2			
		Two explanations of depression from an evolutionary perspective	Outline AO1			
			Outline AO2			
	Topic 2 : Evolutionary explanations of anxiety disorders					
		One explanation of anxiety disorders from anevolutionary perspective	AO1			
			AO2			
		Two explanations of anxiety disorders from an evolutionary perspective	Outline AO1			
			Outline AO2			
Division C : Evolution of intelligence						
	Topic 1 : Evolutionary factors in the development of human intelligence					
		Evolutionary factors in the development of human intelligence	Outline AO1			
			Outline AO2			
	Topic 2 : The relationship between brain size and intelligence					
		Relationship between brain size and intelligence (e.g. the adaptive value of large brains, comparative studies across species)	Outline AO1			
			Outline AO2			

Division	Topics	Revision areas		Basic Under-standing	Good Grasp	Complete Mastery
Division A : Schizophrenia						
	Topic 1 : Clinical characteristics					
		Clinical characteristics of schizophrenia, depression and **one** anxiety disorder	Outline AO1			
			Outline AO2			
	Topic 2 : Biological explanations of schizophrenia					
		Two biological explanations of schizophrenia	Outline AO1			
			Outline AO2			
		More than two biological explanations of schizophrenia	Outline AO1			
			Outline AO2			
	Topic 3 : Psychological explanations of schizophrenia					
		Two psychological explanations of schizophrenia	Outline AO1			
			Outline AO2			
		More than two psychological explanations of schizophrenia	Outline AO1			
			Outline AO2			
Division B : Depression						
	Topic 1 : Biological explanations of depression					
		Two biological explanations of depression	Outline AO1			
			Outline AO2			
		More than two biological explanations of depression	Outline AO1			
			Outline AO2			
	Topic 2 : Psychological explanations of depression					
		Two psychological explanations of depression	Outline AO1			
			Outline AO2			
		More than two psychological explanations of depression	Outline AO1			
			Outline AO2			
Division C : Anxiety disorders						
	Topic 1 : Biological explanations of an anxiety disorder					
		Two biological explanations of **one** anxiety disorder	Outline AO1			
			Outline AO2			
		More than two biological explanations of **one** anxiety disorder	Outline AO1			
			Outline AO2			
	Topic 2 : Psychological explanations of an anxiety disorder					
		Two psychological explanations of **one** anxiety disorder	Outline AO1			
			Outline AO2			
		More than two psychological explanations of **one** anxiety disorder	Outline AO1			

CHAPTER 9 TREATING MENTAL DISORDERS

Division	Topics	Revision areas		Basic Under-standing	Good Grasp	Complete Mastery
Division A : Biological (somatic) therapies						
	Topic 1 : Chemotherapy					
		Use of chemotherapy	AO1			
			AO2			
		Issues surrounding the use of chemotherapy (e.g. appropriateness and effectiveness)	Outline AO1			
			Outline AO2			
	Topic 2 : ECT and psychosurgery					
		Use of ECT and psychosurgery	Outline AO1			
			Outline AO2			
		Issues surrounding the use of ECT and psychosurgery (e.g. appropriateness and effectiveness)	Outline AO1			
			Outline AO2			
Division B : Behavioural therapies						
	Topic 1 : Behavioural therapies based on classical conditioning					
		Two behavioural therapies based on classical conditioning	Outline AO1			
			Outline AO2			
		Issues surrounding the use of behavioural therapies based on classical conditioning (e.g. appropriateness and effectiveness)	Outline AO1			
			Outline AO2			
	Topic 2 : Behavioural therapies based on operant conditioning					
		Two behavioural therapies based on classical conditioning	Outline AO1			
			Outline AO2			
		Issues surrounding the use of behavioural therapies based on classical conditioning (e.g. appropriateness and effectiveness)	Outline AO1			
			Outline AO2			
Division C : Alternatives to biological and behavioural therapies						
	Topic 1 : Psychodynamic therapies					
		Two psychodynamic therapies	Outline AO1			
			Outline AO2			
		Issues surrounding the use of psychodynamic therapies (e.g. appropriateness and effectiveness)	Outline AO1			
			Outline AO2			
	Topic 2 : Cognitive-behavioural					
		Two cognitive-behavioural therapies	Outline AO1			
			Outline AO2			
		Issues surrounding the use of cognitive-behavioural therapies (e.g. appropriateness and effectiveness)	Outline AO1			
			Outline AO2			

REVISION TABLES

Division	Topics	Revision areas		Basic Under-standing	Good Grasp	Complete Mastery
Division A : Issues						
	Topic 1 : Gender bias in psychological theory and research					
		Two types of gender bias	Outline AO1			
		Gender bias in psychological theories	Outline AO1			
			Outline AO2			
		Gender bias in psychological studies	Outline AO1			
			Outline AO2			
	Topic 2 : Cultural bias in psychological theory and research					
		Two types of gender bias	Outline AO1			
		Cultural bias in psychological theories	Outline AO1			
			Outline AO2			
		Cultural bias in psychological studies	Outline AO1			
			Outline AO2			
	Topic 3 : Ethical issues					
		Ethical issues in **two** or more psychological investigations with human participants	Outline AO1			
			Outline AO2			
		Ethics of socially sensitive research	Outline AO1			
			Outline AO2			
	Topic 4 : The use of non-human animals					
		Use of non-human animals in psychologicall investigations	Outline AO1			
			Outline AO2			
		Arguments (both ethical and scientific) for the use of animals in psychological research	Outline AO1			
			Outline AO2			
		Arguments (both ethical and scientific) against the use of animals in psychological research	Outline AO1			
			Outline AO2			
		Constraints on the use of non-human animals in psychological investigations	Outline AO1			
			Outline AO2			
Division B : Debates						
	Topic 1 : Free will and determinism					
		Explain free will and determinism	Outline AO1			
		Free will versus determinism debate with reference to **two** or more psychological theories	Outline AO1			
			Outline AO2			
		Arguments for and against free will	Outline AO1			
			Outline AO2			
		Arguments for and against determinism	Outline AO1			
			Outline AO2			
	Topic 2 : Reductionism					
		Explain reductionism	Outline AO1			
		Examples of reductionism in **two** or more areas of psychology	Outline AO1			
			Outline AO2			
		Arguments for reductionism	Outline AO1			
			Outline AO2			
		Arguments against reductionism	Outline AO1			
			Outline AO2			
	Topic 3 : Psychology as a science					
		Explain 'science' in the context of psychological research	Outline AO1			
		Arguments for the claim the psychology is a science	Outline AO1			
			Outline AO2			
		Arguments against the claim the psychology is a science	Outline AO1			
			Outline AO2			
	Topic 4 : Nature-nurture					
		Explain 'nature' and 'nurture'	Outline AO1			
		Assumptions made about nature and nurture in **two** or more psychological theories	Outline AO1			
			Outline AO2			
		The nature-nurture debate in psychology	Outline AO1			
			Outline AO2			
		Different views regarding the relationship between nature and nurture	Outline AO1			
			Outline AO2			